Prehistory of North America

Prehistory of North America

Jesse D. Jennings

Professor of Anthropology
University of Utah

09.4 - 890

McGraw-Hill Book Company

New York   St. Louis   San Francisco
Toronto   London
Sydney

Cover:
Three copper bracelets in situ, *Burial 47,*
Robbins Mounds, Kentucky. (After W. S. Webb
and Elliot 1942)

Illustrations by Gail Hammond

Prehistory of North America

Preface

My involvement in archeology came about by accident. My graduate training was in anthropology (as is true of all American archeologists) but was aimed at a career in what has come to be known as cultural or social anthropology. However, my research and special study has focused on American prehistory, and this career has been richly rewarding. That I see human behavior dimly and imperfectly through the material of archeology is true; my interest, however, lies not in the artifacts, but in culture history, change and stability, and the causes of these things. As a student of man I view the pots and stonework first as cultural documents. North American prehistory I have learned to see as a series of patterns, not as lists of culture traits. One can view the human adventure in aboriginal America exactly as one would study a Gobelins tapestry or the carving on a Persian mosque or screen; these comprise a terrifyingly complex array of details which readily fade into one another to create an overall design or picture. One can profitably analyze the subtle intricacies of the detail and derive immense satisfaction as well as great knowledge from the study. Or one can be caught up in the patterns which flow across the piece to create its "message" or design. This, too, is a rich experience. While I have spent much time immersed in site, area, and regional archeological detail, my over-riding interest in North American archeology is in its whole effect— its patterned elegance and simplicity—as, through my own eyes, through the eyes of my students, and through the flood of increasingly perceptive literature by a host of colleagues, I have come to see both the details and the relationships I attempt here to narrate.

One of the ironies of writing such a book as this is that the reader learns a story which the author never heard. This book is a distillate of the fieldwork of a thousand hands and the best thought and effort of a hundred minds. It is put together from tens of thousands of pieces of isolated information. The story, as I relate it here, took shape in classrooms, on digs, in random conversations, and at meetings of anthropologists. It has taken me thirty years to learn it and to put the pieces together in this way. Others would assemble the bits differently.

My object, then, is *not* to create an encyclopedic reference work where accurate detail about all local cultures can be found. Nor is it my intent to argue controversial points unduly. Instead, my hope is that by using detail as sparingly as is consistent with understanding, I can impart to readers not only the "flavor" of field work and artifacts, but the exciting order, consistency, and unbelievable efficiency of the many American cultures or traditions as these now lie exposed, literally, by the archeologist's spade and his patient ordering of detail from site to site, region to region, and area to area. Hopefully, too, I can relate the efficiency of the early Americans to the rich land they exploited so that their history can be seen as a blend of cultural tradition and the land's resources as these mutually influenced each other through the centuries.

This text, like many others, grew out of efforts to teach college students. Like many others, it also reflects a teaching philosophy and a series of specific teaching experiences. My classes usually include college sophomores, juniors, seniors, and an occasional graduate student. The basic interests of these students range from anthropology through zoology. Their concern for American prehistory ranges from the superficial to a deadly earnestness. Such heterogeneous groups, though challenging, are hard to teach. This book would fit such a class, I think. I have given short treatment where it is possible without distortion of main points of the story. The narrative approach, with a minimum of jargon, should provide the casual ones with the story they seek, as well as some appreciation for the ways of science. For those whose desire to learn is more profound, key bibliographic clues to the more recent thinking are provided. The book can, I hope, be used as a guide to study as well as a text and can be enjoyed as not the last but the first word on the subject for many readers.

I have tended to restrict the interpretation to material objects and to the conservative interpretations which can be drawn from them. In doing this, I run less risk of mixing the evidence with too facile assumptions about the social or religious or political concomitants of technology, subsistence, and economy. Even so, I have succumbed periodically (but briefly) to the temptation to reconstruct. The reason for eschewing imaginative or analogic flights is my conviction that the novice needs to savor fully the often unspectacular and limited data as they really are. The position in no way derogates interpretive speculation if it be rooted in demonstrable analogs; it is rather to reserve it for a second level of scholarly sophistication which the average reader of this book will not have achieved. For similar reasons, my discussion of the possible relationships between language and prehistory is scant. The correlation of material objects and language is even more tenuous than are the relationships between material culture and social institutions, and, beyond rare mention, the problem of American Indian languages is omitted. Omission of general analysis of the North American variation in physiography and climate is deliberate. These are in the realm of common knowledge and get attention only at the relevant points in the narrative.

I am aware that many earlier works on topics covered in the bibliography have been omitted. My purpose in citing only the latest known to me is that earlier worthwhile works will be brought to the students' attention in the recent studies. Even so, the bibliography is lengthy. Almost without exception I cite only published materials. Although there are many data of extreme importance in the "folklore" of anthropology, relict from the hundreds of excavated but yet unreported sites, the folklore is omitted because a general book should provide documentation which can be consulted.

My contributions to the substantive data incorporated in the text are restricted to research in the American Southeast, the Southwest, the Maya area, the Great Basin, and a stint of "spectator" participation in Plains research. Thus, my debt to colleagues is made manifest.

There is special need to mention my appreciation for the courtesy my colleagues have shown in sending me reprints or off-prints of their technical papers and reports. In these days of burgeoning knowledge, new scientific journals, and an increasing roster of professional anthropologists, no one man could possibly remain fully informed in a field so broad as New World archeology. The importance of the reprint as a mechanism of scholarship cannot be overstated. I mention, too, with equal emphasis, my debt to the museums, universities, and archeological societies that had added me to the mailing list for their scholarly series. This courtesy has provided me with a research library beyond anything I could have hoped to purchase for myself. The value of personal copies of scholarly series, readily available for consultation by oneself and one's students, cannot be calculated. Without these courtesies I could not have undertaken this book.

With the concluding paragraphs of this preface I wish to mention my indebtedness to the several persons who worked so faithfully to put this work into final shape. I mention Mr. Gail Hammond, who brought intense interest, artistic skill, and imagination to the task of illustrating this book. Norma Mikkelsen displayed great patience in checking the accuracy of the bibliographic citations, the bibliography itself, and the congruence between figure captions and text. She also prepared the glossary. Cynthia Thompson and Marilyn Glad took careful and encouraging interest in typing the manuscript through two and sometimes three drafts. For their skill and accuracy I am very appreciative. Finally, I acknowledge the encouragement and patience shown by Jane Jennings, who, in addition to enduring the long period of writing and the slow growth of the manuscript, helped to identify and remove the passages in the final draft where my meaning was most obscure. Without these people, individually and as a team, I would not have had the stamina to finish.

Aside from the basic recognition that this book itself proffers thanks to my colleagues, there are other acknowledgments I wish to make. First, I acknowledge the generosity of Rice University, Robert F. Spencer, and the National Park Service for permission to reuse short passages (in Chapters 4 and 8) which I had previously published in other contexts. Then, and finally, my deepest appreciation goes to three anonymous readers who criticized the December 1966 draft with care and recommended hundreds of improvements. The criticisms ranged from the picayune to the profound, and all were heeded.

Jesse D. Jennings

Contents

Prehistory of North America

1

Distinctions, Definitions, and Background

Man is universally interested in himself, in his ancestors, and in his origins. The omnipresence of creation myths in all cultures of record and a ubiquitous concern with lineages and kin attest this interest. Concern with past events—in this context it can be called archeology—is one form this interest can take. Nevertheless, professional scholars, at one time or another, can become blasé about the elementary data in their field. The archeologist is no exception. He, therefore, is constantly surprised and humbled by the fervent interest almost everyone has in antiquity. Often, it seems, people are interested in antiquity just for its own sake.

Archeology, however, serves many purposes other than reifying mere antiquity. In Europe—where the study of antiquities goes back for centuries—one major motive was sheer patriotism. As nations emerged from the chaotic welter of feudal states, national pride also developed. It became important to demonstrate deep historic continuity and, perhaps, to boast of the ancient but lost glories of one's country. Equally important (and in a sense another expression of patriotism or pride of past) was the Renaissance interest in the ancient art of the Greeks and Romans, an interest which began in the sixteenth century. While the emphasis was upon art and art history, the concern was also with ancient glory. The prestige attached to collecting ancient art was such that noblemen and churchmen alike financed excavation programs and proudly exhibited their beautiful loot—ceramics, statuary, precious stones, and jewelry. Others who could afford these luxuries sent agents to the Mediterranean countries to buy up whatever could be found that was old and beautiful. So much material was accumulated in this search by the dilettanti that by 1763, Johann J. Winckelmann was able to write a significant history of art, a book which further stimulated archeologic studies. These studies came to include architecture and dead languages, as well as portable *objets d'art*. The entire field of study came to be known as "classics"; today there remains the same fascination in what is commonly called "classical" archeology.

Many of the famous collections—the "cabinets of curiosities" of the nobility—grew into world-famous museums all over Europe, particularly after the works of Linneaus and other famous biologists excited interest in natural history among the learned. The natural historians, of course, worked with the collections of natural "curiosities" brought home during the era of world exploration opened by Columbus and his successors. The explorers collected plants, animals, fish and fowl, and native arts and crafts. However, the museums were only hodgepodges until curators and directors began to develop the classifications upon which natural science is still based. In Denmark, government collections of antiquities began in 1797. Within a decade the collections were swamping the Danish National Museum, and a historian, Christian Thomsen, undertook the job of establishing order. Following the ideas of Vedel-Simonsen, he devised a tripartite scheme of cultural succession—the Stone, Bronze, and Iron Ages—and thus established by 1816 the cultural stages still in use in European archeology. Although Thomsen's scheme is now much modified, he is usually identified as the father of modern archeology. Strictly speaking, archeology didn't really emerge as a discipline until the 1830s, when the studies of geologists and paleontologists began to coalesce with the work of the antiquarians.

Archeology Defined

One well-known definition of archeology is that it "reconstructs the past"; another is that it "makes the past live again." Like all slogans, these say either too much or too little, although the implications of both are quite appropriate.

Archeologic research has continuously contributed to the larger field of anthropology. Both European and North American findings have proved fundamental in the growth and content of anthropologic knowledge and theory. Anthropology is generally divided into two fields, physical and cultural. Man is thus defined as a mammalian species (a cultured species, of course, but still mammalian), subject to genetic and biologic study just as any other. Cultural anthropology is concerned with man's behavior in a group; thus it includes the subfields of linguistics, archeology, and ethnology.

For present purposes, archeology can be defined as that portion of cultural anthropology which is concerned with the remnants of now-extinct lifeways, a study devoted to capturing an understanding of vanished cultures, some knowledge of their histories and their relationships to now-extant cultures. Archeology can further be defined as an incomplete extension of history back into time beyond the reach of written records. In the many cases where there is no recorded history of importance (and this involves all of the Americas prior to 1492), the full history, such as it is, must be written through interpretations of archeologic findings. This, of course, provides a continuity and deep chronologic perspective for such modern ethnologic studies as can firmly be connected with archeologic collections of earlier origin. Archeology always has a historical bias, regardless of any other defined aims (see Clark 1957). An important contribution made by archeology is that its findings provide data for artists, architects, or chroniclers. But archeology itself utilizes all these data as documents in the larger task of learning and explaining culture history.

Archeologists can be recognized as cultural anthropologists; they utilize the scientific method. Their work exemplifies many facets of this method: constant concern with repetitive instances and ever-finer detail; descriptive reporting; and unceasing vigilance in noting relationships, in quantifying data, and in ordering these to one organizing system or another in ever-wider comparisons with other areas. In enlisting new technologic aids and interdisciplinary expertise for refined interpretations, in phrasing broader and broader generalizations, in using evidence, and in drawing reasonable inferences about the interlocking relationships of culture traits through time and space, the archeologist is part of the world of science and works within a tradition he shares with most specialists in other fields of modern scholarship. Specialists in other areas of anthropology are equally committed to the scientific method.

Aims

This book has two purposes. The first is to narrate, as "fact," the complex and exciting sequence of events which tell of man's conquest of the New World, or at least of the northern part of the Western Hemisphere. The organization will emphasize a continuity of culture and similarities and relationships through time and over geographic space, as opposed to the regional differences seen and reported by regional specialists. The intent is to dem-

onstrate that a perspective of sufficient breadth reveals in American prehistory a general sequence of culture "stages" recognizable throughout the continent over a 12,000-year period—perhaps even longer. The approach will be a simple narrative (see Swanson 1959), with details, controversies, cultural inventories, and regional differences and likenesses fitted in as the account progresses. By using the stages as an organizing principle, I have avoided the necessity for devising some makeshift "master" classification scheme that would imperfectly reconcile the conceptually different classificatory systems now in use. None of the existing classifications makes the data more available to novices; rather, these schemes are herculean efforts to order masses of regional archeologic data so that broad cultural interpretations can be made. The classifications have been highly successful; in fact, they make this book possible. But appreciation of the subtleties of these schemes requires more information than the novice controls.

The second purpose of this book is to provide chronologic depth and a coherent and reasonable background for the study of the American Indian. The red man has intrigued scholars since the time of Columbus, and the end is not yet in sight. As Wissler (1938) said long ago (and he little suspected the full depth and variety of the American story), the two Americas and the isolated American Indian population provide the most magnificently controlled laboratory for observing human behavior ever to occur on earth. What we, as anthropologists, must do is to understand the end product if we can. Wissler worked at a time when diversity from area to area received great emphasis; even so, he perceived patterns and likenesses and defined the American culture areas. Fascination with the Indian story persists today on a variety of levels. Whether one is interested in Indians only as members of an underprivileged minority, as artists, as quaint relics of an age of savagery, or as targets for missionary zeal, one may find a new appreciation in this account.

Diversity of Aboriginal Cultures in America

Since Columbus' day, the Indian has been speculated about, misunderstood, and misrepresented; he has been ill-treated and exploited, either protected from civilization or forced into its full stream, loved one day and cast off the next, given charity while being robbed of his lands and heritage. From four centuries of such history comes an enormous literature. Despite the overall interest and glamour of the cultures discovered in the Western world, even serious lay students fail to realize the extent to which modern Americans and even Europeans are cultural heirs of the Indian. The diversities, rather than the similarities, have engaged the most attention. The historic Indian did not possess a uniform culture, and this diversity may indeed be the key to the ever-fresh interest. In North America alone, six *major* language stocks are recognized. The total of separate, mutually unintelligible languages exceeds 200. How different these languages were from each other can be exemplified by saying that an English-speaking person can understand Chinese as readily as a Hopi farmer in Arizona could have talked with a Creek warrior from Georgia. The linguistic diversity of the Americas is but one of the elusive aspects of Indian history.

Diversity in other cultural achievements is to be noted in material things. The rich possessions of the military Aztec—large cities; a powerful army; corn, beans, and squash as basic foods; a rich ceramic technology; gems and golden ornaments —are in overwhelming contrast to the shabby and scanty possessions of the

Paiute of Nevada. Yet the Aztec and the Paiute speak dialects of the same great Uto-Aztecan linguistic stock. In sociopolitical organization there is also a vast range. The stratified, self-destroying theocracy of the Natchez, for example, is poles apart from the simple anarchy of the Eskimo.

This diversity has never been fully appreciated by Americans generally; many nonanthropologists, scholars untrained in the observation and analysis of human behavior, have erred in assuming that notions about Indian culture derived from one tribe were valid for other tribes. Nothing could be further from the truth. Language is but one facet of diversity. The social organization, mythology and religion, art motifs, and details of technologies of the Indian tribes ranged over a long and complex set of scales.

The tribal diversity was nonetheless patterned to some degree, as Wissler (1938) and Kroeber (1939) show in their division of the continent into culture areas. A culture area is a geographic area within which the cultures show considerable similarity to each other and lack of similarity to cultures in adjacent areas. There is a strong correlation between culture area and subsistence resources. The culture-area concept carries with it the notion of a "center" where a typical tribe or cluster of tribes provides cultural influences and innovations which diffuse outward with decreasing strength to the less typical tribes of the culture area. The culture areas—such as the Plains, the Arctic, or the Eastern Woodland—do provide a coarse, broad system of classification of the historically observed and reported tribes, a classification based largely on subsistence and material culture. The concept is regarded as a static one, with no great concern for the dimension of time. But Kroeber does emphasize the variation in cultural intensity from area to area and notes that in areas of greatest intensity, climaxes of cultural richness and complexity can be recognized. His identification of cultural climax areas is derived from ethnographic data but tends to agree with archeologic findings, so that some ethnographically delineated culture areas are also fairly accurate demarcations of culture difference and similarity in the prehistoric periods. For example, the climaxes observed archeologically in the Southeast and Southwest were identified by Kroeber from ethnographic data. Ethnographers, as do archeologists, take the culture areas for granted as a useful peg upon which to hang areal generalizations about culture, subsistence, and technology. When the archeologist describes or delineates an archeologic region on the basis of many sites with similar technology and subsistence, he is in effect establishing a prehistoric culture area, although the term is rarely used by archeologists.

Contributions to Modern Civilization

Some mention or acknowledgment ought to be made of the all-pervasive contributions the Indian has made to modern civilization and to the American way of life. Indian heritage enriches our twentieth century American culture, providing much of its individual flavor; world culture and economy are equally indebted to the American Indian. As the Indian vanishes as a racial and cultural entity into the anonymity of modern American citizenship, it seems relevant once more to catalog Indian influence upon our lives today —an influence which, so long as modern civilization lasts, will never disappear. The discovery of America, with its strange new indigenous populations, was, on many counts, one of the greatest events of world history and engendered an immediate worldwide interest which has never waned. As an architect of culture, the Indian contributed in every sphere—even while he faced extinction. In medicine his contributions include cocaine, quinine, and the enema tube. To industry and agriculture he has given corn, rubber, and tobacco, which have worldwide importance. In the American vocabulary, a thousand words such as "succotash," "hominy," "potato," and "tomato" reflect the origin of favorite foods. And 10,000 place names from Tallahassee to Walla Walla proclaim our retention of the musical syllables of many tongues. In literature, the noble red man brought lasting fame to Cooper and Longfellow and much wealth to lesser writers of present-day cinema and television scenarios and slick paperbacks. Of course, in literature the Indian has been both virtuous and vile; in either role he is indispensable to the entertainment world. The sports world owes hockey and lacrosse to the Indian tribes of the Eastern United States; the inspiration behind the Boy Scouts must be credited to the same tribes.

Furthermore, American history until about 1830 is little more than an account of the cooperation and competition of Indians with the whites of many nations for three centuries; the progress of westward expansion, until the 1880s, continued to involve various tribes. It seems somehow fitting that such men as Black Hawk, Tecumseh, Cochise, Geronimo, and Sitting Bull are far better known for their heroic exploits than are the men who finally defeated them and that Sacajewea and Squanto are equally well-known for their heroic pro-white behavior. Even the natural resources of the continent, the prairies and plains of the Midwest or the pine stands of the South, memorialize the fires built for a hundred centuries by the Indians in a deliberate attempt to engineer a terrain fitted to their cherished cultural patterns. Indian trails have become our highways; our towns rest upon the ashes of theirs. In the arts—painting, sculpture, and music—the inspiration of Indian models has been widespread. In short, Americans are far more Indian in thought, language, and action than they realize.

Another important point to be made here is that there is strong evidence that in aboriginal America continuous and long-lived communication and cultural exchange existed between the tribes despite language differences and a few physiographic barriers. Opinions differ as to the nature of this contact. By some students, the contact is seen as very limited, involving trade in luxury items such as copper, seashells (from both oceans), turquoise, catlinite pipes, and the like, over long distances from tribe to tribe. But the dispersal of precious goods may have been the work of professional traders, such as still function in Central America (Tax 1953) and in the South-western states. Another view, one sustained by a host of recorded observations by earlier travelers, is that the Indian was both a roving and a gregarious creature. There was long distance visitation by entire bands or family groups with other tribes (see Lewis and Kneberg 1946). A great awareness of cultural diversity as well as considerable cultural exchange existed over all the continent. There is also overwhelming evidence of intermittent hostility—raids or even pitched battles—between tribes. These hostilities were neither continuous nor universal. Raids conducted for gain in women, horses, scalps, or slaves, were common; but such raids were most frequently initiated by young leaders who could gather and lead other young hotbloods toward a specific objective. Many historically recorded raids were motivated as much for excitement and prestige or sport as for booty.

On the other hand, there is the well-documented practice of long winter visitation by Plains tribes or bands with the Pueblos of Pecos, Taos, and Galisteo. Open

enemies for much of the year, they declared a kind of cold-weather truce during which trading and social intercourse of benefit to both groups took place. Customarily, it was a standard annual event. Cultural exchange was also achieved by some tribes through the common practice of child or woman stealing, followed by adoption into the family of the kidnapper. Sometimes the captives were sold to even more distant tribes. The view that there has always been much contact between the Indian tribes through face-to-face trade, possible friendly visitation, and hostilities is sustained by archeologic discovery. The continued existence, then, of quite different lifeways and of the several culture areas of the continent must be accepted and evaluated as the result of strong factors other than isolation or ignorance of other ideas.

In the foregoing pages there is an apparent discrepancy between the emphasis upon aboriginal diversity and the flat statement that a continent-wide pattern of sequent specializations can be observed. The explanation is that the archeologist inevitably sees a simpler, less variable world because he deals with material culture that bears on economy and subsistence without reference to language, kinship systems, or other intangible aspects of culture. The diversity is seen ethnographically in exactly those non-material aspects of culture least likely to be inferred from archeologic data. Thus, the discrepancy in statements of unity or diversity demonstrates not contradiction but differing data.

Culture

Inevitably, many passages herein will comment upon the nature of culture as this seems justified by the factual material. There is no intent, however, to weave a new theoretical web or to review at length other theories about Indian or any other culture. Nevertheless, it seems unavoidable not to take some position as to the nature of culture at the very outset. Kroeber's (1952b) concept of the superorganic nature of culture as well as White's (1949) *sui generis* view are easy for the archeologist—*qua* archeologist—to work with. This is merely to say that when he deals with cultural debris, that is, the frozen or materialized expressions of vanished technologic, artistic, or religious values, with no social action and no population to obscure the view, he finds it exceedingly easy to accept *Homo sapiens* as a given entity, with culture or the totality of behavior as the one matter of importance. The once-living but anonymous people who possessed these objects and behavior patterns are readily and easily assumed; but the focus of study is the inferable customary behavior which determined the situation in which their individual lives were lived. White's position and his views are easily utilized in archeologic interpretation. Without attempting to defend the point further, it is simply assumed that, wittingly or not, the archeologist at most levels of analysis takes for granted the once-viable population with whose debris he works and "interprets" the debris as quite valid cultural stuff.

The above remarks are not very helpful or useful when one begins to examine an archeologic collection or read technical archeologic monographs. For the prehistorian and other anthropologists, the word "culture" has had so many uses on so many levels of abstraction that it has almost lost its value. It has already been used in this book in the most general way to signify a lifeway and all this implies in technology, philosophy, language, religious custom, social organization, values, world view, law, etc. Obviously the arche-

ologist can't learn all these things from a midden heap. Therefore, *this* meaning of culture won't serve. Nor is the nonanthropologic usage of the term, meaning the finer things of a civilized existence, in any way appropriate. Just what does "culture" seem to mean to an archeologist? Childe (1956) says, in essence, that a culture is a recurrent assemblage of artifact types. Willey and Phillips (1958) are content at one level of discourse to limit it thus: ". . . The term 'culture' usually refers to single technologies or 'assemblages' reflecting a similar economic adjustment shared by a large number of social groups." Krieger (1964) makes a broad and simple archeologic definition: A culture consists of the similar archeologic materials found over a wide region. Highly similar specimens from a small area he calls a "complex." Obviously *one* collection from a single location could in different contexts be referred to as a "complex," a "culture," or a "stage." The problem of terminology is not made any easier by noting that a collection of objects can never do more than merely represent or suggest a lifeway. Therefore, any one of these terms, when used as a label for a collection, requires some degree of interpretation and actually comes to be an abstract statement about a lifeway instead of a group of material objects.

The practice in the pages to follow will be to refer to the specimens from a site or a level within a site as a "complex," "collection," "assemblage," "congery," or some other term which implies a cluster of associated physical objects and their relationships. The word "culture" will be used to express the idea of the unity of, or similarity of, a series of site collections which seem to imply or to prove the existence of a widespread lifeway, involving the same level of technology and a shared exploitive or ecologic base. Examples of this usage would be the Desert culture or the Archaic cultures. "Stage" is an indispensable term, used to raise to even higher abstraction the notion of a unity of culture focus from complex to complex. In "stage" there is an additional connotation of sequence and ranking of cultures by level of complexity toward some terminal or final level. Divorcing the term "stage" from both temporal and spatial connotations is necessary if the term is to be useful. Inventing new terms or adding crippling restrictions or overtones to already useful words is one solution to the problem of terminology, but in this account the effort has been toward a consistent use of "stage," "culture," and "complex," as described above. Although such usage is admittedly imprecise, it approaches that normally employed in the archeologic literature which readers may later consult.

"Stage" and "culture" are seen to be related, but not synonymous, terms; "culture" concerns a group of specific, named units about whose temporal and spatial existence definite data (and/or beliefs) exist. "Stage" lacks *any* temporal and spatial connotations. (Readers interested in terminologic distinctions should consult Swanson 1959; Phillips 1955; Krieger 1953, 1964; Willey and Phillips 1958; and Rouse 1955 among others.)

Archeology and History

The preceding pages make it clear that archeology can, in certain contexts, be considered history. To leave the matter there would be misleading. It is historical, but it isn't exactly history. Most often history is written about events and personages of the past. As such, it must be derived from documents—written documents which reveal the personal lives and actions of leaders and the events which seem to lead to, or result from, such actions. Moreover, much history deals with wars, reforms, campaigns, conflicts

of national internal political interests, economic matters, and such things. History is told in terms of states or populations and is most often revealed through the actions of ruling or dominant classes. The historian is confined in large measure to written records, and the story he puts together is obviously largely controlled by the kind of information he gets out of these records. Although historians do take account of general cultural trends, such as an increase in industrialization and its effect on the lifeway of a country, they are usually concerned with specific persons and their accomplishments; historians also often weigh these accomplishments and evaluate them as to their effect on the state or country. But in the absence of documentation, the academic historian has little to draw upon.

American archeology differs from history, and perhaps benefits from the fact, in that it has no written documents at all. No written language existed in the Americas. The Mexican codices and Mayan hieroglyphs have been called writing, but no competent scholar has yet claimed that these represent a written, phonetic language comparable in flexibility to the written language of even the Sumerians or the Egyptians. Thus, any *pre*history is fleshed out without the distraction and restrictions which written records impose. The North American archeologist can learn of no leaders or prominent men, and there are no chronicles of individual achievements. (Recorded legends provide some historical information about Peruvian and Central American personages, but these are exceptions.) Nor are there detailed day-to-day records of striving against famine, of good crop years, of hard winters, of important battles or successful raids, or of the introduction of technologic innovations such as are available to the prehistorian in other areas of the world. Diaries, religious records, accounts of travel—all are lacking. Since these are the stuff from which history is derived, the archeologist can't be a proper historian.

Nonetheless, he does "write" history and has certain advantages in doing it. Denied written documents, restricted to objects and their relationships, he notes technologic, religious, and other changes in the overall culture as these occur through time. As site after site is dug and reported, the information available increases. If, let us suppose, only one site of a given culture were dug and reported, it would dangle in time and space without connections; it would exist *in vacuo*. If this supposed first site were a cemetery yielding data on burial practices, perhaps information on religion, and some idea (through grave goods) of technology, the full "history" would be scant indeed. If an adjacent site were studied and found to be the associated village, the data on technology would no doubt be fuller; architecture, village plan, and subsistence base could perhaps be added to the description. If yet another sample of the culture came to light in a stratified reoccupied site *under* an altogether different complex of artifacts, the beginnings of knowledge about the relative chronologic position of both complexes would be derived. Thus, as the culture is sampled over and over at site after site—each site having certain unique attributes—a local, then an areal, and even a regional history can be built with increasing confidence. Relationships to other contemporary cultures elsewhere can be inferred from trade objects or other evidence of exchange of ideas. Perhaps even movement of peoples can be shown or reasonably suspected. If culture change through time is regarded as valid history, then prehistory qualifies as history. The lack of documents, the lack of measured, specific points in time when important events occurred, the lack of named personages and their exploits may be an advantage, leaving archeologists to gather

information impartially about all classes of the populace and their lives. The validity and usefulness of this information lie in extending our understanding of human behavior, as well as of human and cultural evolution, deeper into time.

Related to the limitations of archeology as history are its limitations as cultural anthropology. When the ethnologist works with living peoples, he studies the culture as a viable, integrated system with a myriad of interwoven patterns of behavior which make a meaningful environment to those who practice that particular way of life. He studies language; he learns kinship terms and systems; he devotes himself to magical and religious beliefs and notes how these in turn have relevance in hunting, agriculture, economics, law, and government. He inventories the material objects, and he tries to perceive the core values of the culture. Most of these facets of life can be studied through the observed behavior of the people, behavior which is modified by idiosyncratic differences and by age, sex, and experience as well. He, like the historian, must see the culture, but he must see it apart from the persons who actually live it. The ethnologist's difficulty is even greater than that of either the historian or the archeologist because there is so much to see and relate to other things. As interrelationships are perceived, then deeper probing into the significance and value of the behavior to the individual member of the culture must be undertaken.

The archeologist has no such wealth of data and is correspondingly handicapped in seeing the culture whole. The social organization of dead cultures can be dimly seen, as can subsistence, technology, art concepts, architecture, some ceremony, and other categories of values and behavior which leave tangible evidence. But as for language, kinship, detailed religious views, politics, and the like, he has usually no clue. His contribution is held to statements concerning broad cultural events as these can be deduced from the testimony of the tangible remains and their associations.

Relative Chronometry

The prehistorian's interest in the passage of time has been emphasized. If time is thus crucial to archeologic interpretation, the devices for telling time deserve attention. But first a distinction between relative and absolute chronology needs to be drawn. Following Oakley (1953), relative time can be defined as establishing an event or culture as being earlier than, coeval with, or later than, some other event or sequence of events, events lacking a definite age or date in terms of elapsed years or other units of measurement. In short, the event or culture can be placed somewhere in a sequence. Most archeologic dating has been of this relative sort. The stratigraphic principle that layers in the earth are laid down slowly through time with the earliest being the deepest and each successive layer *relatively* younger is crucially important here and forms the basic evidence for most relative chronology. At any one site there may be one or more occupation layers, possibly with alternating bands of sterile fill; in such cases, the stratigraphic sequence is directly observed as a physical phenomenon. The relative sequence of the layers of soil and debris is, therefore, readily established at each archeologic site. But each such sequence from a single site is a unique circumstance revealing only the history of events at that individual location. In order to understand the history of a region, the discrete relative sequences must somehow be fused into a master sequence. Such a sequence can be called "synthetic" or "inferred" stratigraphy and involves the principle of typology. As digging continues through a long-occupied region, it is soon evident that differing

artifact assemblages are collected from site to site. Rarely are all the assemblages represented at each location. With different assemblages (or cultures), identified artifactually and giving evidence of several discrete nonidentical lifeways, the data can be combined to establish a widely applicable relative chronology for the region; it becomes possible, through a typologic comparison of the inventories of objects and traits from each level, to equate or link culture levels across several sites. It is then possible, as shown in Figure 1.1, to build a chronology for increasingly large spatial zones (see also Haury 1955). The cultures represented by A, B, C, etc., in Figure 1.1 represent the observed sequential occurrences at several sites. They are to be understood as comprising similar components, that is, so similar in terms of the material and nonmaterial traits collected, observed, or inferred that they are believed to represent the same lifeway of the same peoples and are, therefore, of the same age. (Typology is thus seen to carry implications of time as well as of culture.) Moreover, cultures A through F may be evolutionary stages

Figure 1.1   *Developing a synthetic regional chronology from a series of stratified sites.*

Actual Stratigraphy

Site	1	2	3	4	5	6	7
Culture	A	B	D	A	B	A	A
	B	C	E	C	D	B	E
	E	E		D		C	F

When matched by culture likeness and level, these sites yield the sequence of cultures A,B,C,D,E,F

A				A		A	A	A
B	B					B	B	B
		C			C		C	C
			D	D	D			D
E	E	E					E	E
							F	F

of one cultural tradition or may represent quite different traditions over a vast span of time, involving varied adaptations to slightly varied environmental circumstances. The sequence is clearly a relative one. A is merely the youngest; F is the oldest. However, if A represents the debris from a culture identified with a historically known culture or tribe, the sequence is safely anchored at one end in calendrical time. For example, in the vicinity of Natchez, Mississippi, an aboriginal archeologic complex containing a few artifacts of French manufacture can be dated as no earlier than 1699 (when St. Catherine's Concession was established north of the central town of the Natchez tribe). Reasonable guesses as to the age of the earlier, entirely aboriginal complexes underlying the 1699 layer can then perhaps be made.

This anchoring of a sequence in the modern year count or calendar, a well-developed procedure in American archeology called the *direct historical* approach, has been utilized in every area. Kroeber's (1916) study of Zuñi potsherds is an example of its application, as were Strong's (1933) work in the Plains, and Collins' (1927) and Ford's (1936) studies of the Lower Mississippi Valley. Scores of others have applied the principle. Strong (1940), Steward (1940), and Steward and Setzler (1938) have explained and advocated the approach, which is standard.

Although more could be said about relative dating (because there are endless nuances and applications of the concept), the paragraphs above will suffice to introduce the problem to the reader.

Chronologic Techniques

Dendrochronology Relative dating based on superposition does not fully satisfy the archeologist's need for precise information. Merely knowing that something is old, or older than something else,

is not enough. If areal or even local studies of cultural change or succession are to be successful, it is necessary to know more precisely how old the cultures are. There is a constant search for techniques with which to determine more and more exactly the age of any site or object. Actually, none of the "precision" techniques gives exact dates: Oakley's (1963) term "chronometric" is properly descriptive of most of them.

Precision can be claimed only for *dendrochronology*, or tree-ring dating. Stallings (1949) and Bannister (1963) have provided the most lucid of the scores of explanations available. Reduced to the simplest terms, tree-ring calendars are based on the belief that each tree-ring represents 1 year's growth (Figure 1.2). Any specimen can be dated by matching its ring pattern against a master calendar of rings, the master being a sequence first built up from many specimens, whose rings are matched backward from living trees known to have been cut in certain years. Tree-ring "pattern" means the sequence of broad and narrow rings which result from favorable (wide-ring) and unfavorable (thin-ring) growing years. "Favorable" implies more rainfall and also involves the amount of sunlight, density of cloud cover, and other factors. These sequences of alternating clusters of broad and narrow rings are shared by all trees over an area, and all of them keep the same "time" throughout their life-span, recording not only each year, but also something about the climate of that year. A tree of unknown antiquity, and unknown cutting or dying date, can be fixed in time by matching its sequence of rings and their pattern with the master chart of wide and thin rings of known date.

But nothing is this simple. Many species do not lay down a ring each year. Others may put on growth on one side of the trunk but not on the other. Still others grow only where there is a constant supply

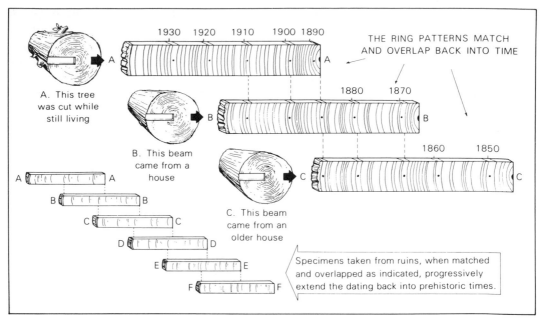

Figure 1.2 *Deriving dates by means of tree-rings. (Modified from Stallings 1949)*

of water and lay down uniform or "complacent" rings, so no pattern develops. Certain pines, possibly red cedar, juniper, sage brush, and a few other trees, yield reliable ring counts. Of all these the western yellow pine is the best timekeeper. It responds very sharply to nuances of rainfall and climate, especially when it is growing in a location where there is no constant supply of groundwater and it is dependent upon annual precipitation. The notoriously variable Western climate contributes to the calendar. The alternating good and bad growth years provide sharp, readily identified, wide and narrow ring patterns. The study of tree-rings as calendars was initiated by Douglass (1929), an astronomer. He trained many students, and dendrochronologic studies are now in progress over the entire world, with many sensitive new species being discovered. At present, the longest master chart of use to archeologists is the one for the American Southwest, a chart which is based on thousands of modern and prehistoric specimens and which goes back to 53 B.C. The specimens on which it is based are among the tens of thousands housed at the Laboratory of Tree-ring Research at the University of Arizona. Figure 1.2 illuminates the system and explains the building of a master chart. When the Southwestern United States is reviewed (Chapter 7), the crucial usefulness of this chronologic system will be better appreciated. Tree-ring studies have been conducted in the Plains (Will 1946; Weakly 1940, 1950), Illinois (Bell 1951), Georgia (Willey 1937), and the Arctic (Giddings 1952), and they have been very helpful. However, the calendars developed from these studies are not as long, and the work of several scholars has been severely criticized on various grounds (for example, Bell 1948). In the Plains, at least, the validity of the criticized studies is slowly being attested by other techniques of dating, to some degree confounding the critics. The bristlecone pine sequence goes back 4,600 years but has had little archeologic application to date.

The major criticism lodged against dendrochronologic findings is aimed not at the calendars per se but at the many dubious interpretations of culture history—interpretations which cannot appropriately be drawn from tree-ring width (for example, the abandonment of the Mesa Verde area in the A.D. 1290s because of drought). Glock (1937), for example, seems to have demonstrated quite adequately that tree-rings measure winter precipitation only; total precipitation is not revealed. Schulman (1956) clearly believes the ring width to be a proper measure of usable water and does sweeping reconstructions of climate on this evidence. Martin (1963) would agree with Glock, as would Fritts (1965), who marshalls increasing evidence that precipitation is only *one* variable controlling tree growth; temperature and cloud cover may be even more important considerations. It is perhaps best for the archeologist to trust the calendar derived from tree-rings for what it is: a count of passing years. Detailed climatologic and other inferences simply cannot yet be drawn on the basis of present knowledge of tree-growth pattern, even though few can resist the temptation.

Astronomy   Elsewhere in the New World, a time count of elapsed days was developed by the Maya. Their inscriptions reveal a precise mathematics and an acute knowledge of astronomy, which they combined in order to keep track of time. The accuracy of the system as used to record celestial events is astonishing, but so far the calendar has not been correlated with our modern Gregorian calendar or year count to everyone's satisfaction. The Mayan calendar and its relation to the Gregorian one, along with the intricacies of Mayan mathematics, make up one of

the most fascinating specialties in American archeology, but do not help us at all in our North American studies.

Radiocarbon   Of greatest general usefulness in developing American and worldwide chronologies is radiocarbon dating, a technique only a few years old and still subject to many doubts (for example, Antevs, various; Bliss 1952; Hunt 1955, 1956). Based on the disintegration of an isotope of carbon, C14, the datings derived are generally regarded as quite accurate. The application of the datings to archeologic situations has often been careless, frequently revealing naïveté about the procedure and formulas necessary for translating radioactivity into years of time. The problems of relating a date or a suite of dates to a culture or an artifact complex are still not fully appreciated by some (Meighan 1956). As dates based on radioactive carbon increase in number, and as students gain sophistication in using them, radiocarbon dating is becoming the sharpest available chronologic tool.

Again, the principle is very simple; the questions arose only after the basic idea was grasped and after the extreme value of radiocarbon for dating human history was perceived. During a study of the isotopes of carbon, the half-life (or rate of decay) of C14 was determined to lie at about 5,570 years. The radioactive C14 is created in the upper atmosphere as cosmic rays bombard nitrogen atoms. The radioactive carbon eventually diffuses evenly throughout the entire biosphere and is taken up directly along with C12 (inert carbon) and C13 by plants making carbohydrates and by marine species that manufacture calcium carbonates for their own shells. As the life cycle continues, plants contribute carbon, some of it radioactive, to the animals that feed upon them and thus all living organic matter contains radioactive carbon. Upon death, carbon intake ceases, but the radioactive carbon continues to decay at the 5,570 years per half-life rate. The carbon is essentially inert after ten half-lives. The rest is simple technology. Dead organic matter can be tested for radioactivity; by means of refined counters, the random emanations per minute can be recorded over a long period (24 to 72 hours is common). The rate of decay, that is, the frequency of the emanations, is then transformed by formula into a statement as to how many years ago the organism died.

In order to put this notion to the test, Libby (1952) ran tests on ancient wooden objects of known age from archeologic collections and other sources. The results were computed and showed ages compatibly close to their known, or reliably estimated, absolute age. The experiment thus sustained the theory on a limited basis. The results, released first informally in 1950, aroused far more excitement in archeologic circles than in the field of chemistry, and a new chronologic "industry" was created. Since those first eight or ten dates were derived, technical refinements in counting have been made; in 1966 there were seventy-one laboratories doing pure research with radioactive carbon and providing hundreds of age determinations on archeologic and geologic specimens. There are also several commercial installations doing similar work for a small fee. A separate annual publication, *Radiocarbon* (established in 1959), is devoted to the annual printing of lists of derived dates, thousands of which have now been run. Radiocarbon counters are now sensitive and accurate enough to measure the carbon content of specimens representing a timespan from ca. A.D. 1500 back to about 40,000 or 50,000 B.C. Thus, prehistorians have a calendar covering all of *Homo sapiens'* time on earth! The best materials for testing appear to be charcoal, uncharred wood, bone, shell, and horn, listed in their order of reliability. Any

organic material can be tested—usually the test involves changing carbon to carbon dioxide after many steps calculated to remove contamination (in fact, reduction to CO_2 is the final step). However, the technicians have most confidence in the results they get from charred plant remains because charcoal is nearly pure carbon, which is chemically quite inert, and because the plant absorbs radiocarbon directly from the atmosphere, where it is created.

Dates are often released by the laboratory as Years Ago with a plus-minus factor: for example, 8950 ±260. Normally, the archeologist adjusts the reading to an A.D. or B.C. date. Both Years Ago and A.D.–B.C. dates are linked to A.D. 1950 as a base line, thereby avoiding the need for knowing the year the ascription was made in order to derive an A.D.–B.C. calendrical date. The plus-minus part of the figure is a statistical statement of uncertainty of 1 standard deviation, based on the nature of counting random events (which the emanations are). Whether the sample was counted 24, 48, 72 hours, or longer, is also involved in calculating the plus-minus figure. All we need know here is that the figure merely says that there are two chances in three that the correct reading of the age of the specimen falls within the plus-minus range. The range for 8950 ±260 is 8690 to 9210. Most archeologists assume the first figure to be accurate and proceed with their interpretations as if no plus-minus computations were involved; this practice will be followed in this book. In some cited cases the apparent stratigraphic discrepancies disappear in the plus-minus ranges.

The theoretical or practical limitations of, and questions about, the method are legion but are given relatively little attention by the archeologists using the data. These fall into about three categories: First, and most important, there is still reasonable doubt whether the cosmic-ray bombardment has been uniform for the past 50,000 years. If variation were proved, it would indicate a fluctuation in the amount of C14 created and distributed around the world for eventual incorporation into organic tissues. If the proportions of C14 to C12 and C13 varied greatly, the radioactivity of organic materials would vary equally and age ascriptions based on emanations measured against those from modern specimens would be in error to the same extent that the production of C14 had varied. This matter is still debated, but one important test has been undertaken. Three European scholars, E. H. Wells, H. Tauber, and K. O. Münnich, made carefully controlled C14 analysis of samples from a giant sequoia cross section which showed over 1,200 annual rings. The samples were tiny cores cut at even (50-year) intervals and were thus of known age. They found that the C14 content of the biosphere has not been constant. There have, in fact, been minor changes in C14 production in cycles of 150 to 200 years. The range of difference in C14 production over the 1,200 years sampled, A.D. 659 to 1859, was only 1.5 percent, not enough to affect the validity of the C14 count, particularly in view of the odds toward accuracy given by the plus-minus readings. This experiment does not entirely solve the problem, being confined to the very recent past, but tends to discount it because the effect of 1.5 percent or even greater variation on extremely old specimens would be negligible, both actually and statistically. There are other theoretical problems, such as the imbalance caused by the presence of countless tons of fossil carbon released into the atmosphere during three centuries of industrialization and the attendant increasing use of fossil fuels that contain only the inert C12. Apparently modern C14 proportion is skewed downward so that the modern woods used as controls actually contain less C14 than was "nor-

mal" 300 years ago and thus form false standards or yardsticks for measurement of emanations. The problem seems to have been resolved by incorporating a correction factor into the formulas used in translating emanation rates into years of elapsed time.

A question of more practical importance about the frequently contradictory radiocarbon readings is the matter of contamination. Contamination of a specimen can occur at any time after death until the moment of testing. Bliss (1952) lists several ways the organic material could be contaminated in "storage" in the ground, such as chemical alteration or biochemical modification. All additions would, of course, be after death and would provide younger carbon dates. Rootlets of modern plants which penetrate charcoal are an often-observed but readily removed contaminant. Hunt (1956) reiterates the fact that many carbon dates show ages which reverse the known stratigraphy. These discrepancies can nearly always be explained as resulting from poor collecting or poor recording or excavating technique, that is, from human error rather than contamination. Even fallout from atomic explosions has apparently contaminated some specimens. For all the above-cited problems and many others, safeguards have been developed and laboratory procedures have been devised to offset, correct, or minimize the danger of false readings. Willis (1963) has written an excellent article dealing with these matters. Human error can, of course, also occur in the laboratory.

I don't want to cast fatal doubts on the method, but I do want to suggest that readers remain somewhat cautious in accepting radiocarbon dates. The space devoted here to questions about the technique is intended to offset somewhat the reliance upon radiocarbon dates in the following chapters. Rarely is *one* radiocarbon date used with confidence. A suite of dates, which reinforce one another in reflecting a local stratigraphy accurately or that have been arrived at by different laboratories on different materials, or even a series of singles which agree in dating several components of a culture is relied upon more heavily than a single date. It should be pointed out quite emphatically that despite all the above qualifications, radiocarbon dates often support "guess dates" arrived at by other means, a fact which in itself generates confidence. Moreover, if radiocarbon proves to be accurate even 51 percent of the time, it has given the greatest precision to chronologic studies of anything since dendrochronology. It has already provided something resembling control in place of guesswork. The unsuspected great age of many American cultures as revealed by radiocarbon has had tremendous impact on American archeology, causing extensive overhaul of previous beliefs. The theoretical importance of the greater time-spans is not even yet fully understood. Prehistorians are deeply in debt to Libby and his colleagues for their yeoman service.

Obsidian Dating   Even newer than radiocarbon is the technique of obsidian dating. This technique is based on the hydration rate, that is, the absorption of water by obsidian, a natural glass. Obsidian is believed to absorb atmospheric water at a constant rate. This absorption causes a cortical change which begins as soon as a fresh surface is formed. The thickness of the cortex is supposed to represent the length of time since the object was chipped, environmental heat being a factor influencing the speed of the process. The technique is not yet out of the experimental stage; variables, other than heat, appear to be involved, and many of the assumptions which underlie the translation of microns

of cortex thickness into Years Ago have not yet been proved. Statements about the method made by Evans and Meggers (1960), Friedman and Smith (1960) and others are repeated and summarized in Friedman, Smith, and Clark (1963). Until the many anomalies and discrepancies in the findings are more convincingly explained, and until regional time scales are arrived at on a more rigorous basis, the method must be regarded as a technique for relative dating.

Less Common Techniques   In other parts of the world, dating is frequently done through evidence of volcanic activity, by other radioactive counts such as potassium-argon, by fluorine content of bone, by pollen analysis (which reflects climatic-geologic conditions), and by other methods. All these yield relative dates only; vulcanism, pollen, and, rarely, fluorine analyses are used when appropriate in dating occasional American finds. In the case of volcanic phenomena, the two obvious situations are the blanketing of archeologic debris with either volcanic ash or lava. Several such instances have been discovered. The remains are clearly older than the explosion. Because of increasingly accurate archeologic chronologies, the discovery of ash over a cultural layer has helped in deriving a chronometric or close relative date for the eruption rather than for the human debris involved! Roaring Springs in Oregon is one famous example. Here an ash fall from Mt. Mazama had sealed, even scorched, some vegetal fiber sandals which were later dated by radiocarbon, thereby establishing a maximum age for the eruption. In Mexico, the famous Copilco and Cuicuilco sites were sealed by a vast lava flow. The age of the covered sites is now known to fall about 200 B.C., thus giving a maximum date for the volcano's last activity.

Fluorine dating is an old but recently

revived technique. Most ground water contains fluorine. Buried bone takes up fluorine; the longer the interment, the greater the fluorine accumulation. However, no chronometric value can be derived from the fluorine content of bone because the fluorine content of water is so variable from place to place. A difference in the concentration in bone from level to deeper level can sometimes be used in interpretation, and significant differences in fluorine content in bones from the *same* level would suggest disturbance, mixing of specimens after digging, or some other confusion. More important, it can reveal deliberately falsified associations. The famous Piltdown Man hoax in England, exposed by Oakley and Weiner (1955), was confirmed by the fluorine test. The most famous use of fluorine dating in North America was in helping establish the contemporaneity of Midland Man, in Texas, with some now-extinct animals. The problem of dating can be pursued in Heizer (1953), or in greater detail in a series of studies in Brothwell and Higgs (1963).

Typology and Cross Dating

There is another constantly employed chronologic device called cross dating, which is an entirely cultural approach rooted in typology. The concept of typology is not unrelated to the biologic concept of species, but it is laden with additional overtones. Discussed, debated, and defined endlessly (for example, Krieger 1944; Wheat, Gifford, and Wasley 1958; Phillips 1958; Rouse 1939; Ford 1954; Hole and Heizer 1965), typology is an important tool for any classifier, because classification usually implies sorting and grouping like objects together. The groups are called types. A "type" is most often defined as a class of objects which share a consistent constellation or combination of similar or identical attributes. The type is therefore an abstraction. The raw data of archeology lend themselves to this treatment. Pottery, whether whole or sherds, stone tools of all sorts, beads and other ornaments, and fabricated bone objects can all be thus ordered. The different classes can be sorted grossly, for example, from a Southwestern site, corrugated pottery in one pile and black-on-white painted in another. Or, sorting can be done on so fine a scale that the corrugated pottery is separated into several heaps, using corrugation width, details of coiling, pinching, etc., as criteria for separation. Similarly, the black-on-white pottery can be subdivided into smaller and smaller clumps on the basis of decoration, vessel form, kind of paint— vegetable or mineral—and other attributes, with pieces in the smaller groupings quite similar in all details. What is important in establishing gross "lumped" or fine "split" types is not whether one black-on-white pot can be distinguished from another, as it obviously can be, but rather what about it is culturally significant? That is, what was the intent of the potter, or flint chipper, or bead maker? What about the bead was important at that time? Here we encounter the crucial question: Was the type, as selected by the sorter, once equally well recognized or regarded as a separate type with prescribed uses by the aboriginal craftsman, or is the type merely a device of convenience for the sorter? Either type is valid, but they must be recognized as having different significance.

I don't intend to belittle the ordering and classifying and naming of the types; no other procedure could possibly isolate and systematize all the specimens and allow inferences about technology, art, culture contact, or culture climax. Establishing types or using those established by others is appropriate procedure for an

time seeming to flow past. Our experience in living makes us aware of past events and their relation to present, if not future, affairs; spatial relationships are no less well understood. Perhaps these dimensions are so early made part of the human mind that they fade into the background of consciousness; if this is true, it may explain the trouble experienced by students in the deliberate recognition of both time and space in dealing with archeologic materials. The problem is intensified by the specificity and unique contents of a single archeologic component. The collection is static, marking a frozen moment of time; at the same time, the objects make up the collection from a single spot. But when the temporal and spatial relationship of this component to an adjacent similar, but not identical, collection must be solved, analysis has shifted from the discrete to the general and poses altogether different problems of manipulation than are involved in mere study of a single collection. Willey and Phillips (1958), as well as Rouse (1939), have full discussions of these matters.

Difficult or not, the intertwined considerations of time and space enter into wellnigh every archeologic statement. Such judgments as "A site is contemporary with B site" or "A site is older than B" weigh evidence and make assumptions about time relationships. No question of culture A influencing or being influenced by culture B can be settled without some chronologic framework and even knowledge of the time when one trait and then another appeared in either or both cultures under study. An interesting example of failure to find a solution to an archeologic question because of time is seen in Ekholm (1953, 1964), where he examines the possibility of transfer (diffusion) of certain traits from Asia to Mesoamerica but can reach no firm conclusion because the precise dates of occurrence in either area cannot be accurately ascertained. If the

Asiatic traits developed 500 years earlier in time than the same traits appeared in America, the eastward influence is at least possible; but if the Asiatic phenomena are even 10 years younger, then the prospect of exportation to the Americas is ruled out, and the problem could then be reversed to ask: Did the traits move as a complex from East to West?

Culture Contact, Change, and Continuity

One of the most troublesome areas in anthropology is the understanding of culture change and its mechanisms. One mechanism, of course, is in the exchange of ideas, or values, or artifacts, or language, or all of these when two expanding cultures come into contact, either directly through geographic contiguity or indirectly through language and precepts. In archeology the matter is especially troublesome because no actual behavior can be observed. Only the testimony of the objects and what can be inferred are at hand as evidence (see Wauchope 1966).

Much nonsense has been written by archeologists about the effects of one culture upon another, partly, it seems, because several concepts such as diffusion, migration, replacement, competition, survival, and perhaps others used in archeologic interpretation are concepts which have been used by biologists and zoologists for centuries but which are not necessarily appropriate in anthropology. Nillson, the Danish zoologist, introduced them into archeologic interpretations about 1830. They are appropriate for nonhuman species but fall far short of adequacy in explaining what the human animal can do. When, for example, one finds ground squirrels occupying a given territory where 50 years ago none existed, the explanation that the species has migrated from elsewhere or that it has spread from a small center over a wider area is highly plausible. But if one finds a distinctive pottery style occuring over an increasingly wider area over a period of time, no such assumption as to migration of either people or pots is automatically valid. Pots, of course, can't move. They may be carried, but they reveal no evidence as to *how* or *why* the carrying was done. Hand-to-hand trade and exchange? Or direct transport from the place of manufacture? More important, however, is the fact that the fashion or style can achieve wider and wider popularity without movement of *either* people or pots. Knowledge transmitted verbally would do the trick. Nearly all explanations of migrations, population mixture or replacement, or progress of pottery across a land should be summarily rejected. If the statements rest only on the evidence of pottery, arrowheads, or house types, the archeologists just don't know. The stand taken here is that much diffusion of culture traits or of full complexes in the Americas involves little more than communication between individuals from two cultures. Diffusion also requires that an innovation be somehow compatible or that it have obvious advantages for the recipient culture. The spread of the horse over the Plains from tribe to tribe, as worked out by Haines (1938a, 1938b), is an example of diffusion of a compatible new artifact and a complex of traits. The object (horse) was very useful to the recipients and was assigned an important place in the culture in accord with Indian values; as a beast of burden it replaced the dog. But even more important, it gave advantages in hunting and raiding and became a symbol of prestige and wealth. Both drastic and trivial changes in prehistoric American Indian cultures must often have occurred in this same fashion, as an idea or complex of ideas and the associated objects diffused to the limits of acceptance without necessarily involving extensive population shifts.

Archeologic finds reveal through artifact styles and types that contacts occurred and that one culture influenced another; this is one of the findings of history. What remains unclear and what will perhaps always be obscure is the mechanism of transport or exchange. Then, too, one may ask: Did culture A actually exert a significant influence on B if the only evidence of contact is the presence of a few pots? That a few examples of a minor art would cause important change in an ongoing lifeway is unthinkable, particularly if the recipient culture B already possessed pottery and a knowledge of its manufacture. However, if culture B had hitherto not known pottery, its introduction could no doubt produce changes in the pattern of B culture; these changes might then be identified as obviously resultant from the new object and the associated technology. But even in such a case, one could not know *how* the first pots were introduced by culture A to culture B.

Whether the *mechanisms* of culture contact can ever be demonstrated through archeologic finds may be doubtful, but the *fact* of contact can be established. Its significance also can be inferred. One must separate, in interpretation, (1) assumptions about *mechanism* from (2) the facts as to artifact presence and (3) the cultural effects of that presence. One can be sure of (2) and make varyingly reasonable inferences about (3), but about (1) there is usually little certainty. [One of the best-documented cases of actual migration of a sizable population is described by Haury (1958) from Point of Pines, where a Kayenta group moved southward from northern Arizona into central Arizona. Their new village is clearly different in architecture from others in the area, and their handicrafts also reveal the Kayenta origin; why the move was made, of course, cannot be proved.]

It is ironic that although archeologists are strongly interested in stability, continuity, and change in culture, no useful theories about culture or culture change have emerged from this interest. Most archeologic writing involves description of data and varyingly extensive comparisons with other sites or cultures and often moves on to statements about influences exchanged between cultures or evidences of culture change, but satisfactory theories about such change have not yet developed. Most archeologists appear to use one of two assumptions about the nature of change. The first appears to be the idea that culture change is a gradual, uniform process which can best be described as complacent. The other view seems to imply change in spurts, followed by periods of quiescence. The spurts would follow introduction of, or local invention of, some new trait—technologic or otherwise. Both views can be defended on the basis of archeologic findings.

Despite the need to understand culture contact, change, continuity, and stability, there have been few efforts to understand the process or to erect systems about it. W. W. Taylor (1948) has dealt well with the matter, as have Willey and Phillips (1958). Perhaps the most useful attempts (certainly for the analysis here) are those arrived at in a series of seminars on American archeology held in 1955 (Wauchope 1956). One (Lathrap 1956) dealt with culture-contact situations which could be observed in archeologic contexts. The seminar recognized and classified eight types of contact, the types being established on the basis of both logic and actual, well-studied examples. The types include situations where an intrusive culture is incorporated into the recipient one, where the intrusive one comes to dominate, where each appears to coexist without marked influence in either direction, and others. The seminar made no attempt to explain why the results varied from case to case. Meeting at the same time, another seminar (Jennings 1956)

dealt with a specific case (the American Southwest), attempting to detect the traits intrusive over a 3,000-year period and to isolate the cases of acceptance or rejection of traits and complexes as these were introduced. At the time, the Southwest was the only culture area well enough known archeologically to permit this kind of analysis. The Southwest seminar has value as a careful effort to outline culture history and to explain culture change. Many of the contact types (Lathrap 1956) are exemplified in the Southwest study. The two reports reinforce each other and can profitably be studied in sequence.

A third session of the seminars concerned itself with stability, a concept which archeologic data can illuminate empirically, although explanations must remain entirely inferential. This seminar was confined to sharply defining certain concepts and to suggesting a carefully developed hypothesis for testing, in the belief that archeologically tested theories could ultimately contribute to broader anthropologic theory. The major concern, analytically, was with the concept of *tradition*, a term which implies persistence of a culture trait or complex of traits over a significant spatial range and in significant time depth. I would argue that persistence can, perhaps, be equated with stability.

One crucial caution must be made now, lest it be overlooked; this caution concerns an assumption often underlying statements about culture change. The assumption, which is unproved, seems to be that changes in details of the attributes of artifacts are an index to significant changes in other aspects of the culture where the objects had their original value. If the student discovers that over an 800-year sequence pottery decoration in a given culture became more flamboyant, that ceramic technology became more efficient, and that other developments related to this minor art appeared, he is immediately faced with the question: Is this an important culture change involving more than ceramics, or does it merely represent a slight intensification of an earlier valuing of pottery? The observed slight change in material specimens may document a certain rigidity, arguing culture stability rather than culture change. How much change in subsistence pattern, architecture, or social organization can be claimed on the basis of prettier, or fussier, or deteriorating pottery décor? Furthermore, if the changes can clearly be traced to another area some distance away, did the donor group that introduced new pottery designs have any real impact on the recipient one, particularly if both cultures are otherwise similar in overall culture pattern? Consideration of the points raised above leads one to be very skeptical of sweeping conclusions about culture changes which are deduced from one class of artifacts. This does not mean that all statements about culture change found in archeologic monographs should be rejected; the evidence and its variety must be weighed against the conclusions. The question: Does the change in artifact assemblage reflect a modification of the genius, the pattern, the structure, or the direction of a culture? is too rarely asked.

Classification

American archeology is still in the fortunate position of lacking a continent-wide classificatory system, fortunate in that the lack of a rigid overall scheme has encouraged the development of a series of locally restricted classifications which, while they can be keyed to one another from region to region, allow for great flexibility. One hopes that the *great* system will be delayed until some of the gaps in knowledge have been filled.

Classification of archeologic data can take several forms. One has been to build up an inventory or list of objects and customs distinguishing each recognized local culture and to arrange the cultures in their known or presumed order. New data can, on the strength of the inventory, be assigned by comparison to one or another of the known divisions in the cultural-chronologic framework. Thus, the new material is absorbed or positioned in the local system of ordering. This is the most common approach to establishing control over a mass of unordered collections (see Griffin 1946). The most popular Southwestern classification, developed at the Pecos Conference of 1927, is of this type. The conference organized the remains of the Anasazi region into eight "periods." These periods, it was argued, were marked by sufficiently different material culture traits to make up distinctive complexes and to warrant separation into periods. The separated complexes thus become statements about *both* time and trait associations. The limitations of such systems are very well outlined by Roberts (1935b) and Brew (1946). In the case of the Southwest, the Pecos classification suffered from the fact that it was made up from far too scanty data; furthermore, the actual chronology was not known, and the system was deemed applicable to an overlarge area. Worst of all, it was so welcome and needed that some students seized upon it as an eternal verity and a valid yardstick far beyond its appropriate geographic range. The classification long ago lost its proper value as an aid to understanding and came to constrict thought by providing ready, if often incorrect, answers (see Steward 1936, 1940, 1941; cf., Aikens 1966b). Similar efforts in other areas of the continent have been briefly restrictive, but to a lesser degree, for example, the Mississippian divisions of Deuel (1935, 1937) or Ford's and Willey's (1941) burial- and temple-mound sequence in the Southeast.

The next most common type of classification, which is of greater usefulness, is the more abstract ordering involving, by the nature of its terminology, some awareness of culture change. Here again the terms often carry implications of *both* time and stage of development. Roberts (1937, 1939a) discarded the Pecos Conference divisions of Basketmaker I, II, III and Pueblo I, II, III, IV, V as the standard culture ladder of the Southwest substituting Basketmaker, Modified Basketmaker, Developmental, Classic, etc. This more flexible plan, by taking account of culture dynamics and acknowledging the development of Pueblo culture along "traditional" lines, recognizes the continuity of a basic cultural adaptation to the arid Southwest. It constitutes a denial of the arbitrary, segmented concept people inevitably derive from the rigid graphic charts which seem to say that "periods" show abrupt change from century to century. Roberts' scheme, although it did not become popular, more accurately describes the changes through time. Much later, Daifuku (1952) suggested a comparable and even more generalized scheme which was applicable to the entire Greater Southwest.

In the first successful article attempting the synthesis of then-available knowledge about the archeology of North America, Griffin (1946) avoided any global classifications; he correlated local culture names and types to arrive at a narrative of culture continuity and change.

In 1958, Willey and Phillips offered a synthesis of the prehistory of the entire New World. Their approach was to define *stages* of cultural development and to classify cultures according to stage. These "stages" could as well be called culture "levels." The terms selected to designate the stages are mixed in concept: Some are interpretive, while others are merely labels. In general outline, the stage sequence resembles the schemes by Roberts and Daifuku, with the important refinement that timespan is *not* imputed to any stage *qua* stage. Time is another dimension. The stages of Willey and Phillips are as follows: Lithic, Archaic, Formative, Classic, Postclassic; these stages will be utilized in later chapters as the major unifying classificatory device. The separate traditions that can be recognized in the stages will be described area by area.

Markedly different from the above is the Midwestern Taxonomic Method, credited largely to Will C. McKern, a system which has been applied to the Plains and over most of the East. The scheme is simple, representing another archeologic modification of a biologic system. Taking account of neither space nor time, it consists in grouping or clustering together those artifacts and trait complexes which appear to be very similar or identical. These clusters of very similar complexes are then compared on a slightly higher level of generality, and those which share a preponderance of traits are again grouped together. Thus, through several increasingly general groupings, the system recalls the biologic charts subsuming species under genera, subfamily, family, etc. The discrete single unit—a single level at a single site—was called the *component,* represented by the inventory of associated objects and traits recovered at any one given site. Of course, at a stratified site more than one component occurred. Components were compared, and were grouped into foci according to their degree of likeness. Each *focus* compared with others nearby was eventually grouped with similar ones into a *phase,* and so on, in increasingly broad and general groupings (McKern 1939).

The introduction of the McKern method led almost instantly to a useful classification of the hundreds of Midwestern sites which had been excavated and reported by then but which were uncontrolled by any system. It soon became evident that the sites of a focus occurred in a closely knit distribution and were probably contemporary. Phases, too, showed quite limited areal spread. At the same time, components of one and another focus were recognized in stratified situations, and a relative chronology was developed. What actually happened was that by ignoring time and space in its concentration upon mere sorting and grouping, the McKern classification brought both spatial and chronologic relationships into sharp relief. The success of the system was such that "focus" has now come to be synonymous with "local culture"; the other groupings have fallen into disuse. Through this scheme, the prehistory of about one-third of the continent was ordered and given meaning in less than a decade, an achievement which marks the McKern taxonomic system as the most important single contribution to method in American archeology. It is true that the system was attacked and criticized and resisted; equally often, it was misunderstood and misused. Often classification was conceived as an end in itself, or the method was applied beyond its usefulness. Even these abuses provided clarification in that the simple logic of the approach was useful even in poor applications. (In this volume the term "focus" will appear only as it is part of the name of a locally delineated complex, a common usage in Plains and Midwest literature.)

Although all the classifications discussed above are of extreme importance in the history of archeologic development, they are of more value to the regional specialist or the professional scholar than they are to the beginner. None fully serves the intent of this book, which is to tell a story as coherently as possible, using all and any available ordering devices which will help make the story clear. In general, the first controlling principle is chronology; the second is cultural likeness or typology. It is obvious that without the use of classifications developed by others, the present approach would not work; however, the classifications as such are not a primary problem in this study.

It is necessary to return to the ambitious synthesis of Willey and Phillips (1958) in order to define some of the terms which will be used later and to touch on other points they make. At the outset, I recommend that readers study early in their archeologic education the introductory section of Willey and Phillips, to say nothing of the material by Hole and Heizer (1965). Both books have excellent expositions of many items touched upon only lightly in this book, but I share many ideas with the four authors. Important differences of viewpoint will also be quite apparent. The remainder of the Willey and Phillips' book is not for novices but can be read with great profit after a little acquaintance with the data.

From that book let us first consider geographic units. The smallest is, of course, the *site*. This unit is the smallest the archeologist works with; its size is extremely variable. The *locality* is again variable, but means what we might call a community or local group. The *region* is viewed as likely to coincide with minor physiographic subdivisions where, at any given time, there is homogeneity of culture. The *area* is large, corresponding perhaps to the culture areas defined by the ethnographer. Willey and Phillips cautiously suggest that the *locality* may be equated with the *community*, while the *region* may be thought of as the *tribe;* this effort to give archeologic units some semblance of social reality was undertaken in order to bring archeologic units into some congruity with other anthropologic concepts as to what elements comprise significant social groupings.

Also of use to us are *horizon* and *tradition*. As seen elsewhere, *tradition* implies persistence through time. This can refer to all the traits of an entire culture or can be restricted to a single complex. Thus, one could speak of the Pueblo tradition, or of an agricultural tradition, or even of a shallow-bowl ceramic tradition. Tradition, then, is a vertical or chronologic concept. *Horizon*, on the other hand, is a spatial continuity of culture traits or complexes which have wide geographic distribution and are known (or believed) to have diffused rapidly over the space where they occur. The notion can be thought of as a horizontal-spatial one, implying contemporaneity; horizon marker traits are normally thought of as coeval, providing time links from one region to another over an area of cultural similarity. Thus, the term "tradition" recognizes the fact of regional cultural stability and persistence, while "horizon" is a practical tool enabling the student to spot close cultural relationships. The horizon markers provide chronologic fixes for developing regional and even areal culture sequences. Figure 1.3, modified from Willey and Phillips, presents their four most important notions.

Archeologic Techniques

At some stage it is necessary to describe how archeology is "done." The question of how is complicated by the fact that almost everyone is already convinced that the requirements are merely picks and shovels, strong backs, and a place to dig. Unfortunately, this is an oversimplification quite difficult to refute because fieldwork doesn't at first blush seem to require much

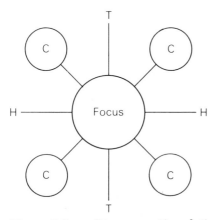

Figure 1.3   *Diagrammatic relationships of archeologic unit concepts: focus, component (C), horizon (HH), and tradition (TT). (Modified from Willey and Phillips 1958)*

beyond interest and leisure time. But fieldwork—the recovery of the artifacts and the noting of relationships—is of utmost and crucial importance because here the control of the information begins and ends. Conclusions are no more valid than the raw information upon which they rest; the data of archeology are recovered from the ground. It is correct, however, to think of fieldwork as being a series of quite simple techniques and procedures, neither difficult nor profound. It is the invisible background of guiding concepts, assumptions, and principles which the observer and recorder possesses as professional intellectual equipment that marks the difference between the collector of data and the antiquarian or mere collector of objects.

The intellectual frame within which proper fieldwork is done includes the concepts of typology, stratigraphy, and culture stage. Recognition of the importance of artifact association and of the need for a record of such associations is essential. An interest in culture history and a knowledge of cultural distribution are also required. Inherent in archeologic interpretation are the many borrowed concepts—for example, migration, diffusion, conquest, and displacement. As used by zoologists, these terms can only imply population shift—actual movement of living creatures. Taxonomic classification, implying genetic relationship, is also taken directly from the zoologists, as is the comparative method. All these have been given new twists and, in some cases, have been refined or extended by anthropologists. For example, the culture area (a geographic concept) is an idea which was given more precise meaning by anthropologists. Diffusion, too, can be seen in two forms—*direct*, meaning actual contact between two different groups, and *stimulus*, in which a new idea or a new technique or a new artifact is transmitted to a new setting verbally or by eyewitness accounts of a strange practice. In addition to the background specified above, the excavator, apparently rooting aimlessly in the ground, usually has specific questions about local or areal cultures and much ordered detail in his mind as he avidly searches for broken pottery and food scraps in long-abandoned midden heaps and crumbled houses.

In the popular mind the archeologist is widely misunderstood. In fact, there are several popular images of the archeologist, as Ascher (1960) discovered by analysis of thirty-four *Life* magazine articles. He finds four themes. The first has to do with discovery of sites; in *Life* this appears to be almost entirely a matter of chance, and everyone can do it. There is some truth in this view; of course, finds made during routine search by professionals do not get much publicity. The second theme is that of the expert; he is called in to give his opinion on something or to undertake a long task of restoration or interpretation. The third theme is that of archeologist-technician; here the time-consuming details of fieldwork sometimes get mentioned. The fourth theme is merely the superlative find and the clever archeologist who achieved the largest or the oldest or the cheapest. Ascher's main point is that the usual public view of the archeologist leaves out the all-important role of culture historian and the training this role requires, emphasizing the concern with objects and persistently depicting the archeologist as merely an expert technician. Small wonder that countless thousands of hobbyists and collectors work assiduously each weekend to find and destroy prehistoric sites. If they can recover objects, they believe themselves to be archeologists. Blame does not accrue exclusively to those whose thoughtless acts of vandalism are daily destroying our prehistoric resources. They do not know they are despoiling unique scientific documents when they destroy a site. Lack of education in conservation and the peculiarly American attitude toward public property, as well as an apathy toward historic or prehistoric treasures, explain the heedless destruction of these resources.

There are a few brilliant exceptions to the above generalization about public disinterest. The Folsom find was made by an untrained man who reported to scientifically competent authorities, as was the related Lindenmeier site. The now-famous Naco and Lehner mammoth finds (Haury, Antevs, and Lance 1953; Haury, Sayles, and Wasley 1959) were made by science-minded ranchers, who recognized the importance of their finds. The famous Midland skull was found by a pipeline welder. Thus, many amateur or weekend archeologists, by knowing the limitations of their training even while they understood the value of their finds, have served science well. At the same time, many amateurs are as competent in observation, as astute in inference, and as aware of scientific values as any professional. They are, in some areas, doing more work of high quality than are the established scholars. In several states there are archeologic societies which undertake large-scale digs, participate in salvage programs, and support publication programs and scientific conservation in every way. To such groups, the world of knowledge owes a tremendous debt because great advances have resulted from their dedication and labor.

The archeologist who directs and records a dig is usually a jack-of-several-trades. Routine archeologic recording requires skill in mapping and photography, a knowledge of earth and soils and their physical attributes, some administrative ability and judgment (Heizer 1958, 1960; Woolley 1960; Childe 1956), and endless patience coupled with a respect for detail. The actual fieldwork is done against a background of training which includes nearly everything touched on in this chapter. It all coalesces in the excavator's mind to form a framework of assumptions, concepts, attitudes, and skills which gives him a posture entirely different from that of the collector.

As he begins an excavation, the recorder accepts one or two conditions: The site is unique; no other is exactly like it. He is ignorant of its contents. Although he may have dug others of the same culture, this specific one is like no other. Ideally, he begins his work as if he were entirely ignorant, with no preconceptions as to what the new site will contain. Assuming ignorance of this particular deposit and taking every care to avoid anticipating that certain phenomena will be present encourages sharper observation and the discovery of subtleties of relationship which would otherwise be lost through a more complacent approach. Every site must be dug on its own terms. Unique in content, individual history, soils, and microgeographic incidents, the site dictates the procedures of its own destruction. And, of course, as he digs the site away, the field archeologist *does* destroy. Upon his astuteness and diligence in observation and recording rests the validity of his conclusions.

It is small wonder, then, that the first sparring with a site is conducted cautiously. The first steps are usually sample cuts—either pits sunk into random (or selected) spots both on the apparent site and off its limits or a test trench dug from the outer limits partway toward the center of the site. These tests reveal conditions such as the nature of the earth to be dealt with, the sequence of culturally relevant and/or natural soils, and many other details that help the digger to understand the site in part and to plan his attack upon it. The test trenches or pits are often called "exploratory," a term neatly expressing their purpose and value. The systematic excavation operation, based on the findings

of the explorations, can be done in several ways. Manuals of procedures are legion (for example, Heizer 1958; Gorenstein 1965), and many special techniques exist (Griffin 1951). All such books are good, but none can possibly meet and cover all the exigencies of every problem the digger meets.

After the first ideas about the contents of a site are gained from exploration, usually the next step is to remove, by careful cutting, the several layers of the site one at a time over a large area of the site, or even over all of it. The cutting away is usually begun carefully at the edge of one of the exploration cuts. "Carefully" does not necessarily mean, either slowly or with tiny tools. Obviously, a 2-foot thick layer of sterile topsoil overlying an ancient campsite could be removed with a bulldozer if "care" were taken to stop before the layer containing the prehistoric data were reached. In fact, a cardinal rule is that one always uses the coarsest tools that will do the work. That is, one does not use shovels if a bulldozer can safely be used, nor a trowel if a shovel will do the trick, and so on. The reasons for this are practical: Archeology is slow at best; any steps which can accelerate the accumulation of data save priceless time for analysis or other excavation. Another reason is the overriding problem of funds. Archeology is increasingly done by hired crews; time wasted on overcautious procedures is translatable into wasted money with reduced research findings per dollar. This does not mean that 2 man-days spent in laboriously tracing the edge of an earthen house floor with a trowel and brush are wasted or that removing fill over a fragile bone artifact grain by grain is improper. On the other hand, to scrape away a large trash heap with a whisk broom or trowel may be senseless rote. What is being argued here is that common sense—not exaggerated meticulousness—is an important ingredient in archeologic work. No procedure, whether "coarse" or "fine," should be followed unless its use is appropriate to the situation and unless it is focused on gaining some specific information. Wendorf (1962) and Wasley (1961) have made some cogent observations about technique, as has Jennings (1957, 1966b).

In some situations, the peeling of layers from a large area is inappropriate or impractical. The removal of a large mound and the cleaning of a large complex of crumbled stone architecture are examples. Here the common procedure is to cut thin slices vertically from top to bottom of the cultural fill. This operation has the primary advantage of speed; at the same time, materials can be readily segregated as to layers, and there is no loss of stratigraphic data. In this technique, horizontal relationships can be kept clear by means of separate maps for every level. The major disadvantage is that one never sees the structural features or other phenomena of an entire occupational level and their associational contexts at one time. The photographic record is thus incomplete; one relies entirely on maps and sketches for the spatial data. Most excavators combine these two basic horizontal and vertical cutting procedures and their many variations on every job, as dictated by the individual site and the data to be recovered.

There is no need to attempt to develop a universal field manual here, even if such a thing were possible. The kinds of sites in the world are legion, and their combinations are numerous. The American archeologist recognizes burial and temple mounds, villages and campsites, cemeteries, refuse or midden heaps, trash pits, tombs, cave deposits, animal kills, irrigation systems, masonry and adobe structures, pit houses, earth lodges, and other situations, as archeologic sites. Each of these requires its own special procedures and precautions. It is easier to dig some

purposeful construction, such as a house or tomb or an earthen mound, than to uncover the randomly accumulated midden, or trash, or occupational deposit because a purposeful construction reveals some system of logic or a pattern of behavior. Its features can to some extent be anticipated and watched for. The random accumulation, however, reveals no plan at all; all relationships *may* be fortuitous, but they can never be assumed to be so in *advance*. The random deposit actually requires more vigilance on the part of the excavator; at the same time, this vigilance is less likely to be rewarded. From the above it is easy to see that archeology is not as simple as the "shovel-and-strong-back" school would have it. On the contrary, fieldwork properly done is slow, tedious, and demanding—to be performed only by the trained and patient man.

Although the archeologist is the superordinate technician in the field, his final report often involves the services of many technicians and scholars from other disciplines. The excellent book, *Science in Archaeology* (Brothwell and Higgs 1963), exemplifies the range of ancillary studies undertaken to enrich archeologic knowledge. The volume contains fifty-five articles by scientists in *other* fields explaining their roles in sharpening anthropologic analysis. The articles do not deal with archeology as such at all but with contributions from nonanthropologists. The authors include dendrochronologists, mammalogists, botanists, metallurgists, radiologists, serologists, and other exotic specialists (see also Jennings and Sharrock 1965; Osborne et al. 1965). Such cooperation is becoming more common as the years pass, with the result that the archeologists must collect more varied data and solicit a wider spectrum of talent during analysis and reporting (W. W. Taylor 1948, 1957). More importantly, these ancillary studies sharpen the perceptions of the excavators and permit subtler inferences; as a result, archeologic conclusions are becoming more precise and probably more valid.

Those thousands of Americans who are interested in prehistory and who wish to see the full story of America's past uncovered should by all means do fieldwork and enjoy their interest. However, they should also align themselves with some organization which has the same educational goals and add their labors and influence in an effective way to the pursuit of this knowledge. Most state archeologic societies emphasize survey—the search for locations—and, in cooperation with state institutions or agencies, file their records and collections in a central place where they are available to all scholars. When sites reported by weekend archeologists are dug by trained men, the local groups often participate and receive training along with the enjoyment of discovery. Cooperation with scholarly institutions means that the data will be preserved and added to the stream of scholarship. Even those persons lacking any great personal interest who chance upon a location are urged to communicate the details of their find to their local university, college, or museum, so that skilled and knowledgeable scholars can take over—to the benefit of all. Americans are not necessarily deliberately destructive of the relics of past days. They are merely unaware of the unique value each site has, and they have not realized that this resource, too, is irreplaceable. The average hobbyist is even ignorant of the several acts—both Federal and state—which provide that the despoliation of antiquities is a felony and punishable by law. It is a monument to Federal apathy that few convictions have been obtained under the 1906 Antiquities Law, although thousands of sites on Federal land have been utterly destroyed. On private lands, destruction has been comparable because public education

about the scientific value of these ancient treasures has been neglected. One hopes that conscientious citizens and scholars can together capture and preserve adequate knowledge before the sites are all destroyed. The race is a close one.

Emergency Archeology

Site destruction comes about in other ways than through deliberate pot hunting, because each new reservoir, highway, airport, pipeline, or subdivision results in tragic losses (Brew 1961; Wendorf 1962). Since 1945, construction in the United States has been so massive that the problem of salvaging prehistoric data thrown into jeopardy by civilization's march has led to a new concept—emergency archeology. This involves a careful survey of the threatened zones and the subsequent excavation of sample sites of each cultural stage represented. The increments to knowledge have been spectacular, and, in some instances, the regional and even areal sequences have been dramatically extended or altered. Some idea of the magnitude of the salvage work is suggested by these figures: Between 1950 and 1960, there were reported in *American Antiquity* alone a total of 250 salvage projects involving 65 institutions. Some were as simple as trenching a proposed new access roadway into an airport. Others involved survey and excavation over a reservoir location 200 miles long on a major river where hundreds of sites were found. By 1960 an informed estimate of Federal salvage costs for emergency archeology exceeded 4 million dollars, to say nothing of private institutional costs and grants from philanthropic organizations. An equal amount was probably spent in the 5 years to 1965, in view of greatly increased road and reservoir construction. One well-known example of vast gain in scientific knowledge resulted from emergency archeology in the Glen Canyon of the Colorado River, where Lake Powell was created in southern Utah. This lake flooded a 186-mile length of the river where some 1,600 archeologic sites were discovered and sampled ahead of inundation. Prior to the emergency work there had been no scientific reports from the region (Jennings 1966b).

Ethnography

Before leaving the matter of interpretation, it is necessary to consider the importance of ethnographic analogies in archeologic detective work. This use of ethnologic knowledge is quite understandable, simple, and proper. It merely needs to be made explicit. In any use of ethnographic analogy, typology is implicit because form is involved; but there is the additional notion that *shared* form implies *similar* function. Thus, when an archeologist finds a clay artifact with a bowl and stem and the bowl is caked with carbon, he has no hesitancy in calling it a pipe. A centrally pierced disc of shell or shiny stone, ½ inch in diameter and wafer-thin is called a bead, and no one questions this. A short, sharp triangle of chipped stone set in a bone or wooden handle is called a knife, and no one doubts. This is so because ethnologic reports contain descriptions of comparable objects used by primitive peoples under direct observation by missionaries, explorers, traders, or scholars. Occasionally, to be sure, the names given artifacts may be in error, but most scholars are content to rest their inferences about culture and their artifacts on ethnographic analogy. In short, a spade is still a spade for most of us. Eggan (1952) has written a classic analysis of the importance of ethnographic analogs for archeologic interpretation.

Historical Sketch

The beginnings of American archeologic study are reasonably clear. However, like most disciplines now associated with universities or colleges and practiced by trained professionals, the field became a specialty over a period of many years and derives its present status from a series of quite fortuitous events, through the labors of a number of American scholars who did not think of themselves as archeologists. In fact, American archeology was intertwined from the outset with the rest of American anthropology as the entire field developed. This adequately explains the fortunate fact that American prehistorians are uniformly trained in general anthropology. Perhaps the paramount reason for this early and continued inclusion of archeology as a special study within the larger field of anthropology is that all early study of man in the New World was focused on the American red man, although for a time the relationship of the ancient objects and monuments to the aboriginals was far from clear.

A strong interest in antiquities existed in North America before 1800. This will surprise some readers because Americans usually think of their intellectual heritage as entirely European-derived. This is not to deny the first American antiquaries their awareness of European scholarship; but as it happened, early American archeologists also knew living Indians. Indian customs, languages, and homelands were familiar to Americans, whereas Europeans had to build a discipline intellectually from scratch, as it were. At best, their knowledge was secondhand. The Americans could and did observe and participate in non- or precivilized behavior. And the founders of American anthropology did just this. The best account of the beginnings of the study of man in the New World is that of Hallowell (1960).

The American interest in antiquities as such predated by several decades any systematic knowledge of geology or paleontology. Thomas Jefferson himself, one of the important figures in early American scholarship, excavated an Indian mound and reported his findings (Heizer 1960; Greene 1959). The time was 1784. Moreover, Jefferson correctly believed that he was excavating an Indian burial site; it was an undertaking aimed at verifying local rumors about the aboriginal purpose of these mounds. However, Jefferson's belief was not shared by others; this was because the intense interest in the mounds, other antiquities, and their authors was not rooted in any curiosity about the American Indian. At the time (the eighteenth century), the earthen structures and the objects discovered were ascribed to the vanished predecessors of the Indians. This belief in a mysteriously vanished race resulted partly from the notion that the Indian was not highly civilized and was incapable of high achievement of any sort and partly from an awareness of the fact that civilizations did fall, to be followed by others. Under the weight of a myth of lost peoples, a theme much labored by popular writers, American archeology moved generally into the doldrums of romance and wild imaginings from Jefferson's time until the late nineteenth century. The myth, of course, had no basis in the evidence of the antiquities themselves or even in the current knowledge of Indian life and custom.

Despite the myth, scattered scholars persisted in gathering information. William Bartram, the famous botanist, recorded scrupulously accurate observations which contributed to both the archeology and the ethnology of the Southeast. The Revolutionary general, Rufus Putnam, had mapped the Marietta, Ohio, earthworks as early as 1788, according to Shetrone (1930). Even though he embraced the lost-race idea, Caleb Atwater in 1820 produced good descriptive material (and an explanatory hypothesis) about antiquities of Ohio and adjacent states. Atwater's work was published by the American Antiquarian Society, which was founded in 1812. Von Humboldt's views on the Mexican prehistoric monuments apparently were known to Atwater.

Whatever the motivation, intense if uninformed interest in the monuments of lost peoples was perhaps at its strongest in America between 1800 and 1860. Expressive of this interest, as well as stimulated by it, were two classic accounts: Stephens' *Incidents of Travel in Yucatán* (1843) and Squier's and Davis' (1848) study of the Mississippi and Ohio valleys. Both are still consulted today. Their authors, in turn, had been stimulated by the equally famous works of Alexander Von Humboldt and J. F. de Waldeck dealing with Mexico. Hallowell calls the Stephens book "an archeological revelation." By means of lucid description, coupled with magnificent illustrations by Frederick Catherwood, it brought the architecture of the Maya to worldwide notice, even though the builders were not then identified as Mayan. (No relationship to Egypt was claimed for the Yucatán monuments at this stage of study, however.)

The efforts of Squier and Davis were of comparable importance. These two men— a newspaperman and a physician, respectively—explored and mapped archeologic sites all over the Middle West. Their work was done in the highest scientific tradition, being concerned with the collection of data, the ordering of these data, and the drawing of tentative comparisons and conclusions. Squier correctly ascribed the ruins to the American Indian.

Despite the above evidence collected by careful scholars before 1850, nearly forty more years passed before it was generally understood that the antiquities of the Americas should properly be credited to the ancestors of the present-day Indians. Carpenter (1950) has interesting comments on the compelling religious reasons for the strength and longevity of the belief in ancient vanished races. He links the low opinion of the American Indians' cultural status which prevailed in the nineteenth century with the doctrine of original sin and man's degeneration from an earlier Golden Age. The concept of degeneration, of course, ran counter to the views of popular writers. For example, Jean-Jacques Rousseau sang of the Noble Savage living a perfect and untroubled life, thus displaying an ignorance equal to that of the exponents of brutish degeneration and vanished glories.

After 1880, government scientists in the Smithsonian Institution—Cyrus Thomas, James Stevenson, Gerard Fowke, William H. Holmes, Charles Rau—as well as museum-connected scholars like Frederic W. Putnam of Harvard, initiated the modern systematic study of American prehistory, unplagued by any doubt that the American remains were of Indian origin. True, their ascription of ruins to this or that modern tribe were, and remain, unproved, but at least their work with the material was not hampered by the myth of vanished giants and lost civilizations. Thomas' huge report of a decade of mound exploration by the Bureau of American Ethnology can be thought of as marking the birth of modern American archeology. The famous Wesley Powell's masterly analysis of the problem of vanished races served as an introduction to Thomas' volume. Together they corrected the misconception as to the relationship of American antiquities to American Indians. In their work urgent problems of research are listed. Raw data are also included. Thomas' findings, although less thoroughly reported than is now the custom, have been consulted and utilized by every succeeding generation of scholars.

Even with the breakthrough achieved by Smithsonian scholars, there was still nothing systematic about the pursuit of archeologic knowledge. What these men really did, perhaps, was to clear a part of the arena for action, action which had already begun in the Middle West and which was growing very strong in the Southwest. The men whose names are associated with this first phase of "modern" archeology are still personally remembered by now-senior scholars. In outlook and aims, however, American study of prehistory was still in the antiquarian stage over most of the continent. Men of that era were essentially collectors until about 1910 or a trifle later. In the Southwest, the first remembered scholars are Adolph F. A. Bandelier, Frank H. Cushing, J. Walter Fewkes, William H. Holmes, Byron Cummings, Edgar L. Hewett, and G. Nordenskiöld. All, energetically but haphazardly, roamed the (then) Western territories and recovered enormous quantities of material in a score of unorganized exploration and collecting trips. These men should not be condemned as unscholarly, even though they do not appear to have had the skills of observation, recording, and scientific synthesis. Rather, they should be credited with providing great stimulus for general appreciation of American prehistory and for having saved vast collections of priceless objects, objects that eventually came to tell part of the story of the Southwestern cultures.

Between 1890 and 1910 or even 1920, the names of important collectors from other parts of North America include Warren K. Moorehead in the Northeastern states, Clarence B. Moore along the Southeastern rivers and coastal waters, Henry Shetrone in the Ohio Valley, William H. Holmes in the East and Southeastern states. All these men thought themselves to be archeologists, but none had formal anthropologic training because there was no place to get such training. The first advanced degree in anthropology in America was awarded by Franz Boas to A. F. Chamberlain from Clark University in 1892. The second was from Harvard by F. W. Putnam to Roland B. Dixon in 1900. Holmes's early experience was in geology; Bandelier was a self-taught student of the primitives; Cummings was a classicist and student of language.

Not to be overlooked for his tremendous influence in American archeology is Aleš Hrdlička, a Bohemian physician who came into the U.S. National Museum in 1898. Hrdlička's contributions are many, but his authoritarian and negative stance on matters of early man—that is, an American population earlier than the historic Indian —was so rigorous and so ably defended that for three decades American scholars gave no serious thought to the possibility that the occupancy of the Americas was anything but recent—no deeper than 2,000 to 3,000 years in time. In this denial of glacial man he was joined by Holmes. Although, prior to 1900, search for evidence of extinct animals in association with man was common enough (see Gross re Koch 1951), these studies languished until about 1930 (see pages 53ff). The Eastern scholars, not suspecting that man had been on the continent since glacial times, gathered materials in a sort of chronologic and cultural vacuum. No great notice was taken of what are now known to have been important differences in mound construction, ceramics, stonework, and other phenomena including stratified remains. Everything was merely "old." The past was flat, like a theater backdrop, and no sequence of cultures was postulated, although, as Griffin (1959) points out, areal differences in cultural remains were recognized.

Somewhat different conditions prevailed in the Southwest. By 1916, Alfred L. Kroeber and Leslie Spier both noted differences in ceramics from ruin to ruin in the Zuñi country and suggested that they pointed to differences in age. Even earlier,

Nels C. Nelson had demonstrated marked differences in the pottery from a deep trash deposit near Santa Fe (Galisteo), New Mexico. The lowest levels containing sherds showed mostly glazed pieces, while the upper, later layers contained unglazed fragments. These clues to culture sequence and change provided by ceramics set a pattern of analysis still dominant in the Southwest, a pattern focusing attention on minor crafts and small antiquities. Alfred V. Kidder, also digging in the Southwest, along with Samuel J. Guernsey verified the presence of the prepottery Basketmakers (so designated by the famous Wetherill ranch family that collected and sold antiquities from the Four Corners area of Colorado, Utah, Arizona, and New Mexico from about 1890 onward). Thus we can see that the Southwestern scholars were well aware of time depth and regional culture differences long before even the likelihood of a comparably deep time scale was suspected for the Eastern remains. Kidder's *An Introduction to the Study of Southwestern Archaeology* (1924) was a summary of what was then known, and its publication closed an era. In it he systematically told what was known about each region. Thus, he identified the geographic provinces where information was lacking and, by so doing, introduced the "problem-oriented" phase of Southwestern study. Contributors to this next phase were Frank H. H. Roberts, Jr., Emil W. Haury, Harold S. Gladwin, E. B. Sayles, Earl H. Morris, John O. Brew, Erik K. Reed, and scores of others. Through their efforts, the Mogollon variant of Pueblo and the entire Hohokam sequence came to be understood, along with refinements of knowledge in the Four Corners and Rio Grande areas, where Kidder's interests lay.

All the Southwestern work after 1927 profited from the Pecos Conference, convened by Kidder, where a tentative list of traits or trait complexes was drawn up for eight sequential stages of Pueblo culture. These began with a logically necessary, but not defined, Basketmaker I stage, followed by Basketmaker II and III, the latter possessing agriculture, pottery, and pit house architecture. Then the Pueblo I, II, III, IV, and V stages were defined. This classification became almost a straitjacket as the tentative notions about stages began to be treated both as rigid yardsticks for identification of new collections and as time periods. The same conference estimated the timespan covered by these stages to be about 4,000 years, that is, reaching back to perhaps 2000 B.C. At that time, all authorities agreed that the Pueblo cultures of the Southwest were, in addition to having begun to develop before the Christian era, probably the oldest of all North American cultures. Even during the gathering of the scholars at Pecos, an important development was in the making —an event which presaged developments in archeology in the latter third of the twentieth century. This was the work of the astronomer Andrew E. Douglass, who was studying tree-rings to learn more about past weather to test a theory about sunspots and weather cycles. A less likely place to turn for an absolute archeologic time scale cannot be imagined. Nonetheless, in 1929 a series of wooden roof beams from Pueblo Bonito collected by Neil M. Judd yielded, as had been hoped, a sequence of rings which overlapped with a short tree-ring calendar built up from rings of living trees and of beams from old historic buildings in the Southwest. By thus extending the ring count deeper into the past, an accurate calendar was established. Soon it was clear that most Southwestern prehistory fell within the Christian era, and the Pueblo's time there was cut in half. Perhaps the important point is less that the calendar came to exist, but that another facet of American study of prehistory was established: The yeoman service of another discipline was enlisted to help unravel the mysteries of man upon

the continent. Turning to experts continued to mark the progress of knowledge from this time on, as evidenced by the contributions of Kirk Bryan, the geologist, and Ernst Antevs, a climatologist and geologist, during the 1930s, followed by an increasing corps of specialists in the period after 1945.

In entering the phase of ordering data, in developing some larger scheme of reference, and in doing extensive comparative work, the scholars in the East and Middle West lagged behind the Southwesterners. The reasons for this lag are various. The Eastern scholars were not trained anthropologists; their interests were more antiquarian than cultural. Furthermore, there were few strong anthropology departments in the colleges and universities, and the few that were chanced to be committed to other fields: for example, Harvard's interest in the Southwest or Columbia's concern with the Northwest coast tribes.

The modern era of archeology so far as the Middle West and East are concerned can be credited to two or three men— Carl Guthe (of the University of Michigan), Fay-Cooper Cole (at the University of Chicago), and Will C. McKern (of the Milwaukee Public Museum). Partially (I have always thought) because of Hrdlička's merciless exposure of careless field observation, all these men saw a need for greater precision in fieldwork and greater detail in the records kept. While the conferees gathered at Pecos in 1927, that same summer Cole called a field conference in Jo Davies County (Illinois), and systematic procedures for mound excavation were agreed upon. By 1930 a handbook had been prepared, setting out what became standard procedures for mound excavation for several years. Refinements and improvements followed, and by 1960 American field techniques had become quite good. Cole's championship of refined field procedures was but one aspect of the series of summer field schools he initiated in 1927 in Fulton County, Illinois. Over about a ten-year period, during which several students received training each year, a series of stratified sites where two or more cultures were represented were dug and *recognized as stratified*. By carefully digging selected sites where the surface remains showed the prospect of variation from nearby sites, Cole developed a culture sequence for a small geographic region in Illinois. This was the first important scientific, problem-oriented, exploratory work done in the East. At the same time, Samuel A. Barrett, followed by McKern, both of the Milwaukee Public Museum, were gathering detailed data from Wisconsin mounds.

But mere data are not enough. They must be ordered or arranged according to some scheme, preferably one which allows wide comparison and detection of similarities or differences in the cultural traits noted in excavation from site to site. McKern pioneered in producing just such a system in 1933. Its almost instant acceptance by Cole and his students, as well as by some other workers in adjacent areas, changed Eastern archeology from antiquarianism to scientific prehistory in only two or three years. It became clear at once that the archeology of the East had great time depth, that there were extreme culture changes in some places, and that the problems of relating one stage to another were far more complex than in the Southwest. Progress in classification and great increases in data came about as the CWA, WPA, and other Depression-spawned agencies of the 1930s diverted manpower to archeology through make-work programs. Thus, by 1946 James B. Griffin attempted a synthesis of then-available knowledge about the entire Eastern United States. This able summary led others to try their hand: Krieger in 1953, Willey and Phillips in 1955. To these can now be added Willey's (1966) fine

synthesis of the prehistory of the Americas, one volume dealing with South America, one with North and Central America.

Since 1945, archeologic field research has gone ahead at an even faster rate, faster than synthesis can keep up with. This surge results almost entirely from the hundreds of emergency jobs of salvaging material threatened by the reservoirs created by big dams all over the North American continent—in Mexico, the United States, and Canada. These dams have created vast lakes in many states. By virtue of congressional recognition of the tragic losses to scholarship in many fields, an army of archeologists has been recovering samples of every prehistoric culture represented in the reservoir areas over much of the United States. The need to salvage a sample of everything has resulted in additions to knowledge exceeding all expectation. Many cultures are now known to have had wider distribution than was thought. Many sections of the continent are now represented by well-controlled information, where in 1950 nothing at all of the prehistory had been available to science. Even where scattered data had existed, intensive work over a restricted area has refined and revised older ideas based on skimpier work. For example, Alexander Lindsay, working in Arizona on the Glen Canyon emergency program, reported more Kayenta (Arizona) sites than all the earlier scholars from Bandelier onward combined. Comparable examples can be adduced in most archeologic provinces. Perhaps one reason these emergency projects have added so spectacularly to knowledge is because they are often located in nonromantic settings. Frequently the objects recovered are few and drab and would never have lured the antiquary-art lover because most collectors prefer their loot to be gaudy. Specimens from the Desert West or the Plains or the Northeast coast would rarely inflame an aesthete's heart. But through emergency action, many such areas are now well known. J. O. Brew and W. Raymond Wood, among others, have made more detailed evaluations of this aspect of salvage work, as has Jennings (1966b).

Guthe (1952) has written a careful history of American archeology covering the period from 1900 to 1950. In it he lists scores of productive local scholars and outlines the increase in public interest, the growth of state archeologic societies, the addition of anthropology departments, and the inauguration of archeologic research by some of these. One major event was the organizing of the Society for American Archaeology in 1934. The society's house organ, *American Antiquity*, became the journal of American prehistory. (Probably one-third of all the citations in this book come from *American Antiquity*.) Guthe also emphasizes the role the several regional conferences have had in accelerating progress in establishing regional understanding. Additional historical notes, differing in interpretation from this account, are to be found in Griffin's (1959) review of the Midwest and W. W. Taylor's (1948, 1954) and McGregor's (1965) material on the Southwest. [Since the above section was written, the best historical review yet to appear has been offered by Wilmsen (1965). Done with great care, this detailed treatment charts the development of trends in both European and American thought about New World prehistory and traces the influence of American and European ideas on each other from the moment of discovery to the present. In general, his account supports the foregoing brief sketch but amplifies it in many important ways, citing a long list of sources in several fields of learning. Wilmsen should by all means be consulted by those interested in the history of ideas.]

Thus, three major phases or eras in the history of American archeology can

readily be isolated. At first, the interest seems to have emphasized antiquarianism within a confused context of mystery and romance but with the artifacts themselves being the focus of interest. The second phase, one of extensive, even systematic collection including excavations, was more correctly focused in that the mystery of authorship was removed and the modern Indian was assumed to have local ancestors. When sufficient data were at hand, study shifted to ordering, classifying, and establishing areal and chronologic ranges for the several recognized cultures.

Finally, in the 1940s broad, areal—even continental—syntheses began to be possible. This book is but another attempt to move one step closer to an understanding of the ebb and flow of human history in the Western Hemisphere. That it is possible even to attempt such an undertaking is testimony to all who have contributed over the two centuries to the available data.

Old World versus New World Archeology

It seems proper to remark that students of American prehistory face a much easier interpretive task than their Old World counterparts. For example, the problem of man's biologic evolution, inextricable from his culture history, does not intrude. Man was fully *sapiens* when he entered the New World. Similarly, he had about completed his slow mastery of stone technology and had learned to live wherever there was available game. He was the dominant species, a predator, from the tip of Africa to the Siberian tundra, and the transition to full exploitation of plant as well as animal resources had begun in the Mesolithic cultures of the Near East in Iraq, Iran, and Palestine. Thus, the deep concern of Eurasian and African scholars with glacial ice and putative pluvials over 2 million years of time arouses no sympathy in Americanist hearts, although the terminal vagaries of the American Pleistocene ice and the climatic oscillations of the Recent bring special trials of their own. Debate about the how and where of first domestication of animals does not occur among Americans, although study of the domestication of indigenous American plants is continuous.

In another important way, the Americanist has a tremendous interpretive advantage in the centuries-old accumulation of ethnographic knowledge of American Indians. From explorers' journals, official reports, missionary *relaciónes,* romantic accounts by travelers, as well as hundreds of scientific ethnologic studies, the American prehistorian can read detailed accounts of the functioning of some historic analog for every culture stage or local substage now known. Possible exceptions in this catalog are the Big Game Hunters, who pursued the mammoth (although the hunters of Tierra del Fuego may approximate the ancient Big Game way of life), and the wealthy Hopewellian priests of the Middle West who lived before the time

of Christ. Without pyramiding examples, one can mention the late woodland subsistence farmers of the East coast who befriended the European immigrants, and the palisaded towns and art-embellished temples of the comfortable Creeks and Natchez of the Southeast as reported by de Soto which preserved the outlines of the Mississippian culture. The farmers of the Plains were found by Lewis and Clark all up and down the Missouri River, while the Archaic stage tribes of the Great Basin, as well as the Southwestern Pueblos and the prestige-burdened Northwest coast tribes, can be studied even today, as can the Eskimo. Conversely, specialists in Middle and South America can readily describe a series of going societies from the records of the Conquest, as these enrich and fill out the archeologic record.

For interpreting the Neolithic, especially the Late Neolithic, the Old World scholars, of course, do have available the millions in Europe, Asia, and Africa who still use Neolithic tools, crops, and technologies and who exhibit social behavior which developed millennia ago. But this must be small solace as they view the stony rubbish of the Paleolithic.

2
Peopling the New World

With the perspective of Chapter 1 behind us, we can turn to the fascinating details of man's conquest of the New World. The first step, if one is to proceed with logic, is to set the stage for the entry. This necessitates an excursion into geology and theories of climate, an assessment of the food resources, and a general statement of other relevant environmental circumstances.

Man is not indigenous to the Americas. His evolutionary development occurred in the Old World, and he entered the Western Hemisphere long after the evolutionary process yielded *Homo sapiens*, between 20,000 and 50,000 years ago, and entered the New World as a generalized physical type resembling no modern group very closely. We think that modern types developed quite recently. When and under what conditions the entry was effected is the concern of this chapter.

Environment

The first factor of several to be recognized is that for man there are literally two environments. One is the natural setting itself, the combination of land, species, and climate as these exist. The second environment is that insulating fabric or blanket of material objects, beliefs, and behavior called culture that man interposes between himself and the world of nature. Because man can and does actively interest himself in modifying the natural setting, his environment is always a blend of natural and cultural elements. Man could not have coped with the American natural setting until his cultural achievements included gear for survival in the crippling rigor of the Arctic. This level had been achieved by 50,000 B.C. and can therefore be taken for granted here. We can go on to the next factor which is, in a sense, a complementary one. What was the environment beyond the protecting cultural one? Here we turn to geologic and climatic conditions.

Man is a product of the Pleistocene geologic epoch, commonly called the Ice Age, a term that is known and meaningful to everyone. Present evidence is that vast ice sheets partially covered the northern areas of both North America and Eurasia several times during this period. The ice was more extensive in North America than anywhere else on the globe. Comparable ice fields still exist in Greenland and in Antarctica. The glaciers formed in northern latitudes (for reasons not yet fully understood) and continued to grow and advance slowly southward for thousands upon thousands of years. The ice sheets, estimated to have been a mile deep at maximum, locked up thousands of cubic miles of water, thereby lowering world ocean levels by as much as 1,000 feet according to some estimates. (Most authorities suggest a lowering of lesser magnitude, but no estimate runs less than 300 feet.) Thus, at the time of maximum glacial extent, the shape of the total visible land area would have differed greatly from modern times, particularly where the wide, shallow continental shelves were expanded. More is known about the Wisconsin advance and its several lobes and oscillations because it was the latest. Less is known of the preceding Nebraskan,

Kansan, and Illinoian advances because each sheet, as it expanded and flowed southward, carried earth and stones and also planed the surface ahead of it, erasing some of the traces of previous ice masses. Figure 2.1 shows the increase in the North American landmass that would have resulted from lowered sea level during the maximum extent of the second major Wisconsin glaciation about 18,000 to 20,000 years ago. Of particular interest is the broad land connection with Asia and the important fact that central and northwest Alaska was never covered by ice.

The Wisconsin sheet is known to have had two major advance-retreat cycles. These are memorialized among other things by ridges of earth called *terminal moraines* that mark the extreme edges of the advance. In these moraines there are boulders quarried by the ice and transported hundreds of miles from the point of origin. Sometimes these moraines overlap and merge to show different periods of advance; *drumlins* are long lateral ridges deposited by the ice, showing different directions of ice movement. The Missouri River bluffs, on the left or east bank in the Dakotas, record the farthest advance of the Wisconsin sheet in this area; in part, the Missouri River is the drainage channel carved by the glacial meltwater.

The story of man in the Americas is probably confined to the last half or even one-third of the Wisconsin period. The first lobes or advances, called Iowan and Tazewell, were followed by a period of complete or near-complete disappearance of ice. This ice-free period, called the Tazewell-Cary, is estimated to have ended at about 25,000 years ago, after which the Cary lobe began to form. As Figure 2.1 shows, the outlines of North America and Asian continental limits were markedly changed during maximum glaciations. The major change was that the two continents blended into one connected landmass. Where the Bering Strait now exists there

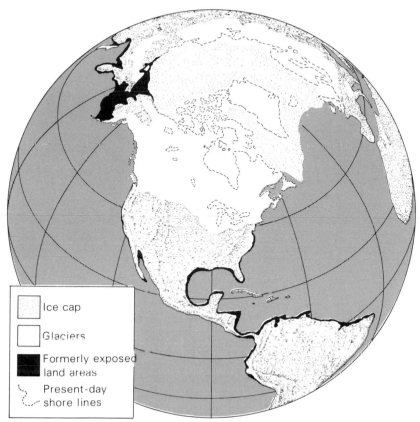

Ice cap

Glaciers

Formerly exposed land areas

Present-day shore lines

Figure 2.1   *Extension of North American shorelines resulting from lowered seas during the second major Wisconsin glaciation. Note land "bridge" across the Bering Strait. (Modified from Haag 1962)*

was a broad land called Beringia some 1,000 miles wide when ice sheets were at maximum size. Thus, there existed no physiographic barrier to movement of any species in either direction. Biologists have long known that the horse and the camel evolved in the Americas and migrated westward, whereas the elephant and the deer (including elk and moose) are Eurasiatic and entered the Americas in an eastward migration. The point is that the broad land bridge was open toll-free many times before and during the Pleistocene. As glaciers melted and waters returned to the sea, the bridge would be narrowed and would finally disappear, reforming as the ice built up again.

As mentioned earlier, man's arrival in North America as *Homo sapiens* means the event must be restricted to the last 50,000 years or less, to the last part of the Wisconsin Ice Age. During the maximum of the Tazewell-Cary interval at 40,000 to 50,000 years ago when the glacial ice was all, or nearly all, gone, the land bridge would have been narrow or nonexistent. So, the first entry of man could only have been effected by scattered individuals or bands during the onset of the Cary sub stage of the Wisconsin period or any time thereafter (Hopkins 1959; Byers 1957; see also Flint 1957; Haag 1962; Chard 1960). This concept is particularly easy to understand if one views the globe from the

Figure 2.2   Pleistocene fauna associated with an arctic environment. A, caribou; B, musk-ox; C, bison; D, mammoth.

North Pole after penciling in a Bering Strait land bridge. More than once in world history a traveler walking east from Siberia could have reached America without realizing it. (In none of the above has account been taken of the frequent crustal upwarping and other tectonic movements which have occurred in the Bering area.)

A third factor to be considered is the climate and resources of Asia, the Beringia bridge, and North America under glacial conditions. Glacial ages are believed to have profoundly affected world climate. Of course, even though the matter can only be studied indirectly, many lines of evidence exist. Such things as fossil pollen, buried timber, the physical properties and chemical content of the earth and soils, the mammalian fossils, and such physiographic elements as old streambeds, ponds, or bogs and the like, all contribute clues to past climates. There is general agreement that the primary effect of the ice sheets and the attendant cold air masses was to push the normal Northern Hemisphere storm, that is, moisture,

paths southward by several degrees of latitude and that the moisture and temperature patterns were drastically different from modern times. The cold air flow from the ice, as it met the warmer, moisture-laden winds from the west or south, probably caused an almost perpetual cold front parallel to the ice edge, as well as greater-than-present precipitation for hundreds of miles to the south. The many fossil lakes of the now-arid Great Basin are seen as evidence of pluvial conditions accompanying the stronger glacial advances. Aside from wet conditions where there is now aridity, the climate nearer the ice would have been chill and damp and often overcast, with a short growing season and limited sunlight. Such climate usually results in a treeless tundra vegetation; streams, lakes, and bogs would have been common as is true of parts of Canada and Alaska today. The fauna associated with the tundra were the mammoth, reindeer (called caribou in America), musk-ox, bison, and many smaller species (Figure 2.2). Tundra-dwelling species oc-

cur in both Asia and America. The environment can be recognized as one rich and attractive to hunters. It would have beckoned to wandering bands as man slowly spread over the Old World. There was probably no great population pressure, although some scholars have argued that there was. It is possible that man was not even consciously exploring or attempting conquest of new lands. More likely, normal hunting pursuits and a slow drifting with game herds opened the Americas to settlement, at a time and at a culture stage no earlier than the terminal Mousterian or Middle Paleolithic of Eurasia. Eiseley's (1955) description of the peopling of the Americas is probably not altogether accurate, but it is one of the most exciting passages in the literature of archeology and conveys a vivid conception of the faunal riches of the era.

J. M. Campbell (1963), while making other points, has written an excellent section in which he demonstrates that the optimum opportunity for man to cross the Bering causeway would probably have oc-

curred shortly after the maximum ice coverage of the final and maximum Wisconsin advance, between 18,000 and 16,000 B.C. The ingenious explanation is rooted in the ecology of the arctic North, where the available prey were tundra animals rather than woodland types. The presence of ice sheets would, as we have seen, have led to the retreat of forests and a resultant increase in total area covered by tundra, as well as a broader Bering Plain. Arguing for the derivation of man (and his tool kit) from eastern Europe via Siberia at the time of maximum ice, Campbell suggests that glacial maxima would not inhibit but rather would encourage the spread of hunting groups. The greater expanse of open or unforested lands would increase the potential hunting ranges; the more numerous game would attract the hunters. Equally intriguing is his point that tundra—wet, boggy, and dotted with lakes—is easy to cross during the cold season and would present no travel difficulties on the American side of the bridge not already solved by the migrants from Eurasia as they sought prey (mammoth, reindeer) common to both continents. His argument, coupled with that of Haynes (1964), would seem to bracket man's entry into the New World between 18,000 and 10,000 B.C. with some certainty. Campbell's derivation of the first American tools as of Levallois-Mousteroid tradition via Siberia rests on data from Kogruk (a surface site) and somewhat uncertain typology, but can be recognized as possible.

In summary, the population of the Americas is believed to have been derived entirely from Asia because: (1) There was there a slowly expanding population of *Homo sapiens*; (2) there was not the slightest physical barrier to the emigration; and (3) the resources and climate of North America and Asia were identical at the point of juncture, imposing no problem of adaptation or cultural adjustment for the migrants. The migration is not thought to have been a steady flow of people. Nor is it reasonable to suspect a series of surges in the earliest stages of the process. Probably a few hundred individuals crossed the bridge and slowly began to drift south and east around the edges of the ice. Their descendants, all unaware, were cut off from return in a few millennia by the narrowing and final disappearance of the bridge: As the glaciers wasted away to open a southward corridor, the sea recaptured the shallow shelves and the Bering bridge itself. It is unfortunate that the complex study of the glacial ages, and particularly of the Wisconsin stage, cannot be given more space here. The very general statement above is adequate for present purposes but omits the myriad of facts upon which it rests. Furthermore, I have not dwelt on the differences of opinion about the interpretation of some of the details, because these do not change the essential conclusions: No informed scholar doubts that man reached the Americas from Siberia by the means and at the time outlined here.

Other Explanations of Man's Presence in North America

Despite the fact that the simple explanation above, developed as it was from the interlocking facts, satisfies most of today's students on logical grounds, there are other views of the origin of native Americans. The hardiest and longest-lived of the theories has been that the American Indian was descended from the lost tribes of Israel. Amerigo Vespucci may have been the first to suggest this after his voyage of 1497. Since then, however, many others have embraced this idea; William Penn and Increase and Cotton Mather believed in the Israelite origin. One of the best-known exponents was James Adair (Williams 1930), whose famous book about the Southeastern Indians (first released in 1775) was widely read. An Indian trader, albeit a literate one, with headquarters in Savannah, Adair seized upon chance linguistic resemblances as evidence of Israelite origin. Linguistic evidence is indeed of tremendous importance in establishing cultural relationships; but to be accepted, it must rest on clear similarity in syntax, grammer, word lists, and recognizable and preserved phonemic (sound) patterns. The objection to the evidence presented by Adair and others is not to the use of linguistics itself but to the citing of coincidental similarities in phonetics or meaning instead of structural similarities. Furthermore, this theory has since been negated in that after intensive scientific study no linguistic evidence of early Hebrew contact has been discovered anywhere in the Americas. Moreover, no fruits, domestic animals, or crops, artifacts, or cultural practices resembling those of the Near East have ever been observed in either of the Americas. Complete lack of tangible evidence—such as the wheel, Old World grains, or domestic animals—makes the theory untenable, to say nothing of the commonsense problem of how a group of herdsmen and gar-

deners with no recorded skills in seaman-
ship could have voyaged to the Americas
all the way from the dry hills of Asia
Minor.

Similar claims that the Welsh or the
Vikings or the Phoenicians settled the
West are based both on chance linguistic
similarities and on legendary (as well as
documented) later voyages of seamen
from these countries. All these theories
are equally groundless and arose before
the development of scientific linguistics
and long before anyone was aware of the
length of time the Western Hemisphere
has been inhabited. However, it is perfectly true that Norsemen visited the
Americas in the A.D. 1000s. They may
even have influenced the cultures of the
Northeast coast Indian tribes, but we may
be sure that the first American was not a
stranded Scandinavian sailor.

Equally without foundation, even verg-
ing upon the ridiculous, are the hardy
myths about lost continents such as Atlantis and Mu. The absurdity of the matter is
manifest when Plato is identified as the
"inventor" of Atlantis, a land "beyond"
(west of) Gibraltar. The legend has remained viable throughout the centuries
and was given new life through a mystic
cult that developed in the late nineteenth
century. The myth is still with us, but no
durable proof has ever been offered,
despite hundreds of books on the subject.
There is no geologic, archeologic, or linguistic evidence to support the existence
of the fabled Atlantis in the New World.
Mu, of course, is a recently "invented"
land; it may be taken even less seriously,
if possible, than Atlantis. The best recent
volume on all these matters is by Wauchope (1962), in which he deals in detail
with the many myths and provides an
extensive bibliography. The Smithsonian
Institution has also prepared a brief statement and bibliography about Atlantis and
Mu. (Wauchope also deals at length with
the way in which the Mormon sect has
worked the Israelite theory and the Ameri-

can aborigines into the basic fabric of
their dogma.)

Gladwin (1947), in explaining the
physical types and culture traits he de-
tects, accepts not only the Siberian migrant
story but later ocean voyages as well. His
hypothesis is that before the time of
Christ, Alexander's fleet sailed East (with
some island layovers) to land somewhere
in Central America and to found the high
cultures there. The objection to this theory
(proposed by Gladwin, I am certain, with
tongue in cheek) is largely that, given the
time of Alexander's conquests, the fleet
would have arrived 1,000 years after the
high cultures of Mexico were well on their
way. (As will be seen later, the basic
notion of pre-A.D. 1 Asiatic contact with
the Americas is tenable.) Gladwin's views
were resisted because of the extreme position he took and the boldness of some of
the other speculations he offered. Furthermore, he wrote at a time when all American archeologists were serenely isolationist
and did not wish to be stirred into changing their views. However, Gladwin and
Heyerdahl (1950) must be credited with
rearousing an older interest in the problem
of trans- or circumpacific contacts in the
millennia before Christ. As will be noted
later, an extensive literature now exists,
and the matter will be reviewed briefly in
Chapter 5 (Eckholm 1953, 1964; Meggers
1964; Estrada and Meggers 1961; Meggers
and Evans 1966; Meggers, Evans, and
Estrada 1965).

Physical Anthropology of the American Indian

Assuming that the Asiatic origin of New
World man via the Bering Strait at the
Homo sapiens stage of evolution provides intellectually satisfying answers to
the basic question, other questions still
remain. Prime among these is the American Indian himself. Although the Indians
of historic times varied in appearance

somewhat from one part of the continent to another, taken as a population, the Indians were more nearly homogeneous and like one another than they were like any other population segment in the rest of the world. If the Indian came from Asia, how can the present absence of Indians in Asia be satisfactorily explained, particularly when most students have viewed the Indian as an American variety of the Asiatic Mongoloid stock? This, then, is the great question: Where did the Indian physical type develop? If it developed on the two American continents, how and under what conditions and from what ingredients?

This question can probably never be answered on empirical grounds, and in this situation theories naturally abound. But there is comfort in noting that physical anthropologists now tend to agree that the American Indian evolved in place; at least, there appears to be agreement as to the homogeneity of the American Indian population. Whether evolution was from a single archaic *sapiens* stock or from the mixture of two or more slightly divergent varieties after the several modern physical types began to evolve, is still debated (Birdsell 1951; Neumann 1952; Hulse 1963; M. T. Newman 1953, 1960, 1962; T. D. Stewart 1960).

Whether the theorist favors a polyhybrid origin or a single genetic stock usually depends upon his conception of the nature of the emigration. If the introduction of people is visualized as a frequent succession of waves or driblets over many centuries, then the notion of polyorigin seems the most plausible. If a small original population in a few closely spaced increments formed the seed stock, then a single genetic reservoir may be assumed. Of course, if the single seed stock were hybrid, then the poly- or dihybrid view would remain valid. (I wish to emphasize that we are discussing the first or parent migration here. The entrants of the past 4,000 years, the Deneid and Eskimos, are not being considered.)

Whatever the genetic attributes of the parent stock may have been, the subsequent development must be understood as having taken place in a situation uniquely American. The human species was not numerous anywhere on earth then, but neither human nor subhuman forms existed in the Americas, and as a result there was no competitive human population. There was an endless land filled with natural riches to be conquered by a tiny, arctic-hardened, cold-screened population of more-than-average toughness and viability. Culturally, they were equipped with a knowledge of flint chipping, possibly of skin-clothing manufacture; they probably sought big game and, at the outset, faced no adaptation problems so far as natural environment was concerned. From the Arctic port of entry, there lay ahead to the east and south increasingly varied environmental zones, more temperate climes, and varied resource complexes. As the original entrants roamed, expanded, and probably rapidly dispersed over the new land, the population remained thin. In response to varied environments (M. T. Newman 1953, 1960), phenotypic differentiation would have occurred and at the same time, in response to isolation, mutation, and genetic drift, genotypic differences would have appeared in small populations. Mayr (1963) makes clear that genetic or genotypic variations on the basic gene endowment in accord with genetic principles would account for the local variation seen in the Indian populations, without destroying or obscuring the basic homogeneity of the American Indian. That the Indian is seen as a variety of the Mongoloid can be explained as being the result of a series of later increments of Mongoloid stock, after it evolved, or the resemblance can be credited to a genetic heritage shared by the Asian Mongoloids and the early Americans, with resultant evolution proceeding along parallel lines. On this latter point the physical anthropologists are much at odds. Some have argued successive waves of emigrants, each later wave being more Mongoloid in type, in order to account for the Mongoloid characteristics visible in modern Indians. Others favor development *in situ* from a tiny and homogeneous population, whether of single stock, dihybrid, or polyhybrid being irrelevant to the argument.

Prior to the 1940s Hrdlička, Dixon, and Hooton were the only ones who seriously studied the problem of Indian origins. Their work (both with living persons and with skeletal material) was often misunderstood. It is now thoroughly outmoded on theoretical grounds. Although some of their findings are still accepted, they were right for the wrong reasons. Among the current theories, Birdsell's (1951) is complex and very interesting. Working entirely with Asiatic and Australian data, Birdsell postulates an eastern Asian population of generalized type which would today be called archaic or primitive Caucasoid. He suggests three varieties, Murrayian, Carpenterian, and Amurian. The enclaved Ainu of Japan are "living fossil" representatives of one such postulated archaic Caucasoid strain. With the explosive appearance of the viable Mongoloids from the Amurian stock in northeast Asia in response to extreme rigors of climate (Coon, Garn, and Birdsell 1950), population pressure pushed the Murrayian and Carpenterians southward, where their descendants are today's Australian aborigines. The same pressure nudged some of the Amurians into the Americas. Birdsell assumes that the later fossil *Homo sapiens* from the Pekin site would be Amurian in type and that the earliest finds in America would also be Amurian. No modern Indians would show morphologic proof of this theory because, he feels, the original traits would have been lost through heavy overlay of recently arrived Mongoloid

populations. Thus, Birdsell, working with morphology and physical form, suggests that the American Indian derives from a generalized variety with a Mongoloid infusion—in short, he is a dihybrid. If Birdsell is correct, some evidence of the Amurian strain should show up in very early American skeletal finds in isolated or bypassed areas.

Neumann (1952), working entirely with small collections of human skeletons recovered archeologically from American sites, arrived at some remarkably parallel ideas independently of Birdsell, although he then viewed the peopling of the Americas as a function of many successive waves. He assumed that he could find a succession of different physical types in isolated or cul-de-sac regions, types memorializing the different increments. He studied small skeletal collections from single levels at selected archeologic sites on the assumption that he would be dealing with a genetically homogeneous, inbred group with the least possible chance of confusion from outside genes. He viewed the main dispersal route as being the Plains east of the Rockies, with the bypassed "pockets" lying to the east and west. The oldest of his types he calls the Otamid; this group is represented by skeletal remains from the Texas Gulf Coast. He, too, sees resemblances between skeletal material from the upper cave of Chou Kou Tien at Pekin and the remains of the Otamid strain. The Otamid skull is long and of only moderate height; it has heavy supraorbital ridges with a slight occipital bulge or "bun-shaped" swelling (see Figure 2.3). Neumann's other types, in order of their presumed appearance after the Otamids, are: (1) Iswanid, (2) Ashiwid, (3) Walcolid, (4) Lenapid, (5) Inuid, (6) Deneid, and (7) Lakotid. The Iswanid (represented by a collection from the Kentucky shellheaps) and Ashiwid (the Southwestern Basketmakers) are known to be old populations, and both resemble the Otamid. The Walcolid and Lenapid are from recent archeologic deposits, whereas the last three of his list are represented by living people. The Inuid are Eskimo, the Deneid are the Athabaskan-speaking tribes of western Canada and the Southwest, and the Lakotid are a Plains mixture of recent origin. Figure 2.3 also shows the distribution of the types (with the exception of the late Lakotid type). Neumann suggests that the distribution argues chronology, the peripheral types being the older ones caught in cultural or geographic cul-de-sacs. Neumann worked with skeletal material, studying the morphology of the bones and the phenotypes rather than the genotypes (which can't be learned from bones). In a later study (1960), he has come to be less certain that his findings presuppose or require as many successive increments as he once thought, and suggests an evolutionary process as satisfactorily explaining the morphologic differences.

Finally, T. D. Stewart (1960) takes an even more explicit stand. He flatly derives the American Indians from the population represented by several eastern Asiatic fossil finds. He argues an early emigration, after which the port of entry was largely sealed off, and ascribes the present homogeneity, and some local variants, to the operation of accepted biologic and genetic principles over a 20,000- to 30,000-year period. He even includes the "climatic control" of Bergmann's and Allen's rules as applied to man by M. T. Newman (1953). The arguments he uses are numerous and various and cannot be detailed here; but he explains certain unique Indian genotypic traits—the Diego blood factor is one example, and the Indian susceptibility to common Eurasiatic diseases (measles, the common cold, tuberculosis) is another—as evidence of long and well-nigh complete isolation of the Indian populations from the rest of *Homo sapiens*.

Stewart acknowledges, of course, the effect of the Deneid and Eskimo arrivals in the recent millennia.

It is very doubtful that any of these views can be proved beyond debate; I tend to favor Stewart's ideas even though he has been accused of having little knowledge of genetics or of evolutionary processes. One support for Stewart's conclusion that "If you've seen one Indian, you've seen them all," is Hulse's (1963) agreement as to the essential homogeneity of the modern Indian, a homogeneity so marked that he can describe the present-day Indians of two continents in one short passage. He reiterates the small gene input, the rigorous filtering effect of the Arctic, and the 16,000,000 square miles of territory lacking human occupancy, and then identifies all these conditions as having been unique in the world. In addition to recognizing several things such as the presence of blood types A and O, with B absent, and citing some evidences of polymorphism, Hulse goes on to describe the Indian as of stocky rather than gracile build regardless of overall stature, which may be either short or tall. The stockiness applies to both sexes. The extent of skin pigmentation is less than seen in the Old World, but the ability to tan is exceptionally high. The eyes are dark, the hair is coarse and straight, and body hair is scant in both sexes. Females often have the Mongoloid fold; incisor teeth are distinctive in the frequency of the shovel shape. The Diego blood factor is essentially unique to Indians, whereas blood types A^2, B, D^u, and r are lacking. The sickle-cell anomaly is not found in Indian blood. The Indian male is rarely bald and rarely becomes gray in old age. Certain hair-whorl patterns and distinctive fingerprint patterns are known.

Santiago Genovés (personal communication, 1966) sees all the above explanations or hypotheses as inadequate and suspect. His views are that the data, which he

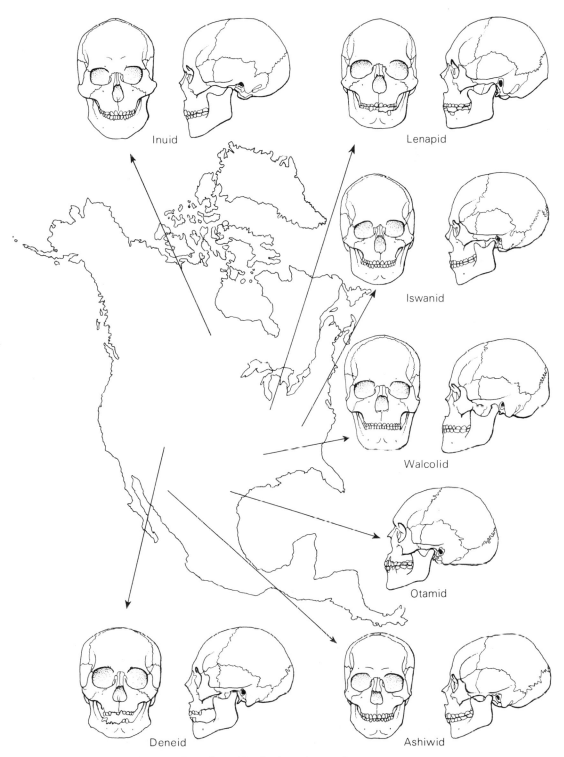

Figure 2.3   *Cranial types found in North America and areas of occurrence. (Modified from Griffin 1952a, Figs. 1, 2, 3, and 4)*

reviews exhaustively, indicate the possibility of several waves of migrants not only at different times but also from different places. He would particularly deny the homogeneity suggested by T. D. Stewart.

In summary, the presence of a unique human population upon the Americas first discovered by the Norse explorers of the eleventh century is a basic assumption. That this homogeneous population derived from a primitive Asiatic human population in the past 10,000 to 40,000 years is viewed as reasonable, but certainly not proved; the "setting" of the genotype in isolation in North and South America is also seen as likely. However, it seems beyond doubt that when and if skeletal specimens of the earliest population are discovered, they will not resemble the modern Indian described by Hulse but will be of a type associated with the Late Paleolithic stages of Eurasian cultures. The Otamids of Texas and the Midland (Texas) specimen approximate the type.

Early Human Remains

If any portion of the material on origins is true, there should be proof scattered over the two Americas, in the form of preserved ancient human skeletons. Many claims of antiquity are made for many finds, but most such claims have not survived expert review. Some have proved to be quite humorous mistakes. Nebraska Man, for example, was announced on the basis of a tooth which was soon identified as being from an extinct peccary!

Students, like other folk, vary greatly in their credulity, and there is perhaps no one list of early finds which archeologists would agree upon. Wormington (1957), in a widely used summary of early finds, evidently accepts a human pelvis found near Natchez (Mississippi) associated with extinct fauna; Minnesota Man; the Torrington (Wyoming) finds; Browns Valley Man and Sauk Valley Man (both in Minnesota); Tepexpan Man (from Mexico); and the Midland (Texas) find. Wormington's discussion indicates that her acceptance of most of these specimens as authentically early is based, in some measure, on the morphology (typology) of the crania, agreeing with Albert E. Jenks and others that dolichocephaly and some primitive features of cranial morphology argue antiquity. T. D. Stewart (1957), relying entirely on form, would accept an even longer list. All the finds cited above [and a long list from South America (Hrdlička et al. 1912)] were made, evaluated, and became varyingly controversial before any of the origin theories cited above were proposed. Hrdlička and those who were influenced by him thought *Homo sapiens* to be a more recent evolutionary form than is now believed; he felt that any specimen that was recognizably human was recent because any truly early form must be expected to be sub-*sapiens*.

On the other hand, archeologists are reluctant to accept most of these finds as representing the first wandering Asiatics. In some cases the finds were made by persons untrained in observation, and one cannot be sure of the context. In others, a complete lack of either artifacts or extinct fauna precludes adducing even ancillary evidence of age; in still others, fluorine or other chemical tests are inconclusive. It seems by far the better part of valor to reject those finds accepted on morphologic grounds only and similarly to disallow those finds where the circumstances of discovery are uncertain or the technical observations inadequate. This leaves us with the Natchez pelvis (which has been lost) and the Midland find in the continental United States. From Mexico, Tepexpan Man, a find widely questioned on the basis of poor field procedures (see de Terra, Romero, and Stewart 1949), was later largely validated by a second study (Arellano 1951). [For a good review of the arguments swirling around these putative "early" men, see Wormington (1957). Her bibliography cites many original sources not specifically mentioned in this selective summary.] The scarcity of human skeletal remains in the Americas may result from the accidents of discovery—the territory *is* large—or from the practice of cremation, which may be a very old one. [Mason and Irwin (1960) have reported a Wisconsin cremation associated with a Scottsbluff point, Scottsbluff being one of the Plano series dating back to 5000 or 6000 B.C.]

Midland Man   In the frustration attendant upon the failure of find after find to satisfy the rigors of scientific control, American scholars have turned with more confidence to the Scharbauer or Midland site in Texas, where what is now the most famous American skull was recovered. Confidence in the find stems not from the clean-cut circumstances of the discovery. It rests, rather on the exhaustive, dogged study of a very complicated situation made by a group of dedicated scholars searching every possible avenue for certainty of provenience. The Midland study has been called a model of the working collaboration between scientists. Even more important, there would be no Midland Man if it had not been for the alertness and good sense of an amateur, Keith Glasscock, who made the original discovery and called in the trained men. May Keith's tribe increase! In two reports Wendorf and his associates (Wendorf, Krieger, and Albritton 1955; Wendorf and Krieger 1959) explain their separate roles in attempting to fix the provenience of the skull and to determine the possible correlations of the associated climate, fauna, and cultural objects.

The study was triggered by Glasscock's search of a "blowout" in a cluster of sand dunes near Midland. Blowouts, which are common in the Plains, are areas where the surface soils and successive lower strata are blown away until a resistant stratum is reached. They vary from a few yards to several miles in area. Many were formed in the Plains states during the terrible dustbowl of the 1930s when, because of continued drought and other factors, the vegetation disappeared and the wind could begin its plucking action. One result of deflation, as this process is called, is that heavy objects in the area—stones, bones, artifacts, beer bottles, or old truck tires—do not blow away but settle down as the earth is blown from beneath them. When deflation finally ceases, the blowout floor is covered with all the objects that had originally been above it. All provenience control is therefore lost. The objects are all now merely surface finds; a beer bottle could be lying beside a mammoth tusk, or a tire might encircle a rusty spur. Hence, even though blowouts often yield prehistoric material, they do not provide reliable clues as to age or original association.

In the deflated zone Glasscock found a crumbling human skull lying partially exposed, apparently weathering out of a bed of gray sand. The blowout was one of several in the dunes. All had little islands and hummocks scattered over their floors. From these little knolls a series of geologic events was deduced, but fitting the evidence together was a complex and tedious labor. Locality 1, where the skull was found, was cut quite deeply into resistant strata. Here the deflating process had removed two layers of sand to expose an ancient lake or streambed. The upper sands, already quite extensively studied by geologists, were the Monahans, a loose, orange-gray sand which dunes readily, and the next lower, the rusty-red Judkins, which is more compact and more resistant to erosion. Visible in some areas under the red component of the Judkins were a calcareous gray sand and, beneath this, an earlier calcareous white sand. These two sands are also part of the Judkins formation. Both the latter could be either lacustrine or riverine deposits. The human skull, heavily mineralized, came from the gray sand, but there was no evidence that it had been intentionally buried (Figure 2.4).

In order to establish an associational context for the human bones, extensive excavation and field study were undertaken, followed by a variety of laboratory tests. Before the work was finally done, the list of collaborators included (aside from the several present or advisory archeologists) paleontologists, photographers, chemists, physicists, geologists, a botanist, physical anthropologists, and palynologists. When the studies were completed, it was determined that the gray sand, the layer which had contained the skull, was older than a Folsom complex found in the upper Judkins sands.

The complex correlations involved cannot concern us here, but the result of the study was that the Midland skull was found to be more than 10,000 years old, and possibly as much as 20,000 years old. Radiocarbon, fluorine, and uranium-daughter tests support the range of dates, as do the extinct-mammal remains and other associations. Eighteen thousand years could be defended on the basis of the test results, but would probably not be generally accepted. (The archeologic contents of the find will be reviewed

later.) The important thing to consider now is the skull. Entirely *sapiens* in form, the small skull fits Neumann's description of the Otamid quite well. Midland "man" was a female about 30 years old. The skull is quite dolichocephalic and in other ways approximates the predicted morphology of the early population. Nothing remindful of the generalized American Indian described earlier by Hulse can be seen. If the woman is in fact an Otamid, as the skull form suggests (even down to the bun-shaped lower occiput), the slight, gracile body build included in Neumann's description may be assumed to accompany the small, smooth, thin-walled skull. Thus, the Midland find seems to confirm in a rather spectacular way the hypotheses of both Birdsell and Neumann because it is more generalized and archaic than it is Mongoloid (Figure 2.5).

Tepexpan Man   There is one other skeletal find in the Americas generally accepted as ancient that must be mentioned. This is the Tepexpan find discovered near Mexico City. Here, after an elaborate experiment in the use of electromagnetic resistivity equipment to locate subsurface phenomena, de Terra found a human skeleton. His statement (de Terra 1949) is a masterpiece of vague reporting. As Black (1949) and Jennings (1950a) have pointed out, the circumstances of the finding are so clouded one can never be sure whether the burial was intrusive into the late Pleistocene sediment where it was found, or whether it was included within the sediment as the latter was deposited. The issue is further confused by the fact that the individual, according to the physical anthropologists (see T. D. Stewart 1949), does not differ morphologically from Recent or even modern Indians. Arellano (1951), using a series of observations (not reported by de Terra), has opined that the Tepexpan skeleton is correctly assigned a terminal Pleistocene date (thus it is not intrusive), and may be

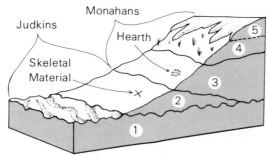

Figure 2.4   *Stratigraphy of Locality 1, Midland (Scharbauer) site. 1, calcareous white sand; 2, gray sand; 3, red sand; 4 and 5, tan sands. (Modified from Wendorf, Krieger, and Albritton 1955)*

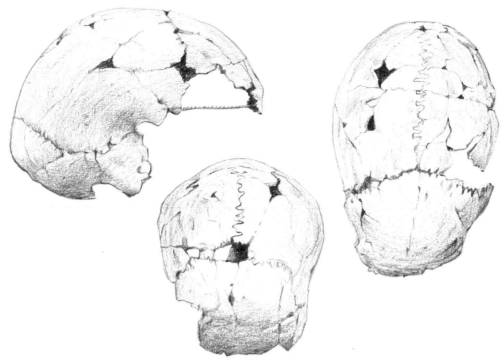

Figure 2.5   Side, back, and top views of the Midland skull.
(After T. D. Stewart 1955)

10,000 or more years old. Many accept his judgment and regard the specimen as evidence that the American Indian had reached an essential homogeneity by that time. Along with Wormington (1957) I hold that the issue remains in doubt.

In sum, the American Indian population is evidently a homogeneous variety, evolved *in situ* in isolation from a primitive, undifferentiated Asiatic population, after entry into the continent sometime during the late Wisconsin phase of the Pleistocene.

History of Study

Realizing that it may be decades before the origin and appearance of the first Americans can be discussed with full evidence at hand, we can now turn to man's handiwork and begin to arrange the evidence and the inferences into some kind of story. As proper archeologists, we can do no better than to begin at the beginning. Therefore, the earliest evidence of man on the continent will be the subject of this section. But first, it is necessary to explain for beginning students the nature of the extensive literature they may decide to sample, where the terms for some of the American cultures are so varied.

The earliest stages of man's career in the Americas are almost invariably referred to either as "Paleo-Indian" or "Early Man." This terminology makes some sense but is largely an artifact of learning rather than logic. The doughty Hrdlička (1907; Hrdlička et al. 1912) systematically evaluated the various finds involving ancient man in America, rejecting them one by one on several grounds. He coined the term "Early Man," the implication being that "early" would probably mean pre-*sapiens* or subhuman. He was resisting not only "earliness" but also "man-ness." For whatever the cause, American prehistory as late as 1930 was allowed very shallow time depth; serious and informed estimates of occupancy were no greater than 3,000 or 4,000 years. The archeologic implications of this situation are quite obvious: All cultural complexes had to be squeezed into this short span. (This factor handicapped all interpretation until radiocarbon dating showed the actual timespan to be much longer.) Even so, scholars accepted the original concept of Early Man as valid, that is, that there was an early cultural stratum. Most thought that there followed a period of no occupancy in the Americas, with a final series of American Indian cultures which made up the bulk of the archeologic story. For this misconception the state of knowledge was again to blame. Until after 1940, there was no clear (or recognized) evidence of a continuum of cultures anywhere in the Americas except after about an estimated 1000 or 2000 B.C. The evolution of thought is summarized in Figure 2.6 (see also Wilmsen 1965). At present it is possible to say that there is no district in the Americas where there is a significant gap in cultural evidence of long occupancy, although there remain regions where the data are scanty or suspect. Wherever research has progressed far enough, it is possible to recognize a con-

tinuum of cultures of known, sequent stages. Aside from Early Man, a classification of no use today because it makes "early" seem to be something other than merely a relative term, there are a host of other schemes which seem somehow to convey: (1) a simultaneous expression of time, (2) an increasing degree of "Indian-ness" or "Mongolianization," and even (3) an implication of culture stage, although these apparent meanings are not explicit. For example, Roberts (1940) uses the term "Paleo-Indian." This probably was intended to emphasize his belief, as opposed to Hrdlička, that the earliest American remains were Indian. Griffin (1946) referred to both "Paleo-Indians" (including more than Roberts did in this rubric) and "Neo-Indians." Suhm, Krieger, and Jelks (1954) used "Paleo-American" and "Neo-American." A. G. Smith (1957) offered "Paleo-," "Meso-," and "Neo-Indian," which Rouse (1964) and others continue to use. Another approach is to give culture names to a regional group of sites having common characteristics. Sellards' (1952) term "Llano" for the elephant hunters of the Plains is a useful example.

As previously noted the only classification that will consistently be employed in this book is the set of stages developed by Willey and Phillips. The earliest stages in their system—the *Lithic,* the *Archaic,* and the *Formative*—will be used, but heavy reliance will also be placed upon the local or regional culture names, since only these can "key" the student into the literature.

	Pre-1900	To 1926	1926-1945	1945 to date
Late	Indian	Indian	Indian	Indian
	Nothing	Nothing	Nothing	Archaic
Early	Early Man	Nothing	Early Man	Early Man

Figure 2.6 *Evolution of scholarly interpretations of American prehistory.*

Climate

Although the differences in climate during Wisconsin times from modern time have been touched upon, it is now necessary to expand on the subject because in archeologic interpretation much—perhaps too much—has been made of the assumed variability of late Pleistocene and Recent climates.

Much of the evidence is, understandably, geologic and is concerned largely with the oscillations (and the effects of these movements) of the later ice lobes in the upper tier of the United States. This is, of course, because the continental ice masses were responsible for weather conditions, so all the climates to the south are functions of the position of the ice. The best sources for the geologic material are Hough (1958), Flint (1957), and Zeuner (1958).

The problem is one of building a reasonable statement from many arguments: There is neither a lack of interest nor a dearth of observations. The extremely complex geologic evidence of climatic change is particularly plentiful; the confusion lies in the interpretation. Difficulty in interpretation has increased since radiocarbon dating was developed. In the pre-1950 era, the last Wisconsin ice advances were estimated by geologists to have ended from 15,000 to 40,000 or more years ago. Now dozens upon dozens of radiocarbon dates, derived from wood from trees buried during glacial advances, show that the last two ice lobes advanced less than 10,000 years ago (Flint 1957). Thus, one of the major advances, the Mankato (or Port Huron, as it is now called), which heralded the end of the Pleistocene in the central United States, occurred apparently after man had entered America. The new conception of a very short Recent period was hard for both the geologists and the archeologists to assimilate. However, the radiocarbon dates seem to have clarified a previously disputed point—whether the pluvial conditions south of the glaciers coexisted with the ice advances. Flint (1957) flatly asserts the synchrony, not only of the pluvial lakes and glaciers, but also of American and Eurasian ice action.

Today, geologists generally accept the many suites of radiocarbon dates as accurate. Hopkins (1959) compresses the entire second half of the Wisconsin into less (?) than 25,000 years. Flint (1957) would agree that the lobes usually identified as the Wisconsin are the Tazewell (maximum at perhaps 20,000 years), Cary (maximum at perhaps 12,000 years), Mankato or Port Huron (maximum at perhaps 10,500 years), and Cochrane (maximum at perhaps 8,000 years). The best available discussion of the Wisconsin ice movements is by Hough (1958). He and Hopkins are essentially in agreement on all points except that Hopkins shortens the later stages even more than Hough (Figure 2.7). The advances are conceived as having occurred rather quickly, requiring only a few centuries—up to 2,000 years in some cases, and the intervals of retreat are believed to have been longer in comparison. The present Recent or Modern era is regarded by some as merely an interval in a Pleistocene era not yet ended. On the other hand, Antevs (various) allows twice the time for all these events, placing the Mankato at about 19,000 years ago, stiffly resisting the validity of the radiocarbon evidence. In dealing with

Years ago	Hopkins chronology	Hough chrononology
8,000	7.	Cochrane
	6. Valders	Valders
10,500	5. Mankato	Two Creeks interval Port Huron (Mankato)
	4. Cary	Cary
20,000	3. Tazewell	Bloomington (late Tazewell)
	2. Iowan	Shelbyville Iowan (early Tazewell)
	1. Farmdale	Farmdale

Figure 2.7   Wisconsin glacial periods. (Modified from Hough 1958; Hopkins 1959)

this matter, the problem facing archeologists is twofold: First, the data employed in reaching geologic conclusions—
land forms, lake levels (fossil and modern), ocean cores, radioactive isotopes,
cross sections, well cores, peat bogs, pollen, etc., along with the assumptions, field
judgments, and assumed connections or
correlations with data from other regions
—are complex and unfamiliar. It is difficult to evaluate the validity of the more
detailed arguments. Second, the geologist
studies spatially widespread phenomena,
painting his geologic canvas with a broad
brush. When asked to assess the details
of a small archeologic site and relate it
to a regional geologic sequence, the geologist is often at a loss because his previous
experience is macro- rather than microscopic in scale. Since the archeologist sees
earth layers in thicknesses of inches and
the geologist is accustomed to dealing with
formations many feet deep, microgeology
often frustrates both of them.

At the time ice flows were advancing
and retreating in response to some kind
of natural rhythm, the rest of North
America presented a different appearance.
Martin's (1958) study of pollen columns,
summarized in the vegetation maps of the
eastern United States in Figures 2.8, 2.9,
and 2.10, reveals climatic change and the
associated expansion and contraction of
biotic communities as a series of floral-
faunal changes synchronized with the slow
ebb and flow of the ice. Tundra, of course,
bespeaks a cold climate too rigorous for
forest. The taiga is a band of coniferous
trees—spruce, fir, balsam, etc.—and to
the south is the Boreal or mixed zone of
transition to the broadleaf, deciduous
forest. The point made by these maps is
that for the past 20,000 years the available
resources of the eastern half of the continent (except for some now-extinct mammals) have not changed. There has been
extensive territorial expansion and contraction, but the life zones remain the
same. This is evidently not true of the

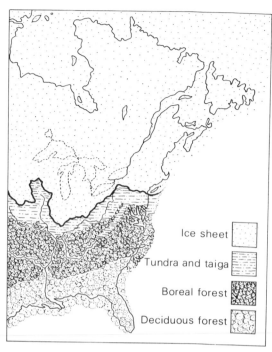

Figure 2.8 *Vegetation zones of eastern
North America during the maximum Wisconsin glaciation ca. 16,000* B.C. *(After Martin
1958)*

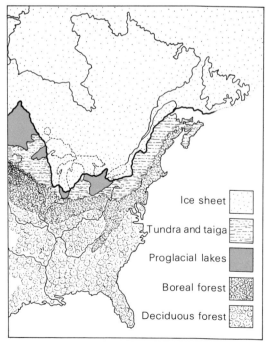

Figure 2.9 *Vegetation zones of eastern
North America during the Valders readvance
ca. 9000* B.C. *(After Martin 1958)*

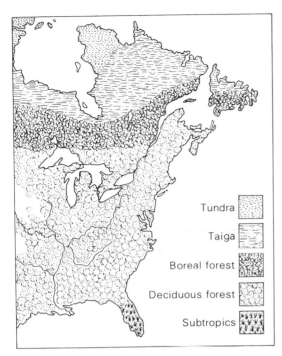

Tundra
Taiga
Boreal forest
Deciduous forest
Subtropics

Figure 2.10   Modern vegetation zones of eastern North America. (After Martin 1958)

Plains and intermontane areas. Here, in what is today grassland and steppe, respectively, and where moisture is scant, pluvial conditions led to the creation of many lakes. In the Great Basin alone, nearly seventy lakes have been identified (Flint 1947). Bonneville was as large as present-day Lake Michigan; Lahontan, too, was large (Figure 2.11). Presumably, prior to 12,000 B.C. the Basin vegetation was ranker and possibly slightly different during the wetter pluvials than today; but after 10,000 B.C. the Basin climate and dependent vegetation and animal resources were not different from now. It can be shown that the effect of the late minor ice advances on the Western climate has been overemphasized, if not exaggerated (see Deevey 1953). Jennings (various) argues that the climate differences if any, would be small, skewed only a trifle toward increased moisture. Slightly more annual precipitation would result only in ranker growth of steppe plants; it would not lead

to a widely different ecosystem or significant change in species proportions. For example, oak, hickory, and walnut might grow along streams and washes where none is found today. Haury (Haury, Sayles, and Wasley 1959) offers documentation of all these points from the Lehner mammoth site. [His conclusions were later fully confirmed by Mehringer and Haynes (1965).] There would also be more marsh plants in the bogs and swampy meadows. In the Plains, the picture is perhaps less clear, but there the endless miles of sunlit and windswept grass are no doubt about as they always were. We know that large beasts which are now extinct dwelt there. These creatures—mammoth, horse, camel, and superbison—subsisted on grass, and the vast herds required large quantities

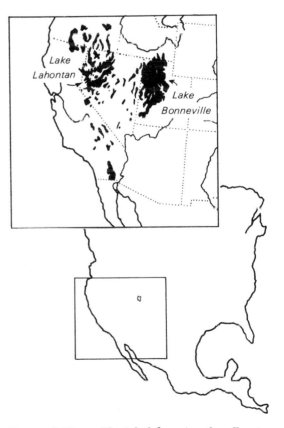

Figure 2.11   Pluvial lakes in the Great Basin. Great Salt Lake (lower map) is present-day remnant of Lake Bonneville. (Modified from Flint 1947)

of it. It is also true that the Plains were well watered. Thousands of huge springs and many streams, shallow bogs, and ponds called *playas* have been located as "fossil" landforms. In the relatively small Llano Estacado (20,000 square miles), where special conditions exist, Wendorf (Wendorf et al. 1961) shows several hundred playas. In fact, some of the Plains archeologic locations reviewed later in this chapter are themselves extinct springs and bog sites.

It is true that the Plains grasslands might have shrunk and/or extended further south in response to the effect on the weather of advancing or retreating ice, but there is no reason to think of the Plains of 15,000 years ago as varying greatly from today. In wetter periods the vegetation would be more lush; nothing

else need change. The above views are not generally held. The argument here for (1) fluctuation of territorial expanse, (2) change in *quantity* rather than *kind* of biota in response to changes in precipitation, and (3) a much slighter effect of recent pluvial conditions than is usually asserted rests partially on archeologic evidence and partially on faunal population data. For example, Hester (1960), as well as Martin (1958) and Jelinek (1957), shows that the extinct large beasts haven't been extinct as long as is often claimed (see Figure 2.12) and that many surviving species were coexistent, in their present form, with the extinct species. This set of herd fauna requires grass! In all fairness, it must be added there is pollen evidence that the Plains may have been savannah (an open grass-shrub-tree land) rather

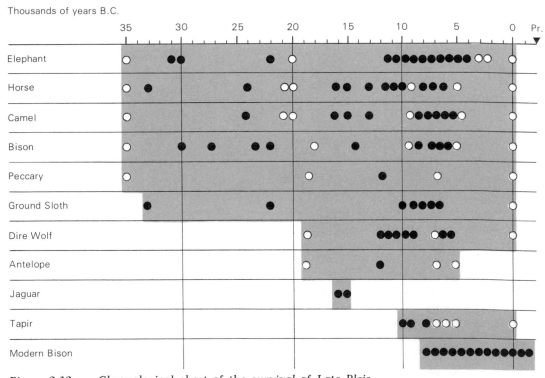

Figure 2.12   *Chronological chart of the survival of Late Pleistocene mammals dated by C14. Black dots are accepted dates; white dots are questioned dates; Pr. means "present." (Modified from Hester 1960)*

than the complete grassland it is today (Wendorf and Hester 1962; Wendorf et al. 1961; Martin 1963). In addition to the pollen records that seem to indicate a scattered woodland situation, O. C. Stewart (1956) summarizes an assortment of evidence to conclude that the Great Plains was created and preserved as grassland by man through the use of fire. Pollen analyses have contributed to the above conclusions, but the study of pollen and the interpretations of the findings are relatively new. At best, the pollen profiles can only suggest, although the chronometric value of pollen studies is rapidly increasing.

Whatever present thought may be, most archeologic interpretations since about 1930 have incorporated the notion of rather drastic climatic and environmental change as the terminal Ice Age climate gave way to modern conditions. The paleoclimatologist Antevs (various) has had the greatest influence in this development. His studies began in the 1920s and have never lagged. His intuitive genius in combining diverse data from clay-varve counts, temperature ranges, river sediments, fossil-lake beaches, and other things, including many an assumption, enabled him to make many acceptable estimates of the age of numerous archeologic sites. These estimates, time after time, were uncannily close to the (supposedly) accurate radiocarbon dates when the latter began to appear. Although Antevs has rejected the geologic radiocarbon dates for the Valders, Port Huron, and Cochrane ice advances as much too recent (the associated, more southerly phenomena would thereby also be older than most now believe), his skill in age estimation gives him a preeminence in the field. However, because he has persisted in regarding the Recent as beginning earlier than it evidently did, his interpretations are now somewhat anachronistic. He has strained to keep all evidence of man's presence in the Recent, when all evidence points to man's arrival and spread during the latest ice movements.

Despite a latter-day inflexibility, Antevs' contributions to the advance of our knowledge are enormous. Perhaps his most important contribution is the concept of the *Neothermal,* which is a set of climatic conditions covering essentially Recent times. Designed to apply primarily to the Plains and the West, the Neothermal embraced three sequent phases characterized by linked temperature-moisture conditions. On the assumption that a generally cool, moist climate is characteristic of pluvial periods, Antevs uses the term "Anathermal"—with conditions cooler and wetter than now—to describe the waning of pluvial intensity as the last glacier ice withdrew. This was followed by the "Altithermal," when conditions were markedly hotter and drier than now. The final "Medithermal" was marked by what are essentially today's conditions of temperature and moisture. As one line of evidence, Antevs points to the widespread Recent alluviation which can be observed, and in some degree correlated, over the western half of the continent. Most of the *evidence* cannot be denied, the extensive alluviation being particularly well documented. The crux of the matter is not alluviation but Antevs' theory of climate. In brief, this proposes that the erosion leading to extensive sedimentation results from very dry conditions that led to the loss of binding vegetation. Thus the Altithermal would equate with widespread heat and drought and the probable disappearance of man from certain areas.

Although widely accepted, the concept of the Altithermal has never been fully satisfactory on a commonsense basis or in explaining all the archeologic finds. These remarks are in no way to be construed as denying the tremendous steps toward understanding of New World prehistory achieved through Antevs' brilliant aid over a 20-year period. His "absolute" datings, based on geologic observations, provided the first reasonable chronologic base available to Western prehistorians (see A. L. Bryan and Gruhn 1964). Only his climatic theory is under review here. The Altithermal may well have been warmer, even drier, than the Anathermal or even than today; the point at issue is whether the dry, hot regime was so intense as to imply centuries of drought. It is not to be doubted that there were cyclic swings from wet to dry within a known range, as there are today, or that periods of severe drought as long as even thirty or forty years have been experienced. Antevs' theory has been questioned increasingly sharply by K. Bryan (1950), Burma (1950), Flint (1957), Aschmann (1958), and Martin (1963). Aschmann and Martin even deny the dryness of the Altithermal. Martin explains the extensive alluviation as resulting from environmental rather than climatic change, the change consisting in a shift from the normal gentle winter precipitation to the summer pattern of frequent, violent rainstorms that still cause quick erosion and sedimentation today despite normal ground cover. A recent extensive review of this problem by Malde (1964) documents twenty or more years of opinion that the evidence points to a hot, dry era—a conclusion which Malde supports. His contribution does nothing to settle the basic problem: That there was heat is not debated; its significance for man is at issue.

This lengthy digression is included in part to aid novices in the reading of primary or secondary sources where Antevs' Altithermal concept has played so dominant a role. The concept of a dry interval is acceptable, but it must be discounted as to intensity and cultural significance (Jennings 1964). In the remainder of this book, the Altithermal will not be used either as a climatic condition or as explanation of cultural fact. Nonetheless, fluctuation of environment (see Schoenwetter 1962) is accepted as common and age-old. The cautions expressed by A. L. Bryan and Gruhn (1964) are exceedingly appropriate here. They remind us that Ana-, Alti-, and Medithermal must be used within the tempering framework of a number of other variables, such as local topography and elevation and the longitude-latitude figures. Nor should the Neothermal subdivisions be regarded as having absolute time values, even though many call them periods. They are merely temperature-moisture ratios or indices describing various conditions.

The intent of this section has been to introduce the complex problem of climate and the accompanying biota of the past 15,000 years. In addition, it has been proposed that the contrast from today's resources is much less than has been claimed and that the normal cyclical changes would require much less drastic adaptation than is often postulated as necessary. Consequently, neither would large sections of the continent ever be devoid of human population, save briefly.

3

The Early Cultures

As yet no mention has been made of the cultural stage that man had achieved when he began the settlement of the Americas. What social organization, what tools or technology did he possess? In short, what cultural baggage did he have? One reason the question has been avoided is that no answer can be given. Sheer logic provides a simple answer, but archeology doesn't confirm it, nor does it provide an alternative. If, as some postulate, man's entry occurred from 20,000 to 40,000 years ago [Haynes (1964) on present evidence restricts man to 11,000 to 11,500 years on the continent], he was undeniably in a Middle or Late Paleolithic Stone Age culture stage, and it would be the eastern Asiatic rather than the Afro-European version of the Paleolithic at that. The fact is that no such assemblage, in proper stratigraphic position, has yet been found. The earliest dated American archeologic specimens (for example, Clovis Fluted points, Figure 3.9) show skill and sophistication in flintwork beyond anything of the same age in either Siberia or northeast Asia and are not equalled there until much later in time.

Logic (or historical necessity) demands that: (1) Recognizable complexes in Asia should match the earliest American remains; or (2) recognizable single ancestral forms, known to have been earlier than any American forms, exist in Asia, or (3) all American tool forms are indigenous inventions. Only alternatives (1) and (2) can be taken seriously. As yet the answer is that we simply don't know!

Despite 50 or more years of search in the Arctic for evidence of man's passage across the Bering land bridge, no reasonable evidence has been found either in Asia or in Alaska as to the tools, stone, bone, or wood which the first men carried. As we have seen, it is possible to bracket man's entry between 23,000 and 9000 B.C. through Hopkins' (1959) correlations of sea levels, ice, and land-bridge width during the last half of the Wisconsin ice age. Why hasn't evidence been found? One very cogent explanation is that most of the evidence may be under water along streams and beaches of land-bridge days. Another is that search may have been for artifact complexes exactly like some of the American ones, instead of for complexes which could be generally typologically antecedent and give rise to American types. There are other problems as well: Siberian and Pacific Coast Asia are not well known archeologically, and the dates ascribed to those sites which have been studied are based on cross dating and typology from European sequences. Although there are enormous difficulties to be reconciled and theories always abound where facts are scant, there are some clues at hand. It may well be decades before clear proof is offered.

The problem has many facets, one of the most important being that two quite distinct cultural traditions are found in Asia. Either one could be the donor for American first beginnings. The Siberian remains are clearly derivative from the Afro-European Paleolithic cultures. The Asiatic Pacific Coast remains are seen as belonging to the ancient Southeast Asian tradition long regarded as different from the European assemblage. Whereas the Afro-European tools can be described as "core" and "flake," the Asian complex is dominated by pebbles or blocks of stone chipped to an edge on one side, called *choppers.*

Given the earlier argument that the first men to cross the Bering bridge should perhaps be identified as being from northeastern Asia, the expectable tool kit would be coastal Asiatic in origin. For this reasonable assumption no good evidence exists, unless it is revealed in the San Dieguito series of artifacts of the California coast and southern deserts. Thus, the other alternative, or central Siberian source, must be invoked. Here Bushnell and McBurney (1959), Griffin (1960b), Wormington (1962), J. M. Campbell (1962a, 1963), and Wilmsen (1964) have obliged. For the Malta site, in the trans-Baikal district, it is possible to estimate from the artifact complex an age of perhaps 20,000 B.C. This is one of the earliest Siberian sites now known, although important later ones are on record. The artifacts at Malta include a series much resembling the Gravettian complex of eastern Europe (Moravia) dated about 24,000 B.C. by radiocarbon. Thus, a Siberian site probably earlier than any of the dated American sites is at least known. All the scholars working on the Siberian origin are concerned with prototypes of certain recognized American tool types and see many resemblances between the trans-Siberian and several American artifact complexes.

The resemblances are in some of the flake tools and specimens that are possibly prototypical for the fine chipped American points or blades called Clovis and Folsom points. Specifically, the interest is focused on a series of chipped stone flakes identified as scrapers, blades, or points which are not chipped to shape but which are flakes knapped from a prepared flint core and used as struck off, with varying amounts of rechipping along the edges of the flake. This technique is in contrast to bifacial chipping, that is, the shaping of a tool by removal of small flakes from both planes of a thin flake. Bifacial chipping usually removes the large flat scars resultant from the manufacture of the original flake. For those interested in the techniques of flint knapping Bordaz (1959) demonstrates several aspects of flintworking, the flaking characteristic of flint, and several ways of producing flakes to a pattern. Figures 3.1 and 3.2 are examples of typical Upper Paleolithic implements recovered from Siberian and American sites.

Wormington (1962), after a review of the Siberian evidence, not all of which is well controlled as to age, is willing to say that the tool kit carried by the migrants into America could have contained chopping tools, flake tools (resembling those of the late Mousterian cultures), discoidal scrapers, crude blades, and perhaps bifacially chipped, leaf-shaped blades. All these would have been percussion-flaked. One difficulty she recognizes lies in the quite late dates ascribed to some of the leaf-shaped, doubled-pointed American blades, the Cascade (northwest America) and Lerma (Mexico). She suggests a

development toward "fineness," beginning with a crude, laurel-leaf–shaped point or blade from Siberia and proceeding to the classic fluted Folsom type (Figure 3.3). The work of A. L. Bryan (1965) should also be consulted in a review of this analysis.

J. M. Campbell (1963) has compared specimens from two Alaskan sites, Kogruk and Naiyuk, to complexes in Siberia and both the Americas. His is the most extensive of the several studies cited and results in the same broad conclusions offered by Wormington. The Kogruk site, which is not fixed in time, yielded almost entirely flake specimens, whereas the Naiyuk showed an odd blend of vaguely Plano-like specimens associated with some trans-Siberian types. Both these authors refer to occasional evidence of fluting but do not view fluting, as seen in the American types, as Asiatic in origin. Wilmsen (1964), who accepts the ideas and data above, has suggested that the actual route

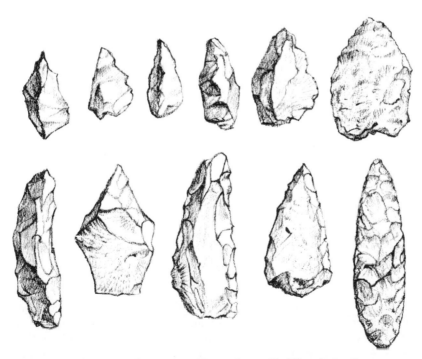

Figure 3.1   *Chipped stone artifacts from Ust'-Kanskaia Cave near Biisk in western Siberia. Approximately one-half size. (After Wormington 1962)*

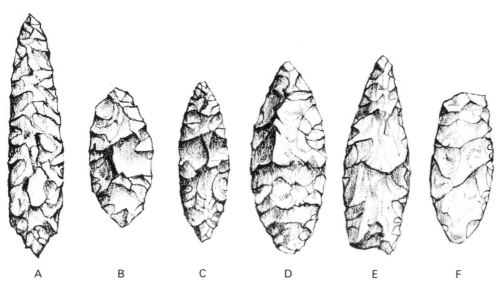

Figure 3.2   *Leaf-shaped points from Siberia and America. A, B, Osipovka site, near Khabarovsk, U.S.S.R.; C, D, DjRi3 site, Fraser Canyon, British Columbia; E, F, from a site near Santa Isabel Iztapan, Mexico. (After Wormington 1962)*

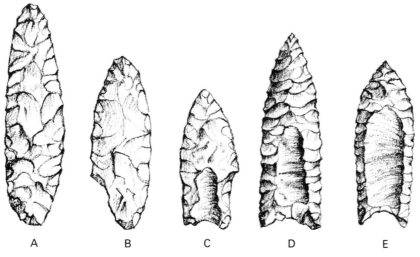

Figure 3.3   *Postulated developmental sequence of projectile point types. A, laurel leaf from Siberia; B, Sandia point; C, fluted Sandia point; D, Clovis Fluted point; E, Folsom point. (After Wormington 1962)*

of migration from Siberia to the Plains can be found in the upland foothills zone, which is continuous from central Siberia to central North America. Given the existence of the Bering bridge, the distribution of the pitifully few relevant sites supports his view.

Authors other than those cited above are working on various aspects of the fascinating problem of first cultural origins. These include Chard (various), Giddings (1963), MacNeish (various), Laughlin (various), and others. Their views, and data, will be introduced later in a more detailed consideration of the Arctic. For all the foregoing speculations the dates are only inferential and the major argument is typologic. Most readers would agree that this material is thin. The data are scant, the artifacts are lacking in crisply diagnostic attributes, and the conclusions are far from convincing—statements with which all the authors cited above would probably concur. What is encouraging is that the question is now being studied within a chronologic framework that makes some sense, given the actual and estimated dates for the earliest accepted American complexes. Nonetheless, complacent acceptance of the possible Siberian origins or even the land bridge (Hunt 1965) should be avoided. In view of our ignorance of eastern Asian Paleolithic data, the different and mutually exclusive tool traditions postulated earlier can perhaps be challenged. There will probably still be discovered in the Asiatic "chopper" area one or more flake industries resembling the European Paleolithic. Should this occur, the argument would be thrown wide open again. The heartening thing now is that the question of origins remains open and that a host of students is meeting the challenge. Thin data and tenuous, farfetched argument can be expected; but as study continues, proof will accumulate.

In summary, most modern scholars accept the trans-Baikal Eurasian Upper Paleolithic as the cultural tradition out of which the earliest American cultures evolved and that evidence of this origin can be seen in the continuous use of a variety of retouched flake tools (in the Llano culture or in the Desert or Western Archaic) over both North and South America into almost modern times. Jennings (1965b) tends to accept a coastal Asian rather than a Siberian origin for the first American artifacts, a view that can still be defended. At the same time, the lack of any real evidence of Asiatic prototypes for the beautifully fluted and pressure-flaked American point and blade

types, as well as some later flint complexes, leaves much of American development to be interpreted as indigenous, as Krieger (1953, 1964) argues.

The Chopper-Scraper Problem

One of the interesting things about the speculations just reviewed concerning the Asiatic base for American cultures is that for some students the answer is, and has long been, at hand, requiring no further discussion. These zealots interpret the widespread chopper-scraper horizon found over much of the two Americas as ample evidence. This complex or culture can be equated on typologic grounds with the Early and Middle Paleolithic of Eurasia. Always percussion-flaked, the specimens are large and crude, and many resemble the sharpened cores and pebbles of the Southeast Asian tradition. Most resemble the core and flake tools of the European Lower Paleolithic (Figures 3.4 and 3.5). Never are there associated projectile points or finely chipped knives or other more specialized tools. Krieger (1964) has assigned the widely distributed complex to a preprojectile point "stage." Although Krieger explicitly denies that his several stages imply a time sequence, he, and most of the others who have tried to assess the profuse material, have thought of the chopper-scraper congeries as a very ancient substratum upon which the American culture sequence is based. Their conviction fulfills both the logic and the typology of the situation.

Why, then, do so few serious students agree that the chopper-scraper substratum can be recognized? The answer is that the sites where the collections have been made simply meet none of the minimum control standards archeologists insist upon for any artifact complex if it is to be deemed truly ancient. These requirements are usually that the data come from a buried site or be sealed by unbroken strata

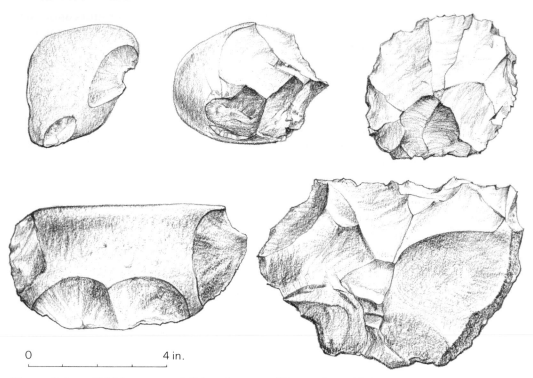

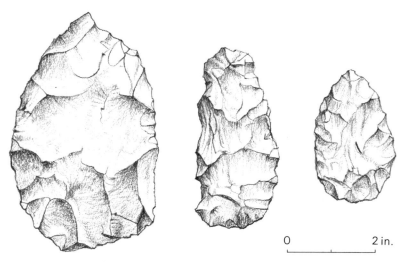

0   4 in.

Figure 3.4   *Pebble core and flake choppers. (Drawn from University of Utah collection, Wyoming and Utah sites)*

0   2 in.

Figure 3.5   *Flaked chopper-scrapers of slightly finer workmanship. (Drawn from University of Utah collection, Pine Spring site, Wyoming)*

of earth; that the stratum of occurrence should be identifiable as a part of, or related to, geologically understood phenomena over a reasonably wide area; that,

preferably, there be association with extinct mammal remains; and, with luck, that there be one or more distinctive artifact types represented in the collection—

specimens comparable to what the paleontologists call "index fossils." Also, since 1950, radiocarbon date ascriptions are sought. Most of the chopper-scraper collections are surface finds and do not fulfill any of the conditions listed above. They may be exceedingly old or they may not, but no indisputable evidence exists. The best-known sites occur in profusion in the western High Plains and the Great Basin.

Krieger, in a sample list, cites over twenty locations in North America and

Figure 3.6 *Chopper-scraper sites and complexes in North America. (Modified from Krieger 1964)*

Mexico (Figure 3.6). While most of the collections consist entirely of stone materials, Krieger would include splinters of leg bones from large animals eroded from wear or use on one or both ends and rare bone tubes made by shearing off the ends of long bones as part of the artifact complex. Generally, the deposits are recovered from river terraces or lake beaches high above present water level or even in situations where there is now no stream or lake at all. Often, too, the specimens are heavily patinated or "varnished" (see Hunt 1954 concerning desert varnish), leading to speculations of great age. Carter (1951) has argued that the cumulative evidence of location, crudity, varnish, and other considerations can well be taken as proof of antiquity. Simpson (1958) is even more positive in her claims. Most archeologists reject or even ignore the entire matter. Some base their rejection on the lack of controls; others appear to reject the idea of a mid-Wisconsin emigration, to say nothing of a *pre*-Wisconsin dating, as the typology of the implements would require. Some, like Jennings (1964, 1965b), express a blind faith that all the claims *could* be true and may one day be substantiated, although this faith seems to weaken as years pass without the emergence of any convincing proof. Others, like William Mulloy (personal communication, 1964) and Sharrock (1966), scoff at the extravagant claims of the proponents, pointing out that comparable specimens can be and have been recovered many times in buried or covered sites in clear association with well-developed projectile point series, milling stones, and other specimens known to be of relatively recent origin. Still others ascribe the crude flaking to natural agencies such as frost or heat, claiming that thermal flaking of certain kinds of flint and chert resembles the results achieved by man. Thus, they deny that these collections are even artifacts (see Ascher and Ascher 1965).

The problem came to recent attention through the work of Renaud (1940, 1947), who was trained in Europe. He became interested in the extensive deposits of these crude specimens in southwest Wyoming, especially on the river terraces on the Blacks Fork of the Green River. Here he found and named the Blacks Fork culture, a complex he describes as displaying close similarity to the Early and Middle Paleolithic cultures of Eurasia. He identifies and figures a pebble industry, numbers of cores resembling fist axes, and extensive examples of Clactonian flaking techniques. This complex of crude pieces he calls the "typical" culture. He recognizes also the later existence of a Peripheral and a Sand Dune culture. Comparable collections were made for many years by Renaud (1940) over a wide area, but no one has taken his claims very seriously. Sharrock (1966) has fully disposed of Renaud's claims through his re-examination of the Blacks Fork area, where he demonstrated the artifacts to be quarry materials. Furthermore, he showed that in one excavated site (Pine Spring, Wyoming), they occur *neatly* stratified over a time range from 6000 B.C. to A.D. 1400.

Carter (1957), a geographer, has been extremely energetic in pursuing the chopper-scraper complex. He claims exceedingly ancient specimens from localities in California near La Jolla and in San Diego. Carter's claims are extravagant, the artifacts are of doubtful authenticity, and the data are neither well controlled nor clearly reported. We can, on the basis of present knowledge, reject out-of-hand the claim of Third Interglacial times as the date of man's arrival in the West. No evidence known to us will support this view. All Carter's claims may be true, but proof must await more rigorous fieldwork and less partisan reporting (see Johnson and Miller 1958, for a detailed negative evaluation of Carter's work).

Another location, which appears at first

glance to be valid, is Santa Rosa Island off the coast of California, where Orr (various) has made several finds. Here dwarf mammoth bones found sometimes lying in reddened earth and deeply buried in sediment give radiocarbon ages ranging from 18,000 to over 25,000 B.C. No artifacts have been found in association with the mammoth bones, although chopper-scraper specimens do occur as isolated finds on the island. There is some doubt that the mammoth bones are burned as claimed. The fascinating prospect of proving men to have been preying on the evidently numerous little mammoth cannot be confirmed until the finds are reported in detail. The presence of man on the island quite early is attested by the radiocarbon date of 8000 B.C. for organic material found beside two human leg-bone fragments at the Arlington Springs site. The bones were in a buried, once marshy, streambed (Orr 1962). There is a wealth of archeologic sites, and a long sequence on Santa Rosa Island as well as an impressive array of radiocarbon dates on shell, charcoal, and other materials. The dates, however, do not apply to anything except the specimens themselves. A cultural inventory and details of recovery have not yet appeared. A visit to the island convinces one that if careful search and excavation were carried out, the prospects for finding artifacts, evidences of fire and of extinct fauna in full association would be excellent. To date, however, this seems not to have happened; therefore, as evidence of man's presence by earlier than 25,000 B.C., these finds must also be awarded a Scotch verdict. In Oregon, Cressman (1960) has found, in a deeply buried context, a crude scraper, but there are no associated artifacts or other evidence of man.

There is no need to continue. Time after time—at Manix Lake (Simpson 1958, 1960), Chapala Lake (Arnold 1957), Tule Springs (Harrington and Simpson 1961),

and other localities—either the finds are surface deposits or the claimed association or age ascriptions dissolve in the face of rigorous reexamination. This study is simultaneously one of the most frustrating researches and one of the most important in American archeology. Some have said that the uncontrolled surface nature of the finds should be ignored (for example, Krieger 1964) because the materials represent a culture *stage* regardless of where found. It is sometimes claimed that although the accumulations are now on the surface, they were, when deposited, on the same surface and were later probably sealed by finer deposits which are now eroded away. It is also argued that the specimens found on what is now the surface may represent one or more living areas in layers higher up in a sediment accumulation now entirely dispersed. For this, again, no proof exists. The person who can lay all claims and doubts to rest (and remove the decades of resistance inertia resultant from doubt) by proving a certain period or time of origin for the chopper-scraper stage will have made a contribution to archeology equal to any to date. Sharrock (1966) has made a strong beginning by clarifying the Blacks Fork situation.

Leaving the acres of surface stones for later study by others, and in the hope that the age and significance of the chopper-scraper complexes will soon be fully understood, we shall now examine some materials recovered under better-controlled conditions. Krieger (1964) briefly reports the fabulous Friesenhahn Cave (Texas) finds. Here, in a sealed cave with a rich bed of Pleistocene fossils, were found chipped flint tools made of flakes with steeply chipped edges. They have not yet been fully reported, although Sellards (1952) has figured one of these pieces. It appears to be an authentic tool. There were also bone tubes, but whether they were made by human hands is questioned.

The associated fauna include elephant, horse, bison, peccary, and dire wolf, all of which are found in association with artifacts in other parts of the Southwest. No radiocarbon date derived from the bones has yet been released.

Perhaps the closest approach to full control over one small collection of the chopper-scraper materials occurred during excavation at the C. W. Harris site in San Diego County (California), which will be described a little later. Here Warren and True (1961) found a mixed artifact complex. A significant number of the specimens can be included in the chopper-scraper class, but there are associated finer pieces. Radiocarbon results are not too clear, but the authors' estimate of 6000 to 8000 B.C. for the lower stratum seems reasonable and can be provisionally accepted. Warren (personal communication, 1965) has continued to study the entire problem and is now testing a hypothesis that there can be found, under controlled conditions, evidence of a consistent scraper-chopper complex dated at 9000 to 12,000 B.C. He assumes that these artifacts were left by Big Game Hunters and that they will be found in the timber-valley ecotone along the Sierra Nevada foothills down into the California desert. This suggestion, which is based on findings at the Harris site, is more conservative and far more reasonable than most of the statements about the complex. However, work in 1965 yielded several radiocarbon dates which fall within the 6000 to 8000 B.C. range estimated earlier.

Related because of uncertain age to the chopper-scraper enigma are the scores of flint and quartzite quarries found over the continent. Holmes (1897) has an exhaustive coverage of a series of quarries between Baltimore and Wilmington and at other places on the fall line, at the inner edge of the coastal plain. The deposits are cobbles or gravels which have been the scene of extensive aboriginal digging and flint knapping. The number of crude specimens that are explained as "blanks" or half-finished tools runs into thousands. These occur in lenticular accumulations that Holmes calls "shop debris," where flakes, broken pieces, and rejected blanks are concentrated. The problem here and at many other quarries, such as the Spanish Diggings in Wyoming, is that pebbles sharpened on one end into well-made fist axes can also be recognized. The quarries may all have been worked for thousands of years and thus may have no affiliation with any one stage. The quarry idea is attractive as an explanation because we know that specific flint deposits have been quarried for thousands of years. For example, Witthoft's (1952) work at the Shoop site (Pennsylvania) certainly indicates that the famed Onondaga (New York) quarries were known and that the materials were transported for many miles in very early times, because a large number of fluted points discovered on the site are made from Onondaga flint. The Shoop site is well over 100 miles from the quarry. Another example is the Alibates (Texas) flint quarry, which was known and used by Texas Indians for centuries. The quarries represent, then, another unsolved problem, a problem which helps confuse the evidence for the chopper-scraper material. There is almost conclusive evidence that the Blacks Fork (Wyoming) deposits are nothing but age-old quarries where some of the artifact "fields" occur at the abundant, black-banded (tiger), flint outcrops.

Concluding this section forces the admission that little has been proved. The intent has been to mention a confusing array of objects, a plethora of claims, and an important problem yet unsolved. Neither the age nor the cultural significance of this complex can be settled here. The answer lies in the ground.

The Big Game Hunters

The title of this section is perhaps misleading; certainly it is arbitrary because all the specimens of the preprojectile stage just discussed are presumed to have been made and used by the takers of big game. In this section, however, most of what is described has been carefully reported and can be set in more definite ecologic contexts. Furthermore, the material is well controlled as to stratigraphy, time, and distribution. Some students, with good arguments, include here the host of "free-floating" complexes from the Western deserts. These complexes, which loom so large in the literature but which are so enigmatic, include the Pinto, Mohave, Silver Lake, Death Valley I, San Dieguito, Amargosa, and Playa, among others. These complexes, their sites, and the speculations about them can most coherently be introduced in the next chapter and will be discussed there.

The Big Game Hunters can be equated with the Paleo-Indian, Paleo-American, Early American Hunter, and Upper Lithic stages mentioned earlier. There are several named complexes and cultures to be described, but the shared criteria are simple and well known. The time range of the specialized hunter stage, determined by repeated radiocarbon testing, extends from perhaps 15,000 to 5000-4000 B.C., with the most reliable dates falling between 9500 and 5000 B.C. The stage began when the available big game was a series of now-extinct species; it persisted through and beyond their extinction, with the later sites yielding exclusively modern fauna. The situation, including the fact of overlap of dates of extinct and modern species, can be readily appreciated in Figure 2.12, taken from Hester (1960). The Big Game Hunters represented in the Western sites are broken into three sequent groups and are given culture names. The earliest is

called the Llano (Sellards 1952), next comes the Folsom, and the latest is the Plano (Jennings 1955). Several Eastern complexes of about the same age can be correlated, on typologic grounds, with these same divisions. The generalized description of these subdivisions of the Big Game stage is short and scant. The sites yield bones—usually from more than one animal—from some or all of the large mammals listed in Figures 2.12 and 3.7. Tools include thin, fine-chipped, laurel-leaf–shaped, biface blades or lance points, scrapers of various sorts, and perhaps burins. For the most part, these sites are confined to the High Plains. They are most often kill sites rather than camps, so the full range of the artifact inventory isn't known. However, sites from the core area (Figure 3.8), as described by Wendorf and Hester (1962), are of two types: campsites and kill sites. Campsites often occur on dunes, and the remains include hearths; broken, split, and charred food bones; chipping debris; and a full complement of flint tools [fluted or unfluted points, channel flakes (debris from the fluting process), hammerstones, several kinds of scrapers made from flakes, and random chips showing wear from use]. Kill sites occur on the banks of former fossil ponds or streams and are often at the base of a cliff or jump-off, where the prey was stampeded to its death; all have been buried by subsequent deposition. The contents are restricted to the skeletons of the animals and the few tools, including the fluted points, used in the killing and butchering processes. A few sites are stratified, yielding evidence of two or even all three cultures from one station. MacHaffie (Montana) and Blackwater Draw, locality 1 (New Mexico) are perhaps the best examples of well-preserved and recorded stratified sites.

If it is possible to generalize so glibly about a 10,000-year-old culture stage that

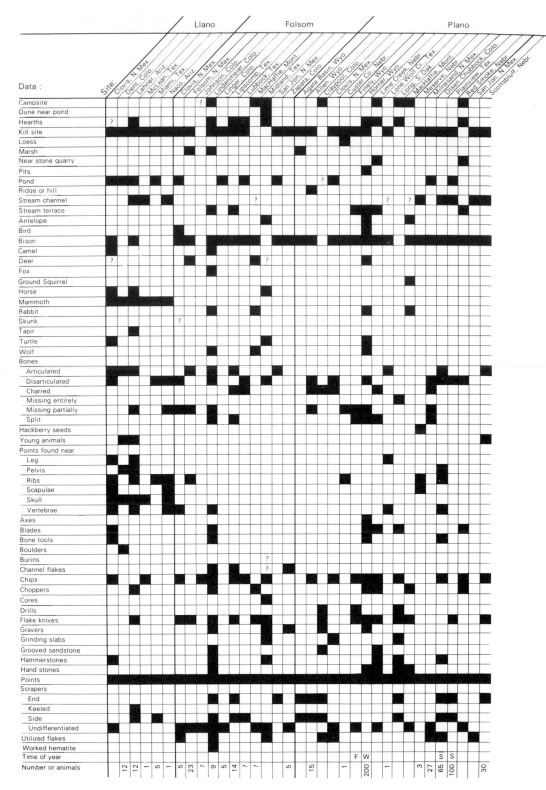

Figure 3.7 *Tabulated characteristics of selected Llano, Folsom, and Plano sites. (Modified from Wendorf and Hester 1962)*

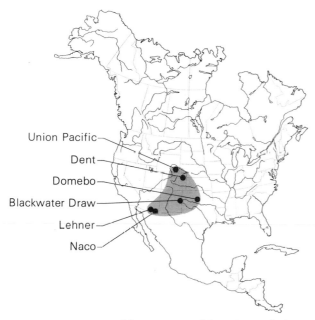

Union Pacific
Dent
Domebo
Blackwater Draw
Lehner
Naco

Figure 3.8   *Core Llano area and locations of sites.*

spans the transition from the Ice Age to the Recent, how do the three subdivisions differ? The Llano, restricted to a small area (Figure 3.8; compare Krieger 1964), is represented by only a few stations where all critics are satisfied as to authenticity. The indices to classification are that the kill always involves the mammoth (but not necessarily exclusively—see the Lehner site below) and that one or more Clovis Fluted points (Figure 3.9) are always found directly with the bones in good "association." These lanceolate points are thin, 3 to 6 inches long, about one-fourth as wide as long, have smooth, if sometimes large, percussion (?) flake scars, and have one or more short flakes removed from the base down the median portion toward the tip. These shallow flake scars give the characteristic "fluting." At present, one would expect to recognize a Llano site from the association of mammoth bones and Clovis Fluted points.

The more numerous Folsom sites always contain remains of one or another of the large-horned extinct bison and the Folsom fluted point (Figure 3.10). The Folsom is also lanceolate; it is made with delicate, pressure-flaked retouch and is thinned by the removal on each face of one long, thin flake almost to the tip. The points are distinct and came to bear the name of the site where they were first discovered. Plano unfluted points are associated with modern fauna, such as bison or antelope (Figure 3.11).

The Folsom point and its importance are such as to warrant a digression. It was at Folsom, New Mexico, that in 1926 and 1927 the remains of twenty-three extinct bison (*Bison antiquus figginsi*) were uncovered in a box canyon with nineteen Folsom fluted points in undisputed association. This single find, dug with care and observed by competent scientists from several institutions, set American prehistory on a new course. Beyond question, here was proof of the coexistence of Pleistocene fauna and toolmaking man.

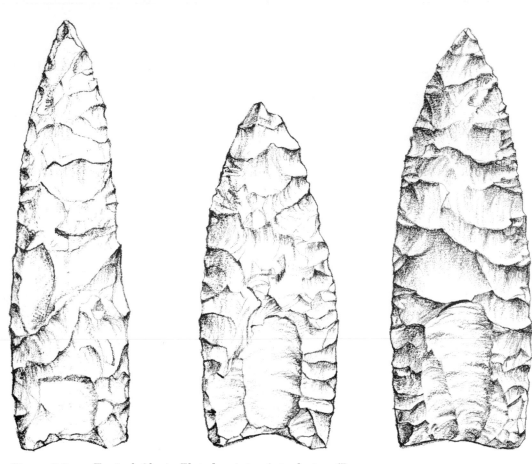

Figure 3.9   *Typical Clovis Fluted points. Actual size. (Drawn from J. A. Eichenberger casts. This and succeeding credits to the Eichenberger casts refer to a collection which is well known to North American archeologists and which can be purchased from the Denver Museum of Natural History)*

The impact of this one discovery, while not instantaneous, ultimately touched off a search for comparable finds which soon led to the discovery and acceptance of the even older Llano complex. As told by Steen (1955), the story of the Folsom discovery is quite romantic. Briefly, it is as follows: The bison-bone bed had evidently been known to a cowhand, George McJunken, since about 1900. He told a family named Schwachheim at Raton, New Mexico, about it because he knew that Carl Schwachheim was an amateur paleontologist. McJunken had died before Schwachheim visited the locality, removed one of the bones, and took it to J. D. Figgins, then director of what is now the Denver Museum of Natural History. Excavation began in 1926, but the world of science ignored Figgins' claim of finding the remains of extinct bison and man-made artifacts together, rejecting rather than investigating the claim. Undeterred, Figgins resumed excavation in 1927. This time he was visited by the archeologists Alfred V. Kidder and Frank H. H. Roberts, Jr., and the paleontologist Barnum Brown. These men saw and agreed that the find was valid. Although it was by no means the first such find [for example, Lone

The Llano Culture

Western Sites The best-known of the Llano culture sites are Blackwater Draw (near Clovis, New Mexico), and the Naco-Lehner duo (in extreme southeastern Arizona). Others, with less claim to authenticity or less fully reported, are listed in Sellards (1952). There are no known precedent Eurasiatic forms for the beautifully chipped Llano and Folsom points. The fluting is believed to be exclusively a New World technique.

Blackwater Draw, locality 1, is described here from Sellards' (1952) account. Wormington (1957) gives a good running résumé of the nearly twenty-year history of exploration, involving numerous observers. The site was once a series of seep springs forming a large, deep pond with a marshy drainage channel (Figure 3.12). The sediment which eventually filled the spring and channel consisted of several contrasting layers, which are diagramed in Figure 3.13. The gray sand yielded elephant remains and the Llano artifacts shown in Figure 3.14.

Additional work at the type "Clovis" (or Blackwater Draw, locality 1) site has shown that the Llano complex can be characterized by another diagnostic artifact called the Clovis blade (Green 1963). While there is doubt as to the exact

Wolf Creek, Texas (Cook 1926)], no other single incident has influenced the study of America's past as much, nor excited such widespread popular interest, as did the Folsom.

After the Folsom discovery (which stimulated search), Plano and Llano sites began to be discovered in quantity. The Plano diagnostic points, while varyingly leaf-shaped, are not fluted and show more variation in form than the preceding Clovis and Folsom fluted types. The associated fauna, or Plano specimens, invariably contain modern species, usually *Bison*.

Figure 3.10 *Folsom fluted points. Actual size. (Drawn from J. A. Eichenberger casts)*

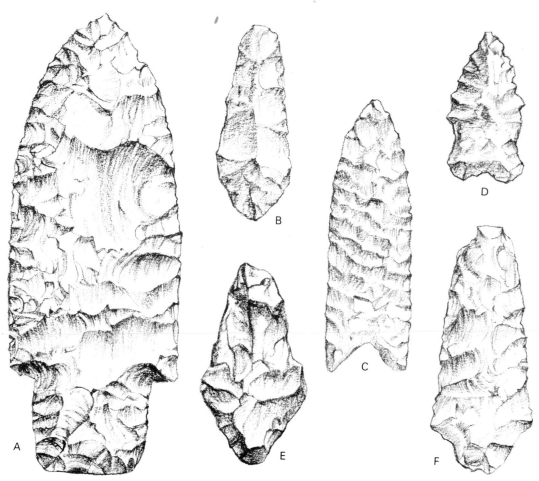

Figure 3.11   *Selected unfluted points. Actual size. A, Alberta;*
B, Lake Mohave; C, Jimmy Allen; D, Pinto Basin; E, Silver Lake;
F, Gypsum Cave. (Drawn from J. A. Eichenberger casts)

provenience, the blades appear to have come from the gray sands whence the Clovis points were derived. The blade discovery came accidentally during gravel-pit operations, and the point of origin of a cache of the blades was inferred from the location of the scattered pieces in freshly deposited spoil dirt left by earth-moving equipment. Green has no hesitancy in assigning the blades to the Llano layer; his position seems sound. Seventeen blades were found (Figure 3.15). They are curved flakes, prismatic in cross section, derived from a well-prepared core. There is no retouch. As Figure 3.16 shows, the preparation of the blade is a fairly sophisticated way of working flint. These blades were probably viewed as finished tools as they came from the core. Their use would have been as knives or scrapers. [The authenticity of the curved flake knives as being of Llano provenience is strengthened by the occurrence of similar blades at a mammoth site nearby, as well as by Haury's (Haury, Sayles, and Wasley 1959) find of similar scrapers at the Lehner site.] Folsom specimens came from the diatomaceous earth, with the carbonaceous silt yielding Plano artifacts. As the stratigraphic chart implies, the geologic processes were complex and have raised many questions, particularly about climate, but these need not detain us here.

Probably the most systematically studied of the Llano sites to date is the Lehner (Arizona) location (Haury, Sayles, and Wasley 1959). Equally well reported, but yielding less information, was the Naco (Arizona) mammoth site (Haury, Antevs, and Lance 1953). Both sites were brought to Haury's attention by laymen whose service to science cannot be overestimated. The Navarretes, Marc and Fred, discovered the Naco site; E. F. Lehner reported the site bearing his name. The sites are close together and very similar. Both are alongside a fossil streambed, sealed over millennia ago by later deposits of sediment. Both had been revealed by modern gullying. At both sites Clovis Fluted points were in direct association with mammoth remains. At Lehner, other creatures—horse, bison, and tapir—were represented. There, too, were evidences of a fire. The nine mammoth and the other animals are believed to have been killed and butchered on the spot. Figure 3.17 shows some of the flaked tools other than projectile points found at the Lehner site. As already indicated, these blades exemplify the Clovis knives as belonging with the Llano complex. The final importance of the Lehner material is that a firm radiocarbon date of about 9500 B.C. can be ascribed. Some would argue that this may be an average age for the Llano in the middle range.

Other generally accepted Llano sites include Miami (Texas), Dent (Colorado), McLean (Texas), and Iztapan (Mexico). At Lindenmeier, too, elephant bones were encountered. There is evidence (for example, Byers 1954) that Lindenmeier is a stratified or twice-occupied site where both Llano and Folsom complexes are found. Thus, for our purposes, Lindenmeier, pending a final report, is also considered to be both a Llano and a Folsom

station. There are other sites where mammoth remains are accompanied by nondiagnostic artifacts. The Union Pacific Mammoth Kill site (Wyoming) is one of these. Here C. Irwin, H. Irwin, and Agogino (1962) report a mammoth which had evidently been trapped in an ancient bog and, they think, had been stoned to death with large boulders. Only two flint tools—not Clovis Fluted points—were with it. The find is authentic enough; the radiocarbon date is 9300 B.C. The Union Pacific site raises an interesting and, as yet, unsolved problem. Are these bog or marsh mammoth kills evidence of a deliberate hunting technique? Did the Llano hunters search out drinking, feeding, or bathing animals and kill them there, where the clutching muck would hamper their movements? Or, as has been suggested, were the animals badly wounded and feverish and did they therefore seek water? Or, as some think, were these animals mired and helpless through their own misjudgment, to be killed when discovered, perhaps by accident, by the hunters? Whatever the answer is, all the now-known Llano sites are associated with fossil bogs and marshes, and it is clear that kills were made in such locations.

The Big Game Hunters are represented at two locations in Mexico as well. At Tepexpan in the Valley of Mexico (see page 52, a human skeleton was found in the same stratum as an articulated mammoth, but not in association; no diagnostic artifacts were found. Because of careless fieldwork there was doubt (later somewhat dispelled) about the validity of this find, and little notice is taken of this discovery. Later, however, and under excellent control a mammoth with associated artifacts was discovered and reported from Santa Isabel, Iztapan, also in the Valley of Mexico. With the Iztapan specimen was a knife vaguely resembling the Plano Scottsbluff type, but the ascribed date is about 9000 B.C., somewhat early for this

type. Nonetheless, there is no doubt as to the validity of this find. It is important as documenting not only the presence of mammoth hunters in Mexico, but also the exceedingly rapid dispersal of the hunters southward as well as to the east from the presumed entry point in the northern Plains. A second Iztapan find also provided some chipped flint knives. These are of nondiagnostic type, but the find again confirms man's presence in Mexico at an early date.

The range of the Western Llano has been extended eastward to the Domebo (Oklahoma) location, where typical Clovis Fluted specimens (Figure 3.18) were found under good control (Leonhardy 1966).

There are many details left untold in the above account. The omissions are made reluctantly because these few Llano sites are perhaps the most exciting in all of American archeology. Aside from being well dated, providing the earliest uncontested evidence of man on the two continents, the sites give rise to fascinating (and no doubt incorrect) mental images of a lone hunter or a small band attempting to slaughter one of these monstrous animals (a mammoth's weight is estimated at 6 to 10 tons) with small flint tools or a few boulders. Probably other animals were more important as prey. All in all, the information on the Llano culture is embarrassingly scanty. The half-dozen sites, scattered over a restricted area, tell us very little. The kill sites only evidence kills. What other tools were possessed? What were the camps like? Were vegetal foods collected and processed?

Reconstruction of the life of the Llano hunters can rest on little solid data. We are left with theory and ethnologic analogs. Even in the areas of subsistence and technology, our knowledge is fragmentary, putting a strain on one's credulity. The few archeologic finds seem to say that only the large animals were taken and that all technology was directed toward the hunt. No observed peoples have ever concentrated upon one species alone, so we must assume a wider subsistence base than the finds can document. One

Figure 3.12   *Blackwater Draw, locality 1, at the time of Llano man.*

can even suspect that the mammoth kills were the exception and that lesser animals were more usually sought. The closest living analog may be the Ona or Yahgan tribes of South America. Among the Ona, the guanaco is the preferred game, but Bridges (1948) tells of their taking birds of several kinds as well as foxes and many rodents. There, evidently, hunting is almost entirely done by lone individuals or small parties. Stealth and slow stalking requiring great skill and patience enable the hunter to get close enough to a large animal to wound it (with an arrow in the case of the Ona). The Llano hunter is presumed to have had the lance or dart and atlatl, but not the bow. Such weapons cannot kill outright. The preferred wound was one into the rib cage and intestines, so that the animal grew weak from loss of blood (largely through internal bleeding) and finally died. Thus the hunter might follow game for several hours, or even days, before the hunt was over. In the Plains, where many tasty vegetable and berry species abound, it is reasonable to assume that the Llano peoples utilized these in season.

If the lone-hunter analogy is sound, it is entirely reasonable to postulate the nuclear or extended family as the effective social and economic unit. Obviously, the population was very sparse; competition for either space or game would not exist, and no raiding or fighting between the tiny groups need be suggested. On the other hand, there were probably sometime concentrations of population, as at Lindenmeier, where the debris is evidently from a camp of some size or of long-continued use, or both. One can postulate continuous capture of waterfowl when and where these were available. Again, the Ona provide a model: Bridges describes night hunting of birds by a group of men carrying torches. The light confused the birds, and they were easily taken with sticks or snares. We may be sure that the quest for food was continuous except when a lucky windfall, such as a mammoth, provided surplus for a few days.

Material possessions would be few,

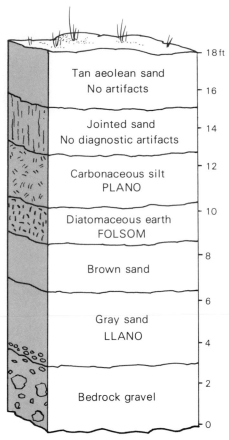

18 ft

Tan aeolean sand
No artifacts

16

Jointed sand
No diagnostic artifacts

14

Carbonaceous silt
PLANO

12

Diatomaceous earth
FOLSOM

10

Brown sand

8

6

Gray sand
LLANO

4

2

Bedrock gravel

0

Figure   3.13   Stratigraphy   of   Blackwater Draw, locality 1. (Modified from Sellards 1952)

probably consisting mostly of tools and weapons used in the endless search for food because the living pattern would have been one of roving and scattered temporary camps, rather than of permanent campsites. The possibility of a permanent camp, however, cannot be ruled out. In game-rich areas, where hunting pressure was not great and was spread across several species, a small family group might live for several seasons at the same spot, hunting selectively in different directions in some sort of established sequence. The clothing of the people was probably confined to fur robes and perhaps footgear. No evidence of artificial shelters has been encountered. We may reasonably

suspect simple brush or grass windbreaks as well as caves or overhangs in restricted areas, but these natural shelters are rare in the Plains. We must assume more-or-less open camps with protection from the weather being afforded by the robes, shelters, and fire. It is recognized that the simple lifeway postulated above goes far beyond the empirical evidence. Additional finds may substantiate the postulated broader subsistence base and a more versatile kit of tools, but there is no likelihood that the effective social unit can be proved archeologically.

Eastern Sites   From the foregoing pages one might suppose that the problem of the Llano culture is confined to the High Plains within the tiny area outlined by the several locations. Such is not the case. Clovis Fluted points occur all over the continent, wherever the land was ice-free 12,000 years ago. Figure 3.19 shows that thousands of these points have been found in the Middle West and East, compared with the dozens found in the Plains. Except for a few locations, all the Eastern finds are uncontrolled surface finds, and no fluted point has been found with elephant remains in the East. Yet we know that the browsing Eastern mastodon (as opposed to the grazing mammoth) was far more common than was the mammoth of the West. (At least, it is represented by more recorded fossil finds.) The problem of the Eastern Llano, its age and its relationship to the Llano of the Plains, has been studied most intensively by three men, Quimby (1960), Byers (1954), and Mason (1962), although Ritchie (1953) and Witthoft (1952) have also made key contributions.

Only the Bull Brook and Debert locations, both reported by Byers, have been sealed deposits; both have also been dated by means of radiocarbon. Moreover, some of the Clovis Fluted points and the other artifacts from the sites are of classic Llano type dated (at the Bull Brook site) at just

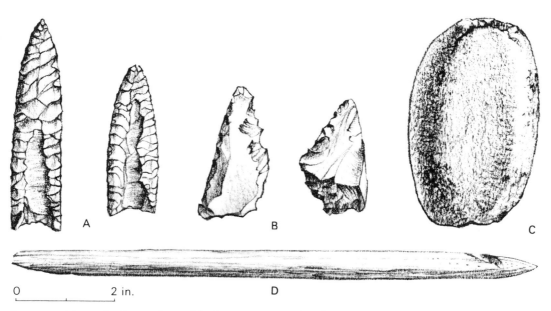

Figure 3.14   *Artifacts from Blackwater Draw, locality 1. A, fluted points; B, scrapers; C, hammerstone; D, worked bone. (After Sellards 1952)*

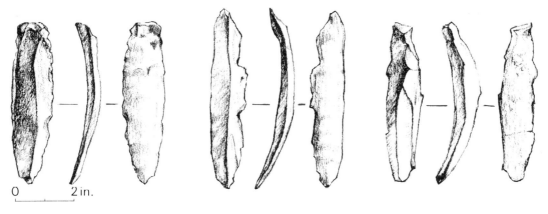

Figure 3.15   *Clovis blades from Blackwater Draw, locality 1. (After Green 1963)*

under 7000 B.C. Byers (1954) not only has described the material but also has convincingly correlated his finds as sharing detailed artifact traits with Lindenmeier (some 2,500 miles distant), as well as with the closer but undated Shoop (Pennsylvania) and Williamson (Virginia) sites of the East. Scholars generally would be willing to extend the Bull Brook dates to the Shoop and Williamson materi-

als. The artifacts found at Bull Brook are shown in Figure 3.20. The startling similarity to Llano artifacts offers the typologic clue that Lindenmeier (the lowest level), Bull Brook, Shoop, and Williamson are perhaps to be equated with Llano rather than with Folsom, as is usually done.

Bull Brook is near Ipswich, Massachusetts. It was discovered during gravel operations (which have since destroyed

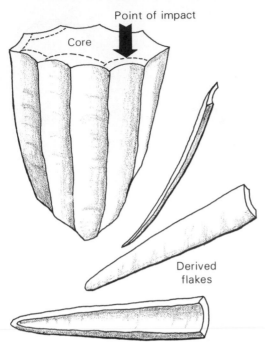

Figure 3.16 *A core-nucleus technique for the production of flake blades. (Modified from Bordaz 1959)*

the site) by W. C. Eldridge and Joseph Vaccaro, members of the Massachusetts Archeological Society. While the micro-geology of the site was puzzling in that no clearly discernible strata or old living surfaces could be detected, the artifacts and charcoal were buried 12 or more inches beneath the surface, and some 1,000 specimens in all were recovered. They tended to occur in concentrations, as if discarded around preferred small camp spots. More than fifty fluted points or fragments were in the collection. The full inventory of specimens includes the Clovis Fluted pieces (which do differ slightly from the Western ones), end scrapers with a spur, flake side scrapers of several sizes including some which again resemble the prismatic-flake Clovis knife, several sharp, pointed little gravers and drills. The cores from which flakes were struck also occur.

At the Debert site in Nova Scotia, which has been partially reported (Byers 1966),

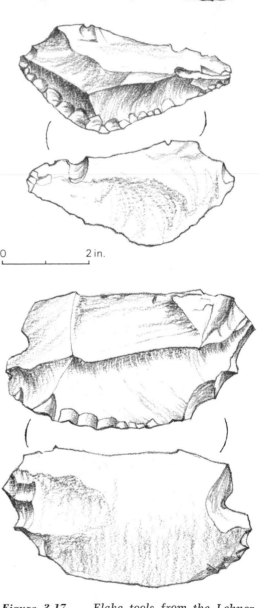

Figure 3.17 *Flake tools from the Lehner site. (After Haury, Sayles, and Wasley 1959)*

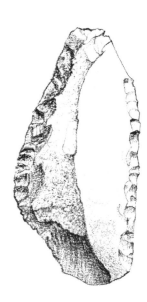

Figure 3.18   *Artifacts from Domebo. Actual size. (Drawn from J. A. Eichenberger casts)*

the Bull Brook assemblage is apparently duplicated. There are 4,000 artifacts from eleven living areas with associated hearths but no faunal associations. The age, derived from charcoal from the hearths, is reported as 9000 to 7000 B.C. The site was occupied when portions of the shrinking ice of the Valders sheet were only 60 miles away and while permafrost existed (Douglas S. Byers, personal communication, 1965). The full significance of this find is yet to be assessed.

Most of the literature on the Eastern fluted points refers generically to Eastern Folsom, or Folsomoid, or Eastern Fluted types or to such local names as Cumberland, Redstone, Dalton, Quad, or Reagan (Figure 3.21). Because the pieces are surface finds, and because none is classic Folsom, the tendency has been to keep any treatment or discussion rather general. In fact, most specimens are more like Clovis Fluted, and a typical Folsom fluted is never found in the East. Since the discovery of Bull Brook, where dates are available, and because there are now enough Western

Clovis Fluted points found *in situ* with mammoth remains which are dated, Quimby and Mason have offered syntheses which conclude that the Llano complex is about the same age wherever it is found; therefore the Eastern version would presumably fall in the same time range as the Western Llano. Mason's (1962) effort is by far the most ambitious and, as a result, can be criticized on several points. Nevertheless it stands as making much overall sense. It is recommended (along with the many criticisms appended to it) as basic to any study of the Llano question. Mason takes account of the ice margins, of the pollen studies, of the facts of distribution, and of the typologic consistency over the entire East to demonstrate that the Big Game Hunter material can be studied specifically and systematically on a continent-wide basis. Mason's position is strengthened by the Debert finds.

Anomalous Situations   Before leaving the Llano complex it is necessary to mention the Sandia Cave finds. The cave is a

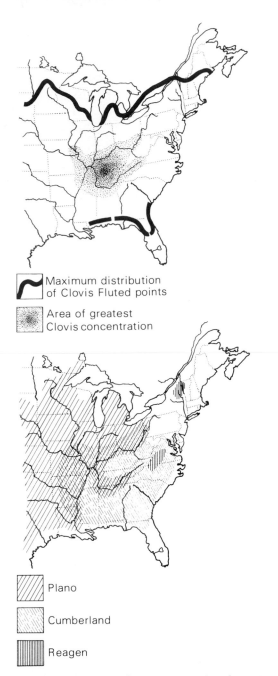

Figure 3.19 *Lithic stage projectile point distribution in eastern North America. (Modified from Mason 1962)*

long, irregular tube, rather than an overhang, in the Sandia Range near Albuquerque, New Mexico. Much argument has surrounded the excavating and reporting of the site, but the situation seems to involve three occupations, each sealed from the other (Hibben 1941), as Figure 3.22 shows. The succession of deposits is the Sandia layer, earliest, Folsom next, and recent (yielding Pueblo pottery) as the latest. The Sandia point is essentially unique. The Sandia Type 1 point has a rounded base; Type 2 has a flat or an indented base and is sometimes thinned by short fluting. Both types are rather crudely chipped. Hibben (1941) views Type 1 as earliest, and Mason (1962) agrees, regarding Type 2 as possibly intermediate between Sandia Type 1 and the Clovis Fluted. The main diagnostic attribute of the point, however, is the well-developed shoulder on one edge (Figure 3.23). These points are accompanied by scrapers, prismatic flakes, and other common tools. The Sandia points occur nowhere else under any semblance of control and are rare in any case. Some archeologists will allow an age of greater than 10,000 years to the Sandia specimens and an even greater age than the Llano complex, but this latter placement cannot be sustained by either stratigraphy or radiocarbon dating. The generalized resemblance of the Sandia point to certain Solutrean points of Europe has led a few Americanists to view the Sandia points as lineal relatives of the Solutre pieces. For our purposes the site and the specimens can be left hanging as unequated with anything else we know. They are merely older than Folsom. The collection will probably eventually be seen as coeval with the Llano because the extinct-mammal associations include mammoth, horse, camel, bison, and mastodon—about the same inventory as at the Lehner site.

Figure 3.20 *Artifacts from Bull Brook. A, B, retouched blades; C, "twist drill"; D, uniface gravers; E, fluted projectile points; F, side scrapers; G, end scrapers with graver spur at edge of blade. (After Byers 1954)*

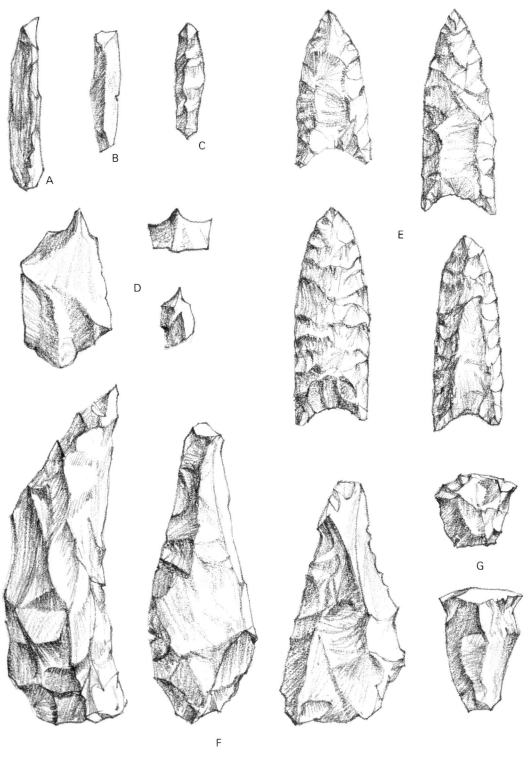

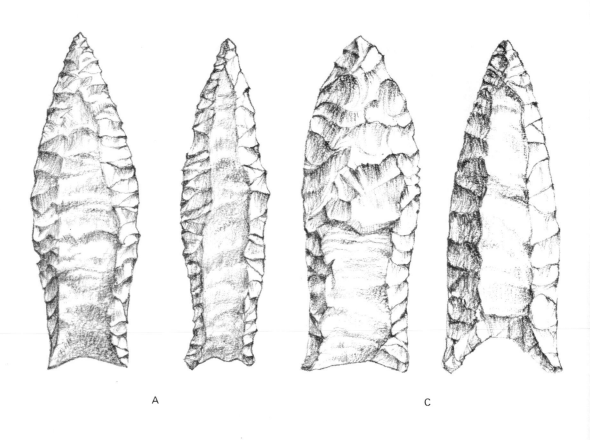

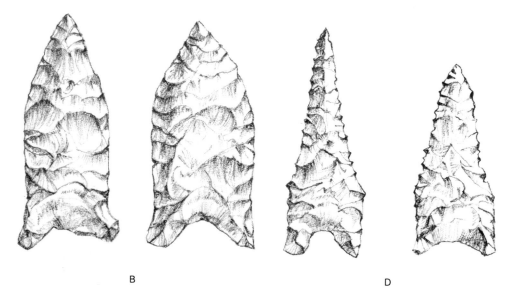

Figure 3.21 *Fluted projectile points from Tennessee. Slightly reduced. A, Cumberland; B, Quad; C, Clovis (so-called); D, Dalton. (After Mason 1962)*

Arguing further for placement of Sandia in the Llano are two bone artifacts found at Sandia, which were made from the leg of a camel. These are thought to have been projectile tips. Similar objects are reported from the Blackwater site. These points would also hint that the collection may belong with the Friesenhahn Cave and other preprojectile-point-stage sites.

Another site which looms large in the literature is Tule Springs. Here, Harrington and Simpson (1961) report charcoal and flint (obsidian) specimens with a radiocarbon ascription of *over* 27,000 B.C. Subsequent work (Shutler 1965) proves this dating of the cultural debris to have been in error. The radiocarbon dates for the very skimpy culture evidence actually cluster around 9000 B.C. (Fergusson and Libby 1964).

Another complex which is hard to place is the "Old Cordilleran" of the Plateau area (Butler 1961). The complex, on typologic grounds, could be included either with the chopper-scraper enigma or with the Desert culture, except for one group of artifacts. This is the double-pointed knife or point called the Cascade (Figure 3.24), which resembles the Lerma point in Mexico and several others. The Cascade point is usually well and neatly chipped, preserving a generally lanceolate form, so the points are not too different from the Agate Basin points of the Plano. The complex should perhaps be placed in the Plano group. Until better chronologic or stratigraphic controls are available, the Plano designation seems appropriate for this complex.

As a conclusion to this section on the Llano phase of the Plains sequence, the study by Haynes (1964) will be summarized. His contribution, using new information along with old, was to demonstrate that there was no ice-free corridor in Canada until about 10,000 B.C. He bases his argument on geologic evidence and on nine or ten of the radiocarbon dates (both new and old) available when

he wrote. The dates from four Llano and five Folsom sites offer dramatic support of this notion, because all are younger than 9500 B.C. (Figure 3.25). Moreover, this same set of dates shows the Llano to have lasted only about 500 years, with Folsom being the longer-lived from 9000 to 7000 B.C. Arguing, then, on the basis of typology (which is dubious in some instances), he 9500 B.C., the Llano phase covered the proposes that within a few centuries after continent south of the ice mass. He then moves on to suggest, using thin data from Alaska, that the fluted points may in fact be earliest there and may even be derivative from some Eurasiatic core-flake complex. These latter ideas are intriguing but are far less convincing than his main thesis, that is, that the Llano phase only appears at 9500 to 10,000 B.C. This important paper separates the data that are essentially proved from speculations that are possible or probable. Nonetheless, Haynes' account, keen as the analysis may be, cannot be taken as the last word on this absorbing problem. To gear students' thinking to so rigorous a denial of Llano man before 10,000 B.C., other than in the extreme northwest of the continent, is to provide chronologic guidelines too tight to allow evaluation of future data. Establishing looser bounds, on both logical and archeologic grounds, seems to be appropriate. However, Haynes expressly states that his paper is concerned with Llano-Folsom phases only; he is completely aware of other evidence for more westerly complexes. The main point is that when Haynes wrote, his evidence supported 9500 B.C. as the extreme limit of time available for human occupancy of the Western Hemisphere. Wendorf (1966) has a thoughtful and restrained review of the climatic restrictions to man's movement into the New World which should be consulted by those much interested in the problem. In the main, his conclusions agree with and support the conclusions of this chapter.

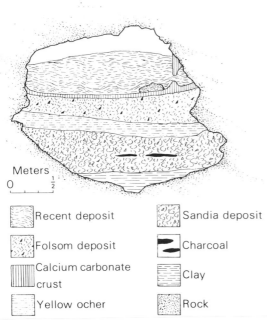

Meters

0 ⟍ ½

⬚ Recent deposit	⬚ Sandia deposit
⬚ Folsom deposit	⬛ Charcoal
⬚ Calcium carbonate crust	⬚ Clay
⬚ Yellow ocher	⬚ Rock

Figure 3.22   Cross section of Sandia Cave. (Modified from Hibben 1941)

The Folsom Culture

The inclusion of the Folsom culture as a separate chapter in the Big Game Hunting sequence is justified on the basis of sentiment rather than logic. On the basis of a dating range of possibly 9000 to 7000 B.C., the presence of extinct fauna and distinctive fluted points, and a concentration in the Plains area, the complex should be regarded as related to, and overlapping with, the Llano, representing no great change in lifeway, despite some artifact change and the new fall or jump hunting technique. Treating it separately here is little more than a gesture memorializing the scientific breakthrough that followed the original Folsom find.

There are several accepted Folsom finds. Folsom (New Mexico) itself (Figure 3.26), Level 2 at Blackwater Draw, locality 1 (New Mexico), Sandia Cave (New Mexico), MacHaffie (Montana), Lindenmeier (Colorado), Lipscomb (Texas), Lubbock

(Texas), and possibly Midland (Texas) all qualify. It will be recalled that Folsom fluted points are usually found in conjunction (although not exclusively) with the fossil wide-horned bison. Most of these are kill sites where small herds of game were either trapped or driven over a fall. Lubbock yields radiocarbon dates of approximately 8000 B.C.

Of the several sites, Lindenmeier will be described at length because it is a campsite, rather than a kill, and yields the widest variety of material objects. [Although the site is usually spoken of as a Folsom site, it appears to be a stratified or mixed site; at any rate, it has yielded both Clovis and Folsom fluted points (see Byers 1954).] The Lindenmeier site, just south of the Wyoming line in Colorado, is the most important of the Folsom sites yet reported. Radiocarbon dates of 8800 B.C., older than the Lubbock date, have been determined from charcoal collected by Haynes and Agogino (1960) some years after the excavation was done (Roberts, various). Aside from its broad importance, the site also stands as a monument to the public-spirited amateurs—C. C., R. G., and A. L. Coffin—who found it and called it to the attention of Roberts (1935a), who then spent several seasons there and provided the information abstracted here.

Although there are several contiguous localities yielding artifacts, and although work continued for several summers, the area of main importance to the story is a deeply buried, sloping stratum of black soil of high organic content, containing bones of extinct bison, modern forms of fox and wolf, and much workshop and campsite debris from a relatively continuous occupancy. This stratum, on the basis of convincing geologic and internal evidence, is interpreted as the shore and gently sloping bed of an ancient marsh or pond into which camp refuse was thrown. Later, the broad valley was silted in by sediment from surrounding ridges and

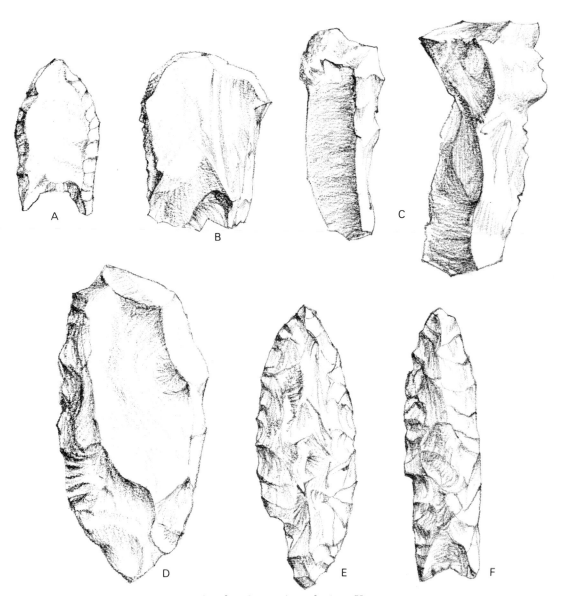

Figure 3.23   *Artifacts from Sandia Cave. Actual size. Upper row, from Folsom deposit: A, Folsom point; B, scraper; C, flake knives. Lower row, from Sandia deposit: D, scraper; E, Sandia Type 1; F, Sandia Type 2. (After Hibben 1941)*

from upstream until the surface was essentially level, with no significant stream flow. When first discovered, the cultural stratum was buried about 2 feet deep near the original shore (?) and about 17 feet deep out toward the center of the bog. The material was revealed by a modern gully which eroded a deep channel and revealed the stratum in the cutbank. The first excavation involved the cutting of a long trench down to the artifact–animal-bone layer (Figure 3.27). No fireplaces, structures, or other evidence of village construction were found. The collection of stone

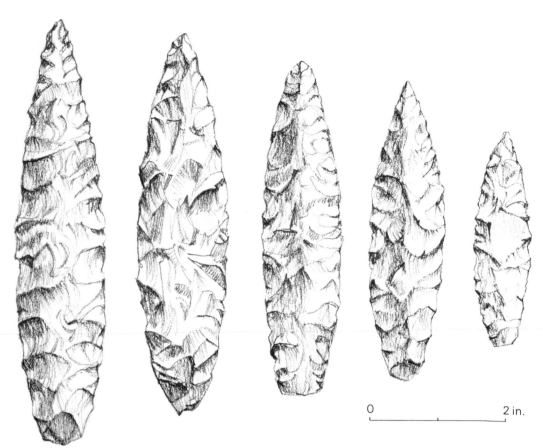

0 _____ 2 in.

Figure 3.24   Cascade points from Cougar Mountain Cave, Oregon. (After Cowles 1960)

artifacts, however, was rich and varied in comparison with other sites of this stage. In addition to small "typical" Folsom fluted points of chalcedony and other "flints," there were several larger specimens. The technically fine Folsom points are quite distinct from the Clovis Fluted of the Llano (Figure 3.28). Aside from being smaller than the typical Clovis piece, less lanceolate in form, and having an indented base with "ears" on each side, the Folsom is characterized by a deep flute on both faces. The fluting results from the removal of a long, thin flake from the base toward the tip. After the fluting flake is removed, the edges of the blade are delicately retouched and, sometimes, ground or dulled toward the base. (This dulling of the edge

is thought to have been necessary in order to attach the point to the haft.) There is much waste flint in the deposit, including long, thin flakes from the flutes, so the location is identified as a flint-knapping site as well as a much-used camp. In addition to the whole and broken Folsom fluted points found scattered in the debris, there were still some in association with partially articulated *Bison figginsii* bones. At other places in the site artifacts were found in context with extinct camel and deer bones as well as with bone from modern antelope. One mammoth tusk was also recovered.

Among the flint tools were a variety of scrapers, including some well-made end or thumbnail types, where a thick flake is given a steeply beveled cutting or scraping edge on one end. Side scrapers are often well-retouched flakes, with less-uniform control of shape. Some of the scrapers illustrated appear to be curved, prismatic pieces resembling the Clovis knife (Figure 3.29). The Lindenmeier specimens show more battering and retouch on the cutting edges than do those from a Clovis locality. Quite numerous pieces are the gravers. These are usually random flakes on one edge of which a tiny, fine, sharp point (for engraving wood and bone?) has been worked with delicate pressure flaking. Some similar specimens with longer projecting points have been called chisels. Knives are broad, thin pieces with parallel sides and retouched edges, generally well made but showing nothing like the delicate skill of the fluted points. Even the flakes removed by the fluting process were used as cutting tools. Some very crude, ax-shaped, rudely chipped forms are called choppers. Other stone items include small hematite chunks used for pigment, grooved sandstone abraders or whetstones for smoothing and sharpening other tools, flat stones used as paint palettes, hammerstones, and some sandstone slabs regarded as hand milling

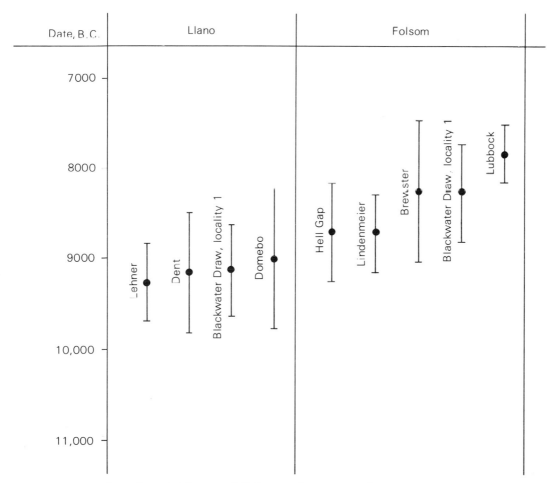

Figure 3.25 *Duration of Llano and Folsom cultures as indicated by C14 dates. (Modified from Haynes 1964)*

Figure 3.26   Reconstruction of the Folsom kill site. (After museum display at Mesa Verde National Park)

stones by Krieger (1964); but neither milling nor food-grinding stones were found. An engraved bone disc may have been an ornament or a gaming piece.

Thus it is possible, on the strength of the Lindenmeier collection, to speak of a Folsom complex of artifacts; but of these artifacts, only the fluted points and the gravers are sufficiently unique in form to have value in diagnosing either culture stage or individual collections as to affiliation. The snubnosed scraper, a beveled knife form, the choppers, and the various side scrapers are found in hundreds of sites throughout the continent in other artifact contexts.

The prismatic knives may not actually be part of the Folsom complex, but they could belong to the Llano tool kit because we have other evidence that Clovis points occurred at Lindenmeier and at Cougar Cave in Oregon (Cowles 1960). Roberts (1936) also reports some Plano types in the upper levels of the dark midden zone, as well as some "unfluted" Folsom speci-

mens. The latter are standard in shape, size, and retouch but are fluted on only one side or not at all. The above account, drawn from several preliminary statements by Roberts, amply documents the importance ascribed to the Lindenmeier site as one of the largest controlled collections of Folsom data.

The "Unfluted" Folsom Point   As mentioned before, stage and age ascriptions are sometimes necessarily made, when other data are lacking, on the basis of artifact typology when diagnostic types occur in otherwise undistinguished congeries. The Folsom fluted point type has often been observed in conjunction with extinct mammals and, on the basis of other evidence, such as being included in sediments known to be early, is known to fall in early Recent times. The presence of Folsom fluted points in a controlled artifact complex is therefore considered to be sufficient evidence of antiquity and would lead to ascribing an age equal to other

Figure 3.27   The Lindenmeier site excavation. Artifacts came from dark layer. (After Roberts 1936)

Folsom collections. But what of the unfluted Folsom points? These points fit the type description closely except for the lack of fluting. Are these also to be assigned to the Folsom culture? The question has arisen at Ventana Cave (Arizona), at Plainview (Texas), at Red Smoke (Nebraska), and at Midland (Texas).

At Midland there was a series of sand strata which included fossil animals and artifacts as well as the famous human skull. The skull came from a layer beneath a rather scanty, artifact-bearing level and could thus be recognized as relatively older. But within the collection were no fully typical diagnostic artifacts. Several (broken and complete) of Folsom shape and size, showing appropriate flintworking

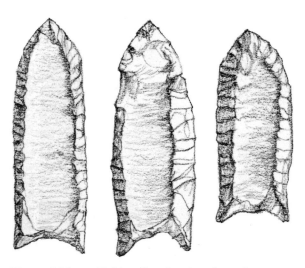

Figure 3.28   Folsom fluted points from Lindenmeier. Approximately actual size. (After Roberts 1936)

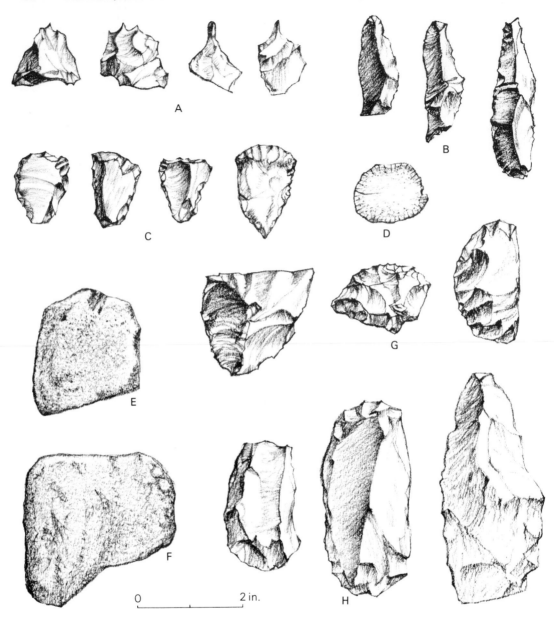

Figure 3.29   *Artifacts from Lindenmeier. A, gravers; B, flake knives or scrapers; C, snubnosed or end scrapers; D, bone disc; E, F, rubbing stones; G, side scrapers; H, quartzite scrapers. (After Roberts 1936)*

techniques but lacking the fluting, were found in addition to a few fluted fragments. The unfluted ones are usually quite thin and perhaps couldn't have been fluted. Are such unfluted points part of the Folsom complex? From the evidence of Lindenmeier, the answer may be a provisional "yes." The question has actually been logically surmounted until better evidence accumulates by giving the Midland specimens a new type name—Midland points, and there the matter rests.

Assuming here, along with Wendorf, Krieger, and Albritton, the authors of the

Midland reports, that the Midland point is a bona fide part of the Folsom complex, a minimum age of 7000 B.C. can be assigned to the Folsom layer at Midland, thus providing a minimum age for the Midland skull. Figure 3.30 shows some unfluted Folsoms from Midland. In addition, the Midland (Scharbauer) site contains a wide variety of extinct faunal forms and seems to have been occupied during the accumulation of some of the gray calcareous sand where the skull was found. In fact, the authors speculate that the individual recovered may have been camping and actually died on the spot. Unfortunately, the artifacts from the stratum where the bones were found are not diagnostic; whether they are Folsom or Llano or something else can't be stated precisely. But the fluorine tests on bone from all three Judkins components show that the layers were laid down rather rapidly, so there is room to argue that the site was there only a few thousand years before the demonstrated Folsom occupancy on top of the Judkins.

This interesting site and the correlation of its geologic-cultural sequence, as interpreted by the scholars who worked there, is presented in Figure 3.31, which is derived and simplified from the original report.

The Folsom lifeway is not an exact duplicate of the one postulated for the Llano. There is evidence of a new and efficient hunting technique, the surround kill, as exemplified at Folsom itself. The evidence suggests that the bison were driven or surprised by several hunters in a cul-de-sac in the arroyo. Or, the beasts may have been wounded during a drive and were hazed into the trap, to die of thirst and weakness in the box end of the gully. Such a technique seems to call for a larger hunting group. It may bespeak intermittent cooperation between hunters from several families, or it may suggest that the social group consisted of several families joined in a permanent band; a director of the hunt, either temporary or of some permanent status, may be inferred.

In portable possessions, camping pattern, clothing and shelter, and simple social organization (except during the hunt), the Folsom hunters no doubt greatly resembled their Llano predecessors.

The Plano Culture

Of the overlapping Big Game Hunter phases, Plano, the latest, is far less crisp and exclusive in its definition. It is characterized by a number of projectile points or knife blades showing a considerable variety of form, although the fine flintwork and the generally lanceolate form of the Llano and Folsom complexes persist. However, the fluting is entirely lost as Folsom disappears. Among the many diagnostic types (point or knife types) are San Jon, Meserve, Milnesand, Browns Valley, Portales, Angostura, Agate Basin, Hanna, Duncan, Midland or unfluted Folsom, Hell Gap, Cascade, Plainview, Scottsbluff, and Eden points (Figures 3.32 through 3.36). The Cody knife is unique (Figure 3.37). As usual, the points are quite often named after the site of first discovery.

The sites bracketed here under Plano

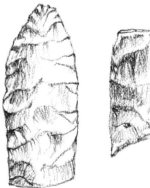

Figure 3.30   Unfluted Folsom points from the Midland (Scharbauer) site. Actual size. (After Wendorf, Krieger, and Albritton 1955)

Event	Deposit	Cultural Association	Fauna	Climate *		
9. Wind erosion	Unit 5 (Monahans)	———	Modern	Tending toward dry (?)	NEOTHERMAL	Medithermal
8. Stabilization of tan sand	———	———?———	———	Moist		Medithermal
7. Deposition and partial erosion of tan aeolian sand	Unit 4 (Monahans)	———	———	Dry		Altithermal
6. Stabilization of red sand dunes; heavy veg., development of soil	———	Folsom and related points	Pronghorn	Cool, moist		Last major Wisconsin ice advance
5. Deposition of red aeolian sand	Unit 3 (Judkins)	———	Horse, turtle, deer or elk, and extinct brocket or antelope	Dry	WISCONSIN GLACIAL	
4. Disappearance of ephemeral lake (?); erosion of bed *b* of Unit 2	———	———	———	Dry		
3. Alternate deposition of gray calcareous sand in either an ephemeral lake or as dunes; erosion of bed *a* of Unit 2	Unit 2 (Judkins)	Human bones, flint chips, scrapers, knives	Horse, bison, extinct brocket or antelope, etc.	Tending toward dry		
2. Drying of lake; erosion of lake bed	———	———	———	Tending toward dry		
1. White calcareous sand deposited in lake	Unit 1 (Judkins)	Cut (?) horse bone; possibly flint chips	Horse, mammoth, camel, peccary, wolf, bison, extinct brocket or antelope, etc.	Cool, wet		

* (Heavy broken lines indicate major reversals in climate)

Figure 3.31 *Sequence of events at the Midland (Scharbauer) site. (Modified from Wendorf, Krieger, and Albritton 1955)*

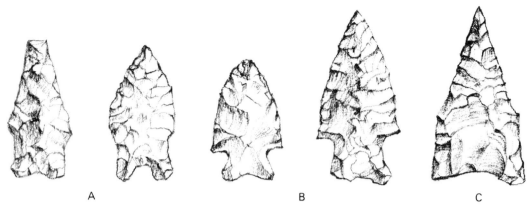

Figure 3.32   *Plano points. Actual size. A, Duncan; B, Hanna;*
C, Meserve. (A, B after R. P. Wheeler 1954; C drawn from J. A.
Eichenberger cast)

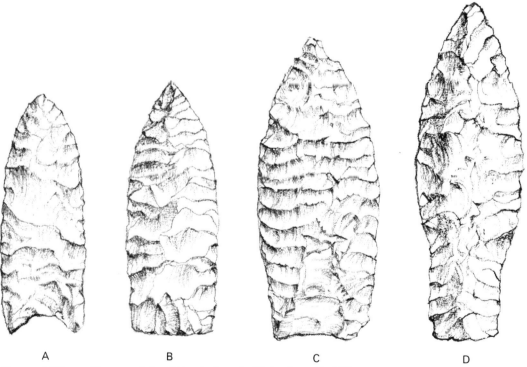

Figure 3.33   *Plano points. Actual size. A, Plainview; B, Milne-*
sand; C, Browns Valley; D, Hell Gap. (A, C, D drawn from J. A.
Eichenberger casts; B after Sellards 1955)

are those generally younger than 7000 to
6500 B.C. Hell Gap and Agate Basin appear
to be a little older (Agogino and Galloway
1965). The collections are characterized
by distinctive lanceolate, unfluted knives
and projectiles (a delicate pattern of long,
thin, pressure-flake scars often characterizes these types). The faunal association is either modern species such as bison,
antelope, wapiti, and lesser rodents, or an

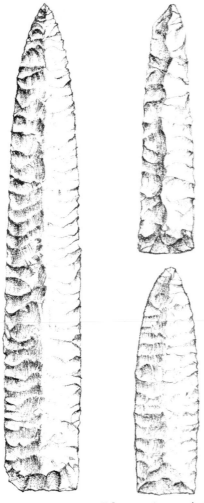

Figure 3.34   *Eden points. Actual size. (Drawn from J. A. Eichenberger casts)*

overlap of extinct and modern species. Such sites occur over a wider area than either Western Llano or Folsom. Typologically, many named point types of the Eastern woodlands (that is, Archaic) would fit the general Plano pattern, but their relationship, apart from their typologic similarity to the Plano types, cannot be assessed yet. [Such points as Dalton, Copena, Colbert, and Lerma would be included here (Figure 3.38).] The most important difference between the Plano grouping and all earlier ones is the occasional presence of flat milling stones with shallow, basin-shaped grinding areas. Associated, of course, is an elliptical hand-held grinding stone or mano—the flat basin slab being the nether millstone and the pebble or mano being the upper stone.

Sites where the Plano is represented are numerous: Red Smoke (Nebraska); Lime Creek (Nebraska); Allan (Nebraska); Milnesand (New Mexico); Long (South Dakota); Plainview (Texas); Finley (Wyoming); Horner (Wyoming); Claypool (Colorado); Portales (New Mexico); Mac-Haffie (Montana); Scottsbluff (Nebraska), lower levels; Graham Cave (Missouri); Levi (Texas); Allen (Wyoming); Damp Cave (Texas); Hell Gap (Wyoming); San Jon (New Mexico); Agate Basin (Wyo-

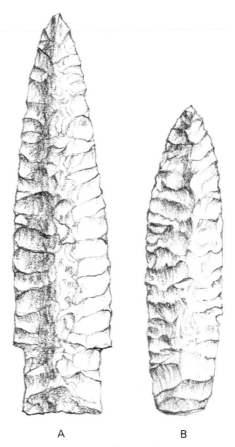

A   B

Figure 3.35   *Other Plano points. Actual size. A, Scottsbluff; B, Agate Basin. (Drawn from J. A. Eichenberger casts)*

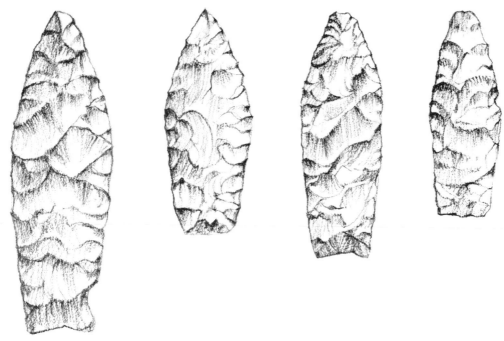

Figure 3.36 Angostura points. Actual size. (After Suhm, Krieger, and Jelks 1954)

Figure 3.37 Cody knife. Actual size. (Drawn from J. A. Eichenberger cast)

ming); and several Canadian sites in Alberta. Midland (Texas), the upper layer, should perhaps be included and possibly the Nebo Hill material from Missouri. The Plains Plano has been incorporated by Krieger (1964) into the Protoarchaic stage, but this tends to obscure the continued special big-game focus of the Plano in its Plains environment.

Among the well-described sites are Lime Creek (Davis 1962) and Red Smoke (Davis 1953). They are close together on Lime Creek, a small tributary of Medicine Creek in south-central Nebraska. Both were deeply buried under deposits of both aeolian and waterborne sediment. Lime Creek was the first discovered in 1947. Discovery resulted from a massive flood which deepened the streambed and exposed a thin stratum (zone I) of artifacts and broken bones at water level under a 50-foot-high bank of loess and alluvial sediment in which several fossil soil zones were visible (Figure 3.39). Eight feet above the basal cultural layer another occupation zone (zone III) was later observed. Although the geology is quite complicated and not yet fully assessed, it is clear that zone I, the lowest, contains debris from a streamside camp. There were 158 chipped stone specimens, of which about 40 were "Lime Creek knives," but no burins or gravers were reported. Hammerstones, sandstone abraders, six triangular, snubnosed scrapers, and flake scrapers were also found. The Lime Creek knives

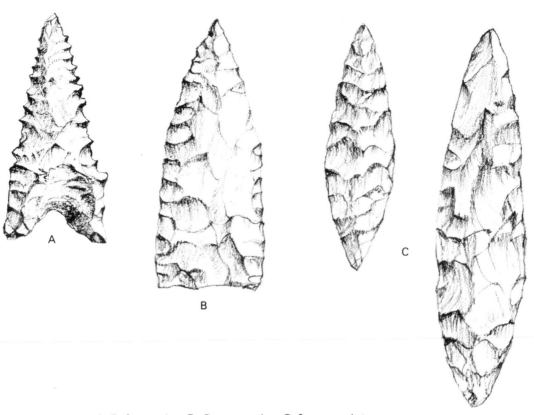

Figure 3.38   *A, Dalton point; B, Copena point; C, Lerma points.*
Actual size. (A drawn from J. A. Eichenberger cast; B after
DeJarnette, Kurjack, and Cambron 1962; C after Suhm, Krieger,
and Jelks 1954)

are large, broad, stemless pieces which are rather crudely chipped, often with a flat or squared-off base and generally parallel sides. They are not very distinctive, but generally comparable pieces occur at MacHaffie and other sites (Figure 3.40). There are, in the collection, three index artifacts. Davis identifies one Milnesand, one Scottsbluff, and one Plainview point. The artifacts are mainly of local jasper; many flakes attest local manufacture. An interesting fact is that the faunal association is dominantly pronghorn antelope and giant beaver, although elk, deer, bison, rodents, raccoon, and coyote are also present in small percentages. It is probable that the marshes or ponds were beaver ponds and that the beaver was

one of the attractions leading to the intermittent use of the site.

From zone III, the highest, only thirty-six artifacts were recovered, but among them were one Plainview and two Milnesand specimens. The faunal association was bison, said to be of an extinct species. Davis emphasizes the change in preferred prey from pronghorn and beaver to bison as evidencing climatic change, but a cultural explanation could be equally valid. No reliable radiocarbon dates are available, but Davis estimates an age of 7000 B.C. for Lime Creek.

At nearby Red Smoke, in sediment almost as deep as at Lime Creek, several occupation surfaces were found. In the preliminary report (Davis 1953), zone 88

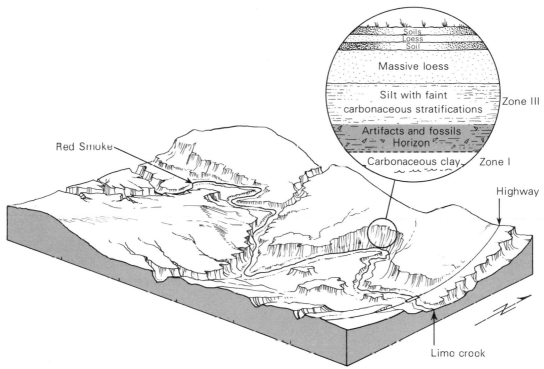

Soils
Loess
Soil
Massive loess
Silt with faint carbonaceous stratifications — Zone III
Artifacts and fossils Horizon — Zone I
Carbonaceous clay — Zone I
Red Smoke
Highway
Lime creek

Figure 3.39   Relief map of the Lime Creek site and cross section of fossil soil zones. Zones I and III are major cultural layers. (After C. B. Schultz, Lueninghoener, and Frankforter 1948)

is described as the richest, having yielded over 500 artifacts and numerous fireplaces. The important diagnostic pieces include both Plainview and Meserve points. A radiocarbon date of 6850 B.C. from zone 92, 4 feet higher than zone 88, shows these two sites to fall in the earliest range of the Plano span, and they may be transitional from Llano-Folsom to Plano.

From the Levi site (Texas) Alexander (1963) recovered several hundred flint specimens, including thirty-two in the Plano tradition. These include pieces resembling Angostura, Meserve, and Plainview specimens. There were also two Lerma points and six resembling those found with the Iztapan mammoth in Mexico. Zone IV was the most productive, yielding exactly half the artifacts from

the site. In addition to fifteen scraper types ranging from well-made oval specimens to irregular flakes showing some use, there were three classes of burins, several prismatic flake scrapers and knives, gravers, five cobbles used as manos, one slab milling stone, and a single short, incised bone tube or bead. This is the most extensive inventory yet reported for any Plano site. Alexander sees resemblances not only to Plano materials but also to certain other sites, such as the Allen site (Holder and Wike 1949), that have been assigned (for example, Jennings 1957) to the Desert or Archaic tradition. Zone II of Levi contained one basal fragment that Alexander identifies as a Clovis point. Two of the burin types were also represented in Zone II. One can agree that Levi, Zone II, may

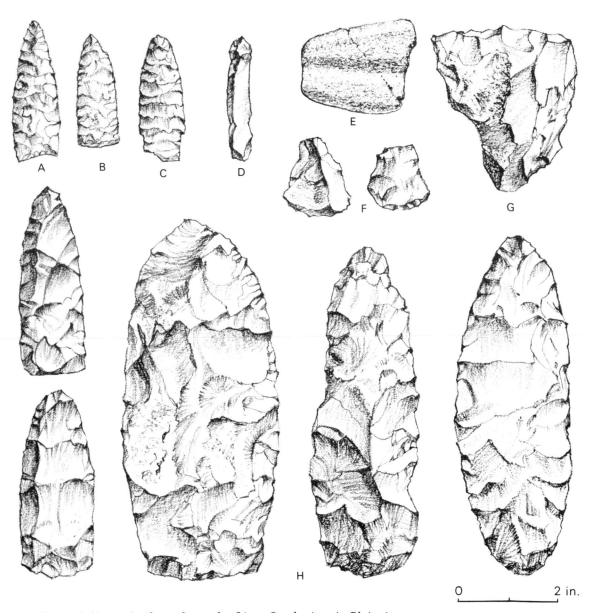

Figure 3.40 *Artifacts from the Lime Creek site. A, Plainview point; B, Milnesand point; C, Scottsbluff point; D, flake scraper; E, grooved abrader; F, end scrapers; G, uniface core chopper; H, five Lime Creek knives. (After Davis 1962)*

in fact represent a transition from Plano to Archaic, as do Graham Cave and other sites in Missouri.

Fauna from Zone IV is chiefly bison and deer, along with rodents, rabbits, and carnivores, whereas Zones I and II contained also horse and tapir. Zone II falls about 8000 B.C.; Zone IV dates range from 7350 to 5400 B.C., with one sample, the deepest, yielding an inconsistent date of 4700 B.C.

Not all the Plano sites have been well reported, even though some are the type localities for certain named projectile or knife types. One, the Eden site in Wyoming, has been extensively studied by geologists, but no full statement of the cultural debris has yet appeared. The Eden point (Figure 3.34) is an especially well-made type, long and slender with smooth, even chipping and a strong median ridge; occasionally, the blade has a slight square shoulder, making a stem and a squared base. Chipping varies; in some pieces the long, ribbony flake scars appear to extend across the entire blade, while in others the flake scars show that shorter, broader flakes were removed from edge to median ridge. The overall form is altogether different in concept and execution from the preceding fluted forms, albeit equally well made. The similarity of Scottsbluff points to Eden is marked. The difference is in the slightly less precise chipping of the Scottsbluff and the stubbier, less graceful blade proportions, heavier shoulders, and shorter stem. That they bear different names should not obscure their probable relationship as variations on a common concept. Another very important site, Horner, lies near Cody, Wyoming. It has never been well reported, but Wormington (1957) has assembled the important facts. There were hearths or fire-stained areas, so it may perhaps have been a village; however, this point isn't clear. Remains of 180 (probably modern) bison were found. Many specimens of both Eden and Scottsbluff points attest the contemporaneity and association of the two types. Other artifacts include scrapers, knives, engraving tools, choppers, hammerstones, and rubbing stones. Here was also found the uniquely distinctive Cody knife (Figure 3.37). This is a sharp cutting blade with an offset or angled stem; chipping is very good; the entire artifact is thin and smooth. Although size varies and blade to stem angles are different in some cases, the basic design remains the same. This knife has come to be regarded as a marker

or index type. The radiocarbon dates, from charred bone and charcoal, agree in placing the Horner site at about 5000 B.C.

Dick and Mountain (1960) have described the Claypool site (Colorado), which yielded many Cody knives; Scottsbluff, Eden, and Plainview points; thumbnail scrapers; drills or perforators of flint; grooved abraders and whetstones; and other nondiagnostic items. The associated fauna are modern species, so Claypool supports the evidence from Horner.

One very distinctive point has been reported by Hughes (1949) from the Ray Long site (South Dakota). This is the Angostura, which is characterized by a long, graceful, lanceolate form with diagonal ripple flaking from edge to edge, no shoulders or stem, and an indented or square base (Figure 3.36). Ray Long is a deeply buried campsite yielding fire areas and an assortment of scrapers, flakes, etc. While the Angostura points, as first described, are quite distinctive, careless typologists have been identifying crude, ill-chipped pieces of vaguely similar form as Angostura in type. The age ascribed by one set of radiocarbon dates places the Long site at about 7000 B.C. Another suite of dates from an area near, but not in, the occupied zone came out at about 5000 B.C. Most scholars would accept the earlier date. Wormington and Forbis (1965) point out that Agate Basin points (Figure 3.35) though larger, less delicately chipped, and of different proportions, are often miscalled Angosturas.

Anomalous and absorbed into the Plano group (perhaps improperly) are some Missouri finds yielding a distinctive knife or projectile point called Nebo Hill. Although heavy and thick, these artifacts seem to fit into the lanceolate tradition which characterized the Plano types (Shippee 1948). These are often surface finds and cannot be interpreted except typologically and hence unconvincingly (Figure 3.41).

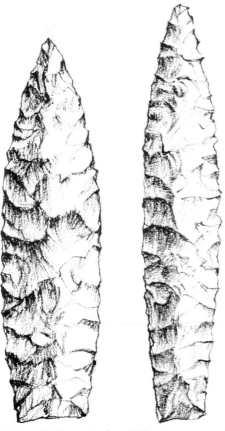

Figure 3.41   *Nebo Hill points. Actual size.*
(Left, after Wormington 1957; right, drawn
from J. A. Eichenberger cast)

Similarly, and also insecurely, one could equate the Lerma points of Mexico and Texas and the Cascade points of the Plateau areas with the Plano in technique of chipping, smooth lanceolate form, and the lack of contrary radiocarbon dates. Their inclusion in the Plano cluster seems to be sound cultural interpretation. Ascribing them to any suspected early chopper-scraper horizon is quite anachronistic in view of the contrast in flint technology. The placement of the Lerma and Cascade points in the Plano grouping is done on admittedly technologic grounds; the one or two radiocarbon dates falling at about 6000 B.C. support this placement. [Since this was written, T. M. Newman (1966) has reported data from Cascadia Cave

which seem to support this interpretation of the Lerma and Cascade as Plano types.]

Milnesand, Portales, and other probable Plano culture sites require mention but are not sufficiently informative to require description here. The possible exception is Milnesand, where a broad, lanceolate, stemless form of point or blade was recovered. This one seems to have wider distribution than some of the more distinctive types.

The fall or jump hunting technique, added to the hunting repertory of the Plains tribes early in Plano times, may be an improvement on the surround of the Folsom. In any case, it persisted, along with the surround, as a basic technique from Plano times until about A.D. 1875. The term "jump" is aptly descriptive, and the technique requires the cooperation of a sizable group of people, close and skilled direction, and advance planning. And, as described by eyewitnesses in the nineteenth century, it was a colorful and exciting event. While the technique was simple in conception, success depended on many factors and on the close cooperation of the hunters. In the Plains, the principle seems to have been to direct a herd of bison toward a precipice or very steeply sloped terrain in order to force the animals over the edge. The key to the process is that herd animals' usual response to the threat of danger is flight, often blind, unreasoned flight, which is called a stampede. The crucial beginning of a jump kill, then, involves turning (or luring with a decoy) a herd of a few hundred animals into the mouth of a wide, V-shaped trap formed by two long lines of men, or cairns of rock, or clumps of brush with people hidden behind them. At the mouth of the V the lines are quite far apart and the animals can be driven by a few men behind them to enter the trap without suspecting the presence of other hunters. When the herd is within the trap, the hunters press close and frighten the animals into a faster pace, and the people in the lines of the V begin to shout, brandish their weapons, wave blankets, and otherwise harass the running herd. The animals go deeper in the trap as they try to escape the hunters, who are on all sides except at the small open end of the V. Terrified, the animals stampede toward the freedom promised by the end of the trap and so plunge, in a cascade of heavy bodies, to their death at the foot of the jump.

The technique involves men, women, and children for stations in the trap and skilled "drivers" who divert a portion of a larger herd into the trap. The technique, of course, works either for foot or for mounted hunters. At the kill site, systematic butchery is carried out. Evidently most of the hides were removed (the tail vertebrae are almost never recovered), and the carcasses were thoroughly dismembered. Ewers (1949) quotes Lewis and Clark's description of a kill location they noted on the Missouri River. Wheat (1967) has an account of the Olsen-Chubbock (Colorado) bison kill site, wherein he reconstructs the route of the drive, describes the butchering procedure, and speculates that the drive occurred in late May because of the presence of bones from quite small calves. In the Olsen-Chubbock situation there was no steep face, but a deep arroyo athwart the path of the stampede, into which the bison fell. The artifacts associated with Olsen-Chubbock were Scottsbluff points.

In areas where the terrain was less broken and no precipice or bluff was available, the trap led to a sturdy corral and the bison were killed as they milled inside the enclosure. The construction of a corral and trap required a large investment of labor; the traps were used year after year. Ewers' account contains a description by a Blackfoot Indian of a surround or corral kill in 1872:

It was in winter. We didn't drive the buffalo over a cliff. We built a corral near the edge of timber toward the bottom of a downhill slope. We made the corral of cottonwood posts set upright in the ground to a height of about 7 feet, and connected by crosspoles of cottonwood or birch tied to the posts with rawhide ropes. All around the corral stakes of cottonwood or birch were laid over the lowest crosspoles. Their butt ends were firmly braced in the ground outside the corral. Their other ends projected about 3 feet or more inside the corral at an angle so that the ends were about the height of a buffalo's body. These ends were sharpened to points, so that if the buffalo tried to break through the corral, after they had been driven into it, they would be impaled on the stakes. From the open side of the corral the fence of poles extended in two wings outward and up the hill. These lines were further extended by piles of cut willows in the shape of little lodges tied together at the tops. These piles were about half as high as a man and were spaced at intervals of several feet. On the hill just above the opening of the corral a number of poles were placed on the ground crosswise of the slope and parallel to each other. The buffalo had to cross these poles to enter the corral. These poles were covered with manure and water which froze and became slippery so that once the buffalo were in the corral they couldn't escape by climbing back up the hill.

Before the drive began a beaver bundle owner handled the sacred buffalo stones in his bundle and prayed. He sang a song, "Give me one head of buffalo or more. Help me to fall the buffalo."

Then the men of the camp rode out on horseback, got around behind a herd of buffalo and drove it toward the corral. A man stood at the top of the hill and gave a signal to the women and children, who were hiding behind the willow piles, when the buffalo were coming. As the buffalo passed them the women and children ran out from their hiding places.

Once inside the corral, the buffalo were killed by men and boys with guns.

The Plainview (Texas) site (Krieger 1947) is probably one of the earliest Plano sites and documents the fall or jump as an early hunting technique. Here, discovered during quarry work, was an extensive bone bed where hundreds of bison

Figure 3.42   *Pleistocene fauna associated with a warmer, drier
climate. A, camel; B, ground sloth; C, tapir; D, dire wolf; E, horse.*

(of probably modern species) had been
driven over a bluff. Among the bones were
a score or more of Plainview points and
other stone tools. The points have parallel
sides, a strong median ridge, and a
squared or concave base; thus they resemble the Folsom form to some degree. There
is no fluting, however, and the chipping
technique is not as fine. These points,
which occur widely in the Plains, are regarded by Krieger as marking the transition from the technology of the Folsom
flintsmiths toward the widespread preference for the lanceolate, medially thicker
points of the Plano cultures.

Wormington suggests that there is a
practical relationship between the associated occurrence of the distinctive,
beveled Meserve points and the Plainview
pieces, in that the Meserve points could
actually be broken Plainview specimens
that were quickly repaired by rechipping
while still hafted. This would account for
the beveling of the cutting edges of the
Meserve point. In some ways, for interpretive purposes, the Meserve has proved
to be the most important of the Plano
types. Aside from having been found in
good association with bison at the Meserve

site (Nebraska), the shape and technique
of chipping are duplicated at the Dalton
(Missouri) site. The more easterly finds
of material that can be equated with the
Plano in stage and age (see Chapter 4)
characteristically contain points resembling the Dalton type. Thus, through
relatively well-controlled finds and associations, the Meserve-Dalton-Nuckolls
link has been used as one of several bases for
both cultural and chronologic conclusions.
One can agree that the general form and
technique of the widely separated examples of the Meserve tradition and their
consistently early occurrence tend to give
validity to this cluster of local types as a
continent-wide, time horizon marker.

Krieger (1964) lumps sites and complexes from all over the continent into a
Protoarchaic stage, a stage which includes
practically all the sites mentioned here
and many others. The generalized, leaf-
shaped, projectile point types are, of
course, found over a far wider range than
the Plano distribution, but the issue to be
considered is that Krieger has included
within the Protoarchaic the Plano Big
Game Hunter tradition, the Archaic full-
exploitive tradition (from both Eastern

and Western areas), and some Arctic complexes not very well known yet. The hallmark of the Protoarchaic Krieger cites as the practice of milling either on slabs or in mortars; it is true that at many sites the mill does, in fact, seem to be a part of the inventory (for example, the Levi site). All these sites might properly be thought of, in their lower levels, as transitional from the Big Game to the Archaic tradition. But to lump them together today, in view of the present state of knowledge, seems to obscure much of value and to jeopardize future classification because the mere act of grouping them obscures the basic big-game economy which in part describes the Plano. On the other hand, as search for buried sites continues in the Middle West and in the East, it is entirely possible that evidence to support Krieger's lumping together of all these sites will be forthcoming.

Plano, defined as are the other subdivisions of the Lithic stage on the basis of typology, fauna, and scattered radiocarbon dates, is the terminal phase of the Big Game Hunter stage. The lack of homogeneous or identical types from site to site and the "expedience grouping" on the basis of dates do not, however, obscure the important fact that the hunting of big game of both extinct and modern species dominated the Plains for perhaps 5,000 years, with an increasingly larger population (at least, the sites become more numerous). The Plano phase takes on additional importance in providing proof of continuous occupancy for this part of the continent.

If typologic evidence is to be accepted, one can see a continent-wide dispersal of Big Game Hunters by, or earlier than, 8000 B.C. This was true east of the Rockies wherever the land was ice-free. There is faint but less-convincing evidence west of the Rockies. In all areas, however, the tradition of the lanceolate blade or point, fluted or unfluted, first coexists with, and finally becomes a part of, the next widespread and long-lived stage called the Archaic, which will engage our attention in Chapter 4.

The Plano cultures bespeak an increasingly complex system of social organization in the jump-kill hunting technique. The subsistence pattern involved the taking and probable preservation of surpluses from the kills. Meat can be preserved either by drying it and by mixing the dried meat with fat and berries in gut or skin bags to make the nutritious pemmican the historic tribes still use. Krieger also suggests that the milling stone for vegetable food began to come into use in Plano times. As far as housing, clothing, and details of social life are concerned, we are no wiser than in the case of the Llano or Folsom peoples.

Extinction

Speculation about the causes of extinction of the mammoth, large long-horned bison, tapir, horse, camel, dire wolf, and giant ground sloth has gone on since before the Folsom find (Figures 2.2 and 3.42). Granting a generally warmer and drier trend from about 15,000 B.C. onward (in the southern and western Plains, at least), it is possible that the big herds found optimum ecologic conditions between 15,000 and 6000 B.C., thus bracketing the timespan in which the Llano and Folsom dates seem to fall. The slight but undoubted continuous changes toward today's climate after 8000 B.C. may have been such as to set up minor but effective ecologic handicaps (as simple, perhaps, as shorter, tougher grasses and fewer or no swamps and bogs where coarser reeds and grasses were available) which slowly gave the biologic advantage to the smaller *Bison bison,* antelope, and elk, so that the bigger creatures were never as numerous as one assumes by analogy with the historic herds. Mysterious plagues or diseases have also been postulated as causes of extinction. While any or all of these causes may be true, the role of man as predator must not be discounted. It is entirely possible that the inroads man made upon the perhaps already dwindling herd populations were enough to destroy the balance of the species or even to reduce the number of individuals in each herd past the minimal group size. This problem of "why extinction?" is quite important to this study but cannot be adequately explained on the basis of present data.

If we knew more about the disappearance of the mammoth and other extinct forms, precise ecologic interpretation might be possible. That there were climatic changes with attendant shifts in flora is a fact not seriously questioned; what we cannot be certain of is just how critical man's role as predator may have been in hastening the extinction of the large animals.

4

The Archaic Stage

So far the glamour of the hunt and the dimly perceived lives of the hunters have held the stage. Imperfectly understood as this phase is, it has been possible to suggest a sequence of population increase and the spread of possibly only a few hundred original individuals over the entire southern half of the continent and deep into Mexico, exploiting both large and small animals to the near-exclusion of other resources. The apparently single-minded focus upon a game-subsistence pattern seems to have been general and long-lived, persisting longest in the Plains area. It seems obvious that this lifeway was successful and quite stable for many generations. No doubt the suggestion of material cultural poverty is overdrawn because the picture is incomplete. Probably there was use of plant products as well as of animal, and the evidence just hasn't been found or noticed yet. One can further argue that, on the basis of present knowledge, the technology was simple, the tools and utensils few, and the sociopolitical organization uncomplicated. The inventory of cultural skills and institutions would be limited to those required for survival in the pursuit of game. One can probably assume some rigorous social controls during the hunt itself, but we know nothing of the size of the effective social unit—whether it was a tribe, a small band, an extended family, or merely a nuclear family.

From this pattern, or at least following it, came a lifeway entirely different in that it was totally exploitive. This concept spread all over the continent, ranging from about 6000 B.C. (earlier in some areas) until the A.D. 1850s in some places. This stage, called the Archaic, has also been described as a foraging pattern of existence. As the range of dates shows, it coexisted with the Folsom and Plano phases. If, as has been suggested, it derives from the chopper-scraper stratum, it would, of course, have ancient roots. Certainly the stage must be defined halfway interpretively, because the artifact assemblages vary so widely that a single definition, on the basis of detailed artifact assemblages, cannot be universally applied. In any case, the Archaic, comprising a myriad of special tools and utensils to meet a varied subsistence base, can be regarded as technologically far more versatile and complex than the preceding stages. Subsistence varied from season to season as it focused first on one species or community of species and then on another, and the artifact inventory was comparably expanded. The variety of technologic skills is reflected by the artifacts and other criteria listed by Willey and Phillips for the Archaic: There are heavy, ground stone woodworking tools necessary for successful occupation of forest environments (axes, adzes, wedges, gouges, etc.); milling equipment in specialized forms (metates, mortars, manos, pestles, etc.); stone vessels (important because they reflect greater permanence of occupancy than in the Lithic); and, as found in particular areas, ground slate points and knives, variously formed polished atlatl weights, plummets, stone tubes or pipes, and stone beads. The chipped stone forms (particularly choppers and scrapers) continue into the Archaic with little modification, but the drill is altogether a new tool found first in the Archaic. Although lanceolate forms continue, there is a greater variety of points, with emphasis on stemmed, corner-notched, and side-notched forms, in that order. The presence of numerous forms—

together and in quantity—of rough-stone items (hammerstones, anvil stones, notched pebbles, saws, abraders, whetstones, etc.) is considered to be a fairly reliable general criterion of the Archaic, as are masses of fire-cracked stones used in pit roasting and stone boiling. Bone, horn, and ivory made into awls, perforators, and needles (indicating basketry and skinworking) or articles such as gorges, pronged fish spears, harpoons, and fishhooks (which attest reliance on marine prey) are abundant in the Archaic as are shell (especially for ornaments) and copper and asphaltum, which first appear in the Archaic. Formalized burials (such as flexed burials in round graves, partial cremation, use of red ocher, and inclusion of grave goods) and village-site refuse accumulations (which, though small in horizonal extent, are often deep enough to indicate considerable temporal continuity) are considered important criteria of the stage; evidence of houses and storage pits is generally lacking.

Despite this inclusive descriptive definition, the Archaic has not always been understood as a continent-wide culture, nor was there an easy acceptance of its definition in subsistence and organizational terms in lieu of the commoner artifactual definition. The first use of the term can be credited to Ritchie (1932), when he applied it as a specific cultural term to the Lamoka complex of New York. Lamoka is a nonceramic collection, containing a distinctive artifact complex found in a shell-midden location. Soon, largely through the studies of Fairbanks (1942) and Haag (1942), Archaic came to be a near synonym for shell-midden cultures found all over the East. Ritchie (1944) then formulated the Archaic as a culture level or stage, and forthwith all nonceramic, nonhorticultural remains were dumped into the category. Griffin (1946) correctly deplored the term but later (1952a) spoke of and defined the stage. Beardsley (1948) had already noted Archaic stage artifacts in the California material and commented upon the possibility of wider relationships. By 1953, Jennings (1953) and Jennings and Norbeck (1955) began to define a Desert culture of Archaic type. In 1955 and 1958 Willey and Phillips sought to reduce the confusion and defined the stage as it is now understood. Jennings and associates (Jennings 1956) recognized the equivalence of the several local Western Archaic complexes, while Jennings (1957) attempted to equate the Desert Archaic with aridity of environment. However, the Archaic can probably best be understood as a fundamental lifeway, not geared to any one ecosystem. Through this approach, regional differences are reduced in importance with the historical implications dominant.

In considering the Archaic, the problem of keeping chronology (especially as it has the ring of certainty when derived from radiocarbon) separate from *stage* becomes acute. Then, too, if the Archaic is defined as above, problems are automatically engendered through the inclusion of several sites which others include in the Protoarchaic, or even label as Paleo-Indian.

In this chapter, it is necessary to begin the regional treatment which will be followed hereafter. Even though one can still think in terms of broad stages, regional difference in artifact inventory becomes more marked in the Archaic stage (and becomes increasingly characteristic as more complex cultures arise). In effect, the differing regional complexes constitute prehistoric culture areas. There are two primary reasons for the regional variations. First, there is the ecologic or subsistence aspect. Given the full-exploitation bias of the Archaic culture, the range in available species between, for example, Alaska, Death Valley, and the Atlantic tidewater area is enormous. If fish and shellfish are a primary game target, fishhooks, nets, and weirs would be commoner utensils than, say, milling stones. By the same token, there would be more tools and ornaments made from shell in Florida shell-mound sites than in a Nebraska site of the same stage. With land fauna being controlled by the flora and flora being controlled by climate, great variation in the specialized tools geared to the specific local resources is to be expected. Second, as the population increased and regional variation accelerated, there is more and more likelihood of local cultural exchange from group to group. Such borrowings would also result in changes in artifact form and in the inventory itself as ideas diffused and afforded cultural stimulus. (In the stages following the Archaic the results of stimulus diffusion become very marked.) This chapter will be developed in regional sections dealing respectively with the Eastern Archaic, the Midwest and Plains (including Texas), and the Desert West (including California and the Intermontane area). These different provinces may be thought of as culture areas but do not exactly fit the concept as originally described.

Forest Efficiency

Interest in the Archaic began in the Eastern area, where, as it turns out, local variants seem to be extremely complex and aren't even yet well sorted out. An advance in the study of the Archaic is represented in Caldwell's (1958) contribution of the concept of *primary forest efficiency*. While his entire thesis has many implications we must ignore here, the core concept is the best organizing principle available for the Archaic of the east half of the continent. In fact, it is useful in any exploration of the persistence of the Archaic stage.

Caldwell explains that in the Eastern

woodlands, a region rich in biotic resources, the peoples of the Archaic stage learned to exploit a wider and wider spectrum of resources with ever-increasing skill until by 2000 B.C. there was a dense population enjoying an optimum adjustment to a generous environment. His phrase, "forest efficiency," means just that, as the peoples harvested in turn, and in season, nuts, fruits, and other vegetable foods while continuously hunting the land and water animals. He suggests that at the beginning of the Archaic, there was local diversity of crude stone tools but that the tool kit was small. As centuries passed, the kinds of species taken increased continuously and there was a multiplication of specialized tools of every sort; technologic skill also increased. The fact that by 2000 B.C. there was much uniformity of material culture over the East he ascribes to a uniformity of growth and a coalescing in adjustment by local peoples rather than seeing it as innovation and diffusion from a single center.

The pattern of living in complete, harmonious parasitism upon the varied offering of the woodlands involved seasonal shifts in subsistence base, or at least the seasonal emphases were cyclical. While deer and other animals might be taken the year round, the various wild plants would beckon at different seasons—nuts in the fall, tender plant greens in the spring, and fruits all summer. In some areas shellfish would supply a year-round staple. Thus, even without the surpluses which come from agriculture, we find that permanent dwelling sites, or at least often-revisited, semipermanent locations, were used as settlements. These were perhaps base communities from which the people moved to exploit and collect and no doubt store surpluses of some seasonal foods. At these base camps or villages deep midden deposits accumulated, containing thousands of discarded tools, the buried bodies of the dead, and tons of food scrap (bones and shell). Coexistent with the large sites are thousands of thin, small sites. These, Caldwell reasons, represent brief occupancy during gathering expeditions. Therefore, primary forest efficiency may imply movement of groups to a schedule; it certainly does not imply an aimless, wandering, nomadic existence. The pattern would be more nearly what Beardsley et al. (Meggers 1956) called "Restricted" or "Central-Based Wandering." There would be a preferred home community (perhaps a winter camp) with movement to well-known locations occurring according to an established pattern. This very pattern of life, albeit less clearly defined and in a more impoverished area, has been ethnographically observed and recorded in the "modern" Archaic-stage tribes of the Great Basin (see Egan in Coon 1948, pages 47–57) and in the Ojibwa of the lake country in Central Canada (for example, Landes 1961). Perhaps we can broaden Caldwell's concept and speak of *Archaic* efficiency, although this modifies his thesis, which contains a partial explanation of the subsequent developments in the East. In the same vein, Swanson (1964) has recently suggested that it might be more useful, both in theory and as an aid to understanding, to disregard the areal terms (Desert, Eastern, etc.) assigned to the Archaic and think instead of *the* American Archaic. One of the implications one sees in his suggestion is that the Archaic was fully efficient, up to the carrying capacity of the land, wherever it spread. Thus it seems reasonable to extend Caldwell's concept, although it was geographically restricted by him to the woodlands, by recasting the idea as Archaic efficiency.

Another part of Caldwell's thesis (see also Griffin 1964) is that the Archaic cultures everywhere become more and more complex and show an ever-increasing inventory of tools through time. Also, the dominant tool types tend to become similar. If, as he thinks, the roots of the Archaic are American rather than Asiatic (in contrast to Willey and Phillips 1958), we would then be left with the notion of scattered groups "growing up together" and slowly influencing each other, becoming more and more interconnected in what he calls the "Archaic Diffusion Sphere." The population density of the continent was probably at the highest point possible under the Archaic lifeway of 2000 B.C. There was easy communication and there was the greatest potential for cultural innovation yet to occur in the New World.

At the close of the Archaic, Caldwell sees the conquest of mere space as completed. Man had succeeded in developing an increasingly efficient set of exploitive techniques. Any changes in lifeway would now perforce occur through innovation, invention, or new ideas diffusing from elsewhere, or all three. Using the concept of Archaic efficiency as an interpretive or organizing principle here makes the entire Archaic stage more readily understood. More importantly, it throws the cultural growth and expansion which occurred into higher relief and gives more meaning to the drab and repetitive artifact complexes with which we must deal.

Efficiency in exploitation implies new techniques of food preparation and, in many aspects of use, of a broadened range of raw materials. One basic innovation is the use of some form of mill for crushing or grinding hard-shelled kernels or nuts. The slab nether millstone and the small upper millstone or mano were used over the West for the grinding of grass seeds from several species. In the East, a stone or wooden (?) pestle was used in stone and wooden mortars to grind nuts and possibly smaller seeds. The mill simultaneously made available new vegetable foods and necessitated new cooking techniques such as those required for making cakes, loaves, or mush.

The utilization of plant fibers made possible the development of textile arts, with the result that mats, baskets, and bags were created from resources previously unused. Coiled basketry making required a few new tools, such as the bone or wooden awl used in the stitching. The availability of baskets expedited gathering, transport, and storage. Mats may imply a notion of greater personal sleeping comfort and the wrapping and storage of objects; or the mats may only have been funerary gear. In the West the flat, shallow, winnowing basket was an essential and highly practical part of the equipment needed in preparing grass seeds for use as food.

Fibers were also used for nets to catch fish, rodents, and even fowl. Vegetable fibers were also used for cordage, perhaps partially replacing skin and sinew in many ways. Cordage for traps, fishlines, and snares would mean that these devices could be prepared in greater numbers with less effort. Also, the variety of devices for taking game of every size may well have increased.

What Archaic efficiency implies, then, is a technology utilizing many raw materials not evident in early cultures, in a series of inventions or innovations. Technologic advance, of course, leads to special, rather than all-purpose, tools (for example, three sizes of snares of a single design for large, medium, and small rodents of similar habits), and increasing skills would lead to refinements in food collecting and conceivably to other special tools. One of the clichés in archeologic thought is that an improved stability or a more dependable and more easily obtained food supply brings leisure time and a concomitant enrichment of life in the areas of religion, aesthetics, and other "finer things." If this occurred in the Archaic cultures, it is not overly apparent, unless burial of the dead or the development of skill in sculpting and polishing stone can be so construed. Perhaps the manufacture of shell beads and pins may be also interpreted in the same vein. Tortoiseshell rattles, common in the East, bespeak either music and the dance or the practice of medicine by shamans; both may be inferred from analogy.

But the major result of increased use of a wider range of species and a better-nourished population seems to have been a population increase and a subsequent expansion of that population, seen in the encroachment of the Eastern Archaic into the Plains and the extension of the Desert Archaic into Mexico and beyond.

Eastern Archaic

There are many reported Archaic sites— too many to describe individually—so a few of the more important will be summarized as representative. "Important" means either that the site was deep and long occupied with clear stratigraphy, or that diagnostic artifacts were found in datable contexts, or that the collections were large or well controlled, or even that the site was reported lucidly and fully. In a few cases, the sites meet all these conditions.

The Stanfield-Worley Bluff Shelter (DeJarnette, Kurjack, and Cambron 1962) is one of the important southern sites and is located in northern Alabama, near Tuscumbia. The circumstances surrounding its excavation merit mention. It was discovered by amateur members of the Alabama Archeological Society and excavated with funds raised by public subscription by the Archeological Research Association of Alabama, Inc. The University of Alabama provided tools, equipment, material, and supervision. Labor was volunteered by students, Boy Scouts, members of the Archeological Society, and other interested parties. The list of donors and participants contains over 300 names. Again, the amateur is to be thanked and congratulated.

The site lies next to a stream under a large overhang 40 to 50 feet wide (or deep) and some 200 feet long. It contained four separable strata. These are labeled zones A through D, D being the lowest. Moreover, zone D was sealed by a sterile silt layer, zone C. Zone A yielded pottery; zone B was late Archaic in stage, lacking pottery; and zone D was early, yielding Dalton points and a small collection of scrapers. The Dalton point is regarded as the Eastern equivalent of the Meserve and other Plano types. The radiocarbon age of zone D was about 7300 B.C. The Dalton (zone D) deposit thus accumulated at, or even slightly earlier than, the time the Plano cultures were beginning to differentiate from the preceding Big Game base. H. T. Irwin (1964), referring specifically to the Western Pinto types, has even argued that the Plano types are actually tools developed in the Eastern woodlands that spread westward during what we shall call here the Transitional stage. Haynes (1964) uses the few radiocarbon dates available to argue the reverse, although his concern stops at the Folsom level.

Although the artifact yield from the Dalton zone was small, there were seven similar, named types recovered. There were three variants on the Dalton-Meserve type (Nuckolls, Colbert, and Greenbriar), Big Sandy I, Hardaway Side Notched, Beaver Lake, and Stanfield Triangular. Despite the various names, these points are not widely different. They are all essentially triangular, with concave bases. Chipping is reasonably smooth, but the overall impression is one of crudeness. The Big Sandy I is important in having irregular side notches, a detail of form which becomes very common in later Archaic developments.

The collection also includes some well-made little gravers (Figure 4.1), the familiar small flakes upon which a tiny, sharp point is prepared by careful chipping, already mentioned from Linden-

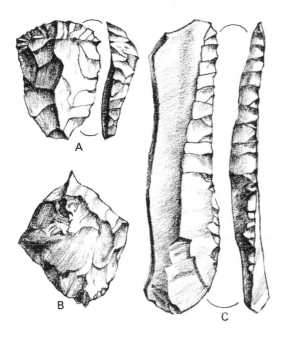

Figure 4.1   *Artifacts from the Stanfield-Worley Bluff Shelter. Approximately actual size. A, chisel end scraper; B, graver; C, uniface or flake knife. (After DeJarnette, Kurjack, and Cambron 1962)*

meier and other Western sites. Comparable gravers are included in all the early collections where they were noticed and saved by the excavator. Being small, rude in outline, and unknown in America until recent years, the likelihood is great that 10,000 gravers have been overlooked and discarded during the decades of excavation. Additional flint tools included long, flat flakes with secondary chipping around the edges to make knives or scrapers. Other, better-modeled scrapers made from thick flakes were rectangular, oval, and triangular in shape. The Dalton food-bone scrap was dominantly white-tailed deer, with terrapin, turkey, and squirrel represented. No tools indicating a concern with vegetable foods were noted.

Although zone D must have been a living site, no hearths or living surfaces were identified. In zones A and B, of less interest here, the artifact take was heavier and can be readily correlated with other reported sites. B was most heavily used;

there were many storage pits and several basin-shaped hearths containing ash and charcoal. Storage pits and hearths are characteristic of zone A as well. The deposit was shallow; the total site depth varied from 5 to 7 feet, with zone B averaging only 6 inches in thickness. Sites in Tennessee (Nuckolls) and Kentucky (Quad) yield large collections of material duplicating the Dalton complex—gravers, variants on the Dalton point, and many scrapers made from prismatic flakes very like the Clovis knives.

North from Stanfield-Worley Shelter, in western Tennessee, is the famous Eva site (Lewis and Lewis 1961). It is an open location on a natural levee along one of the long-abandoned channels of the Tennessee River. The site reveals four strata of significance. The lowest, Stratum V, is dated at 5200 B.C. Strata V and IV yield artifacts of the earliest or Eva component. Stratum III is sterile earth completely sealing the underlying Strata IV and V. Stratum II is the Three Mile component, and Stratum I is the Big Sandy. All the components listed are Archaic. On all levels there were many animal food bones —all of modern species—and on all levels deer accounted for 85 to 92 percent of the bone. Other animals were bear, raccoon, opossum, turkey, and fish. In Three Mile times a heavy occurrence of mussel shell accompanied by a decrease in deer bone represents either a broadening of the subsistence base, a decline in the available number of deer, or a climatic change, or perhaps all of these explanations apply in part. No shell debris was found in the Big Sandy layer. So, at Eva, deer was apparently the year-round staple, and we may assume that the hunting technology was primarily aimed at this prey. Deer provided more than food; it gave dense, solid bone for a variety of tools, also antler for tools and an occasional ornament, sinew for tough cordage or thread, and hide for clothing and other leather goods. In all periods the rich nut crop of the area—

acorn, walnut, and hickory—was probably harvested, but no evidence other than anvil stones from Stratum V and nutstones from I argues for the use of nuts. The artifact complex was rich and varied, with the fewest types coming from the Eva (Strata V and IV) layer. The occurrence of major tool types by level is shown in Table 1. Significant types appear in Figure 4.2.

Table 1   Eva site: major tool types (modified from Lewis and Lewis 1961)

	Stratum I Big Sandy	Stratum II Three Mile	Strata IV and V Eva
Stone, ground and rough:			
Atlatl weights:			
Bicornate			1
Semilunate	1	1	1
Tubular		3	2
Prismoidal	1	2	
Slate gorgets	2		
Tubular pipes	1		
Pestles:			
Cylindrical		1	
Conical	6	6	
Hammers and anvils	2	2	1
Anvils			4
Mullers			3
Mortars(?)	1	1	1
Nutstones	1	1	2
Claystone awl sharpeners		1	2
Whetstones	1	1	
Ocher pigment	7	15	6
Pendants			1
Bone:			
Awls:			
Splinter	24	87	85
Double-tapered		2	5
Deer cannon	1	6	6
Deer ulna	2	2	8
Small-mammal ulna	1	5	3
Turkey tibiotarsus		6	1
Needles	5	20	1
Fishhooks	2	10	3
Raccoon splanchnic hooks	1	3	
Vertebrae necklace	1		

Table 1   (Continued)

	Stratum I Big Sandy	Stratum II Three Mile	Strata IV and V Eva
Bone tubular beads	2	4	4
Beaver-incisor chisels			4
Bear canines, perforated			5
Turtle-shell rattles	1	2	
Antler:			
Scrapers:			
Wide bit	2	4	4
Narrow bit		2	3
Shaft wrenches	1	3	3
Projectile points	3	6	17
Atlatl hooks:			
Small spur		6	
Long spur		1	
Fishhooks			2
Awls or perforators	1	7	5
Flaking tools	10	22	31
Drifts	1	2	1
Scoop scrapers			1

These tools point to specialized uses, most of which can be identified with hunting. The atlatl, of course, was the spearthrower. It was usually a composite object, consisting of a springy wooden shaft about 2 feet long, fitted with a tough hook of antler, often a weight mounted toward the center of the shaft (for balance or better whip action), and a shaped handle or grip with finger loops (W. S. Webb 1946). The spearthrower is in itself an important advance. With it the spear can be thrown farther and with greater accuracy than is possible with the unaided arm. Its use also implies open glades in the woodlands because it cannot be employed in dense growths of timber. The resilient antler tips or tines were used for the delicate work of retouching flint. The large number of awls is often taken as evidence of much leatherworking, but the awls were probably tools for making basketry. They are always common in

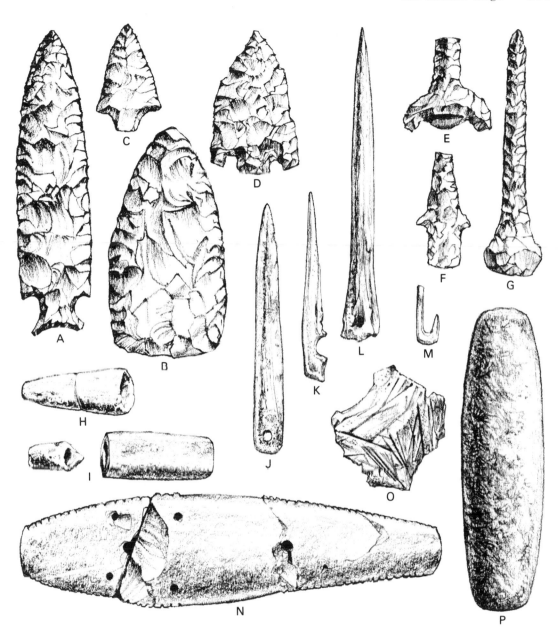

Figure 4.2   *Artifacts from the Eva site. Slightly reduced. A,*
Benton point; B, bifacial blade; C, Morrow point; D, Eva point;
E, F, stemmed drills with Eva base; G, drill; H, tubular pipe; I,
atlatl hook and weight; J, bone needle; K, L, bone awls; M, bone
fishhook; N, gorget; O, sharpening stone; P, pestle. (After Lewis
and Lewis 1961)

sites where basketry itself occurs, and
basketry and weaving are found in early
Archaic sites wherever dry conditions of
deposit permit their survival. That bas-

ketry does not survive in Eastern sites
either in the open or in damp shelters is
merely because of the conditions of local
storage. No other uncharred vegetable

objects survive either. The awls, then, may be a valid clue to a textile and basketry industry rarely mentioned for the Archaic except in the arid West. It just may be that the many Eva *needles* were, in fact, for leatherwork, but most of the *awls* were used in basketry. (This explanation reverses the opinions of the authors of the report.)

The greatest variation, and perhaps specialization, occurs in the stone tools (see Table 2).

There were human burials associated with all levels. A total of 180 were recovered. Forty-seven of these were infants or juveniles, with the remainder adult.

Table 2   Eva site: chipped stone artifacts (modified from Lewis and Lewis 1961)

	Stratum I Big Sandy	Stratum II Three Mile	Strata IV and V Eva
Points:			
Expanded stem	6	5	
Narrow stem	7	3	
Tapered stem	11	4	2
Straight stem	43	23	1
Side-notched	2	9	
Ledbetter	18	5	
Benton	17	1	
Cypress Creek II	1	13	1
Morrow Mt. I	2	11	1
Eva II		11	1
Big Sandy	6	23	2
Sykes	7	3	4
Cypress Creek I	1	3	13
Eva I	2	12	165
Kirk Serrated	3	1	9
Other:			
Biface blades:			
Triangular, large	3	2	131
Other	9	22	43
Scrapers (all classes)	9	16	45
Drills (all classes)	16	21	36
Choppers	6	1	21
Picks	2	2	2

Eighteen large dogs were given formal burial as well. Fourteen of the dogs were from the Three Mile level. None came from the Eva level, so the dog is presumed to have been absent at that time. Usually the dogs as well as the human bodies had been placed in prepared pits; 75 percent (human and dog) were in the fully flexed position. Most came from the Three Mile level, with only seventeen humans from the Eva zone. Sometimes a grave would be dug through an earlier interment and would scatter the bones.

An astonishing thirteen (18 percent) of the adults survived past the age of 60, five even passing 70. The five over 70 were all male. For aboriginals to survive to these ages is unusual. But nearly half the females had died before age 30. They were small, with delicate bone structure, averaging 5 feet 2 inches in height. Males were larger, heavily muscled, and big-boned, with a mean height of 5 feet 6 inches. The crania were high-vaulted, mesocephalic, with medium-heavy brow ridges, wide malar bones, and some alveolar prognathism. Shovel-shaped incisors occurred but were not dominant. They become more numerous in the later levels. No cranial deformation was noted. This physical type corresponds well with other Archaic populations. Certain peculiarities of genetic nature were noted in the Eva site population, such as the large canine teeth found in the later levels. Lewis and Lewis conclude that the basic homogeneity of the skeletal remains from all levels in the site argues for an isolated, inbred group that did not change significantly during the several thousand years the site was used.

At Modoc Rock Shelter in Illinois (Fowler 1959), which is equally as old as the Stanfield-Worley site, a quite different situation obtained. The site, again a protected overhang, contained more than 27 feet of sediment containing artifacts. Four occupation layers were recognized and designated zones I to IV, with zone I being the earliest. The radiocarbon-ascribed age of the basal portion of zone I is 7900 B.C., with the upper levels being dated at around 6200 B.C. The thickness of zone I was over 6 feet. The scanty artifacts in the lowest, 1 foot thick part of zone I included an ovoid knife or scraper, an antler tip, and two small, side-notched points. In the 2 feet immediately above, a bone awl and some awl tips were recovered. In the next-highest levels in the upper part of zone I, there were several kinds of flake scrapers, several bone awls, a variety of stemmed points, ovoid knives, and at least two points resembling the Gypsum and Dalton point types, although the resemblance to the Gypsum point is not very close.

In a comparison of the Modoc with the Stanfield-Worley several interesting differences are noted. At Modoc, the notched points appear before the Dalton, a Plano type, and there is also a larger bone-tool collection. At Modoc, too, the milling stone from zone II bespeaks an early—ca. 6000 B.C.—concern with grinding vegetable food. Admittedly, the collections from Modoc are very small and as such can't be taken too seriously except as they corroborate other finds.

Still another rich Archaic site is Indian Knoll in eastern Kentucky (W. S. Webb 1946). Although the stratigraphy, if present, was not noticed, this site exemplifies the shell-mound Archaic station. The sites of the Lauderdale focus in northern Alabama are also famous examples (W. S. Webb and DeJarnette 1942). Indian Knoll lies on the banks of an old channel of the Green River. It is about 2 acres in extent (450 feet long by 220 feet wide); shell and earth had accumulated to a maximum depth of 8 feet. An incredible amount of debris was recovered. Artifacts exceeded 55,000 in number, while some 880 skeletons were found by Webb. (Previously, C. B. Moore had removed several hundred other burials.) The burials, including twenty-one dogs [these dogs, it is reassur-

ing to know, were right-footed (Skaggs 1946)], were in more than half the cases lightly flexed in round wells or pits (Figure 4.3). Most of the others had been laid on the ground and covered. Many of the human burials had grave offerings and ornaments with them, and most individuals had been smeared with red ocher pigment at the time of burial. In physical type they are very like those described from Eva; they are, moreover, quite homogeneous and provided Neumann (1952)

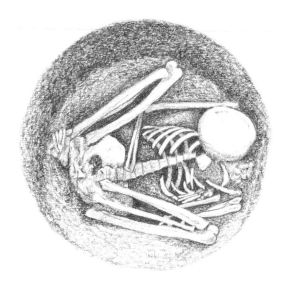

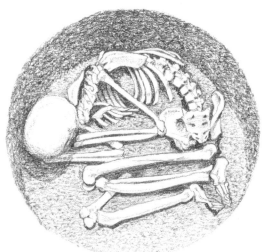

Figure 4.3   *Round grave burials at Indian Knoll, Kentucky. (After W. S. Webb 1946)*

with the inbred type collection on which he based his Iswanid American physical type.

As at Eva, food animals represented in the midden show an overwhelming preference for deer (23,100 pieces of bone out of a total of 25,750), although raccoon, opossum, dog, ground hog, wildcat, and a few rodents were taken. Turkey and goose were the favored birds. Drumfish was also used. Mussel shells were numerous on all levels, indicating that this mollusk probably served as a minor staple. The artifacts were scattered randomly throughout the fill, where they were lost or discarded, although sometimes clusters or caches of almost identical pieces were found, as if the maker or owner had hidden them but never returned to reclaim them. There is a bewildering variety of tools in every material. The list of traits prepared by the author runs over 100 items.

Throughout the site there were prepared clay floors that are presumed to have been living areas. Many fire-reddened zones on these floors marked the hearths. Around the fireplaces were the charred hulls of walnuts, acorns, and hickory nuts in great quantity. Scattered molds of vertical posts set into the clay floors around the burnt areas suggest rude windbreak shelters.

Artifacts can be divided into broad categories based on materials used and on manufacture. There were chipped stone, ground (smoothed) stone, bone, antler, and shell specimens. Chipped-flint objects included quantities of points, usually well chipped and divided into stemmed, sidenotched, and corner-notched types. Stemless ovoid or triangular knives 3 to 4½ inches long were common. Drills of winged and expanding types were numerous, as were a variety of scrapers made from thick, sometimes prismatic, flakes. In all, including fragments, there were over 13,000 flint specimens. A modern-day reporter would have split this collection into many more types, probably giving them specific type names. Ground stone includes atlatl weights of prismatic and bar types, grooved axes, grooved mauls, hammerstones, pestles usually of conical shape, milling stones (lapstones), cupstones or nutstones (slabs with numerous shallow pits 1 to 1½ inches in diameter), a few stone beads, and miscellaneous items such as whetstones and slate discs. In copper, two thin sheets and one bar pendant were found in graves.

Bone awls of many styles, including thousands of splinters, were recovered. There were ulnae of deer and other animals, cannon bones, and tibiae, all used for awls. Flat, spatulate objects were also numerous. Fishhooks; thin, slender pins or bodkins, some with flat heads; tubular beads; larger bone tubes; and other bone tools were also found. Thirty-two rattles, made from box tortoiseshells with pebbles inside, came only from graves. Canine teeth, possibly perforated for necklaces, and beaver-incisor engraving tools round out the list of bone specimens. Antler was used for atlatl tips and handles, boneflaking tools, and projectile points.

Shell was a favorite material for beads (discoidal, tubular, and spherical), rings, gorgets, pendants, atlatl weights, and knob-headed pins. Gorgets and pins were made from marine conch which, of course, had to be imported, as did the several clusters of *Anculosa* and *Olivella* shell sewn on robes or used as beads. Representative specimens of the items cited above appear in Figures 4.4 and 4.5. [As Griffin (1964) has emphasized, the Archaic was *not* a function of the availability of mussel. In fact, the shell industry is typical only where shells are available, whereas Archaic sites are widely distributed.]

The Lauderdale focus sites of Alabama (W. S. Webb and DeJarnette 1942) are equally as rich as the Indian Knoll deposit. The similarities between them are numerous and obvious. Although the deposits span a long time range, the only report of

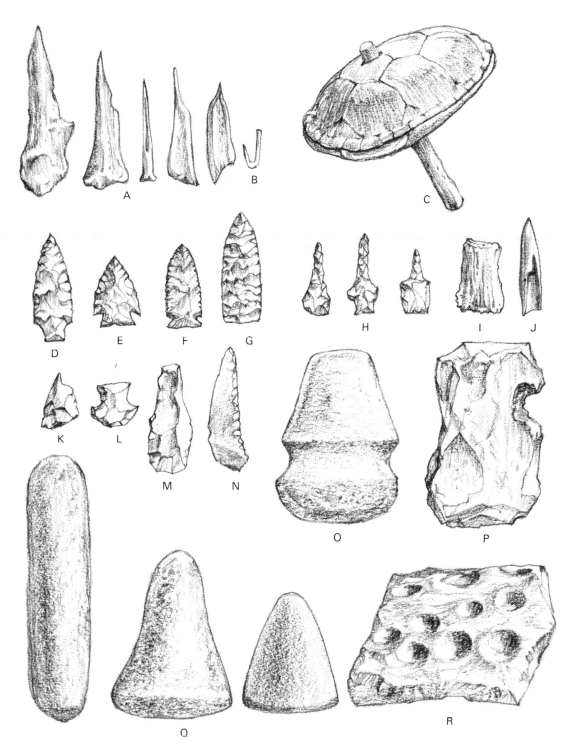

Figure 4.4 *Artifacts from Indian Knoll. Approximately one-fourth size. A, bone awls; B, bone fishhook; C, terrapin-carapace rattle (restored); D–F, projectile points; G, blade; H, drills; I, antler atlatl handle; J, antler projectile point; K, graver; L–N, scrapers; O, grooved ax; P, notched limestone hoe; Q, pestles; R, nutstone. (After W. S. Webb 1946)*

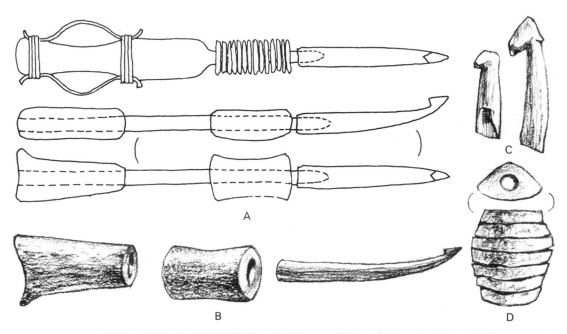

Figure 4.5   *Atlatl parts from Indian Knoll with diagrams of postulated restorations. A, restorations; B, atlatl handle, weight, and hook; C, atlatl hooks; D, shell atlatl weight. (After W. S. Webb 1946)*

the Alabama collection makes no effort to separate the early from the later Archaic complexes. Some of the sites were as much as 16 feet deep and covered many acres. Along with such sites as Turtle Mound near New Smyrna, Florida, they offer conclusive evidence of permanent dwelling places for many people over centuries of use. (In many cases in the riverside locations, thin deposits of silt occur throughout the sites and seal off the lower layers. These silt bands are taken as evidence of brief periods of extremely high water, requiring temporary site abandonment.)

Without adducing further detail, we can now move to a more general view of the Southeastern Archaic as it has been subdivided or systematized by Lewis and Kneberg (1959). Assuming that the Quad, Nuckolls, Stanfield-Worley, and possibly the Russell Cave sites are, as some feel, transitional from the Big Game stage to the Archaic stage and can be called early

Archaic, the comparison of the later sites is easier. Lewis and Kneberg compared the shared material and nonmaterial traits of a series of southern sites and distinguished two traditions: The *Midcontinent* tradition includes components of sites in western Tennessee and Kentucky. The *Eastern* tradition comprises the Alabama, eastern Tennessee, and Georgia sites (see also Fairbanks 1942). Figure 4.6 reproduces the Lewis-Kneberg chart, showing Eva, Three Mile, and Big Sandy phases grouped with Indian Knoll, Parrish, and Ward in Kentucky as the sequence in the West; Lauderdale and Stallings Island fall in the Eastern tradition. The two traditions share a majority of traits, of course, but the Midcontinent shows ocher in graves, terrapin rattles, certain blades and scrapers, stone disc beads, long, cylindrical pestles, bone projectile points, winged and bar atlatl weights (Figure 4.7), and a few other traits, including perforated canine teeth

(W. S. Webb and DeJarnette 1942), not found in the Eastern tradition. Conversely, the Lauderdale sites show the bell-shaped pestle, bone hairpins, bodkins, stone-lined fireplaces, steatite or soapstone vessels, tubular pipes (one tubular pipe came from the latest level of the Eva site) not seen to the north and west. [This, incidentally, is a much shorter list of trait differences than that proposed by W. S. Webb and DeJarnette in 1942 because the inventories have become larger and more nearly resemble one another as more sites have been dug. The reality of these two separate traditions will depend more and more on minor technologic differences; they may

well merge as knowledge increases (for example, in 1940 the antler wrench was not claimed for the West; by 1959, seven occurrences were reported at the Eva site).]

Although the Archaic is represented in Florida and along the Gulf Coast, there has been little or no Archaic material reported in the Lower Mississippi Valley, nor indeed on many of the rivers flowing to the Gulf. As Haag (1961) points out, most authors assume that the stage is represented, but proof was scanty until Gagliano (1963) defined a "normal" sequence ranging from early (transitional) Archaic to modern times. His earliest com-

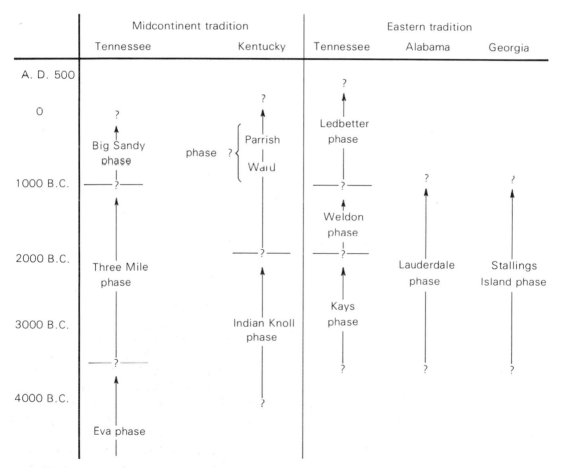

Figure 4.6   *Phases and traditions of the Southeastern Archaic.*
(After Lewis and Kneberg 1959)

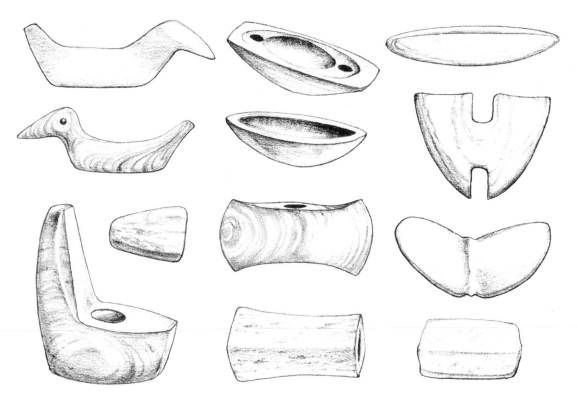

Figure 4.7   *Stone atlatl weights. Slightly less than one-half size. (After Lilly 1937)*

plex is Jones Creek, tenuously dated by radiocarbon at about 4300 B.C. The characteristic Kirk, Dalton, and San Patrice points and flake scrapers and stemmed points are present. Next are the Amite River and Bayou Jasmine phases. The interesting thing about the study, aside from documenting the presence of the Archaic, is that the site locations are closely correlated with landforms. The older sites are inland on the higher ground, and as the Mississippi Delta extended further into the Gulf and new land surfaces appeared, the later sites are successively closer to the sea.

In the Middle West, Archaic sites have also been dug. Here the shell midden is absent and there is a reduction in, or complete absence of, shell as a raw material. Otherwise, the artifacts are quite familiar. An example is the Faulkner site in extreme southern Illinois (MacNeish

1948). An open site on the edge of the Ohio bottoms, it yielded eleven burials and an assortment of flint tools. Bone and shell were missing, having probably long since decayed, as had the human skeletons except for the faintest residual outline. The projectile points, knives, and scrapers, including gravers, are of types already familiar. There were also milling stones (described as mortars and grinding stones). In a comparison with the stone inventory from Indian Knoll, MacNeish shows a close sharing (61 percent) of comparable traits. Presumably, the resemblance would have been even closer had there been other than stone to compare. The Faulkner site also contained a series of trash-filled pits. Some had been used as roasting pits, having fire-reddened earth and fire-cracked stones in the bottom. Others were burial pits. Faulkner thus can be grouped with the Midcontinent tradition. Mayer-Oakes (1951) reports the Starved Rock site, another open site in Illinois where only stone was recovered. He regards the site as transitional because the artifact collection contains both Midcontinent types and lanceolate specimens resembling Plano types. However, the presence of copper fragments would place the upper levels, at least, quite late (Griffin 1964). Other Middle Western local Archaic cultures include the Glacial Kame in Michigan, Red Ocher in Illinois, and the Old Copper of Wisconsin and Michigan.

The so-called "Old Copper culture" has attracted attention for many years because of the wealth of copper tools and weapons which are unique in North America. The collection is now understood as being an Archaic manifestation with these copper tools as an added trait complex. The scraps of copper in other Archaic assemblages are interpreted as trade objects originating in the Old Copper area from copper that was quarried as free or pure copper on the south shore of Lake Superior and on Isle Royale, where quarry sites are numerous and extensive (Bastian 1963). There, pure metal occurs in irregular sheets in crevices and fissures and sometimes in huge float nuggets in the soil. Apparently it was worked into heavy tools, sheets, pins, and ornaments by alternate hammering and annealing. The forms include double-ended awls or pins, square in cross section; spear points with reinforcing rib and long tang; knives and triangular points; a rocker knife blade; harpoons; rings; celts; and massive adz bits (Figure 4.8). All are well made. In form, some pieces resemble slate specimens from Northeastern Archaic stage sites, as Ritchie (1962) reminds us. The specimens are usually surface finds. Excavated sites showing Archaic flint specimens associated with copper are few. Osceola (Ritzenthaler 1946) and Oconto (Ritzen-

thaler and Wittry 1952) are the ones usually cited. There is no connection between this local and special handling of free metal and the complex technology of mining, smelting, and smithing which in other areas of the world had already produced an industry in metallurgy.

The Northeast

In the Northeastern states and provinces, the Archaic cultures show strong local individuality in contrast to the close similarities between the Southeastern and Middle Western remains. Byers (1959) has organized these into two major traditions, the Coastal and the Boreal. Although both are divided into Early and Late, the entire series is later in time than the more southerly cultures. The Coastal, Byers thinks, centered in the tidewater of Virginia and extended its influence northward. Using typology as the major basis for his argument, he describes the basic artifact complex or "kit" as including the following: stemmed and side-notched points and knives, semilunar (rocker) knives, steatite vessels (Late), choppers, grooved axes, gouges, slab milling stones, pestles, and several styles of atlatl weights. There are many sites yielding scanty collections that Byers would assign to the Coastal Archaic, but one, the Boylston Street Fishweir in Boston (Johnson et al. 1942), stands unique in American archeology. Built about 2500 B.C., the 2-acre fish trap was discovered in 1913 during excavations for a building. Renewed excavations in the 1930s provided the opportunity for a detailed study. The weir had been constructed of vertical sticks 4 to 16 feet long, sharpened on one end with a stone ax, and driven into a blue clay bed. The stakes were driven in clusters; the weir consisted of bundles of brush forced down between the stakes, forming a loose fence. Most stakes formed rows but

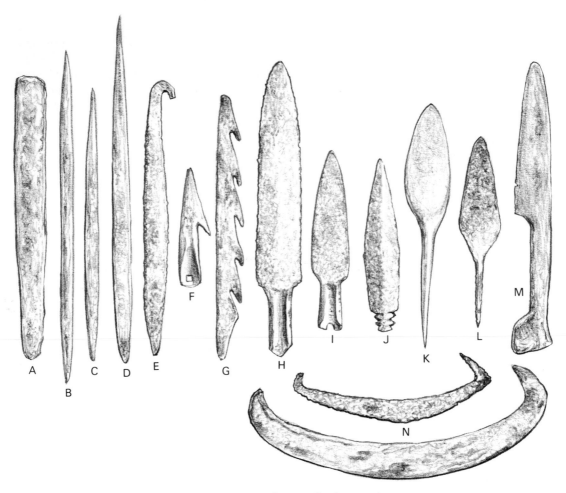

Figure 4.8 *Copper artifacts. Approximately one-third size. A, chisel; B, C, awls; D, E, punches; F, G, harpoons; H–L, spear points; M, knife; N, crescents, probably knives. (After Moorehead 1910, Vol. II)*

other, scattered stakes occurred at random without any pattern. Probably the tops of the stakes were below water level at high tide and stood well in sight at low tide. An estimated 65,000 stakes were required for the 2-acre enclosure. The weir had been constructed at a time when the sea level was much lower. The blue clay stratum into which the stakes were driven lay 16 feet below modern-day sea level (see Figure 4.9). Two layers of brush and many repairs show that the bay was silting up and that it was necessary to place new brush on top of the old as the first layer was partially covered and would not hold the fish.

The permanent fish trap or weir, evidently used all along the Atlantic Coast (see Hariot in Lorant 1946, page 251), was a highly efficient food-gathering mechanism. The traps were usually built in tidal flats or rivers where tide action was strong. Construction involved considerable investment of time and effort, and continuous maintenance was required. The traps were built from thousands of sturdy stakes driven into the muddy bottom in double rows to enclose an area

usually were high enough to be visible except at highest tides. Fish were diverted into the trap by straight "leaders," also of wattle. The leaders might be in a V leading directly to the trap mouth or might be perpendicular to the flow of the current. When the tide receded, the entrapped fish were gathered, either in nets or with spears. Of course, fish could also be left in the trap until needed. The Boylston Weir is important not so much as a weir per se but as evidence of concerted building effort by a nearby community and of constant maintenance work. It gives another insight into the exploitation of an inexhaustible food supply by the members of a permanent settlement. The cost in effort would have been too great for casual or infrequent use. Weirs, often made of brush also, are still quite common on the New England coast, and they, too, require constant maintenance. No doubt, the designs are aboriginal, having been learned from the coast tribes by the earliest European settlers and perpetuated until today.

Another very important site in Massachusetts is the Wapanucket No. 6 (Robbins 1959), dated at about 2300 B.C. The artifact collection fits the Boreal pattern (see Figure 4.10). There are deeply grooved gouges of stone, lugged steatite vessels, plummets or plumb bobs of several styles, winged atlatl weights, bolas stones, grooved axes, a variety of stemmed and notched points and knives, as well as triangular ones. There are milling stones, pestles, and celts. The site contained many pits in which stones and hearths were found. Its importance, however, is derived from what appear to be well-defined twin-post patterns outlining a total of seven round lodges or houses, with an entrance formed by overlapping the walls. If these patterns are actually associated with the artifacts, they are the oldest evidences of house construction in the East, although Ritchie (1965) is confident he has identified a

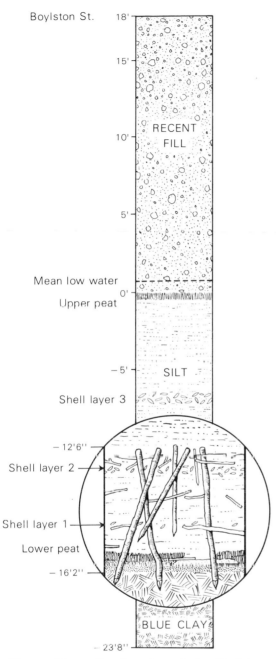

Figure 4.9   Stratigraphy of the Boylston Street Fishweir site. (Modified from Johnson 1942)

several hundred feet in diameter. Brush and flexible withes were placed between the stakes or woven between them in a form of wattlework. The tops of the stakes

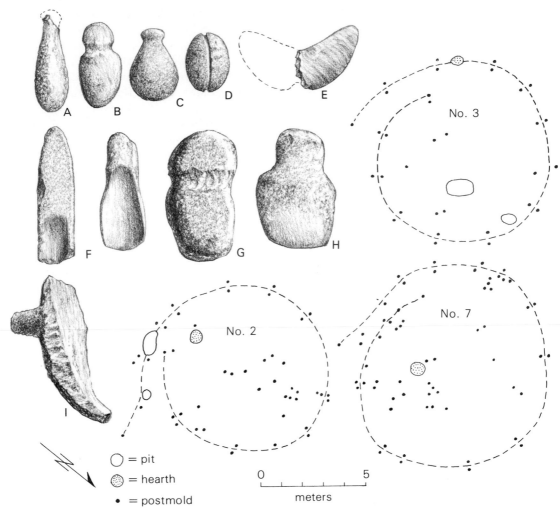

Figure 4.10 *Lodge floor plans and selected associated artifacts found at Wapanucket No. 6. Note southeasterly entry common to all lodges. A–C, plummets; D, bolas stone; E, atlatl weight; F, gouges; G, grooved ax; H, maul; I, steatite pottery fragment. Artifacts approximately one-third size. (After Robbins 1959)*

village of rectangular houses at the Lamoka Lake site in New York. If these are actually houses, they would be about the same age as those at Wapanucket No. 6.

In New York an Archaic series beginning with Lamoka (which is closely allied to the Midcontinent tradition and, therefore, essentially alien in New York) has been identified. Ritchie (1965) has a full description and an ecologic interpretation of the Lamoka material; he alone regards the Lamoka as being an entirely indigenous development but summarizes its similarity to the Kentucky-Tennessee sites. Later is the Laurentian, which is to be grouped with Byers' Boreal, being characterized by ground slate knives and points, polished plummets, ground gouges and adzes of several types, rocker knives, and other traits believed to have diffused from the west (Figure 4.11).

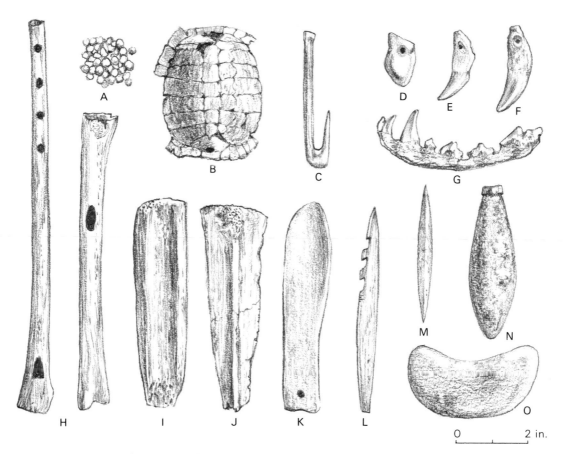

Figure 4.11   *Artifacts from the Frontenac phase of the Lauren-tian tradition. A, B, terrapin-carapace rattle with pebbles; C, bone fishhook; D–F, perforated elk, wolf, and black bear canines; G, wolf mandible with ground off base; H, bone whistles; I, bone gouge; J, deer-scapula scraper; K, antler spoon; L, barbed bone point; M, bone gorge; N, stone plummet; O, atlatl weight. (After Ritchie 1965)*

In view of the complexity of the local cultures, the wide discrepancies in classifi-cation of individual sites, and the lack of consensus among experts as to relation-ships of Archaic complexes from region to region, any effort at classification here seems out of place. For example, Willey and Phillips (1958) emphatically express the idea that the Northeastern and Mari-time Archaic is derived from an Asian circumboreal complex (Spaulding 1946). Griffin (1964), with equal emphasis, denies this, while Byers (1959) seems partially to agree with the Asiatic origin idea. (Willey and Phillips have an excel-lent discussion of the classificatory diffi-culties raised by discrepant chronology, overlapping artifact complexes, and other vexing matters.)

One should note in any debate over origins, however, that the radiocarbon dates from the Southeastern Archaic sites are consistently older than the few North-eastern dates. It seems that whatever the origin of the Archaic may be, it was flourishing in the West and South before it penetrated the Northeast Atlantic Coast territory. It would be foolhardy, at this stage of knowledge, to generate much heated argument over origins, but it seems most consistent with present evidence to propose that the Archaic over most of the continent seems to be indigenous, with the probability that the Boreal and Coastal were influenced from some as yet obscure Canadian complex. Until suspect Asiatic connections can be firmly based on minimal typologic grounds, the problem stands unsolved. Students with special interest in the archeology of the Northeast should consult Ritchie's (1965) account of the archeology of New York State, which appeared after this section was written (although a few references to the volume have been inserted). The ecologic interpretation Ritchie adopted, as well as the wealth of detail included, makes portions of his study especially useful.

(For a chart of the relative chronologic position of the sites mentioned in the preceding section, see Figure 4.12.)

The Midlands

The Archaic developments which are easiest to follow are those in the broad midsection of the continent lying between the Rockies and the Mississippi River, extending from the plains of Saskatchewan and Manitoba to the Texas Gulf. This area encompasses the vast Missouri, Pecos, Arkansas, and Red River drainage basins. Or, as a simpler description, it includes the Western woodlands and the Great Plains. Here, at site after site, the artifact finds reveal a period of transition from the Plano artifacts of 7000 to 5000 B.C. to Archaic tool types already distinguished in the Eastern woodlands.

One of the best known of these is Graham Cave (Missouri), reported by Logan (1952). While there are some contradictory statements about the details of the cave, it is clear that the basal layer yields radiocarbon dates ranging from

2000 B.C.	
	Wapanucket No. 6
2500	Boylston Street Fishweir
	Stallings Island
3000	
	Indian Knoll
	Lamoka
3500	
4000	
	Jones Creek complex
4500	
5000	
	Eva
5500	
6000	Modoc Rock Shelter zone II
6500	
7000	
7500	Stanfield-Worley Bluff Shelter
	Modoc Rock Shelter zone I
8000 B.C.	

Figure 4.12   Chronology of Eastern Archaic sites based on C14 dates.

7700 to 6000 B.C. The cave fill was an accumulation of earth, ash lenses, and living debris, over 7 feet deep. In the lower levels the artifacts were of Plano type, or rather, of types resembling the Plano, including one Dalton point. The dominant projectile points or knives were lanceolate. In the second level (the levels were arbitrary 1-foot cuts) the Plano objects were mixed with those of Eastern Archaic type. Logan would correlate the Archaic types in the collection with the Midcontinent Archaic of Lewis and Kneberg. There were large lanceolate and triangular blades; stemmed and deeply corner-notched points or blades; drills; ovoid and thumbnail end scrapers; flake scrapers; grooved axes, manos, and milling stones; nutstones; a shell pendant; a split bone awl; hammerstones; and an impression (in clay?) of twined weaving. One piece of coiled basketry was also recovered. Bone needles, tubes, spatulas, ulna awls, antler wrenches and flakers, and a perforated wolf canine tooth were also found. In other areas of Missouri—Table Rock and Pomme de Terre reservoirs—the Eastern Archaic is readily recognized at scores of sites. In the Ozarks, however, there is a cluster of rock-shelter sites from which large collections of perishable materials, such as basketry, sandals, wild and domesticated foods, and others, were taken. Typologically these collections resemble the Great Basin specimens (Baerreis 1951). The dating of this enclave of the Desert culture is uncertain, and no explanation of its presence in the Ozarks has been attempted, although Baerreis suggests a possible Cochise (that is, Archaic) origin. Of course, wherever conditions are such as to preserve basketry and other perishables, these are found in Archaic contexts. Examples are Ash Caves in Kentucky (where admittedly the stratigraphy was disturbed) and the Ohio mummy on display in the Ohio State Museum. With the mummy are woven sandals and rabbit-fur cloth which would fit into any Western collection. From Salts Cave in Kentucky, P. J. Watson (1966) figures a woven "slipper" which would usually be called a sandal. From Sheep Shelter, Pennsylvania, much textile material has been recovered (John Senulis, personal communication, 1967). The point here is that the Missouri and Arkansas Ozarks, Kentucky, Ohio, and other dry-storage finds may present a more accurate range of Archaic technology at all the sites. Since the Desert Archaic appears to be older than the Eastern stage, it may be that the Archaic lifeway arose through necessity in the Western deserts and diffused rapidly eastward and southward as big game dis-

appeared and other groups turned to foraging over a wider range of species. This explanation is far too simple, and it cannot be pressed very far without testing. However, it does say something in explanation of several unresolved points of considerable theoretical interest; it is an explanation for which a little evidence exists. [It is interesting to note here that in the caves along the Yellowstone, sandals, rabbit-fur robes, and other specimens occur in profusion—well beyond their previously known eastern range (William Mulloy, personal communication, 1964).] The caves yielding large collections of perishables along the Cimarron and Red Rivers of Oklahoma can also be adduced as evidence of the possible eastern extension of the Desert complex.

Southward, in Oklahoma, Bell and Baerreis (1951) and Baerreis (1959) have noted and segregated a series of Archaic complexes which can be correlated with sites in Missouri in the Table Rock area, such as Bray's (1956) Rice site, as well as with Eastern Archaic sites. In Oklahoma, the complex in question is called the Grove focus. It was possible to divide it into three phases or stages, the earliest going back several thousand years. The three phases, A, B, and C, show accretion in artifact types. The latest, C, yielded pottery as well and is ignored here. The characteristic Grove focus inventory is synthesized from several sites, some of which contained over 12 feet of accumulation. Even though none of the sites was large, the depth of accumulation is taken to indicate (as is the change in artifact lists and frequency) a long period of use or frequent reuse. Bell and Baerreis report the large corner- and side-notched points, with the contracting-, parallel-, and expanding-stem blade or point forms also common. The blades are broad, often having serrated or beveled edges. End and side scrapers, drills and choppers, as well as grooved axes, are also part of the assemblage. The slab milling stones, manos, and mortars reflect an interest in plant foods. In the B level, about the same complex exists, with bone awls and flaking tools and some objects of shell also reported.

Also, in eastern Oklahoma there is the Fourche Maline focus represented by a number of sites; the description of these as well as the artifact list again aligns this focus closely with the Midcontinent Archaic tradition. The locations are middens containing earth, shell in quantity, animal bones, charcoal, fire-cracked stones, fire-reddened areas, and other familiar phenomena, including human and dog burials. Burials are flexed, they have little grave furniture, and they were apparently merely placed on the ground and covered. Only very shallow burial pits were detected. In addition to heavy blades and scrapers, there were celts, full-grooved axes, pendants, gorgets, atlatl weights of several kinds, with the boat shape dominant, and also beads, hammerstones, cupstones, and one pipe fragment. Bone was in common use for many tools, but shell was not utilized as a raw material. Bone was used for awls, bodkins, atlatl hooks with a slot rather than a socket for insertion of the wooden shaft, beads, discs, and rings, as well as for unspecified objects.

From the Rice site (Missouri), Bray (1956) has carefully reported a rather large collection which duplicates the Grove focus inventory. Baerreis (1959) points out that in the Rice site, as well as in the Grove focus sites, there are more lanceolate, vaguely Plano, projectiles or knives in the middle levels than in the earlier strata, a distribution that differs from the finds in Graham Cave and others from the Plains.

The Archaic stage is represented all over Texas (for example, the Levi site, page 101). Over that vast reach of territory, marked changes in the tool types can be noted. There appears to be a transition between, or a blending of, the Eastern Midcontinent Archaic tradition and the

Desert Archaic. Crook and Harris (1952) have described the Carrollton and Elam foci of northeast Texas, adjacent to Oklahoma, emphasizing the similarity of the material to some of the types of the Western deserts.

Kelley (1959) is much more specific in his comparisons and shows the mixed nature of the Balcones phase as it links, through its artifact complex, the Eastern and Desert Archaic traditions. The excellent summary and closely argued Kelley paper is recommended. The Texas Big Bend finds and those by C. B. Cosgrove (1947) in southwestern New Mexico, of course, support Kelley, as do the finds in the lower levels of Tularosa Cave.

As one moves west and north from Missouri, Arkansas, and Oklahoma into the Plains, the reported Archaic sites are less numerous, but those available provide some argument for the blending with the Desert Archaic, such as can be seen quite clearly in the Texas manifestations. The best-known sites are Signal Butte (Nebraska), McKean (Wyoming), Pictograph Cave (Montana), and LoDaisKa (Colorado). These sites (or at least certain levels) would all fall within Mulloy's (1952, 1958) Middle Period.

The most fully reported of these Middle Period sites is the McKean. Here on the Belle Fourche River, Mulloy (1954) found a large, open, well-stratified site in the reservoir area, behind Keyhole Dam. It was located near the river in the lee of a protecting ledge of sandstone. The upper level is radiocarbon-dated at 1450 B.C., the lower level falls perhaps at 3000 to 4000 B.C. In his analysis, Mulloy emphasized the trait similarities shared by the two levels at McKean with one or more complexes at Pictograph Cave, Signal Butte, and Ash Hollow (Nebraska), several early Utah sites, and Birdshead Cave (Montana). From the lower level, level I, which was sealed from the upper level by sterile soil, several diagnostic projectile points were recovered. One was a slender, lanceolate type called the McKean (R. P. Wheeler 1952). McKean points are short, being 2 to 3 inches long, with both base and stem incurving gracefully from a wide midportion. Deftly pressure-chipped and usually with a deeply indented concave base, these are quite distinctive pieces. Other types, many with indented or deeply notched bases, with stems or side notches, also occur. Two of these types, the Duncan and the Hanna, are regarded by R. P. Wheeler (1954) as having diagnostic value in both cultural and chronologic context (Figure 3.32). Most of the blades and points are smaller and better made than is generally true of Eastern Archaic material. There were also snub-nosed end scrapers, spokeshave scrapers, random flake scrapers, round, retouched flake scrapers, and numerous ovoid blades of good workmanship. Manos and milling stones were present. Bone tools were absent, but three tubular bone beads were found. The food bones indicate deer and bison to have been favored prey, but the sample is very small.

The depth of the site is variable, the lower stratum being from 1 to 4 feet below the surface. A total of thirty-four hearths was associated with the lower level. Most of these were irregular lenses of discolored sand and charcoal flecks. A few others were small, shallow basins in the sand lined with small slabs of stone. Charcoal flecks and sand filled the basins. The slabs and peripheral sand were reddened from the heat of continued use. Two cache pits and one human skull burial were also associated with the lower level. The skull fit Neumann's description of his Deneid type. The above artifact assemblage is clearly not like the Eastern Archaic tool kit, but, in the wealth of scrapers, the extensive and frequent use of the sheltered camp, the cache pits, and the milling stones, it is quite readily identified as an Archaic stage component.

At Signal Butte (Strong 1935) and Ash Hollow Cave (Champe 1946), collections

quite like McKean were found. As W. R. Wedel (1964) reminds us, the groups inhabiting these sites depended heavily upon game, and the milling stone was not represented in the archeologic complex. Typologically, however, the complexes otherwise resemble the McKean material. The earliest Scottsbluff layer collections resemble the one from the lower level at McKean, but the layer has a radiocarbon dating of about 1000 B.C., the age of McKean's upper level, a discrepancy not yet resolved. Further west in Montana, from Pictograph Cave, Mulloy (1952, 1958) describes an important sequence which begins with Big Game Hunter debris and proceeds through the Archaic of his Middle Period and on into protohistoric times.

From the foothills west of Denver, the Irwins (1959) have reported a rock shelter—LoDaisKa—which had been repeatedly used as a camp for thousands of years. There were numerous cobblestone areas with ash and charcoal which had seen campfire use, three storage cists, and many artifacts. The charcoal-ash-stone hearths were found in all except the lowest of four separable major layers of accumulation. The natural layers did not exactly coincide with the cultural sequence, a fact which the Irwins ascribe to aboriginal disturbance and mixing. From the earliest deposits two fragments of two lanceolate points of Plano types were recovered.

The major occupancy occurred at the next-highest layer, Complex D, which consists of projectile points; knives; scrapers; gravers; slab milling stones and handstones; bone dice, awls, and beads; mineral pigments; pieces of mica; and other specimens very like those of the Desert Archaic to the west. The Irwins' Complex C contains artifacts similar to those from Western Plains Archaic sites such as McKean and Scottsbluff, and it has been interpreted as a transplanted Desert culture complex expanded out of the Great Basin. Complexes D and C are seen as separate and sequent on typologic and other bases, being blended and mixed instead of sharply separated in the deposit. This lack of separation may argue for continuous occupancy and gradual change in the cultural inventory rather than for mechanical mixing of debris from separate groups. In any case, the LoDaisKa sequence seems to sustain the notion of Plains-Basin contacts at an Archaic stage earlier even than Jennings (1957) has postulated.

Western Archaic

Once across the Rockies, the oldest American Archaic sites of record are encountered. Although only recently labeled the Desert culture (Jennings and Norbeck 1955) and recognized as part of the continent-wide Archaic, the sites and their contents have been longer known and more intensively studied (and speculated about) than any in the West save those of the Pueblo of the Christian era.

On the basis of artifact complexes, several traditions (Figure 4.13) can be readily separated. Coastal California is viewed here as a special case and is considered one of the separable areas. All these areas constitute traditions whose relationships in time and to each other are not yet clear. The first area may need to be modified if yet another Archaic tradition is finally worked out. Such a tradition seems to be taking on a separable identity in the Plateau area, again with an ecologic element in the definition, through the work of Swanson (1962) and Daugherty (1962). Heizer (1964), Jennings (1964), Swanson (1965), and Warren and True (1961) are the latest to have dealt with these problems. Since this was written, Irwin-Williams (1965) has independently postulated (quite convincingly) an "Elementary Southwestern Culture" going back to 3000 B.C. which coin-

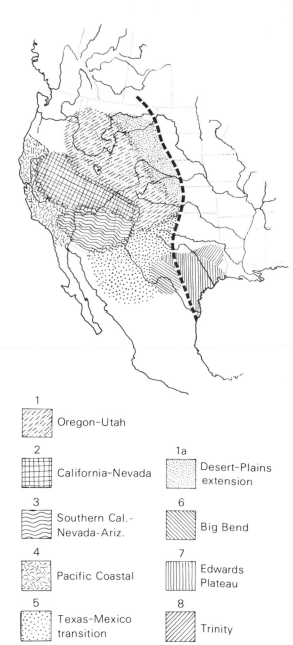

1 Oregon-Utah

2 California-Nevada

3 Southern Cal.-Nevada-Ariz.

4 Pacific Coastal

5 Texas-Mexico transition

1a Desert-Plains extension

6 Big Bend

7 Edwards Plateau

8 Trinity

Figure 4.13 *Areas in the Western Archaic tradition. Dotted line indicates zone of transition between Eastern and Western Archaic.*

cides almost precisely with the southern California-Nevada-Arizona area. Her suggestion is supported by old data and by material from recently excavated sites in northwestern New Mexico.

Before considering the complexes in detail, the very special Western setting needs reviewing. In contrast to the rain-drenched woodlands of the East, or the game-rich Plains and their tree-lined rivers, the Western valleys are bleak and hostile. At no time can one postulate a population as dense as is assigned to the Eastern Archaic climax. The land is arid, the vegetation is sparse, and the animal species are correspondingly limited. Evidently, the present-day conditions of aridity prevailed during all the time when the hunters of the Plains had somewhat moister surroundings, and there is good evidence that the area was never lush during any period of man's use. Earlier, before we can be sure of man's presence, there was more moisture; there were large lakes and, likely, many springs. Nonetheless, the pluvial aspects of the last weak lobes of the Wisconsin ice were obviously negligible west of the Rockies. At least, there is no present evidence for perennial lakes or large rivers over the past 12,000 years other than those now existing. Baumhoff and Heizer (1965) point out that many known Western Archaic sites lie near water sources and believe that this fact of location, as well as the artifacts, argues a lacustrine or riverine focus (specialization) by Archaic populations over most of the West. But such a focus would be inevitable in view of the Archaic concept of total exploitation. To prove an *overriding* lacustrine specialization, it would be necessary to show that no seasonal use of other nonriverine species occurred. Such proof is lacking to date; in fact, evidence to the contrary is common. It is presumed here that the ingenuity and wide exploitive talents of the Westerners were already being tested by 9000 or 10,000 B.C. (For lyrically partisan descriptions of the hardy desert dwellers, see Jennings, various.)

The area where the Desert culture traditions can be recognized encompasses the Great Basin, the Intermontane area, parts of the Colorado Plateau, coastal California, and down across Arizona into the Central Plateau of Mexico; the Desert culture is also represented in the Plains and down into Texas. The fairly consistent complex of stone artifacts differs in a majority of types from the Eastern Archaic complex. As originally defined (Jennings 1957), and as restated (Jennings 1964), the artifacts and lifeway were tied to (perhaps as functions of) an ecologic setting of aridity. But some of the desert types occur deep in the Eastern Archaic zone (J. L. Coe 1952); H. T. Irwin (1964) even argues that these artifact types, especially the indented, base-stemmed points, may in fact have originally been Eastern Archaic types which were popular and hence were adopted by group after group until they achieved a continent-wide distribution. Radiocarbon dates, however, would argue a west-to-east flow of influence.

Despite the certainty implied in Figure 4.13, the areal distinctions between the local Archaic cultures are by no means agreed upon. They should properly be thought of as possible areal clusters, but no one, other than Heizer (1956; Heizer and Krieger 1956) and Cynthia Irwin-Williams (personal communication, 1966), has taken the trouble to begin sorting out the really definitive traits.

Of the areas shown in Figure 4.13, only two are based at this time on detailed study. Only areas 1 and 2 have been established by analysis of individual traits (Heizer 1956; Heizer and Krieger 1956), although area 5, too, has received some careful study by Kelley (1959), among others. Area 3 has a reality of a different sort. In it fall most of the many troublesome, dangling complexes and their apparent derivative cultures. Thus, this area may be the one where controlled evidence of the chopper-scraper industries (mentioned earlier) is to be found. Here, too, are assemblages which lack the fully diagnostic materials of the Desert culture as defined. True, most of the controversial collections are surface finds and dangle unassigned in time; they are not described as to full artifact range and not associated with any faunal assemblage. On typologic evidence they can be fitted into the Desert Archaic and are therefore included here, although many specialists deny the appropriateness of this action. At the same time, the *possibility* that these desert complexes may be transitional from the chopper-scraper substratum is somewhat hopefully acknowledged. The answer is simply not yet available. The named complexes involved here are *not* those in Krieger's (1964) "Pre-Projectile" stage (La Chapala, Manix, Farmington, Las Encinas, and others) because these are disregarded here as being one or more of the following: (1) not artifacts of man, (2) quarry debris, or (3) artifacts, but uncontrolled as to time or association. The southern congeries arbitrarily grouped here into the Archaic are Death Valley I (California), Lake Mohave, San Dieguito, Playa, Amargosa (California), and others which are characterized by a limited inventory of chopper-scraper implements and, in some cases, a variety of projectile and knife types.

Before dealing with the areas separately, it is necessary to orient the reader to the terrain where the Western foragers worked out their version of Archaic efficiency. Except for the Colorado Plateau, certain parts of the Intermontane province, and the Canadian provinces, the Desert West is one of the world's harshest environments. For groups possessing only an aboriginal technology, its human-carrying capacity is limited. Most of the areas delimited in Figure 4.13 can be described as desert, which implies a sagebrush cover and the associated small faunal forms. This is not the full story, however. Parts of the Colorado Plateau are rich in resources, and most of the Western desert

shows rhythmic alternation of steep and short north-south–trending ranges with sage-covered valleys between. Thus in the Great Basin, a foot traveler can move to, and forage in, life zones ranging from Sonoran to the Arctic-Alpine above tree line; within each zone a different inventory of species is available. Thus, over the West, there are more varied seasonal resources than might be supposed. To exploit these resources would necessitate more frequent shifts of residence and probably a much longer annual round than was required of either the woodlands or the Plains foragers. (See Jennings 1957, 1964, for a more detailed treatment of the desert setting and resources.)

Convincing evidence that the Western climate and resources have been almost unchanged since 10,000 B.C., unaffected by the minor glacial activity far to the north and east in the Great Lakes region, suggests that man's entire history in the West has been achieved under essentially today's conditions. Also, as today, during the centuries there existed cycles of variation in the annual rainfall and temperature conditions (and hence in the abundance of species). Documenting this interpretation are Burma (1950), Aschmann (1958), Flint (1947), Schoenwetter (1962, 1966), and Schoenwetter and Eddy (1964). It is assumed here that, at no point in time, did the extreme aridity once claimed for the Altithermal, an aridity that would have made human life impossible, actually characterize the Basin. To this view, Baumhoff and Heizer (1965) take sharp exception, as would William Mulloy (personal communication, 1964), who bases his views on the evidence from the high plains of Wyoming, where the Archaic stage seems to be missing as yet from the 5000 to 3000 B.C. span of time.

The definition of the Desert culture has evolved through several versions as areally greater applications have been attempted and the presence of a continent-wide Archaic was more easily perceived. At present the Desert culture is seen as oriented toward exploitation of all species, as opposed to being concentrated only upon big-game animals. The diagnostic cultural hallmarks have been described as the milling stone and basketry, associated, of course, with scores of flint, bone, and other tools, evidencing an array of special tools for specialized tasks and wide technologic skills. As mentioned earlier, the concept involves more than a tool kit; it implies some basic linkage or correlation between the artifacts and an ecosystem controlled by conditions of aridity.

The most general descriptive definition of the Desert culture content is found in Jennings (1956). Modified, this list includes such traits as an intensive, unrestricted exploitation of species; small-seed harvesting and consequent special cookery of mushes and cakes; fur cloth, woven sandals (sometimes hide moccasins); the atlatl and dart; a wide variety of small projectile points; knives (both large and small); flat and basin nether millstones; crude tools called pulpers; choppers and scrapers; wooden clubs; tubular pipes or sucking tubes; vegetable quids; twined basketry technique first, with coiling soon added; and a high valuing of *Oliva* and *Olivella* shells from California waters. Heizer (1956) and Heizer and Krieger (1956) have listed more detailed, long-persistent core traits involving specific artifact types. This list includes deer-hoof rattles, medicine pouches (which persisted to modern times), twined matting, scapula grass-cutting tools (see Day 1964), perforated bone or antler wrenches, bird-bone whistles, cane arrows with hardwood shafts (late), wooden-handled flint knives, L-shaped scapula awls, digging sticks, solid-shaft fire drills, wooden fire-drill hearths, coiled and twined basketry.

Turning now to the description of selected sites of area 1, among the first to

be reported were the several caves of eastern Oregon—Roaring Spring, Catlow, and Fort Rock being most important (Cressman 1942; Cressman and Kreiger 1940). Together, and usually under good control, the several Oregon caves yielded twined basketry; string; matting; sandals made from tule; fire drills; L-shaped awls; thin milling stones and manos; many atlatls and dart shafts; bone bars (for flaking flint?); bone beads; and a wide variety of projectile points of triangular, notched, and stemmed or stemless lanceolate types. Chipping is usually fine and the pieces are not large. Many end scrapers and other scrapers made from flakes are also found. From Fort Rock Cave, one of the seventy-five woven sandals was radiocarbon dated at over 8100 B.C. Aside from the early date and the frequent sealing of these remains by ancient pumice, these caves gave evidence, which Cressman properly interpreted, for quite early habitation of the desert area at a time (ca. 1940) when scholarly consensus still denied the possibility. With the use of the radiocarbon dating technique in the 1950s, when scores of desert sites yielded dates of 6000 to 8000 B.C., came support for Cressman's interpretation.

Southeast of the Oregon caves in area 1 are a series of sites in Utah. Of these, the best known is Danger Cave (Jennings 1953, 1957) on the western edge of the Great Salt Desert in western Utah. This was a wide-mouthed grotto which had been the scene of intermittent human use from 9000 B.C. until recent times. Its portal was choked by midden by about A.D. 1, so later occupants, including historic Paiute tribesmen, were only able to camp in the slight shelter of the hooded overhang (about eighty sherds of "Shoshoni" pottery, recognized as a recent type, lay in the upper layers of the rock-shelter deposits). Cultural accumulations reached a depth of 13 feet., representing five periods of use (Figure 4.14). Most of the

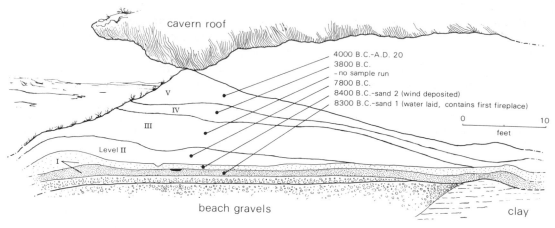

4000 B.C.-A.D. 20
3800 B.C.
– no sample run
7800 B.C.
8400 B.C.-sand 2 (wind deposited)
8300 B.C.-sand 1 (water laid, contains first fireplace)

cavern roof

V

IV

III

Level II

I

0   10
feet

beach gravels   clay

Figure 4.14   *Cross section of Danger Cave, Utah.*

fill was mixed chaff (from pickleweed) and dust from the salt flats where the pickleweed grows. The latter was harvested for its seed, which was parched, milled, and eaten. The debris yielded many artifacts and food bones. With good stratigraphic control, it was possible to see the invention or adoption of new tools as time passed, with the greatest variety occurring in level V. Over sixty knife and projectile point types were isolated and over twenty scraper classes. The radiocarbon age of level I was about 8500 B.C.; that of level II, 7500 B.C.; level III was undated; and that of level IV was 1800 B.C. Samples from level V ranged from 2000 B.C. to A.D. 20. The samples came from within the cave well back from the portal. Materials from the overhang would probably show quite recent dates.

Table 3 shows the increase in classes of artifacts, other than chipped stone, from early to late.

Such simple presence-absence lists tell very little; for example, such things as the shift in basketry techniques from 100 percent twining at 7500 B.C. to 15 percent twining versus 85 percent coiling by 2000 B.C. or the abandonment of hemp (*Apocynum*) for cordage, to be replaced, in turn, by greasewood bark during the last two levels, do not come out. Nonetheless,

the increased tool inventory, as well as the persistence of all basic early items, can be seen. The only knife from level I is vaguely reminiscent of the Plano lanceolate forms but is not a diagnostic named type. Krieger (1964), on the basis of this one point (and the age), argues that level I is referable to the earlier Big Game Hunting stage and is not part of the Desert culture. Level II and later levels show an early preference for the small-to-medium-sized, triangular, stemmed and notched points, with the larger lanceolate or pear-shaped styles gaining in popularity in later layers.

Reminiscent of the chopper-scraper problem are the choppers and scrapers found where end scrapers, side scrapers, a few prismatic knives, and other crude forms occur. A few gravers were also recovered. Generally, in flintwork the Oregon-Utah collections are very similar to each other.

From Danger Cave were recovered over 1,000 flat milling stones and fragments, over 2,000 chipped stone pieces, hundreds of manos or handstones, over a hundred pieces of coiled and twined basketry (and one piece of cloth), netting, horn, bone, wood, antler, shell (including species from the California coast), leather, and minerals such as mica and ocher. Through the accidents of preservation in the dry en-

Table 3 Danger Cave: occurrence of artifacts other than chipped stone (modified from Jennings 1957)

	I	II	III	IV	V
			Levels		
Pottery					x
Wood:					
Dart foreshafts	x		x	x	x
Fire-drill tips			x		x
Fire-drill boards					x
Slabs or "trowels"			x		x
Slab skewers				x	x
Cylinders					x
Gaming sticks					x
Snares (wood and string)					x
Trap springs					x
Arrows					x
Knife handles					x
Bone:					
Splinter awls	x		x	x	x
L-shaped awls			x	x	
Bars			x		x
Tubes (pipes?)			x		x
Spoon?			x		
Needles?				x	x
Tinklers					x
Dice					x
Horn:					
Wrench			x		
Spoon					x
Shell:					
Mussell			x	x	x
Olivella			x		
Pigment:					
Red ocher	x		x	x	x
Yellow	x				x
Clay effigies					x
Millstones, slab	x		x	x	x
Handstones or manos	?		x	x	x
Abraders	x		x	x	x
Etched stone					x
Leather	x		x	x	x
Mica discs	x				x
Quids	x		x	x	x
Cordage	x		x	x	x
Basketry:					
Twining	x		x	x	x
Coiling			x	x	x

vironment, Danger Cave yields one of the most complete Desert culture inventories yet reported. [The cave also differs from some to be mentioned later in being an actual living site where many worn-out tools or weapons or utensils were discarded, as well as food bones and other scrap. Many famous sites seem to have been more heavily used as cache or storage spots (for example, Lovelock) rather than as dwelling places. As a result, Danger has a wider variety of utilitarian objects, whereas the cache sites contain perhaps more "valued" materials (Figures 4.15, 4.16, and 4.17).] Among the debris were various scraps of wood and other plants which were used in perishable utensils. The full list of the plant species identified from 4,000 pieces of artifacts and scraps in the debris numbers over sixty-five—all still found in the area today. Animal species used as food include antelope, bison, mountain sheep, jackrabbit, wood rat, dog (?), bobcat, and desert fox. The mountain sheep was the commonest big game. A few pieces of elk (?) antler were found, but no bones of the big cervids were identified; all these food bones are from modern species. At nearby Juke Box Cave, however, one horse bone was recovered from the bottom of the earliest cultural level. (Since this chapter was written excavation of another dwelling site, Hogup Cave, a few miles east of Danger Cave has been started. Here, in undisturbed, evenly accumulated layers, 14½ feet in total depth, the contents and time span seen at Danger are being duplicated.)

Some 500 miles further east in area 1, LoDaisKa Cave (see page 133) artifacts from Complex D show marked similarity to the Danger Cave collection. LoDaisKa also shares some types with the Uncompahgre (Wormington and Lister 1956) complex, which falls, with LoDaisKa, in area 1 or, more properly, in the gray zone between areas 1 and 2. Hells Midden in extreme northwest Colorado (Lister 1951) is another open site with artifacts closely resembling certain Danger Cave types. LoDaisKa and Hells Midden have the slab milling stone, as do Promontory (Steward 1937) and Deadman (E. R. Smith 1952) Caves in Utah.

In area 2, next south, there are numerous important sites. These include a cluster around Humboldt Lake in west-

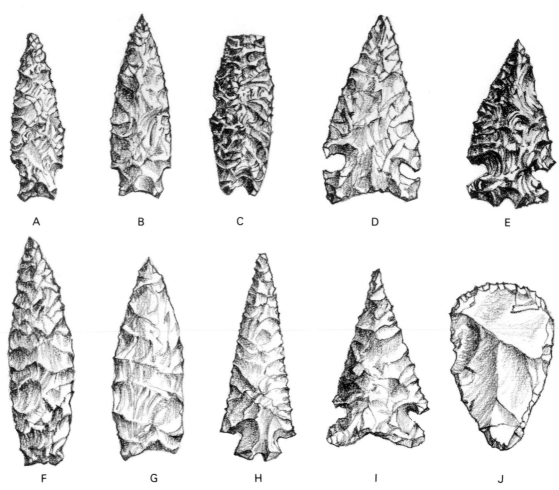

Figure 4.15   *Common stone artifact types from Danger Cave.*
Actual size. A–I, projectile points; J, scraper; K, graver; L, knife;
M, drill; N, basalt knife; O, obsidian knife. (Drawn from Uni-
versity of Utah collection)

central Nevada (Lovelock, Leonard, Humboldt) and the famous Gypsum Cave near
Las Vegas, Nevada. Together the several
sites offer a fairly complete inventory of
the Desert culture artifacts. The first-
mentioned are the remains of a people
whose subsistence focused on the many
lacustrine resources of the shallow, fluc-
tuating lake. Lovelock was one of the
richest sites in the West—a large, irregular cave opening out onto fossil Lake
Lahontan. It was nearly filled with huge
roof spalls weighing many tons and had
been used primarily as a cache site. Love-

lock and Humboldt Caves were dry and,
though sometimes occupied, were used
mainly for caches. Being late in time
(about 2500 B.C. for Lovelock and A.D. 1
for Humboldt), the varied artifacts were
used in a climate very like that of today.
The special items showing lacustrine focus
include duck decoys of tule, fishnets, and
two types of fishhooks, to say nothing of
several dried suckers and chub found in
Humboldt Cave caches. Other artifacts are
more familiar. These include well-made
baskets, both twined and coiled; the
scapula and sheep-horn sickles; fiber san-

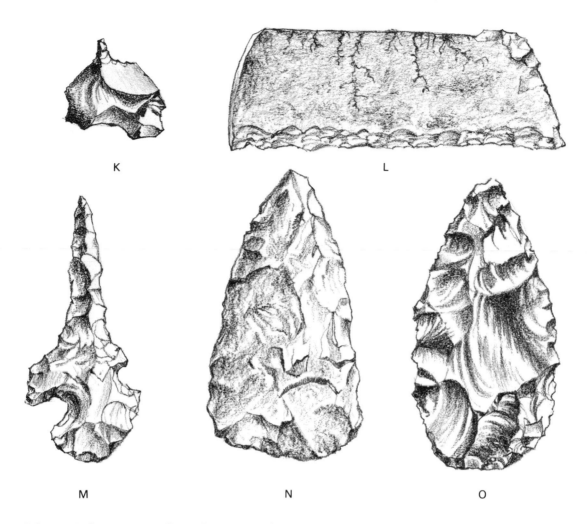

K   L

M   N   O

dals; tubular pipes; flint knives with
wooden handles; bow fragments; and other
evidence of the total exploitive round
(Figures 4.18 and 4.19). Objects very similar to those from Danger Cave include
the L-shaped awls, fine netting, atlatl
foreshafts, fire-drill hearths, skin textiles or blankets, horn spoons and horn
"wrenches," as well as a number of
chipped-flint tools. Humboldt was particularly rich, yielding thirty-one caches.
Most of its cache pits were lined with well-
preserved basket fragments. One contained what appears to be a shaman's kit.
The inventory from Humboldt lists the
following classes: duck decoys of tule;
feather bundles (in fourteen caches);
sickles of mountain-sheep horn; horn
wrenches; scapula sickles or grass cutters;
bone awls, including the L-shaped one
cut from a scapula and other types; bone
needles; fishhooks of two types (both composite); digging sticks; fire drills and
hearths; many composite arrows and
parts; dart shafts; shallow cottonwood
bowls and slabs (trowels?); wooden knife
handles; chipped-flint points, knives, and
scrapers; hammerstones; wicker and coiled
basketry (766 pieces of coiling represented
213 baskets); flexible and rigid twined
basketry (the flexible bags are of a special
type called Catlow twined, described
from the Oregon caves); cordage of all
kinds and sizes; fiber sandals; feather

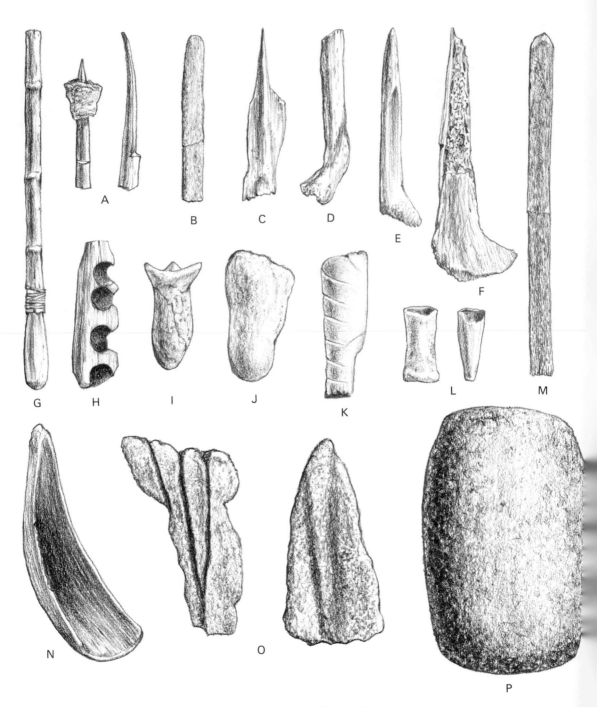

Figure 4.16 *Artifacts from Danger cave. Variable scale. A, wooden pegs; B, worked bone; C–F, bone awls; G, fire drill; H, fire-drill hearth; I, clay effigy, probably a kit fox; J, clay effigy; K, worked bone; L, bone tinklers; M, worked bone; N, horn spoon; O, abrading stones; P, stone mano. (Drawn from University of Utah collection)*

robes; string aprons; pine-nut and *Olivella* beads; bone whistles and tubes; tubular stone pipes; and many fragmentary miscellaneous items. At neither of the above sites was the mano or flat millstone reported, although many occur on nearby open sites around Humboldt Lake. The food bones found in Humboldt Cave show that grebe, pelican, heron, swan, goose, duck, hawk, and raven were taken, as were mountain sheep, deer, jackrabbit, badger, fox, bobcat, marmot, several rats and mice, and muskrat. At Lovelock the mammal list was longer, with weasel, skunk, mink, beaver, wolf, cottontail, and antelope being added; all the species are modern. Raw materials for perishable tools were derived from scores of plants—*Apocynum* (hemp), rush, cane, various grasses, greasewood, willow, cottonwood, and other species—all already cited from Danger Cave. Quids were numerous, also.

From Lovelock the objects were more numerous and varied, being recovered from cache pits (forty) as well as from the fill, but the range of classes is about the same as at Humboldt. On the basis of a trait list with presence or absence noted by level, the Lovelock culture, as it is called, has been divided into an Early-Middle-Late sequence, covering about the last 4,000 years. The list emphasizes the perishable materials, so it is not easy to apply to most sites, but the classes correspond rather neatly with the perishable things found in the upper two layers of Danger Cave. However, on a specific level (for example, in detailed basketry techniques or chipped-flint specimen types), there are fewer correspondences between the Humboldt sites and the Utah-Oregon sites than there are with the Early Basketmaker of the Four Corners area and toward the California coast. These findings remind us that Heizer's (1956) and Heizer and Krieger's (1956) detailed list of "core" elements (page 137) of the Desert culture must be recognized as being drawn from

several sites, most of which are late. Furthermore, like all such synthesized lists, it is not accurate for any one site or for any one time period. More usefully, the Heizer and Krieger lists can be thought of as citing the major traits of what has long been called the Basketmaker I stage or level of the Southwestern sequence. The full-blown Desert culture, with the excellent technology and high exploitive skills implied by the core list, can be recognized from Oregon to Mexico long before Christ, and is the stage at which the catalytic Mexican traits (agriculture, pottery, masonry) diffused northward. It is out of this highly efficient Late stage of the Desert culture that the later "high" (Formative) tradition of the Southwest evolved, never losing the technology nor the close attention to natural species of the earlier stage. (See Martin et al. 1952; C. B. Cosgrove 1947; Reed 1964.) The diffusion of the Desert culture was evidently southward and eastward from the Basin.

Further south, near Las Vegas, Nevada, Etna Cave (S. M. Wheeler 1942) revealed, under good control, horse bones in association with cultural debris. Etna yielded completely typical artifacts of textile and flint in scant quantity but in a good state of preservation. The cave also contained a series of stick figurines of game animals (Figure 4.20), many being impaled upon a spear or lance through the chest cavity. These remarkable little figures have been found in several places along the Grand Canyon and have been dated by radiocarbon. The dates cluster around 1500 B.C. (Schwartz, Lange and deSaussure 1958; Euler and Olson 1965).

Another Las Vegas find seems to show man in conjunction with extinct beasts. This is Gypsum Cave (Harrington 1933), which is among the first of the Western sites to have been excavated. Gypsum Cave is a cluster of irregular rooms connected by the tunnels and passages of a

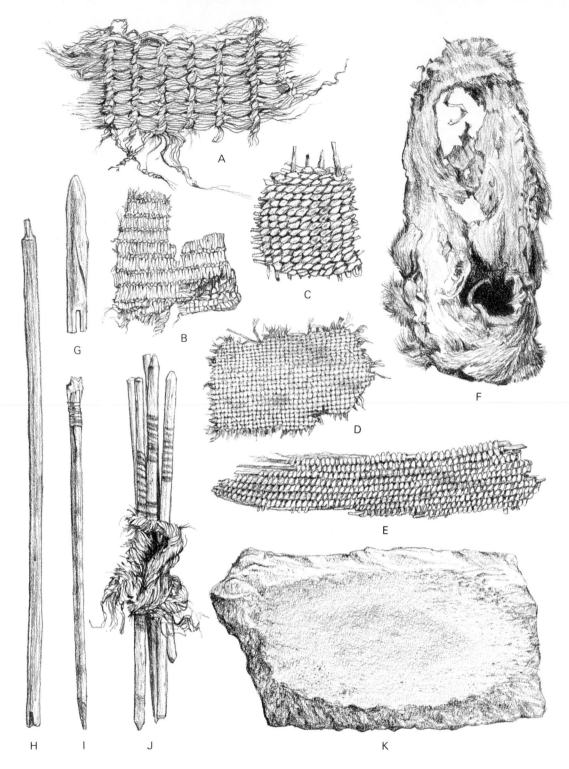

Figure 4.17 *Artifacts from Danger Cave. Variable scale. A, B, twined matting; C, twined basketry; D, coarse cloth; E, coiled basketry; F, hide moccasin; G, wooden knife handle, 4½ inches long; H, dart shaft, 16 inches long; I, arrow shaft with broken projectile point in place, 33 inches long; J, bundle of gaming sticks, 11½ inches long; K, milling stone, 21 inches long. (Drawn from University of Utah collection)*

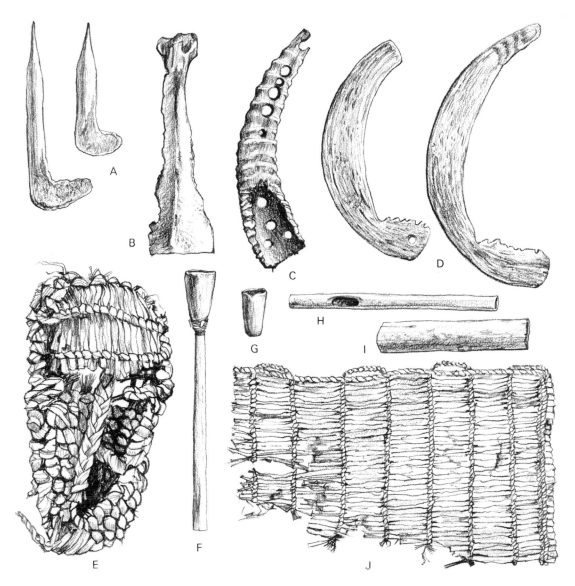

Figure 4.18   Artifacts of the Desert Archaic tradition, California-Nevada (area 2). Variable scale. A, scapula awls; B, scapula grass cutter, 9 inches long; C, worked sheep horn; D, worked horn sickles, 10¼ and 13 inches long; E, tule sandal; F, G, tubular stone pipes (F with stem); H, bird-bone whistle, 6 inches long; I, pelican-bone tube, 4 inches long; J, twined tule mat. (A, B, E, G–J after Heizer and Krieger 1956; C, F after Loud and Harrington 1929; D after Lipe 1960)

natural limestone cave, descending steeply into the mountain from a hooded, shelter-like portal. In the several rooms were extensive deposits of sloth dung along with bones from these extinct giants (see Figure 3.42) and from camel as well. Throughout the cave were artifacts of man, including several fireplaces. The artifacts and the sloth dung were evidently contemporary. The sloth dung, long after

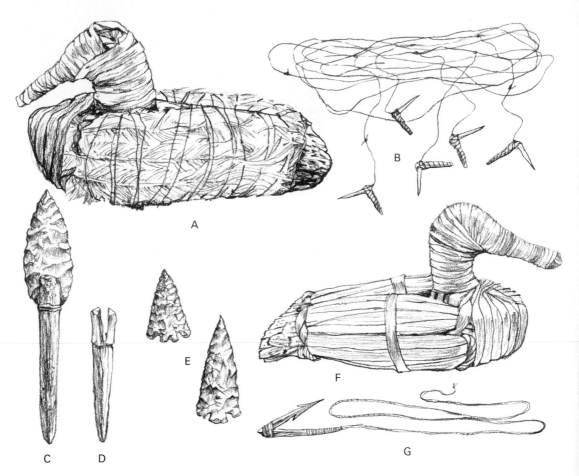

Figure 4.19 Artifacts of the Desert Archaic tradition, California-Nevada (area 2). Approximately one-half size, except decoys much reduced. A, duck decoy of tule and duck feathers; B, fishhooks on setline; C, hafted knife; D, knife handle; E, projectile points; F, tule duck decoy; G, bone fishhook with wooden shank and twined line. (A, B, F after Loud and Harrington 1929; C, D, E, G after Heizer and Krieger 1956)

its recovery, was dated by radiocarbon at 8500 B.C., but none of the wooden or bone artifacts has yet been dated.

The artifacts covered the full range of the Desert culture. Well-preserved, complete atlatl darts tipped with what is regarded by some as a diagnostic type—the Gypsum point—were an important find. There were also many tools of bone, wood, fiber, and stone. Among the diagnostic artifacts were deer-hoof tinklers, compound arrows, bone bars, slab millstones with handstones, scapula cutting or harvesting tools, digging sticks, flint knives

with handles, basketry, and a host of knives and scrapers. Thus, once the sloth association is assessed as possible rather than certain, the collection emerges as quite typical of the Desert culture, readily absorbed by definition. Its inventory aligns it with the Humboldt Lake cluster. It is entirely possible that the sloth-man association at the Gypsum site is fortuitous and that the implied radiocarbon dates ascribed for sloth survival are too recent. Or, it is equally possible that these creatures were never regularly preyed upon and that the mingling of man's artifacts with sloth dung and skeletons was mechanical, resulting from alternate occupancy by the two species. There is no certainty that the sloth was a food animal; there is merely an apparent association.

In area 3, as noted above, the anachronistic sites begin to appear. From extreme south-central Arizona, Ventana Cave (Haury 1950), with 10,000 to 11,000 years of history in its fill, is perhaps the most important document for this area. Undoubtedly a manifestation of the Desert Archaic, its thousands of artifacts do not conform at all closely with the more northerly specimens. Ventana had a complicated geologic history, which was skillfully untangled by Haury and his associates to reveal that the first occupants

left what was called a typically Folsom-stage collection with debris including an unfluted Folsom of generalized shape. [This identification was offered cautiously, and Haury, later (Haynes 1964), came to view the point itself as more properly identified as a small Clovis point, rather than a Folsom type. This is reasonable in view of the radiocarbon date of 9300 B.C., which agrees with the range of other Llano dates.]

Mixed with the Folsom-Llano (?) collections were a crude lot of chopper-scraper forms, most resembling the San Dieguito I (originally called the Malpais complex) from the California desert. (Except for the C. W. Harris site, the original San Dieguito location, Ventana Cave

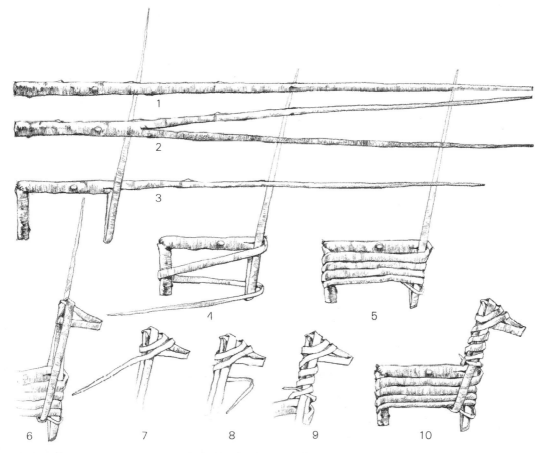

Figure 4.20   *Sequence of steps in making split-twig figure. Approximately one-half size. (After S. M. Wheeler 1942)*

offers the best-controlled chopper-scraper collection available for study.) Figure 4.21 shows the nature of these pieces. Note particularly the grinding stone—possibly a mano or hand milling stone. Both with, and just beneath, the San Dieguito finds

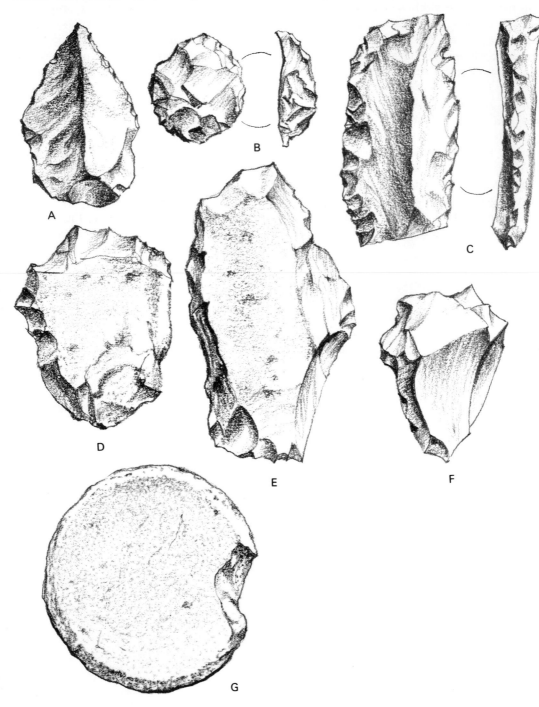

Figure 4.21   *Implements from the lower level of Ventana Cave. Variable scale. A, backed knife; B, worked basalt disc; C, D, E, scrapers; F, chopper; G, mano (?). (After Haury 1950)*

were several extinct large faunal species, the most numerous being the horse. Also present were tapir, four-pronged antelope, sloth, jaguar, kit fox, and dire wolf. Present, too, were modern forms of jackrabbit, prairie dog, coyote, badger, peccary, deer, and bison. The next layers of the deep fill contained a profusion of chipped stone, but because most of the fill was damp, perishables were confined to the uppermost levels, where they were numerous. Although the milling stone was common, the typical one was thick and blocky; the thin-slab was a minority type. The chipped stone points, choppers, scrapers, and knives and other forms on all levels are less deftly made and give an impression of more careless technique. The preferred (or available) material was a coarse basalt, a material much less amenable to pressure-flake finishing than the smooth-grained obsidians, chalcedonies, and cherts preferred throughout areas 1 and 2; this may adequately explain the rough appearance of the Ventana chipped stone.

From the upper fill (which was removed in 50-centimeter layers) there came heavy scrapers and choppers of several styles and many knife and projectile types, as well as gravers and special forms, including a number of drills of chipped stone. These types change through time and show important similarities to the later Desert cultures to the west and to the local sequence called Cochise. Through a comparison of the projectile and knife types which show change up through the midden, Haury correlates the Ventana sequence with the poorly controlled Western sequence subjectively established by Rogers as follows:

Rogers (Haury 1950)	*Rogers (1939)*
Amargosa III	*Amargosa I*
II	*Pinto-Gypsum*
I	
San Dieguito III	*Playa II*
II	*Playa I*
I	*Malpais*

Although there are hundreds of specimens, Haury summarizes the trend as shown in Figure 4.22. Most would agree with his equation of the Ventana and Ventana-Amargosa I with the Mohave manifestations. The later correlation with the Cochise sequence is also generally accepted. The full range of stone types from the three lower levels is summarized in Table 4.

Other stone artifacts, aside from manos and millstones, include the tubular pipe, stone beads, and hoes. Bone awls, fleshers (a broad chisel point on a long bone), and tubes were present, but Haury remarks on the scarcity of bone tools. Because the midden was full of food bones, it is known

SAN PEDRO

CHIRICAHUA-AMARGOSA II

AMARGOSA I

LLANO COMPLEX

Figure 4.22   *Sequence, and cultural affiliation of the projectile point types found in Ventana Cave. (After Haury 1950)*

Table 4   *Ventana Cave: stone artifacts (modified from Haury 1950)*

I   Ventana complex
  A   Stratigraphic position: volcanic debris layer
  B   Tool assemblage:
    1   Projectile points: leaf-shaped, round and concave bases (the latter Folsom-like, 1 recovered)
    2   Knives: curved flakes
    3   Scrapers: discoidal, small core, side (of varying shapes), end, and rough flake
    4   Gravers
    5   Choppers
    6   Planes
    7   Grinding stone (1)
II   Ventana-Amargosa I complex
  A   Stratigraphic position: red sand layer
  B   Tool assemblage:
    1   Projectile points: stemmed: stem parallel-sided or expanding
    2   Knives: amorphous flakes
    3   Scrapers: discoidal, side, end, and rough flake
    4   Planes: oval and elongate
    5   Grinding stones and choppers absent
III   Chiricahua-Amargosa II complex
  A   Stratigraphic position: base of midden, levels 5 to 8
  B   Tool assemblage:
    1   Projectile points:
      a   Leaf-shaped, convex, straight, and concave bases; triangular, straight base; diamond
      b   Stem wider than blade: concave base
      c   Stem narrower than blade: tapering
    2   Scrapers: large, thick flake; oval, thin flaked and keeled; elongate, thin flaked and keeled; pointed, thin flaked and keeled; rectangular, thin flaked and keeled; end, keeled, round and square nosed; hollow, thin and thick flaked and keeled; pointed; discoidal, thin flaked and domed; "thumbnail"
    3   Flake knives
    4   Gravers: thick flakes, prismatic, chisel
    5   Choppers: sharpened flakes, core, and flat pebble
    6   Metates: block and slab forms
    7   Manos: small, single hand type
    8   Pestle: flat and round ended
    9   Ground edge scrapers

that bone survived the dampness; the absence of bone tools is therefore regarded as evidence of limited use of this kind of material.

The lack of perishable specimens prevents close comparisons of the Ventana Cave with sites from areas 1 and 2. The chipped stone itself, however, is sufficiently different, except in the larger choppers and scrapers, to show the reality of the separateness of area 3 from areas 1 and 2. However, the general Desert culture relationships are clear. Haury sees Ventana as a peripheral location where early contact with Desert Archaic peoples from both east and west was followed by dominant western influence, gradually to be replaced with Cochise influence from the east (see Figure 4.23). On typologic grounds alone it seems equally likely that in the Ventana sequence one can see the development of the Cochise sequence out of a substratum clearly derived from the Western deserts, as Jennings (1957) and Meighan (1959a, 1959b) suggest. Such an explanation, if true, emphasizes the unity of the area 3 tradition until, sometime after 1000 B.C. (see Tularosa Cave, page 151), the technologically richer desert manifestations from areas 1 and 2 extend to blanket the entire area. (Although the present concern with Ventana ends at this

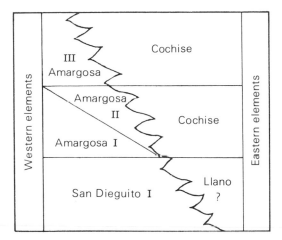

Figure 4.23   Relative dominance of western and eastern Desert Archaic elements at Ventana Cave prior to A.D. *1. (After Haury 1950)*

point, it should be noted that the upper deposits contain remains of late phases of the Cochise cultures, on through the Hohokam stage and into essentially modern times.)

The first of the Desert culture variants (already noted in Ventana) to be described was the Cochise of southeastern Arizona and southwestern New Mexico. In a documentation from several locations on White Water Creek dating back to the 1930s, Sayles and Antevs (1941) describe a three-stage sequence and imply their belief in a "basic pattern" of percussion-flaked tools (the chopper-scraper of this account), which is represented by the earliest Cochise level called Sulphur Spring. This stage, radiocarbon-dated at over 6000 B.C., has a meager inventory: thin, flat milling stones and small manos, percussion-flaked plano-convex tools for chopping and scraping, and little else. These objects are found on deeply buried old land surfaces, now covered by later sediment. The living areas were exposed by recent gullying. Important also is the apparent association with extinct fauna—horse, mammoth, dire wolf—as well as with modern bison, antelope, and coyote. While some have questioned the contemporaneity of the artifacts

and the bones of extinct creatures, the association appears to be valid.

Later in time and from sediments above Sulphur Spring, as well as hearths and middens elsewhere, the Chiricahua Cochise (5000 B.C.) shows a somewhat fuller complement of artifacts, including the milling stones and projectile points. Latest is the San Pedro stage, which endures until the introduction of pottery. In all three stages the stonework can be called crude and shows a general similarity to all early complexes of the southern area. Although the Cochise is important in its own right as a long Archaic sequence, it also seems possible, through both stratigraphy and typology, to show its ancestral relation to the Mogollon phase of the later Pueblo culture. Haury (1950) mentions this, while Martin, Rinaldo, and Antevs (1949) and Martin et al. (1952) insist upon it. Most would agree, but the usual caveat about basing conclusions on the typology of stone artifacts should be mentioned. With the Cochise one should include the Concho complex (Arizona), Lobo (New Mexico), and the Rio Grande-Atrisco sites near Albuquerque.

At Tularosa Cave (Martin et al. 1952), where many classes of perishables were preserved, the transition from Archaic to Formative stage is documented. While the probability exists (Bullard 1962) that during excavation there was some loss of control of provenience in certain areas, the sequence from the lower Chiricahua Cochise stage on up into the Mogollon culture of the Christian era can be accepted. In the prepottery or Cochise levels the stonework was of the same type as elsewhere in area 3; the authors of the Tularosa Cave report explicitly mention, as did Haury, the resemblance to Pinto types from the west. The perishable items were innumerable; Tularosa was one of the richest sites in the West.

From the prepottery levels came the milling stone and small mano; coiled basketry; quids; fiber sandals of wickerwork and leather; moccasins; bone tubular beads; cordage and traps; net bags; cradles; fire drills and hearths; atlatls and darts; chipped points and knives; choppers and hammerstones; drills; gravers; abrading stones; short, stubby bone awls; knife handles and trowels of wood; wooden and bone dice; pigment; skewers; wooden cylinders; and other familiar classes. Specimens of thirty-nine natural floral species exploited for food, tools, and raw materials were recovered. Of these the food plants included yucca seeds, cacti, walnuts, seeds from various grasses, and sunflower and desert primrose seeds. In addition, the prepottery levels yielded maize, beans, squash, and gourds, showing that these cultigens were introduced into a situation where vegetable foods were already an important item of diet before other Middle American traits, such as pottery, had been introduced into the Southwest (by about 300 B.C.). Corn, however, was known much earlier from Bat Cave (New Mexico), not too far and northeast from Tularosa. There Dick (1965) found primitive pod corn, dated at about 3500 B.C., in the lower levels. In successively younger levels, the corn remains demonstrated an evolution toward primitive maize of modern type. The artifacts associated with the corn resemble the Cochise complex. The full significance of this site cannot be assessed. The very early date for such primitive types, this far north in an Archaic context, is unique in the record and has not yet been fully understood. Another open site, well-dug and well-reported, is Cienega Creek (Haury 1957), where the Chiricahua Cochise can be seen to evolve through time into a later form.

To the west, the many presumed early complexes can't be taken too seriously because they are lacking in control. These are the Mohave (E. W. C. Campbell and Campbell 1935; E. W. C. Campbell et al. 1937), Playa, Amargosa, Pinto, and Death

Valley I. These are all interpreted as being Big Game Hunting in focus, and the mano and slab millstone are not usually demonstrated as present. The lack of basketry from open sites is expectable, but if these are to be considered typical Desert culture manifestations, the millstone should be part of the tool kit. The matter of definition must be deferred until more is known of these floating congeries. A start has been made on the problem at the C. W. Harris site in California, which lies outside area 3 but whose contents are entirely typical of area 3 stonework. Warren and True (1961) have reported their pilot excavation there, and they have radiocarbon evidence for ascribing a pre-7000 B.C. date for the lowest level, San Dieguito I. The chipped stone specimens (Figure 4.24) are described as leaf-shaped knives and knife blanks, lenticular in cross section and percussion-chipped. With these items were chopper and scraper pieces as well.

Because this was a buried site and the collections were made under good control, the results and interpretations can be accepted. Further research is being focused on this site and the San Dieguito sequence; this may quickly solve the mishmash of speculation now obscuring the question of the chopper-scraper complexes. If dates consistently older than 9000 B.C. can be obtained at this or any other site, the chopper-scraper substratum can be regarded as established. Warren and True have no hesitancy in postulating a hunting culture different from, and earlier than, the Desert culture, and Warren (1967) develops this idea most convincingly.

Another California site—Stahl (Harrington 1957)—is important on two counts. Here, in a buried and sealed context, was a large collection of projectile points and knives of both the Pinto and the Silver Lake types (Figure 4.25). These were discovered in full association, along with a large number of crude scrapers,

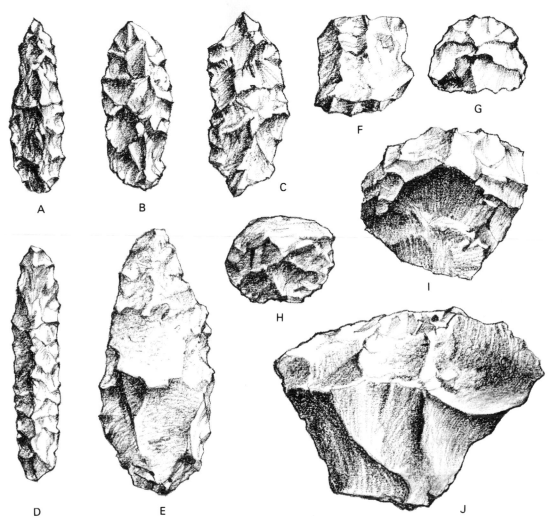

Figure 4.24   *Artifacts from the San Dieguito complex. Much reduced. A–E, knives; F–I, scrapers; J, chopper. (After Warren and True 1961)*

apparently forming a single complex. Thus, the site combines two complexes— Pinto and Silver Lake—previously described and discussed as two separate manifestations. Stahl is also important on another count: There appears to have been a village of seven houses here at a very early date. The houses evidently had been abandoned, had then suffered erosion, and were finally covered in later sediment, so that the postmold patterns originated (at the time of excavation) from a buried and eroded surface. Since the actual level of origin had eroded away, any hard-packed or specially prepared floor and any internal features (for example, fireplaces) had also been removed. What was left, then, were some holes forming regular patterns, with irregular holes inside the pattern; perhaps they were, in fact, houses. If so, others will be found elsewhere and will support the Stahl finds, which at present stand unique in the West. The age of the house level is estimated at

Figure 4.25 *Pinto points. One-half size. (After Harrington 1957)*

1000 to 2000 B.C., but this is not supported by radiocarbon dates.

This section has vacillated in sometimes viewing the chopper-scraper horizon as Archaic and in sometimes favoring the alternative possibility that there is a Big Game Hunting stage earlier than Archaic, as Krieger and Willey and Phillips believe. The few radiocarbon dates which bear on the problem would allow either explanation; Haynes (1964), it will be recalled, insists that all human history in the Americas should be compressed into the last 12,000 years. While there is cultural evidence to the contrary, which he disregards, he could prove to be right, at least about the Plains hunters. But it is likely that earlier radiocarbon dates will be derived from areas 1, 2, or 3 and will show the Great Basin to have been first to cradle Americans, who perhaps arrived by way of a coastal route from northeast Asia with an Asiatic chopper-scraper tool kit. They could have been completely unaware of the continental ice barrier. In any case, as Jennings (1964) suggests, the heavy percentage of crude choppers in all the Archaic complexes may well represent the continuation of ancient tool types from an earlier stage into the Archaic complex.

The California cultures (area 4) west of the deserts are more nearly comparable to the Eastern Archaic stage cultures than to the Great Basin cultures. This is because the special resources—the vast oak groves with their nutritious acorns in the interior and the food wealth of the sea coast—made large semipermanent settlements and heavy population possible on an Archaic exploitive level. In fact, certain California cultures show such high specialization and selectivity in which species are exploited that some see them as having moved out of the Archaic stage into something more complex (see especially Meighan 1959a). Whether to recognize that all the local cultures are Archaic in stage, even sharing certain tools and artifacts with Eastern (Boreal?) Archaic (as pointed out by Beardsley 1948) or whether to assign them some special niche has been much debated. Here they are assumed to be Archaic in stage and to derive from the earlier Basin cultures, probably from area 3 (Heizer 1964). No matter how it is classified, the narrow coastal strip is difficult (if not impossible) to generalize about. From Baja California to Alaska, Heizer (1964) establishes eight subareas, six of them in California, while Meighan (1959a) distinguishes eight in California alone. Recent accounts emphasize the differences among the subareas. This discussion follows Heizer's more recent organization, in which he joins Kroeber and others in explaining the extraordinary variability of California cultures as resultant from the marginal position of California into which population or other pressures pushed remnant groups who "took root" in the varied California microenvironments.

One of the best known and longest lived, from 5000 to 3000 B.C., of the southern coastal California cultures is the LaJolla, a Horizon II or milling stone assemblage

(Wallace 1955)—a rubric which includes other local clusters (designated "facies" by Heizer) called Oak Grove, Little Sycamore, Topanga, and Malaga Cove. The inventory is scanty and not uniform, but pebble choppers; grinding implements (either mortars or the flat slab); large, poorly chipped points; flake scrapers; stone discoidals; shell beads of disc shape; spire-lopped *Olivella*; and both flexed and extended burials, as well as reburials under rock cairns, are more or less shared features. The staple of subsistence was either seeds or shellfish or both, with hunting common to all facies. Dating from perhaps

2000 B.C. to, or into, the Christian era, Wallace proposes the Intermediate or Horizon III, about which less is known; however, the archeology implies a greater concern with hunting than with gathering of vegetable foods, although the mortar and pestle remain in use, with the flat milling slab less common than in Horizon II. The bow and arrow is inferred from the small-sized projectile points, and in some sites the bone awl suggests that basketry was known. Both disc and *Olivella* beads persist. Burial customs are unknown.

In Horizon IV (late prehistoric cul-

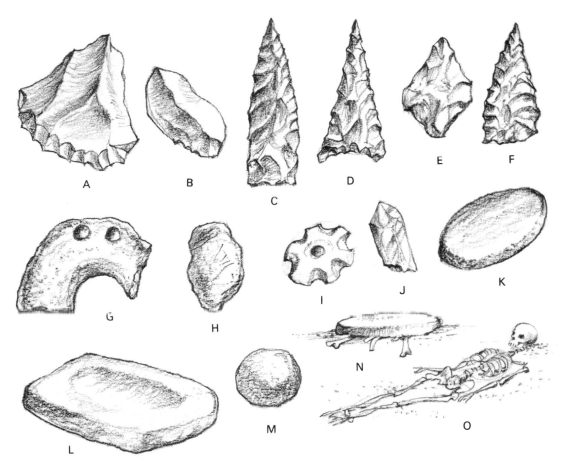

Figure 4.26   *Characteristic traits of the Topanga culture. Variable scale. A, B, scrapers; C–F, projectile points, two-thirds size; G, H, ornaments; I, stone cog; J, worked quartz crystal; K, stone disc; L, metate; M, mano; N, reburial under metate; O, extended burial. (After Meighan 1959a)*

tures), Wallace reports many artifacts added to the roster of material traits: vessels carved from steatite (pottery further south); circular shell fishhooks; burins and bladelets; perforated stones; the use of asphaltum as an adhesive; stone and pottery pipes; many bone tools; and many classes of ornaments in bone, shell, and stone. The bow and arrow seems to become more common; mortuary practice becomes more elaborate and includes cremation. The Canaliño of the Santa Barbara coast is an example of these latest prehistoric local cultures.

Further north, the coastal remains can be divided into about the same horizons, with the array of artifact classes remaining about the same (with notable additions). In the Sacramento area the frequent pendant or charmstone is mentioned along with twined basketry and fiber-tempered burned clay balls, the latter presumed to have been used in "stone" cookery. From the Middle (Intermediate) Horizon many of the southern traits are found, but barbed harpoons and blunt bone tips for arrows show a shift toward fish resources; the charmstones continue. The later cultures—after A.D. 300—are characterized by carryover Middle Horizon objects plus steatite tubular pipes, a variety of abalone-shell beads and ornaments, and much greater emphasis on cremation.

While there are many more local

Figure 4.27 Characteristic traits of the Late Canaliño culture. Variable scale. A, shell fishhooks; B, shell spangles and pendants; C, D, limpet-shell ornaments; E, beads; F–J, spearhead and projectile points, slightly reduced; K, comal; L, M, stone pipes; N, O, arrow shaft straighteners; P, Q, whale effigies; R, paint mortar; S, stone bowl; T, steatite olla; U, sandstone bowl; V, Olivella inlaid sandstone bowl; W–Z, pestles; AA, mortar and pestle; BB, basket; CC, shell beads inlaid in asphaltum; DD, stone dish; EE, burial marker; FF, woven seagrass; GG, tarring pebbles; HH, II, flexed reburials (HH with whale bone). (After Meighan 1959a)

variants distinguished by Heizer, the sample above suffices to define the Archaic-stage level and to demonstrate the overall paucity of the material inventory. In fact, to one not involved in the excavation, analysis, and interpretation of West Coast antiquities, the differences from area to area are less apparent than to those who are close students of the area. This, of course, is true for any area, where the specialist on the spot sees more and sees it differently because regional and district differences are important in understanding the local detailed story. The importance of this aspect of detail is illustrated by the excellent study made by Bennyhoff and Heizer (1958) showing the importance of shell bead types as indices of chronology. Figures 4.26, 4.27, 4.28, and 4.29 (based on similar figures in Meighan 1959a) are included to round out the description of the coastal Archaic. Figure 4.30, also modified from Meighan (1959a), is included as a guide to correlation of the California cultures.

Although the dismissal of area 4 as Archaic can be defended on typologic grounds, it must be repeated that in the Christian era and even into modern times there were California tribes that had become so specialized in reliance on sea animals or the vast acorn crop that their cultures no longer fit the definition of the stage. However, these tribes, with an Archaic technology, had achieved an adaptation permitting a dense population to enjoy a stable, semi- or completely sedentary existence. Heizer (1964) makes this point quite effectively for both California and the Northwest Coast.

Turning now to the Plateau (the north portion of area 1), less information is available and the Archaic affiliations are less clearly established. Although strong Desert culture influence is generally agreed upon, there is considerable debate about other evidence which some scholars think points to quite ancient remains in

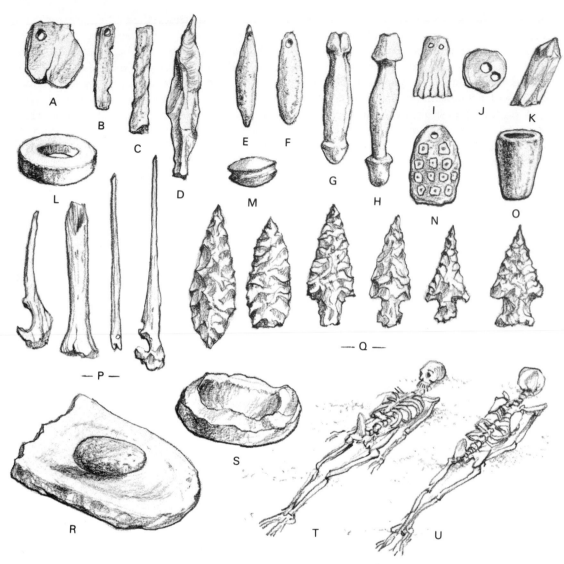

Figure 4.28 Characteristic traits of the Early Central California culture. Variable scale. A, biotite ornament; B, C, slate ornaments; D, "bangle"; E–H, charmstones; I, shell ornament; J, shell disc; K, worked quartz crystal; L, steatite bead; M, clay object; N, shell inlaid turtle-carapace ornament; O, stone pipe; P, bone tools; Q, projectile points, slightly reduced; R, metate and mano; S, mortar; T, U, extended supine and prone burials. (After Meighan 1959a)

the area. The arguments stem largely from ignorance of the area's archeology. Scientific excavation is new in the area (much of it has been of emergency nature), and synthesis by regional experts has only just begun. In any case, the Plateau complexes on all time levels contain much crude flintwork (pebble choppers, chipped scrapers, flake scrapers, etc.), as is true of the area 3 collections. Daugherty suggests that there exists, all over the West, an Intermontane Western tradition whose boundaries, as defined, coincide with those set for the Desert Archaic; the artifacts

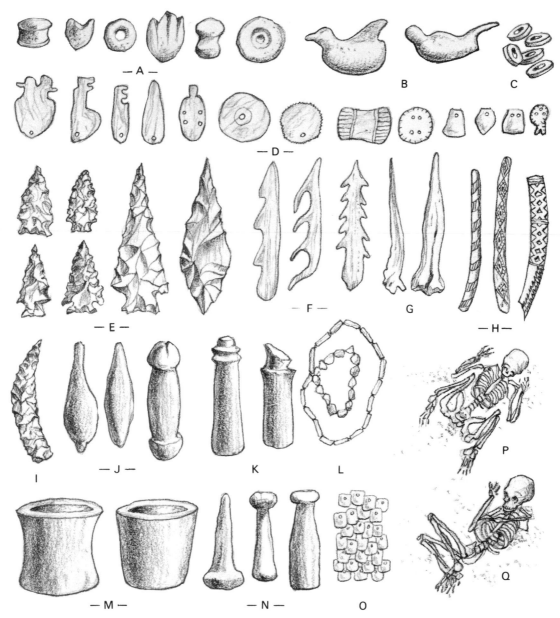

Figure 4.29   *Characteristic traits of the Late Central California culture. Variable scale. A, clay objects; B, clay bird effigies; C, clam-shell disc beads; D, abalone-shell ornaments; E, projectile points, two-thirds size; F, bone spear and gorge hooks; G, bone awls; H, incised bird bones; I, "Stockton curve"; J, charmstones; K, steatite pipes; L, bone and shell necklace; M, mortars; N, pestles; O, shingled Olivella beads; P, Q, back and side flexed burials. (After Meighan 1959a)*

ascribed to it make no consistent pattern (Daugherty 1962). Although Daugherty seems to think of the Intermontane tradition as one aspect of the basal substratum postulated for western North America and as a Big Game-oriented culture, it is not well enough known yet to be precisely defined.

	Northwest	Northeast		North Coast Ranges				Central				South Coast	
	Humboldt	Lassen	Siskiyou-Modoc	Napa Co.	Sonoma	Lake Co.	Mendocino	Coast	Interior	Sierras	Yosemite	Santa Barbara	Los Angeles Ventura
A.D. 1500	Late Prehistoric (Tsurai)	Late (Tommy Tucker, Amedee caves) Upper Karlo	Tule Lake Gillem Bluff Indian Bank	Wooden Valley / Late Goddard	Clear	Lake	Shasta	Drakes Bay	Late Buena Vista	(Vermillion Valley)	Mariposa	Chumash	Malaga Cove IV
A.D. 1000	Early Prehistoric (Patricks Point)							Late Coast / McClure	Late Central Calif.	Kings Beach		Late Canaliño / Early Canaliño	
A.D. 500		Lower Karlo		Early Goddard	Mendocino			Middle Coast	Middle Central Calif.		Tamarack / Crane Flat		Malaga Cove III / Hunting or Intermediate
0			Lairds Bay						Early Buena Vista	Martis		Hunting	Malaga Cove II
2000 B.C.			Narrows					Early Coast	Early Central Calif.				
4000 B.C.								(Stanford Man)	(Capay Man)			Oak Grove	Topanga
6000 B.C.									Tranquillity	Farmington			(Los Angeles Man)

As a summary of the relation of the Plateau to the rest of the West excerpts from Jennings' (1964) statement are quoted below:

After the Cordilleran [or Intermontane cultures] the Desert Archaic lifeway was dominant over the Intermontane area, including the Columbia River drainage, for most of the period from about 6000 B.C. to A.D. 1. Systematic archeological work in the Plateau area is barely begun, but it is evident that local variant cultures will be sorted out for the periods since Christ. One difficulty with the fast-growing literature is that there is less descriptive material than one could desire. Instead, much interpretation, often with an ecological slant, is being offered, but on scant evidence, or on evidence all too briefly summarized. . . . One can accept the statements of the several authors that there are transitional periods in the Plateau, but the evidence is of a restricted sort. One can sense a change more easily than he can demonstrate it from archeological specimens because the changes are generally those resultant from partial adaptation to a specialized subsistence base, but without an abandonment of earlier practices. This specialization, moreover, is usually associated with the adoption of a lacustrine- or riverine-based economy. The accretions to the artifact inventory are not numerous, nor are they very dramatic. . . . Chipped-stone tools are again the major class of artifacts recovered. This single class of artifacts makes detailed cultural interpretation more than hazardous. I incline still to defend the idea that the Desert Archaic as a culture stage persisted in the Intermontane region until the coastal influences—such as mat and plank houses, wood and bone carving, cremation, and scaffold burial—penetrated the interior.

At The Dalles, Cressman (1960) reports a sequence of unusual cultural remains. The basalar stratum, dated by radiocarbon at about 7000 B.C., or slightly earlier, yields quantities of chipped stone, bone, and antler artifacts. Found also were coarse stone tools, burins or gravers, and grooved stone balls, which he calls bolas. The food remains included bones of both land and marine animals, large birds, and fish. This assemblage is represented only in the lowest level. Except for some general similarities to the Pointed Mountain (MacNeish) complex, the early Dalles material stands as different from that found elsewhere in the Columbia drainage and shows an early adaptation to riverine resources [See Sanger 1967].

The Dalles has, however, one way and another, provided a vast amount of material for study. Much has been recovered by amateurs and is relatively uninformative because of poor controls. Butler (1959), however, has attempted to analyze some of the amateur reports and has set up a sequence of complexes covering several thousand years. These complexes rest on his segregation of associated materials as reported by the amateur diggers.

At the basal level Butler places the Congdon I complex—peripherally flaked pebble choppers, cobble choppers, flat grinding slabs, shallow basin-type mortars, scrapers, large triangular side-notched points, some stemmed points, and little else. These, at the Congdon site, were recovered from a midden deposit.

Later in time, in Congdon II, the same tools occur, but to them is added a long list of new types. Included are beads of several kinds of stone (jet, steatite, serpentine, etc.), atlatl weights of galena and stone, tubular and elbow pipes of stone, pendants, crescentic stones, fish gorges, abraders, shaft-smoothers, whetstones, two- and four-notch pebble net sinkers, long conical pestles, basalt adzes, deep mortars, zoömorphic (sheep) sculpture, and numerous projectile points of basin type. This complex was found in a deposit containing many fire-cracked basalt fragments. . . .

The dates ascribed by Butler cover the presumed range of human use of the area. To Indian Well I and its counterparts he allows a period of 8000–5500 B.C.; to Congdon I, II, and other such levels, from 5500 B.C. to A.D. 500, with the time of arrival of boreal traits estimated as 1500–1000 B.C. By A.D. 500 the Wakemap mound series takes over. Wakemap I is characterized by excellent carving in antler and wood, rectangular houses with mat siding, and special fishing equipment. In Wakemap II there are additions. Particularly important are stick dice (a later time-marker in the Plateau) from the Southwest, and a clay figurine cult. Whalebone clubs and "slave-killer" clubs or hammers, as well as very sophisticated sculpture, mark the

Figure 4.30   Correlation of California cultures other than those in area 3 (Southern California-Nevada-Arizona). Sites and skeletal finds are in parentheses. (Modified from Meighan 1959a)

onset of the historic period. Butler sees the Columbia Plateau as being influenced by coastal peoples after about A.D. 500. Others would date the coastal contacts as even earlier.

At Klamath Lake, Cressman (1956) excavated a series of sites and has put together a local sequence which he thinks carries the prehistory of the Klamath area back to 7500 (or even 10,000) years ago. . . . Cressman thinks that he can see the earliest levels as affiliated with (or representing) the Desert Archaic, with an early trend away from the Desert lifeway toward a specialized pattern resultant from a richer and more stable lake and forest environment. This specialization is seen in the early exploitation of fish and mussels. The original foraging exploitive techniques of the Desert Archaic can be noted, however, in the continued heavy reliance on tubers and seeds down into historic time. In the years since Christ, the earth lodge was introduced, and an intensive use of *wocas* (water lilies) for food marks a final local food specialization that characterized the historic Klamath. The two-handed horned mano is a diagnostic Klamath artifact used in the grinding of *wocas* seeds.

As exemplifying the later evidence for the Plateau region, and as exemplification of the extent of the evidence at hand, I use the work of Shiner (1961) at McNary Reservoir in southeast Oregon on the Columbia River. Shiner describes a series of occupations that reflect a simple economy not particularly specialized. At Hat Creek, the earliest site Shiner describes, a typical archaic assemblage occurred. Several choppers, made either from flat pebbles or from large flakes from such cobbles, are characterized as crude. There were a few well-made projectile points and some flake scrapers. Bone was confined to two tubular beads (cross-sections of bird bones), a couple of splinters, and some unidentifiable fragments. The deposit containing these was a midden yielding land mammal (rabbit and deer) bones, and some salmon bone. Considerable use was made of red ocher. At nearby Cold Springs, Shiner reports the same inventory but perceives an improvement in the techniques used in the manufacturing of all artifacts. Notched stones identified as net weights or sinkers appear for the first time. These were simply small pebbles, notched, grooved, or perforated for use with nets. Nets themselves were found, of course. Among the examples, a lanceolate basalt knife becomes more numerous. However, there were many more fishbones in the

midden. Side-notched projectile points of several types appear in the Cold Creek deposits. In the later deposits at this site, marine shell and carved stone (a steatite pendant and a tubular pipe) were found, and a chipped discoid chopper was added. . . . Houses, built over saucer-like excavations, are reported. The houses (interpreted from ethnographic analogy) were light frameworks of wood covered with mats, [but] no real archeologic evidence of superstructure was noted. The circular depressions were about three feet deep and from twenty-five to forty feet in diameter.

House form later shifted to an oval shape, and the size was somewhat reduced; some of the later houses were built of plank. At some time prior to historic contact the characteristic stone club or mallet, carved fetishes, sandstone shaft-smoothers, ornaments made from teeth and claws, and antler digging-stick handles were added to the inventory. Stone bowls and adzes for woodworking appear to be late, as are pestles, shell beads, antler wedges, and beads of stones. These items are recovered from graves at historic sites (e.g., Wallula), where European trade goods were common. At other places in the Plateau, antler wedges are found earlier; they are, in fact, deemed to be quite an old and general North American trait. Roasting ovens and large quantities of burned rock are fairly standard phenomena at most Plateau sites.

Before leaving the Plateau, mention should be made of Swanson, Butler, and Bonnichsen's (1964) intensive study of Birch Creek Valley in eastern Idaho. Swanson attempts to correlate apparent climatic changes with shifts in aboriginal population and accompanying slight changes in the chipped-flint knife and projectile types over a 10,000-year period. This study also involves the reconstruction of extinct biotic assemblages (using faunal remains, pollen sequences, fossil soils, etc.) in what has been called "environmental" archeology, or paleoecology. Swanson's interesting work is rendered less convincing by somewhat dogmatic statements about past geologic events and their correlation with culture change in Birch Creek history. His conclusions suffer, too, from statements about differences in successive cultures whose artifactual differences, at least, are nothing more than type percentage differences (in what is a smooth, local continuum through time) in the popularity of chipped-flint types seen over the entire Great Basin. He describes a culture sequence comprising Birch Creek, believed to be pre-5000 B.C., which is characterized by over 50 percent lanceolate points (Plano types); Bitterroot, 5000 to 1000 B.C., where side-notched points dominate; and Beaverhead (1000 B.C. to A.D. 400), where pieces with a smooth, contracting stem and the small side-notched points come into popularity. Without denying the likelihood that Swanson has correctly assessed local and nondrastic climatic changes through time, one can be highly skeptical of the importance of climatic change alone in effecting the slow change in artifact popularity, which can be seen over the entire West about as he describes it for Birch Creek. For his sequence newly derived radiocarbon dates exist, so there is no doubt of the time depth. Generally, most typologists would agree that the flint collections ascribed to the Birch Creek-Beaverhead sequence do not differ significantly from collections spanning a comparable time range in the rest of area 1.

On the edge of the Plateau, at Wilson Butte Cave, Gruhn (1961) found an interesting succession of occupations showing, successively, Plano types, strong Basin influences, and finally historic Plains affiliations. Gruhn shows, in a detailed report, that the cave contained five separable strata, A to E, with A being recent fill and E the oldest. Stratum C was some 5 feet thick and contained four occupational levels. The lowest, occupation I, was scant, yielding flint scrap, one or two worked bone pieces, and one crudely flaked point or knife blade. Nothing in the level C collection is particularly diagnostic.

Associated with occupation I were horse and camel bones. Occupation II yielded Plano types, with III and IV showing affiliations with both the Desert culture and the Middle Horizon of the High Plains. Later, Gruhn (1965) released a radiocarbon date of 12,500 B.C. derived from bone scrap from occupation I in Stratum C.

Summary

This chapter has touched upon a wealth of archeologic data, referring most of it to what has been called the Archaic stage. The archeologic specimens have not been used to provide a material-culture linkage of all the local complexes through the similarity of the artifacts; rather, the concern has been with the broad subsistence base and the concept of efficiency rather than with any set of tools. Moreover, the principle of efficiency has overridden any originally held notion of consistency of classification. Also, the timespan that a local culture seemed to fit has influenced its inclusion or omission. [Later on, as a summation of the prehistory of North America, the Archaic sites mentioned above will be charted (Figure 9.3).]

This chapter may seem overlong for such drab material, as did Chapter 3, where solid data were so scant. The weighting of Chapters 3 and 4 has been deliberate for two reasons: The first, which is perhaps merely incidental, is that in these two stages, research is extremely active and greater progress is being made than in later ones. The weighting is "where the action is." The second and major reason explains the first. It is simply that unless the origins, evolution, and details of the earlier cultures are known, the later developments cannot be interpreted adequately. This latter point also makes necessary the following chapter.

5

The Mexican Sequence

Archaic

Reserving a review of the Mexican Archaic for a separate treatment, instead of including it in Chapter 4, is necessary because of the special achievement of the Archaic stage peoples of Mexico. These achievements modify all subsequent New World history and must be appreciated before American culture history after about 1500 B.C. can be understood or evaluated.

For information about the Desert culture south of the border there are only a few recent sources because the later monumental remains of the Valley civilizations have been the focus of study since the 1850s, the drab peripheral and earlier material having been disregarded almost entirely until the 1950s. Best known is the work of MacNeish (1958b) in Tamaulipas in northeastern Mexico. After extensive survey and scattered tests in both cave and open sites, MacNeish describes a local series of cultures dated from an estimated (probably slightly overestimated) beginning of 9000 B.C. into the Christian era.

The earliest is called the Diablo phase. Although MacNeish says he uses "phase" as the equivalent of the McKern "component," he actually employs the term to mean widespread local culture. The artifacts are described as pebble choppers, ovoid blades and choppers, flakes and flake scrapers. This is none other than our familiar chopper-scraper substratum resembling in detail the probably ancestral complex in area 3 of the Desert Archaic. Following Diablo is the Lerma, characterized by somewhat the same artifacts plus the double-pointed Lerma point which in this book has been adjudged to be one of the Plano types occurring *after* 7000 B.C. There are also snubnosed end scrapers, some with stems, square-based triangular knives, and semilunar blades (compare the C. W. Harris site). MacNeish estimates the Lerma complex at pre-7000 B.C. In both the Diablo and Lerma, subsistence seemed to be dominantly hunting, although evidence of some gathering also occurs. The next three named levels (Figure 5.1) in the sequence represent nothing more than an Archaic continuum, with new traits appearing in the more recent deposits as accretions to the original complex, a situation seen in

	Sierra de Tamaulipas	Tehuacan
A.D. 700	Los Angeles	Venta Salada
	La Salta	
200 B.C.	Eslabones	Palo Blanco
	Laguna	Santa Maria
900 B.C.		
		Ajalpan
1500 B.C.		
	Almagre	Purron
2300 B.C.		
	La Perra	Abejas
3400 B.C.		
	Nogales	Coxcatlan
5200 B.C.		
		El Riego
7200 B.C.		
	Lerma	Ajuereado

Figure 5.1   *Archaic sequences in Mexico.* (After MacNeish 1958b, 1964)

all other Archaic sites wherever deep deposits have been investigated. These three, Nogales, La Perra, and Almagre, show an increasing dependence on plant foods, with the mortar and handstone and many specialized flint specimens—gravers, spokeshaves, disc scrapers, disc knives set in wooden handles—as well as cordage, basketry, atlatl shafts and darts, and other familiar pieces (including Lerma points) in the Nogales. Almagre yields the same materials except that there are now also villages where wattle-and-daub houses were constructed. Based on the archeologic sample and by means of a crude formula, MacNeish estimates the percentages of the food supply which were derived from gathering and hunting by phase (Figure 5.2). What makes this series important is that remains of domesticated corn and squash were found in deposits from La Perra times! Here, in an Archaic culture concerned with gathering all manner of wild foods, there is evidence of the plants upon which all the high cultures of the New World later came to be dependent in some degree.

Later, MacNeish and a team of supporting specialists made an intensive study of Tehuacan Valley southwest from Mexico City, a study which has not yet been fully reported. Here, he (MacNeish 1964) found a similar sequence of occupations, beginning with the Ajuereado, in which both collecting and hunting (horse, antelope, and many rodents, including jackrabbits) were emphasized and which ended at about 7200 B.C. The pollen evidence is that the environment was identical with that of west Texas today, that is, mesquite and grassland. The animal remains, too, argue the same environment. The flint list included leaf-shaped blades, gravers, end scrapers, and prismatic flake knives. The following phase, El Riego, 7200 to 5200 B.C., seemed to show a denser population which subsisted on about the

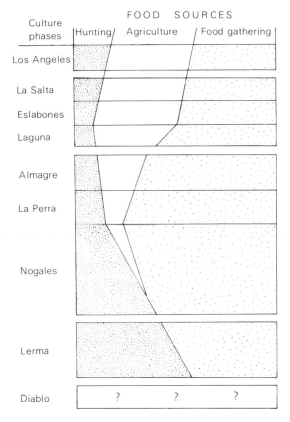

FOOD SOURCES

| Culture phases | Hunting | Agriculture | Food gathering |

Los Angeles

La Salta

Eslabones

Laguna

Almagre

La Perra

Nogales

Lerma

Diablo   ?   ?   ?

Figure 5.2 *Basic food sources in the Sierra de Tamaulipas, charted on a proportional basis. (After MacNeish 1958b)*

same list of foods, except that deer replaced the horse, while cottontail rabbit supplanted the jack. There was no apparent change in climate, but there was a difference in culture: There was either cultivation or collection of squash, chili, and avocados; wild corn and cotton were also present. Throughout the rest of the Tehuacan story—the Coxcatlan (5200 to 3400 B.C.), the Abejas (3400 to 2300 B.C.), and the Purron (2300 to 1500 B.C.) —the full range of staple domesticates appears in the deposits. The milling stone and mortar also appear and remain in use.

The plants collected or cultivated in the Coxcatlan phase were the chili, avocados, squash (all from the preceding phase), plus tepary beans, amaranth (pigweed),

yellow zapote, gourds, and wild corn. In the next, Abejas, phase are added the pumpkin and canavalia (and the domesticated dog). In the Purron, wild maize is replaced by a hybrid corn—maize-*Tripsacum*-teosinte—of essentially modern form. At this time, too, some crude pottery appears in the deposits. Successive phases document the increase in population and the broadening of technologic range which come to characterize the high cultures of Mexico.

These two Mexican series are of importance in demonstrating the slow spread of the idea of domestication of plants and the centuries required for the shift from Archaic foraging to more complete subsistence dependence upon the products of the slowly evolving cultigens. The invention of agriculture by the exploitive foragers of the desert seems well demonstrated by the finds from the Mexican Plateau. The concept of horticulture may somehow have been earlier where there existed techniques for storage and cooking of maize or beans or seeds and fleshy vegetables and tubers, as had long been practiced by most Archaic populations. In the opinion of many experts (see Mangelsdorf, MacNeish, and Willey 1964), American agriculture was begun in Mexico or Mesoamerica, but there must have been several focal points of discovery in a kind of self-stimulating center of innovation.

MacNeish's work in Tehuacan is also of interest in his imaginative, if sketchy, notions about the increasing population of the valley and the accompanying changes in social life, habitation pattern, and technology. While no one would claim that the high cultures of Mexico evolved in Tehuacan Valley, the interpretations made by MacNeish are extremely valuable in understanding how the necessary social and technologic changes might have been made. Based on the size of the sites (open and cave), their frequency, and their contents (plant remains particularly), Mac-Neish outlines the early history of the valley as follows:

1   ***Ajuereado and El Riego***   Wandering microbands (family) moving from wet-season to dry-season camps. Completely cyclical dependence on resources

2   ***Coxcatlan***   Microbands in autumn and winter, with a joining of other microbands in the spring to form macrobands

3   ***Abejas***   Wet-season, semisedentary macroband settlements, with dry-season wandering microbands

The Effects of Domestication

By virtue of having saved the Desert cultures of Mexico till the last, it has been possible to introduce the notion of horti-culture and finally what can be called agriculture. The specialized cultures which will engage attention in various parts of North America after about 1000 B.C. are dependent upon several innovations (hor-ticulture being one of these) resulting from diffusion of ideas and artifacts from Central America. Without this diffusion, the story of American prehistory might well have ended with the Archaic stage. But this did not happen. Indeed, with the invention of farming and the attendant population increase, changes in tech-nology, modification of the social system, the invention of permanent housing, and a host of related cultural phenomena, all of which occurred in Mexico between 5000 to 2000 B.C., the southern Mexican Plateau becomes the dominant source or fountain of innovation and diffusion in the New World, both for North and South America. Thus, during the Archaic stage —from 8000 B.C. for many centuries— the flow of culture and population begun in the Lithic (and earlier chopper-scraper stage?) continued to be from North America to and through Mexico and

Mesoamerica on toward the tip of South America, where it is represented by such finds as Huaca Prieta (Bird 1943) in Peru and Palli Aike and Fells Caves (Bird 1938) farther south at the tip of South America. But with the terminal Archaic periods in Mexico, the cultural initiative passed to the Mexican center. All subsequent devel-opments in North America can usually be traced to the southern Mexican Plateau, except for the Arctic-Sibero-American sphere of specialization. The latter cluster of cultures, of course, developed without reference to plant-domestication. Nor did it exercise influence on the rest of the continent except possibly on the late North-west Coast cultures, which are also very specialized.

American Cultigens

Much hinges on the concept of gardening through which a population is no longer entirely dependent on the vagaries of short-term environmental shifts but can produce and store its own food on a sea-sonal schedule and reduce the total time spent in the food quest. It is therefore desirable to provide a summary statement about American agriculture.

Among the experts (for example, Man-gelsdorf, MacNeish, and Willey 1964) there is no doubt that horticulture or gardening is a Mexican invention. There is no suspicion of the introduction of the idea from Eurasia for two reasons: The first, which is exceedingly cogent, is that *apparent* beginnings of plant domestication in Mexico are coeval with (or might even antedate) the similar, slowly evolving incipient agriculture in Mesopotamia and the Near East, long recognized as the cradle of Eurasiatic and African civiliza-tions. Second, and perhaps less compelling, is the fact that all American domesticates are derived from indigenous American plants (that can still be found wild in many species) and that the cultivation techniques and associated technology are uniquely American in type.

As has often been emphasized (for example, Hallowell 1957; K. M. Stewart 1965), the plants domesticated by the American Indian are of more commercial-industrial importance and are relied upon by more of the world's population than any of the groups derived at the three other centers of domestication (the Near East, Southeast Asia, and western sub-Saharan Africa). A partial list of the American food plants put together by Mangelsdorf, MacNeish, and Willey (1964) is presented in Table 5.

Table 5   Cultivated plants of Middle America (modified from Mangelsdorf, MacNeish, and Willey 1964)

Common Name	Plant Family
Cultivated for their edible seeds	
Amaranth	Amaranthaceae
Apazote	Chenopodiaceae
Bean, common	Leguminosae
Bean, lima	Leguminosae
Bean, runner	Leguminosae
Bean, tepary	Leguminosae
Bean, jack	Leguminosae
Chia	Labiatae
Chia grande	Labiatae
Maize	Gramineae
Panic grass	Gramineae
Peanut*	Leguminosae
Sunflower*	Compositae
Cultivated for their edible roots or tubers	
Coyolxóchitl	Amaryllidaceae
Manioc	Euphorbiaceae
Potato*	Solanaceae
Sweet potato*	Convolvulaceae
Yam bean	Leguminosae
Cultivated for their edible gourdlike fruits	
Chayote	Cucurbitaceae
Squash, cushaw	Cucurbitaceae
Squash, summer	Cucurbitaceae
Squash, walnut	Cucurbitaceae
Other edible fruits	
Anona	Annonaceae
Bullock's-heart	Annonaceae
Cherimoya*	Annonaceae
Ilama	Annonaceae
Soursop	Annonaceae
Sweetsop	Annonaceae
Avocado	Lauraceae
Caujilote	Bignoniaceae

Table 5   (Continued)

Common Name	Plant Family
Capulin cherry	Rosaceae
Tejocote	Rosaceae
Cashew*	Anacardiaceae
Hog plum	Anacardiaceae
Jocote	Anacardiaceae
Coconut*	Palmaceae
Elderberry	Caprifoliaceae
Guava	Myrtaceae
Guayabilla	Myrtaceae
Mammee colorado	Sapotaceae
Sapote, green	Sapotaceae
Sapote, yellow	Sapotaceae
Sapodilla	Sapotaceae
Matasano	Rutaceae
Sapote, white	Rutaceae
Nance	Malpighiaceae
Papaya	Caricaceae
Pineapple*	Bromeliaceae
Pitahaya	Cactaceae
Prickly pear	Cactaceae
Ramón	Moraceae
Sapote, black	Ebenaceae
Herbs and other vegetables	
Chaya	Euphorbiaceae
Chipilín	Leguminosae
Pacaya	Palmaceae
Tepejilote	Palmaceae
Tomato	Solanaceae
Tomato, husk	Solanaceae
Yucca	Liliaceae
Condiments and other flavorings	
Chili pepper	Solanaceae
Vanilla	Orchidaceae
Stimulants and narcotics	
Cacao	Sterculiaceae
Maguey	Amaryllidaceae
Tobacco	Solanaceae
Fiber plants	
Cotton	Malvaceae
Henequen	Amaryllidaceae
Maguey	Amaryllidaceae
Sisal	Amaryllidaceae

* Probably not native to Mesoamerica.

The variety of plants listed in Table 5 testifies to the enormous ingenuity of the American horticulturalists. In further tribute to these early farmers, Anderson (1952) has brilliantly analyzed their gardening techniques and the resultant perpetual harvest. However, despite this wide range of available food, the major domesticates that provided the balanced diet and supported the development and diffusion of American civilizations (?) were squash, beans, and maize, apparently domesticated in that order. All three are evidently capable of rapid speciation, or at least of development into specially hardy variants, to meet such variations in climate as the humid tropics of Yucatan, the icy Andean highlands, and the frost-bitten river bottoms of the American Dakotas. Their very viability and adaptability give them pre-eminence in American prehistory. (Even today millions of the New World population subsist almost entirely on corn.)

Summer squash and pumpkin, *Cucurbita pepo*, seem to have been domesticated by, and possibly before, 5000 B.C. The common wild buffalo gourd (apparently prized for its seed, since it has little flesh and a nauseating odor) was also being taken. The cushaw squash, *Cucurbita moschata*, existed by 2000 B.C. in Peru and only a little later in Tamaulipas. *Cucurbita mixta* includes the popular acorn type and represents a later hybrid. The beans are a different problem. Both the tepary and the runner are still found in both a wild and a domesticated state in Mexico, so the first time of domestication is hard to set. Some indication of their antiquity may be revealed by the age of the common kidney bean (*Phaseolus vulgaris*), which dates back as far as 5,000 years and is a Middle American or Mexican development. Limas are late, appearing to have been domesticated in both South and Central America; in each location, distinctive variants are found.

For maize the data are many and difficult to correlate. Maize has been of such commercial importance that it has been intensively studied for decades by many agricultural specialists whose interests were directed more toward increasing crop yield, developing hardy and special strains, and related objectives, thus leaving the search for origins somewhat neglected. However, corn is now known from palynologic finds to be an ancient Mexican grass. Controlled experiments show it to be much modified by (probably accidental) crossbreedings with *Tripsacum*, another native grass. The maize-*Tripsacum* hybrid is teosinte, now a wild grass, with modern corn evidently resulting from countless later crosses of maize with teosinte, its hybrid offspring.

There is also evidence, both botanic and archeologic, that corn may well have been domesticated separately or concurrently in both Mexico and Peru. Here authorities are divided, but several very productive ancient strains appear to have spread out of South America northward. The sequence of morphologic change during domestication, from primitive wild corn to modern, appears to be somewhat as follows:

1 Male and female parts on the same stem with a few single grains, each partially enclosed in individual husks (glumes)

2 Separate flowers, with the female flower becoming larger and grains packed on an ear

3 Increasing ear size and more kernels, all enclosed tightly in clinging husks

4 Complete dependence on man for survival, as the kernels can no longer scatter naturally (Figure 5.3)

One of the unexplained discoveries about corn and its evolution is the occurrence, in Bat Cave (Dick 1965) in western New Mexico in the proper stratigraphic order, of a series of specimens which exemplify the full evolutionary history of corn from wild, pod, popcorn, on up to modern races. The collection seems to embody the full range of progressively more evolved forms. The date of the earliest occurrence of corn at Bat Cave, 3500 B.C., falls later in time than for the same forms found closer to the center of domestication and poses no problem. What is unexplained is that this is a unique find with no additional evidence

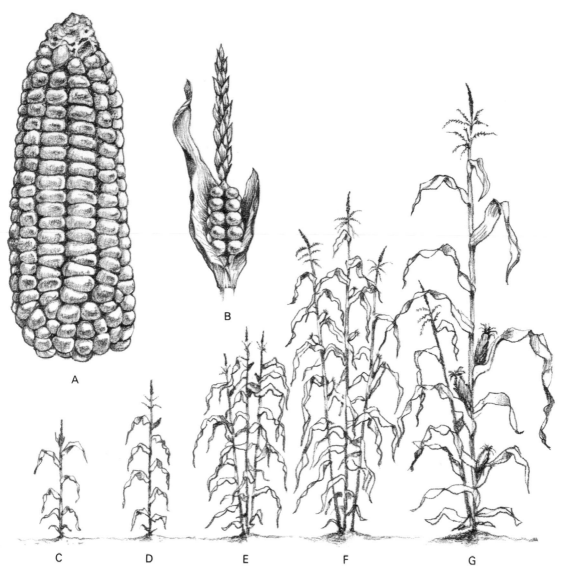

Figure 5.3 *The development of maize in North America. A, typical ear of modern Nal-Tel, actual size; B, reconstruction of wild corn, actual size; C–G, evolution of the maize plant: C, wild pod-popcorn, D, E, improved by hybridization and cultivation; F, after loss of pod-corn gene; G, increased distance between male and female flowers. (A, B after Mangelsdorf, MacNeish, and Galinat 1956, 1964; C–G after Hawkes and Wooley 1963)*

of diffusion and spread in the Southwest of any save the fully evolved recent strains, most of which can be identified with Mexican strains instead of with any local variants seemingly evolved in the Bat Cave area. One can only recognize

the find and note that the cultural context at Bat Cave appears to be a typically Archaic one. The next finds of maize of primitive type occur at Tularosa Cave, where both pod corn and more evolved forms occur. From Mexico, the famed three food species spread to the rest of North America within the limits of climatic possibility, although the idea of agriculture had already diffused since other species—sunflower, amaranth, etc.—were evidently being cultivated in the Middle West ahead of maize.

The North American strains of maize have been identified as deriving from one or another of the Mexican "races." These primitive races—Chapalote, Nal-Tel, Palomero-Toluqueño, and Arrocillo Amarillo—are all popcorns and represent the base from which the later varieties developed, but the routes along which these or their descendents were diffused northward are not known. Failure to find archeologic "way stations" where examples of a Guatemalan race occur on their way to the Southeast means nothing, however. There is no reason to doubt the direct importation of seed stock over wide areas where agriculture was not known in view of the oft-recorded penchant certain tribes had for both aimless and purposeful travel over long distances. The only drawback to the hypothesis of direct transportation over long distances would lie in drastic climatic changes beyond the adaptive ability of the plant. This, as a deterrent to the introduction of plants, has been vastly overemphasized and particularly so in the case of the three hardy staples of America. Experiments with modern ears of the four ancient pod-popcorn races show their ability to mature fully when moved from the low tropics to the high Central American Plateau. Chapalote has been found in the American Southwest, whereas one of the derived races, Harinoso de Ocho (eight-rowed flour corn) is very like the flour corn of the Plains and American Southwest.

Important as corn became once its amazing productivity developed, Armillas (1964) and Wolf (1959) emphasize the earlier and continuing cultivation of the amaranths known to most readers either as the hardy, viable, and fast-maturing weeds farmers call pigweed or careless weed, or as the brilliant red-foliaged ornamental plants. This plant will thrive wherever maize can grow and produces heavy, bushy flowers which, when matured, yield thousands of minute shiny black seeds (Figure 5.4). Amaranth may even yield more grain per area of cultivation than maize, but the ease of harvesting and milling corn, plus 100 percent recovery because the grain is enveloped in the husk may have led to its greater popularity. Nonetheless, amaranth is still used in the American Southwest and in Mexico for certain ritual foods. At the time of the conquest of Mexico, Wolf (1959) reports that the tribute from one Mexican province to the Aztec overlords included 200,000 bushels of amaranth, 280,000 of corn, and 230,000 of beans. Any crop grown in this quantity is of major importance, and the overall value of amaranth in aboriginal American agriculture has probably been insufficiently noted (see Sauer 1950).

The seeds have also been found in both Adena and Hopewell contexts in the Ohio Valley, and one can suspect that amaranth culture may well have been the vehicle by which the concept of horticulture diffused. However, in spite of the fact that earliest agriculture emphasized amaranth along with squash and beans (all with a high yield) until maize had evolved the long cob, studded with grains and protected by enveloping husks, gardening was never more than an adjunct to the subsistence pattern. So, whatever else can be said, fully evolved maize and the beginning of stable, permanent village settlements and a dependence upon food production appear together by 2000 B.C. MacNeish's interpretation of the Tehuacan evidence gives a clue as to what was happening all over central and southern Mexico. Authorities agree that no evidence of village life occurs earlier than the 2000 B.C. date, but at no

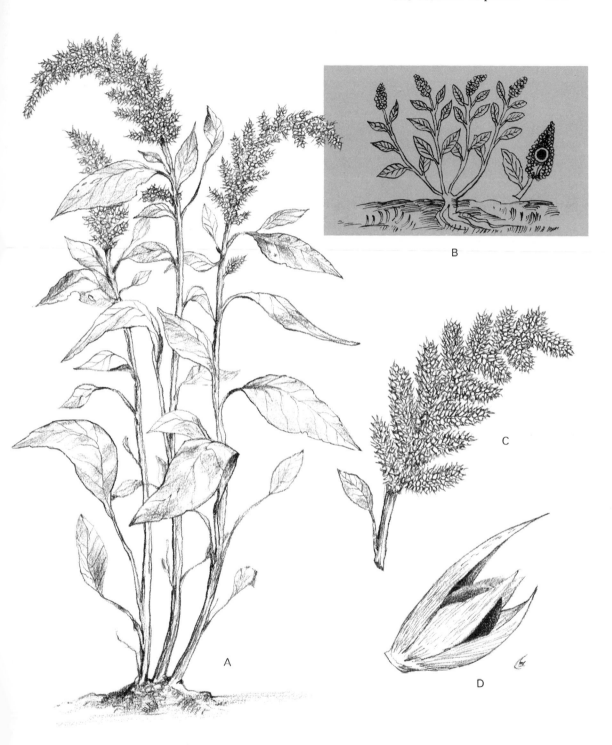

Figure 5.4   *Amaranth. A, mature plant ready for harvest; B, inset of sixteenth-century drawing from Sahagún; C, seed cluster; D, enlarged and actual size views of a single seed. (B after Sahagún 1905)*

place can the very simplest or earliest beginnings of horticulture be pinpointed. The earliest permanent shelters of record include both the pit house and the long-popular jacal—posts or sticks set vertically in rows to form walls after being plastered with mud. The jacal is still used in Mexico and the American Southwest.

Pottery

The first experimentation with pottery is another enigma. The place or reason for the origination of Middle American pottery remains an unsolved problem. If not invented locally, its introduction from somewhere must be postulated, possibly from Ecuador, where it occurs earlier. It could scarcely have come from the north, although an unusual kind of fiber-tempered pottery appears as early as 2500 B.C. (Stoltman 1966) in southeastern North America. Most North American pottery is usually regarded as an Asiatic overland import (McKern 1937; Tolstoy 1953; Griffin 1965) and comes a little later in time. None of the ceramics north of Mexico greatly resembles the Central American types (except in the Southwest, where the ceramics are obviously of Mexican derivation), and no real explanation of the origins of Mexican ceramics may be expected from the north. On the other hand, it is becoming increasingly possible that *all* American pottery may have diffused out of Central America, having been derived ultimately from Southeast Asia. Or, even more likely, two streams of diffusion will be finally sorted out.

Being handmade and open- (not kiln-) fired, Mexican ceramics are hard to derive technically from Southeast Asian prototypes. But since the earliest known ceramic remains are of high technical quality, with no fumbling first attempts yet discovered, the problem is unresolved

and we must beg the question to some extent. The best likelihood is that indisputable proof of trans- or circumpacific introduction sometime earlier than 2000 B.C. will be discovered. Already there are a host of interesting and complicated Central American traits which competent scholars suspect may be Asiatic in first origin. These include whole complexes, such as the ocean-going rafts of Peru, which resemble in detail the deepwater craft of ancient India and Formosa (Edwards 1960). Meggers (1964), Estrada and Meggers (1961), Ekholm (1953, 1964), and many others have contributed to the elucidation of this problem.

Asian Influences

The best case for Asiatic transplant to the New World is presented by Estrada and Meggers (1961). From the Bahia I culture (200 B.C.) from a well-controlled sequence on the Ecuadorian coast, they recovered an associated lot of artifacts whose testimony cannot be disregarded. It is taken here as possible evidence of at least one trans- or circumpacific contact before the time of Christ, when the Central and South American cultures were far from having reached their Classic phases. In Bahia I there are (1) pottery house models depicting house types found from Thailand to Japan, (2) neck rests or pillows noted all over the Old World from 2500 B.C. onward, (3) seated figurines in stylized posture, also distributed from India to Japan, (4) symmetrically graduated panpipes, (5) pottery net weights of distinctive styles, and (6) special earplugs resembling modern golf tees. The coolie yoke is firmly inferred from a decorated pottery spindle whorl, and the Formosan-Indian centerboard, ocean-going raft, still found in South American waters (Edwards 1960) is adduced as the probable vehicle. Estrada and Meggers postulate a trans- (not circum-) pacific voyage (Figure 5.5).

Figure 5.5   *Artifacts from Ecuador with traits suggesting a probable transpacific origin. Variable scale. A, B, pottery house models; C, D, pottery neck rests; F, incised spindle whorl and (E) detail of design showing coolie yoke and tumpline; G, H, figurines with panpipes; I, seated figure with folded legs. (After Estrada and Meggers 1961)*

Earlier, Ekholm (various) had made persuasive cases for other traits but could isolate no such aggregation of associated artifacts. Recognizing that this is no place to argue the details of Asiatic seaborne contact—hence, influence—in Central America in the year 200 B.C., I can only take the position that the Bahia I data constitute adequate proof of one such effective contact: Identically shaped panpipes are still used in South America by aboriginals and occur in Ohio Hopewell by A.D. 200; furthermore, given one voyage, the probability of other earlier and later ones less readily perceived in archeologic debris is increased manyfold (see Ekholm 1964 for the difficulty of such proof). Equally impressive is earlier evidence of contact found in the Ecuadorian culture called Valdivia, apparently nonhorticultural but including a pottery complex which Kidder (1964) and Estrada, Meggers, and Evans (1962) consider equivalent in many details to Middle Jomon pottery (3000 to 2500 B.C.) in Japan. [Meggers, Evans, and Estrada (1965) have given a final report on this material.]

Although no one has yet seriously studied the earliest Central American pottery with the aim of searching for possible or specific Asiatic prototypes at the proper point in time, it is a question which must soon be examined. It is possible even now to suggest, admittedly without adequate proof as yet, that the stimulus of Asiatic thought, religion, art, and architecture is responsible for the flowering of the American high cultures and that it was given at the best possible time, just as the Mexican populations were achieving some horticultural skill with a wide inventory of productive plant species. However, even if the stimulus should prove to be Asiatic—including even the concept of pottery—what Americans did with the varied ideas is uniquely American, with only an occasional trait retaining the Asiatic form by which it is identified.

No "credits" need be denied the Americans. While the question of indigenous versus diffused origin is of crucial importance in the full interpretation of the American story, the task here is less global. The point of the present review of the prehistory of Mexico is to relate the Mexican sequence of cultures to the less complex ones to the north.

Formative Stage

The invention of horticulture and the domestication of plants during the long Archaic stage have been mentioned. MacNeish (1964) reports "very crude crumbly pieces of broken pottery" in the Purron phase in Tehuacan Valley before 1500 B.C. This valley, lying southeast from Mexico City, is within the geographic range of the earliest *well-made* Mexican pottery, found from Vera Cruz across Chiapas to the Pacific Coast in Oaxaca. And, good pottery of Vera Cruz affiliations does occur in the Ajalpan phase just following the Purron in Tehuacan. Worrying further about the inspiration of the first pottery, as it followed close on the heels of horticulture, is beyond the needs of this chapter. Pottery of good quality as early as 2000 B.C. is known in Ecuador, so all Mexican pottery could be derived from the south so far as timing is concerned. The point of major importance is the identification of the cultural effects of the increased food made available by the domestication of maize. The early tangible results are not numerous. There seems to be the emergence of permanent settlements large enough to be called villages, with the first permanent houses, apparently of jacal, by 1500 B.C. (Pit house settlements, however, are claimed by MacNeish in the Abejas phase—3400 to 2300 B.C.—in Tehuacan, so it is perhaps necessary to credit the *concept* of housing to a much earlier stage from a yet unknown source; Eurasian pit houses, of course, go back several millennia B.C.) With the concentration of a rapidly increasing population in villages and the development of fields to be protected, wild game tends to decrease in availability (through a withdrawal from proximity to human beings if for no other reason), and there is marked increase in dependence on produced foods. In the face of heavy demand, even the wild food plants tend to become sparse, and collectors must perforce go farther afield; therefore, plant collecting falls off also and energy is devoted to tending the cultivated plants whose yield is higher. It is this factor of apparent nearly full dependence on the cultigens which marked the boundary between the Archaic and the Formative, so far as human behavior is concerned. Hunting and associated deities decrease in importance. New gods concerned with rain, sunshine, and fertility evolve, and their complex rituals must evolve and be learned, preserved, and administered. Social organization and controls and leadership mechanisms, different from the ones appropriate for foragers, would also evolve to meet the needs of settled groups. Specialists in religion and crafts and administration—even in warfare—develop as population density increases. At least, evidence of these fundamental cultural innovations, which followed so closely on the heels of the early villages, can be read from the archeologic record.

Perhaps the earliest village, Chiapa de Corzo, was sampled by Dixon (1959). He partially uncovered a simple village site where the milling stone, white pottery of good quality, and the figurine cult were present by 1500 B.C. The pottery is especially interesting in that it was decorated by the techniques of brushing and rocker stamping to provide contrasting texture zones on the vessels (Figure 5.6). Rocker stamping, of course, is also found at Valdivia in Ecuador ca. 3000 B.C.

For several reasons, the Middle Formative of the Valley of Mexico is better

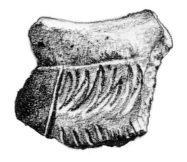

Figure 5.6   *Brushed and rocker-stamped sherds from Chiapas, Mexico. (After Dixon 1959)*

known. One of the great American prehistorians, George Vaillant (various), specifically attacking the problem of what is now called the Formative, worked extensively on a series of sites on the western shores of Lake Texcoco—one of the vast, shallow lakes which long filled the valley where Mexico City now stands (Figure 5.7). He there tested at El Arbolillo and

Figure 5.7   The lake system in the Valley of Mexico during Formative times. (After M. D. Coe 1962)

ca. In the four decades since Vaillant began his study, enough work has been done to allow today's students to see beyond the regional differences and view the Formative as a stage widely distributed over the area from Mexico to Peru (M. D. Coe 1962). The stage draws its importance from the transition it marks from the foraging Archaic cultures to the horticultural, sedentary, stratified societies which dominate the scene from about 1000 B.C. until historic times. Two formative sites of particular interest are Tlatilco (Porter 1953) and LaVenta (Drucker, Heizer, and Squier 1959).

With the passage of time, the Formative, by A.D. 300, had become something else, called the Classic stage. In Mexico, Yucatan, Guatemala, and South America, the village with associated temple and temple grounds was displaced by the elite religious center, supported by a surrounding phalanx of peasant villages. The size of these centers and the grandeur of the pyramid and temple complexes are well known. The city of Teotihuacan, the center at Monte Alban, and the Mayan ruins are examples of the Classic stage. These, however, constitute a separate study and are dismissed here as fascinating but irrelevant for present purposes.

Zacatenco a series of deep midden deposits.

Although Vaillant's test trenches yielded many artifacts—notably clay figurines and pottery—no very useful data about house form or materials, village layout, etc., were obtained. The importance of his finds lies rather in the variety seen in the sophisticated figurines and their changes in form from early (1000 B.C.) to late (A.D. 1). Vaillant used detailed differences in execution of the figurines as a sensitive time scale, and by so doing, focused attention on the problem of the basal Formative stage over all of Central and South Ameri-

North American Formative Stage

The brief digression of this chapter away from North America into Central America and Mexico has been necessary in order to put the North American story into perspective, because all major regional cultural growth and development north of Mexico is directly traceable to the events chronicled for Mexico. It is true that only simple villages of the Formative are represented above the Mexican border and that later Mexican elements were reaching the Southwest and Southeast of the United States as late as A.D. 1000, but all the

Formative specializations of concern to us—Hopewell, Pueblo-Hohokam, and Mississippian—show unmistakable links with the early Formative stage in the years before Christ. It was the diffusion of ideas and concepts, including even religions, which transformed the Archaic in certain favored places into higher, more complex, Formative cultures. Among the traits transmitted (possibly through a program of seaborne colonial expansion or even the establishment of religious or cult centers by bands of priests from the south) were: horticultural technology and, later, the three cultigens—maize, cucurbits, and beans—possibly burial mounds; tobacco and the pipe; certain pottery traits (roulette decoration, alternate bands of plain and textured surface, four-legged pots), as well as the idea of pottery itself; possibly stone masonry; almost certainly the figurine cult; several art motifs; ornaments such as the earspool; the use of conch shell in ceremonies; and other things (see Ford 1966).

The strong early Formative influence of Central America, both in South as well as in North America, has been suspected for many years, but good archeologic proof of diffusion and the routes of dispersal is still lacking. Nonetheless, the suspicions of yesteryear are now widely accepted as true because radiocarbon dating has, since 1950, provided the absolute time scale, pushing the evolution of the Mexican Formative back to 2000 to 1500 B.C. Mexican dates are simply much older than any in North America for remains of the comparable stage. For example, the American Southeast concept of elite centers, where a cadre of priests and apprentices lived, imposing labor and subsistence levies upon a surrounding peasantry, is overwhelmingly Central American in inspiration. Also, increasingly widespread field research has shown the diffused complexes to have existed in Mexico in readily recognizable form at

times early enough to allow a quiet leisurely spread. Botanic evidence is also now at hand. For example, the corn of the Eastern woodlands, Plains, and Anasazi of the Southwest seems to be a strain of flour corn developed and still grown in Guatemala, while the other Southwesterners got their corn direct from Mexico.

Although the ultimate origin of the North American specializations in Mexico and Central America is now being accepted because of radiocarbon dating which shows the time gradient to run from early in Ecuador and to latest in the Ohio Valley of North America, the similarities have been recognized for decades on purely archeologic evidence. Ekholm (various), Newell and Krieger (1949), Phillips (1940), Willoughby (1932), and others since 1950 have emphasized trait similarities. As the long timespan of early Mexican cultures has been perceived and as the archeologic search widens, the earlier suspicion of Mexican origins has changed to certainty as student after student reviews the problem.

Even more important, however, is the basic question of the source of the stimulus received by the original Archaic peoples of Central and South America. Is the evolution of American Indian high cultures an indigenous growth—an evolution inherent in the nature of culture—or are all the high cultures of the New World resultant from a diffusion of ideas, customs, artifacts, and religious-social practices of the Old World? The question is the unresolved one about diffusion as opposed to independent invention, a problem vexing Americanists from the beginning of study. The diffusionists would argue that most elements of material culture and many of nonmaterial culture are invented only once and diffuse outward to such peoples as are receptive to the innovations. Most of the early diffusionists overstated or overemphasized superficial formal similarities and were easily refuted, and Americanists for many decades have usually been militantly of the independent-invention school. Actually, they throw out the baby with the bath in denying Old World contact other than intermittent pulsations from Asia via Siberia. Over the years, argument has generated more heat than light, with evolutionists thoroughly obscuring the primary issue as they showed the course of culture development in Central and South American to parallel, even while it was apparently unrelated to, the histories of Mesopotamia and Southeast Asia. Both schools have been handicapped by ignorance, in that the archeologic data were scant, vast relevant areas of the world were (and remain today) unexplored archeologically, and the crucial factor of time has been under control only in the rarest instances. Now, although it remains unproved, there is little reason to doubt that the stimulus, and some actual origins, of all American cultures (except Eskimo) that follow the Archaic stages can be derived from Southeast Asia and ultimately from the Mesopotamian cradle of civilization. The evidence of North-Central-South American ties, with outward diffusion from South and Central America, can be expected to grow clearer and sharper as research focuses on the many questions about time, routes, mechanisms, and other details of the diffusion process.

The problem of Old World ties has attracted the amateur. Perhaps the best-known writer is Churchward, whose reams of fantasy about Mu can be seen as arch-diffusionism, mixed with mysticism, bias, and no understanding of the nature of culture, or of diffusion, or of the use of evidence. Some of the typologic similarities he sees may be sustained and proved by more critical means, but the mythical country of Mu remains difficult to locate. There are others, uncritical and unskilled in the use of evidence, whose writings also hold a grain of truth. Wauchope (1962) has dealt with some of the more important writers whose intemperate claims have tended to keep the more restrained scholars somewhat stubborn about accepting the possibility of trans- or circumpacific influence. Probably Gladwin (1947), who invoked Alexander's fleet to transport Asian ideas to America, and Heyerdahl (1950), with his theory of American-Polynesian connections, by doing outrageous violence to all "solid" anthropologic knowledge, have been tremendously valuable because their claims resulted in a rethinking and reinspection of the evidence by professional scholars who had no stake in either theory but who wished to discover what may actually have happened. Modern Americanists owe a real debt to both Gladwin and Heyerdahl for reopening the matter. As a final point, Ford (1966) has pyramided ceramic evidence to suggest the early Mesoamerican origins of the Southeastern cultures.

Summary

This chapter was designed to lay the minimum groundwork necessary for an understanding of what happened in three or four areas in North America, north of the Valley of Mexico, after about 2000 B.C., when regional specializations appear. Given the Mesoamerican genius, regardless of whether poorly modeled after Asiatic prototypes or locally developed, the broad unity of the full stream of the later American cultures is readily perceived. Equally plain are the fundamental differences in the earlier Archaic cultures from east to west as the selective acceptance of Mesoamerican innovations allowed each of the major regions to develop unique specializations.

6

Innovation and Change

The transformation of the Mexican Archaic stage into a food-production stage is seen to have happened with considerable rapidity in the second millennium B.C. The consequences of the new technology and subsistence, however dramatic they may have been in Mesoamerica, were equally profound in North America, albeit the diffusion was slow and the changes seem to have been less abrupt. One of the most obvious effects was the abrupt reversal of the cultural flow (which had probably diminished anyhow) from North America southward through Central to South America. With the domestication of plants and the development of horticultural practices and attendant technologic accretions, the cultural initiative shifted to Mesoamerica, with diffusion and stimulus moving both north and south from the central font. Even though the precise sources of the many innovations—horticulture, pottery, house architecture, villages, the temple and elite center, the priest-rulers, the colonizing or missionizing pattern—cannot yet be firmly established, the results are clear. The spread and development of these innovations make up, in fact, the last 2,500 years of the North American story. Assuming that the five stages—Lithic, Archaic, Formative, Classic, and Postclassic—outlined by Willey and Phillips have validity, the distribution and flow of influence can be charted as in

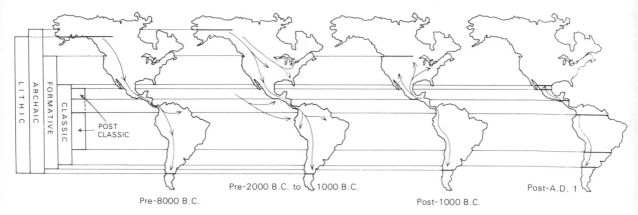

Figure 6.1   *Distribution of prehistoric culture stages and directional flows of influence.*

Figure 6.1. The Lithic stage is observed (or postulated) as basal and the same or a greater distribution can be assigned the Archaic stage. By 2000 B.C. or slightly later the Formative replaces the Archaic in *parts* of both continents. The Formative is a function of horticulture and has a spotty distribution in the lower latitudes on both sides of the Equator. The Classic and Postclassic cover an even smaller area. Figure 6.1 also suggests the routes of cultural transmission and the direction of diffusion.

Using Figure 6.1 as a highly schematic explanation summarizing what seems to have happened, it is possible now to turn back to North America and review the culture that evolved from local Archaic cultures. Formative innovations diffused

northward. In advance, it is necessary to state that the extent of Formative-influenced cultures north of Mexico was quite limited and tended to shrink, rather than expand, after about A.D. 1000 to 1200. For this, as well as for earlier boundary shifts, climatic factors may have been of primary importance (Griffin 1964). It should further be emphasized that the donor areas in Central America were different for eastern North America (Vera Cruz and the Mexican Gulf Coast) from those which contributed to the American Southwest (the Valley of Mexico). Three Formative climaxes occurred in North America. Earliest of these is the Adena-Hopewell-Marksville continuum of the Mississippi and Ohio Valleys from 800 B.C. to ca. A.D. 600 which evolved into the

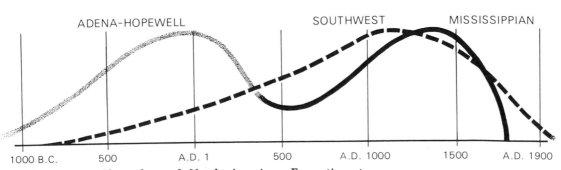

Figure 6.2   *Chronology of North American Formative stage climaxes.*

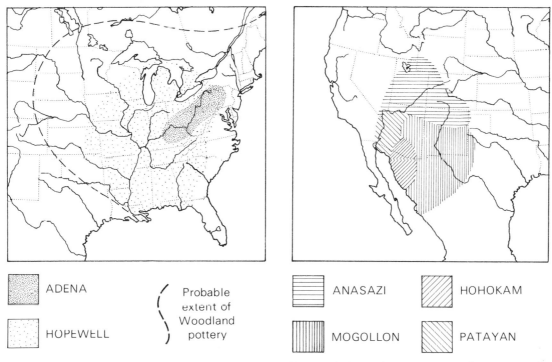

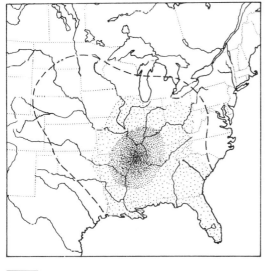

ADENA

HOPEWELL

Probable
extent of
Woodland
pottery

ANASAZI

MOGOLLON

HOHOKAM

PATAYAN

*Figure 6.3   Maximum areal extent of
Adena-Hopewell, Mississippian, and Southwest cultures during their climaxes.*

Mississippian
core area

Major extent
of influence

Extent of
secondary
influence

Mississippian of the Southeast. The Mississippian was at its apogee by perhaps A.D. 1400 to 1500, to disappear by A.D. 1700. In the Southwest, another climax, touched off by developments in the Valley of Mexico, endured from ca. 400 B.C. to modern times and overlapped with both the Eastern high spots. Simply schematized, the peaks in Figure 6.2 imply not only cultural richness and complexity but also territorial maxima as well. The rise, climax, and decline of the three regional specializations constitute the major concern of Chapters 6 and 7. In Figure 6.3, the maximum areal extension of the three climaxes is mapped.

Transition

The transformation of the North American Archaic into something else was a slow, uneven process extending over several centuries. Moreover, the major effect of the cultural accretions which make up the Formative stage, as these diffused in varying strength northward out of Mexico, was largely restricted to the areas where horticulture was possible. Not all the factors influencing the adoption of Mesoamerican ideas by the Archaic stage population can be isolated, but a few are obvious. One, of course, is the mechanical one of climate. Horticulture, a primary element of the Formative by definition, is restricted to the lower latitudes. Pottery is not thus restricted, nor is the building of houses. Elaborate ritual and stratified society need not be tied to food production, nor is a dense population required. Either can arise in situations lacking a controlled food-production technology in very special circumstances. It has been argued, for example (Willey and Phillips 1958; McKern 1956), that the Northwest coast tribes satisfy all the criteria of definition except for the practice of horticulture. The same lack of horticulture, and even of a well-developed ceramic technology, has already been mentioned in connection with the late California Archaic cultures. The California instance, of course, introduces the imponderable factor of the compatibility of an innovation with other aspects of the recipient culture, including the prime question of whether the innovation has any obvious advantages over current practices. Then, too, the manner of transmission of a new idea from donor to recipient culture will bear importantly on the rate and manner of adoption or rejection. These factors and many other relevant ones cannot be firmly isolated or even identified by archeologic means, except in the most speculative terms.

The efficient stability of the Archaic stage variants has been mentioned elsewhere; stability and efficiency continue to mark the transitional regional specializations which grew out of the Archaic, so it is possible to surmise that those innovations that reached the North American Archaic groups were smoothly absorbed into, or grafted upon, the older lifeway, with possibly no major shifts in overall cultural values or orientation toward the natural environment. Each adopting group would adapt all innovations to their local belief systems in somewhat different ways, thus supplying the regional variations in each artifact class or on each technologic complex that can be detected archeologically.

While the transition from the Archaic may have been slow, it can nonetheless be distinguished. It is best understood in the Eastern half of the United States, where, apparently, the first faint contacts with Mesoamerica were felt. Most students, to emphasize the accretions, call the transition stage the Early Woodland. The term "Woodland" is left over from earlier, more general studies, and though of decreasing usefulness, is needed by students as a key to understanding the literature; it will therefore be used at times in this book. For our immediate purposes, the term "transition" seems better to convey what actually happened. The crux of the matter is that the change into the Formative is less a new manifestation than it is the Archaic complex with additions. There is no evidence of drastic cultural modification. In effect, the Archaic ends by definition, since most scholars specify the Archaic stage as lacking in pottery. The presence of ceramic remains, then, arbitrarily marks the beginning of the transition. The not-surprising point to be remembered is that the additions, including pottery, to the Archaic trait list wrought no immediate changes in the overall pattern of life. The transition is marked by the presence of pottery, the use of special cemeteries or low conical or domed earthen mounds for burial, and the introduction of tobacco and a tubular pipe. On the basis of radiocarbon dates it appears that the transition began in the

Eastern United States long before it was felt in the West. Pottery occurs in the deep Southeast by 2500 B.C. (Stoltman 1966). Whether the inspiration for this early pottery came directly from northeast Asia, as argued by McKern (1937), Griffin (1964), and Tolstoy (1953), or whether, as implied above, it came from Mesoamerica, is impossible to determine yet. A strong argument is that of Kehoe (1962), who derives early Eastern American pottery from Scandinavia. The technically poor but distinctive Eastern Woodland pottery resembles nothing yet reported from Mexico, but there are traits—that is, the four-footed vessels seen early in Tchefuncte in the Southeast—which could easily be of Mexican inspiration.

One of the Archaic cultures which may be truly transitional is the Orient of New York. It is represented at several sites, the Stony Brook site (Ritchie 1959) on Long Island being one of the better known. This was a habitation site which yielded radiocarbon dates covering a span from about 1050 to 750 B.C. Plainly Archaic in nature, the subsistence was shellfish-centered, the many midden pits containing remains of oyster, scallop, quahog, long clam, periwinkle, and whelk. Land animals recovered included the white-tailed deer, turkey, box turtle, woodchuck, coon, gray fox, mink, and rodent. The artifacts indicate the Orient phase to be an outgrowth of the Laurentian or Coastal Archaic. What interests us is the presence of some clay pottery and steatite vessels. The steatite vessels are common over much of the Northeast and in some cases were copied in clay after ceramic technology developed. Many steatite vessel shapes occur over the Northeast; all are thought of as being Late Archaic in stage. But at the Orient sites the concurrence by 1000 B.C. of Vinette I clay pottery leads Ritchie (1965) and Griffin (1964) both to speak of the Orient as transitional. Vinette I pottery (Figure 6.4) is not of particularly

high quality, but is evidently the earliest in the Northeast. It has been described by Ritchie (1944) as ". . . moderately thick, coarse to medium grit-tempered gray, black or buff-colored, . . . straight-sided conoidal base vessels, cord or fabric roughened over the entire surface, both outside and inside."

"Temper" is, of course, the nonplastic material (which modern potters call "grog") added to the potter's clay to strengthen the product and minimize shrinkage of pots during drying. The reason for roughening of the surfaces is not understood. It may have been for decoration, but most probably it was a byproduct of manufacture wherein the clay was welded together and compacted by paddling with cord-wrapped or fabric-covered wooden paddles against an anvil or stone inside the vessel. A clear practical advantage would be the much increased surface area for more efficient transfer of heat for cooking. Although not elaborate, the Vinette and other early Northeastern pottery is true pottery, which continues to be of simple shape and crude manufacture until modern times along the East coast and in the Northeast.

While considerable detail about the Orient culture is available, it is the next chronologic sequence that shows the truly transitional changes in the Archaic into what is called Early Woodland by regional specialists. There are many regional versions of this stage. In New York, the Meadowood culture ("phase" in Ritchie's terminology) is a good example. [This account is based on Ritchie's (1965) most recent synthesis.] The culture (Figure 6.5) reveals clear descent from an Archaic base to the west—probably the Red Ocher and Glacial Kame of Illinois and Michigan —in such things as turkey-tail blades; use of red ocher in graves; large caches of mortuary blades; copper awls, beads, and celts; tubular pipes (made of pottery in Meadowood); galena cubes; deep grave

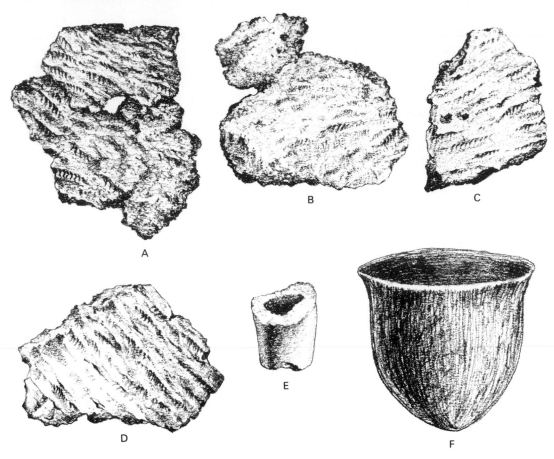

Figure 6.4 *Early Northeast pottery. A–D, pottery sherds of the Vinette I type; E, tubular pottery pipe fragment; F, generalized Vinette I pottery shape. (A–E after Ritchie 1965; F after Griffin 1952a, Fig. 17–D′)*

pits for flexed, bundle, and cremated burials. Its age, by radiocarbon assays, ranges from 1000 to 600 B.C. Most of the data come from burial sites, so no good information on village life is available. Such evidence as there is points to the same kind of pattern seen in the Archaic— hunting, gathering, and fishing. Caches of wild seeds of goosefoot and smartweed, in addition to charred scraps of netting and basketry, appear to support the idea of a mobile, foraging group. The creating of special, if small, cemeteries argues perhaps for a somewhat more sedentary life, but this cannot be proved. The popularity of cremation of the dead has prevented

the preservation of skeletal material, so nothing can be said about the physical type of the people. As the artifacts in Figure 6.5 reveal, the Meadowood material would be identified as an Archaic stage collection, were it not for the presence of pottery.

The widely distributed, crude, surface-textured pottery is important for the definition of stage and poses many problems as to its origin, but its net effect on the Archaic pattern is imperceptible. This is also true of the Southeast, where fiber-tempered pottery occurs (even earlier than in the Woodland cultures discussed above) along the Georgia coast and even on the

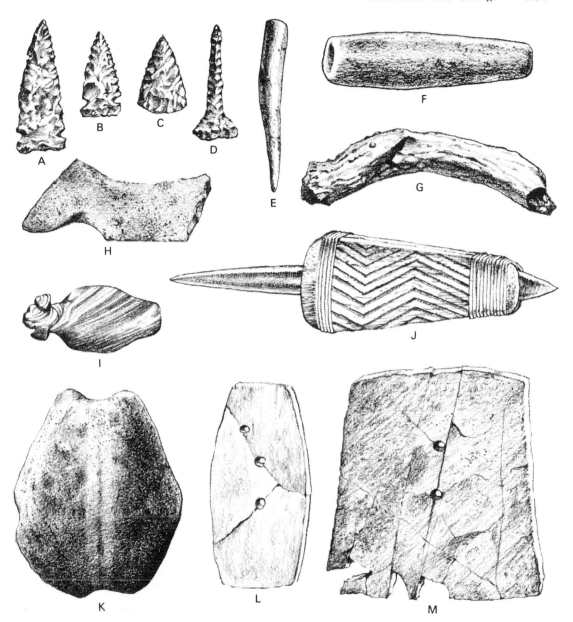

Figure 6.5   *Artifacts of the Meadowood culture. Reduced one half, except J. A–C, projectile points; D, flint drill; E, antler awl; F, tubular pottery pipe; G, cut section of deer antler; H, I, birdstones; J, copper flaking tool in wooden handle (restored), 4½ inches long; K, ovate pebble net sinker with imprint of double cord attachment to net; L, M, stone gorgets. (After Ritchie 1965)*

Tennessee River in Alabama (Figure 6.6). The Tennessee River fiber-tempered types always comprise the earliest ceramic materials in the Alabama area, as is true wherever else fiber occurs. It is also always found in an otherwise Archaic context in the Southeast. Tempering may be grass or Spanish moss or any other available fiber. The thick pottery itself appears to have been molded rather than soft-paddled and

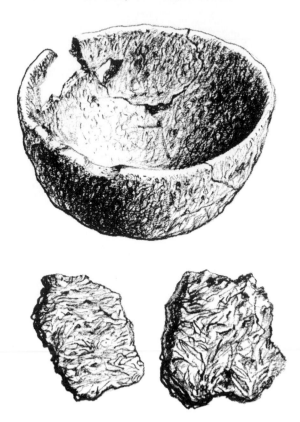

Figure 6.6   *Wheeler Plain vessel shape, and sherds from Alabama. (After Haag 1939)*

list as Early Woodland such assemblages (or sites) as Baumer, Crab Orchard, Black Sand, and Red Ocher (Illinois); Boone (Missouri); Watts Bar and Candy Creek (Tennessee); Tchefuncte (Louisiana); and Glacial Kame (Michigan). There are many others to be found over the East and Southeast, to say nothing of wide, but later, representation over the plains and down into Oklahoma.

The Baumer focus, described from several sites in a restricted area (Cole et al. 1951) in southern Illinois again documents how little the Archaic assemblage is modified in the early steps of the transition. The Baumer site itself lies on a ridge—a prehistoric natural levee of the Ohio River—in the "Black Bottoms" in extreme southern Illinois, an area even now rich in plants, land mammals, fish, and mollusks. Tests revealed that this complex occurred at many sites in the region, basal in all stratigraphic contexts. At Baumer the settlement covered the ridge, an area

is porous; it is not particularly durable or efficient. There are no obvious sources for this unusual ware, so its origin is unexplained. The bowl is the only known shape. Figure 6.7, a study-collection sherd from a Florida site, shows the curious vermiculated channels left twisting across the surface and through the clay (paste) after the fiber is destroyed by the heat of firing.

The transitional stages of nascent Woodland can be found almost everywhere east of the Rockies, in about the same distribution as the Eastern Archaic. And as a generalized "stage," Woodland persisted until historic times over the coastal areas of the Northeast, East, and South, if by this is meant that the Archaic stage multifocus subsistence base continued to be the pattern. The transitional sites are fairly numerous. The authors in Griffin (1952a)

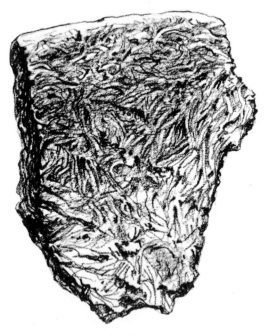

Figure   6.7   Fiber-tempered   sherd   from Florida. (Drawn from University of Utah type sherd collection)

some 1,500 by 300 feet covered with rich humus—black earth—to a depth of about 18 inches. This layer yielded pottery, stone artifacts, and food-bone scrap in quantity. Originating within this layer were many pits—straight-sided, cylindrical, and bell-shaped—which were sometimes lined with clay and which may first have been used for food storage, later to be filled with refuse after they had "soured" or crumbled or otherwise become unsuited for storage. Sometimes the pits were used as graves (during cold weather when the ground was frozen?) after the original storage purpose had been served. The outlines of square houses (?) built of vertical wooden posts were found. These structures were about 16 feet square; posts some 6 inches in diameter were set in individual post-holes at 2-foot intervals. No intrusive features, such as fireplaces or storage pits, were found and no evidence as to roofing techniques was discovered. Artifacts included heavy, stemmed knives or projectile points, a variety of scrapers and disc-shaped cores, the fully grooved ax, the smooth-tapered celt, gorgets of ground stone, and grooved plummets, as shown in Figure 6.8. An unusual artifact type is a large chipped stone, much polished by use, which is thought to have been a digging tool—probably a hoe.

The houses, the hoe, and the pottery are the non-Archaic elements; the pits, the much-chipped stone, and the polished-stone ornaments are seen in older cultures. The pottery is described as consistently coarse and crude. The favored tempering material in the thick, dense paste was crushed limestone, which had often been leached out by the soil acids to leave a pitted surface. Most of the vessels were the deep, globular, narrow-mouthed forms so typical of Woodland pottery. The surface was commonly roughened by impressing with basketry or matting, or the impressions may have been made by pressing a cord-wrapped stick

against the moist clay. The cord marking mentioned earlier also occurs but in reduced percentages. In the comparative treatment of the Baumer focus materials Cole et al. (1951) see the Crab Orchard focus as very similar to Baumer. But in Crab Orchard there are cut carnivore jaws, reel-shaped gorgets, and other objects which appear to belong to a later stage, so it may be that Crab Orchard grew out of the earlier Baumer. During the emergence of the Woodland from the Archaic, the custom of burying important personages (?) in low, domed, earthen mounds appears. The "round-grave" people described long ago by M. R. Harrington (1922) had a similar practice. The Miller I complex (Jennings 1941, 1944) in northeastern Mississippi and the upper levels of the Stallings Island site in Georgia can be assigned to the same transition stage.

While the pottery of the East, as mentioned, is thought to have diffused from Asia, this is far from being proved. The earliest, or fiber-tempered, may be derived from Vera Cruz, but no precursors have been proved. Kehoe (1962) has rather persuasively argued that the point-for-point similarities between Vinette II pottery and that of the Ertebolle peoples of Scandinavia are far too numerous to be overlooked and that Woodland pottery generally may be a direct diffusion from Europe. The timing is right; Ertebolle pottery goes back nearly to 3000 B.C., with the Vinette comfortably later. Ocean transport from Scandinavia would involve very short voyages, with convenient landfalls at the Faeroes, Iceland, and Greenland. Added to this hypothesis about ceramic origins is the appearance in America of mound burial after 1000 B.C., again later than comparable customs appeared in Europe. These reasonable, if novel, conclusions are impressively argued, although the compared traits are general rather than detailed. Lacking airtight evidence for the stereotyped explanation of Asiatic origin,

I am inclined to accept the Kehoe study as being as reasonable as any of the alternatives. Acceptance is particularly easy in view of Lopatin's (1960) study of the typology of sweat bathing, wherein he shows beyond cavil that one trait, the widespread American Indian sweat-bath technology, is entirely Scandinavian in type (Figure 6.9). He cannot, however, utilize chronologic argument because the sweat-bath (vapor-bath) data were largely collected ethnographically in recent years, even though the vapor bath was known in Russia before the beginning of the Christian era. There is archeologic evidence in the Maya area showing the vapor bath to have occurred early in the Christian era, according to Lopatin. His conclusions redocument the fact of Scandinavian contact with northeastern North America before 1492 and thus lend some support to the quite-early contacts proposed by Kehoe. Furthermore, adding to these arguments the fact that burial mounds appear to be earlier in the Midwest than in the Southeast, the distribution of this innovation supports a northerly rather than a southern origin of the custom. Such argument conflicts with the possible derivation of burial mounds from Central America. No verdict can be rendered as yet.

Even though concrete evidence as to the origin of either pottery or the burial-mound complex is lacking, the presence of both does signal the end of the Archaic stage and introduces what may be the beginning of the North American Formative. In this stage, the remains of artifacts generally memorialize the stimulus of

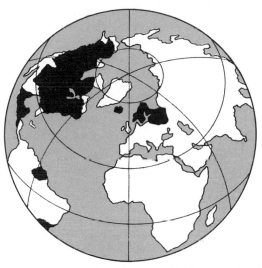

Figure 6.9   *Distribution (black areas) of the sweat bath prior to Russian colonization of Siberia. (After Lopatin 1960)*

Mexican ideas from the south, and the archeologic remains chart the American consequences (adoption) of these influences, however tenuous these may have been or how obscure their paths remain today.

Adena-Hopewell

Adena and Hopewell are essentially contemporary, but are called Early and Middle Woodland by some authors. Ford and Willey (1941) in their early, very insightful summary of Eastern American prehistory speak of two stages, Burial Mound I and II, thus separating the Adena and Hopewell chronologically, partially on burial-mound typology. The distribution of these two cultures coincides to some degree, as do their general traits. Adena, being the simpler, was long thought to be the older of the two. Radiocarbon dates do give the Adenans slight priority and thus it may be ancestral, but the spans show great overlap. Griffin (1964) allows from 1000 B.C. to A.D. 200 for the Adena. Earlier, W. S. Webb and Baby (1957)

Figure 6.8   *Artifacts of the Baumer focus. Variable scale. A, C, projectile points; B, D, scrapers; E, F, hoes; G, I, stone pendants; H, stone gorget; (A–I approximately one-third size); J, plummet stone; K, grooved ax; L, M, idealized pottery forms; N, O, cord-marked sherds; P, typical pit forms in cross section; Q, postmolds of square house plan. (A–I, L–O after Cole et al. 1951; J, K, P, Q after Griffin 1952a, Fig. 96)*

showed a debated radiocarbon-derived span of 800 B.C. to A.D. 800. Ritchie and Dragoo (1960), in discussing the spread of Adena into Maryland and New York (where it is known as Middlesex), tend to accept the 800 B.C. to A.D. 800 timespan. Both the Adena and the Hopewell sites were discovered long ago by assorted diggers; many were excavated before the development of today's more meticulous techniques. As a result of the earlier concern with antiquities rather than with the entire culture, the literature contains a disproportionate amount of description of artifacts and burial complexes and is nearly silent on the other aspects of culture.

The rather full knowledge we have about Adena is largely the result of studies by William S. Webb, who concentrated on this culture for a number of years. His syntheses (Webb and Snow 1945; Webb and Baby 1957) were the best source of data until the work of Dragoo (1963). One of the first impressions the student of Adena-Hopewell gains is the similarity of mortuary practice and artifacts of the two cultures. In view of their overlap in space and their centuries of contemporaneity, this is not surprising. It does mean, however, that distinguishing one from the other rests on the details of mound construction, wealth of artifacts, and the presence of certain classes of artifacts. In all cases, the Hopewell is the more elaborate, richer in artifacts and range of classes; it is marked by an overall greater technologic sophistication.

Sites identified by W. S. Webb and Baby (1957) as Adenan number 222, but this list does not mention the New York and Maryland Middlesex locations. Other authors would place some of the listed sites with Hopewellian. The classic Adena heartland is confined to the central Ohio Valley. Most of the sites fall within 150 miles of Chillicothe, Ohio, extending into Indiana, Kentucky, West Virginia, and Pennsylvania. Many explored by Webb lie near Lexington. The entire complex can be

thought of as extremely restricted; its importance derives from its influence rather than its areal extent, although tenuous Adena connections are seen deep in the Southeast. Many of the sites in the core area are characterized by vast (and unexplained) earthworks. These, as the name implies, are high, narrow ridges of earth, fencing in or enclosing large "fields." The fields may be circular, square, pentagonal, or the earthwork may follow the irregular edges of flat-topped spurs or promontories, but Webb and Snow seem to think only the circular ones may be Adenan. Although Squier and Davis (1848) record hundreds of then-prominent examples, many have disappeared beneath plow and progress. The many near Chillicothe and Miamisburg in 1848 shown by

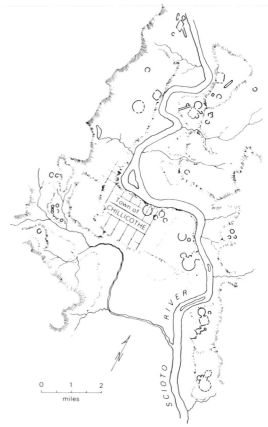

Figure 6.10   *Twelve miles of the Scioto Valley showing earthworks (heavy lines). (After Squier and Davis 1848)*

Squier and Davis give a good idea of their variety of form (Figure 6.10). These earthworks on cliffs and eminences along rivers and creeks are characteristic of both Adena and Hopewell. At Newark, a famous work is partially preserved as a golf course. Two famous Hopewell locations are preserved at Mound City and Great Serpent Parks in Ohio.

Burial mounds—conical or domed—may occur inside the enclosures. Mound groups without associated earthworks are equally common. Some mound groups are built directly over villages. Because both Adena and Hopewell have earthwork associations, the trait is not a diagnostic one. Despite the Formative stage ascription for Adena, there is inconclusive evidence for any but the simplest agriculture, some of which may have been of the demiculti-gens; corn has not been found, nor have beans. Subsistence was still, as in the Archaic, derived from knowledgeable selection from scores of species. The following list is taken from perishable specimens recovered from the dry caves and shelters of Kentucky (Goslin 1957) and from rare preserved pieces from excavated sites. From fecal matter in the caves, several species, not found otherwise, were identified (Jones 1936). The analysis of human fecal matter as an aid in ecologic analysis has become routine, for example, Jennings (1957), Callen (1963), Martin and Sharrock (1964), but the 1936 study by Jones of Newt Kash Shelter vegetal remains was perhaps the first. The feces contained sunflower and goosefoot seed in quantity. Both are thought to have been cultivated. There were also bits of bone and feather, a grasshopper leg, and a beetle fragment in the specimens studied.

The full list of species, presumably food sources, from both excavated sites and caves includes: deer, elk, black bear, dog, raccoon, woodchuck, beaver, opossum, porcupine, otter, fox, wildcat, assorted rodents, turkey, trumpeter swan, ruffed grouse, box turtle, catfish, freshwater mussel, hickory nut, walnut, butternut, acorn, chestnut, pawpaw, honey locust, marsh elder, canary grass, raspberry, and giant ragweed. Probable domesticates were gourd, pumpkin, sunflower, and goosefoot. Again, the bounty of the land offered a wide dietary range. The domestic plants must have been distinctly secondary food sources. It is only fair to point out that the artifacts from eastern Kentucky caves were not particularly special; the food-stuffs identified could equally well have been from Archaic strata, with a few of the associated artifacts apparently of Adena affiliation. Other perishables from the cave sites included wooden pestles, undoubtedly for use in the frequent "hominy holes" (actually mortars in bedrock) in the crushing of nuts and seeds for cookery. Woven moccasins (probably more correctly called sandals) of grass and fiber and beds of grass and leaves were recorded.

There is more information available about the mounds and death rituals of the Adena than about other aspects of the culture. Burial rites tended to interest the early excavators more perhaps than did the mundane matters of foods and handicrafts. The burial mounds are artifically constructed hillocks built laboriously from little individual loads of earth scooped from nearby borrow areas. The small loads were of different colors, depending on the borrow zone; thus, when the mound fill is sectioned, it presents a mottled patchwork of earth colors quite pleasing in its patterned irregularity. The phenomenon of "loading" characterizes most artificial earthen fills. Mound-construction design varies enormously. Some of the smaller ones were built in one stage to cover the body of a single important man. The corpse may have been placed in a simple pit with the mound quickly erected over it after whatever ceremony was involved. In other instances, burial was in large, log-lined pits or may have constituted no more than a clay-lined basin with only some charred or calcined human bones remaining to attest a crematory rite. Some of the larger Adena mounds, such as the Robbins Mounds site (W. S. Webb and Elliott 1942) in Boone County, Kentucky, were built in a series of separate incidents; there were a dozen burials, each covered by an extensive blanket of earth, and with new increments the mounds grew larger and taller. W. S. Webb and Snow (1945) list thirty-five burial traits of varying detail. Aside from the log-tomb burials (Figure 6.11) where one, two, or three individuals in extended position and smeared with red ocher or graphite were interred with grave furniture, there were many variations on the cremation technique. Total cremation occurred in clay-lined basins. Partial burning of the body was usually found in conjunction with a log-lined tomb, and Webb speculates that these latter cases were accidental. The preoccupation with death and fire is remindful of the extensive crematory rites of the Orient and other Archaic cultures to the east of the Adena center.

The round Adena houses are unique in construction. The walls were of paired posts set in the ground to slant outward. The rafters were supported on four sturdy center posts, spaced in a square around the central fire area, and projected well beyond the walls to form generous eaves. The roof may have been of matting or thatch and the walls of flexible withes or cane woven or wattled around the posts. Most of the restoration in Figure 6.12 is conjectural because the construction details were not preserved. The round Adena structures varied greatly in size—from 20 to 80 feet in diameter. Webb doubts that all were roofed. Many were destroyed by fire; the outlines formed by the postholes are frequently encountered under the mounds, as if the burning of a house may have been the first step in construction of a burial mound. Paired posts forming a circle over 100 feet in diameter occur in

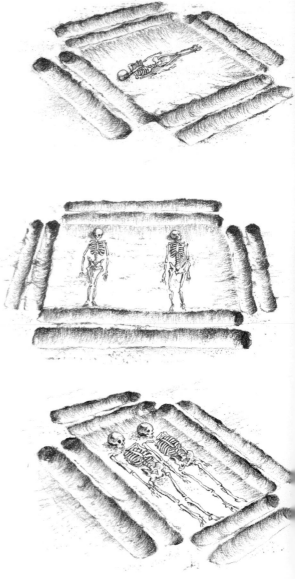

Figure 6.11   *Log tomb burials as excavated at the Robbins Mounds. (After W. S. Webb and Elliott 1942)*

connection with earthworks also. At Mt. Horeb (Kentucky), W. S. Webb (1941b) speaks of a "palisade" over 100 feet in diameter inside a circular earthwork.

Grave goods were not common in the Adena tombs, but those reported are of interest. There were smooth, stone (rarely, copper) gorgets or chest ornaments of

26' diameter

Figure 6.12   Postmold plan and cutaway view of restored Adena house showing probable construction. (After W. S. Webb 1941a)

several shapes—rectangular, lozenge, oval, or reel-shaped. The reel varies in shape but is essentially a rectangular body with four symmetrically flaring arms or prongs (Figure 6.13). The gorgets are quite well made, often being fashioned of banded slate and other striking stone, polished to a high luster.

One of the distinctive Adena artifacts is the engraved tablet; several examples exist. These are rectangular slabs of stone about 3 by 4 inches and ½ inch thick with zoomorphic figures engraved on one or both sides. Birds—probably raptorial—are the commonest form (Figure 6.14), but geometric designs are also found. The cultural function of these tablets is not known; they have been interpreted as stamps for decorating the body or clothing. What is of interest, however, is that the

bird and other motifs are also found later throughout the Hopewell culture, normally on pottery and copper plaques or cutout forms.

The use of pottery as grave furnishings was not an Adena custom, but for ordinary use there was good plain and cord-marked pottery of standard "Woodland" type, that is, the conoidal or round-bottomed jar form, as shown in Figure 6.15. There are also several check-stamped wares, bearing specific type names. The check stamping is done by paddling the soft paste with a grooved wooden paddle; the two sets of grooves are at right angles to each other. The clay is punched in by the raised lands, while the grooves leave the ridges (Figure 6.16). The carved paddle is presumably a development from the cord-wrapped paddle; check stamping is very common at this period and earlier all over the South-east. A special pottery type, Montgomery Incised, is decorated with a nested, incised lozenges design (Figure 6.17). The Adena textile arts were well-developed. Plain and twilled plaiting and several variations on twining have been noted. The textiles have been recovered from open sites, preserved in copper salts when left near, or wrapped around, copper objects. Other artifact classes are not particularly diagnostic. There are awls of several styles; rather heavy chipped knives, points, and scrap-ers; flint hoes; nut- or cupstones; river-mussel pearls; shell beads; spoons from terrapin carapaces; cut animal jaws; celts with a circular cross section; and bowls from human crania. W. S. Webb and Baby report an unusual artifact—the upper jaw of a wolf, cut so that the incisors and canines are intact on a kind of handle

made by carving the palate to a spatulate form. They argue that this is part of an animal mask; the user would have had his upper incisors removed, putting the spat-ula in his mouth through the hole thus created (Figure 6.18). Human skulls thus mutilated have been found, thereby lend-ing credence to the idea.

Of the many Adena sites investigated by Webb and his associates, one of the more complex was the Robbins Mounds near Big Bone, in Boone County, Kentucky (W. S. Webb and Elliott 1942). In it were fifty-two tombs of four types: (1) an earthen-walled enclosure lined with logs and bark with a log roof, (2) a tomb within a for-tuitous cavity made by collapse of the roof of an earlier tomb, (3) a log enclosure on a flat surface, covered by an earthen fill, and (4) a tomb constructed on a slope, by cutting a level floor into the slope.

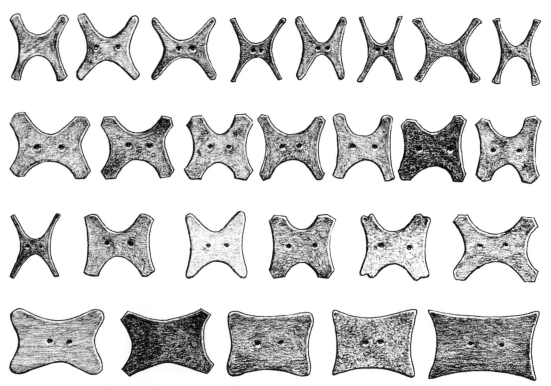

Figure 6.13   *Reel-shaped gorgets. All are reduced to the same vertical height. (After W. S. Webb 1941b)*

Figure 6.14   *Engraved Adena tablets. Bird design elements shown at right center. (After W. S. Webb and Baby 1957)*

Logs were then piled against the one earthen wall but were on the surface on the level, unwalled area. These logs occur on all levels of the mound; the latter had been erected through the addition of six to eight stages or increments, each asso-

ciated with the addition of another tomb. Figure 6.19 shows one cross section, with the relationship of the tombs to building periods plainly evident. Note that no tomb is associated with the low primary mound. This nuclear construction was built upon

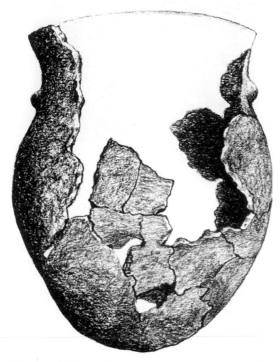

Figure 6.15   Fragmentary pottery vessel, approximately 9 inches high, from the Riley Mound. (After W. S. Webb 1943)

the ashes of a burned circular house of the unique style described above. Many other house patterns of the same type were found elsewhere on the site. Selected Robbins site artifacts are shown in Figure 6.20.

The Adenans appear to have been roundheaded (brachycephalic), whereas the Archaic populations had, as mentioned earlier, longer, slender crania. This roundheadedness has been one reason for thinking of the Adenans as migrant from, perhaps, Mexico. This evidence goes along with the possible Mexican origins of the death mask, the hand-eye and raptor art motifs, and the elaborate burial concepts. Jennings (1965a) halfheartedly suggests that the Adena population was not necessarily roundheaded. Cranial deformation and the attendant facial changes might well account for the obvious morphologic differences they show; the practice of

cranial deformation or accidental cradle-board deformation for the Adena is attested by Snow (1948).

As implied earlier, the Adena is not as important in itself as in its influence, even though it may reflect the first of the Mexican stimuli. Evidently partly ancestral to Hopewell, its influence in its own right extended both south and east. The Tchefuncte site near New Orleans may be related. The several Copena sites in northern Alabama, the Miller I of northeast Mississippi, and the Hamilton focus of eastern Tennessee, as well as the Middlesex of New York, are all related and possibly derivative from the core Adena. W. S. Webb and Baby (1957) seem to have demonstrated the Adena contribution in artifacts and art motifs, and probably in ritual, to all later Eastern cultures. They

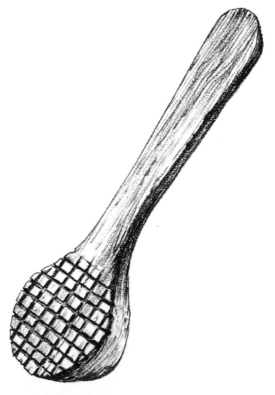

Figure 6.16   Hypothetical construction of carved wooden paddle, eight or nine inches long, used in making check-stamped pottery.

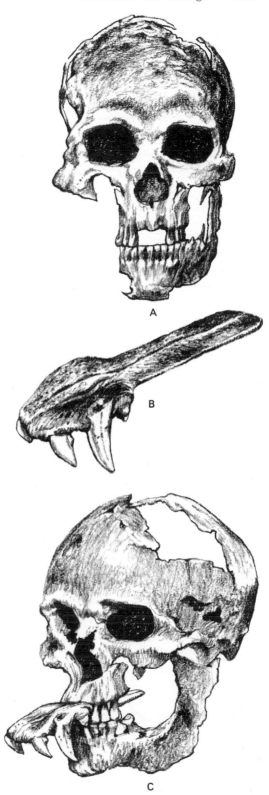

Figure 6.17 *Restored Montgomery Incised vessel, 14½ inches high. (After W. S. Webb and Snow 1945)*

cite as examples the reel-shaped gorget, the hand eye design, the circular-eye death motif, the raptorial bird, the large, circular, shell gorget, and the rectangular gorget. All these motifs and artifacts appear in the Hopewell and in later cultures.

Hopewell

With a general background from the Adena culture and a glimpse at one of the famous sites, the more extensive Hopewell deserves attention. Most of the classic

Figure 6.18 *A, Adena skull with upper incisors missing; B, spatula-shaped artifact made from wolf jaw; C, skull with artifact in gap created by missing teeth. (After W. S. Webb and Baby 1957)*

Figure 6.19   *Cross section of burial mound, Robbins Mounds site, showing several tombs and building levels. (After W. S. Webb and Elliott 1942)*

Hopewell sites were dug during the antiquarian era of study. As a result, there are many data missing from the classic core area in southern Ohio. However, the culture has been the object of continuous study over the Middle West, Northeast, and Southeast, and fuller data are finally available on several, but not all, aspects of the culture. Nevertheless, the full dimensions of the relationship of Adena to Hope-

well are not clear, although the inter-influence is obvious and undebated. Griffin (for example, 1964) perhaps has devoted the most effort to elucidating the Hopewell story.

He (1964) provides a synopsis of his interpretation of the Hopewellian data and establishes a chronology within the culture. Although he recognizes the influence Adena had on Hopewell, he insists that

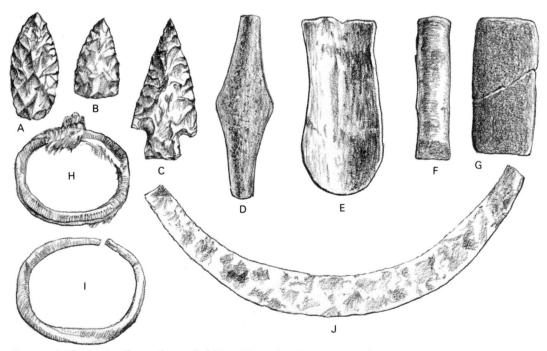

Figure 6.20   *Artifacts from Robbins Mounds. Approximately one-third size. A–C, projectile points; D, gorget; E, spoon made from terrapin carapace; F, tubular pipe with beveled mouthpiece; G, sandstone tablet; H, I, copper bracelets; J, mica crescent. (After W. S. Webb and Elliott 1942)*

this was an ancestral one, discounting the apparent contemporaneity mentioned above. Most of the Hopewell radiocarbon dates acceptable to Griffin fall after 300 B.C. until about A.D. 250. Although Hopewell was discovered and named in Ohio, it is believed to have developed first in Illinois and to have evolved into its classic stage in Ohio. Hopewellian ceramic traits tend to be quite distinctive, as do some other objects, and it is possible for the regional experts to identify scores of related but technically different local centers and to posit the directions and time of diffusion of Hopewell influence. The data are too numerous and the arguments too special for inclusion here (for example, Griffin 1952a, 1958; Struever 1964, 1965). From his detailed analysis, however, Griffin (1964) gives the Illinois center priority because the ceramics seem to be a local development from an earlier Woodland base and because the Ohio platform pipe and copper earspools are missing. Then he sees classic Hopewell resulting from the impact of the Illinois River version upon the Adena population resident in southern Ohio. The burial-mound-and-log-tomb complex was known, however, to the early Illinois Woodland peoples and formed the nucleus of Hopewell ritual. The same Illinoian influence flowed also, he says, to the northeast, north, and west, so that the distinctive Hopewell cast is found in sites in Iowa, Missouri, Wisconsin, Minnesota, Michigan, and even in central Kansas (W. R. Wedel 1943; F. Schultz and Spaulding 1948). In Pennsylvania and New York the Hopewell manifestation is derived from Ohio, as are all the southern versions: The Miller II (Jennings 1944) and Bynum Mounds (Cotter and Corbett 1951) sites are Mississippi examples; the McQuorquodale Mound (Wimberly and Tourtelot 1941) in Alabama, and the Marksville (Fowke 1928; Ford 1951) and Crooks (Ford and Willey 1940) sites of Louisiana

are all famous locations. Best known of the southern derivatives is the Santa Rosa culture of Florida (Willey 1949).

In connection with a general or "average" description of Hopewell culture, it must also be borne in mind that the data reveal less a culture than a cult because the concern with death and the preparation of mortuary furniture led to lavishness in the ritual artifacts. The mounds and their contents have received great attention. The remains—earthworks such as the Newark works (Figure 6.21) and massive two- or three-stage mounds— bespeak a priesthood or priest-rulers who could command corvée labor to support the obligations imposed by the rituals of death. The artisans were superbly competent; there were ceramists, sculptors in stone and bone, skilled flint knappers, and coppersmiths, all possessing exquisite

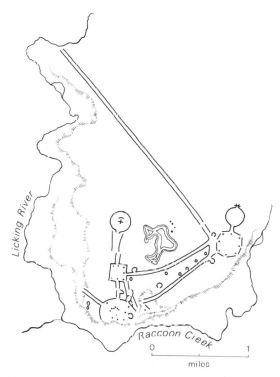

Figure 6.21   Map of the Newark site showing earthworks. (After Prufer 1964)

artistry. This much can be known, but aside from presuming some strong cohesive force—political or religious—and vigorous trade coupled with a rich aesthetic tradition, little is known about the culture (see Prufer 1965). Horticulture is suspected but not widely demonstrated, at least as far as maize is concerned. The subsistence base would seem, then, to have been largely the usual one of wide exploitation of wild species. At one Illinois site, Clear Lake, near Pekin (Fowler 1952), the dominant meat food was deer. Represented in the food scraps were turtle (three species), muskrat, beaver, duck, raccoon, buffalo, elk, turkey, and many rodents. Shellfish—snails and mussels—were well represented, as were catfish, suckers, and bass. From the Apple Creek site (also in Illinois), Struever reports caches of pigweed, lambsquarter, and grape seeds, with hazelnuts, walnuts, and pecans also in evidence. Probably the sunflower, goosefoot, and cucurbits seen in Adena will also one day be reported, as will maize. Prufer (1965) has reported two cobs from the McGraw site in Ohio; this is perhaps the best-controlled evidence to date (Struever 1965).

Village sites have not been extensively explored, so little is known of other mundane matters. A few possible house patterns have been seen. They are rectangular or long, oval postmold patterns with no internal supports. Presumably they were domed mat- or bark-covered structures very like the wigwams of the late Woodland remnant tribes of historic times (Cole and Deuel 1937), but all those described may have been ritual structures.

While the regional variants have a certain reality, all can be identified as Hopewellian, the artifacts serving as index types or even as horizon markers. Until these regional studies began (Morse 1963; Struever 1964, 1965), archeologists had tended to think of the Hopewell as generally uniform in character, with the de-

scriptions tending to represent the classic Ohio version. This traditional approach will be taken in the following paragraphs, and it may be the proper approach; at least, Prufer (1965), in connection with another study, has made the excellent suggestion that the uniformity of Hopewellian cult artifacts is of great cultural importance and not accidental. He sees the cult as imposed upon resident, regionally different, Woodland cultures; such differences in nonmortuary Hopewellian artifacts as occur in the local tradition are irrelevant because Hopewellian influence, spreading as a cult, affected only the mortuary ceremonial complex, leaving the local lifeway otherwise unaffected.

Hopewell mounds tend to be two-stage. The first stage is essentially a low platform prepared to contain a single log tomb [especially in Illinois, for example, the Dickinson Mound site (Walker 1952)] or for a series of crematory basins [in several Ohio mounds, for example, the Harness Mound site (Mills 1907)]. The burials are often accompanied by varied and elaborate grave furnishings. Then the second stage or mantle is applied so that the final earthwork is a conical hillock as much as 100 feet in diameter and from 10 to 40 feet high. It is the grave goods, their material and form, that give the cult its distinctiveness. The raw materials include copper, pipestone, mica, obsidian, meteoric iron, shell, tortoiseshell, shark and alligator teeth, bear teeth, and clay. All are characterized by artisanship of high caliber and by distinctive motifs.

In ceramics (involving the most tractable of materials and one that becomes imperishable when fired), a very sensitive record of aesthetic styles and changes is preserved. The regional styles can be segregated by the knowledgeable, but, in general, Hopewell day-to-day ceramics are merely good-quality Woodland ware, grit-tempered and paddled with a cord paddle or wrapped stick. The usual form was a flat or conoidal base and the familiar flared mouth. But 1 or 2 percent of the pottery—that used in burial ritual—is distinctive. The form was about the same, usually a squat vessel or jar with somewhat constricted neck. The thickened rim was almost always diagonally hatched or crosshatched. Frequently the body of the jar had four symmetric bulging lobes that were relevant in the careful and sometimes repeated design. Designs began below the constricted neck and were worked out in broad, shallow grooves made in the clay with a round, dull-pointed implement. The design was emphasized by texturing either the figure or the background with rocker or roller marks in a zigzag pattern. The raptorial bird and duck designs were common, along with a variety of geometric and cursive designs. Another characteristic design element is a series of nodes formed by pushing a reed or bone tool against the interior to raise a series of spaced bosses or lumps on the exterior near the rim. From clay, too, the beautiful Hopewell figurines were fashioned. Some of the most elaborate come from the Knight Mound group in Illinois (McKern, Titterington, and Griffin 1945). From them the details of headdress, clothing, ornament, and even motor habits can be learned (Figure 6.22). Note the female sitting posture, the big painted beads on ankles and wrist, and the short skirts. Male ornaments and breechclout are also portrayed. (See also Deuel 1952b.)

From the copper, annealed by alternately cold-working and heating into thin sheets, head ornaments, breast ornaments, and many decorative animal forms in repoussé were made. Bicymbal or yo-yo-shaped earspools, beads, panpipes, and flat celts of all sizes were also made from copper. Thin sheets of mica were cut into pleasingly symmetric geometric shapes. Stone platform pipes, often with naturalistic animal and human sculptures of great beauty, occur by the dozens, in caches as well as with important dead. From obsidian the exquisite ceremonial knives and blades were chipped by expert knappers. Another common obsidian object was a small, symmetric, prismatic flake knife. Figures 6.23, 6.24, and 6.25 exemplify in part the richness of the Hopewellian artistry.

From the Wabash Valley, in eastern Illinois, Neumann and Fowler (1952) reported their excavation of the Wilson site. Mound Wh6, 90 feet in diameter and 13 feet high, is a typical two-stage site. Construction was begun by removing the topsoil down to a blue clay subsoil. A tomb 11 by 15 feet was dug into the blue clay; into the center of the tomb a second, deeper pit, 2 by 5 feet, was dug. The spoil dirt was arranged in lunate-shaped "ramparts" around the tomb. Seven extended burials were placed in position, logs were laid over the tomb, and the first stage of the mound was built (Figure 6.23); the second mantle of earth was added soon after.

From Louisiana, Ford and Willey (1940) describe the Crooks site (a southern Hopewell variant called Marksville) as having a flat burial platform erected upon the original surface. Upon this platform 214 burials were made, 168 bodies having already been included in the upper earth fill of the platform itself. A yellow clay dome capped the burial platform and a steeply conical primary mound was constructed. Later the secondary fill was added. In it, in shallow pits, hundreds of other burials were laid. From the site came many fine Hopewellian mortuary pieces, but they are of local manufacture (Figure 6.26). The Marksville site, at Marksville, Louisiana, is one of the most famous Hopewell sites, lending its name to the entire Lower Mississippi Valley complex. Fowke's (1928) excavations there demonstrated the two-stage construction and familiar mortuary function of the mounds. Setzler (1933) figures several Hopewell

Figure 6.22 *Hopewell ceramic figurines. Approximately three-fourths size. (After McKern, Titterington, and Griffin 1945)*

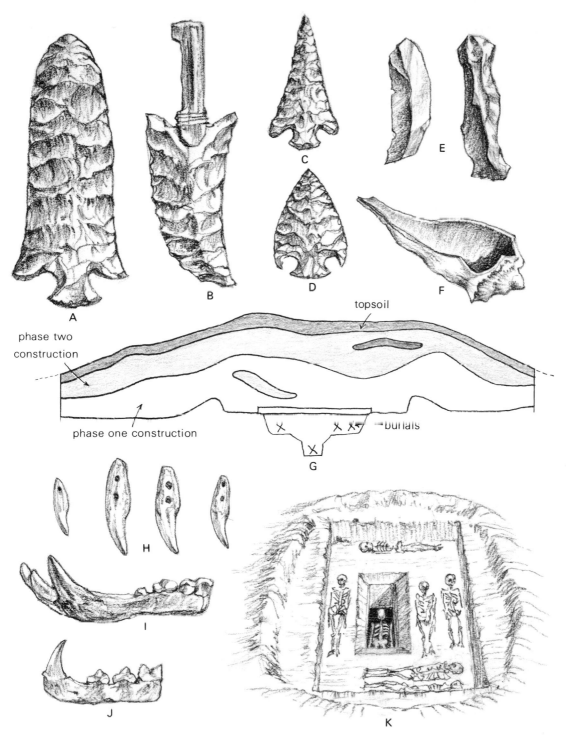

Figure 6.23 *Hopewell artifacts and diagram of burial mound. Variable scale. A, obsidian knife or spearhead; B, obsidian knife, wooden handle (restored); C, D, spearheads; E, flake knives; F, conch-shell dipper; G, cross section of Wh6 burial mound; H, perforated dog, bear, and wolf canines; I, cut bear jaw; J, cut wolf jaw; K, view of central tomb in Wh6 mound. (A–C after Martin, Quimby, and Collier 1947; D after Walker 1952; E after Fowler 1952; F–K after Neumann and Fowler 1952)*

Figure 6.24   *Hopewell stone pipe sculptures. Slightly reduced. A, hawk or eagle attacking a man; B, highly polished platform pipe; C, beaver; D, hawk or eagle tearing at a small bird; E, cougar or wild cat; F, toad; G, bear; H, tufted heron with a small fish. (A, B drawn from University of Wisconsin color slides of original pipes; C–F, H after Squier and Davis 1848; G after Neumann and Fowler 1952)*

Figure 6.25 *Hopewell artifacts. Much reduced scale. Ornaments of sheet mica: A–H (F representing bear claws and G a bird talon); I, stone ear ornament; copper artifacts: J, fish, probably a sucker; K, robe ornament; L, ear ornaments; M, bird with pearl eye; N, ax head; O, bracelets; P, ornament, probably a serpent's head; Q–T, pottery. (A–C after Moorehead 1910, Vol. II; D–P after Martin, Quimby, and Collier 1947; Q after Griffin 1952a, Fig. 32–S; R after Lilly 1937; S after McGregor 1952; T after Griffin 1952b)*

Figure 6.26 *Hopewell pottery types from the Crooks site. A–D, Marksville Plain, 2½ to 3½ inches high; E, F, Marksville Stamped, both 4 inches high; G, H, Marksville Incised, both 4½ inches high. (After Ford and Willey 1940)*

vessels from the Marksville site (Figure 6.27). The Bynum Mounds site in northeastern Mississippi (Cotter and Corbett 1951) is clearly Hopewell-derived. The central sunken tomb and the flat, first-stage mound are both represented in the six mounds at the site. There were large, circular postmold patterns and myriads of unpatterned molds over the village which lay adjacent to the mounds. The circles of posts were large—one was 78 feet in diameter—so there may be doubt as to whether they were for houses; they may have been post enclosures for some unknown use.

The Florida Hopewellian derivative is called Santa Rosa. Usually correlated with the Santa Rosa is a Georgia culture called Swift Creek. (Swift Creek pottery occurs at the McGraw and Wilson sites in Illinois.) Santa Rosa (Willey 1949) shows no big centers nor the elaborate stage-construction mounds. Burials were, of course, in the mounds but were not so

formally interred. It is in the ceramics with distinctive zoning and rocker stamping on somewhat bizarre vessel shapes and in the copper ornaments that the

Figure 6.27 *Typical Hopewell vessel from the Marksville works. Note roulette decorated area outlining design. Approximately one-half size. (After Setzler 1933)*

Hopewellian connections are obvious. Figure 6.28 shows the ceramic evidence. The sites themselves are nondescript shell-heaps with no hint of agriculture. Subsistence evidently continued to emphasize the sea and land mammal and the wild flora characteristic of earlier seacoast dwellers of the Archaic stage. (Thus, Prufer's ideas are supported by the Florida data.) All the Hopewell-tinged local cultures of the South—Marksville, Miller II, Copena, Hamilton, Swift Creek, Santa Rosa—seem to be later than the sites of the core Ohio Valley area. Caldwell (1958) explains the Hopewell spread as an expansion of a generalized northern Woodland tradition into the Middle Eastern tradition area of transitional Archaic, represented by the fabric-marked and check-stamped pottery complexes at such

sites as Baumer, Crab Orchard, Badin, Miller I, etc. (Figure 6.29). His scheme emphasizes the possibility of the local origins of Adena and Hopewell out of the Archaic, with little or no influence from the Mexican area.

One of the northern derivatives of Hopewell of interest to a few scholars is the anomalous Effigy Mound culture of Wisconsin, Illinois, and Iowa. The remains attract attention because of the range of animal forms represented by the low effigy mounds. There are sometimes burials at the "vital" points—hips, head, or heart area—of the animals, but there is only the simplest of grave goods. Burials are either flexed or bundle types. The link with Hopewell is found in ceramics and in the interest in raptors and certain mammals. At one group, Sny-Magill (now a national monument in Iowa), Beaubien (1953) thought two mounds of the group to be Hopewellian in construction and content. McKern has reported several sites of the Effigy culture (McKern 1928; 1930), as well as the Wisconsin Hopewell—locally called the Trempealeau (McKern 1931). Jennings (1965a) and Rowe (1956) have attempted summaries of the Effigy culture. The sites often lie on ridges overlooking a stream valley. The mounds take about a dozen shapes: conical, biconical, oval, linear, panther, bear, bird (goose, raptor), deer, buffalo(?), turtle, lizard, wolf or fox, and beaver. These are arranged in lines or clusters with no regularity as to the forms depicted; the linear and conical ones are mixed with the effigies. The groups may contain dozens of mounds. The Kletzien group had thirty-two; the Nitschke, sixty-two. Rowe argues that the entire enigmatic complex is a very limited local development on a simple Woodland base, thus tending to disallow significant Hopewell contact. Figure 6.30 shows the Nitschke group.

In New York, Ritchie (1965) identifies Hopewell in the artifacts and mounds of

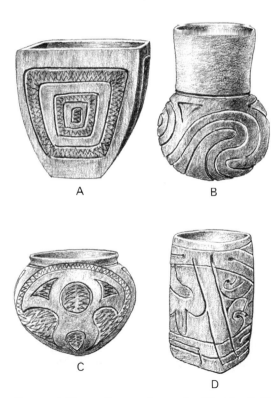

A B

C

D

Figure 6.28   *Pottery from the Florida Gulf Coast. A, C, Alligator Bayou Stamped, 15 and 5 inches high; B, D, Basin Bayou Incised, 6½ and 6 inches high. (After Willey 1949)*

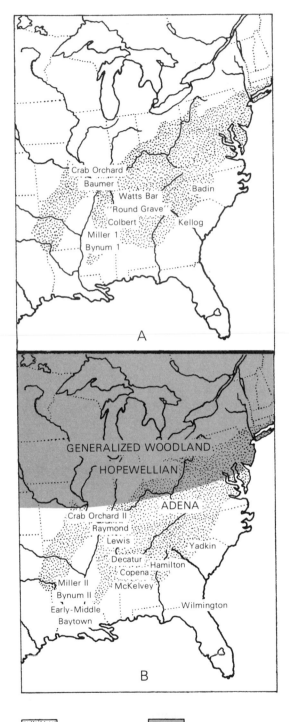

A

B

Deciduous forest

Northern tradition

the Squawkie Hill phase; earlier, he had incorporated this phase in his Point Peninsula culture series. Griffin (1964) also notes the Hopewellian content of the New York finds. Furthermore, he mentions the extension of dentate rocker stamping on pottery well beyond the appearance of other Hopewell traits and also comments on the blurring or fading of the Hopewell complex after about A.D. 250. This is about the time the southern derivatives began to appear and the cultures of the Middle West and East developed stronger regional differences, with many local sequences replacing the more uniform culture characteristic of Hopewell dominance. Even so, as in the widespread dentate pottery decoration, vestiges of Hopewell ancestry can be noted. In New York, for example, the development of late Point Peninsula into Owasco and even historic Iroquois can be tied through a few traits to Hopewell (Griffin 1964).

The Owasco culture of New York, accepted as being ancestral to the Iroquois, is dated at A.D. 1000 to 1300. Several sites have been studied, and it is certain that this late Woodland culture was diversified as to subsistence, with gardening being of some importance. Beans and corn have actually been recovered during excavation but not the cucurbits. Nonetheless, hunting and fishing and gathering continued to be important, as was true even into historic times among the Iroquois. The sites yield charred specimens of many fruit seeds and nuts—apple, cherry, plum, hickory nuts, hazelnuts, acorns, and others. Farming tools included elk-scapula hoes, as well as two types of flint hoe. Food-storage pits are common in some sites.

Several houses comprised the villages,

Figure 6.29   *A, principal foci of the Middle Eastern tradition. B, foci of northern affiliation in the area formerly occupied by the Middle Eastern tradition. (After Caldwell 1958)*

which were sometimes located on water courses or near tidal areas. In late Owasco times the settlements were not on waterways. The houses were made of flexible saplings set in the ground and brought together to a rounded roof. The covering was probably big sheets of elm bark. In form the houses vary, but at the Maxon-Derby and Bates sites the long, communal house is present. Others are rectangular or rounded. The material culture shows no great changes from earlier times except perhaps in the pipes, which are characteristically well made, usually of clay. The shape was similar to modern briars, except that the decorated bowl was usually set at an obtuse angle to the stem rather than at the more familiar right angle. The pottery was usually of the familiar Woodland shape, with more elaborate rim treatment.

By analogy with the descendent Iroquois culture [see Murdock's (1934) short account], it is possible to reconstruct somewhat the living culture of the Owasco. [The archeology of the Iroquois of New York is, of course, also understood (Ritchie 1965).] The Iroquois are thought of as probably the most advanced, politically and culturally, of the Northeastern Woodland tribes, possessing a remarkable representative form of tribal "government." The basis of the tribal and confederacy control was the matrilineal kinship system. The maternal lineage was the effective social unit on all levels. The long house, which a household of families of maternal kindred shared, was dominated by a female acknowledged to be the head of the household line. Husbands of women in the household lived with their wives in the long house but had no rights. Their children, however, were the lineage and belonged "to the house." The males' allegiance was to the lineage and household of their mothers. There were, however, male chiefs who represented households and villages in tribal affairs.

In day-to-day matters there was a strict division of labor, and this probably merely continued an earlier pattern. Men hunted and fished; made weapons and such items as canoes, paddles, snowshoes, bark barrels for food storage, and other wooden objects; built houses; assisted in clearing farm lands; and participated in the harvest. Of course, they were also warriors. Women did the gardening, cooking, caring for children, gathering of wild plant foods (roots, berries, fruits, nuts), made pottery, wove cloth, tailored clothing, and aided the men in some aspects of hunting.

In woodlands, the hunting of deer was usually through the stalking technique by a lone hunter. Stalking involved slow movement by the hunter behind cover (through a thicket or from one bush to another) until he was close enough to be certain he could mortally wound the animal. Often stalking was done with a decoy; a deer head with antlers covered the shoulders or was held in the hand of the bowman as he crept toward the quarry. With the decoy he imitated the movements of a browsing deer until he was close enough for the kill. Traps were of many kinds. The dead fall involved a heavy log which would fall and crush carnivores and bears as they dislodged it in taking a bait or tripping over a trigger string. Bent sapling snares with a looped cord, set in animal trails, were common; even deer and bear can be taken in such a trap. Small loop snares pegged to the ground in runways were used for lesser animals.

The list of wild foods taken is far longer than that recorded for the Owasco because the gathering was observed, rather than inferred from archeologic remains. Vegetables and fruits were dried; fish and venison were dried and smoked. The storage of surplus meat in pits was made possible by lining them with leather. Dried squash and pumpkin were stored in bark-lined pits. Maize was kept in bark barrels. From this wealth of food, a wide variety of tasty

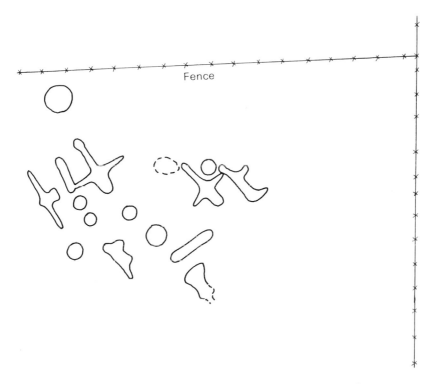

Fence

Figure 6.30   The Nitschke Mound group. Map insert at lower right shows distribution of Effigy Mound culture. (After McKern 1930)

dishes was cooked; many (such as corn bread, hominy, and succotash) are still common American foods. Maple syrup and sugar were important condiments. The Iroquois had a well-developed religion and much ritual, and a comparable development can be assumed for the earlier cultures. Through this brief excursion into the recorded lifeway of a historic tribe, one can look beyond the remains of an archeologic complex and glimpse the daily or even annual rounds of the people as they may have been. The arduous and constant toil required of the American Indian is implicit in the artifacts but can only be savored in an ethnographic account.

Just why the Hopewellian center of dominance shifted southward is unknown, but Griffin (1960a) suggests that it had to do with slight climatic deterioration

from about A.D. 200 to 700. There is no doubt that since A.D. 1 there have been two or three climatic episodes that have been reflected in cultural expansion or regression, especially in marginal areas (see Baerreis and Bryson 1965), and as study continues, it will be possible to see much more precise correlations of climate and culture history.

In general, it can be said that the Woodland tradition originated in the northern, essentially Great Lakes, area by about 1000 B.C. and moved through many transitional stages to climax via Adena into Hopewellian. By A.D. 500, its influence can be traced from the Plains to Nova Scotia, and its characteristic flavor is retained in some of the Northeastern cultures into historic times. Plains ceramics also show the Woodland-tradition effects until quite late in time. Even if Woodland traits can

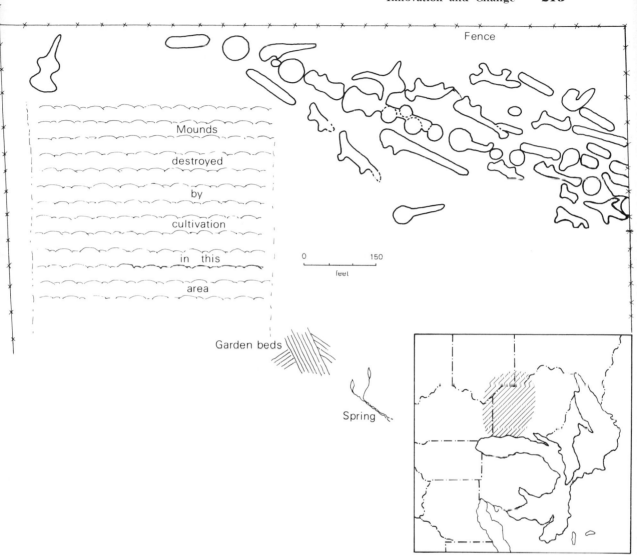

Mounds destroyed by cultivation in this area

Garden beds

Spring

Fence

0   150
feet

be recognized in certain recent tribal cultures, it is emphasized that these later manifestations were much enriched and modified by agriculture and other impulses coming out of the South by A.D. 800 or even earlier.

In the above accounts of Archaic and Woodland stages, no mention has been made of two discoveries in the Lower Mississippi Valley. One is the Jaketown site on the Yazoo River in west-central Mississippi (Ford, Phillips, and Haag 1955), and the other is the Poverty Point site in Louisiana (Ford and Webb 1956). The

Jaketown site was occupied because of an especially favorable location for more than 3,000 years, but the concern here is with its lower, Archaic-stage level. The Poverty Point site appears to have been occupied only during the Archaic stage, with radiocarbon dates covering a 1300 to 200 B.C. span. Both sites have a rich and standard Archaic complex of stone tools and show transition in the presence of conical burial mounds. Objects include tubular pipes of clay and stone; sandstone whetstones and saws; adzes; small celts; atlatl weights of several types; hematite plummets; steatite and sandstone vessels; numerous heavy, stemmed, and notched chipped points; and assorted scrapers. The unusual traits are the "Poverty Point objects" and an extensive microflint industry. The Poverty Point objects are nothing but clay masses of a unique sort. They are thought, on the basis of good evidence at Poverty Point, to have been used in "hot-stone" cookery in a land devoid of stones. The objects are made with no great care. A handful of plastic clay was merely formed into a ball of cylindrical or biconical shape in the hand or between cupped palms, and the object was complete. Finger marks made during the compression and shaping were not obliterated. The clay objects, which occur by the millions, were then fired to a bricklike hardness.

Even more unusual at the two sites was the microflint work. The industry involved the striking of long, prismatic flakes from egg-shaped flint nodules or cores in a manner reminiscent of Eurasiatic Mesolithic industries. From the flakes, perforators, end scrapers, side scrapers, and needles were made. The microflint industry in itself is not news; but to find it so early in the Lower Mississippi Valley is unexpected. The fine flake knives are typical of Ohio Hopewellian and certain arctic cultures (Denbigh) and are found over the Old World. Their occurrence in the American South is nowhere else reported.

The Poverty Point site is also characterized by a vast earthworks composed of five concentric ridges of octagonal shape covering so large an area that it was not recognized as artificial. There was also a possible bird-effigy mound at this site. The fill of the low ridges contains village-site debris, showing no lensing or loading. While the earthworks are reminiscent of Hopewell, they are older than the Ohio works and their relationship is unclear. In fact, the entire Poverty Point site defies acceptable placement in the larger framework of Southeastern prehistory, except

for its Archaic-stage ascription (Figure 6.31).

Without having solved the Poverty Point riddle, we shall move on to the later history of the Southeast. As the northern Hopewell climax passed and the Woodland cultures settled into a peripheral and tranquil mixed Archaic-Formative stage existence, the cultural initiative shifted to the middle reaches of the Mississippi Valley, apparently as a result of strong pulses of stimulus from Mexico upon the resident Woodland cultures.

Interesting as the Hopewellian complex of widespread, distinctive traits may be, there remain many problems of origin and relationship of even more interest for modern scholars. While many see Hopewell (as a cult) growing out of Adena (for example, Dragoo 1963, 1964), with the Adena origins in turn embedded in the Archaic culture (Ritchie 1965), there remains the problem of Hopewell's added flamboyance and rapid spread. And still unsettled is the argument as to whether the raptor, snake, death hand-eye, and other motifs in art or the copper earspools of cymbal type are indigenous or are derivative from Mexico in the centuries before Christ. The burial mound and the two-stage construction in Hopewellian, at least, can be viewed as indigenous to the northern area. With scholars now attacking the Hopewell problem anew (Caldwell and Hall 1964), the entire cultural contour of the Hopewell will soon be modeled in much sharper relief. In the meantime, it stands enigmatic save for its strength and potency in shaping all later Eastern cultures.

Mississippian

Hopewellian derivatives have been identified above as occurring in many parts of the South. The phenomenal southward spread of Hopewell assumes a new importance because a new, final, and the most

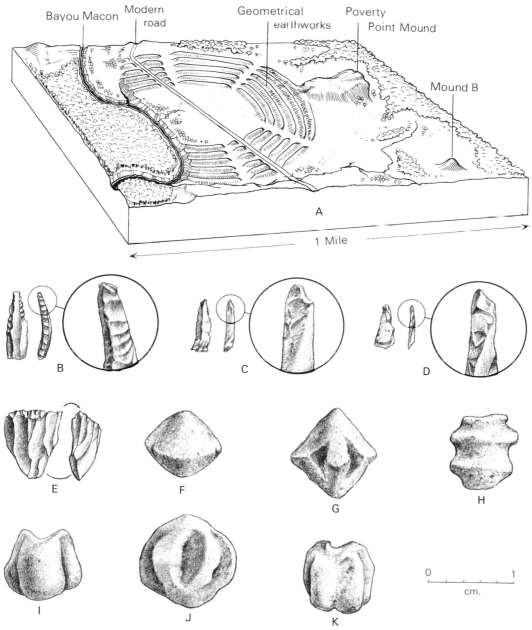

Figure 6.31   A, *relief map of the Poverty Point site. B, experimental "perforator" made and used to cut antler in a test to compare amount and type of wear with Poverty Point "perforators" (C, D); E, microflint core; F–K, common types of baked clay cooking balls. (After Ford and Webb 1956)*

colorful of all American cultures emerges from the southern Hopewell. The transition out of Marksville into something else begins as early as A.D. 400 (Greengo

1964) in western Mississippi in a local culture called Issaquena, named after a site in the Yazoo Basin. Apparently later than the Issaquena phase, the Troyville site (Walker 1936) in Louisiana is another derivative of the Marksville base; the Marksville origins are manifest in details of ceramics and the burial-mound complex. Both the Issaquena and Troyville local complexes are actually Marksville in transition to something else: This is the so-called "Mississippian" culture of the Southeast and Middle West, the dominant American culture from perhaps A.D. 500 to 600 to about A.D. 1650, with vestigial remnants observed and described by French explorers as late as A.D. 1700. In areal extent of influence, ceremonialism, public works, technology, population density, and general richness, the Mississippian is exceeded by no other aboriginal American culture north of Mexico.

Definition or description of the Mississippian in simple terms is impossible because it evolved through many steps in response to both cultural and natural stimuli. Because its evolutionary history is obscure in its details and the area where it "originated" not fully known, and because the extent to which its art is a legacy from the Mexican-influenced Hopewellian, as opposed to direct stimulus from the expanding Mexican civilization after Christ, is uncertain, it is again necessary first to describe the culture in general terms, citing important variances from the "average." Such an approach brings the specialist much anguish and for good reason. There are so many subtleties in every site, and the regional sequences differ so in detail as they vary in distance from the famous blackland delta of western Mississippi that any general account inevitably distorts or misrepresents through omission of relevant detail. But a start must be made somewhere.

In archeologic studies, the Middle Mississippian was first and only a label for a pottery tradition; it was established by Holmes (1903) in his monumental study of the original ceramics of eastern North America. Holmes' term was transferred to the entire culture; the modifying terms Upper and Lower were introduced, not to indicate chronology as an archeologist would expect, but to imply location on the Mississippi River. Actually, it would appear that the culture developed its identifying traits in the Lower and Middle Valley, so the modifiers also proved to have vague chronologic validity. At present, the single term "Mississippian," however ambiguous it may be, is used with occasional modifying references to an Early or Late or Mature phase.

Deuel (1937) listed the diagnostic traits of the Mississippian with simple brevity, but usage has reduced the determinant traits to: crushed shell-tempered pottery, tiny, triangular arrowheads, and the truncated pyramidal mound. Even this definition can be challenged because the pyramidal mound is found at many sites where the pottery is tempered with burned clay and where domed or conical burials are equally characteristic. But why quibble? Surely something can be said to beginning students about the Mississippian.

Despite the vast area where typical sites are found, they did not "cover Dixie like the dew." They are largely confined to the major river valleys of the area where fertile bottom lands, oft-flooded and renewed, made intensive horticulture possible. Our best authorities (Phillips, Ford, and Griffin 1951; Sears 1964) agree that the rich lands from St. Louis (Missouri) to Natchez (Mississippi) are the area of origin, and in this fertile land and its adjacent bluffs and terraces the sites are largest and most numerous (Figure 6.32). All recognize, however, that the Caddo area to the west and the Florida coast had influence upon, and were in turn influenced by, the growth in the central area.

The sheer size of the sites is overwhelming. All are characterized by clusters of mounds, some of which resemble truncated pyramids, arranged around a plaza (Figure 6.33). There may be conical mounds adjacent, but these are arranged

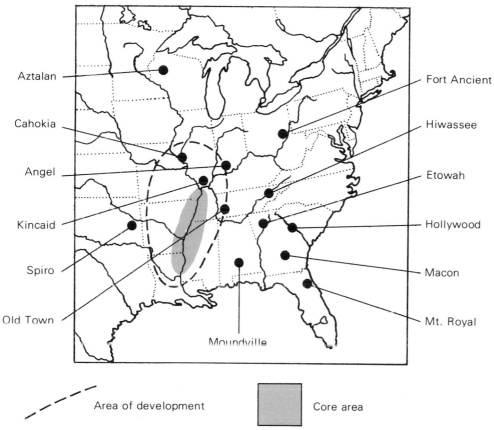

Figure 6.32   *Selected Mississippian sites and foci. Core area includes sites: St. Francis (Ark.), Lake George (Miss.), Greenwood (Miss.), Wycliffe (Ky.), Anna (Miss.), Grand Village of the Natchez (Miss.), Belcher (La.), Greenhouse (La.).*

in no apparent pattern. Many sites, even today after centuries of erosion, reveal an encircling embankment; outside the probably palisaded earthern embankment the borrow pit stood open as a moat at the foot of the earth and post barricade. Villages were not always nearby or inside the palisade. These huge sites must be thought of as being religious centers, such as are presaged in the Hopewellian and are common in Mexico and Central America; these centers were supported by a large dependent population providing both food and millions of man-hours of corvée labor for powerful priest-ruler and artisan governing classes. Sears (1964), as do others, thinks that these large, scattered centers

were coexistent with a "backwoods" population at a simple Woodland—even perhaps an Archaic—culture stage. Certainly there are many apparently contemporary sites untouched or unmarked by identifiable Mississippian influence.

The temple mounds are far more pretentious than the Hopewell burial mounds ever were. These pyramidal earthworks reached enormous size as one increment after another was added to quite sizable nuclei. As many as eight or ten construction phases have been identified in some of the mounds. The flat tops of the mounds supported temples or other structures built of wood and mud and thatch, usually in rectangular form. Exactly as in

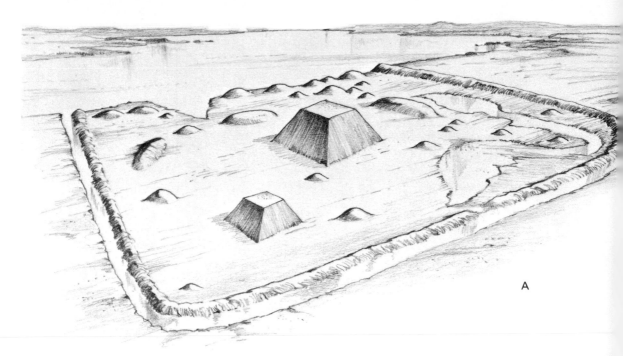

Figure 6.33   *Reconstructed Mississippian mound groups. A, Lake George in the flat "delta" near Holly Bluff, Miss.; B, Anna on the bluffs north of Natchez, Miss. At both sites, dominant pyramid is about sixty feet high. (After Griffin 1952a, Fig. 142–B, C)*

Mexico, the mounds were enlarged by periodic destruction of the temples and the addition of another layer or shell of earth over the entire pyramid, so that a larger, higher structure was created on the same spot to the same pattern. Thus, the larger mounds would resemble the Chinese egg, with each pyramid enveloping an earlier smaller one (Figure 6.34). The mounds, while primarily built to serve as temple bases, often contained burials of important dead accompanied by rich grave furnishings. Professional and layman alike are staggered by the size of the earthworks. The largest known temple mound is at Cahokia (Moorehead 1928; Kelly 1933) in American Bottoms near St. Louis. This artificial hill (Figure 6.35), standing 100 feet high, is 700 by 1,080 feet in basal dimension and covers an area of 16 acres! The major mound at Etowah (Moorehead et al. 1932) is over 60 feet

high and 330 by 380 feet at the base (Figure 6.43). Even at lesser sites a height of 40 to 50 feet for the dominant mound is common. The figure one computes for cubic feet of earth (22,000,000 for Cahokia, 4,300,000 for Etowah—each ounce carried on human backs), when transformed into man-hours, is awesome. Access to the steep-sided mounds was by means of almost equally steep, ramplike stairs into which log steps were sometimes laid. These ramps can still be seen on some of the late sites. Several important sites or portions of them have been preserved as national or state monuments— the Macon group, Etowah, Moundsville, Angel, and part of the Cahokia group are examples, and, as displayed, their evidence of lost glories is indeed eloquent.

Although none of the Mississippian sites has been completely excavated and analyzed in detail, partially because of their

B

great size and the costs of archeologic work, many have been sampled and thousands of beautiful ceramic pieces have been taken from the large cemeteries adjacent to the villages and from the burials of important dead interred through temple floors on the flat summits of the pyramids. Furthermore, each site is littered with broken pottery; tons of sherds have been collected and studied. As any monograph on the subject will demonstrate, we are in the position of knowing more about the minor art of ceramics than about the culture itself. Regional and local chronologies alike are built on pottery differences and likenesses. Sears (1964) lists several sequent ceramic traditions for the Southeast

and tells the entire story with its nuances of areal and regional interinfluence in ceramic terms, as Ford (1936) did in the first systematic study of what came to be called the Mississippian culture. But, restricted as we are in some degree to the ceramics, there are other archeologic data of considerable strength; moreover, the early European explorers saw and, as eyewitnesses, recorded the culture. Thus, we are able at times to infuse the dead evidence with life from ethnographic analogs.

Much is known of the subsistence and technology. Maize agriculture was evidently the base. Squash and beans and some now-wild species were also cultivated or collected. Deer was a major source of meat as well as of hide and bone for raw material. This is to say nothing of the bear, elk, and the same wide spectrum of lesser animals, preyed upon since the earliest Archaic stage, that continued to be important food sources. Freshwater shellfish and fish, especially the drum, were another steady source of protein. Because the sites lie open in an area of much vegetation and heavy rainfall, perishable materials have usually not survived the centuries of alternate wetting and drying unless they had been accidentally charred. So, although adequate evidence for basketry, matting, bark cloth, and skin utensils exists, the preponderance of artifacts is of bone, shell, antler, stone, and fired clay, with copper and other minerals sometimes found. The gardening was done with large hoes of chipped flint weighing several pounds. The shoulder blades of large mammals also made good hoes, as did large bivalve shells. Cutting tools were of fire-hardened cane and chipped stone, as were the hunting tools and weapons. The bow and arrow was the standard weapon; the arrows were tipped with small, triangular, notched chipped points or with bone or antler points. Fish were commonly taken on hooks of copper or bone, very probably on long setlines. A variety of chipped stone tools include knives (with wooden handles), scrapers of many types, drills, and other forms. Shell was used for beads of several types and for cups, hoes, bowls, and dippers; after being pulverized or crushed, it was also widely used as pottery aplastic when available. Ground stone specimens include pipes, celts, axes, adzes, and some millstones, although most milling was done with wooden mortars and pestles. Bone awls, needles, chisels, pins, and arrow wrenches were made in a bewildering variety of forms.

While the above items are relatively standard and resemble to some degree similar items from earlier Woodland cultures, it is in ceramics that diagnostic ma-

terials are especially to be found. Clay, being plastic, is completely responsive to the modeler's touch, and pottery can reveal rigid tradition, or equally easily, the passing whim of the artisan. Mississippian pottery is the most varied in form and decoration and the most sensitive reflector of changing style or other influence of any in America north of Mexico. The skilled potters turned out two general classes of pottery. Perhaps 95 percent was utilitarian. Almost always its surface was plain, although in some areas brushing, fabric imprinting, or even cord marking was practiced. The utilitarian wares were unpainted red or brown or gray, the color being merely a function of firing temperatures and the chemical content of the clay itself. Shell-tempering was also the dominant practice, but other aplastics are noted. One described type (here accepted as typical) is Neeleys Ferry Plain jars, with globular body and recurved rim and a vague shoulder as the most common shape. This vessel shape (Figure 6.36) is the "standard Mississippi jar" (Phillips, Ford, and Griffin 1951). Bowls and bottles are also standard and widespread (Figure 6.37).

There are many secondary features in some classes of the pottery. Loop and strap handles occur (twinned or arcaded). Flat lugs (which were handles), zoomorphic rim ornaments, and appliqued fillets to form conventional animal or human effigies are among the common adornments. The treatment of the plain clay surface is remarkably varied as well. Incising (sometimes engraving), trailing, punctation, or encrusting with clay fillets are among the techniques. Hatching and crosshatching, graceful, cursive, trailed designs, fluting, and zonal whorls and spirals are among the decorative motifs executed on the plastic surface. Many of the designs as well as the techniques themselves can be clearly traced back through the transitional stages —Troyville, Baytown, etc.—to Hopewell originals, although the vessel forms differ from the Woodland models.

The grave-furniture ceramics tend to include more decorated ware (as described above); the use of paint and negative paint is more common, and more effigy jars and bottles are found. As Figure 6.38 demonstrates, many of these pieces are extraordinary examples of ceramic art, whether judged on technologic or on aesthetic grounds. Generally, the Ohio Valley and the Tennessee-Cumberland Valleys provide the most exquisite sculptured effigy bottles, although many specimens are found in the Lower Mississippi Valley as well. In the same Tennessee region, where salt licks abound, the aboriginals manufactured salt in flat pans of very coarse, thick ware. These were always deeply marked with netlike fabric (Figure 6.39). This ware, too, was usually shell-tempered. The pottery skills of the Mississippian artisans were exceeded, it is true, by certain Late or Mature Mississippian Florida coast potters [for example, at Kolomoki, Georgia (Sears 1956)]. However, along with the work of the compulsive potters of the Southwest (being done at about the same time), the thousands of extant Mississippian vessels comprise a rich heritage of aboriginal American art. Mississippian decorative techniques had little influence on the pottery of the extreme Southeast in coastal South Carolina and most of Georgia. There the carved-paddle stamping which began in an Archaic context persisted until the advent of the white man. For the ceramic sequences of the Southeast, Sears (1956, 1964) and Caldwell and McCann (1941) are excellent guides.

The potters were only one part of the artisan group. Engraved and carved shell was used as ornaments and pendants; knobbed hairpins from the columella of conch and beads of tubular, disc, and globular shapes were in great demand and other ornaments were common. From cop-

per, imported from Lake Superior or produced locally in northern Georgia, bracelets, beads, headdresses, and a few awls were made. All attest the presence of craftsmen skilled in other media.

Turning from artifacts to other technology, there are reliable data on architecture. From many reports we know that the Mississippian houses, as well as the temples and council chambers, were soundly built of wood, often with sturdy, vertical, wattled (woven) walls and probably gabled roofs of rafter and thatch. Often the wattled timber elements (flexible canes or withes threaded between, or tied to, posts up to 6 inches in diameter) were plastered with mud inside and out to make a thick, impervious wall, but one that required frequent repair. Posts were set and often wedged in narrow trenches up to 18 inches deep or set in deep individual postholes. Although almost every house shape—square, rectangular, rectangular with rounded corners, oval, and circular—has been found and reported in the literature, most seem to have been square or rectangular. Lewis and Kneberg (1946) show a construction of a vertical-walled post structure with the flexible tips of the posts woven together to make the roof; the result is a loaf-shaped structure resembling the old-fashioned, round-topped trunk. It was probably covered with bark or mats and resembled a wigwam.

Inside the dwellings there was a more or less centrally located fireplace or hearth. This was a shallow pit or basin with a raised, modeled ring of clay which baked to bricklike hardness through use. Often the floor was of specially selected clay, "puddled," or thoroughly wetted and packed down, so that it was exceedingly hard and durable. In some houses (for example, W. S. Webb 1939), raised platforms called "altars" were built along the wall opposite the entrance. Temples or chiefs' houses atop the mounds show about the same interior features, but we

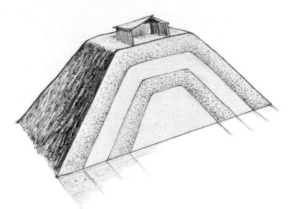

Figure 6.34   *Diagrammatic cross section of an idealized pyramidal mound revealing the construction stages.*

know from sixteenth and seventeenth century accounts that these more special structures had effigy and other adornments on the roof. All in all, the recent literature is of good quality, and the student wishing to specialize in the Southeast

as an area of serious study will find it a stimulating, if still incompletely understood, sequence of cultures, with the Mississippian merely the overwhelming end product of a long process of interaction and interinfluence between the several local cultures.

The Mississippian experienced a particularly vivid climax so far as the cult centers were concerned. The huge sites of the Mature aspects of the culture are characterized less by a conformity of ceramics to definition than by a uniformity of certain other artifacts. Together, these artifacts may testify, after the appearance of the pyramidal mounds, to another thrust of ideas (and artifact design) from Mexico. The cult is referred to as the "Southern Cult," the "Southern Death Cult," or even the "Buzzard Cult." It seems to be almost entirely concerned with death and death symbols. Cult centers are not always typically Mississippian (which is

Figure 6.35   *Cahokia "Monks Mound" (St. Louis, Mo.) with human figure on first level for scale. (After Grimm 1950)*

0   6 in.

Figure 6.36   *Neeleys Ferry Plain jars from Mississippi. (After Phillips, Ford, and Griffin 1951)*

not surprising in view of the lack of a firm definition of what is fully "typical"), but they share the cult complex. The objects are made of copper, shell, polished stone, and some are even of clay. The ceremonial artifacts include copper headdresses, earspools, plaques, celts, and objects of unknown use. From Gulf shell were fashioned large, engraved gorgets, plaques, and pins. Elaborate, well-sculptured stone pipes emphasizing human and animal forms, monolithic axes replicating the stone celt with wooden handle, and round stone plaques are frequent. The motifs include both the raptor and the vulture, the feathered rattlesnake, and a variety of death symbols—the hand-eye, the skull, and the long bone—in many variations. The winged warrior, the spider, the weeping eye, the sun symbol, and many others

are found in every medium. Large, eccentrically shaped blades of skillfully chipped flint are standard cult items. The representations of human sacrifice in pipe sculpture, the daggers in the hands of some of the bird-man warriors or priests, and many of the symbols bespeak a ritual of human sacrifice. Obviously, many of these artifacts and motifs are not new in the South. Some are a legacy from Hopewell and even Adena, as W. S. Webb and Baby (1957) have made clear. On the other hand, the shift to the buzzard and death motif is interpreted by some as evidence of recent strong Mexican cultism, even perhaps of an increment of high-ranking individuals into the South. Others defend it as a climax phenomenon, developed autonomously *in situ* out of the ceremonialism already evident to the north

Figure 6.37   *Mississippian bowls and bottles. A, Neeleys Ferry Plain Bowl; B, C, Bell Plain bowls; D, Old Town Red bowl; E, F, Neeleys Ferry Plain bird-effigy bowls; G, Bell Plain effigy bowl; H, I, Bell Plain human-effigy bowls; J, K, M, Neeleys Ferry Plain bottles; L, Neeleys Ferry or Bell Plain bottle with perforated base. (After Phillips, Ford, and Griffin 1951)*

Figure 6.38   *Mississippian pottery. A–E, variants of Walls Engraved bottles; F–H, Bell Plain frog-effigy vessels; I, Nodena Red and White double bottle; J, Nodena Red and White hooded owl-effigy bottle; K, Bell Plain or Neeleys Ferry stirrup-necked bottle; L, Bell Plain human-effigy bottle; M, N, Bell Plain double bottles; O, Bell Plain modified stirrup-necked bottle; P, Neeleys Ferry Plain double bottle; Q–R, Bell Plain tripod bottles; S, tripod bottle. (After Phillips, Ford, and Griffin 1951)*

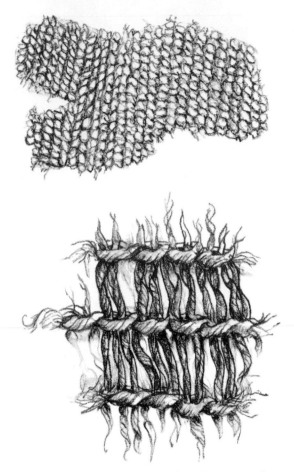

Figure 6.39   *Two examples of twining derived from fabric impressions on Mississippian thick ware. (After Cole et al. 1951)*

there are the famous ceremonial chambers, the one with a "buzzard" altar being unique. Fairbanks (1946) refers to the effigy altar as an eagle, but several "eagle" effigies are strangely vulturelike in outline (for example, the stone mound at Eaton-ton, Georgia, which may not be valid evidence because it has been reconstructed). The several adequately reported Mississippian sites include the Davis site in Texas (Newell and Krieger 1949), Hiwassee Island, Tennessee (Lewis and Kneberg 1946), and Belcher, Louisiana (C. H. Webb 1959); any of these reports is recommended. Kolomoki, Georgia (Sears, various) is also a very interesting site. The stratified Irene site (Caldwell and McMann 1941) on the Georgia coast showed successive building stages for a temple mound, a burial mound, a mortuary–charnel house complex, and a series of palisades. The Irene pottery, all plain or carved-paddle-stamped, is sand- or grit-tempered.

Even in its final stages of decay in the face of European pressures (and donated diseases such as measles, tuberculosis, and the common cold), the bloody strength of Mississippian ritual can be seen in the burial ceremony for the Natchez warrior Tattooed-serpent reported in 1725 with unnerving realism by Du Pratz (in Swanton 1911, pages 144–149; Jennings and Hoebel 1966, pages 232–237, see also below).

Although the above paragraphs and figures can convey an idea of a generalized Mississippian, the shortcomings of this account are legion. No mention, save of scattered sites, has been made of the "Caddo" area of Louisiana, Texas, and Oklahoma, nor has sufficient attention been given to the several Tennessee-Cumberland locations, the Ohio River sites (Kincaid, Angel, and Ft. Ancient), Cahokia itself, or Aztalan. Sears (1964), as well as Caldwell (1958) and the several participants in the Fifth Caddo Conference (T. N. Campbell 1961), all deal with

for some 2,000 years. The debate can't be settled here, although the complete *in situ* development of the cult from an older base is not a generally accepted idea. Figures 6.40 and 6.41 exemplify some of the common cult objects and motifs.

Moundville (Alabama) is one of the famous centers; its mound arrangement and a few of its more famous cult objects are shown in Figure 6.42. Etowah (Georgia) is an equally renowned location. Details of its site and some of its special pieces are presented in Figure 6.43. Note the similarities between Spiro and Etowah axes and macelike artifacts. At Macon (Georgia), which is not a cult center, the complex and unresolved problems of relationships between the several regional Mississippian variants, as well as to the contiguous but non-Mississippian cultures fringing the central area. Nor has any emphasis been placed on the suspicion that the Mature Mississippian sites are probably identifiable with one or more historic tribes. Lewis and Kneberg are convinced that the Dallas focus of Tennessee was the work of the Creek, while the later Mouse Creek focus blends into historic Cherokee, as do the terminal stages of the Etowah-North Georgia sequence. Because there is not space to attempt summaries of the detailed analyses of the ceramic materials and the thoughts of scholars about inter- and intra-areal contacts and sequence, Figure 6.44, modified from Sears (1956), is provided to give a correlation of the named periods recognized over the Southeast area. When the student moves from this account to the detailed literature, he will need to know the several regionally named sequences and how they correlate culturally.

After restudying the output of regional scholars since 1950, I suspect that the term "Mississippian" may have outlived its usefulness. Regional knowledge has progressed so far—much of the study has been of ceramics, it's true—that the term is reduced to an identifying label, useful in pedagogy but not very representative of scholarly concept. Within a few years some specialist will write of southern cultural traditions (not necessarily ceramic) and, by relating these to each other, will redefine or recast and rename the so-called Mississippian. The classification of Temple Mound I and II stages or periods introduced by Ford and Willey (1941) may yet prove to be the best unifying device. So far, Griffin (1967) has treated the problem the most realistically by showing several local subtraditions, such as Caddo, Oneota, Fort Ancient, and South Appalachian.

At the height of its strength, the Mature Mississippian center would have been ex-

citing to visit. The tall mounds towering above the flat river valley, with thatched temples adding several feet of height to the pyramids, would have been visible above the palisade for many miles as one approached along well-worn trails past extensive fields. Carved effigies of birds and other creatures perched on the rounded temple roofs or ridge poles would have given added color, while from each temple there drifted the smoke of an eternal fire. At sunup the priests, in rich regalia and ornaments of copper, shell, and feathers, would offer prayers and greetings to the Sun, calling his blessings on the land.

On festive or ritual days the plaza would be the scene of fiercely fought handball games or complicated dances done to the rhythm of drums and rattles, accompanied by many singers. Dancers, too, would be colorfully dressed in rich costumes and ornaments. The Creek Busk or Green Corn festival of thanksgiving, held on the dance ground even into the twentieth century, probably preserves a faded vestige of the Mississippian splendor. Some of the rituals would have involved purification and long-drawn-out ceremonies of human sacrifice to one or another god, while the people from all supporting villages crowded the plaza to watch the dancers and priests go in procession up the steep stairways to the summit of the mound, where the sacrificial climax was reached.

At other times, the scene at the plaza would involve the death and burial of a priest-ruler. These rituals also involved many days of prescribed processions, feasts, and sacrifice. In the early eighteenth century the French saw and reported a Natchez chieftain's death. The mourning ceremony for the chieftain, Tattooed-serpent, lasted for several days and involved all the Natchez villages. As part of the burial ceremony, the dead man's two wives, his "speaker," his doctor, his head servant, and his pipe bearer were ritually strangled. In addition, several old women who, for one reason or another,

Figure 6.40 *Artifacts from Spiro Mound. Variable scale. A,
shell-inlaid mask of red cedar, 11⅜ inches high; B, monolithic
stone ax, 5½ inches long; C, hafted copper ax, 13 inches long
(pileated woodpecker effigy, shell-inlaid eye); D, turtle-effigy rattle
of red cedar, 6⅞ inches long; E, front and side views of human-
sacrifice clay effigy pipe, 9¾ inches high; F, chipped stone mace,
20 inches long; G, polished stone mace, 13¾ inches long; H,
polished stone spuds, longest is 23 inches; I, human effigy of red
cedar, 11¼ inches high; J, composite animal-bird stone effigy
pipe, 2 inches long at base; K, stone effigy pipe, 9⅞ inches high
(woman with mortar and ear of corn). (After Hamilton 1952)*

had offered their lives, were also strangled. The two wives were buried with Tattooed-serpent in the temple, his speaker and one of the women in front of the temple, and the others were carried to their respective village temples for burial. Then, as was customary, Tattooed-serpent's house was burned. The burial of personages within and near the temple and the subsequent destruction by intentional firing are well-attested archeologically. Had not the Natchez culture been weakened and declining, the next event would probably have been the enlargement of the mound and the building of a new temple.

At intervals there would have been a company of impressed laborers in the plaza engaged in repairing or remodeling the mounds, the plaza, and the priests' dwellings. On rare occasions there would perhaps have been a market where traders bartered with the farmers for local goods in exchange for imported goods. Outside the ceremonial center there would have been extensive fields and many scattered settlements of a few houses each. The fields of maize would have been tended by the women, while the men hunted or conducted raids or manufactured the tools, weapons, utensils, and ornaments. The women probably made the pottery, wove mats and cloth, made moccasins and clothing from deer hides they had tanned, and tended their homes and children in a life of never-ending toil. Except for the frequent ceremonies, festivals, and market days, the daily round of labor for both sexes would have been continuous and arduous and of much the same pattern as reported by the ethnographers Swanton (1911) for the Natchez and Stern (1965) for both the Creek and the Natchez.

The Plains

Because the Plains cultures are also based on both hunting and horticulture, they are included here with the Eastern farmers. A more important reason for their inclusion, however, is that after the Lithic stage the Central Plains story is later than, and a function of, whatever was going on in the fertile, well-watered valleys of the Middle West. This section, moreover, will be short because there is available in W. R. Wedel's (1961) summary one of the few adequate regional syntheses. In most ways, this account will follow his views.

Earlier, Strong (1935) had offered a brilliant synthesis which was the standard until Wedel's summary appeared. Although Strong was able to put the findings of both amateur and professional students into a coherent account, his data were terribly uneven and spotty because of limited research over the vast territory. Jennings (1955) prepared a short, systematic summary, incorporating much new information. This was followed by Wedel's more detailed account, which is based on even more abundant data recovered through the Missouri River Basin Archeological Survey program.

Eastern influences upon the Plains began during the Archaic stage, but by about the time of Christ, the Woodland had diffused into the quite different world of the Plains. The Plains environment has been variously described as "hell on earth" or "not fit for humans." Theodore Roosevelt noted that it was "hard on women and horses." As opposed to the Woodland environment, it is described by W. P. Webb (1931) as ". . . a land of low relief, few trees and little rainfall—of sun and wind and grass." He even goes on to say that there is not so much a Plains *area* as a Plains *environment*. His classic book, dealing with recent American conquest of the Plains, is a gripping adventure story as well as one full of imaginative scholarship. Jennings (1955) has described the Plains thus:

The Plains then is that broad wedge-shaped zone of westward gradation from the fertile well-watered Middle West unto the mountains and deserts of the West. It can be de-

Figure 6.41 *Artifacts from Spiro and Etowah mounds. Variable scale. A, embossed sheet-copper eagle, 11½ inches high; B, embossed sheet-copper human head; C, copper covered earspools; D, embossed sheet-copper feather; E, embossed sheet-copper snake; F, shell gorget of hand symbol, 3⅜ inches high; G, embossed sheet-copper design; H, shell gorget of world symbol with woodpeckers; I, shell design of animal snakes representing world symbol, 8 inches in diameter; J, shell design of two snake dancers, 12⅜ inches long; K, embossed sheet-copper design of dancer wearing eagle paraphernalia, 20 inches long; L, sheet-copper symbol. (A–G, I, J after Hamilton 1952; H, K, L after Willoughby 1932)*

fined on the basis of physiography, geography, climate, vegetation, soil, economy, or many another basis. Figure [6.45] shows a vague "average" Plains region, with the Missouri River Basin superimposed. It is emphasized that this arbitrary set of lines will not now, nor has it ever, offered any barrier to climate or culture. Even as vegetative and climatic zones shift constantly, so will the Plains "environment" shift. The Plains, however, by any definition, falls within the states of Montana, Wyoming, Colorado, New Mexico, Texas, Oklahoma, Kansas, Nebraska, South Dakota, and North Dakota, and parts of the western provinces of Canada.

As for the Missouri River Basin, it comprises better than one-half the Plains area shown in Figure [6.45], in Canada, Montana, Wyoming, Colorado, North and South Dakota, Nebraska, Kansas, Iowa, and Missouri. . . . The Missouri and its hundreds of tributaries spread like the ribs of a giant fan across more than half a million square miles of continental United States. The . . . romantic river and the diversified territory it drains have been described by W. R. Wedel (1947) as ". . . a territory of nearly 530,000 square miles approximately one-sixth the area of the continental United States. . . . The Missouri River itself, from its source at Three Forks, Montana, flows 2,500 miles in a general easterly and southerly direction. . . . The Missouri Basin rises in altitude from about 400 feet above sea level at the mouth of the Missouri to the 10,000- to 14,000-foot snow-capped summits of the continental divide in Montana and Colorado. The watershed consists largely of plains, but in south-central Missouri, in western South Dakota, along the easterly slopes of the Rockies, and elsewhere there are rugged areas of considerable extent. Annual precipitation ranges from 40 inches at the mouth of the Missouri to less than 10 inches in parts of Wyoming and Montana. . . . Native vegetation consists of oak-hickory hardwood forests in the extreme southeast, successively replaced toward the west by tall-grass prairie, shortgrass plains, the sagebrush and desert scrub of Wyoming, and finally the western pine forests of the Rocky Mountains. . . ."

These Plains were long regarded as desert. Even the well informed American does not usually realize that the Plains region, though monotonously level, was not and is not even today, a hostile land. The vast elevated grasslands are veined and broken by a thousand living streams. Immediately over the brink of the deep-cut watercourses the sea of grass

gives over to trees, matted shrubbery, and small meadows. The dual environment—the grassy uplands and the ribbony woodland zones of the countless streams and valleys—provides natural floral and faunal resources of great variety. The variety increased when horticulture came into use by the Plains tribes, and the rich [alluvium of the river bottoms] provided optimum gardening conditions. . . .

[It is well] . . . to remember . . . the wide climatic fluctuation for which the Plains are notorious. The fundamental effects of varying rainfall upon the population of the Plains in the past century were also critically important in the centuries before white men settled the country. There are tree ring records from North Dakota back to A.D. 1406 showing several drouth periods lasting as long as 26 years alternating with long periods of high moisture (Will 1946). Other scanty data show that in western Nebraska the wet-dry cycle was operative before A.D. 1200 (Weakly 1943; W. R. Wedel 1941; Champe 1946). In both of these areas, however, trees survived, so we cannot assume complete desiccation. The Indian technique of farming along the streams and in sheltered valleys must certainly have made their crops less vulnerable to slight climatic variations, or stored surplus might carry them through one or even two crop failures, but the general regional desiccation and erosion resulting from a long drouth would inevitably have decreased crop yield, in addition to causing a sharp decline in the amount of game available because of grass and water shortage (W. R. Wedel 1953). Weakly (1943), for example, tells us that some trees die if moisture is greatly below normal for as little as five years. . . .

At the outset we can recognize the well-established, horticulture-based villages (known from ethnologic accounts such as from Lewis and Clark's visit to the Mandan villages in 1805) as having about a thousand years' span. Cultures varied in detail over the vast area, but in architecture and ceramics they show a Woodland origin, heavily (and early) tinged with Mississippian influences. The earliest Woodland appears to have been the Hopewellian settlement near Kansas City. According to the radiocarbon findings, this village is no older than the Christian era. It is de-

Figure 6.42 *Moundville and associated artifacts. A, reconstruction of site, square pyramid at upper left is almost 60 feet high; B, stone pendant; C, ceremonial disc; D, pottery beaker; E, frog effigy pot; F, G, incised pottery. Artifacts are variable scale. (After Alabama Museum of Natural History 1942)*

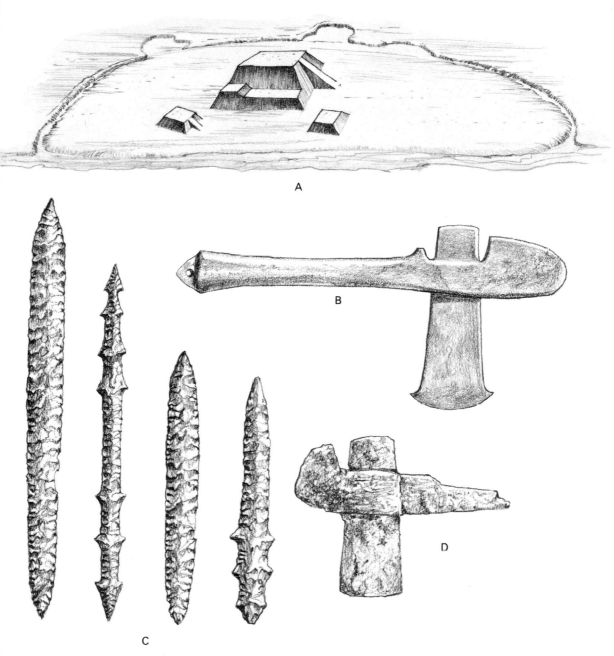

A

B

C

D

Figure 6.43   *Etowah (Georgia) and associated artifacts. A, reconstruction of site with human figure at foot of ramp for scale; B, monolithic stone ax; C, problematical flint forms; D, copper ax head with handle fragment. Artifacts are variable scale. (A after Willoughby 1932; B–D after Moorehead 1932)*

rived from the Illinois Hopewell and lacks the gaudy goods of the classic Ohio version. Further west, in the Central Plains area, three nearly contemporary Woodland complexes have been segregated. The oldest is the Valley focus, followed by the Keith and Loseke Creek foci. They span a period from A.D. 1 to perhaps A.D. 700.

None are spectacular, but all seem to have been slightly touched by Hopewell influence. Kivett (1953) sees some evidence of this in the Valley focus ceramics. Using the Valley material as being typical of the early Plains manifestation of the Woodland, we find the sites to be located on lower terraces beside the minor streams. These appear to have been semipermanent, even seasonal camps. They are small, with shallow deposits and a limited inventory of artifacts. Gardening is by no means proved, but a few corn kernels were found at the type site in Nebraska. Most foods appear to have been wild plants; game animals taken included bison, beaver, deer, badger, and various rodents. Handicrafts were simple. Bone was used for awls, fleshers, or scrapers (for removing flesh from hides) and for beads. Chipping of flint was carelessly done; the usual form was a large, triangular, knife blade or projectile point. Scrapers, ovoid with a steep bit, were also common; probably these were set in a bone or wooden handle. Occasionally a grooved ax occurs.

Pottery, while distinctive, is more durable than beautiful (Figure 6.46). The shape was the familiar Woodland elongated body with a conoidal base, the faint shoulder bulging slightly low on the vessel from a large but constricted mouth. The paste contained sand, grit, or crushed calcite temper, and the vessels were formed by paddling the exterior against the hand used inside as an anvil. The exterior was roughened by the use of a cord-wrapped paddle. While the cord impressions were sometimes irregular or crisscrossed, a pleasing spiral design was also often used. Kivett (1949b) regards this pottery, called Valley Cord Roughened, as the typical and earliest of Plains ceramics. Its distribution is quite wide over the Central Plains. Houses are not well understood. Apparently they were shallow pits over which there may have stood a wooden framework, supporting a hide cover (A. T. Hill and Kivett 1940). The shallow basins representing these houses have a simple central basin for fire, and the floors show scattered postholes for the supporting structures.

Whether the spread of the Woodland and its pottery and the beginnings of horticulture over the Plains are to be seen as representing increasing population pressures in the East or whether a climatic cycle more favorable to gardening was beginning can't yet be known. The important historical fact, however, is that by A.D. 200 to 300 the transition from Archaic toward the horticulture of the Formative was about complete from the Rockies eastward, wherever the cultigens could grow; within only a few centuries, in response to continued stimulus from the East, all the Central Plains states were populated by farmers dwelling in permanent villages. While production of food may have been the key to village prosperity and the population increase, subsistence continued to be drawn equally from the wild species and the cultigens. Probably the richness of the wildlife resources made dependence on this source greater than on the gardens. It is to the gardening cultures of A.D. 700 and later that we now turn.

Apparently the Plains farmers first got the strong thrust of advanced "eastern," that is, Mississippian, ideas in the Middle Missouri area, probably from the "Old Village" level at Cahokia near St. Louis. At least, the strong infusion of architectural styles, ceramics, and cultigens resembles the Old Village pattern. But the temple pyramids and flamboyant art did not appeal to the Plainsmen, so the remains continue to show the drabness of the local Woodland with which the eastern ideas blended. W. R. Wedel (1961) divides the Plains region into five natural areas. These are the Northwestern, Central

Figure 6.44   *Ceramic complexes (and cultures) of the Southeast. (Modified from Sears 1956)*

Region	Cultural sequence (Late → Early)
Texas, La. and Okla.	Fulton aspect; Spiro; Davis-Gahagan
St. Johns	Seminole; Spanish Indian; St. Johns IIc; St. Johns IIb; St. Johns IIa; St. Johns Ib; St. Johns Ia Late; St. Johns Ia Early; Orange
Central Gulf Coast	Seminole; Safety Harbor; Tampa focus; Weeden Island II; Weeden Island I; Perico Island / Santa Rosa-Swift Creek; Deptford; Orange
East Tennessee	Mouse Creek; Dallas; Hiwassee Island; Hamilton; Candy Creek
North Georgia	Cherokee / Lamar; Wilbanks; Etowah I-IV; Woodstock; Napier; Deptford; Fabric marked complex
Savannah Area	?; Spanish Indian; ?; Irene; Savannah; Wilmington; Deptford; Stallings fiber temper
Central Georgia	Creek; Lamar; ?; Macon Plateau; Swift Creek II; Early Swift Creek; Deptford; Fabric marked complex
Kolomoki N. W. Florida	Creek; Lamar; Fort Walton; ?; Kolomoki; Weeden Island Ib; Weeden Island Ia; Santa Rosa-Swift Creek; Deptford; Plain fiber temper
Central Valley	Late Mississippi; Early Mississippi; Late Baytown; Middle Baytown; Early Baytown; Tchula
Lower Valley	Natchez; Plaquemine; Coles Creek; Troyville; Marksville; Tchefuncte

Late — Early

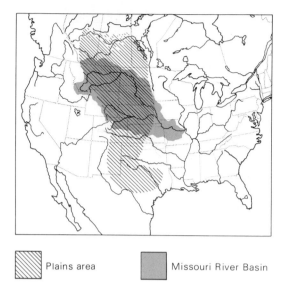

Plains area   Missouri River Basin

Figure 6.45   *Traditional Plains area in re-lation to the Missouri River Basin.* ·

and Southern Plains, the Middle Missouri, and the Northeastern Periphery (Figure 6.47). From all these there are good areal sequences, many named cultures, and some actual, reliable chronology from radiocarbon. Although the Southern, Central, and Northeastern Periphery areas had been studied before the 1930s, the Middle Missouri has been understood only since the emergency work began in 1945. Lehmer (1954a, 1954b) distinguished and described the Middle Missouri area and made an important contribution by pointing out that the early areal distinctions tended to level out by perhaps A.D. 1400 and the cultures of the Plains tended to be more uniform thereafter; this stage of uniformity he called the Coalescent Tradition.

In order to grow corn and beans in the harsh Plains environment, the Plains villagers first had to develop special strains. This may have been deliberate selection by each group, or the plants may have adapted naturally as the concept of horticulture was carried more and more northward. The maize of the Plains was a tough, hardy, dent variety which matured in the short growing season of about 100

days. The cold-resistant, quick-maturing corn that developed from the original, tropical maize is the key to Middle Missouri culture. In a sense, the culture testifies, again, to the genetic flexibility and adaptability of maize itself. Corn farming with these hardy strains is possible almost to the Canadian border. Special resistant strains of beans also developed; the famous Great Northern bean is a historic Mandan variety. (Before 1900, a Mandan (?) Indian gave a handful to a George Will, who operated a seed business in Bismarck, North Dakota. Will discovered that they were hardier and more prolific than any variety then known, and he introduced them to commercial growers; they are now a major commercial crop.) Plains gardening was done in the fertile and easily worked silts of the stream valleys. Probably the work was done by women, as in historic times. The primary tool was the bison scapula, which makes an ideal

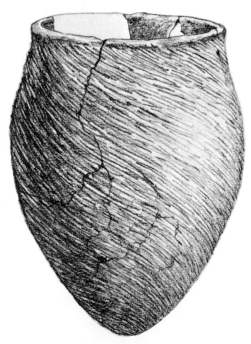

Figure 6.46   *Typical example of Central Plains, Valley focus Woodland pottery. One-third size (After Kivett 1949b)*

hoe when lashed to a handle made from a strong, forked stick. The crops, when harvested, were stored in deep, bell-shaped, cache or storage pits that would hold several bushels. Some were as large as 5 to 6 feet in diameter and equally as deep.

The most distinctive aspect of the Plains culture is the houses. All over the Plains the first houses were rectangular with a narrow entryway. A simple central fire basin was surrounded by four posts set at the corners of an imaginary square; smaller vertical posts formed the low walls. Both the central posts and the wall posts supported plates for the sloping rafters that were laid from the walls to the central framework. The wall and roof covering was of branches or grass over which dirt or sod was placed. The houses were built sometimes in shallow basins or in pits up to 3 or more feet deep. The houses were scattered hither and yon in a loose, unstructured village, located on stream terraces. Kivett (1949a) entirely excavated an Upper Republican village on Medicine Creek which shows the typical random placement of houses very well. In fact, his description is an apt summary of the Upper Republican culture of the western Central Plains.

Returning to the Middle Missouri area, found along the Missouri River from just north of Yankton, South Dakota, to Bismarck, North Dakota, we rely primarily on Lehmer's (various) statements. During excavations at now-inundated sites in the Oahe Reservoir, where the massive earthen dam now stands, he was able to discover the key to a local sequence of village cultures about a thousand years old and extending up to historic times. The key lay at the Dodd site, a complex, stratified location where there had been at least three periods of occupancy. The earliest level, called the Monroe focus, was characterized by distinctive rectangular houses with vertical wall posts in a straight line, with three center supports (for gabled roofs, as

sometimes in the Mississippian) and a fireplace toward the narrow entry ramp. The entry ramp sloped down to meet the sunken floor of the lodge. A striking fact about the Monroe villages was their compactness, with houses more or less aligned along vaguely defined "streets." Houses were located uniformly with the long axis oriented southwest-northeast and the entryway toward the southwest. Artifacts of bone included scapula knives, bison-rib scraper handles, bison–shoulder-blade hoes, and horn scoops or spoons. Chipped stone was represented by small, side-notched projectile points, a vaguely lunate knife, and end scrapers. The grooved maul and grooved arrow-shaft smoother of sandstone were apparently in use too. The major difference from a Woodland artifact assemblage was in the pottery. Although still cord-roughened, it was of better quality, more abundant, and of different form. The basic shape is the globular jar, widemouthed with an everted rim (S-shaped in cross section) and a well-defined

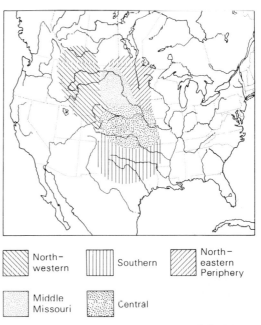

North-western

Southern

North-eastern Periphery

Middle Missouri

Central

Figure 6.47   *Plains regions. (Modified from W. R. Wedel 1961)*

neck above rounded shoulders. There may be strap handles as well. Incised lines occur on the rims, but the rest of the body is cord-paddled.

The Anderson focus, next later than Monroe, is characterized by the same large, rectangular houses, but the details of wall construction differ somewhat. Artifacts are about the same, with one or two additions, including the bone hide flesher or scraper made from the sturdy metapodial of bison (Figure 6.48). Next in time came the Thomas Riggs focus, with rectangular houses and about the same inventory of artifacts.

Later foci include the LaRoche and Stanley, the latter falling within the earliest European contact period. These latter foci showed the round house with an extended entryway. These houses possess, like the Upper Republican houses, the four strong central support posts around the fireplace and were presumably built to a similar design. Portions of the Middle Missouri sequence outlined here have been observed at several stratified sites. One very good example is the Fire Heart Creek location (Lehmer 1966), where the rectangular-to-round house sequence was again observed, and the slight artifact style changes were repeated. In general, the artifact inventory remained quite stable because the tools required to maintain the lifeway remained the same. The many differences from area to area that the specialists can distinguish are in the details. For example, the scapula hoe is found all through the Plains village gardening cultures, but the treatment differed over space and through time. In the Monroe and Anderson foci the glenoid fossa was left on and the scapular spine and the ridge on the posterior border were removed. In the Stanley focus sites the glenoid fossa has been cut away entirely. Similarly, some of the split or beveled bone fleshers are finished with carefully

cut teeth, whereas others have a smooth, chisel-like scraping edge. In the same way, ceramic features in other areas vary from those of Middle Missouri, but all Plains pottery show the general attributes of form, coarse paste, roughened paddled surface, black to gray color, and strong rim described for the Middle Missouri. Figure 6.49 shows the dates ascribed to several individual sites of the later (Extended) Middle Missouri sites. Several of the later villages (Huff, Philip Ranch, and Arzberger sites) are enclosed by extensive earthworks that have regularly spaced bastions. As in the palisaded Mississippian sites, there evidently were heavy log palisades set into the earthen ridges, and the general opinion is that these villages can be described as fortified. The dates of the fortified villages are not precisely known, but they are always late in the sequence. For this reason, some students argue that the concept of fortifying villages is a European innovation, having diffused rapidly westward from the Southeast, where forts of the European conquerors were observed by the Creeks and other tribes. If the bastioned forts were indeed built after European models, the diffusion was very fast, outstripping actual white contact by centuries. The evidence of the Plains is inconclusive, with most dates (tree-ring and radiocarbon) falling around A.D. 1500 —after Columbus' landfall but before extensive colonization of the mainland had begun. Until contrary proof appears, one can regard the fortified villages as having reached the Plains from the Mississippian area and as an indigenous American idea.

In the eastern part of the cultural plains and the lands east of the Missouri River in Iowa and Missouri, the Nebraska and later Oneota cultures bespeak a late Mississippian thrust that well-nigh obscured the Plains influences. The Oneota (M. M. Wedel 1959; Hall 1962) is characterized by shell-tempered pottery with many secondary features and a more varied inventory of artifacts than was true of more westerly Plains cultures.

In the Southern Plains there is a blending of Plains and Southwestern cultures, called Antelope Creek, which Krieger (1946) has described in great detail. In Kansas and southern Nebraska a series of local cultures have been discovered and described by W. R. Wedel (for example, 1936, 1959, and 1961). Among these the Lower Loup focus of Nebraska is identified as descendant from the Upper Republican and as being the archeologic remains of the historic Pawnee tribe. The Oneota is regarded as the remains of the Chiwere-speaking Sioux.

Figure 6.50, modified from W. R. Wedel (1961), shows the several local cultures over the five areas he has established for the Plains region. The contemporaneity of the cultures and their span—from perhaps A.D. 700 to the nineteenth century and continuous white contact—are also brought out. In spite of a now-huge backlog of supporting data and many additional reports yet to appear, there are still problems to be solved in the Plains concerning the relationship and direction of interareal influence. The increments to knowledge since 1945 have come faster in the Plains than in any comparable region in the Americas, and one can predict that it will soon be the best understood of any.

There is cultural, as well as tree-ring and geologic, evidence for an abandonment of the Central Plains in favor of the Middle Missouri area, probably because of lengthy droughts. This movement is seen by Lehmer (1954b) as responsible in large measure for the blending and "leveling" of the cultures of the Plains into the Coalescent Tradition. The sequence of droughts and good years is outlined in Jennings (1955) as follows:

From western Nebraska (Champe 1946;

Weakly 1943), from North Dakota (Will 1946), and from central South Dakota (Meleen 1948) tentative tree ring calendars appear to establish the fact that late 15th century was marked by drouth and by wind storms which moved fantastic quantities of dust. The abandonment of many villages appears to coincide with this period. At least, at many villages the house or lodge remnants are buried under a clean mantle of tan, yellowish, or gray dust, over which the humus and sod of later years developed. These dust deposits vary from one foot thickness in Medicine Creek (Nebraska) sites to 7 feet at the Sommers site (near Pierre, South Dakota). Moreover, tentative tree ring dates on the Sommers site are 1480–1489, plus or minus 10 years. Tree ring records from near Bismarck, North Dakota (Will 1946) show, at this same time, 19 wet years from 1452–71, 14 dry years from 1471–85, 3 wet from 1485–88, 13 dry from 1488–1501, 4 wet from 1501–05, and 13 dry from 1505–18. Thus in the 47 years from 1471–1518 we have 3 long drouth periods totaling 40 years. If these conditions apply down river 300 miles at the Sommers site, we find at least one house (from which the wood specimens came) was built during the end of a dry period, and was abandoned soon enough to be blanketed by 7 feet of dust, presumably whipped up during a subsequent dry spell of long duration or a dust storm of great violence. It should not be forgotten that sites along side the Missouri River (such as Sommers) may have been covered with dust whipped up during low water from extensive bars and flats in the river. It is more likely that the bulk of the Sommers site was established during the 19 wet years from 1452–71. Again, to the west, near Scottsbluff, Nebraska, the small local tree ring record showing long drouths implies that the Upper Republican period ended in that section in the early 1500's. (It should be pointed out that the accuracy of Will's 1946 work with Dakota tree rings has been seriously questioned by Bell 1948, as well as by Lehmer 1954a.)

Although the Woodland base, blended with later Mississippian increments, developed along distinctive lines, the entire region should be viewed, as stated earlier, as derivative almost entirely from the Eastern Woodland.

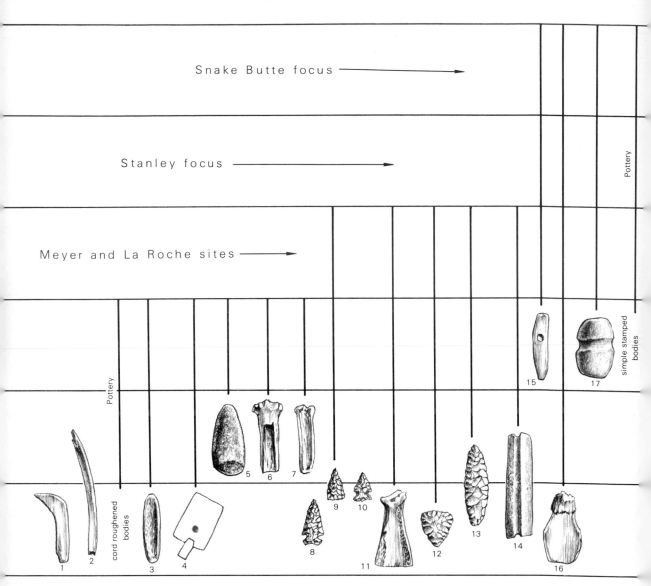

Figure 6.48 *Artifact changes in Middle Missouri sites, Oahe Dam area. 1, scapula knife; 2, bison-rib scraper handle; 3, quill flattener; 4, long rectangular house; 5, celt; 6, pick; 7, flesher; 8– 10, arrow points; 11, scapula hoe; 12, end scraper; 13, knife; 14, arrow-shaft smoother; 15, arrow-shaft wrench; 16, horn scoop; 17, stone maul; 18, 19, knives; 20, end scraper; 21, tenoned bone arrow point; 22, circular house; 23, catlinite elbow pipe; 24, arrow-shaft smoother; 25, arrow-shaft wrench; 26, scapula hoe; 27, brass tinkler; 28, glass beads; 29, knife (metal blade in bone handle); 30, flesher; 31, clasp knife blade, European manufacture; 32, elk-antler scraper haft; 33, snow snake gaming piece. (After Lehmer 1954a)*

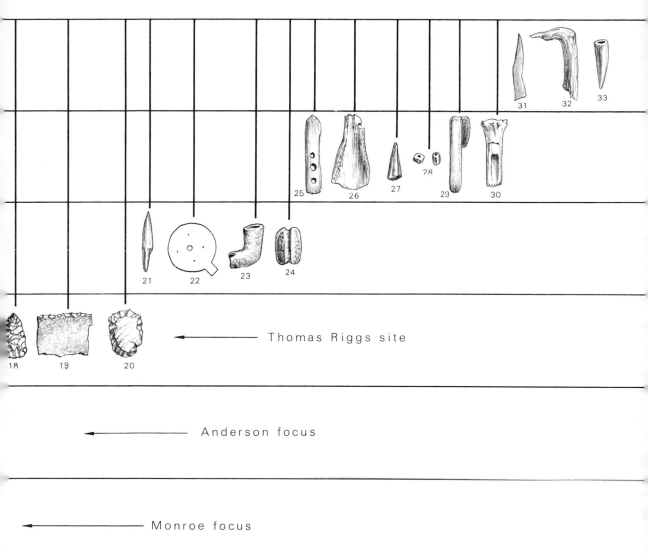

Thomas Riggs site

Anderson focus

Monroe focus

For the Plains village tribes, as elsewhere, the archeologic story does not reveal the complete lives of the people. The earth lodges in the sometimes large villages imply a fully sedentary mode of living that is contradicted by the historic record of several Plains village groups, such as the Pawnee, Arikara, Hidatsa, and Mandan. All these tribes, for example, regularly went on long bison hunts of several weeks' duration. The bison was a major food source for all Plains tribes until its extinction in the late eighteenth century.

The Mandan villages on the Missouri River in North Dakota were observed and often described by a series of explorers. The best known of those who recorded the Mandan customs were Lewis and Clark, who observed them during their historic journey into the American Northwest. The villages were rather large, with several dozen closely spaced earth lodges clustered in no particular order around a central

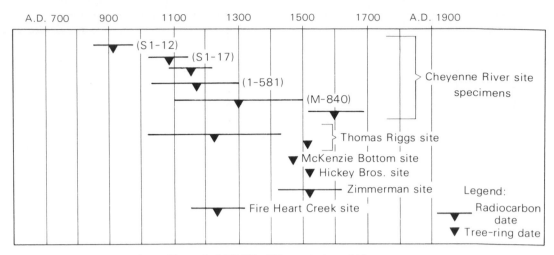

Figure 6.49 *Dates from Extended Middle Missouri sites. (After Lehmer 1966)*

open area, where ceremonies and games were held. Located on terraces above the Missouri River, the villages were protected by high post palisades with a deep ditch just outside. The houses were quite large, ranging from 40 to 80 feet in diameter (Figure 6.51). Several nuclear families occupied each lodge; the families were members of the same extended family of a matrilineal kinsgroup. The villages were almost deserted during the summer hunt and again during the winter, when temporary quarters were taken up in protected wooded areas in the valley, where game and firewood were more plentiful.

The lodges were round and built of timber, with earth and sod covering in the familiar Plains pattern. The size of the structures necessitated large center posts as the major supports; rafters radiated outward from the crossbeams of the four center posts to plates upon the shorter posts set at the edge of the circular floor. Upon the rafters, willows and grass or thatch were spread to support the earth covering. The roof was open in the square area formed by the central crossbeams on the center posts. This opening was the only source of sunlight and was also the smoke hole. In bad weather, a shield—

sometimes it was one of the round buffalo-hide bull-boats used for ferrying the river—was placed over the smoke hole. There was a short, covered entryway also made of timber and earth. The arrangement of facilities inside the lodge was evidently more or less standard. The fire was within the square formed by the central supports. There were curtained bunklike beds around the back or side walls. On the right of the fire area or behind the fire opposite the entrance was a family shrine or altar where ceremonial objects were kept. At other locations would be a sweat bath, a stall for a favorite horse and food for him, food-storage areas, and extra clothing. Buffalo-robe seats were ranged around the fire. In the floor were deep, jug-shaped storage pits for corn and other food (Figure 6.52). Outside the lodges were innumerable scaffolds or racks for drying both vegetable and meat products.

Although the lodges were roomy and comfortable, they would not have fitted modern conceptions of creature comfort or sanitation. One of these villages was described by an early visitor as "filthy," with "villainous smells everywhere assailing" him. He complained of the swarming dogs and children and described the vil-

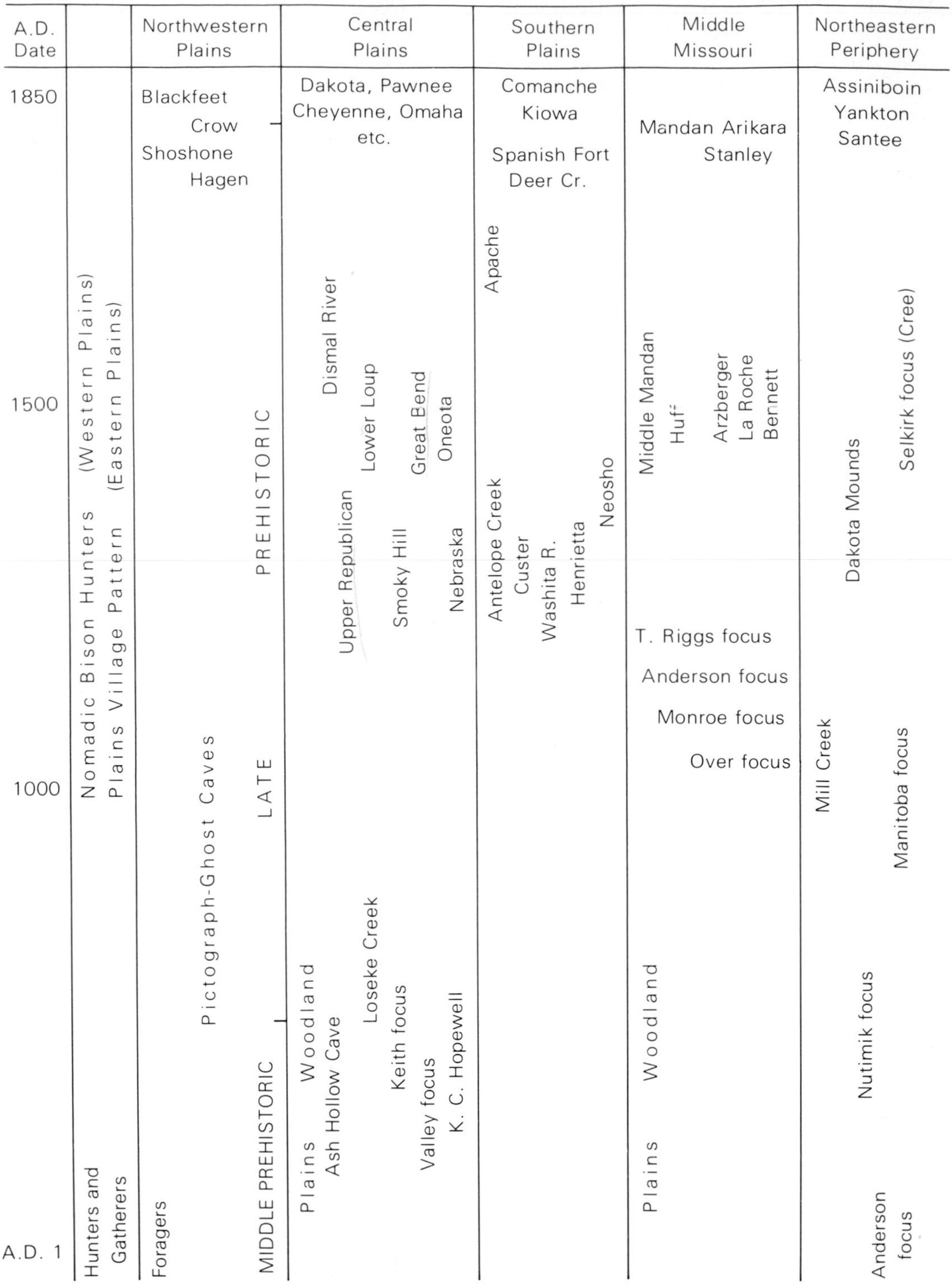

A.D. Date		Northwestern Plains	Central Plains	Southern Plains	Middle Missouri	Northeastern Periphery
1850		Blackfeet Crow Shoshone Hagen	Dakota, Pawnee Cheyenne, Omaha etc.	Comanche Kiowa Spanish Fort Deer Cr.	Mandan Arikara Stanley	Assiniboin Yankton Santee
1500			Dismal River Lower Loup Great Bend Oneota Upper Republican Smoky Hill Nebraska	Apache Antelope Creek Custer Washita R. Henrietta Neosho	Middle Mandan Huf² Arzberger La Roche Bennett	Dakota Mounds Selkirk focus (Cree)
1000					T. Riggs focus Anderson focus Monroe focus Over focus	Mill Creek Manitoba focus
A.D. 1			Plains Woodland Ash Hollow Cave Loseke Creek Keith focus Valley focus K. C. Hopewell		Plains Woodland	Nutimik focus Anderson focus

Column 2 (vertical labels): Hunters and Gatherers; Foragers; Nomadic Bison Hunters (Western Plains); Plains Village Pattern (Eastern Plains); Pictograph-Ghost Caves; PREHISTORIC; LATE; MIDDLE PREHISTORIC

Figure 6.50 *Chart of approximate time relationships of selected archeological sites and complexes in the Plains areas since* A.D. *1. (Modified from W. R. Wedel 1961)*

lage as a hogpen. This description can be supported on archeologic grounds because thick midden or garbage dumps are scattered all through the village. Often one can associate a midden area with a specific lodge. The towns would have been malodorous quagmires after a rainstorm, with only slightly less stench in dry seasons.

The Mandan artifact list, of course, reflects both hunting and horticulture, the latter involving the sunflower as well as the familiar maize. Tobacco, important in ritual and ceremony, was grown by the men; the rest of the gardening was done by the women and children on small plots in the loose, rich soils of the Missouri River Valley floor. The gardening tools

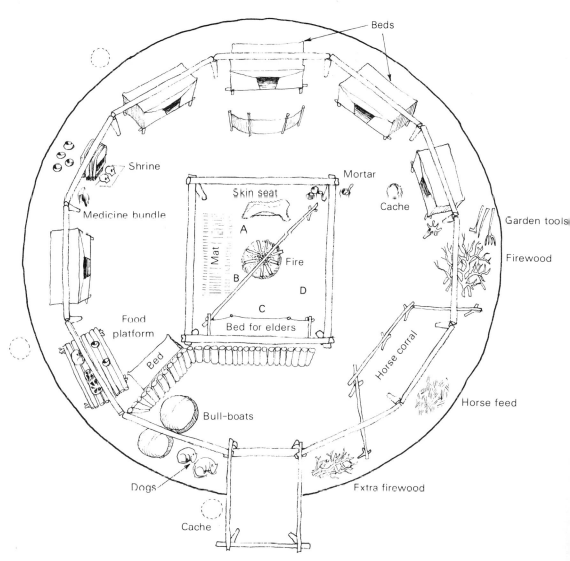

Figure 6.51   *Diagram of a twelve-post Hidatsa earth lodge. A, B, places of honor for guests; C, grandfather's place to make arrows; D, cook's place. The cooking kettle was suspended from diagonal pole over the fireplace. (After Lowie 1954)*

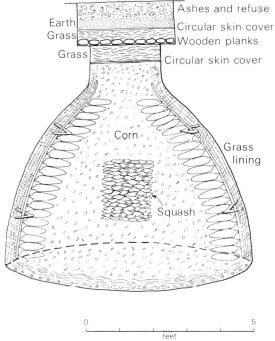

Ashes and refuse
Earth
Grass Circular skin cover
Wooden planks
Grass Circular skin cover
Corn
Grass lining
Squash

0   5
feet

Figure 6.52 Cross section of Hidatsa cache pit. (After Lowie 1954)

included a wooden digging stick, a bison-scapula hoe, and an elk-antler or willow-branch rake. Corn and beans were planted together, with sunflower around the edges of the field. Squash was grown in separate patches. Agriculture was surrounded with ritual and ceremony to provide supernatural aid in production. In addition to gardening, the women tanned skins, made clothing of all sorts, made pottery of good quality, gathered wood, did much of the work of house building and maintenance, cared for children, prepared food, and did other chores. The men hunted, fought if need be, performed many important ceremonies, and competed in games and contests. When necessary, they assisted the women in the heavier labor of harvest and construction.

Given the near-certainty of ample food from the inexhaustible herds and the products of the fertile valley gardens, the Mandan had a rich ceremonial life centered on the vision quest and a number of "medicine" bundles that gave various kinds of "power." Some bundles were quite specific in their effect on crop fertility or weather; others had to do with curing disease. Self-torture was an important element in the religion and was a dominant theme in some of the ceremonies.

7

The Southwest

Many readers will welcome a chapter about the Southwest because so many people have seen and loved its grandeur, its mist-softened mountains, its shimmering heats, and its lavender sunset charm. Within the lure of the Southwest are included the enclaved Pueblo Indian tribes along the Rio Grande and on the high mesas of the desert, peoples whose timeless cultures seem so admirably suited to a harsh, but not necessarily hostile, environment. Those who treasure the colorful tribesmen almost as part of the natural land-scape offer unwitting tribute to these ingenious folk who have so long successfully exploited an unwatered waste. This respect is justified by the record, a record that this chapter will summarize.

Travelers to the Southwest know the famous prehistoric ruins of Mesa Verde National Park and many national monuments such as Chaco Canyon, Casa Grande, and Bandelier. In these, and at many an unprotected site, the multistoried buildings offer thrilling testimony to a numerous people of long ago. These were people, more-over, who had mastered many skills of survival and whose technology was complex and its products strong and beautiful to all eyes. Inter-esting, too, is the fact that these ancient Southwesterners worked out their destiny separately and a little later than their countrymen east of the mountains (see Chapter 6). The prime source of South-west inspiration and stimulus again can be located in Mexico to the south, whence came the origins of excellent pottery, the cultivated crops, possibly some religious ideas, and other practices. However, the staunch conservatives of the region evidently rejected the Mexican concept of priest-rulers, of tribute to powerful centers, and of militant political structure.

By continental standards the Southwest culture area is quite small. Reed (1964) describes the Southwest as extending north-south "from Durango, Colorado, to Durango, Mexico, and from Las Vegas, New Mexico, to Las Vegas, Nevada" on the east-west axis, but most of its area of dominance falls within the states of New Mexico and Arizona with some of northern Mexico and southern Colorado and southern Utah added. Within this restricted zone there developed one of the three Formative-stage climaxes of North America, and for many people it carries the most interest of any. The chronologic relationships and the durations of the Hopewell, Mississippian, and Southwestern developments are shown in Figures 6.2 and 9.2.

The Southwest tribes, both prehistoric and modern, were gardeners from before the Christian era. They were thrifty, skillful exploiters of land and available water; the crops were corn, beans, squash, and cotton. Other food plants now regarded as weeds, such as amaranth, sunflower, Rocky Mountain beeweed, and wild potatoes and tomatoes, were cultivated (or at least encouraged) and were equally important to the aboriginal gardening economy. What is often forgotten is that the Southwestern farmer depended upon hundreds of wild species as heavily as upon the cultigens. The cultigens made possible a denser population, it's true, and were probably of crucial importance to subsistence. Nonetheless, the success of the Southwestern cultures was the result of a complex year-round exploitation of all available species, as was true all over the continent.

This Western symbiosis of man and biota is the familiar but often forgotten legacy from the Archaic cultures, overlooked because of the emphasis given to the very *fact* of food production and the cultural effects of the gardening complex. Jennings (1966b) has a detailed discussion of the aboriginal ecology of the Glen Canyon area in southeastern Utah. Over 300 species were collected there in the yearly round, and it is clear that horticulture need not be thought of as having been the sole source of food. At the same time, even the existence of extensive gardening in the American Southwest is a minor miracle. No large part of the region is truly suitable for dry-farm operations, even with the most modern techniques. But modern agricultural practices are so different from the aboriginal ones that there is no validity in the comparison. One can ask: How did a food-producing culture operate where agriculture is not possible? Here the answer is found in the ethnographic analogs— the practices observed among modern tribes—and in the archeologic data. The success of the Southwestern farmer was due to a series of realistic techniques for the exploitation of limited water, several of which are described by Hack (1942). These techniques, in use today, probably included in aboriginal times floodwater irrigation of several types, sand-dune or subsurface irrigation, and seepage springs watering colluvial soils. To the above must be added actual water impoundment and distribution in essentially the modern manner in the Salt and Gila Valleys of southern Arizona (for example, Woodbury 1960; Midvale 1965) by the Hohokam and apparently in the Pueblo areas in New Mexico, Utah, and Arizona (Herold 1961; Rohn 1963; Lindsay 1961; and Sharrock, Dibble, and Anderson 1961). In mountainous areas the use of loose-stone check dams across the minor drainages effectively slowed down rainwater runoff, providing additional watered areas and simultaneously trapping soil behind the dams to form what can be called terraces. These little terraces, called *trinchera* plots, though often only a few feet in area, would add precious garden space where, with luck, a few plants could be grown. Thus, in some areas, most of the gardening activity was a function of a myriad of small, scattered plots where the soil and water could be brought together. In Glen Canyon, Adams, Lindsay, and Turner (1961) even found narrow, masonry-enclosed terraces built on a narrow sandstone ledge with trash and dirt brought in to take advantage of a weak seepage along the base of a cliff.

Planting techniques were also special. The seed corn was planted early, ten or twelve kernels to a spot, in deep holes where groundwater ensured germination and the deep planting afforded protection from late frosts in the northern provinces. These seedings, called hills, were widely, even irregularly, spaced over the plot, so that the limited water was not divided between too many plants. The stalks, because of the lack of water, did not grow more than 3 or 4 feet high and the hill of perhaps a dozen plants resembled a bush. The outer leaves took the brunt of the dry, hot winds of summer, protecting the inner plants that produced the several ears of corn harvested from each hill (Figure 7.1).

The scientific record of Southwest pre-

Figure 7.1   *Typical Hopi corn field. (After Judd 1954)*

history is found in hundreds of monographs and thousands of articles. The detailed literature is well-nigh inexhaustible. The region has perhaps the longest history of intensive study of any north of Mexico, and many important contributions to archeologic theory and study have come out of this long period of scholarly concern (see Chapter 1). As was true of the Southeast, much attention has been paid to the ceramic arts. As a result of long study and because many ruins and living tribes are accessible to visitors, the cultures of the Southwest are not complete mysteries but are widely known and understood. Because of the general familiarity of the region, this chapter will be somewhat curtailed and perhaps even faintly unorthodox in places; the aim is again to present the outline of knowledge instead of the details an areal or regional specialist perceives.

As is obvious, the key to understanding the Southwest lies in water and its use in gardening (Haury 1956). For some, this makes it easiest to see all the Southwest as one cultural tradition showing areal variation in some aspects of culture. This unitary view can be defended and at one level of discussion is useful and valid, particularly in a long-range consideration of the local prehistory. Normally, however, three contemporary major traditions or cultures are recognized and are treated as separate, even through their intertwined origins are well understood. This three-tradition division will be followed here. These major divisions are the Mogollon or Western Pueblo, the descendent and more widespread Anasazi Pueblo of the northern Southwest, and the areally restricted Hohokam group, which was confined to the Salt and Gila River drainages of southern Arizona.

All three evolved from the Desert Archaic cultures upon stimulus from Mexico. The Archaic-stage beginnings are manifest in many things, ranging from the ingenious exploitation of resources to many details of technology, settlement pattern, and the like. That the Mogollon, Anasazi, and Hohokam reacted to the same stimuli may be true, but each tradition evolved in different directions, partly because of different environmental conditions, and each can readily be distinguished by the specialists. These environmental forces are most obvious in the terrain itself. In the Mogollon province, where the transition from the Archaic stage to horticulture first occurred, we find some of the most rugged country in the Southwest. In the core area along the New Mexico-Arizona border there are steep mountains and narrow valleys where little arable land exists. Here, few extensive villages ever developed. Wendorf (1956) makes clear the physiographic reasons for the lack of large population centers. The difficulties of large-scale gardening were offset by the rich biotic offerings in the relatively well-watered mountains, and there seems to have been a greater reliance on wild species than in the other traditions. The year-round climate, too, was milder and showed a less extreme temperature range than in either the Hohokam or the Anasazi heartlands.

The Anasazi flourished to the north in the Colorado plateaus, an area characterized by high mesas and many deep canyons with swift, clear streams in often narrow valleys. Temperatures range from below zero to the high 90s throughout the year, and unseasonable frosts are frequent. The tablelands, being well watered, now support forests of pine, pinyon, and juniper and much associated game. At lower elevations shrub and grasslands are dominant. Gardening appears to have been on a dry-farming basis in the higher, better-watered locations and on a combined dry-farm–irrigation basis at lower elevations. (Even now the highlands between Monticello, Utah, and Cortez, Colorado, support a vast commercial bean-farming operation using modern dry-farm techniques.)

The Hohokam were restricted to the desertlands along the lower Salt and middle Gila Rivers (plus a few of their tributaries) and utilized these waters for large-scale irrigation. The modern city of Phoenix, Arizona, is built upon the ruins of many Hohokam settlements and the complex system of irrigation ditches that made life possible. The major canals of the Hohokam system underwent constant repair and modification. The biotic resources in these two valleys were undoubtedly much restricted, even as today, and of the three traditions, the Hohokam were probably the most dependent upon their fields for food, although the historic Pima derived about half their subsistence from wild species.

As described above, the Southwestern cultures are established as representing a subsistence pattern wherein gardening and gathering are in a complex balance in a land where farming is difficult, if not unreasonable. The environmental settings of the three range from Colorado's green mesas to the sere wastes of Arizona's deserts. All are derived from earlier Archaic cultures and preserve the technology of the early foraging stage. All depended on the careful use of limited water. We can now turn our attention to the individual cultures mapped in Figure 7.2.

The Mogollon

The transition to the horticultural stage is documented largely from the Mogollon data, derived from a series of sites in southwest New Mexico which have been systematically studied for many years. Haury (1936) first defined the Mogollon tradition. Other major contributions have been made by Martin and various associates (for example, Martin et al. 1952, 1956, 1962, 1964; Martin, Rinaldo, and Bluhm 1954; Martin, Rinaldo, and Barter

1957) and Wheat (1955). Developing out of the Chiricahua and San Pedro Cochise Archaic (Haury 1957; Martin, Rinaldo, and Antevs 1949), the Mogollon transition had well begun by 1000 B.C. and possibly before. Evidence from Bat Cave (Dick 1965) and Tularosa Cave (Martin et al. 1952) suggests that the Cochise peoples were harvesting primitive corn by 2000 B.C. By 1000 B.C., however, squash and beans were evidently also available. While the origins of domesticated plants and the techniques of horticulture are clearly Mexican, the New Mexico finds document the northward diffusion of the plants even during their long period of evolution from the wild state. With horticulture in rudimentary form compatibly grafted onto the Cochise Archaic base of gathering and milling vegetable foods, the transition was complete by 300 B.C. (Martin et al. 1952), when pottery was introduced to the Mogollones, again from the south. [Bullard (1962) challenges the accuracy of the date of pottery acquisition on archeologic grounds.]

By definition, then, the Mogollon begins when horticulture *and* a knowledge of ceramics have appeared. As early as 1934, Mera had referred to the "southern brownware complex" as distinct from the northern Pueblo. Haury (1936), in reporting the Harris and Mogollon sites (New Mexico), offered the name "Mogollon" and documented Mera's earlier suggestion that the southern brownware pattern or tradition was sufficiently distinctive to warrant separating it from the then-better-known, more northerly Anasazi. He was able to sort out and describe four sequent phases for which he listed characteristic diagnostic traits. As research continued, the Mogollon was seen not only as separable from, but also in some ways ancestral to, other Southwestern groups. At the same time, the sequent stages of the culture were extended and refined; Haury's four stages within the Mogollon were the

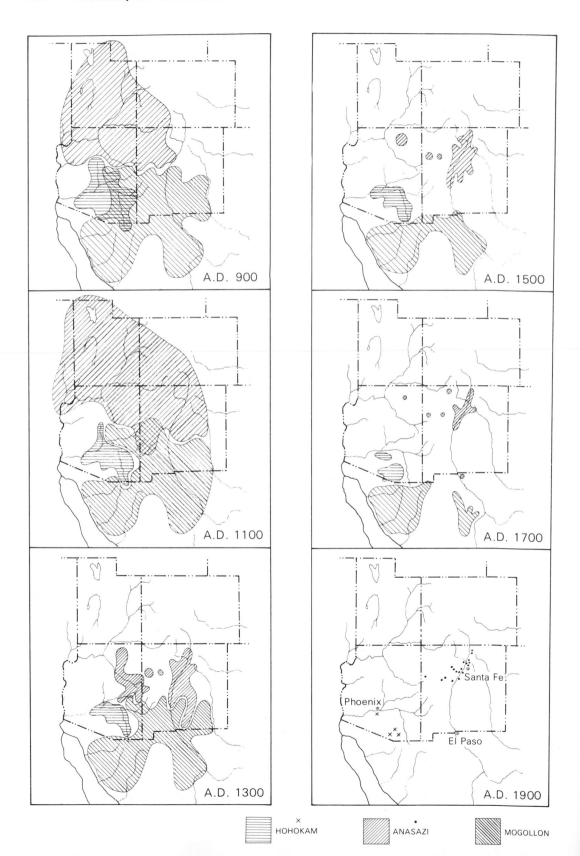

A.D. 900

A.D. 1500

A.D. 1100

A.D. 1700

A.D. 1300

A.D. 1900

Santa Fe

Phoenix

El Paso

× HOHOKAM   • ANASAZI   MOGOLLON

Georgetown phase, the earliest with little or no *painted* pottery, followed by the San Francisco, the Three Circle, and, last, the Mimbres. Estimated dates were ascribed to these phases for lack of tree-ring or other dating material. Martin (1959) was able, 20 years later, to add for the Reserve area of New Mexico the Pine Lawn Period, from 300 B.C. to A.D. 500; Georgetown, A.D. 500 to 700; San Francisco, A.D. 700 to 900; Three Circle, A.D. 900 to 1000; Reserve, A.D. 1000 to 1100; Tularosa, A.D. 1100 to 1200; and, last, Foote Canyon, A.D. 1200 to 1350. The dates are derived from a combination of radiocarbon dates, tree-rings, and estimates drawn from aboriginal trade goods. At the close of the Foote Canyon phase the Reserve area was abandoned, and later Mogollon settlements are to the north and west. There is general agreement that the modern Zuñi are remnant Mogollones.

In order to attempt a synthesis of the Mogollon data, Wheat (1955) ignored phase names and reduced the local phases of the several subareas to a simple, widespread series of *numbered* periods: Mogollon 1: 300 B.C. to A.D. 400; Mogollon 2: A.D. 400 to 600; Mogollon 3: A.D. 600 to 900; Mogollon 4: A.D. 900 to 1100; Mogollon 5: A.D. 1100 to 1350. The earlier dates are drawn from Tularosa Cave, where the Archaic (Cochise) base complex was represented in the lower levels, as were the basic cultigens; occupancy of the cave continued until about A.D. 1100. In addition to spanning most of Mogollon history in the Reserve district, the cave yielded a rich inventory of stone, ceramic, and perishable artifacts; these data also allowed the listing of many more specific Mogollon traits than had been possible before. Martin et al. (1952) provide a detailed listing of material and nonmaterial

Figure 7.2 *Approximate extent of Southwest cultures at two-hundred-year intervals. (After Jennings 1956)*

culture traits, making it necessary to report here only the classes of materials recovered. Wickerwork sandals are earliest, this having been the dominant technique in Pine Lawn times; plaited work was dominant by the Reserve period. Ornaments included bracelets of shell; tubular bone beads; and pendants of wood, shell, stone, and bone. String aprons and both fur and feather robes were present. Milling tools included several metate styles and mortars, with varied handstone types. Snares, digging sticks, bows and arrows, and many chipped flint forms as well as netting were among the food-getting artifacts. Foods, aside from cultigens and wild game, included yucca, cactus, walnuts, acorns, grass, and sunflower seeds, but amaranth was not mentioned. Textiles abounded; there were cradles; carrying nets; tumpline straps; twilled, twined, and coiled baskets; twilled and twined matting; cotton cloth; netting; and the blankets mentioned earlier. Antler and bone tools are: awls, notched ribs, fleshers, punches, hammers, flakers, and wrenches. Wood was used for tool handles; scoops; trowels; awls; ladles; lapboards; spatulas; weaving tools, including spindles and whorls; flutes (reed); dice; and many other articles, including the painted *tablitas* used in headdresses (?). Tubular pipes of stone and clay were replaced by reed cigarettes. Figurines were common in both human and animal forms. Pottery was increasingly abundant; the earliest was a brown ware of good quality, called Alma Plain, a ware whose manufacture continued for more than 1000 years. Companion types are Alma Roughened and Alma Red. The above list of portable artifacts is, of course, not complete, but testifies to a heavy Archaic carry-over in the tool and utensil inventory.

In all phases save the late Reserve, the dwelling of the Mogollones was the semi-subterranean house or pit house, but no uniformity in design can be detected in the early phases. Wheat establishes eighteen architectural patterns in the range. Suffice it to say that the houses were usually built in shallow pits with a narrow passageway or ramp descending from the ground level. Many were rounded, but D-shaped, kidney-shaped, or rectangular ones also occur. Figure 7.3 shows three phases of house form and construction from the Harris village. Built of wood, the houses may have been mat- or reed-covered or plastered with mud. In Mogollon 1 times the houses varied greatly in size, had rough, uneven floors pocked with holes and pits, and were generally crudely executed. In later times, the pit houses

were more uniform in size and more rectangular in shape, a form which persisted through Mogollon 5 until after A.D. 1100. At this time, the stone masonry of the Anasazi was introduced, and the pit house almost disappeared. The Mogollon villages were often occupied over very long periods; at the Harris site, Haury (1936) found house-style changes over three phases in a well-defined stratigraphy (Figure 7.4). While continuous use cannot be proved, it is deemed likely on ceramic evidence. To be noted is the loose and unstructured village layout (Reed 1956; Wendorf 1956), which is characteristic of the Mogollon settlements in all phases,

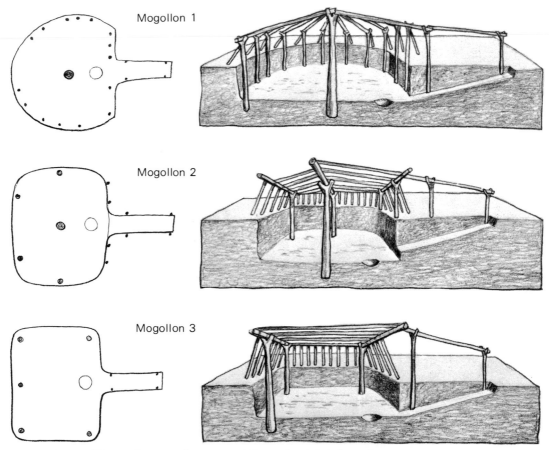

Mogollon 1

Mogollon 2

Mogollon 3

Figure 7.3   *Floor plans and cross sections (postulated roof constructions) of Mogollon houses at the Harris village site. (After Haury 1936)*

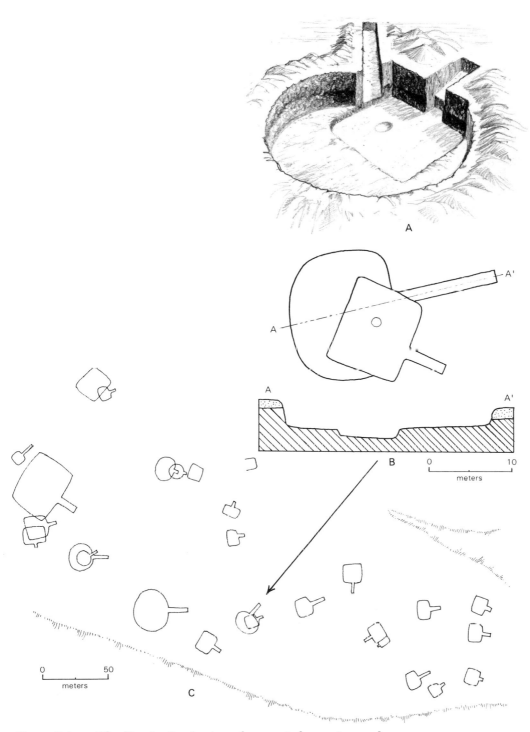

Figure 7.4   *The Harris site. A, view of excavated superimposed
pit houses; B, plan and cross section of A; C, map of village and
location of A. (After Haury 1936)*

until the introduction of masonry. The elevated location of Harris is also typical. Haury (1936), as well as Martin et al. (1952), emphasizes the occasional large houses found at Mogollon villages during all the period phases. These are regarded as having been ceremonial structures, being larger than, but resembling, the dwellings. Whether they were communal meeting places is difficult to determine; certainly they bear little formal resemblance to the famous kivas of the Anasazi, other than being built in deep pits. By Mogollon 5 the ceremonial (?) structures were entirely subterranean.

Perhaps the most famous Mogollon settlement is that at Point of Pines in Arizona. Lying just west of the Arizona–New Mexico line on the San Carlos Apache Reservation, the general region contains over 200 sites. These sites span some thousands of years of aboriginal use, from the Archaic of the Cienega Creek site (Haury 1957) until almost modern times. The area was systematically studied for more than a decade by members of a permanent field school, where dozens of professional archeologists began their training.

One of the Point of Pines sites is Crooked Ridge Village (Wheat 1954). The site, about 6,000 feet above sea level, was settled by A.D. 100 and was continuously occupied until A.D. 900. The low, broad ridge is aligned almost north-south; the village lay on the gently sloping eastern side. Culinary water, always a problem, was obtained from walk-in wells along the stream to the east (Wheat 1952). These walk-in wells were, in essence, deep reservoirs which collected subsurface water flowing along an impervious blue clay toward the intermittent streams of the area. (Somewhat similar wells were identified at the Cienega Creek site; hence in the area the technique goes back into the Archaic stage of at least 2000 B.C.) Wheat excavated over twenty pit houses

of varied shapes and sizes and two ceremonial structures. There were several cases of pit house superposition, and on this evidence, as well as on ceramic and other data, Wheat demonstrates a long occupancy for the village. The houses were true pit houses, resembling the sequence from the more easterly Mogollon. The quadrilateral house with a simple entry ramp was commonest (fifteen examples), with four others showing vestibule entryways and three with an annex from the south side. The floors were pocked with pits (for storage?) and were otherwise irregular. Most houses had four major supports; replacement of posts during use sometimes resulted in there being more than four at the time of excavation. Figure 7.5 shows the pit and floor of Pit house 1 at Crooked Ridge. (The inner, deeper pit in Figure 7.5 is the original size of the floor. The secondary shelf is an artifact of the excavation procedure, where exploration was extended beyond the original walls.) Figure 7.6 shows Wheat's restoration of the sturdy framework of the superstructure. Many variations on this basic design are also suggested. Figure 7.7 shows the largest pit house (number 19); the shallow trench enclosing the central area and divided firepit is an interesting and unusual feature. Without discussing the entirely typi-

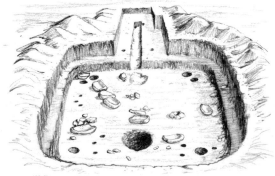

Figure 7.5   *View of excavated pit house in Crooked Ridge Village. Floor is approximately 18 feet wide and 15 feet long. Note metates on floor. (After Wheat 1954)*

Figure 7.6   *Postulated roof construction, seen in cross section, of a four-support Mogollon house, Crooked Ridge Village. (After Wheat 1954)*

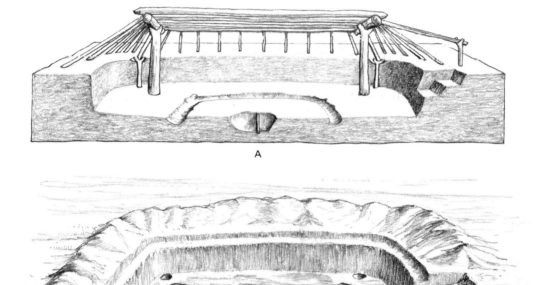

A

B

Figure 7.7   *Mogollon ceremonial pit house at Crooked Ridge Village. A, postulated roof structure seen in cross section; B, view of excavated pit, approximately 30 feet square. (After Wheat 1954)*

cal artifacts (and some exotic goods from nearby areas), the site as a unit can be noted as having contributed significantly to the understanding of Mogollon architecture. Wheat estimates that only one-fourth of the site was dug, with about seventy-five structures yet to be examined.

Published description has tended to emphasize the Mogollon pit house and the fact that many northern Pueblo or Anasazi traits were derived from the Mogollones as early as A.D. 400 (for example, Dittert, Hester, and Eddy 1961; Jennings 1966b), but it must be emphasized that by A.D. 900 Anasazi traits were spreading back to the south. Foremost were the concept of stone masonry and the manufacture of black on white pottery (see Wheat 1955). Thus, by about A.D. 1100, a superficial areal uniformity, mentioned by many authors, can be recognized as the Anasazi and Mogollon come to share more and more traits, but the internal consistency and distinctiveness of each culture never disappeared.

The Mogollon culture as such continued over a wide area, including the Jornada Branch in eastern New Mexico and into Texas (Lehmer 1938) until about A.D. 1400, when a noticeable contraction can be charted. Following Reed (1946, 1950a, 1950b, 1955), Martin and Rinaldo (1960) identify the historic Zuñi tribe as likely the remnant of Mogollon. Their argument rests on careful study of ceramics as well as on more general traits. Sites of interest in the period later than A.D. 900 on into the fifteenth century include the Table Rock, dated at A.D. 1350 (Martin and Rinaldo 1960), and Hooper Ranch, A.D. 1200 to 1375 (Martin, Rinaldo, and Longacre 1961), among many others in eastern Arizona on the headwaters of the Little Colorado. Reed's analyses of the Western Pueblo reveal the extent to which it is a blend or fusion of Anasazi and Mogollon. (See also Rinaldo 1964.)

Anasazi influences were conspicuous in the southern part of the Mogollon region in the Mimbres area. The large, compact villages of stone masonry, adobe houses, and distinctive black on white pottery have long been famous. The Swarts Ruin (H. S. Cosgrove and Cosgrove 1932) and the Mattocks Ruin (Nesbitt 1931) are two well-known sites. The much-prized pottery is characterized by graceful life forms —insect, animal, and human—and many bawdy scenes from folktales and mythology, featuring such characters as the humpbacked flute player. Despite the Anasazi element in ceramics and architecture, the Mogollones of the Mimbres area retained a simplicity and a backwoods quality at variance with the more flamboyant technology of the Hohokam and Anasazi.

The Hohokam

Neighbors to the Mogollon in Arizona, the Hohokam are also clearly derived from the Archaic Cochise cultures (Haury 1950) and were concentrated in the desert lands of the Salt and Gila River Valleys. The two streams head in the Mogollon homeland but in their middle reaches pass through some of the driest deserts of North America. Here gardeners could not survive without irrigation; the irrigation works of the Hohokam are the most sophisticated to be found north of Mexico. While the ditch systems run for miles (Midvale 1965), they have not been, nor can they be, adequately studied. Extensive modern agricultural practices have destroyed most of the evidence, but two (observed before 1900) near Phoenix were over 10 miles long, swinging out from the river intake to bring water to fields quite distant from the river. When sectioned, these ditches proved to be wide channels—sometimes lined with clay—either U- or V-shaped. One, reported by Woodbury (1960), is 12 feet deep by 18 feet across. Although the extensive canal systems are estimated to fall after A.D. 800, there seems no doubt that an earlier, less elaborate network of canals existed. Whether the entire idea was an import from Mexico or was an indigenous development is still an unsettled point. The Hohokam occupied a very small area, constituting the most distinctive of any of the Southwestern traditions. Nonetheless, in its earliest phases, the Hohokam resembled the Mogollon to some degree. The most famous Hohokam site is Snaketown (Gladwin et al. 1937 and Gladwin 1937), although other sites have been excavated and reported (Haury 1932). The students divide the culture into four major periods; in each are one or more finer divisions called phases. These periods or stages can be tenuously correlated with the Mogollon and Anasazi sequence, but, as yet, neither tree-ring nor radiocarbon dates are available. The oldest period is called the Pioneer (Vahki, Estrella, Sweetwater, and Snaketown phases); the Colonial (Gila Butte and Santa Cruz) came next, then the Sedentary (Sacaton and Santan), followed by the final or Classic period (Soho and Civano).

The Pioneer period is dated from about 100 B.C. to A.D. 500 to 600 and is thus roughly equivalent to Wheat's Mogollon 1. While the ceramics included a red ware, as in Mogollon, they were largely of unslipped buff ware and made by paddle-and-anvil technique instead of by the coil-and-scrape method of the Mogollon. In the earliest or Vahki phase, the houses were large and rectangular with four central support posts. A few of these resembled the Mogollon houses in that they were true pit houses; this means the wall posts or leaners were set on the ground surface, so that the pit edge was inside the house and constituted a part of the wall. After the Vahki phase, however, all the houses came to be set into shallower pits and were less pit houses than houses

in a pit, because the vertical wall poles were set inside the excavation-pit edges instead of on the ground surface outside the pit. Thus, a different architectural principle was involved. The pole framework of the house was covered with smaller branches and grass, and mud was applied as the final element. The sloping roofs may have been thatched, but flat ones were mud-plastered. Annual repair of roofs and walls would have been necessary. Figure 7.8 presents the evolutionary house sequence at Snaketown. The village layout tended to be loose and scattered, as in Mogollon, until Classic times.

Distinctiveness in ceramics also begins in the Pioneer period. The basic ware is the buff mentioned earlier, with simple bowls and widemouthed ollas being the dominant forms. The surfaces were undecorated. Painted decoration, red on gray or red on buff, soon appeared and remained the dominant Hohokam decorative motif. Thereafter, unique pottery forms also appeared, the commonest being a hemispheric jar with small mouth, swelling outward toward the base, with the greatest diameter being only an inch or two above the flat base (Figure 7.9). Out of the flat bowl shape a shallow plate evolved, and some tripod and tetrapod legs on shallow bowls appeared in Sedentary times. The major shapes are presented in Figure 7.10. Figure 7.9 also shows one of the favored decorative styles—the endless repetition of zoomorphic designs, both realistic and stylized. The common stone tools for cutting, digging, and other tasks are about the same as found elsewhere among the gardeners of the region and show the relationship to earlier Archaic forms. The metate, if not basin-shaped, is troughed, but tends to be thick and shovel-shaped. The usual inventory of chipped stone and bone tools persist as elsewhere. Few perishable artifacts were recovered from the open sites, so data about basketry, textiles, wood, or skin objects are rare or

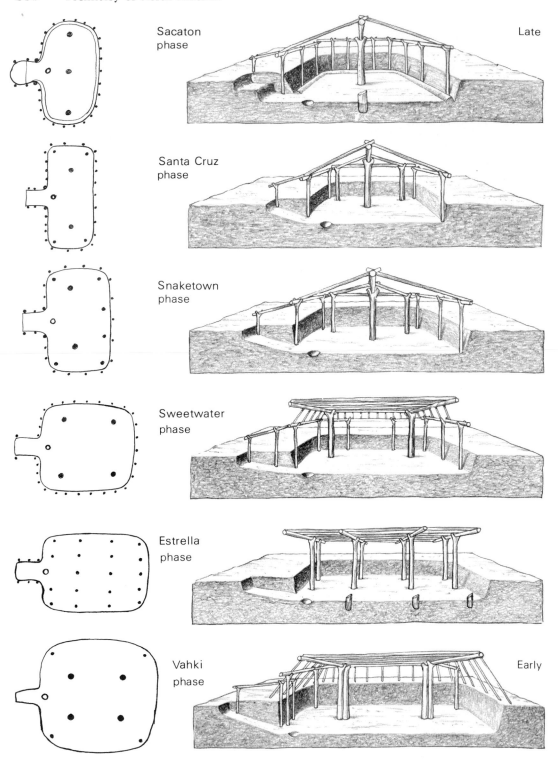

Sacaton phase — Late

Santa Cruz phase

Snaketown phase

Sweetwater phase

Estrella phase

Vahki phase — Early

Figure 7.8 *Floor plans and cross sections (postulated roof constructions) of Hohokam houses at Snaketown arranged in an evolutionary sequence. (After Sayles 1937a)*

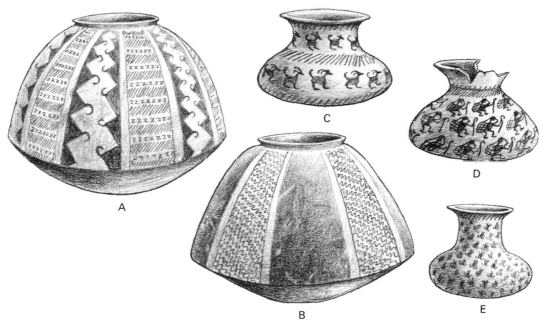

Figure 7.9 *Examples of Hohokam decorated pottery. A, B, Sacaton Red-on-buff, both approximately 18½ inches high and 25½ inches in diameter; C–E, Santa Cruz Red on buff, all about 5½ inches high. (A, B after Haury 1937c; C–E after Wasley and Johnson 1965)*

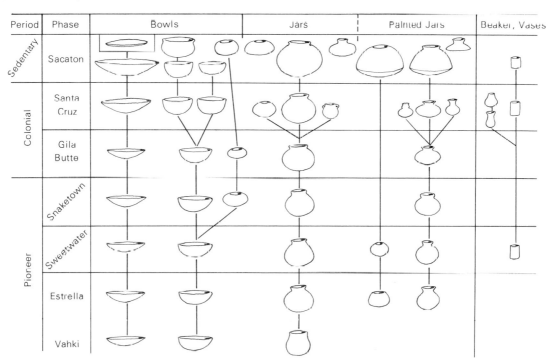

Figure 7.10 *Evolution of dominant Hohokam vessel forms. (After Haury 1937c)*

derived from charred and otherwise preserved fragments. The three-quarters–grooved ax is a common and distinctive form, as are graceful, thick-walled bowls carved from stone.

The most distinctive aspect of the Hohokam, however, is found in other than workaday artifacts. These special artifacts also attest to the stronger and quite direct stimulus and contact the Hohokam received from Mexico. It has even been argued that this was a Mexican colonial territory because of the irrigation, the pottery tradition, and the distinctive artifacts. As opposed to the notion of an actual Mexican population, an equally strong opinion prefers to interpret the Hohokam as an indigenous development receiving strong and frequent stimuli from Mexico. The exotic items include decorated, flat-stone paint palettes; stone effigy bowls (sometimes in the Chac-Mool style); exquisite rings, bracelets, and pendants of acid-etched shell; inlaid mosaic mirrors of pyrites on a round slate backing; copper bells; beads of stone (turquoise, steatite); and other items. Here, too, the life forms were the dominant decorative themes. Lizards, frogs, turtles, bears, and various birds are forms commonly depicted. There was also a figurine cult, exemplified by realistic, if crudely modeled, baked-clay female statuettes, with the facial features executed in vaguely Mexican techniques. However, in view of the early popularity of the female figurine in Anasazi and Fremont cultures to the north, the Mexican origin of this trait may be challenged. Figure 7.11 exemplifies a few of these unique artifacts. The bells, of course, are of great interest, being among the few objects of smelted and cast metal found north of Mexico. They are made by the Mexican lost-wax casting technique and appear to be actual imports. Even more convincing, if more evidence is needed of the southern affiliation of Hohokam, are the stepped pyramids and the ball courts. The outstanding examples of the Hohokam court are found at Snaketown in the Sedentary period and in the Painted Rocks Reservoir area (Sacaton phase), although about thirty are known over all the Southwest (Wasley and Johnson 1965). The ball court is an oval depression with arcing earthen embankments on each side. At the Gatlin site the puddled *caliche* playing floor was about 100 feet long and 35 feet wide. After a period of disuse, the floor had been replaced once, and the sloping floor edges had been repaired or remodeled several times. The game is presumed to have resembled the Central American ball game; center and end markers of stone or even small basins modeled in the floor are found. Two rubber balls have even been found, but not in association with a court.

At the Gatlin site (Wasley 1960) there was also a platform mound or truncated pyramid which had been rebuilt and enlarged several times. Although made of mud and surfaced with *caliche* plaster, the structure can be likened to nothing but the stone-faced platforms of Mexico, which were substructures for temples as in the Southeast. At the Gatlin site and many others, crematory basins where calcined human bones are found attest the universal and continuing practice of cremation instead of burial.

Figure 7.11   *Hohokam artifacts from Snaketown. Variable scale. Stone effigies: A, duck; B, mountain sheep (?), 2½ inches high; C, lizard, 3 inches in diameter; D, horned toad, 9 inches long; E, turtle, 4½ inches long; F–I, cut and etched (G) shell ornaments; J, shell bracelet; K, stone-backed plaque, or mirror, 4½ inches in diameter, encrusted with iron pyrites; L, Q, R (from Tempe, Arizona), three views of plaque, 4⅓ inches in diameter, similar to K: L, plaque in original wrapping; Q, front of plaque showing pyrite polygons; R, back of plaque; M–O, clay figurines (M is 4½ inches high); P, copper bell, ⅜ inches high; S–V, stone palettes, 7 to 12½ inches long. (A–E after Sayles 1937b; F–V after Haury 1937a, b, d, e)*

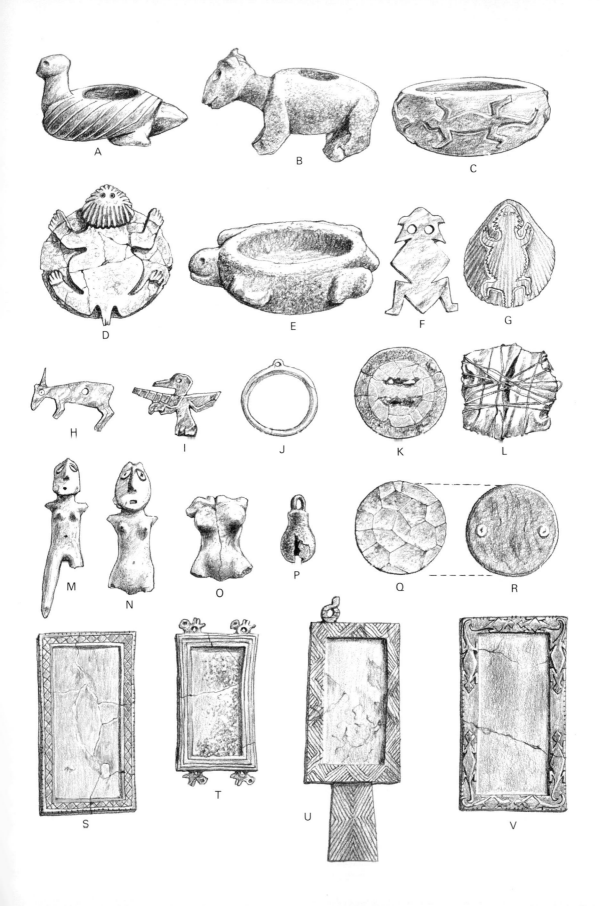

While the details of this culture are well set out and its affiliations much discussed, more field study is needed if the exact nature and origin of its Mexican stimuli are to be identified. And its ultimate fate is not yet fully known, although most specialists see the modern Pima-Papago as the remnant Hohokam. Students interested in beginning detailed study of this most intriguing and least understood of the Southwestern cultures first should consult Gladwin et al. (1937), Haury (1945, 1950), Wheat (1955), Wasley and Johnson (1965), and Schroeder (1965, 1966). Snaketown has recently been extensively reexcavated (E. W. Haury, personal communication, 1966), and many new data about the early periods were recovered. This restudy and the inevitable reevaluation of older findings should illuminate many now-obscure points about this small but important ancient people.

The Anasazi

By far the most extensive Southwestern culture was the Anasazi, which developed after stimulus from the more southerly Mogollon. The area of the Anasazi which is best known and which is often regarded as typical is the Four Corners area, where Utah, Colorado, Arizona, and New Mexico share a common boundary point. The Mesa Verdeans, although they are on the northern frontier, are *the* Anasazi for most laymen and many students. Their fabled cliff houses stir the imaginations of hundreds of thousands each year, having been a lodestone for visitors since their discovery in the nineteenth century (Figure 7.12). It must be remembered, however, that these grandeurs grew out of the Desert cultures in response to the spread of Mogollon traits—red-brown pottery, pit houses, and the cultigens so important in the American Formatve stage—and that the cliff houses are merely a very special

end product evolving from simple beginnings; they are not the whole story.

The Anasazi territory is broken today into the San Juan area, the Chaco-de Chelly Canyons axis, the vast Kayenta-Virgin territory, and, some would say, the Fremont and Sevier-Fremont, which covers most of Utah (Figure 7.13). [The appropriateness of including the Fremont as Anasazi has been effectively challenged (Aikens 1966a) and will be touched on later.] The Anasazi have been described in some detail by Wormington (1956); Martin, Quimby, and Collier (1947); McGregor (1965); and by Reed in brief summaries (1946, 1964), the latter dealing with the entire Southwest. These authors all drew on an enormous literature and have succeeded in summarizing the available evidence according to their individual interests and biases.

Intensive study of the Southwest was begun in the Four Corners area primarily because of the Wetherills, a clan of rancher-explorer-collectors who brought the wonders of Mesa Verde to the attention of the world about 1890. They, too, noted the sequence from early nonpottery deposits into the later ceramic-using, stone-architecture sites, and Richard Wetherill even gave the term "Basketmaker" to the prepottery levels. As a result of several decades of study, Kidder (1924) was able to write a comprehensive introduction to the Southwest; in this he summarized some of the discrete data of the Anasazi. Furthermore, he pinpointed the several subareas (for example, the Hohokam), where knowledge was insufficient for systematic appraisal. Thus, his brilliant book became a guide to study. Through the writing of this volume Kidder came to realize that better ordering of the Anasazi regional data was possible. Accordingly, in 1927 he called a conference of Southwestern specialists at Pecos, New Mexico (where he was then excavating). There a basic classification was devised.

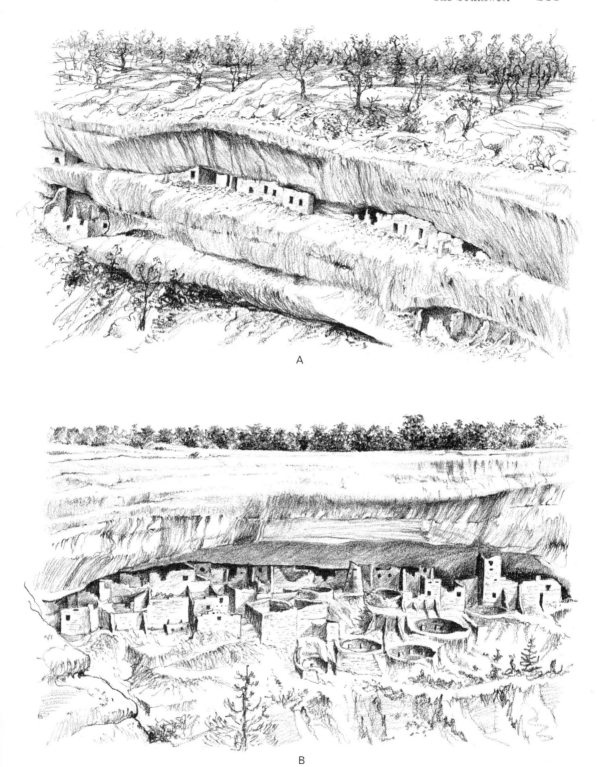

A

B

Figure 7.12   *Mesa Verde. A, Double House; B, Cliff Palace.*
(After D. Watson 1950)

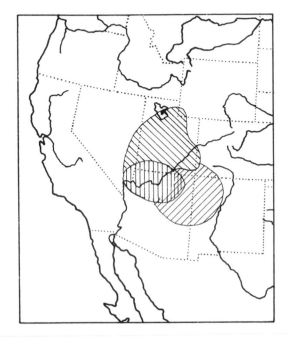

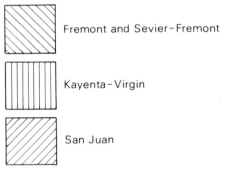

Fremont and Sevier-Fremont

Kayenta-Virgin

San Juan

Figure 7.13   *Anasazi subprovinces.*

It is still used by students today. The classification was intended to be tentative and flexible, but accepted uncritically, it all too soon became rigid and was applied as a yardstick to all the Southwest beyond its limits of applicability (see Brew 1946; Roberts 1935b; and Jennings 1966b). The classification was the first one developed in America from intensive fieldwork. It was based on sequential cultural development, but has come to be used as if it were entirely chronologic. Prehistoric time was broken into eight segments, and these "periods" were separated on the basis of traits present

or absent in the collections. The periods were as follows, with dates which were established long after the 1927 conference:

Latest:	*Pueblo V*	A.D. *1700 to the present*
	Pueblo IV	A.D. *1300–1700*
	Pueblo III	A.D. *1100–1300*
	Pueblo II	A.D. *800/850–1100*
	Pueblo I	A.D. *750–900 (where it exists)*
	Basketmaker III	A.D. *450–750*
	Basketmaker II	A.D. *1–500*
Earliest:	*Basketmaker I*	*pre-*A.D. *1*

Basketmaker I was hypothesized in 1927 as a logical necessity since knowledge then ended with Basketmaker II. The widespread Desert culture has long since been accepted as filling the gap, forming the base with the requisite traits upon which pottery, horticulture, etc., were grafted.

Roberts (1935b, 1937) recognized the rigidity of the Pecos classification and attempted to loosen it by combining some of the stages and supplying semi-interpretive names. Contrasted, the systems are:

Roberts	**Pecos**
Historic	*Pueblo V*
Regressive (and Renaissance)	*Pueblo IV*
Great (Classic)	*Pueblo III*
Developmental	*{Pueblo II* *{Pueblo I*
Modified Basketmaker	*Basketmaker III*
Basketmaker	*{Basketmaker II* *{Basketmaker I*

With the classification, Roberts (1937) later provided a detailed trait list; at the same time, he issued a warning about the dangers of mistaking a classification as the "truth" rather than using it as a temporary device or tool for analysis and interpretation. Roberts' excellent suggestions were not widely accepted in practice, and most students still use the Pecos classification today. The significance of the periods has shifted from content to chronology, probably because there is so much variation in the detailed trait associations from one district to another.

Initial Basketmaker II is now dated at about the time of Christ, persisting until about A.D. 500. Its identifying traits are familiar, being those cited for the Desert culture (Chapter 4) and equally remindful of the early Mogollon material from Tularosa Cave. The sites are most often to be found in caves, alcoves, or overhangs. In such situations, the perishable artifacts are preserved, as are the bodies of the dead. The practice of skull deformation, which later proved popular, had not yet appeared.

The difference between Basketmaker II and the preceding Archaic is not in the basic inventory of objects—woven sandals, basketry, cloth of several types, wooden scoops or trowels, clubs and assorted bone and chipped stone tools, string aprons, cordage of all kinds, fur blankets and skins, atlatls, darts, gaming pieces or dice, bone whistles, crude figurines—but in the addition of new traits. These are horticulture (corn and squash) and a unique style of architecture. The corn is of a different strain from the earliest Mogollon variety.

The dwelling architecture of Basketmaker II is unique. The dwellings were rounded, shallow basins, some 12 to 18 feet in diameter, with the walls made of horizontal logs laid in mud mortar. Evidently the walls sloped or curved toward a domed top; entry was through a side door. These structures have been reported at the Talus Village site (Morris and Burgh 1954), where a sizable village was uncovered, and at a few other locations in the same drainage area near Durango, Colorado. The houses were built on shelves or terraces constructed by cutting a level floor into the sloping rubble against the cliffs. The resultant area was, therefore, level with the surface at one edge and sunk 2 or 3 feet below the sloping surface on the other side toward the cliff. The houses cannot be thought of as pit houses; the log "masonry" was built on the leveled area, and the structures may be thought of as surface dwellings. There were no fireplaces as such; "heating" pits, full of fire-cracked and mottled stones, which must have been heated out-of-doors, are the rule. These pits are lined with mud plaster or are merely unmodified basins with no secondary features. No fires were kept. At least reddening of the clay, which is characteristic of true fireplaces, was lacking. There were cists and storage pits dug into the irregular floors. And there were many carefully made storage cists outside the houses; some were of clay and others carefully lined and floored with flagstones.

The Durango villages were occupied for some 200 years (from A.D. 50 to 260), and the houses were rebuilt, or new ones were built over old ones, several times. Morris and Burgh point out that these structures are quite reminiscent of the Mogollon in many ways, and after an analysis of all traits, they opine that both the early Mogollon and the Basketmaker II were similar enough to have derived from a common base. Bullard (1962) would probably agree. Be that as it may, the origin and diffusion of the pit house or earth lodge in the Americas are not yet known, although the concept is known from the Arctic southward.

The Durango log-and-mortar technique has not been found elsewhere. Even so, it is usually spoken of as being typical of Basketmaker II. Not too far from Durango, at Navajo Reservoir near Farmington, New Mexico, Dittert, Eddy, and Dickey (1963) and Eddy (1961) report surface structures with peculiar cobble "aprons" which they identify as Basketmaker II houses of the Los Pinos phase (A.D. 1 to 400). Horizontal logs around the edges of the oval floor area are very like the Durango finds. Moreover, the Los Pinos phase sites yielded a small amount of polished

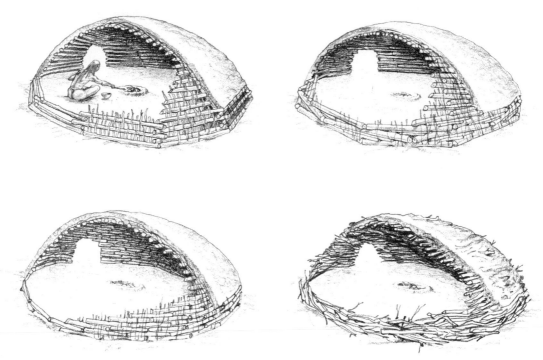

Figure 7.14   Four postulated reconstructions, other than log and mortar, of Basketmaker II dwellings (cutaway views). Floors are approximately 15 feet in diameter.

brown pottery of fair quality, resembling the Mogollon wares of the time. This is the earliest true pottery reported from the Four Corners area. Maize was also discovered at these New Mexico sites.

The Basketmaker III house type is much better known and is represented by numerous excavated examples. Bullard (1962) presents the best extant analysis of pit house architecture. He provides a summary of the Basketmaker III pit house (and of later periods to A.D. 900). Perhaps his most cogent observation is that ". . . every pit house . . . is to a certain extent different from every other." Nonetheless, one can generalize that both Basketmaker III and Pueblo I pit houses tended toward the rectangular ("square with rounded sides") and were actually semisubterranean, the roof being erected over a room carved deep into the earth as much as 3 or 4 feet. Certain special

features were normally present, such as a tunnel entrance leading from an antechamber to the main room, southeast orientation, four post roof supports, and benches around the walls. Later, the antechamber gave way to the ventilator, and the posts were replaced by roof-supporting pilasters set on the bench. Finally, the kiva, the subterranean ceremonial structure, which was not used for habitation, evidently evolved from the pit house as surface masonry structures came to serve as dwellings by A.D. 700 in the San Juan Anasazi area. But to the west—in the Kayenta and more westerly districts—the pit house remained a popular architectural form until the end of the thirteenth century.

The basic Anasazi settlement pattern developed during Basketmaker III. This is a village orientation along a southeast-northwest axis; the storage bins or cists were the "back" of the settlement, with

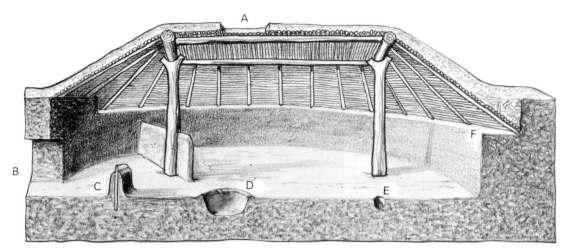

Figure 7.15   *Postulated reconstruction (cross section) of a late Basketmaker III pit house. A, hatchway and smokehole; B, tunnel entrance to antechamber; C, deflector; D, firepit; E, sipapu; F, bench. (After Lancaster and Watson 1954)*

the pit houses to the southeast and with the midden area and burial ground again southeast of the dwellings. When the clustered above-ground houses first developed, they were to the northwest, with the pit houses, or kivas, and the refuse toward the southeast (Reed 1956). Figure 7.15 is a cross section of a late Basketmaker III pit house at Mesa Verde (Lancaster and Watson 1954) showing many of the same features as the kiva (Figure 7.16). The classic kiva form is restricted to the San Juan Anasazi, but rectangular structures believed to have had the same function are found in the Kayenta and other western districts. Pit house architectural details have come to be understood as important in establishing district relationships over the Southwest. Bullard (1962), for example, has analyzed these details and tends to view the pit house as having diffused from the Anasazi area southward. This position opposes that of Wheat (1955) mentioned earlier. In another context, Aikens (1966b) uses pit house and other architectural detail to clarify the Kayenta-Virgin relationships.

But the Southwest is noted more for

above-ground dwellings than for pit houses. After A.D. 900, except in the Fremont and Kayenta regions, the tendency toward large settlements of contiguous rooms or, more accurately, clusters of contiguous rooms, became the rule. The clustering of dwellings and storage rooms with a kiva to the south or southeast has been interpreted as evidence of a pattern of clan or subclan or even family residence. Even though the town or village may have consisted of many houses, the clustered groupings almost certainly preserved family or lineage integrity. This interpretation is largely drawn from ethnologic analogy, but Longacre (1964b) has convincingly demonstrated its probable archeologic validity in an interesting analysis of the ceramic debris from a series of subsettlements at the Carter Ranch site in Arizona. J. N. Hill (1966) has reported similar findings.

By A.D. 1100, Mesa Verde, Chaco Canyon, Canyon de Chelly, and southeastern Utah were densely populated, and the fabled "cities" and cliff dwellings were developed. These are villages where the masonry surface structures became multi-

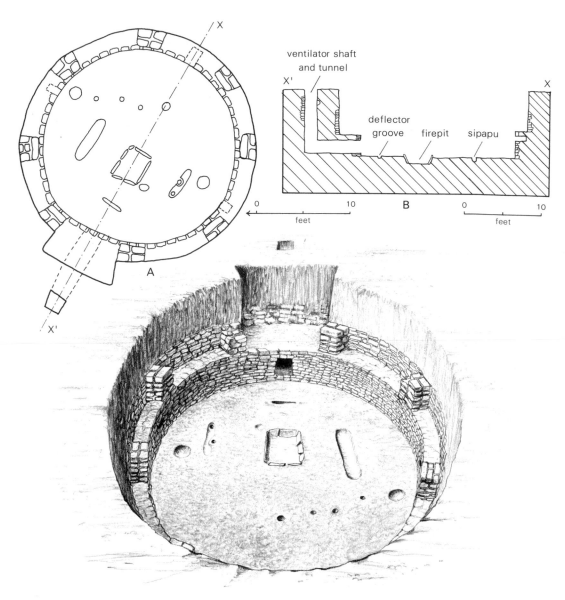

Figure 7.16   *Pueblo II kiva at Mesa Verde National Park. A, plan view; B, cross section; C, view of excavated kiva. (After Lancaster and Pinkley 1954)*

story as population tended to concentrate. Outside the Four Corners area, where Mesa Verde National Park and Aztec National Monument preserve several large buildings, the most spectacular of several large sites is Pueblo Bonito in the fertile Chaco River Valley (Figure 7.17). Located within a national monument, Bonito is known to thousands. It was dug by Neil Judd in the 1920s and is reported in great detail (1954, 1964). The major ruin is a vast, D-shaped or semicircular apartment of 800 rooms, rising to four or five stories around the rim of the arc. The arms of the arc were connected by a long wall to create an enclosure; two large plazas were

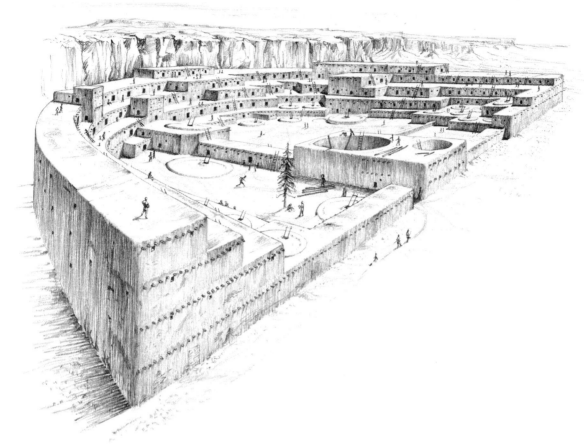

Figure 7.17 *Pueblo Bonito as it may have appeared about* A.D. *1050. (After Judd 1964)*

developed within the enclosed area (Figure 7.18). Although the structure was a honeycomb of rooms, there were kivas in the plazas and even incorporated out of sight throughout the rooms, so the concept of clan settlements and clan kivas is again supported here. Figure 7.19 shows a variety of Pueblo Bonito artifacts.

The richness of the Anasazi begins to be seen in Basketmaker III times in the beautiful sandals woven of finespun string in several colors; decorated, loose-coiled basketry; twined and netted bags; elaborate atlatls and carved throwing sticks; and true fired gray pottery. Designs were sometimes painted on the bowl interiors, but most of the pottery is plain. The brown or red-brown wares of the Basketmaker

II were displaced by the gray, and the dominant Anasazi ceramic style continued to be white or gray, with decoration done in black. The subsistence base was broadened by the addition of beans to the cultigens by the end of Basketmaker II, and apparently the domestication of turkeys also occurred this early.

The differences between Basketmaker III and Pueblo I are negligible, being largely a matter of ceramics. The "period" is actually restricted to a small area in the Anasazi heartland and has little validity elsewhere.

Brew (1946) remarks on the transitional nature of Pueblo I as a time when the pit house remained common but the trend toward surface architecture grew

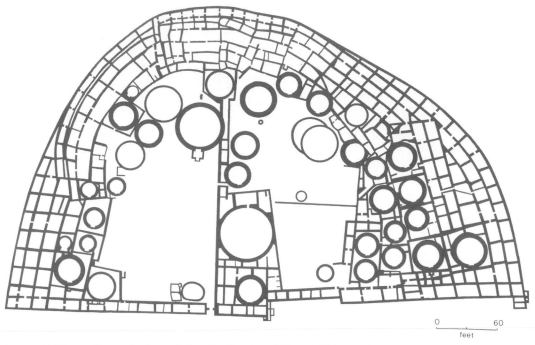

0 ⊢——————⊣ 60
feet

Figure 7.18   *Ground plan of Pueblo Bonito. (After Judd 1964)*

stronger. Bullard (1962) also comments on this aspect of Pueblo I. But it is at this time that the Pueblo ceramics are the most varied. In addition to the fine ware of plain gray, black on white, and black on red and the introduction of a "slip" and corrugated neck bands on culinary pottery, there is a complex of bizarre vessel shapes, possibly borrowed from the Mississippian cultures of the Arkansas Valley. These include trilobed vessels with constricted neck, duck- and gourd-effigy pots, stirrup-spouted vessels, and other forms not found elsewhere in the Southwest (Jennings 1956). The jacal construction, which begins to appear in the Pueblo I, also may very well be a Mississippian trait, known there as wattle-and-daub, but this seems far less likely. Other additions to the Pueblo I trait list include cotton cloth and the practice of cranial deformation— a steeply angled flattening of the occipital area—resulting probably from the use of a rigid cradleboard. Both the cotton and

the cranial flattening (of a milder sort) appear earlier in Mogollon.

It was during Pueblo II, after about A.D. 850, however, that the distinctive flavor of the Anasazi, as well as its vast areal extent, developed. The pit house dropped from favor (but did not disap-

Figure 7.19   *Selected artifacts from Pueblo Bonito. Variable scale. A–C, shell ornaments; D, jet ornament, 2½ inches long; E, F, bone dice, 1 inch long; G, jet ring (bird has turquoise inset wings); H, copper bells; I, turquoise bird effigy, 2 inches high; J, ceramic bear effigy; K, turquoise pendants, 1 inch long; L, turquoise bead; M, turquoise necklace; N, bone scrapers with jet and turquoise inlay, 6½ and 5 inches long; O, wooden snake effigy, 12¾ inches long; P, three bone awls, 4½ to 7¾ inches long; Q, bone needle, 2¾ inches long; R, flint knife, 7¼ inches long; S, projectile points; T, fragment of ceremonial staff; U, black on white bowl, 2¾ inches high, 7 inches in diameter; V, stone pipe, 3½ inches long; W, pottery pipe, 3½ inches long; X, Old Bonitian pot, 13½ inches high; Y, bifurcated basket, 15½ inches high, 12 inches wide. (After Judd 1954)*

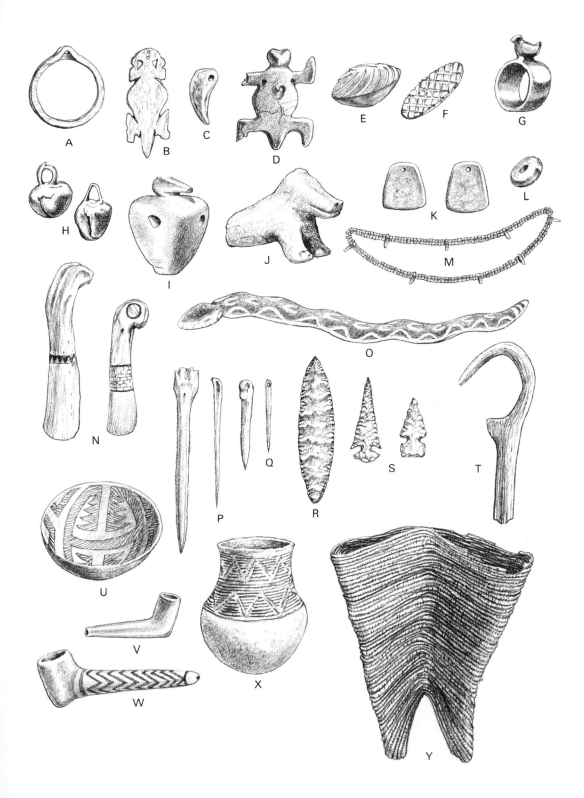

pear, particularly in the western or Kayenta province, where it persisted until A.D. 1300), and the typical architecture became the block or arc of contiguous rooms with the frontal kiva.

The spread of Anasazi influence can perhaps be credited particularly to a somewhat favorable rainfall pattern (Baerreis and Bryson 1965; compare Schoenwetter and Eddy 1964; Schoenwetter 1966) and possibly to new strains of cultigens. But credit must also go to the Anasazi family or lineage farmstead pattern of life. Small ruins occur by the thousands wherever there was water to put on the fertile soil; thus, the population spread as family after family "hived off" to make new stands and the culture spread far beyond the favored areas where the land could support heavy aboriginal use (Jennings 1966b).

In Pueblo II ceramics there is an increased use of coarse, wavy corrugations over the full surface of cooking vessels. The use of decoration increased on most vessels except on the cooking wares. The open-ended metate, the increased use of cotton, coiled basketry, the bow and arrow—all are found with some stylistic and decorative changes; but as Woodbury (1954) has said, the form and overall inventory of Anasazi tools and implements change remarkably little through time. The major stylistic changes are found in the pottery. The appearance, period of popularity, and disappearance of distinctive pottery styles or types have been extensively studied and are well charted. Ceramics have provided the clues to regional boundaries and evidence of interregional communication, and they also form the backbone of the chronologic system. Breternitz (1963) has compiled an excellent index to the many diagnostic pottery types, their span of popularity (usually deduced from association with ruins datable by dendrochronology), and the chronologic "clustering" of certain types. The

undecorated wares enjoyed long life-spans and are not very useful in either cultural period or chronologic ascriptions, although corrugation techniques tend to have some diagnostic usefulness.

Whether the viability of Pueblo II was real or whether its spread was entirely an environmental phenomenon, the fact of areal dominance cannot be denied. In some areas Pueblo II can be thought of lasting until the thirteenth century, while in the core district Pueblo III developed into the climax most people know about. It is in Pueblo III that the large settlements and multistory "communal" dwellings appear—at Mesa Verde, Chaco and de Chelly Canyons, and at two sites, Betatakin and Keet Seel, in the Kayenta. And it is at this time that the spread of masonry southward and an intrusion of some Hohokam influences northward led to a kind of leveling off of all the Southwest traditions that Reed (1964), Wheat (1955), and others speak of. This leveling off or uniformity is real enough but does not obscure the comparable reality of certain minor districts—Patayan, Salado, Sinagua—where regional specialists have perceived local blendings of a distinctive nature.

Because of the impact the large Pueblo III settlements have always had on laymen, the reports of their excellence are often more enthusiastic than accurate. However glowingly it may be described, Anasazi (or other Southwestern) masonry architecture was neither very sophisticated nor particularly good. The mortar was mud, and the building stones were whatever lay at hand. Although masonry was often coursed and the stones were sometimes shaped, the structures usually reveal little planning or foresight, and no special engineering principles (such as the arch or cantilever span) were achieved. The unit of construction was a single, four-sided cell or boxlike room. Its walls were stones laid in mud mortar. Mud sometimes makes up 30 or 40 percent of the volume. The room width was controlled by the length of available timbers strong enough to span the walls to support a roof of mud placed upon a platform of sticks and bark or grass athwart the major beams (Figure 7.20). Given this cellular module (and walls of sufficient strength), one could raise a structure to two, three, four, or five stories in height and extend it infinitely horizontally simply by adding more single cells or units, that is, rooms. Most ruins testify to accretional growth, room by room, as each new room abuted and shared one or more walls with an earlier room or rooms. Even the symmetric and smoothly terraced Pueblo Bonito shows several periods of accretion by the users. In effect, these were like all other aboriginal dwellings, handmade from locally available materials by the user (or his spouse) to a pattern but to no rigid detailed specifications. Where stone was lacking, jacal was used, or coursed adobe alone. No great effort to create artistic textured effects is noted, except in the Chaco area, where textured, decorative facing techniques in a distinctly Mexican manner are found. These techniques, as well as the Great Kivas of the district (Ferdon 1955), may be ideas borrowed from Mexico. Usually the walls were covered with mud plaster so that the masonry was not visible, and one has the impression that the niceties of stonemasonry were ignored. To point out the simplicity of the architecture is not to deprecate it; the appropriateness of the structures for

Figure 7.20 *Postulated, somewhat idealized, reconstruction of room interior at Pueblo Bonito. (After Judd 1964)*

the environment, their sturdiness, and the formal charm of those that still survive impress all beholders.

In crafts, Pueblo III can be thought of as an age of specialization. The quality of the already-good pottery improved, and the famous Mesa Verde mug was added to the list of vessel forms. Polychrome painting and black paint on yellow and orange extended the color range. Decorations were elaborate and meticulously executed. In each district, distinctive styles developed, and the different ceramic types are readily identifiable. There was much trade in pottery during this time indicating, perhaps, widespread popularity of different styles. Culinary vessels became increasingly elaborate in the fine, often patterned, coiling over all the exterior. While pottery became more exuberant, the textiles tended to be undecorated, albeit well made, except for cotton cloth, where complex, lacelike, loom-made designs became the mode.

The collections from Pueblo III sites are enormous in their bulk. The artifacts range from cobbles used as hammerstones to exquisite ornaments of turquoise and turquoise mosaics. Tools of bone, stone, wood, and antler occur by thousands. Textiles—mats, bags, baskets, sandals, nets, cordage, aprons, robes, blankets—demonstrate great skill and artistry. Personal ornaments such as pendants, bracelets, or beads, as well as religious objects, are found by the hundreds. Typical Pueblo II and III objects are shown in Figures 7.21 and 7.22.

The closing years of Pueblo III were marked by extreme contraction of Anasazi territory; all of Utah, much of northern Arizona, and Colorado seem to have been abandoned. Some Kayentans seem to have migrated to east-central Arizona, generally, while the Anasazi shrank almost to the limits of the Rio Grande Valley. Although the extent of the cultural areas shown in Figure 7.2 is based largely on ceramic data, these data are sufficient to convey the shocking suddenness of the weakening of all Southwestern cultures. Just why this sudden contraction should have occurred is not known.

Reasons suggested include a long drought, the pressure of "enemy peoples," or a change in precipitation pattern from winter to summer rain, with a disastrous attendant flooding-and-gullying cycle which made horticulture difficult. All these lack proof, although Schoenwetter (various) and Jennings (1966b) summarize evidence of frequent summer floods on a scale that would ensure repeated crop failures in some areas. For even part-time gardeners, successive crop losses would ensure privation and the death of the very young and aged as rations grew shorter. The work of Fritts, Smith, and Stokes (1965) does not entirely support Schoenwetter's conclusions (see Chapter 9).

As for enemy peoples, there is evidence for attack and slaughter of members of a settlement at some locations, but most ruins reveal little violence at the time of abandonment, with many valuable items being left behind intact. Of course, foot travelers cannot carry many household furnishings on a long trek, so the discarding of pottery vessels, tools, and clothing when a starving, weakened family abandoned its home forever would not be surprising. Even so, there could have been alien "pressure" without warfare as the Shoshonean-speaking tribes of the Great Basin spilled over into Utah, Colorado, and Arizona. This is known to have occurred about six- to eight-hundred years ago, a time coincident with the southward movement of the Anasazi. In the face of double demand the attrition of the natural resources could have begun with the "Shoshonean" entry. There would also have been additional pressure, such as crop raids and miscellaneous thievery, that the newly arrived Great Basin foragers could have put on the Pueblo populations. Simi-

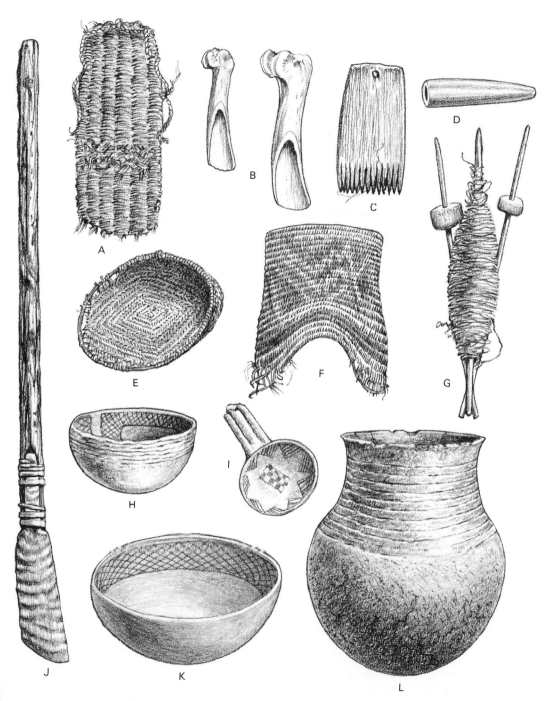

Figure 7.21 *Pueblo II artifacts. Variable scale. A, woven sandal; B, bone scrapers; C, wooden comb; D, stone pipe; E, winnowing basket; F, bifurcated basket; G, spindle and weighted whorls; H, black on white bowl; I, black on white ladle (broken handle); J, digging stick with sheep-horn blade (restored); K, black on red bowl; L, utility vessel. (Drawn from University of Utah collection)*

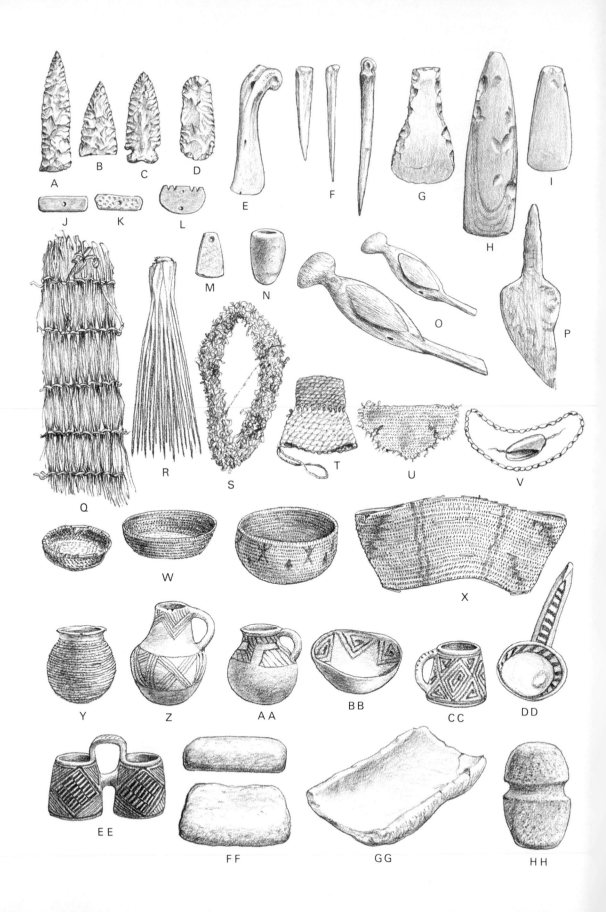

Table 6   Comparison of Mesa Verde and Sinagua culture traits (modified from Reed 1964)

	Mesa Verde	*Sinagua*
Residential architecture	Very large to very small pueblos, well built of selected and worked stone, arranged consistently in a front-oriented plan	Pueblos of generally inferior masonry with no particular orientation, no front or back
Ceremonial structures	Specialized kivas, quite distinct from domiciliary rooms, generally circular, with standard features; also various peculiar buildings	None definitely recognizable (in a few pueblos, for example, Tuzigoot, a rectangular chamber larger than other rooms, with a few special features, and very possibly a kiva)
Utility (culinary) pottery	Gray, all-over-indented corrugated, scraped (no use of paddle and anvil), unpolished	Polished, smooth brown- and redware, finished with paddle and anvil
Painted pottery	A distinct type of fine black on white	None locally made; imported Anasazi vessels
Stone axes	Full-grooved for a wrapped haft, only the cutting edge ground, made of river pebbles	Well-made, polished, three-quarters grooved (for a J-shaped haft), worked all over, of hard volcanic rock
Artificial (cradleboard) deformation of the skull	Both lambdoid and vertical occipital types	Exclusively vertical
Burial of the dead	Both flexed and extended inhumation, the former predominating	Uniformly extended inhumation
Turkeys	Domesticated, or at the very least kept and eaten	Wild turkeys occasionally hunted (or captured for feathers?), probably not eaten

lar pressure may well have been felt in the Hohokam and Sinagua areas as the

Figure 7.22   Pueblo III artifacts. Variable scale. A–C, points; D, stone scraper; E, bone scraper; F, bone awls; G–I, polished stone celts or hoes; J, K, bone gaming pieces; L, stone gaming piece; M, stone ornament; N, stone pipe; O, carved wooden birds; P, wooden utensil; Q, fragment of woven mat; R, yucca bundle used as hair brush (?); S, skein of cotton string; T, woven bag of dog and human hair; U, twilled cotton fabric; V, string of Olivella beads and enlarged view of shell; W, baskets; X, fragment of carrying basket; Y, corrugated pot; Z, black on red jar; AA, black on white pot; BB, black on white bowl; CC, Mesa Verde Black-on-white mug; DD, Mesa Verde Black-on-white ladle; EE, black on white twin mug; FF, manos; GG, metate; HH, fully grooved stone ax. (Drawn from University of Utah collection)

Yuman-speaking tribes pressed eastward from California at about this same time. If enemy pressure is conceived thus, instead of as warfare, present data make this speculation defensible. Actually, no single explanation is especially convincing, and the full explanation of the shrinkage of Pueblo territory is not known.

While the San Juan Anasazi were in full climax in Pueblo III, the provincial areas were by no means as impressive. Reed (1964) makes this clear for the Sinagua of central Arizona by means of a contrasting list, presented here as Table 6.

The story of Pueblo IV is one of territorial contraction and consequent increase in population in restricted areas. As Figure 7.2 reveals, by A.D. 1500, Pueblo settlements were only to be found in the Upper Rio Grande Valley, the Acoma and Zuñi districts, and the Hopi villages. Two outstanding advances in ceramic technology were the use of metallic glazes, in both the Zuñi district and in the Rio Grande Valley, and the development of the Hopi Sikyatki Polychrome, featuring (Mexican-inspired?) graceful, realistic designs in lieu of the early geometric motifs (Reed 1964). Some of the finest pottery north of Mexico was produced at this time. The ancient settlement pattern—storage-dwelling-midden axis—gave way to the enclosed or central-plaza village plan.

Pueblo V is primarily a story of European contact and the stresses of acculturation with the Spanish, with the Indians in continuous, varyingly intense cooperation or conflict. The Pueblo tribes became even more conservative, retaining their languages, religion, and other traditions in the face of economic, military, and religious pressures. Resistance in 1680 took the form of outright revolt, and the Southwest was free of Spaniards, including priests, until 1692. In the sphere of material culture the Indian groups were more receptive. European crops, domestic animals, iron tools and weapons, and some architectural features were accepted from the conquerors; but in all other things the Pueblo preserved their old ways remarkably intact, although the shrinkage of territory and the decrease in population trends continued under Spanish and, later, American rule (Reed 1954).

These decreases in territory and population during late Pueblo IV and V can now be more certainly credited in part to enemy peoples. Some time before A.D. 1500 (Gunnerson 1956), the nonagricultural Athabaskan tribes came into the Southwest from the north and east. These emigrants are known today as the several Apache bands and the numerous Navajo. By A.D. 1500, the land was, as mentioned

earlier, largely empty of permanent settlements and the Navajo and Apache began to spread into these "empty" spaces. They also put heavy raiding pressures on the usually unwarlike Pueblo. The newcomers not only took food and women, but also borrowed many traits, such as horticulture and weaving and elements of religion. In fact, the most impressive trait of the Navajo, as a tribe, is their adaptability. Their religion, their material culture (including weaving and metal smithing), their pastoral life of sheep rearing, and their settlement patterns are a blend of their original culture with elements from all the peoples they have touched. As pastoralists moving in a seasonal rhythm, the Navajo achieved a sort of symbiosis, albeit sometimes uneasy, with the sedentary Pueblo, with each group exploiting somewhat different ecologic niches.

Archeologic evidence of these latest aboriginal entrants into the Southwest is scanty, but some data are at hand. Perhaps the two most thorough-going archeologic studies of Navajo sites are those by Hester and Shiner (1963) from the San Juan River Valley in New Mexico and Colorado and by Keur (1941) of Big Bead Mesa, also in northwestern New Mexico.

Hester and Shiner report several locations which are consistently located on the edge of the first or second terrace or bench above the river floodplain. The timespan falls from A.D. 1550 to perhaps 1775. The remains are divided into three phases—the Dinetah (A.D. 1550 to 1696), the Gobernador (1696 to 1775), and the Refugee Pueblo. (The late, fairly heavy, Pueblo admixture came as the Pueblo fled northward from the reprisals following the Pueblo Revolt of the 1680s.) The typical Navajo site shows evidence of one or more hogans and limited debris. The normal living pattern is, and presumably was, a cluster of two or three hogans sheltering an extended family. The clusters are widely scattered; only in modern times have "The People" developed the loose settlements of a dozen or so hogans a few hundred feet apart along a wash.

The hogan traditionally had a tripod frame of forked posts with sticks and branches forming the walls of the tipi-shaped dwelling. An entryway opened to the east (Figure 7.23). It contained a basin-shaped or even flat fireplace in an oval, saucer-shaped floor and rarely other internal features. Outdoor firepits, a shade or ramada, and metate rests accompany the hogans. This style is often called the summer hogan. Another, more durable, design was a circular structure of stone. Cribbed logs, resulting in a hexagonal or octagonal shape, have commonly been used in recent years. Near each settlement the one or more small "hogans" are the remains of sweat lodges. Artifacts are scant and rarely diagnostic, except pottery, which in many attributes resembles Woodland pottery in shape, surface texturing, coarse temper, and general crudity. The pottery offers some support for the idea

that the Athabaskans reached the Southwest by way of the Plains (Figure 7.24). Hester (1962) gives a summary of research done to date and outlines the many problems yet unsolved in Navajo archeology. He also provides a complete list, in tabular form, of the few scholars who have concerned themselves with Navajo archeologic studies. Only two have done extensive excavation; the score of others contented themselves with survey, so the entire field still awaits systematic attention.

Summary

Little, other than mention, need be said about the several outlying Southwestern provinces. Regional specialists identify the Fremont and Sevier-Fremont of Utah. The Virgin in Utah and Nevada is a part of the Kayenta. These and the Patayan, the Jornada, and even other local variants, are all so clearly derivative from one or

Figure 7.23   *Typical Navajo hogan. (After Mindeleff 1898)*

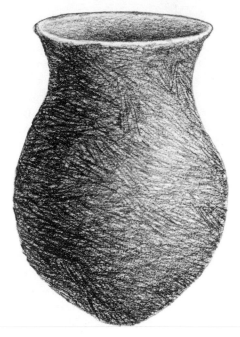

Figure 7.24   Navajo utility vessel (restored). Approximately 12 inches high. (After Keur 1941)

another of the major traditions that further description seems unnecessary. An exception can be made in the case of the Fremont of Utah, however. Described first by Morss (1931), the Utah material has been recognized as showing many Northern Plains traits, as has the presumably late Promontory culture of northern Utah (Steward 1937). Aikens (1966a), with new data, has greatly strengthened the hypothesis of a Plains origin for Fremont and has also showed undoubted Promontory-Fremont contemporaneity. Thus, he would label the Fremont as basically a Plains thrust into the Southwest, with the Anasazi overlay—gray and black on gray pottery, a variety of pit house, aboveground structures, and little else—indicative of much less Southwestern dominance than earlier students had thought. Nondescript and "average" Southwestern in quality as the usual Fremont ceramic artifacts are (see Figure 7.25), the figurine cult (and related pictograph complex) is one

of the distinctive aspects of the culture (Figure 7.26).

The Southwest traditions represent the third of the climaxes reached in aboriginal North America as a result of the introduction of horticulture, pottery, and other traits from Mexico. A synthetic summary covering the period A.D. 450 to 1450, modified from Jennings (1956), is outlined below:

1 Settlements
   a Some areas of dense population
   b Pit houses and jacals
   c Surface masonry or adobe structures
   d Granaries
   e Sedentary or semisedentary habitat, permanent villages
   f Specialized religious structures
   g Tendency toward patterned settlements
2 Subsistence
   a Close adaptation to environment as revealed in hunting and use of native resources
   b Agriculture, minor at first, but increasing in importance
   c Domesticated animals: turkeys, dogs
   d Irrigation, floodwater farming, or other evidences of some sort of controlled or planned water supply
3 Artifact inventory
   a Pottery, in general characterized by use of color in decoration rather than surface treatment (exception: corrugation)
   b Bow and arrow; projectile points quite variable but in general small,

Figure 7.25   Fremont artifacts. Variable scale. A, bone splinter awl; B–D, bone awls; E, antler flaking tool; F, bone gaming pieces; G, points; H, shaft scraper; I, K, scrapers; J, perforated clay disc; L, rough hammerstone; M–O, stone balls (N coated half with red ocher, half with black pigment); P, bone necklace; Q, twisted bark rope; R, leather moccasins; S, pot and enlarged view of applique treatment; T, small pot; U, Ivie Creek Black-on-white bowl; V, pot with applique at rim and restricted waist; W, pottery jar. (Drawn from University of Utah collection)

A   B   C   D   E   F   G   H

I   J   K

L   M   N   O

P   Q   S

R   T   U   V   W

notched, pressure-flaked, with preference for fine-grained rocks with a conchoidal fracture such as obsidian and chalcedony

c Grooved ax; maul
d Extensive use of marine shell for ornament
e Trade in, or for, turquoise, lignite,

Figure 7.26   *Fremont clay figurines. A–C, Pillings Cave, Utah; D–G, University of Utah collection. A, B, D, one-half size; C, E–G, two-thirds size. (A–F after Morss 1954, 1957; G after Aikens 1966a)*

feathers, and other objects of value; generally "luxury" items (ornamental, ceremonial)

f Weaving, use of textiles

g Rather coarse coiled basketry, twilled basketry

h Trough metates (or slab metates in mealing bins); characteristic grinding implements

i Great variability in bone tools: awls, flakers, wedges; in general, absence of harpoons or barbed bone implements

j Figurines, not abundant but found throughout the region

k Pipes and cane cigarettes, use of tobacco

4 Social features

a Weakly stratified society; strong class structure not evidenced (as compared with the Southeast United States, for example)

b Some social control, as evidenced by irrigation projects, great kivas, and other works requiring community effort

c A general tendency toward ceremonial elaboration and reliance upon religious controls (crop-increase rites and so forth) rather than upon political controls (raiding or conquest)

d Despite large settlements, no particular evidence for a militaristic city-state such as is found in Mexico and the Near East

e Relatively limited warfare mostly confined to local raiding

f Some development of mortuary complex including specially prepared graves and mortuary offerings; no marked status differences observable in mortuary practices

g Little evidence of human sacrifice or the taking of human trophies

h Adaptability and receptivity to foreign ideas, but with strong integration of new traits into existing patterns

The features which represent dominant holdovers from the Desert culture are:

1 General close adaptation to local environmental features

2 Techniques of food preparation

3 Tendency toward community with little social stratification

4 Weakly developed ideas of conquest

8

The Arctic

While the entire sequence of arctic cultures might, with some justi-
fication, have been considered Archaic in stage, they are reserved
for separate description because they do not precisely fit the Archaic
definition of "total exploitation." Admittedly, the vegetal resources of
the area are not lush, nor are they available the year round, but
during the short summer season there grows a variety of edible
species but rarely utilized (Spencer 1965a). The subsistence base is
almost entirely restricted to the animals of land, sea, and air. A
second and more important reason for the separate treatment is
that the arctic cultures show little relationship to any other American
cultures in either artifacts or economy, which is not surprising in
view of the special and rigorous arctic environment. The arctic
adaptation seems to have evolved in place from very early beginnings
with little evidence of exchange with any of the more southerly
cultures we have examined. From the outset, the arctic cultures
turned toward the sea as the primary food source. Along with specialized equipment for sea hunting, the arctic climate required many
special tools for working, traveling, and living in the snowy wastes.

The physical type of the Eskimo population is recognized as distinct from all other American Indian types and is usually regarded
as being the result of a spread of Siberian Mongoloid stock (the

Inuid of Neumann) into the arctic area in the last 3,000 to 4,000 years. The equally distinctive language, Eskaleut, is usually explained in the same way, but Dumond (1965) offers evidence (see page 319) which suggests that the idea of recent immigration from Asia may be in error.

The dean of Arctic archeologists, Collins (1964), reminds us that two of the major problems in American archeology are set in the Arctic—the entry of man into the New World and the origin of Eskimo culture. The first of these problems has been outlined (Chapter 3), leaving the equally complex problem of Eskimo culture to be dealt with here. The Arctic has an enormous extent. Figure 8.1, a polar view, shows the thousands of miles of coastline, the hundreds of islands, and the long inlets and stretches of open water, to say nothing of tens of thousands of square miles of landmass. In this account, Alaska is of such primary concern that the following description of the peninsula seems appropriate.

Alaska can be divided into three geographic regions. Southern Alaska is mountainous and heavily glaciated. The mountain ranges are geographically younger and lower in elevation in the western part of the Alaskan peninsula and in the Aleutian Islands than are the mainland ranges to the east. Volcanic activity has been frequent—at least forty-seven eruptions have been recorded since 1760. The broad valleys and low mountain ranges of the interior are in sharp contrast to southern Alaskan topography. The Yukon River is the most extensive drainage system of the interior, heading in southeast Yukon and finally flowing into the Bering Sea at Norton Bay. The Kuskokwim River drains the southwest flank of the Alaskan Range and finally flows into the Bering Sea at Kuskokwim Bay.

North of the Yukon Valley lies the Brooks Range, which provides a barrier between the interior and arctic Alaska.

This large mountain range, an extension of the Rocky Mountain system, is rugged and barren. It ranges in altitude from 9,000 feet near the Canadian border to 3,000 feet in its western portion, near the Bering Sea. The 8-mile-wide range offers one principal pass, the Anaktuvuk, to the Yukon Valley. The arctic slope, north of the Brooks Range, is a crescent-shaped tundra. The coastal waters are shallow, and the land is flat, with innumerable shallow lakes. The frozen tundra of the winter becomes swampy and impassable in the summer.

The climate varies widely from the mild, moist weather of southeast Alaska to the dry, cold, windswept weather of the arctic slope. The mountains of southeast Alaska intercept moisture-laden winds of the Pacific, causing abnormally heavy snowfall, with the result that the glaciation of Alaska has been confined essentially to this area. The effects of the Japanese Current account for the mild climate of the southern Alaskan coastal belt. The Aleutian Islands remain cool in the summer, with more-or-less continuous rain throughout the year. The climate of the interior of Alaska is continental. The winters resemble those of the Plains states; temperatures are seldom severe.

North of the Aleutians, the Japanese Current is dissipated in the Bering Sea, and thus its effect is not felt north of the Pribilof Islands. These islands closely approximate the southern boundary of the winter ice fields. From October to August the Arctic Ocean is locked by ice. The arctic slope is windswept, but summer and early autumn are fairly mild. Spring and late autumn afford the best conditions for movement on the land. Permafrost solidifies the land of the entire arctic slope and about half the Yukon Valley, as well as small areas in southern Alaska.

The flora of Alaska is alpine. The interior, especially along the waterways, has large spruce forests, mixed with bal-

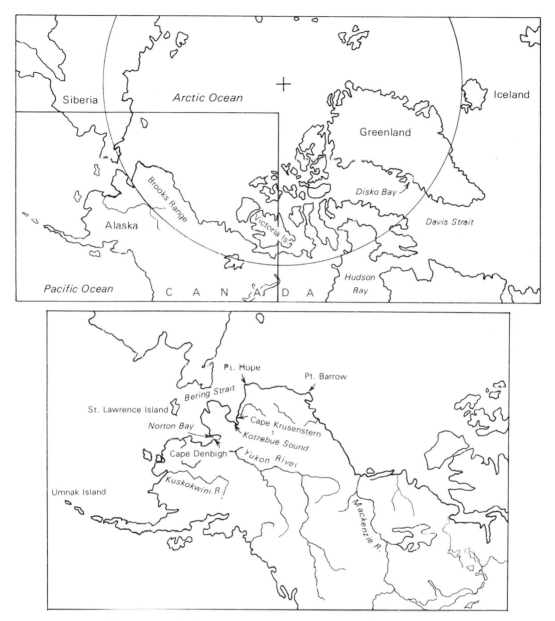

Figure 8.1   *Polar view of the Arctic and enlarged map of Alaskan peninsula.*

sam, poplar, and birch. The milder climate of the south permits the growth of hemlock, whereas willow shrubs, grasses, mosses, and lichens thrive on the arctic slope. Throughout the entire area animal life is plentiful. The sea yields salmon, halibut, cod, crab, sea otter, sea lion, seal, walrus, and whale. Bear, moose, elk, and numerous small, fur-bearing animals abound in the interior, while caribou inhabit the arctic slope and occasionally penetrate the interior.

Although during the Ice Age there was extensive glaciation of Canada, extending southward, no similar ice sheet covered Alaska. The glaciers that were formed centered in the mountain masses and radiated down drainage systems to the sea. The interior was free from ice and was probably filled with fauna. However, glacial deposits were left in the interior, carried by water from melting glaciers. Evidence points to the contemporaneity of the last great Alaskan ice advance with the Wisconsin stage, but the interglacial stages that have been recognized for the Wisconsin have not been fully correlated in Alaska.

Research on the early cultures of the Canadian-Alaskan-Arctic area has only just begun. Here the data are thinly scattered, not yet fully understood, and somewhat obscured by disputes over their probable relationship to better-known materials. The most useful of recent sources about the Arctic in general are two symposia (F. H. West 1963a; J. M. Campbell 1962b) wherein several authorities report their findings and views. Indicative of the state of knowledge are the flatly contradictory positions several experienced students take (compare F. H. West 1963b and MacNeish 1963), and the different chronological and cultural schemes of MacNeish and Giddings discussed below (compare Figures 8.2 and 8.3).

Among the least conservative of the synthesized sequences for Alaska and northwest Canada are MacNeish's (1963) suggestions. Using data from surveys and on the basis of typology, he proposes a basal culture called British Mountain, estimated to be possibly older than 10,000 B.C., then a Flint Creek or Cordilleran at 7000 B.C., a Northern Plano tradition covering a span of 3,000 years, with a Microblade and Small Tool tradition closing this pre-Eskimoid series. Figure 8.2 shows the time and territorial relationships of these traditions. In the same volume, Giddings (1963) handles the Alaskan evidence somewhat more conservatively. His

sequence of cultures (Figure 8.3) represents in the main a series of excavated sites which provide a sequence that is generally accepted. Figure 8.3 is interesting also in that it highlights the long life and wide distribution of Plano-like flint types throughout the arctic complex.

As for the evidence for the antiquity of the British Mountain culture, it is tenuous indeed, being derived entirely from surface material (J. M. Campbell 1959, 1961) or disturbed stratigraphy (MacNeish 1963). On the basis of mere typology, it must be considered here as unproved. At the Kogruk site (Figure 8.4), J. M. Campbell (1962a) sees in the artifacts evidence of trans-Siberian influence from the Mousterian cultures of Eurasia. The similarity of these objects to many other collections of choppers, flakes, and scrapers is not denied, but to argue for either time or cultural ascription on such evidence is not very convincing. One can accept a vague similarity in technology to Levallois-Mousterian flint technology, but this is not a particularly definitive thing in itself. Commenting on this same general problem, Chard (1963) reviews the evidence and arguments and offers the reasonable suggestion that the earliest tool tradition in the Americas might well be a blend of eastern European technology, via Siberia, and the East Asian chopper tradition; he has long insisted that the latter is beyond any doubt present in the Western Hemisphere.

After the debated British Mountain remains, which should probably be ascribed to the Big Game Hunter stage, MacNeish and several other authors recognize many Plano-type projectile points which also imply a Big Game stage. Collins (1964) recognizes the long time which these types seem to span in referring to the phenomenon of "arctic retardation," or lag. Since these types can most economically be explained as having diffused northwestward into the Arctic from the Plains, as Wor-

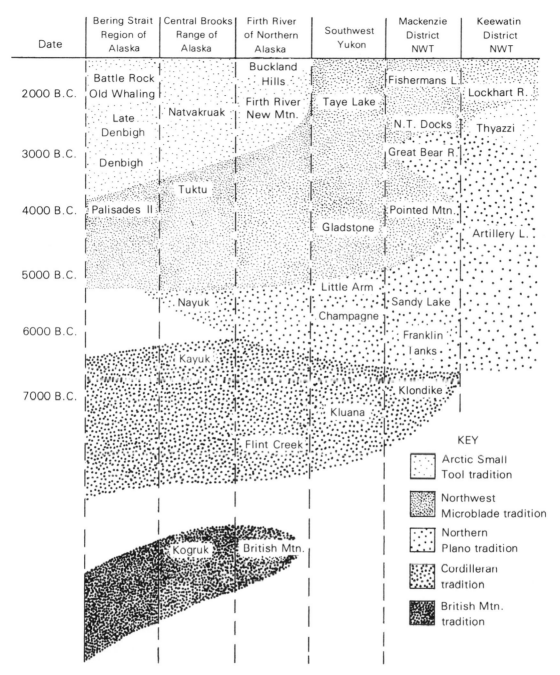

Date	Bering Strait Region of Alaska	Central Brooks Range of Alaska	Firth River of Northern Alaska	Southwest Yukon	Mackenzie District NWT	Keewatin District NWT
2000 B.C.	Battle Rock Old Whaling	Natvakruak	Buckland Hills Firth River New Mtn.	Taye Lake	Fishermans L.	Lockhart R.
	Late Denbigh				N.T. Docks	Thyazzi
3000 B.C.	Denbigh				Great Bear R.	
4000 B.C.	Palisades II	Tuktu		Gladstone	Pointed Mtn.	Artillery L.
5000 B.C.				Little Arm		
		Nayuk		Champagne	Sandy Lake	
6000 B.C.		Kayuk			Franklin Tanks	
7000 B.C.				Kluana	Klondike	
			Flint Creek			
	Kogruk		British Mtn.			

KEY

Arctic Small Tool tradition

Northwest Microblade tradition

Northern Plano tradition

Cordilleran tradition

British Mtn. tradition

Figure 8.2 *Early traditions in arctic America according to MacNeish. (After MacNeish 1963)*

mington and Forbis (1965) do, they can be dismissed with bare mention along with MacNeish's Flint Creek and Plano stages, which should probably be combined as one. The frequently forgotten finds of Plano Angostura and Agate Basin specimens reported by Rainey (1939) were reputedly associated with extinct large fauna as deep as 60 feet in frozen silt near Fairbanks. These were uncovered during

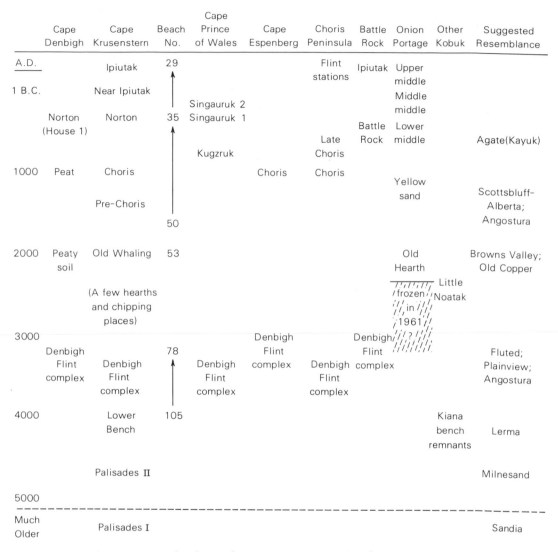

Figure 8.3   *Arctic sites and culture phases containing projectile points similar to forms found in central United States and Canada. (After Giddings 1963)*

gold-dredging operations, so the provenience and actual association must be questioned, particularly since no other such finds have been made.

Giddings' (1960a, 1960b) Palisades I and II from Cape Krusenstern are evidently of considerable age, but again the evidence is inferential. The complex consists of small, side-notched, and stemmed points crudely chipped from flint. As Figure 8.5 shows, the pieces resemble Archaic specimens much more than they share the form and chipping characteristics of the apparently later Plano. Moreover, the Palisades flint collection had been exposed so long that it showed cortical change or decomposition, although this alone cannot constitute evidence of antiquity. What makes this complex important is its location near a series of parallel beaches where, in horizontal beach "stratigraphy," the remains of modern Eskimo houses

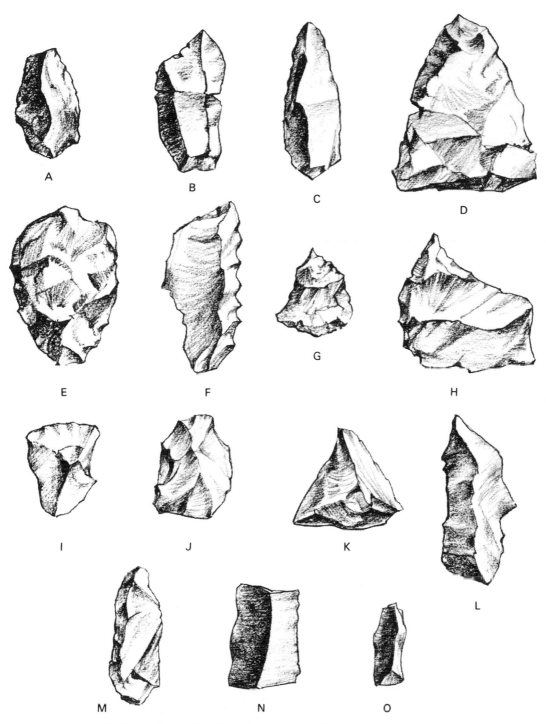

Figure 8.4 *Artifacts from the Kogruk complex. Slightly reduced. A–C, points or end blades; D, biface; E, double-edged side scraper; F, saw; G, H, gravers; I, J, knife-like tools; K, remnant flake core; L–O, blades and microblades. (After J. M. Campbell 1962a)*

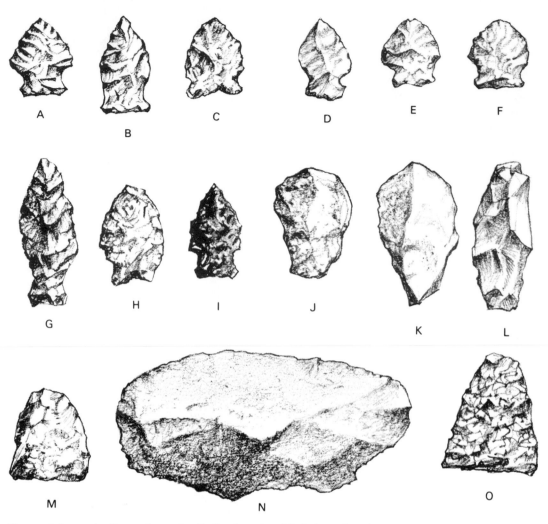

Figure 8.5   *Artifacts from the Palisades site. Slightly reduced.*
A–I, side-notched projectile points; J–M, crude flakes; N, ax-like
flake; O, biface knife fragment. (After Giddings 1962)

occur on the present beach, with older cultural remains (known from other stratigraphic situations to be earlier) occurring on successively higher beaches, reaching further and further inland. With the sea so important to arctic dwellers, the beaches are the preferred dwelling sites; but beaches "recede" inland as new ones of gravel are built up by heavy seas in the areas where conditions are right. The new beaches then become dwelling sites. Thus, through centuries, the older remains are increasingly distant inland from the cur-

rently occupied beach, and a reliable time sequence is built up on the basis of the horizontal relationship of the materials. Figure 8.6 shows Cape Krusenstern, the parallel beaches, and the location of the Palisades, Norton-Choris, Old Whaling, and Denbigh Flint finds made there. Col-

Figure 8.6   *Cape Krusenstern and loci of*
early arctic cultures. A, Palisades; B, Old
Whaling; C, Norton-Choris; D, Denbigh Flint.
Map insert shows location of the Cape. (After
Giddings 1960b)

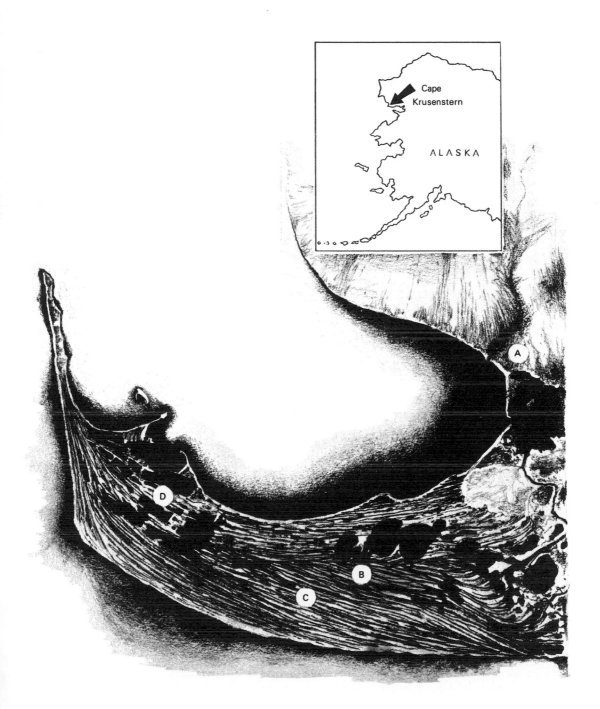

lins has also remarked and relied upon beach stratigraphy elsewhere in the Arctic.

For the Denbigh Flint complex, adequate description and evidence of good control are available in Giddings' (1951, 1964) reports. The Arctic Small Tool and MacNeish's Northwest Microblade traditions would include the Denbigh Flint complex, the Denbigh being one of the type assemblages. First described from a shallow but well-sealed deposit in extreme western Alaska on Norton Bay (see Figure 8.1), a long-known but ignored congery of arctic types and flint techniques was rediscovered beneath evidence of later and already described cultures. The Denbigh complex was one already first described from the Campus site at Fairbanks by Nelson (1937), consisting of chipped crescentic blades or knives; blades or points; delicate little burins made from fine, prismatic flakes; other burins from large, irregular flakes; flake scrapers; harpoon blades; faintly fluted points; and some lanceolate blades remindful of Eden points (Figure 8.7). Noteworthy are the fine ripple diagonal flaking and the use of prismatic flakes. Nelson saw the closest typologic parallels to be with the Siberian Mesolithic sites near Lake Baikal. This assessment still stands as acceptable.

Aside from the stratigraphy and its role in reminding Arctic scholars of the American occurrence of this complex, the Denbigh site is important in providing a hitherto lacking time depth for the arctic cultures in that it yielded radiocarbon dates of over 3500 B.C. Since Giddings' (1951) preliminary report, other locations yielding evidence of the Denbigh Flint complex have been found; search for even older materials has been continued with some success—for example, the Palisades material. As would be expected, the new culture contributed tools and technology to the later cultures of the Arctic. However, since the first report of Denbigh, Laughlin (1963a) and Laughlin and Marsh (1954)

have reported much early occupancy of Umnak Island and other islands of the Aleutian chain.

Given the distribution of the ice at 10,000 B.C. (Figure 8.8), one would expect the earliest evidence of man to occur on Beringia or in the valleys of the Yukon and MacKenzie in Alaska. Any coastal sites of that period would long ago have been inundated, but the eastern islands of the Aleutian chain should reveal evidence of early populations and old technologies, entrapped by the rising sea which turned their mountainous homeland into a series of islands. Such seems to be the case. Laughlin reports a site on Anangula Island where a distinctly East Asiatic core, lamellar flake, and burin industry dated at 6500 B.C. and older was found (1963a). Thus, Japanese-East Asian connections are to some degree confirmed by the Anangula finds. This flake industry, much antedating the Denbigh Flint complex, may, however, be ancestral to it. The Anangula industry may document the arrival of Aleuts in Beringia at a time when land access was entirely feasible, although the possibility of sea travel cannot be ruled out on present evidence.

As for the later Aleutian cultures, Laughlin (1963a) offers a summary which effectively documents the rich faunal resources—from the open sea, the intertidal zone, and the shore—available to the Aleutian Islanders for more than 4,000 years, a period marked by extremely little change in tool type or subsistence focus. From 2000 B.C. onward, these cultures exploited the whale, walrus, sea lion, seal, sea otter, and many birds (at huge rookeries), as well as many species of fish and shellfish. The game, in his words, extended "from whales to whelks." The richness of the land was not reflected in the artifacts; while numerous, specialized, and well-manufactured, they were not elaborate. The art is simple, albeit distinctive in some aspects. The major classes of artifacts

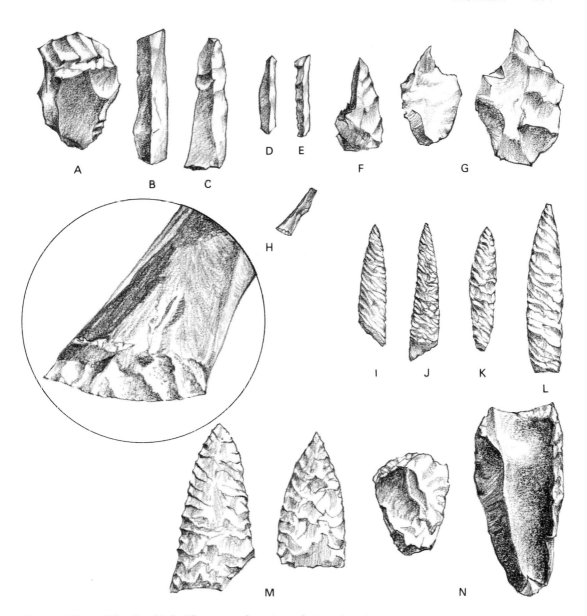

Figure 8.7　　*The Denbigh Flint complex. Actual size. A, microblade core; B–D, microblades; E, burin spall; F, angle burin; G, beaked burins; H, burin spall and much enlarged view showing retouched cutting edge; I, J, side blades; K, L, end blades; M, harpoon blades; N, scrapers. (After Giddings 1964)*

from the earliest levels at the Chaluka site on Umnak Island are presented in Table 7.

Even slate was chipped, not rubbed or ground. At this early date, Laughlin identifies the presence of critical Eskimo

traits. These are the harpoons, fish spears, pronged bird spears, chipped ulus and knives, lamps, fishhooks, and bolas. Skin boats, atlatls, lamellar flakes, and woodworking are present but are not restricted to Eskimo culture. Lacking are ceramics,

Table 7   *Chaluka site: major classes of artifacts (modified from Laughlin 1963a)*

Stone	Bone and Ivory
Bolas	Compound fishhooks
Net sinkers	Spearheads (including three-pronged
Projectile points	bird spears)
Thrusting points	Harpoon heads (including toggleheads)
Ulus of chipped stone	Foreshafts
Tanged knives	Two-piece sockets
Choppers	Wedges
Nonlamellar scrapers and gravers	Awls, pins, etc.
Lamellar scrapers and gravers	Sea-otter-bone tools
Drills	Flakers
Adz blades	Labrets
Pounding, grinding, and polishing stones	Image of the diety
Paint metates, rubbing stones, and red	Adz heads
ocher	Bone dishes
Lamps	Root diggers
Pots (stone dishes or bowls)	Needles (including eyed)
House-wall stones	

sleds, burins, and equipment associated with ice hunting. After about 2000 B.C. the concern of arctic prehistory is with those cultures that are largely dependent on sea-mammal hunting and a technology of considerable complexity.

There are major difficulties of two kinds

Figure 8.8   *Probable distribution of man (shaded area) and ice sheets at about 10,000 B.C. (Modified from Haynes 1964)*

encountered in studying arctic archeology. One, of an entirely practical nature, is the difficulty of excavation itself. The sites are normally in areas of permafrost. This means that the excavations proceed very slowly; once the surface few inches are removed, the subsequent excavation consists of daily removal of an inch or two or three of thawed soil and refuse as new surfaces are exposed. The soil is wet, and the stench is strong as food scraps, bone, human fecal matter, and other items in the midden, frozen solid for millennia, thaw and give off their characteristic odors. This same frost, however, preserves everything else discarded. Organic as well as inorganic objects survive. As a result, the "take" in artifacts is very large and constitutes a very complete inventory of material objects, even though many are worn-out or broken. This complete recovery of objects is an advantage because the recorded ethnographic analogs allow the archeologist to know the function of almost every object he finds. He can make shrewd inferences as to its uses and as to its value in the culture. However, the plentitude of specimens raises other problems in classification, analysis, and interpretation because of the sheer amount available.

The second problem is inherent in the artifacts themselves. This is the fact that almost no typologic changes or differences occur in most of them over long spans of time. This uniformity is not surprising in a rigorous environment with a series of cultures clearly evolving from earlier ones in the same area. The typologic sameness must result simply from the fact that a tool designed for some special task and found satisfactory for that operation will usually not be changed so long as need for it exists; in the Arctic, the need continues. In the Arctic, too, there is need for scores of special tools (for example, ice picks, snow knives, snow goggles), so the analyst is confronted with hundreds of artifact classes and many types within the classes. Only a few of these types give diagnostic clues to time. As a result, the novice is bewildered by the fact that so little of the artifactual bulk provides indices to time or even to local cultures at first—or second—glance.

Although the Arctic has been a subject of anthropologic interest since the late nineteenth century, relatively few scholars have been involved, and the accumulation of data has been slow. Even so, most of the arctic coast, subarctic Canada, and Greenland have at least been sampled. Best known, however, are the Bering Sea area, the northern coast of Alaska, and the Chukchi (Chukotsky) Peninsula. Since 1945, interior Alaska and the Aleutians have received attention. Considering how large the area is, the general chronologic framework is quite well established. There are three reasons for this firm chronology. First, sites were often reused and show cultural change and succession through hundreds of years of time in the deep deposits. Frequent reoccupancy occurs, of course, at protected or elevated or otherwise favorable locations near the sea and provides the basic relative ages of the layers. A second time control, also resulting from the necessity for living near the sea where the food mammals are, is found in those cases, mentioned above, where new beachlines are built up by currents and eddies during storms. The third control is, of course, the radiocarbon technique, which has provided a scattering of dates for the sequence of complexes whose relative ages are already known in the situations described above. (The abundance of organic remains makes it possible to get radiocarbon dates from almost any arctic site.) With three such chronologic cross checks, the arctic time scale is probably as reliable as any in North America.

The Eskimo and pre-Eskimo remains from about 500 B.C. onward are found in both northeastern Siberia and Alaska; these cultures have usually been regarded as Siberian in origin. But, as mentioned above, there are earlier remains that also show a sea-mammal orientation and a similar set of traits not represented (or not yet recognized) in Asia. A much-simplified sequence derived from both Collins (1964) and Giddings (1964) makes the situation clear (Figure 8.9). The figure shows several important things. Thule, for example, is progressively earlier toward the west; hence it can be viewed as a Bering Sea-Siberian development ultimately blanketing the entire Arctic. A second important point is that the continuum from Old Whaling Culture to Thule in the Choris-Norton tradition has about 4,000 years' depth and antedates the more complex and highly developed Maritime tradition. Thus, although much in Eskimo culture of the last 2,000 years has long been labeled as Eurasiatic in origin (Collins 1954, 1960; Giddings 1960a; Rudenko 1961), it must also be noted that pre-Eskimo cultures in Alaska and Canada made major contributions to Eskimo culture. The present Eskimo way of life is therefore by no means *merely* a Siberian transplant, but may combine some Old World elements with earlier New World traits, the latter no doubt once Asiatic but not Eskimo (for example, the Denbigh Flint complex).

	Asia and Alaska (Maritime tradition)	Aleut– Pacific Coast (Southern tradition)	Alaska (Choris–Norton tradition)	Canada and Greenland (Dorset tradition)
Present				
	Eskimo	Athabaskan	Eskimo	Eskimo
	↑			
A.D. 1000	Thule		Thule	Thule
	↑			
	Punuk	Kachemak III		
	↑		Birnirk	
	Birnirk			
	↑		Ipiutak	Dorset
		Kachemak II	Near Ipiutak	
A.D. 1				
	Old Bering Sea			
			Norton	
	Okvik			
500 B.C.				
				Sarqaq
1000 B.C.		Kachemak I (Marpole)		
			Choris	
			Old Whaling culture	
2000 B.C.				
			Denbigh Flint	
3000 B.C.				
		Microblade		
Earlier than 3000 B.C.			Palisades I, II	

Figure 8.9   Chronologic chart of Eskimo and pre-Eskimo cultures. (Modified from Collins 1964; Giddings 1964)

For Alaska itself, the longest series of culture sequences represented in one area is that reported by Giddings (1960b, 1964) from Cape Krusenstern (compare, Borden 1967). Here the succession runs from the earliest locally known cultures, Palisades I and II, to modern Eskimo. After Palisades and Denbigh Flint comes the Old Whaling culture at 2000 B.C., and the Choris at around 1000 B.C., followed by Norton and Near Ipiutak. Artifacts from the last four show the whale-hunting orientation, the subterranean house, the use of ground-slate implements, the stone lamp, and even pottery for Choris and Norton. The sequence in Figure 8.10 summarizes these important points. It should be mentioned that the Old Whaling artifacts show no similarity to the antecedent Small Tool or Denbigh complex, so their origins must be sought elsewhere. Note that Ipiutak (which will be discussed later) is atypical in most of the diagnostic respects. Figure 8.11 shows some typical Old Whaling artifacts, and Figure 8.12 presents typical items from the Norton stratum at Cape Denbigh. The Norton objects are characteristically crude and rough, revealing nothing of the artistic emphasis of the later Maritime tradition. Only the chipped stone was well done, and some care was taken with the coarse and simple pottery. One might hope that the Norton pottery would shed some light on the origins of the pottery of Eastern United States, but this hope is apparently vain, primarily because pottery appears later in the Arctic, than in the Eastern woodlands. For some reason, most people are surprised that any pottery should occur in the Arctic, perhaps because ceramics were once thought to accompany agriculture. The Norton pottery is thick and heavy, and though frequently not well fired, it is surprisingly sturdy. The usual vessel is a flat-bottomed, bucket-shaped form, which may be plain or paddled with a check or curious linear stamp or which may show incising or linear-stamp decoration. The coarse and flaky paste was tempered either with vegetal fiber and feathers or with coarse sand or with all three.

Slatework, particularly, was merely roughed out and used, unsmoothed. Houses were large and substantial, heated by lamps and fireplaces, the latter being rare in the Arctic. At the major Norton site, no drum pieces, engraved bone, sled or boat parts, or evidences of ceremonialism were recovered. This may represent the accidents of preservation but because of these lacks, the culture is regarded as distinctive (in its impoverishment) from others except the Near Ipiutak at the more northerly Point Hope. The Old Whaling culture is represented by an old beach site on Cape Krusenstern, where five deep winter houses in a compact group and five summer lodges appear to represent a permanent village. The presence of much whalebone for house construction and many large flint blades argues for the whaling industry's having been dominant. The full tool inventory must await more excavation and reporting.

More sites of the Maritime tradition have been worked and described, so the entire sequence from the quite-restricted Bering Sea area is more fully known than any other. Collins has synthesized this material at intervals; in this book I use his latest (1964) statement, which identifies four traditions. Thus, following Collins (1960, 1964), I shall review the three Arctic traditions. The best known is the Northern Maritime, thought by Collins to be derived from Asia. The second is the Southern, and the third is the Dorset. The latter two are older and seem to be less affected by the presumed Asiatic influences of the past two millennia, although both are regarded as being Eskimo. All these traditions tend to fuse by mutually influencing one another, with a final dominance of a uniform culture, the Thule, which spreads at about A.D. 800 to 900

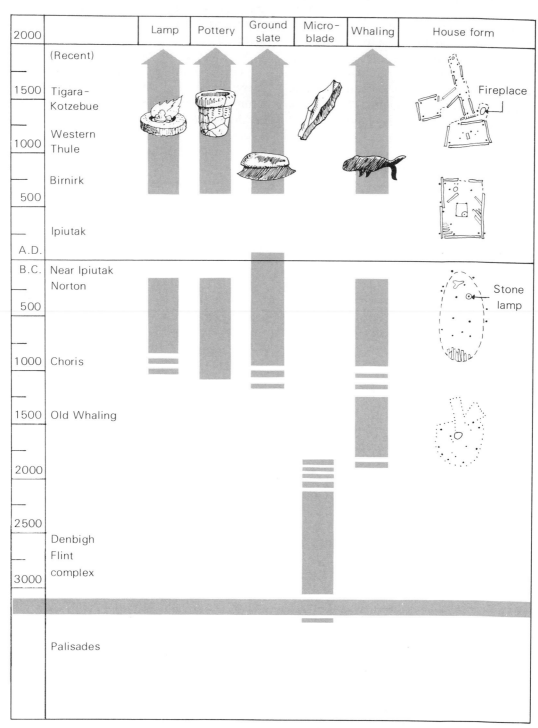

Figure 8.10   *Alaskan cultural sequences and artifact traits.*
(After Giddings 1960b)

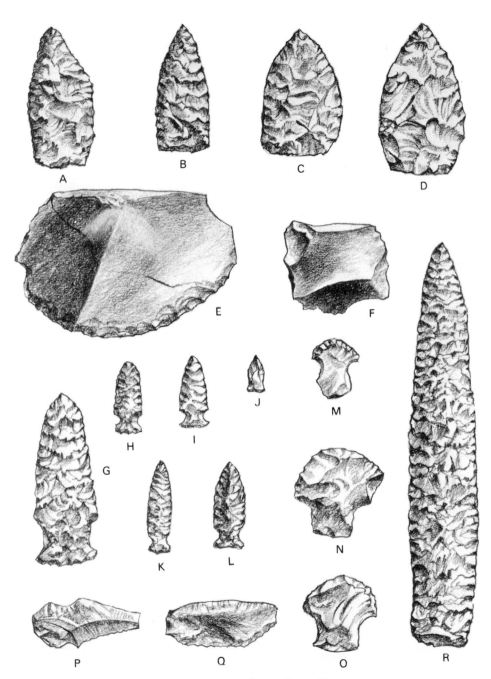

Figure 8.11 *Old Whaling artifacts from Cape Krusenstern. Variable scale. A–D, harpoon (?) points; E, ulu; F, adz head (unique form); G–L, side-notched projectile points; M–O, notched scrapers; P, notched knife blade; Q, flake knife; R, lance blade. (After Giddings 1962)*

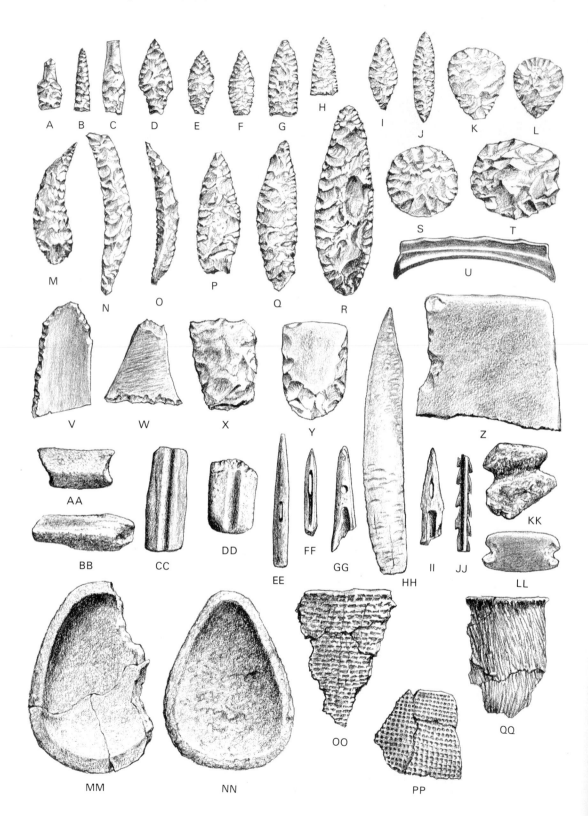

from Norton Sound to Greenland and is ancestral to modern Eskimo cultures. Despite the great similarity in form of the artifacts from one period to another, there are a few index classes or types having diagnostic cultural and chronologic value. These few are readily identifiable by the experienced student. One such class is the harpoon head, which undergoes marked formal and decorative simplification from early to late. The formal changes are shown in Figure 8.13. Another is the "winged object" (possibly used as a stabilizing device on harpoons, functioning in somewhat the same way as the vanes on a rocket or the fletching of an arrow), which grows more elaborate in middle cultures and quite simple in the latest (Figure 8.14). Needlecases, arrowheads, and other artifact classes undergo comparably slight changes in appearance through time and can be used in reaching judgments as to age and affiliation of a collection or a site.

The Northern Maritime Tradition

The Maritime tradition was and still is focused on the sea—walrus, seals, and whales were the primary game. The whale

Figure 8.12   Norton artifacts from Cape Denbigh. Variable scale. A–C, drill bits; D–H, projectile points; I, J, side blades; K, L, biface end scrapers; M–O, flake knives; P, lance point; Q, R, biface blades; S, T, discoidal scrapers; U, labret; V, W, slate knife fragments; X, Y, adz blades; (A–Y approximately one-half size); Z, grindstone, one-fourth size; AA, BB, five-sided whetstones; CC, DD, sandstone shaft smoothers; EE, antler harpoon foreshaft; FF, antler arrowhead fragment; GG, antler harpoon head; HH, ivory harpoon or ice pick, 8½ inches long; II, antler harpoon head; JJ, leister prong fragment, one-half size; KK, LL, stone net sinkers; MM, NN, stone lamps, both 10 inches long; OO, PP, Norton Check Stamped sherds, actual size; QQ, Norton Linear Stamped sherd, actual size. (A–NN after Giddings 1964; OO–QQ after Griffin and Wilmeth 1964)

provides considerable food and has a dominant position in ceremonial life and religion, but the other two species are the standby staples. The entire tradition shares

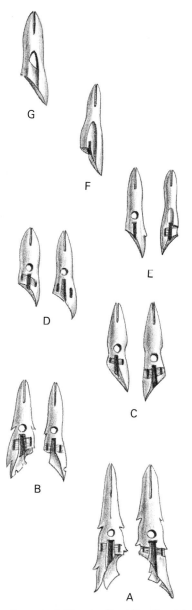

Figure 8.13   Developmental changes in harpoon heads from elaborate older forms (A) to a simple modern type (G). Details of engraved art motifs have been omitted. A, Old Bering Sea; B, Old Bering Sea–early Punuk; C–E, Punuk; F, protohistoric; G, modern. (After Collins 1964)

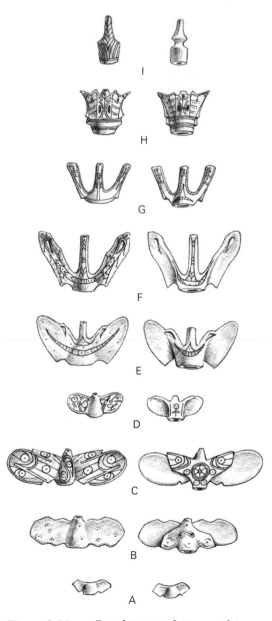

Figure 8.14 *Developmental stages of ivory "winged objects" from Old Bering Sea (A–D) to late Punuk (E–I) cultures. (After Collins 1964)*

the shoreside settlement pattern of permanent villages of rectangular subterranean houses with long entrance passages used for storage. A typical early house at Miyowagh on St. Lawrence Island was 18 by 22 feet in dimension, with an entryway

(including an antechamber) 27 feet long. The entryway sloped downward toward the house so that one crawled from the passageway up into the house. The entryway and house were paved with stone; its walls and roof were made of whalebone jaws, scapulae, skulls, and ribs and of timbers and stones (Figure 8.15). Old Bering Sea period homes were smaller than houses of later periods. Figure 8.16 presents a modern Point Barrow Eskimo house showing the interior arrangement of furnishings and the mode of entrance; the details are undoubtedly similar to those of the prehistoric use of space.

The artifacts of hunting are numerous and of quite specific use. The basic weapon was the harpoon, an ingenious and complex device. It was made of wood, ivory, bone, and sinew or hide strips so that after the quarry was struck, the shaft and foreshaft came loose, leaving the head and point imbedded in the animal; the prey exhausted itself pulling air-filled bladders and a circular drag fastened to the long line attached to the head of the harpoon. In addition to helping as a drag, the bladder served as a marker buoy so that the hunters could follow the wounded game (Figure 8.17). Hunting was done from both the kayak and the open umiak. The bow and arrow was used, as was the atlatl. Light, pronged, bird darts were used with both weapons. Collins (1960) lists other general traits such as skin boats, hand sleds (dog-drawn later), toboggans of baleen, implements of rubbed slate, as well as chipped bone, lamps of both pottery and stone, adzes, mattocks, the crescent-shaped ulu or woman's knife, snow goggles, needlecases, ivory and wooden dolls, and the tambourine drum. Both skin boats—the decked kayak or men's boat and the open umiak—are, of course, quite ancient. Toy models, as well as broken pieces of both kinds of craft, are recovered archeologically (Figure 8.18). (See also D in Figure 8.20.)

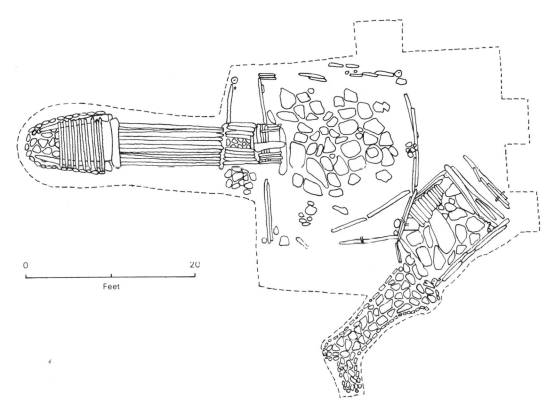

0 _____ 20

Feet

Figure 8.15   *Ground plans of houses (corner of larger house*
superimposed over smaller one) excavated on St. Lawrence Island.
(After Collins 1937)

Despite the subsistence emphasis on sea mammals (and the corollary preference for permanent coastal villages), there was an equal, seasonal interest in land animals, particularly the caribou and musk-ox, where the latter were available. The evidence is that, even as today, there was extensive summer hunting of caribou; aside from hides (which were preferred for clothing) and meat, antler was needed as raw material for numerous tools. Collins (1964) and Spencer (1959) agree that the alternate preying upon land and sea creatures has always been a fundamental part of Eskimo culture, although emphasis on land animals would be greater in the east and along the north arctic coast than on the Bering Sea.

One of the type-sites of the Early Punuk-Birnirk culture is Birnirk itself, near Point Barrow. Ford (1959) presents a complete, detailed report of excavations there. Collins' (1937) classic report on St. Lawrence Island is also important for beginning students. Ford describes the Eskimo as "gadget-burdened"; his inventory of tools and other artifacts securely documents the statement. From a village of twelve or thirteen houses, he partially excavated seven house mounds. The houses were rectangular, subterranean, wooden structures with a domed roof, sodded over and with a long, sunken entryway—all standard features. The raised sleeping platform at the back of the house was also standard even then. The trash heaps lay on each side of the entrance.

From the houses, the fill over them, and the midden pits, Ford recovered thousands of specimens. These by class or type alone

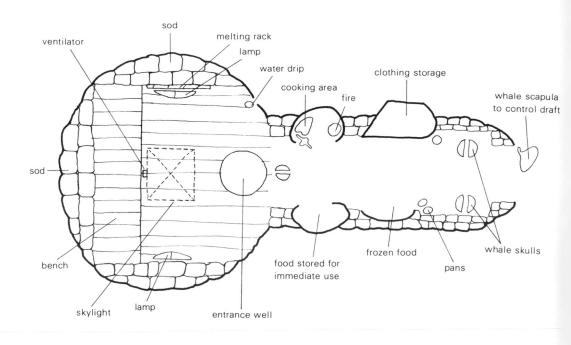

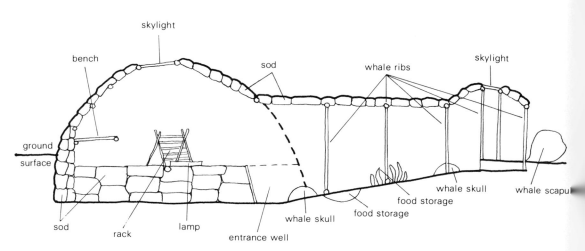

Figure 8.16   *Floor plan and cross section of a Point Barrow Maritime Eskimo house. (After Spencer 1959)*

make a long list. The stylistic variations within the classes of gadgets are also numerous. Ford (1959) describes the following items under *hunting equipment:* harpoon heads (nineteen types), harpoon blades, foreshafts, socket pieces, shafts, harpoon finger rests, ice picks, lances, lance points, seal float bars, mouthpieces and plugs, wound plugs and pins, ice scoops (two types), seal scratchers, seal killers, rattles, dragline handles, atlatl-dart shafts, bladder darts, inflation nozzles,

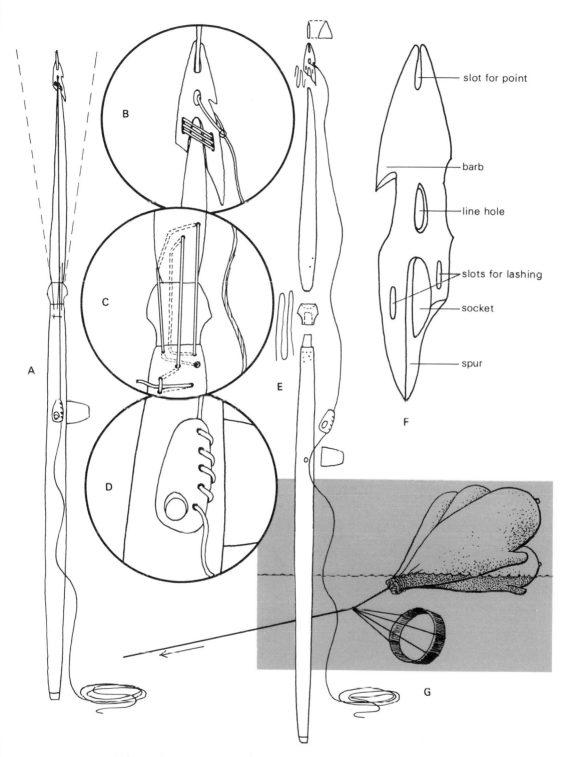

slot for point

barb

line hole

slots for lashing

socket

spur

Figure 8.17 *Eskimo harpoon. A, assembled harpoon (dotted lines indicate flexibility of foreshaft); B, harpoon head; C, flexible joint showing shaft, shaft head, and foreshaft lashed together; D, line retainer secured to shaft by knob; E, component parts of harpoon; F, idealized harpoon head; G, sealskin floats and drag attached to end of line. (A–E, G after Boas 1888; F after Rudenko 1961)*

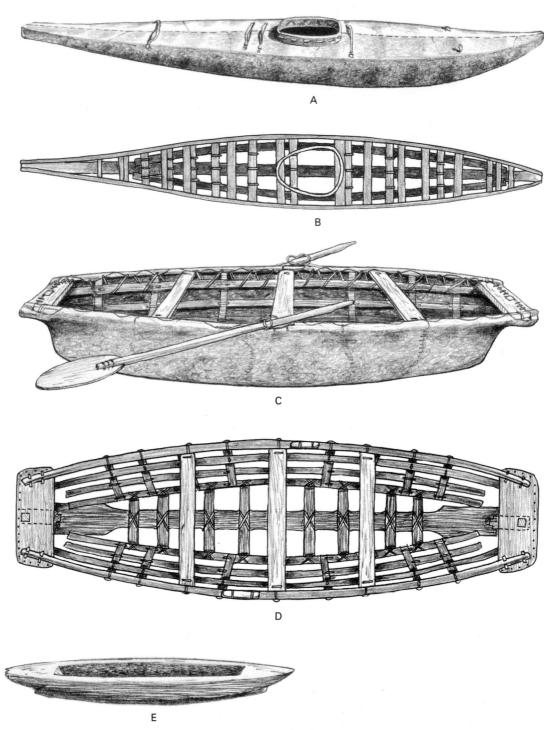

Figure 8.18 *A, B, kayak and plan view of framework; C, D, umiak and plan view of framework; E, toy wooden model of umiak. (A–D after Boas 1888; E after Rudenko 1961)*

bird-dart points, bows and arrows, arrow-shafts, bone arrowpoints (sixteen types), chipped flint points, wrist guards, arrow-shaft wrenches, feather-cutting boards, and bolas balls (three classes). *Fishing gear* includes spears, gillhooks and gorges, and fishhooks. *Transportation* involved toboggans, sleds, kayaks, umiaks, and their many parts. Miscellaneous gear for travel includes snow-probe ferrules, snow knives, snow shovels, ice-staff rings, and snow goggles.

Materials classed as *men's tools* involve men's knives (three types); whetstones; engraving tools; flint flakers; bow drills; fire sets; baleen (whalebone) shovels, mattocks, and picks; adzes; splitting wedges; blubber hooks; and the component parts of all of these. Finally, consideration of *women's tools and utensils*—from wooden buckets to needles and needlecases of bone, through ornaments, clothing, toys, and musical instruments—stretches the list even further.

At the several sites near Gambell on St. Lawrence Island, Collins (1937) recovered specimens by the thousands. His collections duplicate the classes and types reported for Birnirk. Figures 8.19 and 8.20, both taken from Collins, exemplify common artifacts. The Maritime tradition ends with the spread of the Thule culture, which rapidly replaced all other arctic forms, with modern Eskimo culture stemming from the Thule.

Related to Old Bering Sea but anomalous in many respects is the famous site of Ipiutak, excavated by Larsen and Rainey (1948). The village is huge—some 600 houses are arranged along streets, a feature reported nowhere else as yet. The semisubterranean houses are up to 20 feet square. There is no stratigraphy, midden is thin, and the artifacts are very uniform, so a relatively short use at about A.D. 300 to 400 is postulated for the settlement. The lack of certain hunting tools—float plugs, wound plugs, meat- and boathooks,

fishhooks and sinkers, rubbed-slate blades—and of other artifacts, including pottery, lamps, bow drills, ice creepers, and ivory sled runners, argues for less emphasis on sea hunting; however, other sea weapons—harpoons and salmon spears—are present, as well as scores of other familiar artifacts. Aside from its ambiguous cultural connections, the site is primarily famed for the delicacy and elaborateness of its art forms, most of which were recovered from a large cemetery. Collins thinks the art pieces are parts of shamans' kits. Collins also emphasizes the chipped stonework which is reminiscent of Denbigh Flint; he would derive the stone tradition from Denbigh; thus, Ipiutak could represent a blend of Denbigh and Maritime (Figure 8.21).

The Southern Tradition

The second tradition Collins identifies is the Southern—the Pacific Coast and the Aleut. (He combines the Choris-Norton sequence with the Southern tradition on the basis of some of their shared traits.) The Southern tradition is older than the Maritime; Kachemak Bay I is dated at about 750 B.C., older than Okvik by some years, and the Choris is even older, being dated at 1000 B.C. or earlier. Although only two or three sites from the southern coast of Alaska are fully reported, connections with Laughlin's (1963a) Paleo-Aleut and with Asia, including Japan, are noted. Collins (1960) lists the features which give a distinctive stamp to these cultures as ". . . oval and round stone lamps, whaling with poisoned lance, the detachable barbed head with hole in tang more important than the toggle harpoon head, composite fishhooks and stone sinkers, specialized forms of slate blades, emphasis on decoration of clothing and the person, high development of woodworking, painting, and especially of weaving." He also

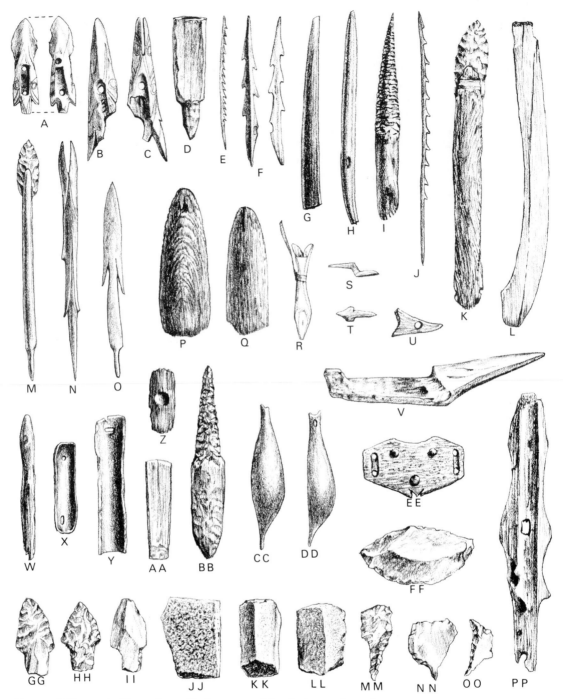

Figure 8.19   *Artifacts from St. Lawrence Island. Approximately one-third size. A–C, ivory harpoon heads; D, ivory harpoon socket piece; E, ivory fish spear point; F, ivory side prongs for bird darts; G, ivory harpoon foreshaft fragment; H, ivory harpoon foreshaft; I, ivory ice pick; J, ivory fish spear point; K, hafted knife; L, wooden adz handle; M–O, arrowheads; P, Q, wooden wound plugs; R, walrus-tusk knife sharpener; S, T, ivory pegs for end of throwing board; U, ivory finger rest for harpoon shaft; V, ivory meathook; W, wooden drill shaft; X, Y, ivory fat scrapers; Z, ivory drill mouthpiece; AA, ivory wedge; BB, ivory ice pick; CC, DD, ivory fishline sinkers; EE, bone ice creeper; FF, ulu blade; GG–II, knife blades; JJ–LL, rubbing stones; MM, hand drill; NN, OO, gravers; PP, fragmentary throwing board. (After Collins 1937)*

points out that these cultures become less and less Eskimoid in recent times because of influences from inland and more southerly Indian tribes.

The possibility that the early origins of the entire Eskimo complex come from the Aleutian-Alaskan Pacific Coast–British Columbia axis is strongly supported by Borden (1962), who analyzes new Northwest coast data to show anew that occupancy of the Northwest coast (and undoubtedly of the Aleutians) goes back to perhaps 6000 B.C. At a deep site (DjRi3 on the Fraser River, British Columbia), he has discovered five sequent occupations. The next-to-oldest yields a date of 6200 B.C., with the oldest estimated at 9000 B.C. These earliest occupations Borden equates with the finds at The Dalles, where Cressman (1960) demonstrates the existence of a flourishing riverine economy (salmon and seal) at an equally early time on the Columbia River further south. Borden also documents the presence of well-made rubbed-slate knives and points in the Marpole and Locarno Beach phases (ca. 950 B.C. to A.D. 200), long before these replace the chipped stone of Okvik and Old Bering Sea to the north; the technique he derives from the Baikal area of Siberia, where it is known by the fourth millennium B.C., earlier even than it is found in the Eastern Archaic. In sum, Borden also sees the Southern tradition as older than the Maritime and regards the sea-riverine adaptation as one made by peoples much earlier than those of Okvik or later times. The early contribution of Denbigh and other microflint complexes is also recognized by Borden; probably these complexes reached the Canadian coast from the interior of Canada. Thus, there is little doubt that the Southern tradition had developed a distinctive Eskimo flavor very much ahead of the Alaskan Eskimo pattern. Figure 8.22 shows some distinctive items from Marpole and Locarno Beach sites dating back to 800 B.C. and found all over the central and eastern Arctic.

The Dorset Tradition

The third tradition discussed by Collins is the Dorset. Distinctly in the Small Tool tradition, the Dorset is confined to interior and eastern Canada. It represents the diffusion of the Mesolithic flake industry over the subarctic before the characteristic Eskimoid tradition developed. East coast distribution is from Greenland to Nova Scotia, and it is found around Hudson Bay. The earliest of the tradition is called Sarqaq, a simple and as yet little-studied phase dated about 1000 B.C., at a time when the Eskimo tradition was already in its formative stages on the Pacific side of the continent. The artifacts of Sarqaq include bone harpoon heads and oval chipped flint blades, as well as tiny burins, notched points, and microblades made of the delicate, curved flakes.

In Dorset the range of weapon and tool types is greater; there is an increase in size of the blades and points, and slate begins to replace chipped stone. In Dorset times, the stone lamp, snow knives, and other Eskimoid traits are added to the products as these evolved from the Sarqaq base. Except for these few additions, Dorset, although fully adapted to the Arctic, is non-Eskimoid. The preferred game was the same—seal, walrus, polar bear, caribou, birds, and fish (the whale was not available)—but the entire inventory of gear was simpler and less specialized. The houses, however, were semisubterranean and rectangular, and somewhat smaller than the Eskimo ones. Collins' (1956) excavated T1, an early (675 B.C.) Dorset site at Native Point. It is located on an ancient gravel ridge; several old beachlines lie between it and the present beach. No house ruins were found. Although it is known that Dorset houses were rectangular, stone-and-sod structures, this location yielded only midden or waste deposits. Spread fairly well over a very large (30-acre) area, the midden averaged about a foot thick; the midden was only sampled

in several places. Debris over so large an area (and some internal evidence) argues for a seaside camping site over a long period. The site was quite informative in view of the limited excavation; only nineteen 5-foot-square pits were sunk at random over the area. From these pits in the shallow midden accumulation came an incredible 25,000 animal bones and several thousand artifacts of stone, bone, and ivory, although the wooden objects that must once have been there were not preserved. Seal made up 66 percent of the bones, with caribou only 0.8 percent. The adjacent Sadlermiut site (where the Sadlermiut Eskimo group lived until their extinction in 1903) yielded the same percentage of seal bones, but over 11 percent of caribou. Modern Eskimo have the dog and could return from the interior with caribou meat on sleds. The Dorset people, lacking the dog, may have consumed the caribou they took at the kill location or may have brought back only the meat.

Artifacts of chipped stone were most numerous. There were classes or types not usually found in all Dorset sites, but of Dorset style and size. These included triangular arrowheads, side blades, micro-

blades and backed blades (the latter two made from prismatic flakes), burins, gouges, gravers, spall implements (tiny slivers of chert), as well as a host of scraper types. All of these objects were very small. Arrowheads were as small as ¼ inch long; microblades were as small as ¼ to ½ inch long by ⅛ inch wide; spalls were even tinier. The material of bone and ivory was no exception to the rule of microsize. Harpoon heads were less than 2 inches in length; needles were as short as 1 inch.

Later Dorset materials came to resemble the western arctic cultures but retained much evidence of the Arctic Small Tool origin until it was entirely submerged in the eastward flow of the Thule that blanketed the Arctic in a few hundred years, after about A.D. 1000. Collins thinks that some remnant Dorset peoples persisted until somewhat later, but in modern Eskimo remains in the area there is barely a trace except in one or two weapons (harpoon and lance) found in the central Arctic. In the southern part of the Dorset area there is a mixing of Dorset with the Boreal Archaic of the Northwestern United States.

Figure 8.20   Artifacts from St. Lawrence Island. Variable scale. A, ivory vessel, 7½ inches long; B, C, wooden snow goggles, 5 inches long; D, toy wooden kayak, 5½ inches long; E, drum handle and rim fragment; F, antler spoon, 3 inches long; G, antler ladle, 5½ inches long; H, ivory browband, 2 inches long; I, ivory comb, 2 inches high; J, bark doll, 2½ inches high; K, bone drill point, 2½ inches long; L, M, ivory awls, 3½ and 5 inches long; N, baleen ice scoop, 7 inches long; O, bone ladle, 10½ inches long; P, wooden pottery paddle, 11¼ inches long; Q, R, hafted slate knives; S, baleen vessel; T, wooden pail handle; U, wooden bow drill; (Q–U one-third size); V, W, slate ulus, wooden handles, 3 and 6 inches long; X, pottery lamp, one-fourth size; Y, toy wooden bow, 10 inches long; Z, AA, ivory sledge shoes, 10 and 6 inches long; BB, toy wooden sledge runner, 3½ inches long; CC, DD, ivory sledge runners, 25 and 20 inches long; EE, bone snow shovel, 8½ inches high. (After Collins 1937)

The Thule

The Thule culture developed out of the Birnirk phase and spread rapidly along the northern coast. There was evidently some local development in the central Arctic and a recent return flow of influence from these sites back to northern Alaska. Collins (1964) summarizes the Thule situation thus:

The Thule culture has many points of similarity with Western Eskimo culture, particularly Point Barrow. . . . The most typical elements of the prehistoric Canadian Thule culture (soapstone lamps and cooking pots, wick ledges on pottery lamps, trace buckles and swivels for the dog harness, woman's knife handle with central hole,

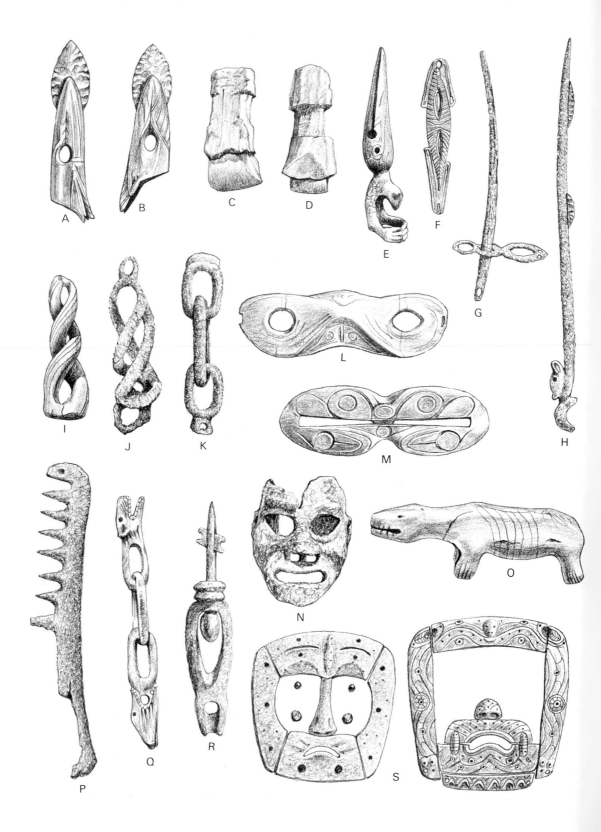

small knobs on the tangs of bone arrowheads, drilled lashing holes and rivet holes on harpoon heads, and flat-based ivory bird figures) are equally prominent at modern and protohistoric sites in northern Alaska. . . .

An Ethnographic Sketch

To visualize the annual round of arctic cultures for the past 3,000 years we have only to consult any standard ethnology of a modern tribe. Spencer (1959, 1965a), in describing the Eskimo of Northern Alaska at Point Barrow, gives particular emphasis to a complex technology and to the details of the continuous food quest. He also emphasizes the Mesolithic genius of the culture and the considerable time depth already documented.

For the Point Barrow tribesmen, whaling is of dominant importance. The bowhead whale, the largest extant mammal, comes in herds in April and provides a focus for Eskimo life. The whale is not the only food source, but it is the center of social and ceremonial life. Whaling only occupied two months (April and May) of the year, after leads opened in the ice, and required the cooperative effort of all the men of a village. Preparation for the hunt involved ritual purification and the performance of magical rites to ensure success, to say nothing of making new hunting gear and new clothing. The hunt itself was a solemn affair without the laughter, joking, and teasing the Eskimo so enjoy. Pursuit of the prey was a hazardous opera-

Figure 8.21   Ipiutak artifacts. Variable scale. A, B, harpoon heads; C, D, adz heads with slate blades; E, ivory openwork carving; F, ivory ornament; G, H, ivory lance heads or daggers; I, ivory swivel; J, ivory openwork carving, K, ornamental linked ivory object; L, M, ivory snow goggles; N, human effigy of antler; O, ivory polar bear effigy; P, unidentified ivory implement; Q, ornamental linked object; R, swivel; S, mask-like ivory carvings usually found associated with burials. (After Larsen and Rainey 1948)

tion carried out in the fragile, open umiak, paddled by six or eight men. The harpooner sat in the bow; success depended on his skill and on the strength of his magic songs. The skill of the steersman was equally important. When a whale was sighted, the boat was brought alongside the powerful animal, and the harpooner sank one or more sharp blades wherever he could. The whale would usually sound, dragging the floats attached to the harpoon headlines. When he surfaced for air, more harpoons were sunk and more floats thus attached. When he was weakened by slight loss of blood and the effort of dragging several floats, the boat was brought close enough for the harpooner to thrust the killing lance time after time into the heart and lung cavity. The kill was the high point of danger, with the animal wallowing in pain and threshing the water with his broad flukes. Success required the utmost coordination of the crew's efforts. When dead, the whale was towed to the beach, and there his 60-ton carcass was cut up and divided with ceremonial thanksgiving among all members of the village. Most of it was stored in pits (into the permafrost zone) for winter. Even one whale was a good catch; four or five per season was enough to ensure a happy winter.

By the end of whaling, full summer had come and the villagers dispersed to summer work of their choice. In any case, the work was food collection and storage. Spencer describes one family whose summer round—June to October—exemplifies the pattern: After whaling, the hunter loads his umiak with clothing, fishnets, harpoons, and sled. The dogs, straining along the shore, pull the boat upstream for several days until a fishing station is reached. Here he leaves the women and children to catch and store fish until he returns. After killing some caribou for meat and skins, he goes back to the coast, where he assists in a walrus hunt and

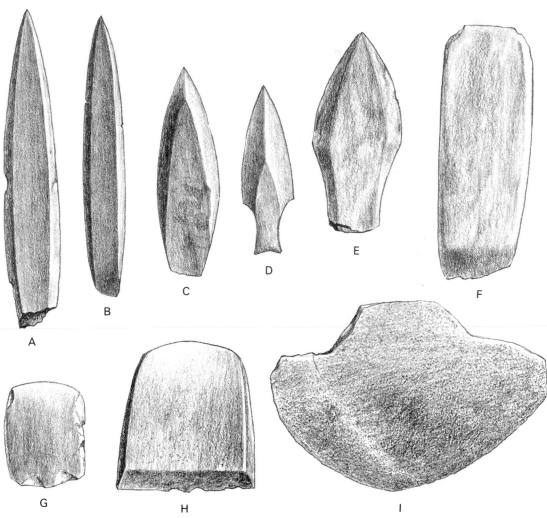

Figure 8.22   *Marpole and Locarno Beach artifacts from the Fraser delta region. Approximately one-half size. A–D, ground-slate points, E, double-edged end blade of ground slate; F–H, adz blades; I, ground-slate ulu. (After Borden 1962)*

finally goes with other men on a trading trip along the coast. By September, he returns to the fishing camp and with the first snow, loads the umiak, gear, and family onto the dogsled and returns to the subterranean winter house. He then makes many trips to the fish camp by dogsled to bring the fish and caribou meat to the village for winter food. Thus, as the winter night closes in, there are literally tons of animal food stored, but the hunting continues, along with repairing and making new gear for the hunt. Seals, small land animals, and birds, while available, are sought throughout the winter until the spring, when the round begins again with the whale hunt. Such is the life of the Eskimo hunter.

The Eskimo woman has equally arduous tasks and responsibilities. She devotes much time to tanning skins and tailoring the clothing and footgear all the family require. She cooks, cares for the house, tends and teaches her little daughters, and participates sometimes in food gathering.

While not emphasized here, the Eskimo have a rich mythology and an important ceremonial life. Stories are told, dances and feasts are common, and there is considerable social exchange during the winter months, but the kinship and other social bonds are loose. Families may move from one village to another in order to be with friends or to avoid constant contact with a disliked person. The social ties are more likely to relate to cooperative work needs and ceremony than to any village or group allegiance.

Men and women both age rapidly under the stresses of arctic life, with its many dangers and demands. Survival requires continuous concern with the upkeep of tools, utensils, and other gear and with food. There is no recorded evidence of game or environmental management except in the many ceremonies aimed at placating and increasing the sea mammals through ritual and magic. Such is the age-old picture of arctic life.

Language

The basic language stock was Eskaleut, with Eskimo having evidently separated from Aleut before 2000 B.C. Eskimo later divided into two branches called Yupik and Inupik, with Yupik restricted to southern mainland Alaska and Inupik spreading all the way to Greenland. Dumond (1965) has compared the genetic relationships of Eskimoan dialects and their distribution with the archeologic data from the Arctic. His conclusion partially reverses orthodox thought. He sets the Eskimoan-Aleutian language separation from basic Eskaleut at 4000 to 6000 B.C. (estimated on glottochronologic grounds) and denies that the Eskimo are Asian in any recent sense. Moreover, he would argue that the popu-

lation (mentioned earlier) from Anangula Island spoke Eskaleut and that they spread thence as carriers of what evolved into the Arctic Small Tool tradition and finally into modern Eskimo. In short, the Eskimo are entirely an American people. What this implies is that the core of all the arctic culture sequence is equally indigenous, having evolved *in situ* on the continent. By his analysis, he has pinpointed areas where archeologic assemblages, clearly ancestral to the cultures after A.D. 1, should be sought.

Although his argument is dominantly linguistic, its implications for further archeologic work are far reaching. If, as Borden has suggested, and as Dumond would no doubt agree, there is much evidence of indigenous evolution of the Eskimo cultures in the New World, scholars perhaps can be persuaded to look less toward coastal Siberia for Eskimo origins and may arrive at more convincing interpretations of the entire arctic sequence. However, Dumond's position takes no account of the appearance of a new physical type in the arctic population after about 2000 B.C. A heavy influence of Siberian genes can hardly be denied.

Summary

Despite nearly a century of study, it was possible only a few years ago to say that the Arctic showed no trace of early habitation because only Eskimoid remains were then known, or at least they alone were accepted. Generations of scholars searching for material that could be proved to be ancestral to other, more southerly American cultures or that could shed any light at all on American origins were continuously disappointed. As this chapter has shown, all this has changed since about 1945. There is even some hope that the cultures of the very first entrants to the New World will be identified (Chapter 3).

Furthermore, there is no doubt that the course of local cultural development can be charted from about 6000 B.C., as cultural increments from both Siberia and Northeast Asia (Japan) were added and spread across the arctic area. There are many nuances to be argued as the details of local cultures and individual sites are studied and compared; but there is increasing agreement among scholars as to the broad outlines of the 8,000 years of arctic history as summarized above. It is probable, too, that connections will be found between the earlier arctic cultures and those of the Indian cultures in the rest of the Americas, even though there has been no progress as yet in this direction. In any case, the American Arctic documents an ingenuity and tenacity of cultural adaptation to a special and dangerous environment not matched elsewhere on the continent.

9
Summation

In the foregoing pages it has been necessary to point to gaps in knowledge in large geographic areas where data are very scanty and to otherwise qualify the history related in this book. One important by-product readers may gain from mention of these gaps and qualifications is an awareness of how many important studies are yet to be made in North American prehistory and how fresh and challenging a field of study and research the subdiscipline of American prehistory truly is. In view of the many gaps in knowledge, it seems appropriate to close this book with a definition of one or two of the important problems, the mention of a few trends, a myopic glance into the future, and a general summary of all that has gone before.

Needed Research

The most vexing handicap in the telling of the story of America's past is the lack of precise data about the time and place of man's entry into the Western Hemisphere. Search for this information, instead of being declared to be impossible and finished, has only just begun. Students interested in either or both biologic and cultural evolution would find this a most relevant area in which to pursue their own researches. Related and only slightly less important is the problem of the origin of the American material culture. What tool kit, in what paleolithic tradition, did man possess at the time of first entry? Is my faith, expressed in earlier chapters, that there is in America an East Asian chopper-scraper substratum valid or even likely to be proved either valid or invalid? Or, is the derivation of the entire American chipped stone inventory from Central Siberia and ultimately from Europe more easily defended? This problem, of course, is greatly complicated by the dearth of information and even more by the strong probability that the relevant data are beneath 90 meters of seawater somewhere in Beringia. However, this problem will engage the attention of arctic specialists for many years and could prove to be the basis for a richly rewarding professional career for younger students interested in either of the dual problems of man and his cultural environment.

Still in the field of material culture, there is the question hinted at so often in Chapter 4 about the Archaic stage. There it was emphasized that our knowledge of the Eastern Midlands and Plains Archaic manifestations is confined to stone implements, whereas in the arid West, the dry caves yield a wide array of perishable artifacts as well. But in the Ash Caves of Kentucky and the Ozark caves of Missouri and Arkansas (and in rare but fortunate finds of carbonized material in open sites of the East), there are sandals, blankets, basketry, nets, and other evidence suggesting that the Archaic may indeed have been much richer and far more uniform from coast to coast than has hitherto been recognized. Should the Archaic turn out to be quite uniform in its total inventory of both perishable and nonperishable objects and overall technology, as is suggested here, this would strengthen the concept of Archaic efficiency and would eliminate the many apparent differences

in subsistence and other technology which appear in the trait lists and which seem to separate the provinces of East and West. It would even demonstrate the sometimes-challenged validity of the concept that the Archaic was indeed a uniform and highly stable culture.

Related to this question of Archaic uniformity is the geographic problem of exactly what is to be found in Canada. When, in fact, did the last glacial ice melt and make the present terrain available to man? How widespread is the Canadian Archaic stage, and what are its attributes? The work of MacNeish in the Arctic, of Wormington and Forbis in the central prairie area, and of Borden along the Pacific Coast demonstrates that there is a wealth of material. It remains to be discovered, excavated in quantity, and studied on a regional basis and compared with the better-known materials south of the Canadian border.

Yet another and very important question of origins remains open: This is merely the discovery of, or the satisfactory deducing of, the origins of the Woodland cultures of the eastern two-thirds of the continent. The evidence that the earliest Woodland is an indigenous development is not at all convincing; on the other hand, speculations as to Asiatic, Scandinavian, or Central American origins are not much more robust. A very rewarding study could be built around the quest for Woodland "origins" as data become more precise and ancillary sciences come more and more to the assistance of the archeologist in his interpretations. A similar and crucially important problem in need of continued study is the matter of trans- or circumpacific contact in the second and third millennia before Christ. In Chapter 5 there is a brief summary of what is known today. But I would expect a fruitful collaboration between specialists in Southeastern Asia, Oceania, and South

America to result in much firmer data that would allow positive statements on this point.

If, as has been postulated, all the Eastern cultures after 1000 B.C. are derivative from Mexico and Central America, it should be possible to find the roots, the time, and the mechanism of contact. On this score speculation reigns (see Ford 1966). The student who can adduce satisfactory evidence bearing on any of the above points would at one stroke make a major contribution in one of the most obscure areas and fill a most crippling gap in knowledge. Connected with this task, but nearer solution, is the ordering, along some more useful classificatory scheme, of the Southeastern cultures which replaced the southern Hopewellian ones. The term "Mississippian," unless completely redefined, is well-nigh useless. Redefinition and probable segmentation of the concept or the development of a substitute one is imperative before even the specialist will be able to talk simply and coherently about Southeastern prehistory.

A less pressing problem, but one of continuing importance in any interpretation, is the diffusion of the concept of agriculture, to say nothing of the routes of dispersal of the several American cultigens. It is not sufficient to note that there are several strains of corn, primitive and modern, and that maize was cultivated from the Canadian border to the Chilean mountains. Many nuances in cultural interpretation and historical connections would be instantly clarified if the history of the dispersal of maize were understood. It may be that this history can never be completely clear. Cutler (1966) reminds us that the history of corn is incredibly complicated, involving an ancient natural mixture and hybridization of three grasses—maize, *Tripsacum*, and *Manisuris*. One of the hybrids was teosinte, which entered into later crosses, so we know that modern maize is many times a mixture. Study over several decades has given students of the matter confidence in the genetic history and relationship of many varieties (called races) and their appearance in time in the Mexican area, but the routes of dispersal of these strains are still not understood. One specific problem is the relationship, if any, of the flour and dent corns of the East and Southeast to the very special dent, called Fremont dent, of Utah. Even the origin of this special variety is debated. Cutler sees it as a Mexican dent, introduced into Utah by some pathway along the western edge of Arizona, thence to spread over most of Utah. Galinat and Gunnerson (1963), on the other hand, derive the Fremont dent from a teosinte and primitive Chapalote race admixture with the flint and flour corns called Pima-Papago. Given the complexity of the genetic history and the spotty occurrence of archeologic specimens, a fully satisfactory statement about the introduction of maize to either the Southwest or the East may never be developed.

But most important of all is simply the continuous demand for more raw data. It is not enough for younger generations of students interested in synthesis merely to reexamine old collections and rethink older interpretations. It is imperative that synthesis based on present knowledge be continuously enriched and refined by new information. Hence, it seems obvious that ceaseless excavation geared toward problems which emerge from the restudy and reevaluation of old work must be undertaken by the succeeding generations of students as they build upon the less-than-perfect labors of earlier scholars. Archeologic techniques are becoming somewhat more precise, and new procedures are being developed to answer new questions. Nonetheless, archeology is first, last, and always a function of competent fieldwork and observation. Furthermore, it follows that future students will be asking more acute questions, and these must be answered from data not yet uncovered. All will agree, I think, that fieldwork and new raw data constitute the crying need in American prehistory. Here a terribly practical aspect must be considered. In the face of dam construction, airport extension, interstate highway construction, and the growth of suburbia, to say nothing of the opening of new farmlands, no hour passes without the destruction of one more site, one more unique document in America's past. Unless the tempo of archeologic fieldwork is stepped up, the end of archeologic investigation in many areas of America is already in sight. The number of sites is finite, each is different, and they are disappearing at an alarming rate. Then, too, as indicated variously in earlier chapters, there are large geographic areas where systematic study has simply not yet been initiated. There are rich intellectual rewards for the investigator who carries on archeologic exploration in unstudied areas. Moreover, surprises and reversals of interpretation are still possible even in the better-known regions. An example is seen in the comfortable and widely accepted interpretation of the Fremont cultures of the eastern Great Basin and Colorado plateaus. When Morss (1931) first identified and described the culture, he interpreted it as being a dilute or hybrid manifestation of the Anasazi of the Southwest. Morss and subsequent students, with experience primarily in the Southwest, continued to make the same interpretation, noting but dismissing the many anomalous traits which did not fit this assumption. Aikens (1966a), as a result of archeologic investigations in the extreme northern part of Utah (Aikens had no great personal involvement in the study of Southwestern prehistory), proposed the alternative hypothesis that the Fremont cultures were primarily of western Plains origin with a superficial overlay of Southwestern traits as one moved further south toward the Anasazi heartland. This is but one example of the results of the reinspection of old material by a younger student with a different background and a minimum of new raw data. In connection with Aikens's work, one can mention the prehistoric Yurok material reported by Elsasser and Heizer (1966) from northern California. Apparently this culture shares an astonishing number of material traits with the Fremont-Promontory of northern Utah; thus, with just two new excavations, a hitherto completely unsuspected link between the western High Plains and the California Coast was exposed.

As another instance of how far from finished the gathering of data is, I note the Onion Portage site on the Kobuk River in northwestern Alaska. Here there is a deep succession of cultural layers, with the earliest giving a radiocarbon date of 6200 B.C. (Borden 1967). The importance of the find cannot yet be assessed, but it is the earliest absolute (?) dated archeologic collection in any part of the Arctic except the Aleutians. It will, undoubtedly, greatly modify current interpretations of arctic prehistory. In sum, more fieldwork is the outstanding need in American archeology today.

Connected with the above, but more fine-focused, is the lack of firm identification of historic tribes with recognized prehistoric or proto-historic archeologic manifestations. As Figure 9.1 shows, this is not true for all of North America, but an astonishing number of tribes or protohistoric groups have not yet been tied through the historical approach to local sequences going back deep into time. There are many reasons for this, including the fact that, outside of the Southeast and Southwest and one or two areas

Eskimo

Mandan, Arikara

Paiute and Washo

Yokuts and other
California tribes

Navajo and various
Pueblo tribes

Pima and Papago

Pawnee

Iroquois

Osage, Ponca
Omaha, Oto

Cherokee

Creek

Chickasaw

Choctaw

Natchez

Caddo

Figure 9.1　*Some historic tribes for which there are archeologic records.*

of the Plains, the archeologic determinants of a given historic tribe's culture are nondescript or nondiagnostic. Even though many historic campsites and village locations can be identified from historical documentary sources, there is often no continuity in the artifact inven

tory between the historic and prehistoric material, and firm identification is not possible.

One sadly neglected area is that of close collaboration between physical anthropologists and archeologists. As a result, it is almost impossible to speak with confidence about the physical types associated with various archeologic stages in several major regions. Exceptions to this are to be found in the Southwest, where specialists have been able to document a morphologically unchanged population in the Southwestern area for 2,000 to 3,000 years. Equally well established appear to be the stable midcontinent Archaic populations reported by W. S. Webb and Snow (1945) and Lewis and Kneberg (1946) from two well-documented sites. The failure of physical and cultural anthropologists to collaborate on this highly important point can be explained historically, but at the moment, this stands as one of the most challenging fields into which a student could move. There is evidence that more and more attention will be given to this problem. The question is not so much whether it is possible to describe a given population; there are data available, but trends in current physical anthropologic study are in other directions. Many series of skeletal remains have already been studied and reported, but this has been done more or less in a vacuum. Since the work of Neumann (1952), no study, save that of Bass (1964) has undertaken any interpretation of the variation in skeletal morphology which can be seen through time and across the continent.

Trends

Perhaps the most important trend in North American prehistoric interpretation is paleoecology, or environmental archeology. To call this a new trend is to overstate the case. Archeologists have traditionally attempted to understand the natural environment in which a culture under study flourished. But the fruitfulness of collaboration between scientists from several scholarly fields has through the years become more and more appar-

ent and, as a result, the decades since World War II have shown an intensification of this effort to reconstruct the microenvironments where a culture was successful. The increased effectiveness of this aspect of archeologic interpretation has resulted in large measure from the recruitment of ancillary scientists across the whole spectrum of scholarship. Brothwell and Higgs (1963) dramatically exemplify the number of approaches which have been of aid in refining the conclusions of the anthropologist and in rendering more subtle and, presumably, more accurate interpretations. Their book includes fifty-four articles by students in the following fields:

Geology	Anatomy
Nuclear physics	Dermatology
Geodesy and	Pathology
geophysics	Wool industry
Marine science	Metallurgy
Forestry	Natural history
Botany	Radiocarbon
Entomology and	Classical archeology
plant pathology	History of art
Zoology	Ancient monuments
Domestic animal	Archeology and
research	anthropology
Veterinary anatomy	Ancient glass

This is only one aspect of paleoecologic interpretation. Raikes and Dyson (1961), in an intensive study of the utilization of scarce water in Baluchistan, have rather firmly demonstrated that the Harappan cultures flourished in an environment and climate probably identical to that of today; this is a complete reversal of the romantic and entirely erroneous interpretations of the first cadre of investigators. In America, Mehringer and Haynes (1965) have been able to demonstrate that when the Llano hunters were preying upon the mammoth, southern Arizona had a climate and a set of biotic resources no different from 1960. This modifies some earlier ideas. Here, too, must be mentioned the work of Martin (1963) and Schoenwetter (1962), who by means of palynology combined with geologic evidence, propose that the abandonment of the Anasazi area may have been a function not of drought, but rather of a change in rainfall regimen (less winter but more summer precipitation) which made horticulture hazardous and difficult. Fritts, Smith, and Stokes (1965) cannot agree with this notion because their data from several species of trees on the Mesa Verde show that at the height of the "Great Drought" there was no increase in summer rainfall to offset a drier winter. Thus, even with finer tools and new outlooks, the question of Anasazi abandonment of the Four Corners area lies unresolved.

Also in the broad area of paleoecology is the hitherto-neglected matter of aboriginal land management. The meaning of this phrase in connection with aboriginal America is obvious if one assumes that the American Indian developed a culture geared to a given environment. Part of the adaptation would involve preserving the environment at its optimum productivity. For example, there is a wealth of evidence, both chronologic and biologic, that the Southern Indians for centuries preserved all over the Southeastern United States an ecologic subclimax wherein the pine was the dominant forest species in an area where the "unmanaged" final climax forest is a mixed hardwood complex. Swanton (1946) documents the perpetuation of the pine subclimax by means of annual, even semiannual, fires. That this was an ancient practice is manifested by the fact that certain species of pine can not propagate without intermittent firing of the woods. Byers (1946) believes that the northeastern woodlands Indians preserved the hardwood forest there with open glades scattered through it also by means of fire. In both cases, the prime source of meat was the deer, and there was also need for garden patches. O. C. Stewart (1956) has summarized a great deal of research on his part, indicating his belief that the Great Plains themselves, if not developed entirely by means of fire, were at least held in grasses against the westward migration of the woodlands by frequent firing. Connected with the problem of woodland management is the shifting pattern of slash-and-burn, dibble agriculture. Ritchie (1965) suggests, on the basis of archeologic and ethnographic evidence, that the Indian fields were exhausted after 6 to 8 years of use and were abandoned for new land. This apparently necessitated the actual moving of the village to new ground. In the course of a few years the forest closed in on the abandoned fields, and eventually these could be cleared and utilized once more. Under such an arrangement the territory required for the support of a single agricultural village would be five to ten times larger than a comparable settlement where fertilization and crop rotation were practiced. It may be doubted whether archeologic data will often be precise enough to permit detailed conclusions about land management, but I would expect more to be discovered than has been the case to date. Judging by the work of Arrhenius (1963) in Scandinavia, one could predict that, with the aid of soil scientists and chemists, it should be possible to discover the actual outline and location of ancient Indian fields. An abortive effort along this line has been reported by Sharrock et al. (1964). Another important aspect of land management is suggested by Hickerson (1965) in his study of the deer harvest in the buffer zones in the northern Woodland area.

A very recent and even startling development is the paleosociology being attempted by Deetz (1965), Longacre (1964a, 1964b, 1966), and J. N. Hill (1966), among others. Based on archeologic debris associated with discrete structures, Deetz makes a good case for the breakdown of matrilineity among the

Arikara in protohistoric times. Also using sherd counts and individual dwelling units, Longacre has made some convincing inferences about clan affiliations and marriage preferences at a site in New Mexico at about 1200 A.D. A. L. McPherron (personal communication, 1965) uses the changes in ceramic styles (combined with ethnographic data) over a 600-year span at the Juntunen site in Michigan to infer that an assymetric cross-cousin marriage preference and virilocal residence characterized the population of the area. Even with the aid of ethnographic and historical documents, however, the validity of extensive inferences about social behavior is exceedingly shaky, as Trigger (1967) demonstrates in a detailed and thoughtful evaluation of "settlement [pattern] archeology." The study of settlement patterns (Willey 1956) has for decades provided an approach for comparative ordering of such data as dwelling size, village arrangement (houses scattered or close together in clusters), presence of fortifications and house arrangement within the palisades, and the change or retention of a pattern through time. These data permit inferences as to population density, pressures of enemy groups, improved subsistence technology, political institutions, kinship groupings, a shift in subsistence base, and even the appearance of artisan or craftsman or other classes. Proof of the accuracy of such inferences is another matter; the value of the concept and the reality of its strict limitations must be accepted simultaneously, as Trigger's study of Iroquois warfare shows. Several of the studies above included the use of modern technical research equipment in that statistical analyses were made with the aid of computer hardware.

Because of the necessity for new data and the refinements in interpretation made possible by ancillary sciences, there is an increased tendency toward under-taking complete excavations of large sites. The Amerind Foundation work at Casas Grandes is an example. Here, in cooperation with the Mexican government, C. C. Dipeso (personal communication, 1965) spent 2 continuous years of fieldwork with a large crew of laborers and discovered a large town, an extensive irrigation system, and a distinctive settlement pattern not previously discovered in the 80 years the Casas Grandes culture has been known and discussed. Similarly, Haury in a massive "revisit" to Snaketown revealed a settlement pattern, a network of canals often rebuilt, and many aspects of material culture the earlier sampling (Gladwin et al. 1937) had not revealed. Of course, it is not entirely surprising that a dragnet operation should reveal more than the sampling technique. The work of Lewis and Kneberg (1946) at Hiwassee Island laid bare a complete sequence of occupancy for an estimated 4,000-year period. The Hiwassee operation essentially "stripped" the entire island. The fruitfulness of the long-term, thoroughgoing excavation of a single site or a small district has also been demonstrated in Mesoamerica, in the work at Mayapan (Pollock et al. 1962).

Another major manifestation of the dragnet operation is the emergency work occasioned by construction of dams and the creation of reservoirs. Enforced full-scale study of an arbitrary area has resulted in astonishing gains for scholarship, and the salvage programs, through their very productiveness, have probably encouraged the present trend toward dragnet operations. Furthermore, since the establishment of the National Science Foundation, the scholar is able to envision and plan a large operation because the Foundation has been extremely generous in providing funds for well-conceived archeologic research programs on the grander scale. Through its support of worthy projects, the Foundation has strengthened and stimulated improved research design, to say nothing of accelerating the rate of increase in knowledge of crucial importance in the understanding of man's American past. Without discrediting either the agencies that have sponsored and financed the invaluable emergency excavation programs or the National Science Foundation in its encouragement of pure research, the intensified research in American prehistory after 1945 is the contribution of the well-known Wenner-Gren Foundation for Anthropological Research. This generous, private foundation disperses funds for all kinds of worthy programs in research and publication in anthropology, but it has been particularly generous in grants for American prehistory. The inspired pattern of grant giving is what has made Wenner-Gren support so valuable: The grants are small but numerous, aimed at exploratory research. The largest grants are for new ideas. Some of the most crucial data in archeology are directly referable to Wenner-Gren monies; support for the years of pilot study and perfecting of the radiocarbon dating process is but one example. Foundation assistance is manifold and includes institutional help and publication of data. In truth, the current popularity, strength and progress of anthropology can in large part be credited to the Wenner-Gren Foundation and its grants-in-aid of research since World War II. The Foundation was particularly important in the expansion of research and interest from 1945 to 1953.

Finally, and perhaps given all the above, the most important trend I can recognize today is the concern of the younger students with reanalysis, reevaluation, and reinterpretation of earlier work. Some of the more impatient young scholars refer to the "new archeology." This term seems to imply the utilization of new "theoretical" viewpoints (which are less theories than new hypotheses or restate-

ments of old assumptions) and the assistance of the ancillary sciences along with the old data and old ideas. Certainly interpretations are becoming more precise because they rest on finer detail; they are also more interesting. This reevaluation trend is perhaps the best proof available that the archeologist is a scientist. Only through reexamination of the old in the light of the new can a discipline progress toward research that is sharply focused and more detailed in its conclusions. In the process of developing the new archeology, the younger students tend to be sometimes impatient with, and carpingly critical of, older generations and their many shortcomings. Here, methinks, they are in error. The short history of archeologic study and the spotty nature of its data must be remembered. It should also be remembered that earlier generations of students had first to collect the data, a task they accepted. As they continued to collect and describe (and in many cases to misunderstand and misinterpret), the corpus of data slowly increased. Without the bumbling and shortsighted work of their predecessors, the ofttimes brilliant current generation of scholars would have nothing to work with. They would instead be left grubbing in the earth, gathering enough data for their successors to review and reinterpret and with which to create some other version of the "new" archeology. At all costs, all archeologists need to remember that, like Antaeus, they must continue to "touch the earth" or they will lose their strength and potency. Advance in knowledge rests on both field and laboratory labors.

Connected with the effort to identify more convincingly the archeologic remains of historic and protohistoric named tribes is the increasing likelihood that the archeologists and the linguists could collaborate in a study of the diffusion and dispersal of the more recent American Indian cultures. Here the work of Swadesh (various) must be mentioned as being of paramount importance. Using the techniques of glottochronology, the linguists can apparently pinpoint more and more accurately the time when dialect groups became separated from others of the same language stock. As an example, the work of Lamb (1958) and Goss (1965) is of great importance in Western archeology. They seem to have demonstrated beyond debate that tribes speaking the Shoshonean dialect were separated from other Uto-Aztecan-speaking groups at about the time of Christ, somewhere in the southern Great Basin of the West. Additional study shows that the spread of the Shoshonean-speaking groups was northward and eastward in a kind of sweeping arc spreading out from the spot of separation, until the Ute reached their extreme eastern prehistoric limits by about A.D. 1600. The work of Haas (1941, 1958) with the Southeastern and Gulf Coast languages seems to show a distinct, if distant, relationship between the Muskogean-, Caddoan-, and Algonkian-speaking tribes. It is interesting to note that the distribution of these languages at the time of the discovery of America coincided almost exactly with the distribution of horticulture in the East. At present, I am unable to do more than point out the interpretive possibilities of a combined archeologic-linguistic study. Griffin (1964), W. W. Taylor (1961), and Swadesh (1964) have made worthwhile attempts to correlate archeologic finds either with tribes and/or with language groups, but at the moment of writing, the data seem far too inadequate for convincing arguments to be mounted. Nonetheless, the importance of this kind of collaborative study must not be underestimated. Spencer (1965b), writing entirely from the linguist's point of view, has made a few cogent speculations about the whole problem and seems to support Swadesh's opinion that the apparently diverse and unre-

lated major linguistic phyla perceived in the American Indian languages will ultimately be shown to be derived from a single stock. He does not include the Athabaskan and Eskimo languages, whose more recent Asiatic origins are regarded as demonstrated, although Dumond (1965) challenges the findings in the case of Eskaleut.

The Future

Although the use of the crystal ball might prove to be helpful, even with its aid there can be no infallible clues to the direction archeologic study will take in America in the next few decades. Nonetheless, certain developments seem clearly indicated. First of all, there is no doubt that the emphasis will remain, as it has for some 30 years, on the search for origins because of the understandable urge students have to push knowledge further and further back into time on the one hand and the need to know the facts of the "beginnings" on the other. This book itself reflects this emphasis because it has been drawn from current journals and monographs; as a result, the two chapters dealing with the Lithic and Archaic stages are longer and contain more controversial material than the chapters dealing with the more recent and far more complex cultures. This weighting accurately reflects the proportion of effort being expended in study and research. All this being true, we can expect the emphasis to remain on the early stages, and our understanding of these will become increasingly complete. At the same time, the renewal of interest in the Mississippian cultures of the South will draw more students than have recently been involved, partly because of the challenge of the present need for reclassification and reanalysis which was emphasized in Chapter 6 and partly because of the availability of generous grants for the increasingly expensive task of excavating large sites. Available funds have already encouraged the attack upon large, important, Southeastern locations which previously could not be attempted because of excessive costs.

There is little doubt of the crying need for more, careful, "dirt" archeology as analytic study more and more pinpoints the lack of data about the several sequent stages over the entire continent. Somehow the concern with the use of ancillary data in interpretation, the development of computer analysis, and other important new ideas have led to a temporary downgrading in some quarters of the basic archeologic activity, that is, *digging*. There is evidence that this distaste for dirt is a passing phenomenon, and there is no real doubt that the younger students will again understand and appreciate the need for the collection of new data in order to verify or disprove the increasingly complex web of hypotheses resultant from reinvestigation and reanalysis of older work.

Inevitable in all the above is the hoped-for development of more coherent theories of culture and culture change that will provide sharper analytic tools for the archeologist. At present, no significant body of theory rooted in data can be isolated in the manipulation of archeologic material. It is true that there are many assumptions, many of them unstated, to be found in archeologic writings. But aside from Willey, Phillips, Rouse, and perhaps one or two others, no systematic effort to develop even rudimentary archeologic theory has been made. Hence, we can expect much more theory, some of it useful, to develop.

Perhaps too obvious to require special mention is the ever-present concern with increasingly precise chronology. It is not enough for Griffin to perceive certain formal similarities between the ceramics of the Mississippi Valley and those of the Anasazi in the Four Corners area. This observation raises a question with no answer until it is possible to say that these forms appeared first either in the Mississippi Valley or at the Four Corners. Once both complexes are securely dated, one may then safely make inferences as to the direction of diffusion. Until a greater network of accurately dated sites is developed, many historical reconstructions as to influence or the direction and flow of ideas must remain speculative.

There is no present evidence that the emergency demands for salvaging archeologic materials in the face of construction will diminish. Almost every week there comes notice of a new dam, a new canal, or a new highway which will jeopardize or completely destroy a series of prehistoric locations. Continued concern with emergency tasks, is, in the long run, a good thing and can only result in much-needed data. At the same time, it has the effect of robbing the emergency excavator of the opportunity to review, compare, and deliberate in order to formulate interpretive and synthetic conclusions from the reams of descriptive literature resulting from emergency projects. No matter how motivated or how brilliant the scholar may be in synthesis or second-level interpretation, his best efforts are achieved in contemplative leisure rather than under the duress of deadlines and of construction completion dates.

One of the more romantic aspects of the new archeology is a function of technologic advance. The perfecting of scuba diving gear and the sporting aspects of this activity have led to the development of what is widely known as underwater archeology. Numerous "expeditions" have been organized in both Old World and New World waters. To date, most of the researches have had to do with buried cities or sunken vessels, as would be expected in the waters of the Mediterranean and western European coast. Similar riches await discovery in the Caribbean area of the New World. More mundane finds include a large deposit of stone mortars and metates off the coast of California (Tuthill and Allanson 1954), the recovery of Mayan gold from Yucatan *cenotes,* and related aboriginal finds along continental coasts. As was implied in the opening chapters, it is almost a certainty that much aboriginal history does lie on now-submerged land surfaces, but the likelihood that an aboriginal camp or midden deposit would withstand years of attack by breakers as the seawater slowly rose is terribly remote. Nonetheless, enthusiasts are doing more and more exploring, and the possibility of important discoveries must not be discounted in advance. Emery and Edwards (1966) expect underwater vehicles to prove useful in this activity. (Evidence of the popularity of this new branch of prehistoric research is the fact that at the Royal Ontario Museum in 1965 the second conference on underwater archeology lasted for three days and involved something like thirty-five featured speakers on diverse subjects ranging from ancient ship construction to manned undersea stations.) Both the popular press and our technical journals are carrying an increasing amount of material on this activity. At present the interest seems to be more antiquarian than scientific, but a shift in attitude toward solving problems in North American prehistory can be noted.

Of possible importance in cultural theory and perhaps worthy of reexamination are the comments by scholars about the stability of aboriginal American cultures. The arctic succession, the ubiquitous Archaic, and the Southwestern traditions all show this attribute. It is true that archeology provides little more than a technologic and subsistence model (Piggott 1965; Clark 1957). It is not reason-able to suggest that the subsistence pattern is an entirely valid index to other aspects of culture, but the concept of stability (conservativeness) in subsistence is generally applicable. The notion here is that stability can be correlated with efficiency. This is to say that once a satisfactory and balanced exploitive technique is achieved by a population (a proper wedding of resources and technology), there is no reason for change in either the technology or the "management" practices so long as climatic and other factors are constant, regardless of linguistic or social changes. And in any concept of efficiency, the additional concept of aboriginal ecologic "management" must be included. As Byers (1946), O. C. Stewart (1956), and Swanton (1946) have shown, the American Indian, and the historic Woodland tribes in particular, had developed an efficient management policy which preserved an optimum ecologic subclimax environment which was of maximum efficiency. This is emphatically not a doctrine of "environmental determinism." It is, rather, a reverse doctrine of ecologic management giving man an active, consonant role in manipulating the environment toward specific, well-understood, optimal ends in a well-balanced ecosystem. Of course, the rigor of environment would restrict the range of both innovation—as in the Arctic—and adoption of diffused ideas—as in the well-nigh perfectly balanced subsistence base of California coastal cultures. The argument for stability, however, rests more on the continent-wide Archaic cultures found in the temperate zones (where management practices *other* than those utilized are possible) than on extreme, climatically limited situations.

One can doubt that origins of New World horticulture will be pinpointed very accurately. That many now-domesticated species were once collected in the wild state (Chapter 5) is not debated; but when the species were first tended, annually planted, and deliberately selected toward improved yield or hardiness cannot be proved. Furthermore, even in the case of maize, one cannot argue convincingly for a full horticultural technology until the time when the maize cobs and grains were completely enclosed in the tough envelope of multiple husks, and the species became entirely dependent upon man for its propagation. This, of course, occurred after the many hybridizations with other grasses. This hybridization is as likely to have resulted from accidents of nature as from deliberate actions of Archaic-stage aborigines.

In this connection, it is interesting to note also that after the introduction of horticulture to North America, the evidence shows man to be much more dependent on minor climatic changes in rainfall and temperature than was true in the Archaic stage. In short, once he accepts dependency upon a vegetable-food-production technology, man significantly and immediately limits his range of adaptability and binds himself to an environment where cultigens can survive. His range is determined not by human adaptability and resourcefulness but by the adaptive attributes of the species with which he develops a mutual dependence. (The vegetable species, within limits, can also be manipulated by man.)

Underlying these remarks is an acceptance of innovative stimulus of either Asiatic or Scandinavian Neolithic origin upon the Eastern Archaic (Chapter 4) and the extreme probability of Southeast Asian and/or Japanese contact in Ecuador by 3000 B.C. (Chapter 5). This position represents not so much a decision to take sides in a diffusion–versus–independent-invention controversy as an attempt to read and interpret economically the limited evidence of stability as it can be weighed in 1966. Whether the concept of stability survives review and testing is not

important. It does pinpoint the fact that the data of North American archeology, as seen on a continental scale, suggest that the selectively equable climate of most of the New World, in its near-perfect isolation from the more climatically stressful Eurasiatic landmass, and its short occupancy by man made it in fact the natural laboratory suggested by Wissler. One implication of this general conclusion is that, lacking significant stress (for example, climatic change, overpopulation), innovators are rare and change is extremely slow in the absence of cultural contributions from external sources. The point here is that in the New World, the Archaic—that is, a Mesolithic ecosystem—was continent-wide and stable and was probably supporting a large population in an efficient symbiosis with other species and *would have continued indefinitely.* The regional changes remarked after 2000 B.C. (Chapters 5, 6, and 7) can thus probably be credited less to innovation than to stimulus from the Old World.

Recapitulation

Although it would be possible to continue citing tentative new advances in research and interpretive approaches, this is the place to attempt a concise summary of the foregoing pages. Being restrained, as we have been by evidence, this volume envisions man's first dispersal in the New World as having occurred at about 10,000 B.C. That there may have been occupancy earlier—perhaps by 25,000 B.C.—is envisioned as a good possibility (for example, Müller-Beck 1966). Whether this earlier date will eventually be sustained or not, we are on reasonably solid ground with the 10,000 B.C. date. The first entrants are presented as probably having been a dihybrid stock in which the emerging Mongoloid race was blended with an

Archaic Caucasoid strain. It is presumed that from an early and small population and a restricted gene reservoir, the basic American Indian stock evolved in the New World. Additional increments of Mongoloids after about 4000 to 3000 B.C. are also assumed. Again, the numbers would probably have been small.

Although the material culture and technology of the original emigrants cannot be identified with certainty, in this book it has been proposed that they were at an essentially Late Paleolithic stage with a tool complex derived from the Eastern Asian chopper-scraper technology. Again, this has not been demonstrated beyond debate (see Warren 1967). Upon this hypothetical but logically necessary base, one can identify three later general stages in the culture development in the New World. These are charted as in Figure 9.2, the earliest being the Lithic, which blends into an Archaic, to be followed in restricted areas by what has been called the Formative. The Lithic, Archaic, and Formative can be identified on both continents. In Central America and South America, in quite restricted areas, Classic and Postclassic civilizations are recognized.

The developmental history which has been documented occurred on two large continental landmasses that offered every climatic extreme from arctic to tropic and that lacked major barriers to communication. Even though modern man thinks in terms of roads and passes and marshes and lakes, many of which are barriers to the wheels of progress, the aborigine had no such problems. Judging by the distribution of the cultural debris, man filled the continent as population increased, and there is every evidence of far-flung communication at all time levels. This account has frequently offered cultural explanations in an ecologic context and has argued that with optimum management at a given technical level, the land was

fruitful and that cultural stability on the *technologic* level is an outstanding trait of American aboriginal history.

The Lithic was primarily characterized as being focused on big game with a small but highly diagnostic tool kit. The Archaic, much better represented in the archeologic record, has an opposite definition in that it is described as utilizing a much broader subsistence base, exploiting in season and in turn the widest possible spectrum of species with some diagnostic artifacts and many skills. The milling stone or mortar implies the use of hard-skinned seeds and nuts as one class of food staple. The continent-wide presence of cordage, basketry, sandals, and cloth textiles (wherever dry storage preserved these) and a wide variety of stone tools bespeak a large tool kit containing special items for special tasks. It was during the Archaic period that agriculture, or at least the domestication of many indigenous American plants, was begun in the highlands of Mexico. Significant contacts with Southeast Asia and/or Japan are credited with the introduction into this Archaic stratum or stage of certain ideas which led to, or stimulated, the increase in food production through gardening, with consequent increases in population and development of the Formative cultures. This evidently occurred in Central America. Diffusion of these complexes resulted in the so-called "high cultures" of North America in the Midwest, Southeast, and Southwest. Because these cultures were restricted to the climatic zones in which corn, beans, and squash would prosper, it was noted that over much of the continent the culture remained in an essentially Archaic stage until white contact, persisting in the Desert West until the twentieth century. This distribution and persistence in time remind us that the Archaic, at an essentially Meso- or early Neolithic level of technology, is perhaps the most adaptable lifeway ever developed

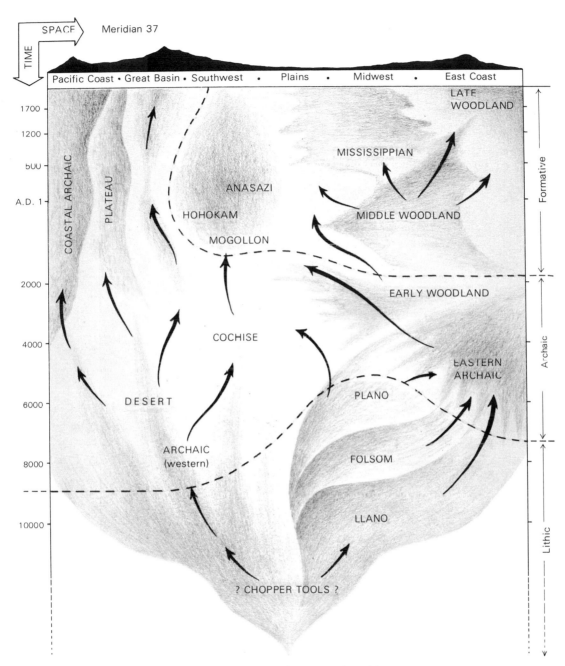

Figure 9.2   *General succession, in time and space, of prehistoric cultures in North America.*

by man. As soon as man commits himself to food production, he simultaneously commits himself to the narrow geographic range where his staples can grow. In short, there is little or no climatic control on an Archaic population, in that the Archaic subsistence base was inclusive rather than exclusive, whereas with a Formative, agriculture-based subsistence pattern, environment does determine

Chronological chart of North American archaeological cultures and phases (dates in A.D./B.C.)

Date	Arctic and Pacific Coast	Plateau and Great Basin	Southwest and Mexico	Plains	Midwest and Mississippi River drainage	East Coast
A.D. 1800	TIGARA-KOTZEBUE; LATE CANALIÑO / LATE CENTRAL CALIF.		REFUGEE; *Big Bead Mesa*; GOBERNADOR P.V	STANLEY	Natchez Village	
1600			DINETAH	DISMAL R. / LOWER LOUP / ONEOTA / SELKIRK / LA ROCHE	Dodd; *Huff / Arzberger / Sommers / Zimmerman / McKenzie Bottom / Hickey Bros.*	
1400			*Table Rock* P.IV	UPPER REPUBLICAN / NEBRASKA / ANTELOPE CR.	Belcher Md.	
1200			Hooper Ranch / FOOTE CANYON / CLASSIC P.III / MOGOLLON V / TULAROSA	THOMAS RIGGS / ANDERSON	Moundville / Ft. Ancient; *Thomas Riggs / Fire Heart Cr.*	
1000	THULE		RESERVE / MOGOLLON IV / SEDENTARY / *P. Bonito* / THREE CIRCLE P.II / P.I	MONROE	Etowah / Hiwassee Is.	
				MANITOBA	*Cheyenne R.*	
800	KACHEMAK III; PUNUK / BIRNIRK		SAN FRANCISCO		*Aztalan / Cahokia / Apple Cr.*	
			VENTA SALADA / LOS ANGELES	LOSEKE		
600			MOGOLLON III			
400	HORIZON IV		COLONIAL BM. III / MOGOLLON II / GEORGETOWN	NUTIMIK; KEITH	*L. George / McGraw*	
200	*Ipiutak*		*Talus Village* / Crooked Ridge; LA SALTA		*Spiro / Kincaid*	OWASCO
A.D. / B.C.	DORSET IPIUTAK / KACHEMAK II / NEAR IPIUTAK	*Danger V* / *Humboldt*	BM. II LOS PINOS / BM. I (postulated)	VALLEY / ANDERSON (Woodland)	*Angel / Kolomoki*	
B.C. 200	OLD BERING SEA / NORTON		PIONEER; PALO BLANCO / ESLABONES	Ash Hollow	Marksville / LEDBETTER; *HOPEWELL*	
400	OKVIK		MOGOLLON I / PINE LAWN / *Tularosa Cave* / *Snaketown*			
600	C. Krusensternito A.D. 1180		SANTA MARIA / LAGUNA		BIG SANDY	
800	*Choris* / *T1*					
1000	MARPOLE LOCARNO BEACH / KACHEMAK I / SAROAQ CHORIS	BEAVERHEAD	L. Texcoco	BAUMER; Signal Butte	*ADENA*; MEADOWOOD	*Stony Brook*
		Etna	AJALPAN; *Chiapa de Corzo*	*McKean* (upper)	Poverty Pt. / WELDON / *Osceola*	
2000	OLD WHALING *Stahl*; EARLY CENTRAL CALIF. INTERMEDIATE (HORIZON III)	*Danger IV*	SAN PEDRO; PURRON / ALMAGRE		LAUDERDALE / THREE MILE / STALLINGS IS.	*Wapanucket No. 6*

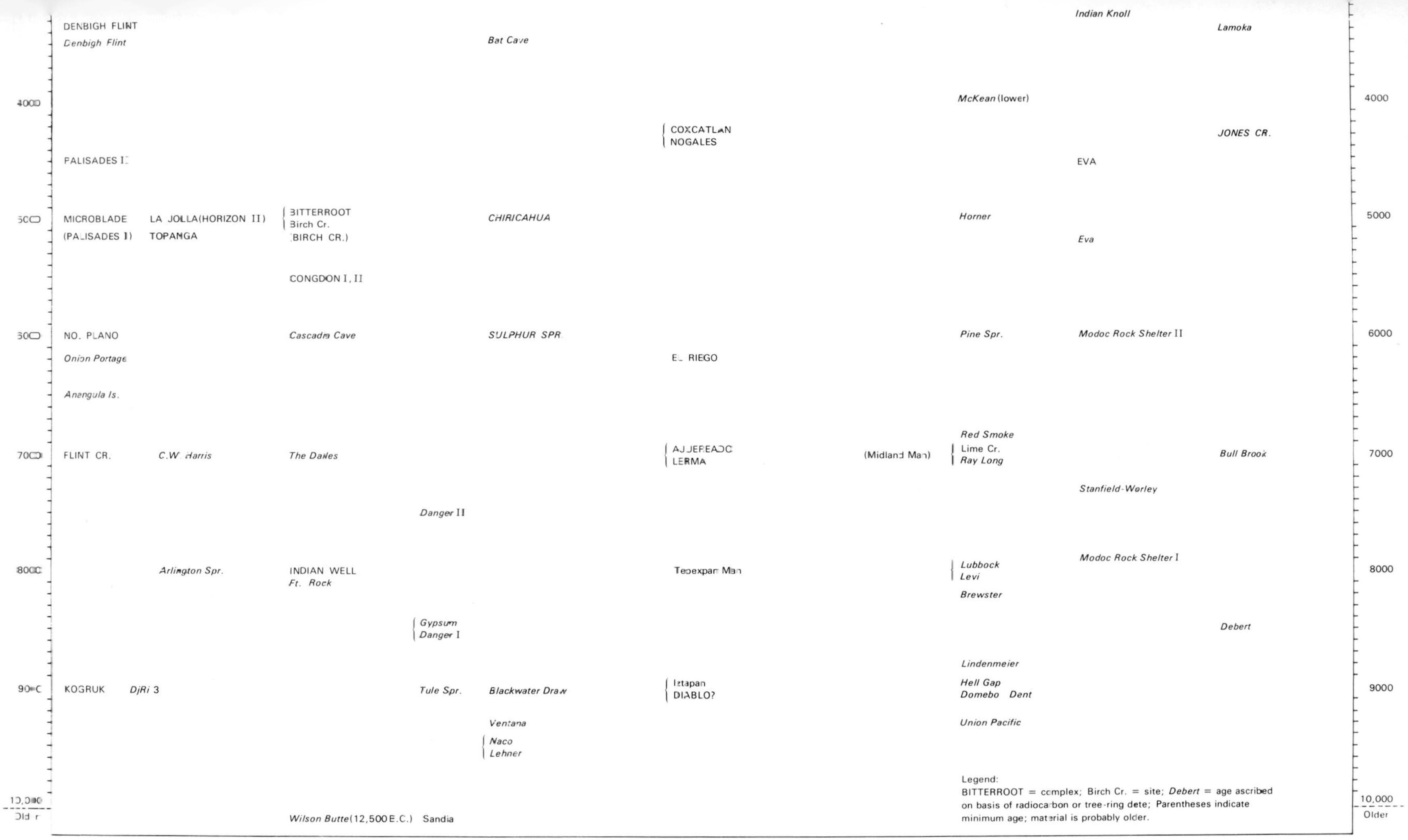

Figure 9.3 Chronology of selected sites and complexes cited in the text.

Top scale: 4000 5000 6000 7000 8000 9000 10,000 Older

DENBIGH FLINT
Denbigh Flint

PALISADES II
MICROBLADE
(PALISADES I)
LA JOLLA (HORIZON II) TOPANGA
CONGDON I, II
NO. PLANO
Onion Portage
Anangula Is.
FLINT CR.
KOGRUK
DjRi 3

Wilson Butte (12,500 B.C.) Sandia

Bat Cave
CHIRICAHUA
SULPHUR SPR
Danger II
Cascade Cave
The Dalles C.W. *Harris*
INDIAN WELL *Ft. Rock*
Arlington Spr.
{ *Gypsum* / *Danger I* }
Blackwater Draw *Tule Spr.*
Ventana
{ *Naco* / *Lehner* }

{ COXCATLAN / NOGALES }
E. RIEGO
{ AJUEREADO / LERMA }
Tepexpan Man
{ Iztapan / DIABLO? }

McKean (lower)
Horner
Eva
Pine Spr.
Red Smoke
Lime Cr.
Ray Long
(Midland Man)
{ *Lubbock* / *Levi* }
Brewster
Lindenmeier
Hell Gap *Domebo Dent*
Union Pacific

Indian Knoll
EVA
Modoc Rock Shelter II
Stanfield-Worley
Modoc Rock Shelter I

Lamoka
JONES CR.
Bull Brook
Debert

Legend:
BITTERROOT = complex; Birch Cr. = site; *Debert* = age ascribed on basis of radiocarbon or tree-ring date; Parentheses indicate minimum age; material is probably older.

Bottom scale: 4000 5000 6000 7000 8000 9000 12,000 Older

range and, in turn, restricts the culture alternatives open to the population (see Leeds and Vayda 1965).

The reader who has followed the evidence and the arguments can at this stage appreciate the simple dignity of the pattern of man's achievements on the North American continent. For me and many students the broad and general sequence of stages is exciting in its sheer depth and what might be called its inevitability.

Even more exciting are the ingenuity and skill the aboriginal displayed in exploiting the riches of the continent with increasing success. Whether the concept of Archaic efficiency is acceptable to all is an open question, but it is hoped that no reader will fail to appreciate the achievements of the American Indian as they were worked out over twelve millennia before the explorations and conquests by the Old World nations in the fifteenth and sixteenth centuries.

Glossary

Adz A stone tool with a thinned, convex cutting edge which is hafted at right angles to a handle (compare **Ax**). Used mainly for woodworking, rarely as a weapon.

Adobe Mud used as mortar in aboriginal masonry. More recently, an unfired, sun-dried brick made from clay mixed with vegetal fibers and used in the Southwest and Mexico as a building material.

Alluvium Sand, gravel, or soil deposited by running water as it loses velocity on flood plains of streams or in valley floors.

Antler Flaker An implement made from an antler tip or tine and used in pressure flaking (q.v.) stone.

Antler Wrench See **Wrench, Arrow.**

Arrow Wrench See **Wrench, Arrow.**

Artifact Any object made by human hands.

Asphaltum A black to brown mineral pitch used as an adhesive for hafting purposes and for applying decorations on objects.

Atlatl A short board or stick, 20 to 24 inches long, fitted with a handle on one end and a groove or peg at the other, used in throwing a dart or lance. Widely used in the New World.

Awl, Splinter An awl made from a splintered section of an animal's long bone (often the cannon bone).

Ax A stone implement with a sharp, cutting edge to be used for chopping or crushing chores. It is usually grooved for hafting to a handle; "fully grooved" means the groove encircles the ax and "three-quarters-grooved" means the groove runs around three sides. An ax is hafted with the cutting edge in line with the handle (compare **Adz**). An ungrooved ax is often called a celt (q.v.); and an ax that was to be held in the hand is often called a fist or hand ax.

Baleen The horny substance found in the mouths of certain whales (especially the right whale) which serves as a strainer to collect and retain food. It grows from the whale's upper jaw in fringelike plates from 2 to 12 feet long and is used as a raw material for utilitarian and ornamental objects.

Bannerstone A polished stone artifact (usually perforated), having a variety of forms (winged, boat-, bird-, or animal-shaped, etc.), probably used as an atlatl weight but which may have had a ceremonial function as well.

Basalt   A form of igneous rock which is compact and dark gray to black. Used for many ground stone (q.v.) implements.

Bergmann's and Allen's Rules   Bergmann's law is that there is a tendency for birds and mammals living in cold areas to have greater body bulk than their close relatives living in warmer areas. Allen's law is that there is a tendency for birds and mammals living in cold areas to have shorter appendages than their close relatives living in warmer areas.

Beringia   The land bridge that existed between Siberia and Alaska during the Ice Age.

Biotite   A type of mica (q.v.), generally black or dark green, used primarily for ornaments or for decorative purposes.

Birdstone   See **Bannerstone.**

Bladder Dart   A dart, used in hunting seals, with a bladder float attached to serve as a drag as well as a marker buoy.

Blade   A long, narrow flake (q.v.) with parallel sides, sometimes called a lamellar flake. Blades are usually struck from a prepared core (q.v.). Small specimens are called microblades.

Blade, Backed   A cutting-scraping stone tool with one blunted edge to protect the user's fingers. This term is also used for a curved, stone implement with a prominent ridge on the convex side.

Blank   An unfinished stone tool partially worked to the shape and size of the intended implement. It is possible that blanks were stockpiled for later completion.

Bodkin   A long pin or awl made of bone or copper for making holes in fabric. Also, a blunted needle with a large eye.

Bolas   A hunting weapon consisting of two or more grooved stone balls tied on separate thongs to a longer line. It was thrown at the legs of animals and at birds in flight, entangling them and preventing their escape.

Bone Tube   A short section of hollow bone believed to have been used by shamans (q.v.) in curing ceremonies to suck out the causes of illness or pain.

Boreal   The northern and mountainous areas of North America, Central America, and Greenland where the mean temperature of the hottest season does not exceed 64.4°F and characterized by coniferous forests.

Brachycephalic   Short- or broad-headed (compare **Mesocephalic** and **Dolichocephalic**).

Browband   An Eskimo ornament to be worn across the forehead.

Bull-boat   A tub-shaped boat made from a whole buffalo skin stretched tightly over a light willow frame. Used by the Plains Indians.

Burial, Bundle   Reburial of defleshed and disarticulated bones tied or wrapped together in a bundle.

Burial, Extended   A form of burial in which the body rests in a supine or prone position with legs extended and arms at the side.

Burial, Flexed   A form of burial in which the arms and/or legs are bent up against the body.

Burin   A flake or blade (qq.v.) stone tool with a small, angled chisel edge or a sharp, beaked point used for sculpturing and engraving purposes.

Calcite   Calcium carbonate (q.v.) which has crystallized. Used (crushed) as temper for ceramics.

Calcium Carbonate   The substance of limestone. Often found in caves, where it can have sealed cultural deposits and protected them from disturbances.

Caliche   A crust of calcium carbonate (q.v.) that forms within and/or on top of arid and semiarid soils.

Catlinite   A red, indurated clay found in the Upper Missouri region and used for making tobacco pipes. Also called pipestone.

Celt   An ungrooved ax (q.v.) used mainly for woodworking. It is often shaped somewhat like a chisel (q.v.) but with a broader blade.

Chalcedony   A variety of quartz with a waxlike luster used for chipped stone (q.v.) implements.

Charmstone   Any stone object believed by the owner or wearer to bring good fortune or to ward off danger, etc.

Check-stamped   A design of small, impressed squares used in decorating pottery vessels and produced by a paddling or stamping technique.

Chert   An impure flint (q.v.), usually brown or gray-black, used for chipped stone (q.v.) implements.

Chipped Stone   Stone artifacts manufactured by percussion and/or pressure flaking (qq.v.) techniques. Chipped stone implements are predominantly used as projectiles and as cutting or skinning tools.

Chisel   A celtlike (q.v.) implement with a narrow blade chipped to a thin edge. Used mainly for woodworking.

Chopper An axlike (q.v.) implement which is worked only on one edge.

Coiling Both a pottery and a basketry manufacturing technique. In pottery: Long, finger-sized rolls of clay are added one on top of another in a circular fashion starting at the bottom of the pot and continuing up to the desired height. The inner and outer surfaces are then smoothed. In basketry: A spirally coiled foundation of warp strands is sewn together in horizontal rows, the weft strands looping over the warp strands in an overcast stitch.

Comal A pottery griddle used to cook such things as tortillas.

Cooking Ball See *Stone Boiling.*

Core A stone from which flakes have been removed to make implements. A prepared core is one which has been purposefully worked so that the shape of flakes or blades (qq.v.) can be controlled.

Corrugated A type of coiled (q.v.) pottery found in the Southwest in which the outer surface, instead of being smoothed, is finished by letting the edges of the clay coils overlap to create a scalloped effect. This type of pottery was used as utility ware.

Coursed An architectural technique in which stones or bricks are arranged in continuous horizontal rows.

Cupstone See *Nutstone.*

Deflector A floor structure of uncertain function found in early Southwestern pit houses and (later) in kivas. It was always constructed between the firepit and the tunnel or ventilator shaft and probably served as a draft control for the fire.

Dibble Agriculture A primitive form of planting crops utilizing a pointed stick (dibble) for making holes in the ground into which seeds were dropped. (See also *Slash and Burn.*)

Dolichocephalic Long- or narrow-headed. Since most early human forms are dolichocephalic, it is believed to be an earlier form than the brachycephalic or the mesocephalic (qq.v.).

Drift A blunt-edged bone tool probably used to enlarge holes in skins or textiles.

Drill The stone bit attached to the end of a drill stick which is rotated rapidly, as in the bow drill (q.v.), to perforate dense materials. This term also refers to any device used for drilling purposes or for making fire, in which case a drill stick without a bit is used (see *Drill, Fire*).

Drill, Bow A drilling device which is operated by twisting the string of a bow around the drill stick and moving the bow back and forth rapidly. Used in perforating bone, stone, ivory, etc., and in making fire.

Drill, Fire A device for making fire, consisting of a drill stick which is twirled rapidly in a small pit in a piece of wood (the hearth). The friction creates heated sawdust which eventually begins to glow and will ignite a piece of tinder of shredded dry grass or other vegetal fibers.

Drill, Twist A chipped stone drill (q.v.) bit with a beveled, pointed end similar to the modern metal-cutting drill.

Earspool A spool-shaped ornament to be worn in the ear lobe.

Fist Ax See *Ax.*

Flake The thin, flattened piece removed from a stone by pressure or percussion-flaking (qq.v.) techniques. Flake tools are usually retouched (q.v.).

Flesher A blunted stone or bone tool used to scrape off flesh and fat from the inner surface of a hide.

Flint A variety of quartz, gray to brown or black, used for chipped stone (q.v.) implements. Although harder than steel, it is easy to work, making it a valuable raw material for stone tools.

Galena A lead ore, bluish-gray with a metallic luster. Crystals and lumps were used by the mound builders of the Mississippi Valley for ornaments and for trading purposes.

Gaming Piece An artifact believed to have been used in any aboriginal game of chance and skill.

Genotype A physical type determined by the genetic characters shared by a group of individuals (compare *Phenotype*).

Glottochronology The chronologic study of languages by comparing their basic vocabularies sampled at different times in order to discover relationships and common origins between languages.

Gorge A small, double-pointed implement which is attached to a line and used to catch small animals and fish. It is usually baited with meat or fat; when taken, it imbeds itself crosswise in the throat of the game.

Gorget An ornament which is usually worn over the chest and which is perforated for attaching to clothing or suspending on a cord.

Gouge A chisel (q.v.) with a scoop-shaped cutting edge to be used in woodworking, for removing bone marrow, etc.

Graver A small trimming or cutting tool with a sharp point or edge used for woodworking.

Great Basin The area of internal drainage in the Western United States comprising Nevada, eastern California, southeastern Oregon, and western Utah.

Great Plains Generally, the area lying east of the Rocky Mountains and west of the Mississippi-Missouri Valley and usually characterized as a treeless, semiarid, flat grassland.

Ground Stone Stone artifacts manufactured by pecking and abrading techniques. Usually included in this category are grinding and pounding implements such as the mano, metate, mortar, and pestle (qq.v.), as well as pipes and statuary pieces.

Hammerstone A rounded stone to be used as a hammer and which is sometimes grooved (see *Ax*) for hafting to a handle. Usually ungrooved, however, it has a variety of forms ranging from a crudely shaped sphere to a finely ground ovoid with a battered end.

Handstone See *Mano.*

Hearth, Fire See *Drill, Fire.*

Hematite See *Ocher.*

High Plains The outwash belt along the eastern base of the Rocky Mountains, creating broad, flat uplands which extend from the southern boundary of South Dakota almost to the Rio Grande.

Ice Creeper A roughened or spiked piece of ivory or bone to be attached to the bottom of the Eskimo's footgear to facilitate movements while hunting on the ice.

Incising A method of decorating pottery vessels by cutting the design in the wet clay surface with a sharp implement.

In situ A Latin phrase meaning "in place." Archeologically, it refers to an artifact (q.v.) or object being found in its original, undisturbed position. Items found *in situ* provide an opportunity for establishing firm stratigraphic or other associations for dating purposes.

Interstadial The period between glacial phases of a major glaciation.

Jasper An opaque, uncrystalline variety of quartz, found in many bright colors, used for ornaments and chipped stone (q.v.) implements.

Jet A velvet-black stone (fossilized conifer) which takes a high polish. Used for decorative purposes and for jewelry.

Kayak The arctic canoe, which has an enclosed cockpit and is covered and decked, usually with sealskin (hair removed).

Labret An ornamental plug to be worn in the lower lip.

Lacustrine Of or pertaining to a lake or an inland sea (for example, the deposits, the flora, and fauna).

Lamellar See *Blade.*

Lanceolate Shaped like a lance, being tapered at one or both ends. In archeological usage the term usually refers to long slender chipped stone points or knives pointed at one or both ends.

Lapstone See *Milling Stone.*

Leister A fish spear with at least three barbed prongs.

Lignite A brownish-black coal used for jewelry and other ornaments.

Limpet A marine mollusk whose low, conical shell was used for ornamental and decorative purposes.

Llano Estacado (Staked Plains) A vast plateau in western Texas and eastern New Mexico of approximately 20,000 square miles and bounded on three sides by nearly vertical escarpments from 500 to 1,000 feet in height. The location of several early sites, including Blackwater Draw, Plainview, and Scharbauer (Midland).

Loess An unstratified deposit of windblown sand or clay, yellow or buff, which occurs on the flanks of glacial maxima. Although fertile, the extremely fine soil makes agriculture difficult.

Lost Wax A casting process in which a clay model is coated with wax and then covered over with clay. When the mold is heated, the wax melts, leaving a hollow space between the core and outer mold. The casting material is poured into the space and after it has hardened, the inner and outer clay is removed.

Mace A club with side projections at one end which could have been used as an offensive weapon, but which may have had only ceremonial use.

Mano The upper stone used on a metate (q.v.) to grind corn and other grains. "Handstone" is another term used for the upper millstone. A handstone is generally associated with the milling stone (q.v.) and is moved in a circular or a back-and-forth motion. The mano is moved only back and forth.

Mattock A stone pickax with broad ends used to loosen soil and for grubbing and digging purposes.

Maul A stone implement with blunted or rounded edges to be used as a hammer for heavy work such as driving wedges, breaking stone, etc., or for lighter work such as pounding seeds or for pecking and flaking operations. It may be grooved (see *Ax*) for hafting to a handle.

Mesocephalic Referring to a head of medium breadth (compare *Dolichocephalic* and *Brachycephalic*).

Metate The lower part of a milling stone (q.v.), usually made of semiporous stone, and found associated with agriculture for grinding corn and other grains. The upper part of the mill is the mano (q.v.).

Mica Any of a group of crystalline silicates characterized by perfect cleavage so that they separate into paper-thin sheets. Used primarily for ornaments or for decorative purposes.

Microblade See *Blade.*

Midden The accumulation of refuse near a habitation site or dwelling.

Milling Stone A general term for all types of stones used as the lower part of a grinding mill. It may be flat, or slightly or deeply hollowed out. Small specimens are often called lapstones. Specifically, it is not associated with agriculture, being used to crush wild seeds (compare *Metate*). The upper part of the mill is the handstone or mano (q.v.).

Mortar A heavy, deeply basined stone or wooden bowl used with a pestle (q.v.) to pulverize various materials and foodstuffs.

Mouthpiece, Seal Float A perforated wooden or ivory plug to be lashed into small openings cut in the skin of a harpooned seal. Air could then be blown through the perforation to inflate small areas between the blubber and muscles. The mouthpiece could then be stoppered, the captured air acting as a float to keep the seal buoyant while being towed. (See also *Wound Plug.*)

Muller See *Pestle.*

Negative Painting A method of painting designs on pottery by covering the background elements of the design with wax and then painting the rest of the design with the desired colors. During the firing process, the wax melts, leaving the lighter color of the clay outlining the design.

Nutstone A flat slab or a boulder with small depressions to hold nuts for cracking.

Obsidian Volcanic glass, which, because it can be worked to an extremely sharp edge and point, is highly prized for chipped stone (q.v.) implements. Also, because of its reflective qualities when in thin, flat sections, it was used for mirrors in Mesoamerica.

Ocher A ferruginous clay or earth ranging from yellow to brown, used as a pigment. Red ocher (hematite) is very often used for ceremonial purposes.

Olivella A genus of marine univalves, found on the North American Pacific Coast and in the Gulf of Mexico, whose shell was widely used as money and for making necklaces.

Olla A Spanish term used in the Southwest for the widemouthed water jar.

Ossuary A depository (a place or a receptacle) for the bones of the dead. Usually refers to a place where several individuals are buried.

Palynology The study of past vegetation and climates through microscopic and C14 analyses of pollen recovered from stratified soil zones.

Percussion Flaking The technique of shaping a stone by striking it with another stone, a heavy bone, or a piece of wood. If a finer finished tool was desired, the surface and edges were further worked by pressure flaking (q.v.).

Perforator A problematic stone artifact (q.v.) that was once thought to have been used as an awl, but which may be a knife or blade (q.v.) dulled from use.

Permafrost Permanently frozen subsoil, found in the tundra (q.v.) areas of the arctic region.

Pestle A club-shaped implement used to pulverize various materials in a mortar (q.v.). Also called a muller.

Phenotype A physical type determined by visible characteristics rather than genetic or hereditary characteristics (compare *Genotype*).

Pick A bar-shaped stone implement with a blunt point at each end to be used in piercing operations. Otherwise, it is functionally similar to the ax (q.v.).

Pipestone See *Catlinite.*

Plane A stone artifact with a flat base, a humped back, and a sharp edge which may have been used for woodworking, but is probably a used core (q.v.) from which thin flakes have been struck.

Plateau, Columbia The area between the Cascade and Rocky Mountains in the Western United States, comprising southern and western Idaho and eastern Oregon and Washington and containing the drainage system of the Snake and Columbia rivers.

Playa In an arid region, a shallow basin or dry lake bed in which water from rain or runoff collects and stays until it evaporates.

Plummet Stone A top-shaped weight used in various ways: in spinning as a whorl weight, in fishing as a net sinker, in construction as a plumb bob, etc.

Pluvial   Of or pertaining to rain. Also refers to the wetter periods during a major, extended dry period.

Pod Corn   A type of Indian corn with each kernel covered by a husk.

Pressure Flaking   The technique of removing flakes (q.v.) from a stone by pressing a blunt, pointed implement of antler or bone against the edge being worked. This method permits greater control over the size and direction of the flakes removed than does percussion flaking (q.v.).

Prognathism, Alveolar   Projection of the facial bones in the region of the teeth.

Provenience   The location of an artifact (q.v.) or object described in terms of map grids, stratified levels, and/or depth from ground surface. It provides for a scientific control of artifacts and associations once the items have been removed from the context of the site.

Pulper   A conical, blunt-ended stone implement whose use has not been definitely determined. It could be a reject or a worn-out tool. (See also *Plane*.)

Quartzite   A compact, granular rock composed of quartz, used for chipped stone (q.v.) implements.

Quid   A piece of vegetal matter (yucca, tule, corn husk, etc.) that was chewed to extract the juice and nutriment and then spat out.

Quill Flattener   A bone implement used to flatten porcupine quills so they could be used for decorative purposes.

Retouch   Secondary flaking of a stone implement to remove surface irregularities and to refine or modify the cutting edge. Always done by pressure flaking (q.v.).

Rocker-stamped   A design of connecting zigzag lines used in decorating pottery vessels and produced by rocking a sharp-edged implement back and forth on the wet clay surface.

Roulette   An incised (q.v.), punctated design used in decorating pottery vessels and produced by a rocker-stamping (q.v.) technique.

Rubbing Stone   A small, smoothed stone, often found stained with red pigment, whose use is uncertain.

Scraper   A stone implement used to remove fat from the under side of a skin, to smooth wood, to scrape leather, etc. Different types are described in terms of the shape and/or position of the cutting edge: side scraper, end scraper, snubnosed scraper, thumbnail scraper, scoop scraper, etc.

Seal Killer   A round stone, often attached to a leather thong or encased in a rawhide net, used to club seals to death once they were harpooned.

Seal Scratcher   A long, pronged implement used to decoy seals at their breathing holes in the ice. Often, seal claws were attached to the prongs to better imitate the sound that might be made by another seal.

Serpentine   A magnesium silicate stone, dull green and often mottled, used for ornaments.

Setline   A long, heavy fishing line to which a series of short lines, with attached baited hooks, is attached at intervals.

Shaft Wrench   See *Wrench, Arrow*.

Shaman   A medicine man or any individual who used his supernatural powers to cure ailments or to interpret strange phenomena. Rarely, these powers were also used to inflict harm or cause disaster.

Sherd   A broken piece of a pottery vessel. The most durable of archeologic specimens.

Sipapu   The Southwest Indian's name for the small, circular pit in the floors of the early pit houses and the later kivas. The Indians believe that their original ancestors came up into the world through the sipapu.

Slash and Burn   A means of clearing ground for planting crops by cutting down the ground cover and burning it. The resulting ashes also enriched the soil. Usually associated with dibble agriculture (q.v.).

Slate   A dense, fine-grained rock used for sculptured pieces, as well as for sharply edged tools.

Slip   A thin, surface coat of very fine, untempered clay in liquid form which is applied to the surface of pottery prior to firing.

Soapstone   See *Steatite*.

Spokeshave   A scraper (q.v.) with a rounded notch in the edge used for such chores as scraping arrow shafts.

Spud   A shovel-shaped implement probably used for digging purposes, but which, eventually, may have had only ceremonial use.

Steatite   A variety of talc, grayish-green or brown, used for pots and other utilitarian items. Also called soapstone.

Stockton Curve   A crescentic, chipped-obsidian (q.v.) artifact considered a diagnostic trait (q.v.) of the Late Central California culture. Its specific use is unknown.

Stone Boiling   A method of cooking by dropping hot stones or clay balls into a basket or container filled with liquid and/or the substance to be cooked. This method was used when the cooking vessel couldn't be placed directly over the fire.

Taiga The swampy, coniferous forest area which begins to the south of the zone where the tundra (q.v.) ends.

Throwing Board Another term for the atlatl (q.v.) or spear thrower.

Tinkler A small conical or cylindrical ornament probably worn together as a fringe on a garment or as a garter.

Trailing A variant technique of incising (q.v.) a design on pottery vessels by making broad, U-shaped lines in the wet clay surface.

Trait A diagnostic artifact (q.v.) or characteristic element of a culture.

Tule A bulrush or reed found in the Southwest, California, and Mexico, used for making such things as mats, sandals, decoys, etc. It was also chewed (see **Quid**).

Tumpline A cord or strap placed across the forehead or the chest to support burdens carried on the back.

Tundra The treeless plain within the Arctic Circle which is marshy in summer and frozen in winter. The subsoil is permanently frozen, but the surface soil supports mosses and lichens.

Turquoise A blue to greenish-gray, aluminum phosphate stone highly valued for jewelry and other decorative purposes in the Southwest.

Twilling A weaving technique in which the weft strands are taken over one or two warp strands and then under two or more. Each row is subsequently offset one warp strand, and the visual effect achieved is that of a series of steps or stairs.

Twining A weaving technique utilizing parallel warp strands between which two weft strands are threaded in and out, one weft going over the warp as the other goes under. The wefts are twisted together in half turns between each warp, making a strong, smooth weave.

Ulu The Eskimo woman's knife which has a semicircular blade usually fitted into a slotted wooden handle.

Umiak The flat-bottomed, open, arctic boat which has a wooden frame covered with walrus hide. It is not as maneuverable as the kayak (q.v.).

Varve A regular, annual layer of silt and clay formed in lakes fed by melting glacier water. Since each varve in the laminated bed is the result of one summer's melting and represents one year, the number of years required for deposition can be determined by counting the varves.

Wattle-and-Daub A construction technique in which a frame of poles and interwoven twigs is plastered with mud or a similar substance.

Wicker A type of weaving in which the flexible, slender weft strands are passed over and under the more rigid and thicker warp strands. The most elementary of the weaving techniques.

Winnowing Basket A shallow, tray-shaped basket in which dry foodstuffs were tossed so the wind could carry away the chaff or unwanted portion. It was also used to separate fine and coarse particles of clay.

Wooden Cylinder A straight, peeled stick with the ends cut off at right angles to the length and carefully smoothed. Has been variously described as a noseplug, gaming stick, or toggle.

Wound Plug A tapered plug to be inserted in the wound of a harpooned seal to stop the flow of blood. Probably also used to close up small openings which were cut in the animal's skin so that air could be blown into small spaces between the blubber and muscles. The pockets of air, trapped beneath the skin, kept the animal afloat while being towed. (See also **Mouthpiece, Seal Float.**)

Wrench, Arrow (Shaft) A device for straightening arrow shafts. Made of stone, bone, ivory, or antler, it was fashioned either with a small, pierced hole or with a circular hook through which the shaft could be pulled.

Yucca A member of the lily family, with long, sharply pointed, fibrous leaves, found in arid and semiarid regions. The fleshy leaves were chewed (see **Quid**); the fibers were used for utilitarian purposes; and the sap from the roots, which sudses when mixed with water, was used as soap and shampoo.

Bibliography

Adams, William Y., Alexander J. Lindsay, Jr., and Christy G. Turner, II
  1961 Survey and Excavations in Lower Glen Canyon, 1952–1958. *Museum of Northern Arizona Bulletin*, No. 36, *Glen Canyon Series*, No. 3. Flagstaff.

Agogino, George A., and Eugene Galloway
  1965 The Sister's Hill Site: A Hell Gap Site in North-central Wyoming. *Plains Anthropologist*, Vol. 10, No. 29, pp. 190–195. Lincoln.

Aikens, C. Melvin
  1966a Fremont-Promontory-Plains Relationships. *University of Utah Anthropological Papers*, No. 82. Salt Lake City.
  1966b Virgin-Kayenta Cultural Relationships. *University of Utah Anthropological Papers*, No. 79, *Glen Canyon Series*, No. 29. Salt Lake City.

Alabama Museum of Natural History
  1942 Mound State Monument, Moundville, Alabama. *Alabama Museum of Natural History, Museum Paper*, No. 20. Moundville.

Alexander, Herbert L., Jr.
  1963 The Levi Site: A Paleo-Indian Campsite in Central Texas. *American Antiquity*, Vol. 28, No. 4, pp. 510–528. Salt Lake City.

Anderson, Edgar
  1952 *Plants, Man and Life.* Little, Brown and Company, Boston.

Antevs, Ernst
  1925 On the Pleistocene History of the Great Basin. *In* "Quaternary Climates." *Carnegie Institution of Washington Publication*, No. 352, pp. 51–114. Washington.
  1935 The Spread of Aboriginal Man to North America. *Geographical Review*, Vol. 25, No. 2, pp. 302–309. New York.
  1937 Climate and Early Man in North America. *In Early Man*, George G. MacCurdy (ed.), pp. 125–132. J. B. Lippincott Company, Philadelphia.
  1941 Age of the Cochise Culture Stages. *In* "The Cochise Culture," E. B. Sayles and Ernst Antevs. *Medallion Papers*, No. 29, pp. 31–56. Gila Pueblo, Globe, Arizona.
  1948 Climatic Changes by Pre-white Man. *In* "The Great Basin with Emphasis on Glacial and Postglacial Times." *Bulletin of the University of Utah*, Vol. 38, No. 20, *Biological Series*,

Vol. 10, No. 7, pp. 168–191. Salt Lake City.

1950a Conditions of Deposition and Erosion by Streams in Dry Regions of the Great Plains. *In* "Proceedings of the Sixth Plains Archeological Conference, 1948," Jesse D. Jennings (ed.). *University of Utah Anthropological Papers*, No. 11, pp. 42–45a. Salt Lake City.

1950b Postglacial Climatic History of the Great Plains and Dating the Records of Man. *In* "Proceedings of the Sixth Plains Archeological Conference, 1948," Jesse D. Jennings (ed.). *University of Utah Anthropological Papers*, No. 11, pp. 46–50. Salt Lake City.

1952a Cenozoic Climates of the Great Basin. *Geologischen Rundschau*, Bd. 40, Heft 1, pp. 94–108. Stuttgart.

1952b Climatic History and the Antiquity of Man in California. *In* "Symposium of the Antiquity of Man in California," Walter Goldschmidt (ed.). *Reports of the University of California Archaeological Survey*, No. 16, pp. 23–31. Berkeley.

1955a Geologic-climatic Dating in the West. *American Antiquity*, Vol. 20, No. 4, Pt. 1, pp. 317–335. Salt Lake City.

1955b Geologic-climatic Method of Dating. *In* "Geochronology," Terah L. Smiley (ed.). *University of Arizona Bulletin*, Vol. 26, No. 2, *Physical Science Bulletin*, No. 2, pp. 151–169. Tucson.

1955c Varve and Radiocarbon Chronologies Appraised by Pollen Data. *Journal of Geology*, Vol. 63, No. 5, pp. 495–499. Chicago.

1956 Review of: *Climatic Change: Evidence, Causes, and Effects*, Harlow Shapley (ed.). *American Antiquity*, Vol. 21, No. 4, pp. 423–424. Salt Lake City.

1957 Geological Tests of the Varve and Radiocarbon Chronologies. *Journal of Geology*, Vol. 65, No. 2, pp. 129–148. Chicago.

1959 Geologic Age of the Lehner Mammoth Site. *American Antiquity*, Vol. 25, No. 1, pp. 31–34. Salt Lake City.

1962 Late Quaternary Climates in Arizona. *American Antiquity*, Vol. 28, No. 2, pp. 193–198. Salt Lake City.

Arellano, A. R. V.
1951 Some New Aspects of the Tepexpan Man Case. *Bulletin of the Texas Archeological and Paleontological Society*, Vol. 22, pp. 217–225. Lubbock.

Armillas, Pedro
1964 Northern Mesoamerica. *In Prehistoric Man in the New World*, Jesse D. Jennings and Edward Norbeck (eds.), pp. 291–329. *Rice University Semicentennial Publications*, The University of Chicago Press, Chicago.

Arnold, Brigham A.
1957 Late Pleistocene and Recent Changes in Land Forms, Climate, and Archaeology in Central Baja California. *University of California Publications in Geography*, Vol. 10, No. 4, pp. 201–318. Berkeley.

Arrhenius, Olof
1963 Investigation of Soil from Old Indian Sites. *Ethnos*, Nos. 2–4, pp. 122–136. Ethnographical Museum of Sweden, Stockholm.

Ascher, Robert
1960 Archaeology and the Public Image. *American Antiquity*, Vol. 25, No. 3, pp. 402–403. Salt Lake City.

Ascher, Robert, and Marcia Ascher
1965 Recognizing the Emergence of Man. *Science*, Vol. 147, No. 3655, pp. 243–250. Washington.

Aschmann, Homer H.
1958 Great Basin Climates in Relation to Human Occupance. *In* "Current Views on Great Basin Archaeology." *Reports of the University of California Archaeological Survey*, No. 42, pp. 23–40. Berkeley.

Baerreis, David A.
1951 The Preceramic Horizons of Northeastern Oklahoma. *University of Michigan, Museum of Anthropology, Anthropological Papers*, No. 6. Ann Arbor.

1959 The Archaic as Seen from the Ozark Region. *American Antiquity*, Vol. 24, No. 3, pp. 270–275. Salt Lake City.

Baerreis, David A., and Reid A. Bryson
1965 Climatic Episodes and the Dating of the Mississippian Cultures. *Wisconsin Archeologist*, n.s., Vol. 46, No. 4, pp. 203–220. Milwaukee.

Bannister, Bryant
1963 Dendrochronology. *In Science in Archaeology*, Don Brothwell and Eric Higgs (eds.), pp. 162–176. Basic Books, Inc., Publishers, New York.

Bass, William M., III
1964 The Variation in Physical Types of the Prehistoric Plains Indians. *Memoir*, No. 1. *Plains Anthropologist*, Vol. 9, No. 24, pp. 65–145. Lincoln.

Bastian, Tyler J.
1963 *Prehistoric Copper Mining in Isle Royale National Park, Michigan.* Unpublished master's thesis, Depart-

ment of Anthropology, University of Utah, Salt Lake City.

Baumhoff, Martin A., and Robert F. Heizer
1965 Postglacial Climate and Archaeology in the Desert West. *In The Quaternary of the United States*, Part I: *Geology*, H. E. Wright, Jr., and David G. Frey (eds.), pp. 697–707. Princeton University Press, Princeton.

Beardsley, Richard K.
1948 Culture Sequences in Central California Archaeology. *American Antiquity*, Vol. 14, No. 1, pp. 1–28. Salt Lake City.

Beaubien, Paul L.
1953 Cultural Variation within Two Woodland Mound Groups of Northeastern Iowa. *American Antiquity*, Vol. 19, No. 1, pp. 56–66. Salt Lake City.

Bell, Robert E.
1948 Review of: "Tree Ring Studies in North Dakota," George F. Will. *American Anthropologist*, Vol. 50, No. 1, Pt. 1, pp. 104–108. Menasha.
1951 Dendrochronology at the Kincaid Site. Appendix I *in Kincaid: A Prehistoric Illinois Metropolis*, Fay-Cooper Cole et al., pp. 233–292. *Publications in Anthropology, Archaeological Series*, The University of Chicago Press, Chicago.

Bell, Robert E., and David A. Baerreis
1951 A Survey of Oklahoma Archaeology. *Bulletin of the Texas Archeological and Paleontological Society*, Vol. 22, pp. 7–100. Lubbock.

Bennyhoff, James A.
1958 The Desert West: A Trial Correlation of Culture and Chronology. *In* "Current Views on Great Basin Archaeology." *Reports of the University of California Archaeological Survey*, No. 42, pp. 98–113. Berkeley.

Bennyhoff, James A., and Robert F. Heizer
1958 Cross-dating Great Basin Sites by Californian Shell Beads. *In* "Current Views on Great Basin Archaeology." *Reports of the University of California Archaeological Survey*, No. 42, pp. 60–93. Berkeley.

Bird, Junius B.
1938 Antiquity and Migrations of the Early Inhabitants of Patagonia. *Geographical Review*, Vol. 28, No. 2, pp. 250–275. New York.
1943 Excavations in Northern Chile. *Anthropological Papers of the American Museum of Natural History*, Vol. 38, Pt. 4, pp. 171–316. New York.

Birdsell, Joseph B.
1951 The Problem of the Early Peopling of the Americas as Viewed from Asia. *In Papers on the Physical Anthropology of the American Indian*, William S. Laughlin (ed.), pp. 1–68. The Viking Fund, Inc., New York.

Black, Glenn A.
1949 "Tepexpan Man," a Critique of Method. *American Antiquity*, Vol. 14, No. 4, pp. 344–346. Salt Lake City.

Bliss, Wesley L.
1952 Radiocarbon Contamination. *American Antiquity*, Vol. 17, No. 3, pp. 250–251. Salt Lake City.

Boas, Franz
1888 The Central Eskimo. *Bureau of Ethnology, 6th Annual Report*, pp 399–669. Washington.

Bordaz, Jacques
1959 First Tools of Mankind, Parts I and II. *Natural History*, Vol. 68, No. 1, pp. 36–51; Vol. 68, No. 2, pp. 92–103. New York.

Borden, Charles E.
1962 West Coast Crossties with Alaska. *In* "Prehistoric Cultural Relations between the Arctic and Temperate Zones of North America," John M. Campbell (ed.). *Arctic Institute of North America Technical Paper*, No. 11, pp. 9–19. Montreal.
1967 Archaeology *In Britannica Book of the Year, 1967*, pp. 100–103. William Benton, Chicago.

Bray, Robert T.
1956 The Culture-complexes and Sequence at the Rice Site (23SN200), Stone County, Missouri. *Missouri Archaeologist*, Vol. 18, Nos. 1–2, pp. 46–134. Columbia.

Breternitz, David A.
1963 *The Archaeological Interpretation of Tree-ring Specimens for Dating Southwestern Ceramic Styles*. Unpublished doctoral dissertation, Department of Anthropology, University of Arizona, Tucson.

Brew, John O.
1946 Archaeology of Alkali Ridge, Southeastern Utah. *Papers of the Peabody Museum of American Archaeology and Ethnology*, Vol. 21. Cambridge.
1961 Emergency Archaeology: Salvage in Advance of Technological Progress. *Proceedings of the American Philosophical Society*, Vol. 105, No. 1, pp. 1–10. Philadelphia.

Bridges, E. Lucas
1948 *Uttermost Part of the Earth*. E. P. Dutton & Co., Inc., New York.

Brothwell, Don, and Eric Higgs (eds.)
1963 *Science in Archaeology: A Comprehensive Survey of Progress and Research*. Basic Books, Inc., Publishers, New York.

Bryan, Alan L.
1965 Paleo-American Prehistory. *Occasional Papers of the Idaho State University Museum,* No. 16. Pocatello.

Bryan, Alan L., and **Ruth Gruhn**
1964 Problems Relating to the Neo-thermal Climatic Sequence. *American Antiquity,* Vol. 29, No. 3, pp. 307–315. Salt Lake City.

Bryan, Kirk
1950 Geological Interpretation of the Deposits. *In The Stratigraphy and Archaeology of Ventana Cave,* Emil Haury et al., pp. 75–126. The University of New Mexico and University of Arizona Presses, Albuquerque and Tucson.

Bullard, William R., Jr.
1962 The Cerro Colorado Site and Pithouse Architecture in the Southwestern United States Prior to A.D. 900. *Papers of the Peabody Museum of Archaeology and Ethnology,* Vol. 44, No. 2. Cambridge.

Burma, Benjamin H.
1950 Erosion and Sedimentation in the Great Plains: A Criticism of Dr. Antevs' Conference Papers. *In* "Proceedings of the Sixth Plains Archeological Conference, 1948," Jesse D. Jennings (ed.). *University of Utah Anthropological Papers,* No. 11, pp. 52–55. Salt Lake City.

Bushnell, Geoffrey, and **Charles McBurney**
1959 New World Origins Seen from the Old World. *Antiquity,* Vol. 33, No. 130, pp. 93–101. Gloucester, England.

Butler, B. Robert
1959 Lower Columbia Valley Archaeology: A Survey and Appraisal of Some Major Archaeological Resources. *Tebiwa,* Vol. 2, No. 2, pp. 6–24. Idaho State University Museum, Pocatello.
1961 The Old Cordilleran Culture in the Pacific Northwest. *Occasional Papers of the Idaho State College Museum,* No. 5. Pocatello.

Byers, Douglas S.
1946 The Environment of the Northeast. *In* "Man in Northeastern North America," Frederick Johnson (ed.). *Papers of the Robert S. Peabody Foundation for Archaeology,* Vol. 3, pp. 3–32. Andover, Massachusetts.
1954 Bull Brook—A Fluted Point Site in Ipswich, Massachusetts. *American Antiquity,* Vol. 19, No. 4, pp. 343–351. Salt Lake City.
1957 The Bering Bridge—Some Speculations. *Ethnos,* Nos. 1–2, pp. 20–26. Ethnographical Museum of Sweden, Stockholm.
1959 The Eastern Archaic: Some Problems and Hypotheses. *American Antiquity,* Vol. 24, No. 3, pp. 233–256. Salt Lake City.
1966 *The Debert Paleo-Indian Site.* A Guide for Stop No. 11, Field Trip No. 4. Geological Association of Canada, Mineralogical Association of Canada, Ottawa.

Caldwell, Joseph R.
1958 Trend and Tradition in the Prehistory of the Eastern United States. *American Anthropologist,* Vol. 60, No. 6, Pt. 2, *American Anthropological Association Memoir,* No. 88; and *Illinois State Museum Scientific Papers,* Vol. 10. Menasha.

Caldwell, Joseph R., and **Robert L. Hall (eds.)**
1964 Hopewellian Studies. *Illinois State Museum Scientific Papers,* Vol. 12. Springfield.

Caldwell, Joseph R., and **Catherine McCann**
1941 *Irene Mound Site, Chatham County, Georgia.* University of Georgia Press, Athens.

Callen, Eric O.
1963 Diet as Revealed by Coprolites. *In Science in Archaeology,* Don Brothwell and Eric Higgs (eds.), pp. 186–194. Basic Books, Inc., Publishers, New York.

Campbell, Elizabeth W. C., et al.
1937 The Archaeology of Pleistocene Lake Mohave: A Symposium. *Southwest Museum Papers,* No. 11. Los Angeles.

Campbell, Elizabeth W. C., and **William H. Campbell**
1935 The Pinto Basin Site: An Ancient Aboriginal Camping Ground in the California Desert. *Southwest Museum Papers,* No. 9. Los Angeles.

Campbell, John M.
1959 The Kayuk Complex of Arctic Alaska. *American Antiquity,* Vol. 25, No. 1, pp. 94–105. Salt Lake City.
1961 The Kogruk Complex of Anaktuvuk Pass, Alaska. *Anthropologica,* n.s., Vol. 3, No. 1, pp. 1–18. Ottawa.
1962a Cultural Succession at Anaktuvuk Pass, Arctic Alaska. *In* "Prehistoric Cultural Relations between the Arctic and Temperate Zones of North America," John M. Campbell (ed.). *Arctic Institute of North America Technical Paper,* No. 11, pp. 39–54. Montreal.
1962b (ed.) Prehistoric Cultural Relations between the Arctic and Temperate Zones of North America. *Arctic Institute of North America Technical Paper,* No. 11. Montreal.
1963 Ancient Alaska and Paleolithic Europe. *In* "Early Man in the Western

American Arctic: A Symposium," Frederick H. West (ed.). *Anthropological Papers of the University of Alaska*, Vol. 10, No. 2, pp. 29–49. College.

Campbell, Thomas N. (ed.)
1961 Symposium: Relationships between the Caddoan Area and Neighboring Areas. *Bulletin of the Texas Archeological Society*, Vol. 31, for 1960, pp. 1–151. Austin.

Carnegie Institution of Washington
1925 Quaternary Climates. *Carnegie Institution of Washington Publication*, No. 352. Washington.

Carpenter, Edmund S.
1950 The Role of Archeology in the Nineteenth Century Controversy between Developmentalism and Degeneration. *Pennsylvania Archaeologist*, Vol. 20, Nos. 1–2, pp. 5–18. Philadelphia.

Carter, George F.
1951 Man in America: A Criticism of Scientific Thought. *Scientific Monthly*, Vol. 73, No. 5, pp. 297–307. Washington.
1957 *Pleistocene Man at San Diego.* The Johns Hopkins Press, Baltimore.

Champe, John L.
1946 Ash Hollow Cave. *University of Nebraska Studies*, n.s., No. 1. Lincoln.

Champe, John L., et al.
1949 Proceedings of the Fifth Plains Conference for Archeology. *University of Nebraska, Laboratory of Anthropology Note Book*, No. 1. Lincoln.

Chang, Kwang-Chih
1967 *Rethinking Archaeology.* Random House, Inc., New York.

Chard, Chester S.
1956 The Oldest Sites of Northeast Siberia. *American Antiquity*, Vol. 21, No. 4, pp. 405–409. Salt Lake City.
1959a New World Origins: A Reappraisal. *Antiquity*, Vol. 33, No. 129, pp. 44–49. Gloucester, England.
1959b Old World Sources for Early Lithic Cultures. *Actas del XXXIII Congreso Internacional de Americanistas*, Tomo 1, pp. 314–320. San José, Costa Rica.
1960 Routes to Bering Strait. *American Antiquity*, Vol. 26, No. 2, pp. 283–285. Salt Lake City.
1963 The Old World Roots: Review and Speculations. *In* "Early Man in the Western American Arctic: A Symposium," Frederick H. West (ed.). *Anthropological Papers of the University of Alaska*, Vol. 10, No. 2, pp. 115–121. College.

Childe, V. Gordon
1956 *Piecing Together the Past: The Interpretation of Archaeological Data.* Routledge & Kegan Paul, Ltd., London.

Clark, Grahame
1957 *Archaeology and Society.* Harvard University Press, Cambridge.

Coe, Joffre L.
1952 The Cultural Sequence of the Carolina Piedmont. *In Archaeology of Eastern United States*, James B. Griffin (ed.), pp. 301–311. The University of Chicago Press, Chicago.

Coe, Michael D.
1962 *Mexico.* Thames and Hudson, London.

Cole, Fay-Cooper, et al.
1951 *Kincaid: A Prehistoric Illinois Metropolis. Publications in Anthropology, Archaeological Series*, The University of Chicago Press, Chicago.
1956 Papers of the Third Great Basin Archeological Conference. *University of Utah Anthropological Papers*, No. 26. Salt Lake City.

Cole, Fay-Cooper, and Thorne Deuel
1937 *Rediscovering Illinois: Archaeological Explorations in and around Fulton County.* The University of Chicago Press, Chicago.

Collins, Henry B., Jr.
1927 Potsherds from Choctaw Village Sites in Mississippi. *Journal of the Washington Academy of Science*, Vol. 17, No. 10, pp. 259–263. Washington.
1937 Archeology of St. Lawrence Island, Alaska. *Smithsonian Miscellaneous Collections*, Vol. 96, No. 1. Washington.
1952 (ed.) Science in Alaska: Selected Papers of the Alaskan Science Conference of the National Academy of Sciences–National Research Council, Washington, November 9–11, 1950. *Arctic Institute of North America Special Publication*, No. 1. Washington.
1954 Arctic Area: Indigenous Period. *Program of the History of America*, I, No. 2. *Instituto Panamericano de Geografía e Historia Publicación*, Num. 160, *Comisión de Historia Publicación*, Num. 68. Mexico, D. F.
1956 The T 1 Site at Native Point, Southampton Island, N.W.T. *Anthropological Papers of the University of Alaska*, Vol. 4, No. 2, pp. 63–89. College.
1960 Comments. *In* "The Archeology of Bering Strait," James L. Giddings, Jr. *Current Anthropology*, Vol. 1, No. 2, pp. 131–136. Chicago.
1963 Paleo-Indian Artifacts in Alaska: An Example of Cultural Retardation in the Arctic. *In* "Early Man in the Western American Arctic: A Symposium,"

Frederick H. West (ed.). *Anthropological Papers of the University of Alaska*, Vol. 10, No. 2, pp. 13–18. College.
1964   The Arctic and Subarctic. *In Prehistoric Man in the New World*, Jesse D. Jennings and Edward Norbeck (eds.), pp. 85–114. *Rice University Semicentennial Publications*, The University of Chicago Press, Chicago.

Cook, Harold J.
1926   The Antiquity of Man in America. *Scientific American*, Vol. 135, No. 5, pp. 334–336. New York.

Coon, Carleton S.
1948   *A Reader in General Anthropology*. Holt, Rinehart and Winston, Inc., New York.

Coon, Carleton S., Stanley M. Garn, and **Joseph B. Birdsell**
1950   Races—A Study of the Problems of Race Formation in Man. *American Lecture Series Publication*, No. 77. Charles C. Thomas, Springfield.

Cosgrove, Cornelius B.
1947   Caves of the Upper Gila and Hueco Areas in New Mexico and Texas. *Papers of the Peabody Museum of American Archaeology and Ethnology*, Vol. 24, No. 2. Cambridge.

Cosgrove, Harriet S., and **Cornelius B. Cosgrove**
1932   The Swarts Ruin: A Typical Mimbres Site in Southwestern New Mexico. *Papers of the Peabody Museum of American Archaeology and Ethnology*, Vol. 15, No. 1. Cambridge.

Cotter, John L., and **John M. Corbett**
1951   Archeology of the Bynum Mounds, Mississippi. *National Park Service Archeological Research Series*, No. 1. Washington.

Cowles, John
1960   *Cougar Mountain Cave in South Central Oregon*. Privately printed, Rainier, Oregon.

Cressman, Luther S.
1942   Archaeological Researches in the Northern Great Basin. *Carnegie Institution of Washington Publication*, No. 538. Washington.
1956   Klamath Prehistory: The Prehistory of the Culture of the Klamath Lake Area, Oregon. *Transactions of the American Philosophical Society*, n.s., Vol. 46, Pt. 4, pp. 374–513. Philadelphia.
1960   Cultural Sequences at The Dalles, Oregon: A Contribution to Pacific Northwest Prehistory. *Transactions of the American Philosophical Society*, n.s., Vol. 50, Pt. 10. Philadelphia.

Cressman, Luther S., and **Alex D. Krieger**
1940   Atlatls and Associated Artifacts from Southcentral Oregon. *In* "Early Man in Oregon: Archeological Studies in the Northern Great Basin," Luther S. Cressman, Howell Williams, and Alex D. Krieger (eds.). *University of Oregon Monographs, Studies in Anthropology*, No. 3, pp. 16–52. Eugene.

Cressman, Luther S., Howell Williams, and **Alex D. Krieger (eds.)**
1940   Early Man in Oregon: Archeological Studies in the Northern Great Basin. *University of Oregon Monographs, Studies in Anthropology*, No. 3. Eugene.

Crook, Wilson W., Jr., and **R. K. Harris**
1952   Trinity Aspect of the Archaic Horizon: The Carrollton and Elam Foci. *Bulletin of the Texas Archeological and Paleontological Society*, Vol. 23, pp. 7–38. Lubbock.

Cutler, Hugh C.
1966   Corn, Cucurbits and Cotton from Glen Canyon. *University of Utah Anthropological Papers*, No. 80, *Glen Canyon Series*, No. 30. Salt Lake City.

Daifuku, Hiroshi
1952   A New Conceptual Scheme for Prehistoric Cultures in the Southwestern United States. *American Anthropologist*, Vol. 54, No. 2, Pt. 1, pp. 191–200. Menasha.

Daugherty, Richard D.
1962   The Intermontane Western Tradition. *American Antiquity*, Vol. 28, No. 2, pp. 144–150. Salt Lake City.

Davis, E. Mott
1953   Recent Data from Two Paleo-Indian Sites on Medicine Creek, Nebraska. *American Antiquity*, Vol. 18, No. 4, pp. 380–386. Salt Lake City.
1962   Archeology of the Lime Creek Site in Southwestern Nebraska. *Special Publication of the University of Nebraska State Museum*, No. 3. Lincoln.

Day, Kent C.
1964   Thorne Cave, Northeastern Utah: Archaeology. *American Antiquity*, Vol. 30, No. 1, pp. 50–59. Salt Lake City.

Deetz, James
1965   The Dynamics of Stylistic Change in Arikara Ceramics. *Illinois Studies in Anthropology*, No. 4. Urbana.

Deevey, Edward S., Jr.
1953   Paleolimnology and Climate. *In Climatic Change: Evidence, Causes, and Effects*, Harlow Shapley (ed.), pp. 273–318. Harvard University Press, Cambridge.

DeJarnette, David L., Edward B. Kurjack, and **James W. Cambron**
1962   Stanfield-Worley Bluff Shelter

Excavations. *Journal of Alabama Archaeology*, Vol. 8, Nos. 1 and 2, pp. 1–111. University.

De Laguna, Frederica (ed.)
1960 *Selected Papers from the American Anthropologist, 1888–1920*. Harper & Row, Publishers, Incorporated, New York.

de Terra, Helmut
1949 Early Man in Mexico. *In* "Tepexpan Man," Helmut de Terra, Javier Romero, and T. Dale Stewart. *Viking Fund Publications in Anthropology*, No. 11, pp. 11–86. New York.

de Terra, Helmut, Javier Romero, and
T. Dale Stewart
1949 Tepexpan Man. *Viking Fund Publications in Anthropology*, No. 11. New York.

Deuel, Thorne
1935 Basic Cultures of the Mississippi Valley. *American Anthropologist*, Vol. 37, No. 3, pp. 429–445. Menasha.
1937 The Application of a Classificatory Method to Mississippi Valley Archaeology. Appendix I *in Rediscovering Illinois*, Fay-Cooper Cole and Thorne Deuel, pp. 207–219. The University of Chicago Press, Chicago.
1952a (ed.) Hopewellian Communities in Illinois. *Illinois State Museum Scientific Papers*, Vol. 5. Springfield.
1952b Hopewellian Dress in Illinois. *In Archeology of Eastern United States*, James B. Griffin (ed.), pp. 165–175. The University of Chicago Press, Chicago.

Dick, Herbert W.
1965 Bat Cave. *School of American Research Monograph*, No. 27. Santa Fe.

Dick, Herbert W., and Bert Mountain
1960 The Claypool Site: A Cody Complex Site in Northeastern Colorado. *American Antiquity*, Vol. 26, No. 2, pp. 223–235. Salt Lake City.

Dittert, Alfred E., Jr., Frank W. Eddy, and
Beth L. Dickey
1963 Evidences of Early Ceramic Phases in the Navajo Reservoir District. *El Palacio*, Vol. 70, Nos. 1–2, pp. 5–12. Santa Fe.

Dittert, Alfred E., Jr., Jim J. Hester, and
Frank W. Eddy
1961 An Archaeological Survey of the Navajo Reservoir District, Northwestern New Mexico. *School of American Research and the Museum of New Mexico Monograph*, No. 23, *Navajo Project Studies*, No. 2. Santa Fe.

Dixon, Keith A.
1959 Ceramics from Two Preclassic Periods at Chiapa de Corzo, Chiapas,

Mexico. *Publications of the New World Archaeological Foundation*, No. 4, *Paper*, No. 5, Orinda, California.

Douglass, Andrew E.
1929 The Secret of the Southwest Solved by Talkative Tree Rings. *National Geographic Magazine*, Vol. 56, No. 6, pp. 737–770. Washington.

Dragoo, Don W.
1963 Mounds for the Dead: An Analysis of the Adena Culture. *Annals of the Carnegie Museum*, Vol. 37. Pittsburgh.
1964 The Development of Adena Culture and Its Role in the Formation of Ohio Hopewell. Paper No. 1 *in* "Hopewellian Studies," Joseph R. Caldwell and Robert L. Hall (eds.). *Illinois State Museum Scientific Papers*, Vol. 12, pp. 1–34. Springfield.

Drucker, Philip, Robert F. Heizer, and
Robert J. Squier
1959 Excavations at La Venta, Tabasco, 1955. *Bureau of American Ethnology Bulletin*, No. 170. Washington.

Dumond, Don E.
1965 On Eskaleutian Linguistics, Archaeology, and Prehistory. *American Anthropologist*, Vol. 67, No. 5, Pt. 1, pp. 1231–1257. Menasha.

Eddy, Frank W.
1961 Excavations at Los Pinos Phase Sites in the Navajo Reservoir District. *Museum of New Mexico Papers in Anthropology*, No. 4, *Navajo Project Studies*, No. 4. Santa Fe.

Edwards, Clinton R.
1960 Sailing Rafts of Sechura: History and Problems of Origin. *Southwestern Journal of Anthropology*, Vol. 16, No. 3, pp. 368–391. Albuquerque.

Eggan, Fred R.
1952 The Ethnological Cultures and Their Archeological Backgrounds. *In Archeology of Eastern United States*, James B. Griffin (ed.), pp. 35–45. The University of Chicago Press, Chicago.

Eiseley, Loren C.
1955 The Paleo-Indians: Their Survival and Diffusion. *In New Interpretations of Aboriginal American Culture History*, Betty J. Meggers and Clifford Evans (eds.), pp. 1–11. The Anthropological Society of Washington, Washington.

Ekholm, Gordon F.
1942 Excavations at Guasave, Sinaloa, Mexico. *Anthropological Papers of the American Museum of Natural History*, Vol. 38, Pt. 2, pp. 23–139. New York.
1944 Excavations at Tampico and

Panuco in the Huasteca, Mexico. *Anthropological Papers of the American Museum of Natural History*, Vol. 38, Pt. 5, pp. 319–509. New York.

1953   A Possible Focus of Asiatic Influence in the Late Classic Cultures of Mesoamerica. *In* "Asia and North America: Transpacific Contacts," Marian W. Smith (ed.). *American Antiquity*, Vol. 18, Pt. 2, *Memoirs of the Society for American Archaeology*, No. 9, pp. 72–97. Salt Lake City.

1955   The New Orientation toward Problems of Asiatic-American Relationships. *In New Interpretations of Aboriginal American Culture History*, Betty J. Meggers and Clifford Evans (eds.), pp. 95–109. The Anthropological Society of Washington, Washington.

1964   Transpacific Contacts. *In Prehistoric Man in the New World*, Jesse D. Jennings and Edward Norbeck (eds.), pp. 489–510. *Rice University Semicentennial Publications*, The University of Chicago Press, Chicago.

Elsasser, Albert B., and **Robert F. Heizer**
1966   Excavation of Two Northwestern California Coastal Sites. *Reports of the University of California Archaeological Survey*, No. 67, pp. v–149. Berkeley.

Emery, K. O., and **R. L. Edwards**
1966   Archaeological Potential of the Atlantic Continental Shelf. *American Antiquity*, Vol. 31, No. 5, Pt. 1, pp. 733–737. Salt Lake City.

Estrada, Emilio, and **Betty J. Meggers**
1961   A Complex of Traits of Probable Transpacific Origin on the Coast of Ecuador. *American Anthropologist*, Vol. 63, No. 5, Pt. 1, pp. 913–939. Menasha.

Estrada, Emilio, Betty J. Meggers, and **Clifford Evans**
1962   Possible Transpacific Contact on the Coast of Ecuador. *Science*, Vol. 135, No. 3501, pp. 371–372. Washington.

Euler, Robert C., and **Alan P. Olson**
1965   Split-twig Figurines from Northern Arizona: New Radiocarbon Dates. *Science*, Vol. 148, No. 3668, pp. 368–369. Washington.

Evans, Clifford, and **Betty J. Meggers**
1960   A New Dating Method Using Obsidian: Part II, an Archaeological Evaluation of the Method. *American Antiquity*, Vol. 25, No. 4, pp. 523–537. Salt Lake City.

Ewers, John C.
1949   The Last Bison Drives of the Blackfoot Indians. *Journal of the Washington Academy of Sciences*, Vol. 39, No. 11, pp. 355–360. Washington.

Fairbanks, Charles H.
1942   The Taxonomic Position of Stalling's Island, Georgia. *American Antiquity*, Vol. 7, No. 3, pp. 223–231. Salt Lake City.

1946   The Macon Earth Lodge. *American Antiquity*, Vol. 12, No. 2, pp. 94–108. Salt Lake City.

Ferdon, Edwin N., Jr.
1955   A Trial Survey of Mexican-Southwestern Architectural Parallels. *School of American Research Monograph*, No. 21. Santa Fe.

Fergusson, G. J., and **Willard F. Libby**
1964   UCLA Radiocarbon Dates, III. *Radiocarbon*, Vol. 6, pp. 318–339. New Haven.

Flint, Richard F.
1947   *Glacial Geology and the Pleistocene Epoch.* John Wiley & Sons, Inc., New York.

1957   *Glacial and Pleistocene Geology.* John Wiley & Sons, Inc., New York.

Ford, James A.
1936   Analysis of Indian Village Site Collections from Louisiana and Mississippi. *Louisiana Geological Survey, Anthropological Study*, No. 2. New Orleans.

1951   Greenhouse: A Troyville-Coles Creek Period Site in Avoyelles Parish, Louisiana. *Anthropological Papers of the American Museum of Natural History*, Vol. 44, Pt. 1, pp. 1–132. New York.

1954   On the Concept of Types: The Type Concept Revisited. *American Anthropologist*, Vol. 56, No. 1, pp. 42–54. Menasha.

1959   Eskimo Prehistory in the Vicinity of Point Barrow, Alaska. *Anthropological Papers of the American Museum of Natural History*, Vol. 47, Pt. 1, pp. 1–272. New York.

1966   Early Formative Cultures in Georgia and Florida. *American Antiquity*, Vol. 31, No. 6, pp. 781–799. Salt Lake City.

Ford, James A., Philip Phillips, and **William G. Haag**
1955   The Jaketown Site in West-central Mississippi. *Anthropological Papers of the American Museum of Natural History*, Vol. 45, Pt. 1, pp. 1–164. New York.

Ford, James A., and **Clarence H. Webb**
1956   Poverty Point, a Late Archaic Site in Louisiana. *Anthropological Papers of the American Museum of Natural History*, Vol. 46, Pt. 1, pp. 1–136. New York.

Ford, James A., and **Gordon R. Willey**
1940   Crooks Site, a Marksville Period

Burial Mound in LaSalle Parish, Louisiana. *Louisiana Geological Survey, Anthropological Study,* No. 3. New Orleans.
1941 An Interpretation of the Prehistory of the Eastern United States. *American Anthropologist,* Vol. 43, No. 3, Pt. 1, pp. 325–363. Menasha.

Fowke, Gerard
1928 Archeological Investigations— II. *Bureau of American Ethnology, 44th Annual Report,* pp. 399–540. Washington.

Fowler, Melvin L.
1952 The Clear Lake Site: Hopewellian Occupation. Paper No. 4 *in* "Hopewellian Communities in Illinois," Thorne Deuel (ed.). *Illinois State Museum Scientific Papers,* Vol. 5, pp. 131–174. Springfield.
1959 Modoc Rock Shelter: An Early Archaic Site in Southern Illinois. *American Antiquity,* Vol. 24, No. 3, pp. 257–270. Salt Lake City.

Friedman, Irving, and Robert L. Smith
1960 A New Dating Method Using Obsidian: Part I, the Development of the Method. *American Antiquity,* Vol. 25, No. 4, pp. 476–522. Salt Lake City.

Friedman, Irving, Robert L. Smith, and Donovan Clark
1963 Obsidian Dating. *In Science in Archaeology,* Don Brothwell and Eric Higgs (eds.), pp. 47–58. Basic Books, Inc., Publishers, New York.

Fritts, Harold C.
1965 Tree-ring Evidence for Climatic Changes in Western North America. *Monthly Weather Review,* Vol. 93, No. 7, pp. 421–443. Washington.

Fritts, Harold C., David G. Smith, and Marvin A. Stokes
1965 The Biological Model for Paleoclimatic Interpretation of Mesa Verde Tree-ring Series. *In* "Contributions of the Wetherill Mesa Archeological Project," Douglas Osborne et al. *American Antiquity,* Vol. 31, No. 2, Pt. 2, *Memoirs of the Society for American Archaeology,* No. 19, pp. 101–121. Salt Lake City.

Cagliano, Sherwood M.
1963 A Survey of Preceramic Occupations in Portions of South Louisiana and South Mississippi. *United States Gulf Coastal Studies, Technical Report,* No. 16, Pt. E; *Coastal Studies Institute Contribution,* No. 63 7, pp. 105 132. Baton Rouge. (Also published in *Florida Anthropologist,* Vol. 16, No. 4. Tallahassee.)

Galinat, Walton C., and James H. Gunnerson
1963 Spread of Eight-rowed Maize

from the Prehistoric Southwest. *Harvard University, Botanical Museum Leaflets,* Vol. 20, No. 5, pp. 117–160. Cambridge.

Giddings, James L., Jr.
1951 The Denbigh Flint Complex. *American Antiquity,* Vol. 16, No. 3, pp. 193–203. Salt Lake City.
1952 *The Arctic Woodland Culture of the Kobuk River.* University of Pennsylvania, University Museum, Museum Monographs, Philadelphia.
1960a The Archeology of Bering Strait. *Current Anthropology,* Vol. 1, No. 2, pp. 121–130. Chicago.
1960b First Traces of Man in the Arctic. *Natural History,* Vol. 69, No. 9, pp. 10–19. New York.
1962 Side-notched Points near Bering Strait. *In* "Prehistoric Cultural Relations between the Arctic and Temperate Zones of North America," John M. Campbell (ed.). *Arctic Institute of North America Technical Paper,* No. 11, pp. 35–38. Montreal.
1963 Some Arctic Spear Points and Their Counterparts. *In* "Early Man in the Western American Arctic: A Symposium," Frederick H. West (ed.). *Anthropological Papers of the University of Alaska,* Vol. 10, No. 2, pp. 1–12. College.
1964 *The Archeology of Cape Denbigh.* Brown University Press, Providence.

Gladwin, Harold S.
1937 Excavations at Snaketown, II: Comparisons and Theories. *Medallion Papers,* No. 26. Gila Pueblo, Globe, Arizona.
1947 *Men Out of Asia.* Whittlesey House (McGraw-Hill Book Company), New York.

Gladwin, Harold S., et al.
1937 Excavations at Snaketown: Material Culture. *Medallion Papers,* No. 25. Gila Pueblo, Globe, Arizona.

Glock, Waldo S.
1937 Principles and Methods of Tree-ring Analysis. *Carnegie Institution of Washington Publication,* No. 486. Washington.

Goldschmidt, Walter (ed.)
1952 Symposium of the Antiquity of Man in California. Presented before the Southwestern Anthropological Association, Los Angeles, California, October 27, 1951. *Reports of the University of California Archaeological Survey,* No. 16. Berkeley.

Gorenstein, Shirley
1965 *Introduction to Archaeology.*

Basic Books, Inc., Publishers, New York.

Goslin, Robert M.
1957 Food of the Adena People. *In The Adena People, No. 2,* William S. Webb and Raymond S. Baby, pp. 41–46. Published for the Ohio Historical Society by the Ohio State University Press, Columbus.

Goss, James A.
1965 Ute Linguistics and Anasazi Abandonment of the Four Corners Area. *In* "Contributions of the Wetherill Mesa Archeological Project," Douglas Osborne et al. *American Antiquity,* Vol. 31, No. 2, Pt. 2, *Memoirs of the Society for American Archaeology,* No. 19, pp. 73–81. Salt Lake City.

Green, F. E.
1963 The Clovis Blades: An Important Addition to the Llano Complex. *American Antiquity,* Vol. 29, No. 2, pp. 145–165. Salt Lake City.

Greene, John C.
1959 *The Death of Adam.* Iowa State University Press, Ames.

Greengo, Robert E.
1964 Issaquena: An Archaeological Phase in the Yazoo Basin of the Lower Mississippi Valley. *American Antiquity,* Vol. 30, No. 2, Pt. 2, *Memoirs of the Society for American Archaeology,* No. 18. Salt Lake City.

Griffin, James B.
1946 Cultural Change and Continuity in Eastern United States Archaeology. *In* "Man in Northeastern North America," Frederick Johnson (ed.). *Papers of the Robert S. Peabody Foundation for Archaeology,* Vol. 3, pp. 37–95. Andover, Massachusetts.
1951 (ed.) Essays on Archaeological Methods: Proceedings of a Conference Held under Auspices of the Viking Fund. *University of Michigan, Museum of Anthropology, Anthropological Papers,* No. 8. Ann Arbor.
1952a (ed.) *Archeology of Eastern United States.* The University of Chicago Press, Chicago.
1952b Some Early and Middle Woodland Pottery Types in Illinois. Paper No. 3 *in* "Hopewellian Communities in Illinois," Thorne Deuel (ed.). *Illinois State Museum Scientific Papers,* Vol. 5, pp. 93–129. Springfield.
1958 The Chronological Position of the Hopewellian Culture in the Eastern United States. *University of Michigan, Museum of Anthropology, Anthropological Papers,* No. 12. Ann Arbor.
1959 The Pursuit of Archeology in

the United States. *American Anthropologist,* Vol. 61, No. 3, pp. 379–389. Menasha.
1960a Climatic Change: A Contributory Cause of the Growth and Decline of Northern Hopewellian Culture. *Wisconsin Archeologist,* n.s., Vol. 41, No. 2, pp. 21–33. Milwaukee.
1960b Some Prehistoric Connections between Siberia and America. *Science,* Vol. 131, No. 3403, pp. 801–812. Washington.
1964 The Northeast Woodlands Area. *In Prehistoric Man in the New World,* Jesse D. Jennings and Edward Norbeck (eds.), pp. 223–258. *Rice University Semicentennial Publications,* The University of Chicago Press, Chicago.
1965 Ceramic Complexity and Cultural Development: The Eastern United States as a Case Study. *In* "Ceramics and Man," Frederick R. Matson (ed.). *Viking Fund Publications in Anthropology,* No. 41, pp. 104–113. New York.
1967 Eastern North American Archaeology: A Summary. *Science,* Vol. 156, No. 3772, pp. 175–191. Washington.

Griffin, James B., and Roscoe H. Wilmeth, Jr.
1964 The Ceramic Complexes at Iyatayet. Appendix I *in The Archeology of Cape Denbigh,* James L. Giddings, Jr., pp. 271–303. Brown University Press, Providence.

Grimm, R. E. (ed.)
1950 *Cahokia Brought to Life: An Artifactual Story of America's Great Monument.* The Greater St. Louis Archaeological Society, St. Louis.

Gross, Hugo G.
1951 Mastodons, Mammoths and Man in America. *Bulletin of the Texas Archeological and Paleontological Society,* Vol. 22, pp. 101–131. Lubbock.

Gruhn, Ruth
1961 The Archaeology of Wilson Butte Cave, South-central Idaho. *Occasional Papers of the Idaho State College Museum,* No. 6. Pocatello.
1965 Two Early Radiocarbon Dates from the Lower Levels of Wilson Butte Cave, South-central Idaho. *Tebiwa,* Idaho State University Museum, Vol. 8. No. 2, p. 57. Pocatello.

Gunnerson, Dolores A.
1956 The Southern Athabascans: Their Arrival in the Southwest. *El Palacio,* Vol. 63, Nos. 11–12, pp. 346–365. Santa Fe.

Guthe, Carl E.
1952 Twenty-five Years of Archeology in Eastern United States. *In Archeology of Eastern United States,*

James B. Griffin (ed.), pp. 1–12. The University of Chicago Press, Chicago.

Haag, William G.
1939 (ed.) *Southeastern Archaeological Conference News Letter*, Vol. 1, Lexington, Kentucky.
1942 Early Horizons in the Southeast. *American Antiquity*, Vol. 7, No. 3, pp. 209–222. Salt Lake City.
1961 The Archaic of the Lower Mississippi Valley. *American Antiquity*, Vol. 26, No. 3, Pt. 1, pp. 317–323. Salt Lake City.
1962 The Bering Strait Land Bridge. *Scientific American*, Vol. 206, No. 1, pp. 112–123. New York.

Haas, Mary R.
1941 The Classification of the Muskogean Languages. *In Language, Culture, and Personality*, Leslie Spier, A. Irving Hallowell, and Stanley S. Newman (eds.), pp. 41–56. Sapir Memorial Publication Fund, Menasha.
1958 A New Linguistic Relationship in North America: Algonkian and the Gulf Languages. *Southwestern Journal of Anthropology*. Vol. 14, No. 3, pp. 231–264. Albuquerque.

Hack, John T.
1942 The Changing Physical Environment of the Hopi Indians of Arizona. *Papers of the Peabody Museum of American Archaeology and Ethnology*, Vol. 35, No. 1, *Reports of the Awatovi Expedition*, No. 1. Cambridge.

Hadleigh-West, Frederick
See West, Frederick H.

Haines, Francis
1938a The Northward Spread of Horses among the Plains Indians. *American Anthropologist*, Vol. 40, No. 3, pp. 429–437. Menasha.
1938b Where Did the Plains Indians Get Their Horses? *American Anthropologist*, Vol. 40, No. 1, pp. 112–117. Menasha.

Hall, Robert L.
1962 *The Archeology of Carcajou Point*. 2 vols. The University of Wisconsin Press, Madison.

Hallowell, A. Irving
1957 The Backwash of the Frontier: The Impact of the Indian on American Culture. *In The Frontier in Perspective*, Walker D. Wyman and Clifton B. Kroeber (eds.), pp. 229–257. The University of Wisconsin Press, Madison. (Also published in *Readings in Anthropology*, 2d ed., Jesse D. Jennings and E. Adamson Hoebel, pp. 348–361. McGraw-Hill Book Company, New York.)
1960 The Beginnings of Anthropology in America. *In Selected Papers from the American Anthropologist, 1888–1920*, Frederica De Laguna (ed.), pp. 1–90. Harper & Row, Publishers, Incorporated, New York.

Hamilton, Henry W.
1952 The Spiro Mound. *Missouri Archaeologist*, Vol. 14. Columbia.

Harrington, Mark R.
1922 Cherokee and Earlier Remains on Upper Tennessee River. *Indian Notes and Monographs, Miscellaneous*, No. 24. Museum of the American Indian, New York.
1933 Gypsum Cave, Nevada. *Southwest Museum Papers*, No. 8. Los Angeles.
1957 A Pinto Site at Little Lake, California. *Southwest Museum Papers*, No. 17. Los Angeles.

Harrington, Mark R., and Ruth D. Simpson
1961 Tule Springs, Nevada, with Other Evidences of Pleistocene Man in North America. *Southwest Museum Papers*, No. 18. Los Angeles.

Haury, Emil W.
1932 Roosevelt:9:6, a Hohokam Site of the Colonial Period. *Medallion Papers*, No. 11. Gila Pueblo, Globe, Arizona.
1936 The Mogollon Culture of Southwestern New Mexico. *Medallion Papers*, No. 20. Gila Pueblo, Globe, Arizona.
1937a Figurines and Miscellaneous Clay Objects. *In* "Excavations at Snaketown: Material Culture," Harold S. Gladwin et al. *Medallion Papers*, No. 25, pp. 233–245. Gila Pueblo, Globe, Arizona.
1937b Minerals and Metals. *In* "Excavations at Snaketown: Material Culture," Harold S. Gladwin et al. *Medallion Papers*, No. 25, pp. 163–167. Gila Pueblo, Globe, Arizona.
1937c Pottery Types at Snaketown. *In* "Excavations at Snaketown: Material Culture," Harold S. Gladwin et al. *Medallion Papers*, No. 25, pp. 169–229. Gila Pueblo, Globe, Arizona.
1937d Shell. *In* "Excavations at Snaketown: Material Culture," by Harold S. Gladwin et al. *Medallion Papers*, No. 25, pp. 135–153. Gila Pueblo, Globe, Arizona.
1937e Stone Palettes and Ornaments. *In* "Excavations at Snaketown: Material Culture," Harold S. Gladwin, et al. *Medallion Papers*, No. 25, pp. 121–134. Gila Pueblo, Globe, Arizona.
1945 The Problem of Contacts between the Southwestern United States and Mexico. *Southwestern Journal of Anthropology*, Vol. 1, No. 1, pp. 55–74. Albuquerque.

1950 *The Stratigraphy and Archae-ology of Ventana Cave, Arizona.* The University of New Mexico and University of Arizona Presses, Albuquerque and Tucson.

1954 (ed.) Southwest Issue. *American Anthropologist,* Vol. 56, No. 4, Pt. 1, pp. i–ii, 529–731. Menasha.

1955 Archaeological Stratigraphy. *In* "Geochronology," Terah L. Smiley (ed.). *University of Arizona Bulletin,* Vol. 26, No. 2, *Physical Science Bulletin,* No. 2, pp. 126–134. Tucson.

1956 Speculations on Prehistoric Settlement Patterns in the Southwest. *In* "Prehistoric Settlement Patterns in the New World," Gordon R. Willey (ed.). *Viking Fund Publications in Anthropology,* No. 23, pp. 3–10. New York.

1957 An Alluvial Site on the San Carlos Indian Reservation, Arizona. *American Antiquity,* Vol. 23, No. 1, pp. 2–27. Salt Lake City.

1958 Evidence at Point of Pines for a Prehistoric Migration from Northern Arizona. *In* "Migrations in New World Culture History," Raymond H. Thompson (ed.). *University of Arizona Bulletin,* Vol. 29, No. 2, *Social Science Bulletin,* No. 27, pp. 1–6. Tucson.

Haury, Emil W., Ernst Antevs, and John F. Lance
1953 Artifacts with Mammoth Remains, Naco, Arizona; I, II, III. *American Antiquity,* Vol. 19, No. 1, pp. 1–24. Salt Lake City.

Haury, Emil W., Edwin B. Sayles, and William W. Wasley
1959 The Lehner Mammoth Site, Southeastern Arizona. *American Antiquity,* Vol. 25, No. 1, pp. 2–30. Salt Lake City.

Hawkes, Jacquetta, and Sir Leonard Woolley
1963 *Prehistory and the Beginnings of Civilization.* Volume I of *History of Mankind,* International Commission for a History of the Scientific and Cultural Development of Mankind. Harper & Row, Publishers, Incorporated, New York.

Hay, Clarence L., et al. (eds.)
1940 *The Maya and Their Neighbors.* Appleton-Century-Crofts, Inc., New York.

Haynes, C. Vance, Jr.
1964 Fluted Projectile Points: Their Age and Dispersion. *Science,* Vol. 145, No. 3639, pp. 1408–1413. Washington.

Haynes, C. Vance, Jr., and George Agogino
1960 Geological Significance of a New Radiocarbon Date from the Lindenmeier Site. *Proceedings of the Denver Museum of Natural History,* No. 9. Denver.

Heizer, Robert F.
1953 Long-range Dating in Archeology. *In Anthropology Today,* Alfred L. Kroeber et al., pp. 3–42. The University of Chicago Press, Chicago.

1956 Recent Cave Explorations in the Lower Humboldt Valley, Nevada. *Papers on California Archaeology,* No. 42, *Reports of the University of California Archaeological Survey,* No. 33, pp. 50–57. Berkeley.

1958 (ed.) *A Guide to Archaeological Field Methods,* 3d rev. ed. National Press, Palo Alto.

1960 (ed.) *The Archaeologist at Work, a Source Book in Archaeological Method and Interpretation.* Harper & Row Publishers, Incorporated, New York.

1964 The Western Coast of North America. *In Prehistoric Man in the New World,* Jesse D. Jennings and Edward Norbeck (eds.), pp. 117–148. *Rice University Semicentennial Publications,* The University of Chicago Press, Chicago.

Heizer, Robert F., and Alex D. Krieger
1956 The Archaeology of Humboldt Cave, Churchill County, Nevada. *University of California Publications in American Archaeology and Ethnology,* Vol. 47, No. 1, pp. 1–190. Berkeley.

Herold, Joyce
1961 Prehistoric Settlement and Physical Environment in the Mesa Verde Area. *University of Utah Anthropological Papers,* No. 53. Salt Lake City.

Hester, James J.
1960 Late Pleistocene Extinction and Radiocarbon Dating. *American Antiquity,* Vol. 26, No. 1, pp. 58–77. Salt Lake City.

1962 Early Navajo Migrations and Acculturation in the Southwest. *Museum of New Mexico Papers in Anthropology,* No. 6, *Navajo Project Studies,* No. 5. Santa Fe.

Hester, James J., and Joel L. Shiner
1963 Studies at Navajo Period Sites in the Navajo Reservoir District. *Museum of New Mexico Papers in Anthropology,* No. 9, *Navajo Project Studies,* No. 8. Santa Fe.

Heyerdahl, Thor
1950 *Kon-Tiki: Across the Pacific by Raft.* Translated by F. H. Lyon. Rand McNally & Company, Chicago.

Hibben, Frank C.
1941 Evidences of Early Occupation in Sandia Cave, New Mexico, and Other Sites in the Sandia-Manzano

Region. *Smithsonian Miscellaneous Collections,* Vol. 99, No. 23. Washington.

Hickerson, Harold
1965 The Virginia Deer and Intertribal Buffer Zones in the Upper Mississippi Valley. *In* "Man, Culture, and Animals," Anthony Leeds and Andrew P. Vayda (eds.). *American Association for the Advancement of Science Publication,* No. 78, pp. 43–65. Washington.

Hill, Asa T., and **Marvin Kivett**
1940 Woodland-like Manifestations in Nebraska. *Nebraska History.* Vol. 21, No. 3, pp. 143–243. Lincoln.

Hill, James N.
1966 A Prehistoric Community in Eastern Arizona. *Southwestern Journal of Anthropology,* Vol. 22, No. 1, pp. 9–30. Albuquerque.

Holder, Preston, and **Joyce Wike**
1949 The Frontier Culture Complex: A Preliminary Report on a Prehistoric Hunters' Camp in Southwestern Nebraska. *American Antiquity,* Vol. 14, No. 4, Pt. 1, pp. 260–266. Salt Lake City.

Hole, Frank, and **Robert F. Heizer**
1965 An Introduction to Prehistoric Archeology. Holt, Rinehart and Winston, Inc., New York.

Holmes, William H.
1897 Stone Implements of the Potomac-Chesapeake Tidewater Province. *Bureau of Ethnology, 15th Annual Report,* pp. 3–152. Washington.
1903 Aboriginal Pottery of the Eastern United States. *Bureau of American Ethnology, 20th Annual Report,* pp. 1–201. Washington.

Hopkins, David M.
1959 Cenozoic History of the Bering Land Bridge. *Science,* Vol. 129, No. 3362, pp. 1519–1528. Washington.

Hough, Jack L.
1958 Geology of the Great Lakes. The University of Illinois Press, Urbana.

Hrdlička, Aleš
1907 Skeletal Remains Suggesting or Attributed to Early Man in North America. *Bureau of American Ethnology Bulletin,* No. 33. Washington.

Hrdlička, Aleš, et al.
1912 Early Man in South America. *Bureau of American Ethnology Bulletin,* No. 52. Washington.

Hubbs, Carl L. (ed.)
1958 Zoogeography. *American Association for the Advancement of Science Publication,* No. 51. Washington.

Hughes, Jack T.
1949 Investigations in Western South Dakota and Northeastern Wyoming. *American Antiquity,* Vol. 14, No. 4, Pt. 1, pp. 266–277. Salt Lake City.

Hulse, Frederick S.
1963 The Human Species. Random House, Inc., New York.

Hunt, Charles B.
1954 Desert Varnish. *Science,* Vol. 120, No. 3109, pp. 183–184. Washington.
1955 Radiocarbon Dating in the Light of Stratigraphy and Weathering Processes. *Scientific Monthly,* Vol. 81, No. 5, pp. 240–247. Washington.
1956 A Skeptic's View of Radiocarbon Dates. Paper No. 3 *in* "Papers of the Third Great Basin Archeological Conference," Fay-Cooper Cole et al. *University of Utah Anthropological Papers,* No. 26, pp. 35–46. Salt Lake City.
1965 Quaternary Geology Reviewed. *Science,* Vol. 150, No. 3692, pp. 47–50. Washington.

International Commission for a History of the Scientific and Cultural Development of Mankind
1963– History of Mankind. Harper & Row, Publishers, Incorporated, New York. (Published to date: Vol. I, *Prehistory and the Beginnings of Civilization,* Jacquetta Hawkes and Sir Leonard Woolley.)

Irwin, Cynthia, Henry Irwin, and
George Agogino
1962 Wyoming Muck Tells of Battle: Ice Age Man vs. Mammoth. *National Geographic Magazine,* Vol. 121, No. 6, pp. 829–837. Washington.

Irwin, Henry J., and **Cynthia C. Irwin**
1959 Excavations at the LoDaisKa Site. *Proceedings of the Denver Museum of Natural History,* No. 8. Denver.

Irwin, Henry T.
1964 Possible Eastern Connections for the San Jose-Pinto Basin Complex. *American Antiquity,* Vol. 29, No. 4, pp. 496–497. Salt Lake City.

Irwin-Williams, Cynthia
1965 The Elementary Southwestern Culture: The Configuration of Late Preceramic Development in the Southwestern United States. Paper presented at the 64th annual meeting of the American Anthropological Association, Denver.

Jelinek, Arthur J.
1957 Pleistocene Faunas and Early Man. *Papers of the Michigan Academy of Science, Arts, and Letters,* Vol. 42, (1956 meeting), pp. 225–237. Ann Arbor.

Jennings, Jesse D.
1941 Chickasaw and Earlier Indian

Cultures of Northeast Mississippi. *Journal of Mississippi History,* Vol. 3, No. 3, pp. 155–226. Jackson.

1944 The Archaeological Survey of the Natchez Trace. *American Antiquity,* Vol. 9, No. 4, pp. 408–414. Salt Lake City.

1950a On the Validity of Tepexpan Man. *Bulletin of the Texas Archeological and Paleontological Society,* Vol. 21, pp. 105–110. Lubbock.

1950b (ed.) Proceedings of the Sixth Plains Archeological Conference, 1948. *University of Utah Anthropological Papers,* No. 11. Salt Lake City.

1953 Danger Cave: A Progress Summary. *El Palacio,* Vol. 60, No. 5, pp. 179–213. Santa Fe.

1955 *The Archeology of the Plains: An Assessment (with Special Reference to the Missouri River Basin).* Prepared in fulfillment of Memorandum of Agreement No. 14-10-0100-287, dated June 1, 1954, between the National Park Service and the University of Utah. Department of Anthropology, University of Utah, Salt Lake City. (Limited distribution.)

1956 (ed.) The American Southwest: A Problem in Cultural Isolation. *In* "Seminars in Archaeology: 1955," Robert Wauchope (ed.). *American Antiquity,* Vol. 22, No. 2, Pt. 2, *Memoirs of the Society for American Archaeology,* No. 11, pp. 59–127. Salt Lake City.

1957 Danger Cave. *University of Utah Anthropological Papers,* No. 27. Salt Lake City. (Also published in *American Antiquity,* Vol. 23, No. 2, Pt. 2, *Memoirs of the Society for American Archaeology,* No. 14. Salt Lake City.)

1964 The Desert West. *In Prehistoric Man in the New World,* Jesse D. Jennings and Edward Norbeck (eds.), pp. 149–174. *Rice University Semicentennial Publications,* The University of Chicago Press, Chicago.

1965a Later Specializations. *In The Native Americans,* Robert F. Spencer, Jesse D. Jennings et al., pp. 57–99. Harper & Row, Publishers, Incorporated, New York.

1965b Perspective. *In The Native Americans,* Robert F. Spencer, Jesse D. Jennings et al., pp. 7–56. Harper & Row, Publishers, Incorporated, New York.

1966a Early Man in the Desert West. *Proceedings, VII Congress, International Association for Quaternary Research,* Vol. 15, *Quaternaria,* Vol. 8, pp. 81–89. Rome.

1966b Glen Canyon: A Summary. *University of Utah Anthropological Papers,* No. 81, *Glen Canyon Series,* No. 31. Salt Lake City.

Jennings, Jesse D., and **E. Adamson Hoebel**
1966 *Readings in Anthropology,* 2d ed. McGraw-Hill Book Company, New York.

Jennings, Jesse D., and **Edward Norbeck**
1955 Great Basin Prehistory: A Review. *American Antiquity,* Vol. 21, No. 1, pp. 1–11. Salt Lake City.

1964 (eds.) *Prehistoric Man in the New World. Rice Semicentennial Publications,* The University of Chicago Press, Chicago.

Jennings, Jesse D., and **Floyd W. Sharrock**
1965 The Glen Canyon: A Multi-discipline Project. *Utah Historical Quarterly,* Vol. 33, No. 1, pp. 35–50. Salt Lake City.

Johnson, Frederick
1942 The Excavation of the Fishweir. Part I *in* "The Boylston Street Fishweir," Frederick Johnson et al. *Papers of the Robert S. Peabody Foundation for Archaeology,* Vol. 2, pp. 11–38. Andover, Massachusetts.

1946 (ed.) Man in Northeastern North America. *Papers of the Robert S. Peabody Foundation for Archaeology,* Vol. 3. Andover, Massachusetts.

Johnson, Frederick, et al.
1942 The Boylston Street Fishweir. *Papers of the Robert S. Peabody Foundation for Archaeology.* Vol. 2. Andover, Massachusetts.

Johnson, Frederick, and **John P. Miller**
1958 Review of: *Pleistocene Man at San Diego,* George F. Carter. *American Antiquity,* Vol. 24, No. 2, pp. 206–210. Salt Lake City.

Jones, Volney H.
1936 The Vegetal Remains of Newt Kash Hollow. *In* "Rock Shelters in Menifee County, Kentucky," William S. Webb and William D. Funkhouser. *University of Kentucky Reports in Archaeology and Anthropology,* Vol. 3, No. 4, pp. 147–165. Lexington.

Judd, Neil M.
1954 The Material Culture of Pueblo Bonito. *Smithsonian Miscellaneous Collections,* Vol. 124. Washington.

1964 The Architecture of Pueblo Bonito. *Smithsonian Miscellaneous Collections,* Vol. 147, No. 1. Washington.

Kehoe, Alice B.
1962 A Hypothesis on the Origin of Northeastern American Pottery. *South-*

western Journal of Anthropology, Vol. 18, No. 1, pp. 20–29. Albuquerque.

Kelley, J. Charles
1959 The Desert Cultures and the Balcones Phase: Archaic Manifestations in the Southwest and Texas. *American Antiquity,* Vol. 24, No. 3, pp. 276–288. Salt Lake City.

Kelly, Arthur R.
1933 Some Problems of Recent Cahokia Archaeology. *Transactions of the Illinois State Academy of Science,* Vol. 25, No. 4, pp. 101–103. Springfield.

Kenyon, Bruce
1959 The Inverhuron Site, Bruce County, Ontario, 1957. *Royal Ontario Museum, Art and Archaeology Division, Occasional Paper,* No. 1. Toronto.

Keur, Dorothy L.
1941 Big Bead Mesa. *American Antiquity,* Vol. 7, No. 2, Pt. 2, *Memoirs of the Society for American Archaeology,* No. 1. Salt Lake City.

Kidder, Alfred V.
1924 An Introduction to the Study of Southwestern Archaeology. *Papers of the Southwestern Expedition,* No. 1. Published for the Phillips Academy by the Yale University Press, New Haven.

Kidder, Alfred, II
1964 South American High Cultures. *In Prehistoric Man in the New World,* Jesse D. Jennings and Edward Norbeck (eds.), pp. 451–486. *Rice University Semicentennial Publications,* The University of Chicago Press, Chicago.

Kivett, Marvin F.
1949a Archaeological Investigations in Medicine Creek Reservoir, Nebraska. *American Antiquity,* Vol. 14, No. 4, Pt. 1, pp. 278–284. Salt Lake City.

1949b A Woodland Pottery Type from Nebraska. *In* "Proceedings of the Fifth Plains Conference for Archeology," John L. Champe et al. *University of Nebraska, Laboratory of Anthropology Note Book,* No. 1, pp. 67–69. Lincoln.

1953 The Woodruff Ossuary, a Prehistoric Burial Site in Phillips County, Kansas. *River Basin Surveys Papers,* No. 3. *Bureau of American Ethnology Bulletin,* No. 154, pp. 103–141. Washington.

Krieger, Alex D.
1944 The Typological Concept. *American Antiquity,* Vol. 9, No. 3, pp. 271–288. Salt Lake City.

1946 Culture Complexes and Chronology in Northern Texas with Extension of Puebloan Datings to the Missis

sippi Valley. *University of Texas Publication,* No. 4640. Austin.

1947 Artifacts from the Plainview Bison Bed. *In* "Fossil Bison and Associated Artifacts from Plainview, Texas," Elias H. Sellards, Glen L. Evans, and Grayson E. Mead. *Bulletin of the Geological Society of America,* Vol. 58, No. 10, pp. 938–954. New York.

1953 New World Culture History: Anglo America. *In Anthropology Today,* Alfred L. Kroeber et al., pp. 238–264. The University of Chicago Press, Chicago.

1964 Early Man in the New World. *In Prehistoric Man in the New World,* Jesse D. Jennings and Edward Norbeck (eds.), pp. 23–81. *Rice University Semicentennial Publications,* The University of Chicago Press, Chicago.

Kroeber, Alfred L.
1916 Zuñi Potsherds. *Anthropological Papers of the American Museum of Natural History,* Vol. 18, Pt. 1, pp. 1–37. New York.

1939 Cultural and Natural Areas of Native North America. *University of California Publications in American Archaeology and Ethnology,* Vol. 38. Berkeley.

1952a *The Nature of Culture.* The University of Chicago Press, Chicago.

1952b The Superorganic (1917). *In The Nature of Culture,* Alfred L. Kroeber, pp. 22–51. The University of Chicago Press, Chicago.

Kroeber, Alfred L., et al.
1953 *Anthropology Today.* The University of Chicago Press, Chicago.

Lamb, Sydney M.
1958 Linguistic Prehistory in the Great Basin. *International Journal of American Linguistics,* Vol. 24, No. 2, pp. 95–100. Baltimore.

Lancaster, James A., et al.
1954 Archeological Excavations in Mesa Verde National Park, Colorado, 1950. *National Park Service Archeological Research Series,* No. 2. Washington.

Lancaster, James A., and Jean M. Pinkley
1954 Excavation at Site 16 of Three Pueblo II Mesa-Top Ruins. *In* "Archeological Excavations in Mesa Verde National Park, Colorado, 1950," James A. Lancaster et al. *National Park Service Archeological Research Series,* No. 2, pp. 23–86. Washington.

Lancaster, James A., and Don Watson
1954 Excavation of Two Late Basketmaker III Pithouses. *In* "Archeological

Excavations in Mesa Verde National Park, Colorado, 1950," James A. Lancaster et al. *National Park Service Archeological Research Series*, No. 2, pp. 7–22. Washington.

Landes, Ruth
1961   The Ojibwa of Canada. *In Cooperation and Competition among Primitive Peoples*, Margaret Mead (ed.), pp. 87–126. Beacon Press, Boston. (Revised paperback edition.)

Larsen, Helge E., and **Froelich G. Rainey**
1948   Ipiutak and the Arctic Whale Hunting Culture. *Anthropological Papers of the American Museum of Natural History*, Vol. 42. New York.

Lathrap, Donald W. (ed.)
1956   An Archaeological Classification of Culture Contact Situations. *In* "Seminars in Archaeology: 1955," Robert Wauchope (ed.). *American Antiquity*, Vol. 22, No. 2, Pt. 2, *Memoirs of the Society for American Archaeology*, No. 11, pp. 1–30. Salt Lake City.

Laughlin, William S.
1951   (ed.)   *Papers on the Physical Anthropology of the American Indian.* Delivered at the Fourth Viking Fund Summer Seminar in Physical Anthropology Held at the Viking Fund, September, 1949. The Viking Fund, Inc., New York.
1952   Contemporary Problems in the Anthropology of Southern Alaska. *In* "Science in Alaska," Henry B. Collins (ed.). *Arctic Institute of North America Special Publication*, No. 1, pp. 66–84. Washington.
1962a   Bering Strait to Puget Sound: Dichotomy and Affinity between Eskimo-Aleuts and American Indians. *In* "Prehistoric Cultural Relations between the Arctic and Temperate Zones of North America," John M. Campbell (ed.). *Arctic Institute of North America Technical Paper*, No. 11, pp. 113–125. Montreal.
1962b   Generic Problems and New Evidence in the Anthropology of the Eskimo-Aleut Stock. *In* "Prehistoric Cultural Relations between the Arctic and Temperate Zones of North America," John M. Campbell (ed.). *Arctic Institute of North America Technical Paper*, No. 11, pp. 100–112. Montreal.
1963a   The Earliest Aleuts. *In* "Early Man in the Western American Arctic: A Symposium," Frederick H. West (ed.). *Anthropological Papers of the University of Alaska*, Vol. 10, No. 2, pp. 73–91. College.
1963b   Eskimos and Aleuts: Their

Origins and Evolution. *Science*, Vol. 142, No. 3593, pp. 633–645. Washington.

Laughlin, William S., and **Gordon H. Marsh**
1954   The Lamellar Flake Manufacturing Site on Anangula Island in the Aleutians. *American Antiquity*, Vol. 20, No. 1, pp. 27–39. Salt Lake City.

Leeds, Anthony, and **Andrew P. Vayda (eds.)**
1965   Man, Culture, and Animals. *American Association for the Advancement of Science Publication*, No. 78. Washington.

Lehmer, Donald J.
1938   The Jornada Branch of the Mogollon. *University of Arizona Bulletin*, Vol. 19, No. 2, *Social Science Bulletin*, No. 17. Tucson.
1954a   Archeological Investigations in the Oahe Dam Area, South Dakota, 1950–1951. *River Basin Surveys Papers*, No. 7. *Bureau of American Ethnology Bulletin*, No. 158. Washington.
1954b   The Sedentary Horizon of the Northern Plains. *Southwestern Journal of Anthropology*, Vol. 10, No. 2, pp. 139–159. Albuquerque.
1966   The Fire Heart Creek Site. *Smithsonian Institution River Basin Surveys, Publications in Salvage Archeology*, No. 1. Lincoln.

Lehmer, Donald J., and **Warren W. Caldwell**
1966   Horizon and Tradition in the Northern Plains. *American Antiquity*, Vol. 31, No. 4, pp. 511–516. Salt Lake City.

Leonhardy, Frank C.
1966   Domebo: A Paleo-Indian Mammoth Kill in the Prairie-Plains. *Contributions of the Museum of the Great Plains*, No. 1. Lawton, Oklahoma.

Lewis, Thomas M. N., and **Madeline Kneberg**
1946   Hiwassee Island: An Archaeological Account of Four Tennessee Indian Peoples. University of Tennessee Press, Knoxville.
1959   The Archaic Culture in the Middle South. *American Antiquity*, Vol. 25, No. 2, pp. 161–183. Salt Lake City.

Lewis, Thomas M. N., and **Madeline K. Lewis**
1961   *Eva, an Archaic Site.* University of Tennessee Press, Knoxville.

Libby, Willard F.
1952   *Radiocarbon Dating.* The University of Chicago Press, Chicago. (2d ed. published in 1955.)

Lilly, Eli
1937   *Prehistoric Antiquities of Indiana.* Indiana Historical Society, Indianapolis.

Lindsay, Alexander J., Jr.
1961 The Beaver Creek Agricultural Community on the San Juan River, Utah. *American Antiquity*, Vol. 27, No. 2, pp. 174–187. Salt Lake City.

Lipe, William D.
1960 1958 Excavations, Glen Canyon Area. *University of Utah Anthropological Papers*, No. 44, *Glen Canyon Series*, No. 11. Salt Lake City.

Lister, Robert H.
1951 Excavations at Hells Midden, Dinosaur National Monument. *University of Colorado Studies, Series in Anthropology*, No. 3. Boulder.

Logan, Wilfred D.
1952 Graham Cave: An Archaic Site in Montgomery County, Missouri. *Missouri Archeological Society Memoir*, No. 2. Columbia.

Longacre, William A.
1964a Archeology as Anthropology: A Case Study. *Science*, Vol. 144, No. 3625, pp. 1454–1455. Washington.
1964b Sociological Implications of the Ceramic Analysis. *In* "Chapters in the Prehistory of Eastern Arizona, II," Paul S. Martin et al. *Fieldiana: Anthropology*, Vol. 55, pp. 155–170. Chicago.
1966 Changing Patterns of Social Integration: A Prehistoric Example from the American Southwest. *American Anthropologist*, Vol. 68, No. 1, pp. 94–102. Menasha.

Lopatin, Ivan A.
1960 Origin of the Native American Steam Bath. *American Anthropologist*, Vol. 62, No. 6, pp. 977–993. Menasha.

Lorant, Stefan (ed.)
1946 *The New World: The First Pictures of America*. Duell, Sloan & Pearce, Inc., New York.

Loud, Llewellyn L., and Mark R. Harrington
1929 Lovelock Cave. *University of California Publications in American Archaeology and Ethnology*, Vol. 25, No. 1, pp. i–183. Berkeley.

Lowie, Robert H.
1954 Indians of the Plains. *American Museum of Natural History Anthropological Handbook*, No. 1. New York.

MacCurdy, George Grant (ed.)
1937 *Early Man; As Depicted by Leading Authorities at the International Symposium, the Academy of Natural Sciences, Philadelphia, March 1937*. J. B. Lippincott Company, Philadelphia.

MacNeish, Richard S.
1948 The Pre-pottery Faulkner Site of Southern Illinois. *American Antiquity*, Vol. 13, No. 3, pp. 232–243. Salt Lake City.
1954 The Pointed Mountain Site near Fort Liard, Northwest Territories, Canada. *American Antiquity*, Vol. 19, No. 3, pp. 234–253. Salt Lake City.
1956a The Engigstciak Site on the Yukon Arctic Coast. *Anthropological Papers of the University of Alaska*, Vol. 4, No. 2, pp. 91–111. College.
1956b Two Archaeological Sites on Great Bear Lake, Northwest Territories, Canada. *National Museum of Canada Annual Report, 1953–4, Bulletin*, No. 136, pp. 54–84. Ottawa.
1958a An Introduction to the Archaeology of Southeast Manitoba. *National Museum of Canada Bulletin*, No. 157, *Anthropological Series*, No. 44. Ottawa.
1958b Preliminary Archaeological Investigations in the Sierra de Tamaulipas, Mexico. *Transactions of the American Philosophical Society*, n.s., Vol. 48, Pt. 6. Philadelphia.
1959a Men Out of Asia; As Seen from the Northwest Yukon. *Anthropological Papers of the University of Alaska*, Vol. 7, No. 2, pp. 41–70. College.
1959b A Speculative Framework of Northern North American Prehistory as of April, 1959. *Anthropologica*, n.s., Vol. 1, Nos. 1 and 2, pp. 7–23. Ottawa.
1962 Recent Finds in the Yukon Territory of Canada. *In* "Prehistoric Cultural Relations between the Arctic and Temperate Zones of North America," John M. Campbell (ed.). *Arctic Institute of North America Technical Paper*, No. 11, pp. 20–26. Montreal.
1963 The Early Peopling of the New World—As Seen from the Southwestern Yukon. *In* "Early Man in the Western American Arctic: A Symposium," Frederick H. West (ed.). *Anthropological Papers of the University of Alaska*, Vol. 10, No. 2, pp. 93–106. College.
1964 Ancient Mesoamerican Civilization. *Science*, Vol. 143, No. 3606, pp. 531–537. Washington.

Malde, Harold E.
1964 Environment and Man in Arid America. *Science*, Vol. 145, No. 3628, pp. 123–129. Washington.

Mangelsdorf, Paul C., Richard S. MacNeish, and Walton C. Galinat
1956 Archaeological Evidence on the Diffusion and Evolution of Maize in Northeastern Mexico. *Harvard University, Botanical Museum Leaflets*, Vol. 17, No. 5, pp. 125–150. Cambridge.

1964 Domestication of Corn. *Science,* Vol. 143, No. 3606, pp. 538–545. Washington.

Mangelsdorf, Paul C., Richard S. MacNeish, and **Gordon R. Willey**
1964 Origins of Agriculture in Middle America. *In Natural Environment and Early Cultures,* Robert C. West (ed.), pp. 427–445. Volume I of *Handbook of Middle American Indians,* Robert Wauchope (ed.). University of Texas Press, Austin.

Martin, Paul S.
1958 Pleistocene Ecology and Biogeography of North America. *In* "Zoogeography," Carl L. Hubbs (ed.). *American Association for the Advancement of Science Publication,* No. 51, pp. 375–420. Washington.
1959 Digging into History. *Chicago Natural History Museum Popular Series, Anthropology,* No. 38. Chicago.
1963 *The Last 10,000 Years: A Fossil Pollen Record of the American Southwest.* University of Arizona Press, Tucson.

Martin, Paul S., et al.
1952 Mogollon Cultural Continuity and Change. *Fieldiana: Anthropology,* Vol. 40. Chicago.
1956 Higgins Flat Pueblo, Western New Mexico. *Fieldiana: Anthropology,* Vol. 45. Chicago.
1962 Chapters in the Prehistory of Eastern Arizona, I. *Fieldiana: Anthropology,* Vol. 53. Chicago.
1964 Chapters in the Prehistory of Eastern Arizona, II. *Fieldiana: Anthropology,* Vol. 55. Chicago.

Martin, Paul S., George I. Quimby, and **Donald Collier**
1947 *Indians Before Columbus: Twenty Thousand Years of North American History Revealed by Archeology.* The University of Chicago Press, Chicago.

Martin, Paul S., and **John B. Rinaldo**
1960 Table Rock Pueblo, Arizona. *Fieldiana: Anthropology,* Vol. 51, No. 2, pp. 129–298. Chicago.

Martin, Paul S., John B. Rinaldo, and **Ernst Antevs**
1949 Cochise and Mogollon Sites: Pine Lawn Valley, Western New Mexico. *Fieldiana: Anthropology,* Vol. 38, No. 1, pp. 1–232. Chicago.

Martin, Paul S., John B. Rinaldo, and **Eloise R. Barter**
1957 Late Mogollon Communities: Four Sites of the Tularosa Phase, Western New Mexico. *Fieldiana: Anthropology,* Vol. 49, No. 1, pp. 1–144. Chicago.

Martin, Paul S., John B. Rinaldo, and **Elaine Bluhm**
1954 Caves of the Reserve Area. *Fieldiana: Anthropology,* Vol. 42. Chicago.

Martin, Paul S., John B. Rinaldo, and **William A. Longacre**
1961 Mineral Creek Site and Hooper Ranch Pueblo, Eastern Arizona. *Fieldiana: Anthropology,* Vol. 52. Chicago.

Martin, Paul S., and **Floyd W. Sharrock**
1964 Pollen Analysis of Prehistoric Human Feces: A New Approach to Ethnobotany. *American Antiquity,* Vol. 30, No. 2, Pt. 1, pp. 168–180. Salt Lake City.

Mason, Ronald J.
1962 The Paleo-Indian Tradition in Eastern North America. *Current Anthropology,* Vol. 3, No. 3, pp. 227–278. Chicago.

Mason, Ronald J., and **Carol Irwin**
1960 An Eden-Scottsbluff Burial in Northeastern Wisconsin. *American Antiquity,* Vol. 26, No. 1, pp. 43–57. Salt Lake City.

Matson, Frederick R. (ed.)
1965 Ceramics and Man. *Viking Fund Publications in Anthropology,* No. 41. New York.

Mayer-Oakes, William J.
1951 Starved Rock Archaic, a Prepottery Horizon from Northern Illinois. *American Antiquity,* Vol. 16, No. 4, pp. 313–324. Salt Lake City.

Mayr, Ernst
1963 *Animal Species and Evolution.* The Belknap Press, Harvard University Press, Cambridge.

McGregor, John C.
1952 The Havana Site. Paper No. 2 *in* "Hopewellian Communities in Illinois," Thorne Deuel (ed.). *Illinois State Museum Scientific Papers,* Vol. 5, pp. 43–91. Springfield.
1965 *Southwestern Archaeology,* 2d ed. The University of Illinois Press, Urbana.

McKern, William C.
1928 The Neale and McClaughry Mound Groups. *Bulletin of the Public Museum of the City of Milwaukee,* Vol. 3, No. 3, pp. 215–416. Milwaukee.
1930 The Kletzien and Nitschke Mound Groups. *Bulletin of the Public Museum of the City of Milwaukee,* Vol. 3, No. 4, pp. 417–572. Milwaukee.
1931 A Wisconsin Variant of the Hopewell Culture. *Bulletin of the Public Museum of the City of Milwaukee,* Vol. 10, No. 2, pp. 185–328. Milwaukee.

1937 An Hypothesis for the Asiatic Origin of the Woodland Culture Pattern. *American Antiquity*, Vol. 3, No. 2, pp. 138–143. Salt Lake City.

1939 The Midwestern Taxonomic Method as an Aid to Archaeological Culture Study. *American Antiquity*, Vol. 4, No. 4, pp. 301–313. Salt Lake City.

1956 On Willey and Phillips' "Method and Theory in American Archeology." *American Anthropologist*, Vol. 58, No. 2, pp. 360–361. Menasha.

McKern, William C., Paul F. Titterington, and **James B. Griffin**
1945 Painted Pottery Figurines from Illinois. *American Antiquity*, Vol. 10, No. 3, pp. 295–302. Salt Lake City.

Mead, Margaret (ed.)
1961 *Cooperation and Competition among Primitive Peoples.* Beacon Press, Boston. (Revised, paperback edition.)

Meggers, Betty J.
1956 (ed.) Functional and Evolutionary Implications of Community Patterning. *In* "Seminars in Archaeology: 1955," Robert Wauchope (ed.). *American Antiquity*, Vol. 22, No. 2, Pt. 2, *Memoirs of the Society for American Archaeology*, No. 11, pp. 129–157. Salt Lake City.

1964 North and South American Cultural Connections and Convergences. *In Prehistoric Man in the New World*, Jesse D. Jennings and Edward Norbeck (eds.), pp. 511–526. *Rice University Semicentennial Publications*, The University of Chicago Press, Chicago.

Meggers, Betty J., and **Clifford Evans**
1955 (eds.) *New Interpretations of Aboriginal American Culture History.* The Anthropological Society of Washington, Washington.

1966 A Transpacific Contact in 3000 B.C. *Scientific American*, Vol. 214, No. 1, pp. 28–35. New York.

Meggers, Betty J., Clifford Evans, and **Emilio Estrada**
1965 Early Formative Period of Coastal Ecuador: The Valdivia and Machalilla Phases. *Smithsonian Contributions to Anthropology*, Vol. 1. Washington.

Mehringer, Peter J., Jr., and **C. Vance Haynes, Jr.**
1965 The Pollen Evidence for the Environment of Early Man and Extinct Mammals at the Lehner Mammoth Site, Southeastern Arizona. *American Antiquity*, Vol. 31, No. 1, pp. 17–23. Salt Lake City.

Meighan, Clement W.
1956 Responsibilities of the Archeologist in Using the Radiocarbon Method. Paper No. 5 *in* "Papers of the Third Great Basin Archeological Conference," Fay-Cooper Cole et al. *University of Utah Anthropological Papers*, No. 26, pp. 48–53. Salt Lake City.

1959a California Cultures and the Concept of an Archaic Stage. *American Antiquity*, Vol. 24, No. 3, pp. 289–305. Salt Lake City.

1959b Varieties of Prehistoric Cultures in the Great Basin Region. *Masterkey*, Vol. 33, No. 2, pp. 46–59. Los Angeles.

Meleen, Elmer E.
1948 A Report on an Investigation of the LaRoche Site, Stanley County, South Dakota. *University of South Dakota Museum Archaeological Studies, Circular*, No. 5. Vermillion.

Mera, Harry P.
1934 Observations on the Archaeology of Petrified Forest National Monument. *Laboratory of Anthropology Technical Series, Bulletin*, No. 7. Santa Fe.

Midvale, Frank
1965 Prehistoric Irrigation of the Casa Grande Ruins Area. *Kiva*, Vol. 30, No. 3, pp. 82–86. Tucson.

Mills, William C.
1907 The Explorations of the Edwin Harness Mound. *Ohio Archaeological and Historical Quarterly*, Vol. 16, No. 2, pp. 113–193. Columbus.

Mindeleff, Cosmos
1898 Navaho Houses. *Bureau of American Ethnology, 17th Annual Report*, pp. 469–517. Washington.

Moorehead, Warren K.
1910 *The Stone Age in North America.* 2 vols. Houghton Mifflin Company, Boston.

1928 Explorations of 1922, 1923, 1924, and 1927. *In* "The Cahokia Mounds," Part I. *University of Illinois Bulletin*, Vol. 26, No. 4, pp. 7–106. Urbana.

1932 Description of Excavations, Mound C. *In Etowah Papers*, Warren K. Moorehead et al., pp. 68–87. Published for the Phillips Academy by the Yale University Press, New Haven.

Moorehead, Warren K., et al.
1932 *Etowah Papers.* Published for the Phillips Academy by the Yale University Press, New Haven.

Morris, Earl H., and **Robert F. Burgh**
1954 Basket Maker II Sites near Durango, Colorado. *Carnegie Institu-*

tion of Washington Publication, No. 604. Washington.

Morse, Dan F.
1963 The Steuben Village and Mounds, a Multicomponent Late Hopewell Site in Illinois. *University of Michigan, Museum of Anthropology, Anthropological Papers*, No. 21. Ann Arbor.

Morss, Noel
1931 The Ancient Culture of the Fremont River in Utah: Report on the Explorations under the Claflin-Emerson Fund, 1928–29. *Papers of the Peabody Museum of American Archaeology and Ethnology*, Vol. 12, No. 3. Cambridge.
1954 Clay Figurines of the American Southwest. *Papers of the Peabody Museum of American Archaeology and Ethnology*, Vol. 49, No. 1. Cambridge.
1957 Figurines. Appendix I *in* "Two Fremont Sites and Their Position in Southwestern Prehistory," Dee C. Taylor. *University of Utah Anthropological Papers*, No. 29, pp. 167–170. Salt Lake City.

Müller-Beck, Hansjürgen
1966 Paleohunters in America: Origins and Diffusion. *Science*, Vol. 152, No. 3726, pp. 1191–1210. Washington.

Mulloy, William B.
1952 The Northern Plains. *In Archeology of Eastern United States*, James B. Griffin (ed.), pp. 124–138. The University of Chicago Press, Chicago.
1954 The McKean Site. *Southwestern Journal of Anthropology*, Vol. 10, No. 4, pp. 432–460. Albuquerque.
1958 A Preliminary Historical Outline for the Northwestern Plains. *University of Wyoming Publications*, Vol. 22, No. 1, pp. i–235. Laramie.

Murdock, George Peter
1934 *Our Primitive Contemporaries.* The Macmillan Company, New York.

National Park Service
1955 *A Survey of Archaeology and History in the Arkansas-White-Red River Basins.* Washington.

Nelson, Nels C.
1937 Notes on Cultural Relations between Asia and America. *American Antiquity*, Vol. 2, No. 4, pp. 267–272. Salt Lake City.

Nesbitt, Paul H.
1931 The Ancient Mimbreños, Based on Investigations at the Mattocks Ruin, Mimbres Valley, New Mexico. *Logan Museum Publications in An-thropology, Bulletin*, No. 4. Beloit, Wisconsin.

Neumann, Georg K.
1952 Archeology and Race in the American Indian. *In Archeology of Eastern United States*, James B. Griffin (ed.), pp. 13–34. The University of Chicago Press, Chicago.
1960 Origins of the Indians of the Middle Mississippi Area. *Proceedings of the Indiana Academy of Sciences*, Vol. 69, pp. 66–68. Indianapolis.

Neumann, Georg K., and Melvin L. Fowler
1952 Hopewellian Sites in the Lower Wabash Valley. Paper No. 5 *in* "Hopewellian Communities in Illinois," Thorne Deuel (ed.). *Illinois State Museum Scientific Papers*, Vol. 5, pp. 175–248. Springfield.

Newell, H. Perry, and Alex D. Krieger
1949 The George C. Davis Site, Cherokee County, Texas. *American Antiquity*, Vol. 14, No. 4, Pt. 2, *Memoirs of the Society for American Archaeology*, No. 5. Salt Lake City.

Newman, Marshall T.
1953 The Application of Ecological Rules to the Racial Anthropology of the Aboriginal New World. *American Anthropologist*, Vol. 55, No. 3, pp. 311–327. Menasha.
1960 Adaptation in the Physique of American Aborigines to Nutritional Factors. *Human Biology*, Vol. 32, No. 3, pp. 288–313. Detroit.
1962 Evolutionary Changes in Body Size and Head Form in American Indians. *American Anthropologist*, Vol. 64, No. 2, pp. 237–257. Menasha.

Newman, Thomas M.
1966 Cascadia Cave. *Occasional Papers of the Idaho State University Museum*, No. 18. Pocatello.

Oakley, Kenneth P.
1953 Dating Fossil Human Remains. *In Anthropology Today*, Alfred L. Kroeber et al., pp. 43–56. The University of Chicago Press, Chicago.
1963 Analytical Methods of Dating Bones. *In Science in Archaeology*, Don Brothwell and Eric Higgs (eds.), pp. 24–34. Basic Books, Inc., Publishers, New York.

Oakley, Kenneth P., and Joseph S. Weiner
1955 Piltdown Man. *American Scientist*, Vol. 43, No. 4, pp. 573–583. Easton, Pennsylvania.

Orr, Phil C.
1956a Dwarf Mammoths and Man on Santa Rosa Island. Paper No. 8, *in* "Papers of the Third Great Basin Archeological Conference," Fay-Cooper Cole et al. *University of Utah Anthro-*

pological Papers, No. 26, pp. 74–81. Salt Lake City.

1956b Radiocarbon Dates from Santa Rosa Island, I. *Santa Barbara Museum of Natural History, Department of Anthropology Bulletin*, No. 2. Santa Barbara.

1960 Radiocarbon Dates from Santa Rosa Island, II. *Santa Barbara Museum of Natural History, Department of Anthropology Bulletin*, No. 3. Santa Barbara.

1962 The Arlington Spring Site, Santa Rosa Island, California. *American Antiquity*, Vol. 27, No. 3, pp. 417–419. Salt Lake City.

Osborne, Douglas, et al.
1965 Contributions of the Wetherill Mesa Archeological Project. *American Antiquity*, Vol. 31, No. 2, Pt. 2, *Memoirs of the Society for American Archaeology*, No. 19. Salt Lake City.

Phillips, Philip
1940 Middle American Influences on the Archaeology of the Southeastern United States. *In The Maya and Their Neighbors*, Clarence L. Hay et al. (eds.), pp. 349–367. Appleton-Century-Crofts, Inc., New York.

1955 American Archaeology and General Anthropological Theory. *Southwestern Journal of Anthropology*, Vol. 11, No. 3, pp. 246–250. Albuquerque.

1958 Application of the Wheat-Gifford-Wasley Taxonomy to Eastern Ceramics. *American Antiquity*, Vol. 24, No. 2, pp. 117–125. Salt Lake City.

Phillips, Philip, James A. Ford, and
James B. Griffin
1951 Archaeological Survey in the Lower Mississippi Alluvial Valley, 1940–1947. *Papers of the Peabody Museum of American Archaeology and Ethnology*, Vol. 25. Cambridge.

Piggott, Stuart
1965 *Ancient Europe from the Beginnings of Agriculture to Classical Antiquity*. Aldine Publishing Company, Chicago.

Pollock, Harry E. D., et al.
1962 Mayapan, Yucatan, Mexico. *Carnegie Institution of Washington Publication*, No. 619. Washington.

Porter, Muriel N.
1953 Tlatilco and the Pre-classic Cultures of the New World. *Viking Fund Publications in Anthropology*, No. 19. New York.

Prufer, Olaf H.
1964 The Hopewell Cult. *Scientific American*, Vol. 211, No. 6, pp. 90–102. New York.

1965 The McGraw Site: A Study in Hopewellian Dynamics. *Cleveland Museum of Natural History Scientific Publications*, n.s., Vol. 4, No. 1. Cleveland.

Quimby, George I.
1960 *Indian Life in the Upper Great Lakes, 11,000 B.C. to A.D. 1800*. The University of Chicago Press, Chicago.

Raikes, Robert L., and Robert H. Dyson, Jr.
1961 The Prehistoric Climate of Baluchistan and the Indus Valley. *American Anthropologist*, Vol. 63, No. 2, Pt. 1, pp. 265–281. Menasha.

Rainey, Froelich G.
1939 Archaeology in Central Alaska. *Anthropological Papers of the American Museum of Natural History*, Vol. 36, Pt. 4, pp. 351–405. New York.

Rands, Robert L.
1953 The Water Lily in Maya Art: A Complex of Alleged Asiatic Origin. *Anthropological Papers*, No. 34. *Bureau of American Ethnology Bulletin*, No. 151, pp. 75–153. Washington.

Reed, Erik K.
1946 The Distinctive Features and Distribution of the San Juan Anasazi Culture. *Southwestern Journal of Anthropology*, Vol. 2, No. 3, pp. 295–305. Albuquerque.

1950a Eastern-central Arizona Archaeology in Relation to the Western Pueblos. *Southwestern Journal of Anthropology*, Vol. 6, No. 2, pp. 120–138. Albuquerque.

1950b Population Shifts in the Pre-Spanish Southwest. *Bulletin of the Texas Archeological and Paleontological Society*, Vol. 21, pp. 90–96. Lubbock.

1954 Transition to History in the Pueblo Southwest. *American Anthropologist*, Vol. 56, No. 4, Pt. 1, pp. 592–603. Menasha.

1955 Painted Pottery and Zuñi History. *Southwestern Journal of Anthropology*, Vol. 11, No. 2, pp. 178–193. Albuquerque.

1956 Types of Village-plan Layouts in the Southwest. *In* "Prehistoric Settlement Patterns in the New World," Gordon R. Willey (ed.). *Viking Fund Publications in Anthropology*, No. 23, pp. 11–17. New York.

1964 The Greater Southwest. *In Prehistoric Man in the New World*, Jesse D. Jennings and Edward Norbeck (eds.), pp. 175–191. *Rice University Semicentennial Publications*, The University of Chicago Press, Chicago.

Renaud, Etienne B.
1940 Further Research Work in the

Blacks Fork Basin, Southwest Wyoming. *Archaeological Survey of the High Western Plains, 12th Report.* Department of Anthropology, University of Denver, Denver.
1947 *Archaeology of the High Western Plains: Seventeen Years of Archaeological Research.* Department of Anthropology, University of Denver, Denver.

Rinaldo, John B.
1964 Notes on the Origins of Historic Zuñi Culture. *Kiva,* Vol. 29, No. 4, pp. 86–98. Tucson.

Ritchie, William A.
1932 The Lamoka Lake Site. *Researches and Transactions of the New York State Archeological Association, Lewis H. Morgan Chapter,* Vol. 7, No. 4, pp. 79–134. Rochester.
1944 The Pre-Iroquoian Occupations of New York State. *Rochester Museum of Arts and Sciences Memoir,* No. 1, Rochester.
1953 A Probable Paleo-Indian Site in Vermont. *American Antiquity,* Vol. 18, No. 3, pp. 249–258. Salt Lake City.
1959 The Stony Brook Site and Its Relation to Archaic and Transitional Cultures on Long Island. *New York State Museum and Science Service Bulletin,* No. 372. Albany.
1962 Northeastern Crossties with the Arctic. *In* "Prehistoric Cultural Relations between the Arctic and Temperate Zones of North America," John M. Campbell (ed.). *Arctic Institute of North America Technical Paper,* No. 11, pp. 96–99. Montreal.
1965 *The Archaeology of New York State.* Natural History Press, Garden City, New York.

Ritchie, William A., and Don W. Dragoo
1960 The Eastern Dispersal of Adena. *New York State Museum and Science Service Bulletin,* No. 379. Albany.

Ritzenthaler, Robert
1946 The Osceola Site: An "Old Copper" Site near Potosi, Wisconsin. *Wisconsin Archeologist,* n.s., Vol. 27, No. 3, pp. 53–70. Milwaukee.

Ritzenthaler, Robert E., and Warren L. Wittry
1952 The Oconto Site—An Old Copper Manifestation. *Wisconsin Archeologist,* n.s., Vol. 33, No. 4, pp. 199–223. Milwaukee.

Robbins, Maurice
1959 *Wapanucket No. 6, an Archaic Village in Middleboro, Massachusetts.* Massachusetts Archaeological Society, Inc., Cohannet Chapter, Attleboro.

Roberts, Frank H. H., Jr.
1935a A Folsom Complex: Preliminary Report on Investigations at the Lindenmeier Site in Northern Colorado. *Smithsonian Miscellaneous Collections,* Vol. 94, No. 4. Washington.
1935b A Survey of Southwestern Archaeology. *American Anthropologist,* Vol. 37, No. 1, pp. 1–35. Menasha.
1936 Additional Information on the Folsom Complex: Report on the Second Season's Investigations at the Lindenmeier Site in Northern Colorado. *Smithsonian Miscellaneous Collections,* Vol. 95, No. 10. Washington.
1937 Archaeology in the Southwest. *American Antiquity,* Vol. 3, No. 1, pp. 3–33. Salt Lake City.
1938 The Lindenmeier Site in Northern Colorado Contributes Additional Data on the Folsom Complex. *Explorations and Field-work of the Smithsonian Institution in 1937,* pp. 115–118. Washington.
1939a Archeological Remains in the Whitewater District, Eastern Arizona. Part I: House Types. *Bureau of American Ethnology Bulletin,* No. 121. Washington.
1939b The Folsom Problem in American Archeology. *Annual Report of the Board of Regents of the Smithsonian Institution . . . for the Year Ending June 30, 1938,* pp. 531–546. Washington.
1940 Developments in the Problem of the North American Paleo-Indian. *In* "Essays in Historical Anthropology of North America." *Smithsonian Miscellaneous Collections,* Vol. 100, pp. 51–116. Washington.

Rogers, Malcolm J.
1939 Early Lithic Industries of the Lower Basin of the Colorado River and Adjacent Desert Areas. *San Diego Museum Papers,* No. 3. San Diego.

Rohn, Arthur H.
1963 Prehistoric Soil and Water Conservation on Chapin Mesa, Southwestern Colorado. *American Antiquity,* Vol. 28, No. 4, pp. 441–455. Salt Lake City.

Rouse, Irving
1939 Prehistory in Haiti: A Study in Method. *Yale University Publications in Anthropology,* No. 21. New Haven.
1953 The Strategy of Culture History. *In Anthropology Today,* Alfred L. Kroeber et al., pp. 57–76. The University of Chicago Press, Chicago.
1955 On the Correlation of Phases of Culture. *American Anthropologist,* Vol. 57, No. 4, pp. 713–722. Menasha.

1964 The Caribbean Area. *In Prehistoric Man in the New World*, Jesse D. Jennings and Edward Norbeck (eds.), pp. 389–417. *Rice University Semicentennial Publications*, The University of Chicago Press, Chicago.

Rowe, Chandler W.
1956 The Effigy Mound Culture of Wisconsin. *Milwaukee Public Museum Publications in Anthropology*, No. 3. Milwaukee.

Rudenko, Sergei I.
1961 The Ancient Culture of the Bering Sea and the Eskimo Problem. Translated by Paul Tolstoy. *Arctic Institute of North America, Anthropology of the North: Translations from Russian Sources*, No. 1. Published for the Arctic Institute of North America by the University of Toronto Press, Toronto.

Sahagún, Bernardino de
1905 *Codex Florentino;* Illustrations for Sahagún's *Historia de las Cosas de Nueva España*, Francisco del Paso y Troncoso (ed.), Vol. 5. Hauser and Menet, Madrid.

Sanger, David
1967 Prehistory of the Pacific Northwest Plateau as Seen from the Interior of British Columbia. *American Antiquity*, Vol. 32, No. 2, pp. 186–197. Salt Lake City.

Sauer, Jonathan, D.
1950 The Grain Amaranths: A Survey of Their History and Classification. *Annals of the Missouri Botanical Garden*, Vol. 37, pp. 561–632. St. Louis.

Sayles, Edwin B.
1937a Houses. In "Excavations at Snaketown: Material Culture," Harold S. Gladwin et al. *Medallion Papers*, No. 25, pp. 59–90. Gila Pueblo, Globe, Arizona.
1937b Stone Implements and Bowls. In "Excavations at Snaketown: Material Culture," Harold S. Gladwin et al. *Medallion Papers*, No. 25, pp. 101–120. Gila Pueblo, Globe, Arizona.

Sayles, Edwin B., and Ernst Antevs
1941 The Cochise Culture. *Medallion Papers*, No. 29. Gila Pueblo, Globe, Arizona.

Schoenwetter, James
1962 The Pollen Analysis of Eighteen Archaeological Sites in Arizona and New Mexico. In "Chapters in the Prehistory of Eastern Arizona, I," Paul S. Martin et al. *Fieldiana: Anthropology*, Vol. 53, pp. 168–209. Chicago.
1966 A Re-evaluation of the Navajo Reservoir Pollen Chronology. *El Palacio*, Vol. 73, No. 1, pp. 19–26. Santa Fe.

Schoenwetter, James, and Frank W. Eddy
1964 Alluvial and Palynological Reconstruction of Environments, Navajo Reservoir District. *Museum of New Mexico Papers in Anthropology*, No. 13, *Navajo Project Studies*, No. 11. Santa Fe.

Schroeder, Albert H.
1965 Unregulated Diffusion from Mexico into the Southwest Prior to A.D. 700. *American Antiquity*, Vol. 30, No. 3, pp. 297–309. Salt Lake City.
1966 Pattern Diffusion from Mexico into the Southwest after A.D. 600. *American Antiquity*, Vol. 31, No. 5, Pt. 1, pp. 683–704. Salt Lake City.

Schulman, Edmund
1956 *Dendroclimatic Changes in Semiarid America.* University of Arizona Press, Tucson.

Schultz, C. Bertrand, Gilbert C. Lueninghoener, and W. D. Frankforter
1948 Preliminary Geomorphological Studies of the Lime Creek Area. *Bulletin of the University of Nebraska State Museum*, Vol. 3, No. 4, Pt. 1, pp. 31–42. Lincoln.

Schultz, Floyd, and Albert C. Spaulding
1948 A Hopewellian Burial Site in the Lower Republican Valley, Kansas. *American Antiquity*, Vol. 13, No. 4, Pt. 1, pp. 306–313. Salt Lake City.

Schwartz, Douglas W., Arthur L. Lange, and Raymond deSaussure
1958 Split-twig Figurines in the Grand Canyon. *American Antiquity*, Vol. 23, No. 3, pp. 264–274. Salt Lake City.

Sears, William H.
1951a Excavations at Kolomoki, Season I—1948. *University of Georgia Series in Anthropology*, No. 2. Athens.
1951b Excavations at Kolomoki, Season II—1950, Mound E. *University of Georgia Series in Anthropology*, No. 3. Athens.
1953 Excavations at Kolomoki, Season III and IV, Mound D. *University of Georgia Series in Anthropology*, No. 4. Athens.
1956 Excavations at Kolomoki, Final Report. *University of Georgia Series in Anthropology*, No. 5. Athens.
1964 The Southeastern United States. *In Prehistoric Man in the New World*, Jesse D. Jennings and Edward Norbeck (eds.), pp. 259–287. *Rice University Semicentennial Publications*, The University of Chicago Press, Chicago.

Sellards, Elias H.
1952 *Early Man in America.* University of Texas Press, Austin.

1955 Fossil Bison and Associated Artifacts from Milnesand, New Mexico. *American Antiquity*, Vol. 20, No. 4, Pt. 1, pp. 336–344. Salt Lake City.

Sellards, Elias H., Glen L. Evans, and Grayson E. Meade
1947 Fossil Bison and Associated Artifacts from Plainview, Texas. *Bulletin of the Geological Society of America*, Vol. 58, No. 10, pp. 927–954. New York.

Setzler, Frank M.
1933 Pottery of the Hopewell Type from Louisiana. *Proceedings of the U.S. National Museum*, Vol. 82, Art. 22, pp. 1–21. Washington.

Shapley, Harlow (ed.)
1953 *Climatic Change: Evidence, Causes, and Effects.* Harvard University Press, Cambridge.

Sharrock, Floyd W.
1966 Prehistoric Occupation Patterns in Southwest Wyoming and Cultural Relationships with the Great Basin and Plains Culture Areas. *University of Utah Anthropological Papers*, No. 77. Salt Lake City.

Sharrock, Floyd W., et al.
1964 1962 Excavations, Glen Canyon Area. *University of Utah Anthropological Papers*, No. 73, *Glen Canyon Series*, No. 25. Salt Lake City.

Sharrock, Floyd W., David S. Dibble, and *Keith M. Anderson*
1961 The Creeping Dune Irrigation Site in Glen Canyon, Utah. *American Antiquity*, Vol. 27, No. 2, pp. 188–202. Salt Lake City.

Shetrone, Henry C.
1930 *The Mound Builders.* Appleton-Century-Crofts, Inc., New York.

Shiner, Joel L.
1961 The McNary Reservoir: A Study in Plateau Archeology. *River Basin Surveys Papers*, No. 23. *Bureau of American Ethnology Bulletin*, No. 179, pp. 149–266. Washington.

Shippee, James M.
1948 Nebo Hill, a Lithic Complex in Western Missouri. *American Antiquity*, Vol. 14, No. 1, pp. 28–32. Salt Lake City.

Shutler, Richard, Jr.
1965 Tule Springs Expedition. *Current Anthropology*, Vol. 6, No. 1, pp. 110–111. Chicago.

Simpson, Ruth D.
1958 The Manix Lake Archeological Survey. *Masterkey*, Vol. 32, No. 1, pp. 4–10. Los Angeles.
1960 Archeological Survey of the Eastern Calico Mountains. *Masterkey*, Vol. 34, No. 1, pp. 25–35. Los Angeles.

Skaggs, Opal
1946 A Study of the Dog Skeletons from Indian Knoll with Special Reference to the Coyote. *In* "Indian Knoll, Site Oh2, Ohio County, Kentucky," William S. Webb. *University of Kentucky Reports in Anthropology and Archaeology*, Vol. 4, No. 3, Pt. 1, pp. 341–355. Lexington.

Smiley, Terah L. (ed.)
1955 Geochronology. *University of Arizona Bulletin*, Vol. 26, No. 2, *Physical Science Bulletin*, No. 2. Tucson.

Smith, Arthur G.
1957 Suggested Change in Nomenclature of the Major American Time Periods. *American Antiquity*, Vol. 23, No. 2, Pt. 1, p. 169. Salt Lake City.

Smith, Elmer R.
1952 The Archeology of Deadman Cave, Utah: A Revision. *University of Utah Anthropological Papers*, No. 10. Salt Lake City.

Smith, Marian W. (ed.)
1953 Asia and North America: Transpacific Contacts. *American Antiquity*, Vol. 18, No. 3, Pt. 2, *Memoirs of the Society for American Archaeology*, No. 9. Salt Lake City.

Smithsonian Institution
1940 Essays in Historical Anthropology of North America: Published in Honor of John R. Swanton. *Smithsonian Miscellaneous Collections*, Vol. 100. Washington.

Snow, Charles E.
1948 Indian Knoll Skeletons of Site Oh2, Ohio County, Kentucky. *University of Kentucky Reports in Anthropology [and Archaeology]*, Vol. 4, No. 3, Pt. 2, pp. 367–555. Lexington.

Spaulding, Albert C.
1946 Northeastern Archaeology and General Trends in the Northern Forest Zone. *In* "Man in Northeastern North America," Frederick Johnson (ed.). *Papers of the Robert S. Peabody Foundation for Archaeology*, Vol. 3, pp. 143–167. Andover.

Spencer, Robert F.
1959 The North Alaskan Eskimo: A Study in Ecology and Society. *Bureau of American Ethnology Bulletin*, No. 171. Washington.
1965a Arctic and Sub-Arctic in Native America. *In The Native Americans*, Robert F. Spencer, Jesse D. Jennings, et al., pp. 119–167. Harper & Row, Publishers, Incorporated, New York.
1965b Language—American Babel, pp. 100–111. *In the Native Americans*,

Robert F. Spencer, Jesse D. Jennings et al. Harper & Row, Publishers, Incorporated, New York.

Spencer, Robert F., Jesse D. Jennings et al.
1965 *The Native Americans: Prehistory and Ethnology of the North American Indians.* Harper & Row, Publishers, Incorporated, New York.

Spier, Leslie, A. Irving Hallowell, and **Stanley S. Newman (eds.)**
1941 *Language, Culture, and Personality: Essays in Memory of Edward Sapir.* Sapir Memorial Publication Fund, Menasha.

Squier, Ephraim G., and **Edwin H. Davis**
1848 Ancient Monuments of the Mississippi Valley. *Smithsonian Contributions to Knowledge,* Vol. 1. Washington.

Stallings, William S., Jr.
1949 Dating Prehistoric Ruins by Tree-rings. *Laboratory of Anthropology General Series, Bulletin,* No. 8 (1939), Santa Fe. (Revised edition published by the Tree-ring Society with the cooperation of the Laboratory of Tree-ring Research, Tucson.)

Steen, Charlie R.
1955 Prehistoric Man in the AWR River Basins. *In A Survey of Archaeology and History in the Arkansas-White-Red River Basins,* pp. 1–34. National Park Service, Washington.

Stephens, John L.
1843 *Incidents of Travel in Yucatán.* Harper and Brothers, New York.

Stern, Theodore C.
1965 The Southeast. *In The Native Americans,* Robert F. Spencer, Jesse D. Jennings et al., pp. 402–434. Harper & Row, Publishers, Incorporated, New York.

Steward, Julian H.
1936 Pueblo Material Culture in Western Utah. *University of New Mexico Bulletin,* No. 287, *Anthropological Series,* Vol. 1, No. 3. Albuquerque.
1937 Ancient Caves of the Great Salt Lake Region. *Bureau of American Ethnology Bulletin,* No. 116. Washington.
1940 Native Cultures of the Intermontane (Great Basin) Area. *In* "Essays in Historical Anthropology of North America." *Smithsonian Miscellaneous Collections,* Vol. 100, pp. 445–502. Washington.
1941 Archaeological Reconnaissance of Southern Utah. *Anthropological Papers,* No. 18. *Bureau of American Ethnology Bulletin,* No. 128, pp. 275–356. Washington.

Steward, Julian H., and **Frank M. Setzler**
1938 Function and Configuration in Archaeology. *American Antiquity,* Vol. 4, No. 1, pp. 4–10. Salt Lake City.

Stewart, Kenneth M.
1965 American Indian Heritage: Retrospect and Prospect. *In The Native Americans,* Robert F. Spencer, Jesse D. Jennings et al., pp. 490–506. Harper & Row, Publishers, Incorporated, New York.

Stewart, Omer C.
1956 Fire as the First Great Force Employed by Man. *In Man's Role in Changing the Face of the Earth,* William L. Thomas, Jr. (ed.), pp. 115–133. The University of Chicago Press, Chicago.

Stewart, T. Dale
1949 Comparisons between Tepexpan Man and Other Early Americans. *In* "Tepexpan Man," Helmut de Terra, Javier Romero, and T. Dale Stewart. *Viking Fund Publications in Anthropology,* No. 11, pp. 137–145. New York.
1955 Description of the Human Skeletal Remains. *In The Midland Discovery,* Fred Wendorf, Alex D. Krieger, and Claude C. Albritton, pp. 77–90. University of Texas Press, Austin.
1957 American Neanderthaloids. *In* "Symposium Commemorating the Hundredth Anniversary of the Discovery of Neanderthal Man," B. H. Willier (ed.). *Quarterly Review of Biology,* Vol. 32, No. 4, pp. 364–369. Baltimore.
1960 A Physical Anthropologist's View of the Peopling of the New World. *Southwestern Journal of Anthropology,* Vol. 16, No. 3, pp. 259–273. Albuquerque.

Stoltman, James B.
1966 New Radiocarbon Dates for Southeastern Fiber-tempered Pottery. *American Antiquity,* Vol. 31, No. 6, pp. 872–874. Salt Lake City.

Strong, William D.
1933 Studying the Arikara and Their Neighbors on the Upper Missouri. *Explorations and Field-work of the Smithsonian Institution in 1932,* pp. 73–76. Washington.
1935 An Introduction to Nebraska Archeology. *Smithsonian Miscellaneous Collections,* Vol. 93, No. 10. Washington.
1940 From History to Prehistory in the Northern Great Plains. *In* "Essays in Historical Anthropology of North America." *Smithsonian Miscellaneous*

Collections, Vol. 100, pp. 353–394. Washington.

Struever, Stuart
1964 The Hopewell Interaction Sphere in Riverine-western Great Lakes Culture History. Paper No. 3 *in* "Hopewellian Studies," Joseph R. Caldwell and Robert L. Hall (eds.). *Illinois State Museum Scientific Papers*, Vol. 12, pp. 85–106. Springfield.
1965 Middle Woodland Culture History in the Great Lakes Riverine Area. *American Antiquity*, Vol. 31, No. 2, Pt. 1, pp. 211–223. Salt Lake City.

Suhm, Dee Ann, Alex D. Krieger, and Edward B. Jelks
1954 An Introductory Handbook of Texas Archeology. *Bulletin of the Texas Archeological Society*, Vol. 25. Austin.

Swadesh, Morris
1954 Time Depths of American Linguistic Groupings. *American Anthropologist*, Vol. 56, No. 3, pp. 361–364. Menasha.
1964 Linguistic Overview. *In Prehistoric Man in the New World*, Jesse D. Jennings and Edward Norbeck (eds.), pp. 527–556. *Rice University Semicentennial Publications*, The University of Chicago Press, Chicago.

Swanson, Earl H., Jr.
1959 Theory and History in American Archaeology. *Southwestern Journal of Anthropology*, Vol. 15, No. 2, pp. 120–124. Albuquerque.
1962 The Emergence of Plateau Culture. *Occasional Papers of the Idaho State College Museum*, No. 8. Pocatello.
1964 *The Idea of an American Archaic*. Unpublished manuscript. Paper presented at the Great Basin Anthropological Conference, Reno, Nevada.
1965 Archaeological Explorations in Southwestern Idaho. *American Antiquity*, Vol. 31, No. 1, pp. 24–37. Salt Lake City.

Swanson, Earl H., Jr., B. Robert Butler, and Robson Bonnichsen
1964 Birch Creek Papers No. 2: Natural and Cultural Stratigraphy in the Birch Creek Valley of Eastern Idaho. *Occasional Papers of the Idaho State University Museum*, No. 14. Pocatello.

Swanton, John R.
1911 Indian Tribes of the Lower Mississippi Valley and Adjacent Coast of the Gulf of Mexico. *Bureau of American Ethnology Bulletin*, No. 43. Washington.
1946 The Indians of the Southeastern United States. *Bureau of American Ethnology Bulletin*, No. 137. Washington.

Tax, Sol
1953 Penny Capitalism, a Guatemalan Indian Economy. *Smithsonian Institution, Institute of Social Anthropology Publication*, No. 16. Washington.

Taylor, Dee C.
1957 Two Fremont Sites and Their Position in Southwestern Prehistory. *University of Utah Anthropological Papers*, No. 29. Salt Lake City.

Taylor, Walter W.
1948 A Study of Archeology. *American Anthropologist*, Vol. 50, No. 3, Pt. 2, American Anthropological Association Memoir, No. 69. Menasha.
1954 Southwestern Archeology, Its History and Theory. *American Anthropologist*, Vol. 56, No. 4, pp. 561–570. Menasha.
1957 (ed.) The Identification of Nonartifactual Archaeological Materials. *National Academy of Sciences, National Research Council Publication*, No. 565. Washington.
1961 Archaeology and Language in Western North America. *American Antiquity*, Vol. 27, No. 1, pp. 71–81. Salt Lake City.

Thomas, William L., Jr. (ed.)
1956 *Man's Role in Changing the Face of the Earth*. The University of Chicago Press, Chicago.

Thompson, Raymond H. (ed.)
1958 Migrations in New World Culture History. *University of Arizona Bulletin*, Vol. 29, No. 2, Social Science Bulletin, No. 27. Tucson.

Tolstoy, Paul
1953 Some Amerasian Pottery Traits in North Asian Prehistory. *American Antiquity*, Vol. 19, No. 1, pp. 25–39. Salt Lake City.

Trigger, Bruce G.
1967 Settlement Archaeology—Its Goals and Promise. *American Antiquity*, Vol. 32, No. 2, pp. 149–160. Salt Lake City.

Tuthill, Carr, and A. A. Allanson
1954 Ocean-bottom Artifacts. *Masterkey*, Vol. 28, No. 6, pp. 222–232. Los Angeles.

University of California, Department of Anthropology
1958 Current Views on Great Basin Archaeology. *Reports of the University of California Archaeological Survey*, No. 42. Berkeley.

University of Illinois
1928 The Cahokia Mounds. *Univer-*

sity of Illinois Bulletin, Vol. 26, No. 4. Urbana.

University of Utah
1948 The Great Basin with Emphasis on Glacial and Postglacial Times. *Bulletin of the University of Utah*, Vol. 38, No. 20, *Biological Series*, Vol. 10, No. 7. Salt Lake City.

Vaillant, George C.
1930 Excavations at Zacatenco. *Anthropological Papers of the American Museum of Natural History*, Vol. 32, Pt. 1, pp. 1–197. New York.

1931 Excavations at Ticoman. *Anthropological Papers of the American Museum of Natural History*, Vol. 32, Pt. 2, pp. 199–439. New York.

1935a Early Cultures of the Valley of Mexico: Results of the Stratigraphical Project of the American Museum of Natural History in the Valley of Mexico, 1928–1933. *Anthropological Papers of the American Museum of Natural History*, Vol. 35, Pt. 3, pp. 281–328. New York.

1935b Excavations at El Arbolillo. *Anthropological Papers of the American Museum of Natural History*, Vol. 35, Pt. 2, pp. 137–279. New York.

1950 *The Aztecs of Mexico: Origin, Rise and Fall of the Aztec Nation.* Penguin Books, Inc., Baltimore.

Walker, Winslow M.
1936 The Troyville Mounds, Catahoula Parish, La. *Bureau of American Ethnology Bulletin*, No. 113. Washington.

1952 The Dickison Mound Group, Peoria County. Paper No. 1 *in* "Hopewellian Communities in Illinois," Thorne Deuel (ed.). *Illinois State Museum Scientific Papers*, Vol. 5, pp. 13–41. Springfield.

Wallace, William J.
1955 A Suggested Chronology for Southern California Coastal Archaeology. *Southwestern Journal of Anthropology*, Vol. 11, No. 3, pp. 214–230. Albuquerque.

Warren, Claude N.
1967 The San Dieguito Complex: A Review and Hypothesis. *American Antiquity*, Vol. 32, No. 2, pp. 168–185. Salt Lake City.

Warren, Claude N., and D. L. True
1961 The San Dieguito Complex and Its Place in California Prehistory. *Archaeological Survey Annual Report, 1960–1961*, pp. 246–337. Department of Anthropology and Sociology, University of California, Los Angeles.

Wasley, William W.
1960 A Hohokam Platform Mound at the Gatlin Site, Gila Bend, Arizona. *American Antiquity*, Vol. 26, No. 2, pp. 244–262. Salt Lake City.

1961 Techniques and Tools of Salvage. *Archaeology*, Vol. 14, No. 4, pp. 283–286. New York.

Wasley, William W., and Alfred E. Johnson
1965 Salvage Archaeology in Painted Rocks Reservoir, Western Arizona. *Anthropological Papers of the University of Arizona*, No. 9. Tucson.

Watson, Don
1950 *Cliff Dwellings of the Mesa Verde: A Story in Pictures.* Mesa Verde National Park, Mesa Verde Museum Association, Colorado.

Watson, Patty J.
1966 Prehistoric Miners of Salts Cave, Kentucky. *Archaeology*, Vol. 19, No. 4, pp. 237–243. New York.

Wauchope, Robert
1956 (ed.) Seminars in Archaeology: 1955. *American Antiquity*, Vol. 22, No. 2, Pt. 2, *Memoirs of the Society for American Archaeology*, No. 11. Salt Lake City.

1962 *Lost Tribes and Sunken Continents: Myth and Method in the Study of American Indians.* The University of Chicago Press, Chicago.

1964– (ed.) *Handbook of Middle American Indians.* University of Texas Press, Austin. [Published to date: Vol. I, *Natural Environment and Early Cultures*, Robert C. West (ed.); Vols. II and III, *Archaeology of Southern Mesoamerica*, Pts. 1 and 2, Gordon R. Willey (ed.).]

1966 Archaeological Survey of Northern Georgia with a Test of Some Cultural Hypotheses. *American Antiquity*, Vol. 31, No. 5, Pt. 2, *Memoirs of the Society for American Archaeology*, No. 21. Salt Lake City.

Weakly, Harry E.
1940 Tree-rings as a Record of Precipitation in Western Nebraska. *Tree-ring Bulletin*, Vol. 6, No. 3, pp. 18–19. Tucson.

1943 A Tree-ring Record of Precipitation in Western Nebraska. *Journal of Forestry*, Vol. 41, No. 11, pp. 816–819. Washington.

1950 Dendrochronology and Its Climatic Implications in the Central Plains. *In* "Proceedings of the Sixth Plains Archeological Conference, 1948," Jesse D. Jennings (ed.). *University of Utah Anthropological Papers*, No. 11, pp. 90–94. Salt Lake City.

Webb, Clarence H.
1959 The Belcher Mound: A Strati-

fied Caddoan Site in Caddo Parish, Louisiana. *American Antiquity*, Vol. 24, No. 4, Pt. 2, *Memoirs of the Society for American Archaeology*, No. 16. Salt Lake City.

Webb, Walter P.
1931   *The Great Plains*. Ginn and Company, Boston.

Webb, William S.
1939   An Archaeological Survey of Wheeler Basin on the Tennessee River in Northern Alabama. *Bureau of American Ethnology Bulletin*, No. 122. Washington.
1941a   The Morgan Stone Mound, Site 15, Bath County, Kentucky. *University of Kentucky Reports in Anthropology and Archaeology*, Vol. 5, No. 3, pp. 219–291. Lexington.
1941b   Mt. Horeb Earthworks, Site 1, and the Drake Mound, Site 11, Fayette County, Kentucky. *University of Kentucky Reports in Anthropology and Archaeology*, Vol. 5, No. 2, pp. 135–218. Lexington.
1943   The Riley Mound, Site Be 15, and the Landing Mound, Site Be 17, Boone County, Kentucky. *University of Kentucky Reports in Anthropology and Archaeology*, Vol. 5, No. 7, pp. 581–697. Lexington.
1946   Indian Knoll, Site Oh2, Ohio County, Kentucky. *University of Kentucky Reports in Anthropology and Archaeology*, Vol. 4, No. 3, Pt. 1, pp. 111–365. Lexington.

Webb, William S., and Raymond S. Baby
1957   *The Adena People, No. 2*. Published for the Ohio Historical Society by the Ohio State University Press, Columbus.

Webb, William S., and David L. DeJarnette
1942   An Archeological Survey of Pickwick Basin in the Adjacent Portions of the States of Alabama, Mississippi and Tennessee. *Bureau of American Ethnology Bulletin*, No. 129. Washington.

Webb, William S., and John B. Elliott
1942   The Robbins Mounds, Sites Be 3 and Be 14, Boone County, Kentucky. *University of Kentucky Reports in Anthropology and Archaeology*, Vol. 5, No. 5, pp. 373–499. Lexington.

Webb, William S., and W. D. Funkhouser
1936   Rock Shelters in Menifee County, Kentucky. *University of Kentucky Reports in Archaeology and Anthropology*, Vol. 3, No. 4, pp. 101–167. Lexington.

Webb, William S., and Charles E. Snow
1945   The Adena People. *University of Kentucky Reports in Anthropology and Archaeology*, Vol. 6. Lexington.

Wedel, Mildred M.
1959   Oneota Sites on the Upper Iowa River. *Missouri Archaeologist*, Vol. 21, Nos. 2–4. Columbia.

Wedel, Waldo R.
1936   An Introduction to Pawnee Archeology. *Bureau of American Ethnology Bulletin*, No. 112. Washington.
1941   Environment and Native Subsistence Economies in the Central Great Plains. *Smithsonian Miscellaneous Collections*, Vol. 101, No. 3. Washington.
1943   Archeological Investigations in Platte and Clay Counties, Missouri. *U. S. National Museum Bulletin*, No. 183. Washington.
1947   Prehistory and Environment in the Central Great Plains. *Transactions of the Kansas Academy of Science*, Vol. 50, No. 1, pp. 1–18. Kansas City.
1953   Some Aspects of Human Ecology in the Central Plains. *American Anthropologist*, Vol. 55, No. 4, pp. 499–514. Menasha.
1959   An Introduction to Kansas Archeology. *Bureau of American Ethnology Bulletin*, No. 174. Washington.
1961   *Prehistoric Man on the Great Plains*. University of Oklahoma Press, Norman.
1964   The Great Plains. *In Prehistoric Man in the New World*, Jesse D. Jennings and Edward Norbeck (eds.), pp. 193–220. *Rice University Semicentennial Publications*, The University of Chicago Press, Chicago.

Wendorf, Fred
1956   Some Distributions of Settlement Patterns in the Pueblo Southwest. *In* "Prehistoric Settlement Patterns in the New World," Gordon R. Willey (ed.). *Viking Fund Publications in Anthropology*, No. 23, pp. 18–25. New York.
1962   *A Guide for Salvage Archaeology*. Museum of New Mexico, Santa Fe.
1966   Early Man in the New World: Problems of Migration. *American Naturalist*, Vol. 100, No. 912, pp. 253–270. Lancaster.

Wendorf, Fred, et al.
1961   Paleoecology of the Llano Estacado. *Fort Burgwin Research Center Publication*, No. 1. Santa Fe.

Wendorf, Fred, and James J. Hester
1962   Early Man's Utilization of the Great Plains Environment. *American Antiquity*, Vol. 28, No. 2, pp. 159–171. Salt Lake City.

Wendorf, Fred, and Alex D. Krieger
1959   New Light on the Midland Discovery. *American Antiquity*, Vol. 25, No. 1, pp. 66–78. Salt Lake City.

Wendorf, Fred, Alex D. Krieger, and
Claude C. Albritton
1955 *The Midland Discovery: A Report on the Pleistocene Human Remains from Midland, Texas.* University of Texas Press, Austin.

West, Frederick H.
1963a (ed.) Early Man in the Western American Arctic: A Symposium. *Anthropological Papers of the University of Alaska,* Vol. 10, No. 2. College.
1963b Leaf-shaped Points in the Western Arctic. *In* "Early Man in the Western American Arctic: A Symposium," Frederick H. West (ed.). *Anthropological Papers of the University of Alaska,* Vol. 10, No. 2, pp. 51–62. College.

West, Robert C. (ed.)
1964 *Natural Environment and Early Cultures.* Volume I of *Handbook of Middle American Indians,* Robert Wauchope (ed.). University of Texas Press, Austin.

Wheat, Joe Ben
1952 Prehistoric Water Sources of the Point of Pines Area. *American Antiquity,* Vol. 17, No. 3, pp. 185–196. Salt Lake City
1954 Crooked Ridge Village (Arizona W:10:15). *University of Arizona Bulletin,* Vol. 25, No. 3, *Social Science Bulletin,* No. 24. Tucson.
1955 Mogollon Culture Prior to A.D. 1000. *American Antiquity,* Vol. 20, No. 4, Pt. 2, *Memoirs of the Society for American Archaeology,* No. 10. Salt Lake City. (Also published in *American Anthropologist,* Vol. 57, No. 2, Pt. 3, *American Anthropological Association Memoir,* No. 82. Menasha.)
1967 A Paleo-Indian Bison Kill. *Scientific American,* Vol. 216, No. 1, pp. 44–52. New York.

Wheat, Joe Ben, James C. Gifford, and
William W. Wasley
1958 Ceramic Variety, Type Cluster, and Ceramic System in Southwestern Pottery Analysis. *American Antiquity,* Vol. 24, No. 1, pp. 34–47. Salt Lake City.

Wheeler, Richard P.
1952 A Note on the "McKean Lanceolate Point." *Plains Archeological Conference News Letter,* Vol. 4, No. 4, pp. 39–44. Lincoln. (Reprinted February, 1961.)
1954 Duncan and Hanna Points. *Plains Anthropologist,* No. 1, pp. 7–14. Lincoln.

Wheeler, S. M.
1942 *Archeology of Etna Cave, Lin-*

coln County, Nevada. Nevada State Park Commission, Carson City.

White, Leslie A.
1949 *The Science of Culture.* Grove Press, Inc., New York.

Will, George F.
1946 Tree Ring Studies in North Dakota. *North Dakota Agricultural College, Agricultural Experiment Station Bulletin,* No. 338. Fargo.

Willey, Gordon R.
1937 Notes on Central Georgia Dendrochronology. *Tree-ring Bulletin,* Vol. 4, No. 2, pp. 6–8. Tucson.
1949 Archeology of the Florida Gulf Coast. *Smithsonian Miscellaneous Collections,* Vol. 113. Washington.
1956 (ed.) Prehistoric Settlement Patterns in the New World. *Viking Fund Publications in Anthropology,* No. 23. New York.
1966 *An Introduction to American Archaeology.* Vol. I, *North and Middle America.* Prentice-Hall, Inc., Englewood Cliffs, New Jersey.

Willey, Gordon R., and **Philip Phillips**
1955 Method and Theory in American Archeology II: Historical-Developmental Interpretation. *American Anthropologist,* Vol. 57, No. 4, pp. 723–819. Menasha.
1958 *Method and Theory in American Archaeology.* The University of Chicago Press, Chicago.

Williams, Samuel Cole (ed.)
1930 *Adair's History of the American Indians.* Watauga Press, Johnson City, Tennessee.

Willier, Benjamin H. (ed.)
1957 Symposium Commemorating the Hundredth Anniversary of the Discovery of Neanderthal Man. *Quarterly Review of Biology,* Vol. 32, No. 4, pp. 323–451. Baltimore.

Willis, E. H.
1963 Radiocarbon Dating. *In Science in Archaeology,* Don Brothwell and Eric Higgs (eds.), pp. 35–46. Basic Books, Inc., Publishers, New York.

Willoughby, Charles C.
1932 Notes on the History and Symbolism of the Muskhogeans and the People of Etowah. *In Etowah Papers,* Warren K. Moorehead et al., pp. 7–66. Published for the Phillips Academy by the Yale University Press, New Haven.

Wilmsen, Edwin N.
1964 Flake Tools in the American Arctic: Some Speculations. *American Antiquity,* Vol. 29, No. 3, pp. 338–344. Salt Lake City.
1965 An Outline of Early Man Studies in the United States. *Ameri-*

can Antiquity, Vol. 31, No. 2, Pt. 1, pp. 172–192. Salt Lake City.

Wimberly, Steve B., and **Harry A. Tourtelot**
1941   The McQuorquodale Mound: A Manifestation of the Hopewellian Phase in South Alabama. *Geological Survey of Alabama Museum Paper,* No. 19. University.

Wissler, Clark
1938   *The American Indian,* 3d ed. Oxford University Press, Fair Lawn, New Jersey.

Witthoft, John
1952   A Paleo-Indian Site in Eastern Pennsylvania: An Early Hunting Culture. *Proceedings of the American Philosophical Society,* Vol. 96, No. 4, pp. 464–495. Philadelphia.

Wolf, Eric R.
1959   *Sons of the Shaking Earth.* The University of Chicago Press, Chicago.

Woodbury, Richard B.
1954   Prehistoric Stone Implements of Northeastern Arizona. *Papers of the Peabody Museum of American Archaeology and Ethnology,* Vol. 34, *Reports of the Awatovi Expedition,* No. 6. Cambridge.
1960   The Hohokam Canals at Pueblo Grande, Arizona. *American Antiquity,* Vol. 26, No. 2, pp. 267–270. Salt Lake City.
1961   Prehistoric Agriculture at Point of Pines, Arizona. *American Antiquity,* Vol. 26, No. 3, Pt. 2, *Memoirs of the Society for American Archaeology,* No. 17. Salt Lake City.

Woolley, Leonard
1960   *Digging Up the Past,* 2d ed. Penguin Books, Inc., Baltimore.

Wormington, H. Marie
1956   Prehistoric Indians of the Southwest, 3d ed. *Denver Museum of Natural History Popular Series,* No. 7. Denver.
1957   Ancient Man in North America, 4th rev. ed. *Denver Museum of Natural History Popular Series,* No. 4. Denver.
1962   A Survey of Early American Prehistory. *American Scientist,* Vol. 50, No. 1, pp. 230–242. Easton, Pennsylvania.

Wormington, H. Marie, and
Richard G. Forbis
1965   An Introduction to the Archaeology of Alberta, Canada. *Proceedings of the Denver Museum of Natural History,* No. 11. Denver.

Wormington, H. Marie and **Robert H. Lister**
1956   Archaeological Investigations on the Uncompahgre Plateau in West Central Colorado. *Proceedings of the Denver Museum of Natural History,* No. 2. Denver.

Wright, Herbert E., Jr., and **David G. Frey (eds.)**
1965   *The Quaternary of the United States: A Review Volume for the VII Congress of the International Association for Quaternary Research.* Princeton University Press, Princeton.

Zeuner, Frederick E.
1958   *Dating the Past: An Introduction to Geochronology.* 4th rev. ed., enlarged. Methuen & Co., Ltd., London.

Index

Page numbers in *italics* refer to illustrations.

Pottery, Basketmaker II, 268
  black on white, 258
  chronologies based on, 219
  and culture change, 21, 22
  as diagnostic material, 220
  Early Northeast, *186*
  Florida Gulf Coast, *209*
  gray, 271
  Hohokam, 259, *261*
  Hopewell, *208*
  Hopi Sikyatki Polychrome, 280
  Irene, 226
  Middle American, 174
  Mississippian, 220, *225*
  Montgomery Incised, 196, *199*
  Navajo, 281
  Norton, 301
  of Plains, 234, 237, 238
  Pueblo, 84, 272
  Pueblo II, 274
  and transition, 184–185
  in typology, 17–18
  Valley focus, *236*
  "Woodland" type, 189, 195, 202–203
  (*See also* Ceramics)
Poverty Point site, Louisiana, 213
  objects from, *214*
  relief map, *215*
Powell, Wesley, 33
Pre-Eskimo cultures, 290, 299
Prehistoric cultures, North American, general succession of, *335*
Prehistory, absence of written records, 8
Preprojectile stage, 71
Pribilof Islands, 288
Priest-rulers, 201, 217, 248
  burial of, 227
Priests, 179, 227
Projectile points, 68, 95, 106, 130, *149*, 152
  development of, *64*
  diagnostic, 132–133
  fluted, *86*
  Lithic stage distribution, *84*
  Plano-type, 290
Promontory Cave, Utah, 139, 282
Protoarchaic stage, 106, 107
Pueblo, Mogollon variant, 34
  Western, 258
Pueblo I, transitional nature of, 271
Pueblo I-V divisions, 24, 35
Pueblo II, 272
  artifacts from, *277*
  viability of, 274

Pueblo III, 274
  as age of specialization in crafts, 276
  artifacts from, 276, *278*
Pueblo V, European contact of, 280
Pueblo Bonito site, 270, *271*, 275
  artifacts from, *273*
  ground plan of, *272*
  room interior, *275*
Pueblo culture, 24
  sequential stages of, 34–35
Pueblo Revolt of 1680's, 280
Pueblo territory, shrinkage of, 279
Pueblo tribes, 247
Pumpkin (crop), 170
Purron phase of Tehuacan, 167, 176
Putnam, Frederic W., 33, 34
Putnam, Rufus, 32
Pyramdis, stepped, 262

Quarries, flint and quartzite, 70

Rabbit, cottontail, 167
Race, vanished, belief in, 32, 33
Radioactivity, testing for, 14
Radiocarbon (publication), 14
Radiocarbon counters, 14
Radiocarbon dating, 13–16, 67, 69, 137, 179
  and glacial advances, 55
Rainfall, varying, 231, 327
Rainfall pattern, and Anasazi influence, 274
  and weakening of Southwestern cultures, 276
Random deposits, 29
Ray Long site, 103
Recent period, new conception of, 55
Red Ocher in burials, 119
Red Ocher culture, Illinois, 125, 185
Red Smoke site, 93, 99
Reed, Erik K., 34
Region, as geographic unit, 25
Regional complexes, as prehistoric culture areas, 111
Regional conferences, 37
Reindeer (*see* Caribou)
Religious centers, 178, 179, 217
Research, archeologic, 2
Reserve area, New Mexico, 253

Reservoir areas, samples from, 36
Resources, natural, attrition of, 276
  seasonal, Western, 136
Revolt of Southwest against Spaniards, 280
Rice site, Missouri, 131, 132
Rio Grande-Atrisco sites, New Mexico, 151
Ritual, Mississippian, 226, 227
Riverine economy, 313
Riverine focus of Archaic populations, 135
Roaring Spring site, Oregon, 16, 137
Robbins Mounds site, Kentucky, 194, 196
  artifacts from, *200*
Roberts, Frank H. H., Jr., 34, 74
  classification of, 24, 266
Rock-shelter sites, Ozarks, 131, 133
Rocker stamping (pottery), 208
  dentate, 210
Romance and American archeology, 32
Rooms, contiguous, 269
Roundheadedness of Adenans, 198
Rousseau, Jean-Jacques, 33
Royal Ontario Museum, 332

Sadlermiut site, 315
St. Catherine's Concession, 1
St. Lawrence Island, artifacts from, *312, 314*
Salvage projects, 30, 37
San Dieguito complex, 136
  artifacts from, 62, *153*
San Dieguito I site, 147, 152
San Francisco phase, 253
San Juan Anasazi, 269, 279
San Pedro Cochise Archaic, 251
San Pedro stage of Desert culture, 151
Sandals, Basketmaker III, 271
Sandia Cave finds, 83–86, *88*, 89
Sands, layers of, 51
Santa Rosa Island, 69, 208
Sarqaq tradition, 313
Sauk Valley Man, 50
Savannah, 58
Sayles, E. B., 34
Scandinavia, contact with North America, 191
  as source of pottery, 185, 189